Lecture Notes in Artificial Intelligence   12568

Subseries of Lecture Notes in Computer Science

More information about this subseries at http://www.springer.com/series/1244

Takahiro Uchiya · Quan Bai ·
Iván Marsá Maestre (Eds.)

PRIMA 2020: Principles and Practice of Multi-Agent Systems

23rd International Conference
Nagoya, Japan, November 18–20, 2020
Proceedings

 Springer

Editors
Takahiro Uchiya
Nagoya Institute of Technology
Nagoya, Japan

Quan Bai ⓘ
University of Tasmania
Tasmania, TAS, Australia

Iván Marsá Maestre
University of Alcalá
Alcala de Henares, Spain

ISSN 0302-9743   ISSN 1611-3349 (electronic)
Lecture Notes in Artificial Intelligence
ISBN 978-3-030-69321-3   ISBN 978-3-030-69322-0 (eBook)
https://doi.org/10.1007/978-3-030-69322-0

LNCS Sublibrary: SL7 – Artificial Intelligence

This Springer imprint is published by the registered company Springer Nature Switzerland AG
The registered company address is: Gewerbestrasse 11, 6330 Cham, Switzerland

Preface

Welcome to the proceedings of the 23rd International Conference on Principles and Practice of Multi-Agent Systems (PRIMA 2020) held online, during November 18–20, 2020. Originally started as a regional (Asia-Pacific) workshop in 1998, PRIMA has become one of the leading and most influential scientific conferences for research on multi-agent systems. Each year since 2009, PRIMA has brought together active researchers, developers, and practitioners from both academia and industry to showcase, share, and promote research in several domains, ranging from foundations of agent theory and engineering aspects of agent systems, to emerging interdisciplinary areas of agent-based research. PRIMA's previous editions were held in Nagoya, Japan (2009), Kolkata, India (2010), Wollongong, Australia (2011), Kuching, Malaysia (2012), Dunedin, New Zealand (2013), Gold Coast, Australia (2014), Bertinoro, Italy (2015), Phuket, Thailand (2016), Nice, France (2017), Tokyo, Japan (2018), and Torino, Italy (2019).

This year, we received 50 full paper submissions from 20 countries. Each submission was carefully reviewed by at least three members of the Program Committee (PC) composed of 91 prominent world-class researchers. In addition, 14 sub-reviewers were called upon to review submissions. The review period was followed by PC discussions. At the end of the reviewing process, authors received the technical reviews. PRIMA 2020 accepted 19 full papers (an acceptance rate of 38%) and 15 submissions were selected to appear as short papers. The 1st International Workshop on Frontiers of Multi-Agent Systems (FMAS 2020) was included in PRIMA 2020. Four papers were accepted to be presented at FMAS 2020. In total, 19 full papers and 13 short papers are included in these proceedings.

In addition to the paper presentations, the conference included two tutorials: the first by Yasser Mohammad, and the second by Catholijn M. Jonker and Reyhan Aydogan. Also, the conference included one keynote speech, by Prof. Catholijn Jonker, and conference included two invited talks, by Prof. Bo An and Prof. Taiki Todo.

We would like to thank all the individuals and institutions that supported PRIMA 2020. Mainly we thank the authors for submitting high-quality research papers, confirming PRIMA's reputation as a leading international conference in multi-agent systems. We are indebted to our PC and SPC members and additional reviewers for spending their valuable time to provide careful reviews and recommendations on the submissions, and for taking part in follow-up discussions. We also thank EasyChair for the use of their conference management system.

November 2020

Takayuki Ito
Minjie Zhang
Takahiro Uchiya
Quan Bai
Iván Marsá Maestre

Organization

Conference Chairs

Takayuki Ito — Kyoto University, Japan
Minjie Zhang — University of Wollongong, Australia

Program Chairs

Takahiro Uchiya — Nagoya Institute of Technology, Japan
Quan Bai — University of Tasmania, Australia
Iván Marsá Maestre — University of Alcalá, Spain

Publication Chair

Toshihiro Matsui — Nagoya Institute of Technology, Japan

Workshop and Tutorial Chairs

Tokuro Matsuo — Advanced Institute of Industrial Technology, Japan
Rafik Hadfi — Kyoto University, Japan
Reyhan Aydogan — Ozyegin University, Turkey

Financial, Sponsorship, and Local Arrangement Chairs

Takayuki Ito — Kyoto University, Japan
Takanobu Otsuka — Nagoya Institute of Technology, Japan
Ahmed Moustafa — Nagoya Institute of Technology, Japan
Shun Okuhara — Kyoto University, Japan

PRIMA Steering Committee

Guido Governatori (Chair) — Data61, Australia
Takayuki Ito (Deputy Chair) — Kyoto University, Japan
Aditya Ghose (Immediate Past Chair) — University of Wollongong, Australia
Abdul Sattar (Treasurer) — Griffith University, Australia
Makoto Yokoo (Chair Emeritus) — Kyushu University, Japan
Hoa Dam — University of Wollongong, Australia
Jeremy Pitt — Imperial College London, UK
Yang Xu — University of Electronic Science and Technology of China, China

Jane Hsu	National Taiwan University, Taiwan
Andrea Omicini	Università di Bologna, Italy
Qingliang Chen	Jinan University, China
Paolo Torroni	Università di Bologna, Italy
Serena Villata	Inria Sophia Antipolis, France
Katsutoshi Hirayama	Kobe University, Japan
Matteo Baldoni	University of Torino, Italy
Amit K. Chopra	Lancaster University, UK
Tran Cao Son	New Mexico State University, USA
Michael Mäs	Karlsruhe Institute of Technology, Germany
Leon van der Torre	University of Luxembourg, Luxembourg
Ana Bazzan	Universidade Federal do Rio Grande do Sul, Brazil
João Leite	Universidade NOVA de Lisboa, Portugal
Bo An	Nanyang Technological University, Singapore
Itsuki Noda	AIST, Japan
Tony Savarimuthu	University of Otago, New Zealand
Nir Oren	University of Aberdeen, UK
Tim Miller	University of Melbourne, Australia
Yuko Sakurai	AIST, Japan

Program Committee

Thomas Ågotnes	University of Bergen, Norway
Mohammad Al-Zinati	Jordan University of Science and Technology, Jordan
Ryuta Arisaka	Kyoto University, Japan
Reyhan Aydogan	Ozyegin University, Turkey
Cristina Baroglio	Università di Torino, Italy
Federico Bergenti	Università degli Studi di Parma, Italy
Floris Bex	Utrecht University, Netherlands
Stefano Bistarelli	Università di Perugia, Italy
Olivier Boissier	Laboratoire Hubert Curien CNRS UMR 5516, France
Daniela Briola	University of Milano-Bicocca, Italy
Luciano Cavalcante Siebert	Delft University of Technology, Netherlands
Rem Collier	UCD, Ireland
Silvano Colombo Tosatto	University of Luxembourg, Luxembourg
Stefania Costantini	University of L'Aquila, Italy
Matteo Cristani	University of Verona, Italy
Luis Cruz-Piris	Universidad de Alcalá, Spain
Célia Da Costa Pereira	Université Nice Sophia Anipolis, France
Mehdi Dastani	Utrecht University, Netherlands
Paul Davidsson	Malmö University, Sweden
Dave De Jonge	IIIA-CSIC, Spain
Dario Della Monica	Università degli Studi di Udine, Italy
Yves Demazeau	CNRS – LIG, France
Barbara Dunin-Keplicz	University of Warsaw, Poland
Animesh Dutta	NIT Durgapur, India

Rino Falcone	Institute of Cognitive Sciences and Technologies-CNR, Italy
Susel Fernández	University of Alcalá, Spain
Angelo Ferrando	The University of Manchester, United Kingdom
Nicoletta Fornara	Università della Svizzera italiana, Switzerland
Katsuhide Fujita	Tokyo University of Agriculture and Technology, Japan
Naoki Fukuta	Shizuoka University, Japan
Rustam Galimullin	University of Bergen, Norway
Mingyu Guo	The University of Adelaide, Australia
Rafik Hadfi	Kyoto University, Japan
Hiromitsu Hattori	Ritsumeikan University, Japan
Koen Hindriks	Vrije Universiteit Amsterdam, Netherlands
Shohei Kato	Nagoya Institute of Technology, Japan
Weihua Li	Auckland University of Technology, New Zealand
Beishui Liao	Zhejiang University, China
Donghui Lin	Kyoto University, Japan
Emiliano Lorini	IRIT, France
Xudong Luo	Guangxi Normal University, China
Elisa Marengo	Free University of Bozen-Bolzano, Italy
Shigeo Matsubara	Osaka University, Japan
Toshihiro Matsui	Nagoya Institute of Technology, Japan
David Mercier	Université d'Artois, France
Roberto Micalizio	Universita' di Torino, Italy
Tim Miller	The University of Melbourne, Australia
Yasser Mohammad	NEC Corporation, Japan
Stefania Monica	Università degli Studi di Parma, Italy
Koichi Moriyama	Nagoya Insitute of Technology, Japan
Ahmed Moustafa	Nagoya Institute of Technology, Japan
Jörg P. Müller	TU Clausthal, Germany
Shun Okuhara	Kyoto University, Japan
Andrea Omicini	Università di Bologna, Italy
Hirotaka Ono	Nagoya University, Japan
Nir Oren	University of Aberdeen, United Kingdom
Takanobu Otsuka	Nagoya Institute of Technology, Japan
Tadachika Ozono	Nagoya Institute of Technology, Japan
Julian Padget	University of Bath, United Kingdom
Agostino Poggi	University of Parma, Italy
R. Ramanujam	Institute of Mathematical Sciences, India
Alessandro Ricci	University of Bologna, Italy
Luca Sabatucci	ICAR-CNR, Italy
Francesco Santini	University of Perugia, Italy
Giuseppe Sarnè	University Mediterranea of Reggio Calabria, Italy
Ken Satoh	National Institute of Informatics, Japan
Francois Schwarzentruber	École normale supérieure de Rennes, France
Valeria Seidita	Università degli Studi di Palermo, Italy

Shun Shiramatsu	Nagoya Institute of Technology, Japan
Ronal Singh	The University of Melbourne, Australia
Tran Cao Son	New Mexico State University, United States of America
Xing Su	Beijing University of Technology, Australia
Toshiharu Sugawara	Waseda University, Japan
Stefano Tedeschi	Università degli Studi di Torino, Italy
Alice Toniolo	University of St Andrews, United Kingdom
Behnam Torabi	The University of Texas at Dallas, United States of America
Jan Treur	Vrije Universiteit Amsterdam, Netherlands
Leon van der Torre	University of Luxembourg, Luxembourg
Giuseppe Vizzari	University of Milano-Bicocca, Italy
Yì Nicholas Wáng	Zhejiang University, China
Brendon J. Woodford	University of Otago, New Zealand
Yi Yang	Deakin University, Australia
William Yeoh	Washington University in St. Louis, United States of America
Makoto Yokoo	Kyushu University, Japan
Neil Yorke-Smith	Delft University of Technology, Netherlands
Weiwei Yuan	Nanjing University of Aeronautics and Astronautics, China
Dongmo Zhang	Western Sydney University, Australia

Additional Reviewers

Furkan Arslan	Naoyuki Nide
Flavien Balbo	Tiago Oliveira
Annemarie Borg	Charith Pereras
Filippo Cantucci	S. P. Suresh
Moinul Morshed Porag Chowdhury	Andrzej Szałas
Davide Dell'Anna	Francesco Tiezzi
Onur Keskin	Shihan Wang
Jieting Luo	

Contents

Full Papers

Implementation of Real Data for Financial Market Simulation Using
Clustering, Deep Learning, and Artificial Financial Market. 3
   Masanori Hirano, Hiroyasu Matsushima, Kiyoshi Izumi,
   and Hiroki Sakaji

Hybrid Dynamic Programming for Simultaneous Coalition Structure
Generation and Assignment 19
   Fredrik Präntare and Fredrik Heintz

A Socio-psychological Approach to Simulate Trust and Reputation
in Modal Choices 34
   Khoa Nguyen and René Schumann

Reasoning About Trustworthiness in Cyber-Physical Systems Using
Ontology-Based Representation and ASP. 51
   Thanh Hai Nguyen, Tran Cao Son, Matthew Bundas,
   Marcello Balduccini, Kathleen Campbell Garwood,
   and Edward R. Griffor

Optimal Deterministic Time-Based Policy in Automated Negotiation 68
   Yasser Mohammad

Agent Simulation of Collision Avoidance Based on Meta-strategy Model. . . . 84
   Norifumi Watanabe and Kensuke Miyamoto

The Smart Appliance Scheduling Problem: A Bayesian Optimization
Approach. 100
   Atena M. Tabakhi, William Yeoh, and Ferdinando Fioretto

Distance-Based Heuristic Solvers for Cooperative Path Planning
with Heterogeneous Agents 116
   Keisuke Otaki, Satoshi Koide, Ayano Okoso, and Tomoki Nishi

Policy Advisory Module for Exploration Hindrance Problem in Multi-agent
Deep Reinforcement Learning. 133
   Jiahao Peng and Toshiharu Sugawara

Analysis of Coordination Structures of Partially Observing Cooperative
Agents by Multi-agent Deep Q-Learning 150
   Ken Smith, Yuki Miyashita, and Toshiharu Sugawara

Policy Adaptive Multi-agent Deep Deterministic Policy Gradient   165
  Yixiang Wang and Feng Wu

Multi-agent Planning with High-Level Human Guidance   182
  Feng Wu, Shlomo Zilberstein, and Nicholas R. Jennings

Preference Elicitation in Assumption-Based Argumentation   199
  Quratul-ain Mahesar, Nir Oren, and Wamberto W. Vasconcelos

Declarative Preferences in Reactive BDI Agents   215
  Mostafa Mohajeri Parizi, Giovanni Sileno, and Tom van Engers

Predicting the Priority of Social Situations for Personal Assistant Agents   231
  Ilir Kola, Myrthe L. Tielman, Catholijn M. Jonker,
  and M. Birna van Riemsdijk

Mutex Propagation for SAT-based Multi-agent Path Finding   248
  Pavel Surynek, Jiaoyang Li, Han Zhang, T. K. Satish Kumar,
  and Sven Koenig

A SMT-based Implementation for Safety Checking of Parameterized
Multi-Agent Systems   259
  Paolo Felli, Alessandro Gianola, and Marco Montali

A Goal-Based Framework for Supporting Medical Assistance:
The Case of Chronic Diseases   281
  Milene Santos Teixeira, Célia da Costa Pereira, and Mauro Dragoni

Optimal Control of Pedestrian Flows by Congestion Forecasts Satisfying
User Equilibrium Conditions   299
  Hiroaki Yamada and Naoyuki Kamiyama

Short Papers

Automated Negotiation Mechanism and Strategy for Compensational
Vehicular Platooning   317
  Sînziana-Maria Sebe, Tim Baarslag, and Jörg P. Müller

A Cognitive Agent Framework in Information Retrieval: Using User
Beliefs to Customize Results   325
  Dima El Zein and Célia da Costa Pereira

Deep Reinforcement Learning for Pedestrian Guidance   334
  Hitoshi Shimizu, Takanori Hara, and Tomoharu Iwata

NegMAS: A Platform for Automated Negotiations   343
  Yasser Mohammad, Shinji Nakadai, and Amy Greenwald

Simulation of Unintentional Collusion Caused by Auto Pricing in Supply
Chain Markets   352
    Masanori Hirano, Hiroyasu Matsushima, Kiyoshi Izumi,
    and Taisei Mukai

Construct an Artificial Population with Urban and Rural Population
Differences Considered: To Support Long-Term Care System Evaluation
by Agent-Based Simulation   360
    Shuang Chang and Hiroshi Deguchi

Multi-Agent Path Finding with Destination Choice   368
    Ayano Okoso, Keisuke Otaki, and Tomoki Nishi

Abductive Design of BDI Agent-Based Digital Twins of Organizations   377
    Ahmad Alelaimat, Aditya Ghose, and Hoa Khanh Dam

Beliefs, Time and Space: A Language for the Yōkai Board Game.   386
    Dominique Longin, Emiliano Lorini, and Frédéric Maris

Argumentation-Based Explanations of Multimorbidity Treatment Plans   394
    Qurat-ul-ain Shaheen, Alice Toniolo, and Juliana K. F. Bowles

The Persistence of False Memory: Brain in a Vat Despite Perfect Clocks. . . .   403
    Thomas Schlögl, Ulrich Schmid, and Roman Kuznets

Box-Office Prediction Based on Essential Features Extracted
from Agent-Based Modeling.   412
    Koh Satoh and Shigeo Matsubara

Short Duration Aggregate Statistical Model Checking
for Multi-Agent Systems   420
    Ramesh Yenda and M. V. Panduranga Rao

Author Index   429

Full Papers

Implementation of Real Data for Financial Market Simulation Using Clustering, Deep Learning, and Artificial Financial Market

Masanori Hirano[1]([✉]) [iD], Hiroyasu Matsushima[2] [iD], Kiyoshi Izumi[1], and Hiroki Sakaji[1]

[1] School of Engineering, The University of Tokyo, Tokyo, Japan
hirano@g.ecc.u-tokyo.ac.jp, {izumi,sakaji}@sys.t.u-tokyo.ac.jp
[2] Center for Data Science Education and Research, Shiga University, Shiga, Japan
hiroyasu-matsushima@biwako.shiga-u.ac.jp
https://mhirano.jp/

Abstract. In this paper, we propose a new scheme for implementing the machine-learned trader-agent model in financial market simulations based on real data. The implementation is only focused on the high-frequency-trader market-making (HFT-MM) strategy. We first extract order data of HFT-MM traders from the real order data by clustering. Then, using the data, we build a deep learning model. Using the model, we build an HFT-MM trader model for simulations. In the simulations, we compared our new model and a traditional HFT-MM trader model in terms of divergence of the ordering behaviors. Our new trader model outperforms the traditional model. Moreover, we also found an obstacle of combination of data and simulation.

Keywords: Artificial financial market · Multi-agent simulation · Machine learning · Deep learning · Data mining · High-frequency trade · Market-making · Clustering

1 Introduction

Today, there are increasing systemic risks in the financial market. It is because the complexity of the financial market has been increasing. The financial crisis of 2007–2008 was one of the most famous examples of systemic risks. The beginning of the crisis was subprime mortgages. However, the fails in subprime mortgages spread widely, and it also affected stock markets. The other example of those risks is flash crashes. The most famous flash crash was the 2010 Flash Crash in the U.S. stock market on May 6, 2010. S&P 500 and Dow Jones Industrial Average rapidly dropped. The main reason for this crash was said to be one big sell order. Additionally, many algorithmic sell orders followed the big sell orders, and it was said to cause a significant crash. Supposedly the improvements of information technologies are attributed to risks in the financial market. However, the ground truth of these crashes has not been revealed.

T. Uchiya et al. (Eds.): PRIMA 2020, LNAI 12568, pp. 3–18, 2021.
https://doi.org/10.1007/978-3-030-69322-0_1

Although the prediction for these risks is essential, it has significant difficulties. There are two types of approaches to deal with these risks. One is data analysis. The approach of data analysis aims to find what happened during incidents, such as flash crashes, or to find the future risk seeds. Nevertheless, only using data, what we can find is only based on records. That is, data analysis cannot reveal future potential incidents that have never known or charted. The other approach is multi-agent simulations for financial markets. One of the significant benefits of multi-agent simulations is that it can test hypothetical situations. For example, Mizuta et al. [15] revealed the effect of tick size (the minimum ordering price unit) by using artificial financial markets. The artificial financial market is a virtual financial market on a computer, and it can test any situation. The change in tick size cannot be tested in the real financial market. Thus, in such a test, multi-agent simulation is beneficial.

However, the case studies using artificial market simulation are limited. It is because artificial market simulations cannot be trusted. The main problem is that many models employed in artificial markets are hand-made. So, there is a good chance that humans miss some real traders' behaviors during model-building.

Previously, Hirano et al. [5] showed the differences between actual data and simulated data. According to this study, the current simulation model can not completely reproduce an important feature in real markets.

Thus, building more realistic and trustworthy models is necessary. To do so, we should combine the benefits of both data analysis and multi-agent simulations. Recently, a lot of simulation study, such as [15], has already employed real data. However, usually, in these studies, data are only used for tuning parameters in models to fit their simulation results to the real data. Moreover, even in these studies, simulations employed human-made models. So, this type of data usage is not enough to make realistic and trustworthy models.

In this paper, we show the new way to combine a data-driven approach and a model-driven approach, i.e., multi-agent simulations, in financial market simulation. To evaluate the outcome of this combination, we only focused on a specific type of traders. The trader type is high-frequency trading market-making (HFT-MM) traders. In the HFT-MM strategy, traders make many frequent limit orders on the millisecond time scale. The profits are made by simultaneously placing bids (buy orders) and asks (sell orders) near the best prices. During HFT-MM operations, traders are at risk of price fluctuations. The usual profits they can get is limited to the spread between the best bid and ask. However, once the price moves dramatically, traders can lose greater than the spread. Thus, as a hedge against risk, the HFT-MM strategy must closely monitor price changes. The reason we focused on HFT-MM was it was very recognizable in the ordering data. Moreover, the usual HFT-MM model had already been established in previous work [1]. Therefore, it was suitable for a comparison between a traditional model-driven approach and our new model.

Our new model was validated to outperform the traditional model. This is the biggest contribution, and it can help future model building for multi-agent simulation. In addition, an obstacle to the combination was also identified.

2 Related Works

Considerable work trying to predict future-market performance are available. Several researchers have used support vector machines to predict prices or price indices [10,11]. Some studies have also used deep learning to predict market prices, movements, or turning points [4,17,23]. Moreover, Wang et al. [25] proposed CLVSA, which is a model for predicting price trends in financial markets based on long short-term memory (LSTM) and Seq2seq deep learning models. Tashiro and Izumi [18] proposed a short-term price prediction model using millisecond time scale order data and an LSTM network [8]. Further, the author recently extended this method [19] using a convolution neural network (CNN) [12].

Other types of approaches exist that can find distinct patterns in financial markets. Nanex [16] mined and reported some distinguishing ordering patterns from order data. Cont [3] obtained stylized facts of real financial markets with statistical analytics. Miyazaki et al. [13] detected illegal orders and trades by applying a Gaussian mixture model to raw ordering data.

Considerable work exist on multi-agent simulations for financial markets. Mizuta [14] demonstrated that multi-agent simulations of financial markets could contribute to the implementation of rules and regulations of actual financial markets. Torii et al. [21] used this approach to reveal how the flow of a price shock was transferred to other stocks. Their study was based on [2], who presented stylized trader models including fundamental, chartist, and noise factors. Mizuta et al. [15] tested the effect of tick size, i.e., the price unit for orders, which led to a discussion of tick-size devaluation in the Tokyo Stock Exchange (TSE). Hirano et al. [6,7] assessed the effect of regulating the capital adequacy ratio (CAR) based on the Basel regulatory framework and observed the risk of market price shock and depression caused by CAR regulation. As a platform for artificial market simulation, Torii et al. [22] proposed the platform "Plham." In this study, we have partially used the updated "PlhamJ" platform [20].

Moreover, some studies have focused on HFT or HFT-MM strategies. Hosaka [9] performed an HFT analysis based on the same data used in this study and found that many of the HFTs in the TSE market were executing market-making orders. Uno et al. [24] proposed a method of clustering traders based on financial market data (which we extended in this study) and demonstrated that it could identify the orders of traders employing distinctive strategies such as HFT-MM. Also, Hirano et al. [5] extended the method and compared actual data and simulated data. According to this study, the current simulation model can not completely reproduce an important feature in real markets. This study also bases on the works by Hirano et al. [5] and Uno et al. [24].

Researches focused on an agent model of HFT-MM also exist. Other researchers later built and demonstrated a model of HFT-MM traders [1] based on equations that considered market ordering strength, current fundamental prices, and trader inventories. Hirano *et al.* [5], we mentioned in the previous paragraph, also focused on the behavior of HFT-MM based on [1]. In this study, we also focused on reproducing the behavior of HFT-MM in simulations.

3   Data and Extracting HFT-MM Orders

In our study, we used two kinds of data on the Tokyo Stock Exchange (TSE). One is the FLEX Standard, which contains the order book information. The other is order book reproduction data. This data contains all complete orders and masked trader information and enables us to trace traders' behaviors. We used ordering data of HFT-MM traders, which is extracted from order book reproduction data. The way of the extraction is explained in the following.

FLEX Standard is only used for building our new model. However, ordering data of HFT-MM traders is used both for building our new model and for evaluation and comparison. The ordering data from January 2015 to July 2015 was used for building our new model. On the other hand, the ordering data from August 2015 was used for evaluation and comparison.

In the following, we explain the extraction of HFT-MM trader's ordering data from the order book reproduction data. Although order book reproduction data has masked traders' information, it cannot help us to identify the type or strategy of traders. So, to extract ordering data of HFT-MM only, we used a clustering analysis base on [24]. In our paper, we extended the method [24] in terms of the usage of the executed and market order ratio.

At first, we calculated the (ActionsPerTicker) for each trader:

$$(\text{ActionsPerTicker}) = \frac{(\text{newOrders}) + (\text{changeOrders}) + (\text{cancelOrders})}{(\text{numTickers})}.$$

Here, we calculate the index for each business day and we employ the median of the indices of business days in the data. Then to extract HFT only, we filter traders by (ActionsPerTicker) > 100. This gave us a total of 181 traders. Then, we also calculated the following indices for each trader on each day.

– Absolute inventory ratio:

$$(\text{InventoryRatio}) = \underset{\text{ticker}}{\text{Median}} \left(\left| \frac{(\text{soldVol.})_{\text{ticker}} - (\text{boughtVol.})_{\text{ticker}}}{(\text{soldVol.})_{\text{ticker}} + (\text{boughtVol.})_{\text{ticker}}} \right| \right) \qquad (1)$$

– Ratio of executed orders to all orders:

$$(\text{ExecutedRatio}) = \frac{(\text{executedOrders})}{(\text{newOrders})}. \qquad (2)$$

– Ratio of canceled orders to all orders:

$$(\text{CancelRatio}) = \frac{(\text{cancelOrders})}{(\text{newOrders})}. \tag{3}$$

– Ratio of market orders to all orders:

$$(\text{MarketOrderRatio}) = \frac{(\text{marketOrders})}{(\text{newOrders})}. \tag{4}$$

– Natural logarithm of the number of tickers traded per one gateway called virtual server (VS)[1]:

$$(\text{TickerPerVSLOG}) = \ln\left\{ \frac{(\text{numTikcer})}{(\text{numVS})} \right\}. \tag{5}$$

– Natural logarithm of the number of actions per ticker:

$$(\text{ActionsPerTickerLOG}) = \ln(\text{ActionsPerTicker}). \tag{6}$$

After calculating these indices for each day, we took the median values. These indices are corresponding to the features of HFT-MM, i.e., low inventory ratios (InventoryRatio), low executed ratios (ExecutedRatio), high cancel ratios (CancelRatio), and very low market order ratios (MarketOrderRatio). Then, we normalized all indices over traders before clustering analysis. The clustering analysis we employed was hierarchical clustering with Ward's method, Euclidean distances, and a limit of ten clusters.

As a result, we found one cluster which satisfies all criteria for HFT-MM, i.e., low inventory ratios (InventoryRatio), low executed ratios (ExecutedRatio), high cancel ratios (CancelRatio), and very low market order ratios (MarketOrderRatio). In the cluster, there are seven traders. To ensure that these seven traders employ the HFT-MM strategy, we confirmed it by plotting their ordering histories and stock prices. Thus, finally, we got the ordering data of HFT-MM.

4   Trader Models

4.1   Stylized Trader Model

We build a stylized trade model based on [21], which was based on [2]. At time t, a stylized trader agent i decides its trading actions based on the following. This type of agent has three factors in deciding its actions. The three factors are fundamental, chartist, and noise factors. First, agents calculate these three factors.

---

[1] Usually, due to the limitation of transactions per one VS, traders use multiple VS.

– Fundamental factor:

$$F_t^i = \frac{1}{\tau^{*i}} \ln \left\{ \frac{p^*_{(t-100)}}{p_{(t-100)}} \right\},\tag{7}$$

where τ^{*i} is agent i's mean-reversion-time constant, p_t^* is the fundamental price at the time t, and p_t is the price at time t. Stylized trader agents have an information time delay (the details will be explained in Sect. 5); therefore, they always refer to the information from 100 steps earlier.

– Chartist factor:

$$C_t^i = \frac{1}{\tau^i} \sum_{j=1}^{\tau^i} r_{(t-100-j)} = \frac{1}{\tau^i} \sum_{j=1}^{\tau^i} \ln \frac{p_{(t-100-j)}}{p_{(t-100-j-1)}},\tag{8}$$

where τ^i is agent i's time window size and r_t is the logarithm return at time t.

– Noise factor:

$$N_t^i \sim \mathcal{N}(0, \sigma),\tag{9}$$

denoting that N_t^i obeys a normal distribution with zero mean and variance $(\sigma)^2$.

Then, agents calculate the weighted average of these three factors.

$$\widehat{r_t^i} = \frac{1}{w_F^i + w_C^i + w_N^i} \left(w_F^i F_t^i + w_C^i C_t^i + w_N^i N_t^i \right),\tag{10}$$

where w_F^i, w_C^i, w_N^i are the weights of agent i for each factor.

In the next step, the expected price of agent i is calculated using the following equation:

$$\widehat{p_t^i} = p_{(t-100)} \exp \left(\widehat{r_t^i} \tau^i \right).\tag{11}$$

Then, using a fixed margin of $k^i \in [0, 1]$, the actual order prices are determined using the following rules.

– If $\widehat{p_t^i} > p_t$, agent i places a bid at the price

$$\min \left\{ \widehat{p_t^i}(1 - k^i), p_t^{\text{bid}} \right\}.\tag{12}$$

– If $\widehat{p_t^i} < p_t$, agent i places an ask at the price

$$\max \left\{ \widehat{p_t^i}(1 + k^i), p_t^{\text{ask}} \right\}.\tag{13}$$

Here, p_t^{bid} and p_t^{ask} are the best bid prices and the best ask price, respectively.

In addition to the price calculation above, we implemented a cancel routine. It is because the original model [21] aimed to regenerate limited stylized facts in financial markets and ignore the order book state. So, the model without cancel routine accumulated its order too much. Thus, we decide to add a cancel routine to the model. The routine is very simple: stylized traders cancel all orders before making new orders.

The parameters that we employed for this type of trader are $w_F^i \sim Ex(1.0), w_C^i \sim Ex(1.0), w_C^i \sim Ex(0.1), \sigma = 0.001, \tau^* \in [50, 100]$, and $\tau \in [100, 200]$. Apart from weights, we mainly determined these parameters based on the work of [21]. Here, $Ex(\lambda)$ indicated an exponential distribution with an expected value of λ.

4.2   Traditional HFT-MM Trader Model

The HFT-MM trader agents in this study were based on [1]. At time t, agent i calculates the ask and bid prices as the following.

1. Calculate agent i's mid-price:

$$\widehat{p_{mid,t}^i} = p_t^* - \gamma^i \left(\widehat{\sigma^i}\right)^2 T^i q_t^i, \tag{14}$$

where γ^i is agent i's risk hedge level, $\widehat{\sigma^i}$ is agent i's observed standard deviation in the last τ^i steps, τ^i is agent i's time window size as defined previously, T^i is the time until their strategy is optimized, and q_t^i is agent i's inventory. T^i is the parameter in the optimization process for deriving this equation, which we set to 1.

2. Agent i's price interval between ask and bid:

$$\delta_t^i = \gamma^i \left(\widehat{\sigma^i}\right)^2 T^i + \frac{2}{\gamma^i} \ln\left(1 + \frac{\gamma^i}{k}\right), \tag{15}$$

where k is a parameter for the order arrival time, which depends on $Ex(k)$. In this simulation, we employed $k = 1.5$, which was the same as that used in [1].

3. Agent i's bid and ask price is calculated as

$$\widehat{p_t^{bid}} = \widehat{p_{mid,t}^i} - \frac{\delta_t^i}{2}, \quad \widehat{p_t^{ask}} = \widehat{p_{mid,t}^i} + \frac{\delta_t^i}{2}. \tag{16}$$

4. Then, agent i places a bid at the following price

$$\min\left\{\widehat{p_t^{bid}}, p_t^{bid}\right\}, \tag{17}$$

where p_t^{bid} is the best bid price, and agent i places an ask at the following price

$$\max\left\{\widehat{p_t^{ask}}, p_t^{ask}\right\}, \tag{18}$$

where p_t^{ask} is the best ask price.

In addition to the calculation above, we added cancel routine. First, agents cancel orders whose prices are worse than $\widehat{p_t^{bid}}$ and $\widehat{p_t^{ask}}$. Second, we set the maximum numbers of either bids or asks to 10. If ten orders exist on the order books, agents cancel the oldest order. Moreover, all orders will expire after a certain time. The expiration period is the same as the time window sizes of the agents.

4.3   HFT-MM Machine Learned (ML) Trader Model

As our newly proposed model, we build an HFT-MM ML model. Here, we used two kinds of data. One is detailed ordering data of HFT-MM. The data details are explained in Sect. 3. The other is data called FLEX Standard. FLEX Standard is the order book data in TSE. And it contains the real-time order volume at prices such as ask/bid market, the best, second, third, $\cdots$, and eighth bid/ask, and the over. So, we used this data as the inputs representing market states.

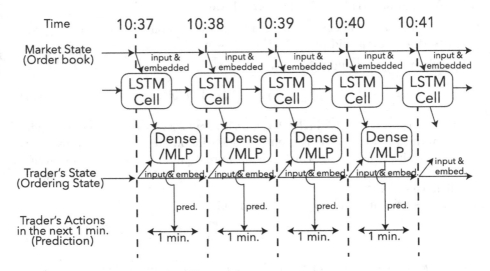

Fig. 1. Overview of our deep learning model. This takes the market state and a trader's ordering state during a one-minute interval as the input and predicts the trader's actions over the next one minute.

Figure 1 gives an overview of our model. This model is a kind of deep learning model to predict the future behavior of the traders. In this model, we employed an LSTM [8] for processing time-series market states.

As a market state, we input data from FLEX Standard. The orders are divided into 18 classes: (1) best bid, (2–8) 1–7 tick(s) below the best bid, (9) 8 or more ticks below the best bid, (10) best ask, (11–17) 1–7 tick(s) above the best ask, and (18) 8 or more ticks above the best ask. Inputs data are turned into percentages of all volumes on the order book. In addition to these 18 classes, we include two features describing the best bid and ask prices. Thus, LSTM receives a total of 20 input features.

As another input representing the traders' ordering state, we input the detailed order data of HFT-MM. This data contains the orders' placement state at each minute. The 18 classes exists: (1) best bid, (2–8) 1–7 tick(s) below the best bid, (9) 8 or more ticks below the best bid, (10) best ask, (11–17) 1–7 tick(s) above the best ask, (18) 8 or more ticks above the best ask. These values are also the percentage of all volume of the current trader's orders, but when there is no existing order, these values are 0.0.

After the processing by LSTM and Dense/MLP layer in Fig. 1, our model predicts the probabilities of the actions in the next minute. The 21 possible ordering actions are (1) above best bid, (2) best bid, (3–9) 1–7 tick(s) below the best bid, (10) 8 or more ticks below the best bid, (11) below best ask, (12) best ask, (13–19) 1–7 tick(s) above the best ask, (20) 8 or more ticks above the best ask, and (21) other (do nothing). For the prediction, we used the softmax layer. And, for the model training, we used Adam optimizer and loss function of mean squared error (MSE).

The model details are tuned in hyperparameter tuning. Here, we divided the data into 90% training and 10% validation sets. The data was from January 2015 to July 2015 (143 business days). As a result, LSTM with a hidden layer size of 523 with an embedded size of 505, a dense layer with an embedded size of 310, and a ReLU activation function are employed.

Using the trained ML model, we build a model for simulations. As inputs for the model, we made the same inputs in simulations as the inputs in machine learning. Then, through the ML model, we can get the predicted probabilities of the next action of HFT-MM traders. However, these outputs have limited numbers of action classes, as we mentioned above. Some classes, (1) above best bid, (10) 8 or more ticks below the best bid, (11) below best ask, or (20) 8 or more ticks above the best ask, do not have enough information to decide a specific trading action. Thus, we added the action criteria. If the prediction is (1) or (11), the trader bid/ask $n(n \in [1, 2, 3, 4])$ ticks above/below the best price at the probability corresponding to $\sum_{k=n}^{4} \frac{1}{4k}$. If the prediction is (10) or (20), the trader bid/ask $n(n \in [8, 9, 10, 11])$ ticks below/above the best price at the probability of a quarter. In other words, if the prediction is (1) or (11), the probabilities of actions for 1, 2, 3, 4 ticks above/below the best price are $25/48, 13/48, 7/48, 1/16$, respectively. It corresponds to `randInt(randInt(4))+1`. If the prediction is (10) or (20), the probabilities of actions for 8, 9, 10, 11 ticks below/above the best price are $1/4$ at each action.

5 Simulations

We ran two types of simulations.

1. 1,000 stylized traders vs. 1 traditional HFT-MM trader
2. 1,000 stylized traders vs. 1 HFT-MM ML trader

Stylized trader agent has the opportunity to place orders only every 100 steps. These opportunities do not simultaneously arrive. For example, agent 1 has opportunities in the first step of every 100 steps, and agent 2 has opportunities in the second step of every 100 steps. In addition, as mentioned in Sect. 4.1, stylized traders can access market information with a delay of 100 steps. On the other hand, two types of HFT-MM trader models can place their orders at any time. They also can immediately access any information from the market.

These correspond to the differences between the access speed to markets of HFT-MM and stylized traders, i.e., ordering speed and speed of accessing and processing market information. In the real market, HFT-MM traders locate their Algo ordering servers in the space provided by stock exchange markets to reduce information and ordering latencies.

The market mechanism is the continuous double auction system. We implemented this mechanism in our simulation using the platform known as "PlhamJ" [20]. We set the market start price to 1000. Moreover, fundamental price movement accords to a geometric Brownian motion (GBM) with a standard deviation of 0.0001. We obtained this setting empirically by investigating real intra-day price changes, which were roughly 1%. The tick size was set to 1.

When the simulations start, all the stylized trader agents had 50 shares. In the simulation, 100 steps existed before the artificial market opening, 500 steps to market stabilization, and 10,000 steps in the test.

Moreover, we ran 21 simulations for each type of simulation. It is because the number of business days in August 2015, which is the test period in our study, was 21.

After running 21 simulations for each type of simulation, we compared the 21 data from the simulations and 21 data from real data in August 2015. In the analysis, we focused on how far the number of ticks was between the best price and the trader's orders. It is because, here, we should analyze the HFT-MM trader's behavior in real markets and simulations. The key feature of the HFT-MM trader's behavior is the price of their bids/asks. Thus, in this paper, we show the comparisons and statistical tests in HFT-MM traders' bids/asks prices.

6 Results

6.1 Comparison of Ordering Price Distribution

We first compare the ordering price distribution of HFT-MM.

The results are shown in Fig. 2. In this figure, the horizontal axis represents ticks between the best price and the ordering price. If the order is bid, the horizontal axis indicates the number of ticks of the order below the best bid, and the minus tick indicates that the order is placed above the best bid. On the other hand, if the order is ask, the horizontal axis indicates the number of ticks of the order above the best ask, and the minus tick indicates that the order was placed below the best ask. The vertical axis indicates the relative frequencies among order volumes, which are placed between −5 ticks and 15 ticks.

This result roughly suggests that the traditional HFT-MM trader model cannot replicate the tail of the ordering price distribution among ticks in a range from 5 to 12. Moreover, the traditional model far more frequently places its orders at the best price (at the 0 tick in the figure) than actual data. However, by only using this plot, we cannot judge which model is better. Therefore, as the next step, we introduce a statistical test.

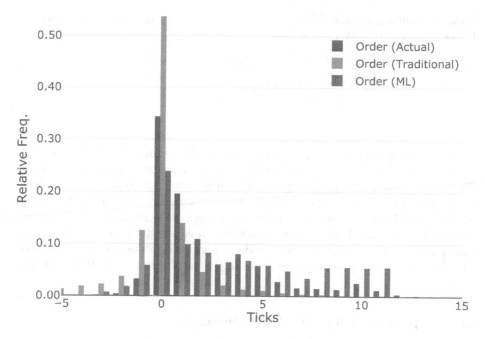

Fig. 2. Ordering Price Distribution. The horizontal axis represents the ticks between the best price and the ordering price. The minus ticks denote that the orders were placed above the best bid or below the best ask. The vertical axis represents the relative frequency among order volumes, which are placed between −5 ticks and 15 ticks. The blue bars correspond to the results from actual data from the 21 business days in August 2015; the orange bars correspond to the results from 21 simulations1 with the traditional HFT-MM trader model; the green bars correspond to the results from 21 simulation2 with the HFT-MM ML model. (Color figure online)

6.2   Comparison by Kullback–Leibler Divergence

As a statistical metric for the divergence between two distribution of the actual data and the data from simulations, we employ Kullback–Leibler divergence. Kullback–Leibler divergence is defined by

$$D_{KL}(P, Q) = \sum_{x \in \mathbb{X}} P(x) \log_2 \left(\frac{P(x)}{Q(x)} \right),\qquad(19)$$

where x represents ticks in Fig. 2, and $\mathbb{X}$ is $[-5, -4, \cdots, 15]$, $Q(x)$ represents relative frequency of actual data at x ticks of 21 business days, and $P(x)$ represents relative frequency of simulation data from only one try in 21 tries. $D_{KL}(P, Q)$ is calculated for each of the 21 simulations. Subsequently, we calculate the mean and standard errors for $D_{KL}(P, Q)$ between actual data and the traditional HFT-MM trader and HFT-MM ML models. The results are shown in Table 1.

Table 1. Kullback–Leibler divergences between the actual data and the traditional HFT-MM trader HFT-MM ML models.

Q	P	D_{KL}
Actual	Traditional	0.730009 ± 0.119884
Actual	ML	0.648459 ± 0.957854

According to Table 1, the HFT-MM ML model marginally outperformed the traditional HFT-MM trader model with respect to its fitness for actual data. The less Kullback–Leibler divergence, the more similar two distributions are. And if P and Q are the same, Kullback–Leibler divergence would be 0. So, the less Kullback–Leibler divergence means the better result. However, the standard error of the Kullback–Leibler divergence between actual data and the data from simulations with the HFT-MM ML model is significant. Therefore, in the next subsection, we conduct a deeper analysis of the results from the HFT-MM ML model.

6.3 Deep Analysis for ML Model Simulation

To identify the cause of the significant variance, we plot the frequency distribution of the Kullback–Leibler divergence in Fig. 3.

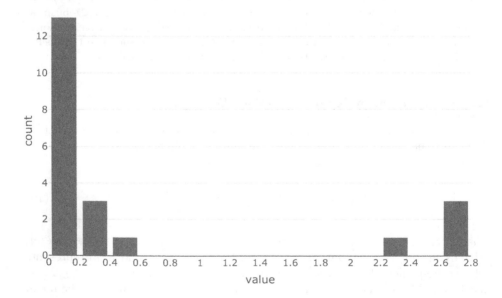

Fig. 3. Histogram of the Kullback–Leibler divergences between the actual data and the data simulated by the HFT-MM ML model. There are 21 results in total.

As shown in the Fig. 3, the Kullback–Leibler divergence exceeded 2.2 in four out of the 21 simulations. As a result of the investigation of these four situations, their ordering price distribution of HFT-MM was found to be completely different from real data. In all of these failure cases, the HFT-MM ML model published a lot of orders whose prices are far more than eight ticks from the best price. These actions are obviously inappropriate as HFT-MM traders' actions. Therefore, we decided to omit the four simulations whose Kullback–Leibler divergences were significant and more than 2.2. Subsequently, we conducted the same analyses like those in Sect. 6.1 and 6.2.

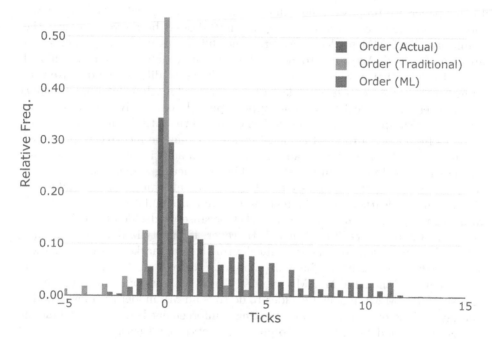

Fig. 4. Ordering Price Distribution. The blue bars correspond to the results from actual data from 21 business days in August 2015; the orange bars correspond to the results from 21 simulations1 with the traditional HFT-MM trader model; the green bars correspond to the results from 17 simulations2 with the HFT-MM ML model (four simulations2 are omitted). (Color figure online)

The results after excluding the errant simulations are shown in Fig. 4 and Table 2. In Fig. 4, the fitness of the HFT-MM ML model for the actual data is much better than that without omission. This improvement is confirmed in Table 2. The Kullback–Leibler divergence between the actual data and the HFT-MM ML model is considerably improved by omitting the four simulations. The four omitted simulations not only decrease the standard error but also decrease the mean.

Table 2. Kullback–Leibler divergences between the actual data and the traditional HFT-MM trader HFT-MM ML models with omissions.

Q	P	D_{KL}
Actual	Traditional	0.730009 ± 0.119884
Actual	ML (w/ omissions)	0.186192 ± 0.085099

7 Discussion

In this paper, we proposed a new simulation model using real data and the ML model. According to the results, this attempt showed better results than the traditional HFT-MM model. However, some difficulties in the implementation are also identified. According to Sect. 6.3, some simulations with our new model showed results that were worse than those with the traditional model. We presume that this was because of the lack of robustness of machine learning. Usually, machine learning is weak for out-of-sample inputs. In our study, simulations can make out-of-sample states. Therefore, if the state of the artificial financial market deviates from that of the real financial market, it may be incorrectly processed by our ML model. Even if we train our model with additional training data, we will not be able to cover all the states while conducting simulations. However, we assume that some solutions exist. One is that all things while conducting simulations are learned from the real market. In our simulation, only the HFT-MM ML trader learns from the real market because we decided to compare the new model and the traditional model. However, if the stylized traders are also replaced with the stylized traders trained with the real market data, the market states in the simulations will be more similar to the real market. It can improve the response of the HFT-MM ML models. The other solution is making a more robust HFT-MM ML model. One idea to do so is an ML model with fewer nodes and layers. The other idea is implementing reinforcement learning to the model to ensure the model can be used to pursue investment returns.

In future work, we should conduct additional implementations. First, our clustering method should be generalized, and we should make the method applicable to the traders other than HFTs. Second, machine learning models can process more detailed data, including orders placed over eight ticks from the best price. Finally, we should test deep learning architectures other than LSTM and MLP.

8 Conclusion

In this paper, we have developed a new model for the artificial financial market. The model represents HFT-MM and is built by using real traders' ordering data of HFT-MM. We ran simulations and compared our new HFT-MM ML model and the traditional HFT-MM model. Our HFT-MM ML model marginally outperformed the traditional HFT-MM model. The problem of implementing an ML model to simulations was identified. Omitting a few numbers of failed simulations, our ML model showed promising performance. We also identified important goals for future work, such as improving the robustness of the ML model.

Acknowledgement. We thank the Japan Exchange Group, Inc. for providing the data. This research was supported by MEXT via Exploratory Challenges on Post-K computer (study on multilayered multiscale space-time simulations for social and economic phenomena). This research also used the computational resources of the HPCI system provided by the Information Technology Center at The University of Tokyo, and the Joint Center for Advanced High Performance Computing (JCAHPC) through the HPCI System Research Project (Project ID: hp190150).

References

1. Avellaneda, M., Stoikov, S.: High-frequency trading in a limit order book. Quant. Finance **8**(3), 217–224 (2008). https://doi.org/10.1080/14697680701381228
2. Chiarella, C., Iori, G.: A simulation analysis of the microstructure of double auction markets. Quant. Finance **2**(5), 346–353 (2002). https://doi.org/10.1088/1469-7688/2/5/303
3. Cont, R.: Empirical properties of asset returns: stylized facts and statistical issues. Quant. Finance **1**(2), 223–236 (2001)
4. Dixon, M.F., Polson, N.G., Sokolov, V.O.: Deep learning for spatio-temporal modeling: dynamic traffic flows and high frequency trading. Quant. Finance **19**(4), 549–570 (2019)
5. Hirano, M., Izumi, K., Matsushima, H., Sakaji, H.: Comparing actual and simulated HFT traders' behavior for agent design. J. Artif. Soc. Soc. Simul. **23**(3), 6 (2020). https://doi.org/10.18564/jasss.4304. http://jasss.soc.surrey.ac.uk/23/3/6.html
6. Hirano, M., Izumi, K., Sakaji, H., Shimada, T., Matsushima, H.: Impact assessments of the CAR regulation using artificial markets. Proc. Int. Workshop Artif. Market **2018**, 43–58 (2018)
7. Hirano, M., Izumi, K., Shimada, T., Matsushima, H., Sakaji, H.: Impact analysis of financial regulation on multi-asset markets using artificial market simulations. J. Risk Financ. Manage. **13**(4), 75 (2020). 10.3390/jrfm13040075. https://www.mdpi.com/1911-8074/13/4/75
8. Hochreiter, S., Schmidhuber, J.: Long short-term memory. Neural Comput. **9**(8), 1735–1780 (1997)
9. Hosaka, G.: Analysis of High-frequency Trading at Tokyo Stock Exchange (2014). https://www.jpx.co.jp/corporate/research-study/working-paper/tvdivq0000008q5y-att/JPX_working_paper_No.4.pdf
10. Kercheval, A.N., Zhang, Y.: Modelling high-frequency limit order book dynamics with support vector machines. Quant. Finance **15**(8), 1315–1329 (2015)
11. Kim, K.j.: Financial time series forecasting using support vector machines. Neurocomputing **55**, 307–319 (2003)
12. Krizhevsky, A., Sutskever, I., Hinton, G.: ImageNet classification with deep convolutional neural networks. In: Advances in Neural Information Processing Systems, vol. 25, NeurIPS 2012, pp. 1097–1105 (2012)

13. Miyazaki, B., Izumi, K., Toriumi, F., Takahashi, R.: Change detection of orders in stock markets using a Gaussian mixture model. Intell. Syst. Account. Finance Manage. **21**(3), 169–191 (2014)
14. Mizuta, T.: An Agent-based Model for Designing a Financial Market that Works Well (2019). http://arxiv.org/abs/1906.06000
15. Mizuta, T., et al.: Effects of price regulations and dark pools on financial market stability: an investigation by multiagent simulations. Intell. Syst. Account. Finance Manage. **23**(1–2), 97–120 (2016). https://doi.org/10.1002/isaf.1374
16. Nanex: Nanex - Market Crop Circle of The Day (2010). http://www.nanex.net/FlashCrash/CCircleDay.html
17. Sirignano, J.A.: Deep learning for limit order books. Quant. Finance **19**(4), 549–570 (2019)
18. Tashiro, D., Izumi, K.: Estimating stock orders using deep learning and high frequency data. In: Proceedings of the 31nd Annual Conference of the Japanese Society for Artificial, pp. 2D2-2 (2017). (in Japanese)
19. Tashiro, D., Matsushima, H., Izumi, K., Sakaji, H.: Encoding of high-frequency order information and prediction of short-term stock price by deep learning. Quant. Finance **19**(9), 1499–1506 (2019)
20. Torii, T., et al.: PlhamJ (2019). https://github.com/plham/plhamJ
21. Torii, T., Izumi, K., Yamada, K.: Shock transfer by arbitrage trading: analysis using multi-asset artificial market. Evol. Inst. Econ. Rev. **12**(2), 395–412 (2015)
22. Torii, T., Kamada, T., Izumi, K., Yamada, K.: Platform design for large-scale artificial market simulation and preliminary evaluation on the K computer. Artif. Life Robot. **22**(3), 301–307 (2017)
23. Tsantekidis, A., Passalis, N., Tefas, A., Kanniainen, J., Gabbouj, M., Iosifidis, A.: Using deep learning to detect price change indications in financial markets. In: Proceedings of the 25th European Signal Processing Conference, pp. 2580–2584 (2017)
24. Uno, J., Goshima, K., Tobe, R.: Cluster analysis of trading behavior: an attempt to extract HFT. In: The 12th Annual Conference of Japanese Association of Behavioral Economics and Finance (2018). (in Japanese)
25. Wang, J., Sun, T., Liu, B., Cao, Y., Zhu, H.: CLVSA: a convolutional lstm based variational sequence-to-sequence model with attention for predicting trends of financial markets. In: Proceedings of the Twenty-Eighth International Joint Conference on Artificial Intelligence (IJCAI-19), pp. 3705–3711 (2019)

Hybrid Dynamic Programming for Simultaneous Coalition Structure Generation and Assignment

Fredrik Präntare[✉] [ID] and Fredrik Heintz[ID]

Linköping University, 581 83 Linköping, Sweden
{fredrik.prantare,fredrik.heintz}@liu.se

Abstract. We present, analyze and benchmark two algorithms for simultaneous coalition structure generation and assignment: one based entirely on dynamic programming, and one anytime hybrid approach that uses branch-and-bound together with dynamic programming. To evaluate the algorithms' performance, we benchmark them against both CPLEX (an industry-grade solver) and the state-of-the-art using difficult randomized data sets of varying distribution and complexity. Our results show that our hybrid algorithm greatly outperforms CPLEX, pure dynamic programming and the current state-of-the-art in all of our benchmarks. For example, when solving one of the most difficult problem sets, our hybrid approach finds optimum in roughly 0.1% of the time that the current best method needs, and it generates 98% efficient interim solutions in milliseconds in all of our anytime benchmarks; a considerable improvement over what previous methods can achieve.

Keywords: Combinatorial assignment · Dynamic programming · Coalition formation · Coalition structure generation · Games with alternatives.

1 Introduction

Forming teams of agents and coordinating them is central to many applications in both artificial intelligence and operations research. In cooperative game theory, this is known as *coalition formation*—the process by which heterogeneous agents group together to achieve some goal. Central to this endeavor is: i) optimally partitioning the set of agents into disjoint groups—an optimization problem known as *coalition structure generation* (CSG) [11,13]; and ii) deciding on the teams' individual goals, which can be modelled as a *linear assignment* problem [2,4]. Combining these problems, and solving them simultaneously, can potentially both reduce a problem's computational complexity and increase the agents' aggregated potential utility and performance [6]. This combined CSG and linear assignment problem is a general case of utilitarian combinatorial assignment, and it is known as *simultaneous coalition structure generation and assignment* (SCSGA) in the multi-agent research community.

© Springer Nature Switzerland AG 2021
T. Uchiya et al. (Eds.): PRIMA 2020, LNAI 12568, pp. 19–33, 2021.
https://doi.org/10.1007/978-3-030-69322-0_2

Technically, from a game theoretic perspective, SCSGA is a CSG problem for *games with alternatives* [1]. In this game type, there is a set of agents $A = \{a_1, ..., a_n\}$, and several alternatives $t_1, ..., t_m$, of which each agent must choose exactly one, with $C_i \subseteq \{a_1, ..., a_n\}$ defined to be the set of agents who choose alternative t_i. The vector $\langle C_1, ..., C_m \rangle$ thus constitutes an ordered coalition structure over A. In SCSGA, the goal is to find an ordered coalition structure that maximizes welfare in such contexts.

Moreover, SCSGA algorithms have a range of potential different applications in many domains. They can for example be used to deploy personnel to different locations and/or allocate alternatives to agents (examples include utilitarian course allocation and winner determination in combinatorial auctions). SCSGA is also the only CSG paradigm in the literature that has been demonstrated for use in a real-world commercial application to improve agents' coordination capabilities, wherein it has been used to optimally form and deploy teams of agents to different geospatial regions [5]. However, the state-of-the-art algorithm can only solve problems with severely limited inputs with up to roughly 20 agents in reasonable time. Although this algorithm performs fairly well in practice and greatly outperforms the industry-grade solver CPLEX, it suffers from there being no proven guarantee that it can find an optimum without first evaluating all the m^n possible feasible solutions. [7]

To address these issues, we develop an algorithm with a proven worst-case time complexity better (lower) than $\mathcal{O}(m^n)$, and devise a second algorithm that finds both optimal and anytime (interim) solutions faster than the state-of-the-art. More specifically, we focus on the paradigm *dynamic programming* to accomplish this, and investigate how dynamic programming can be combined with branch-and-bound to obtain the best features of both. Against this background, our two main contributions that advances the state-of-the-art are the following:

- We develop, present and benchmark *DP*—a simple, easy-to-implement dynamic programming algorithm for SCSGA. We also analyze it, and prove its correctness and worst-case time/memory complexity, consequently showing that it has the lowest worst-case time complexity proven in the literature.
- We develop and present *HY*—a hybrid optimal anytime SCSGA algorithm that uses dynamic programming together with branch-and-bound. Subsequently, we empirically show that our hybrid algorithm greatly outperforms both current state-of-the-art and the industry-grade solver CPLEX in all of our benchmarks. We also provide empirical data that shows that the hybrid algorithm is more robust to the distribution of values compared to the state-of-the-art.

The remainder of this paper is structured as follows. We begin by presenting related work in Sect. 2. Then, in Sect. 3, we define the basic concepts that we use throughout this report. In Sect. 4, we describe our pure dynamic programming algorithm, and in Sect. 5 we show how we combine dynamic programming techniques with branch-and-bound. In Sect. 6, we present our experiments. Finally, in Sect. 7, we conclude with a summary.

2   Related Work

The only optimal algorithm in the literature that has been developed for the SCSGA problem is the aforementioned branch-and-bound algorithm. (We improve on this work by combining it with dynamic programming to construct a stronger hybrid algorithm.) Apart from this, a plethora of different optimal algorithms have been developed for the closely related *characteristic function game* CSG problem. The first algorithm presented for it used dynamic programming [14], which [8] then improved upon by finding ways to guarantee optimality while making fewer evaluations. These algorithms both run in $\mathcal{O}(3^n)$ for n agents, and have the disadvantage that they produce no interim solutions—i.e., they generate no solution at all if they are terminated before completion. Subsequently, [12] presented an anytime tree search algorithm based on branch-and-bound that circumvented this issue, but at the cost of a much worse worst-case time complexity of $\mathcal{O}(n^n)$. In addition to these algorithms, several hybrid algorithms have been proposed. They fuse earlier methods in an attempt to obtain the best features of their constituent parts [3,9,10].

However, all of these CSG algorithms were specifically designed for problems without alternatives. Consequently, they: a) only consider *unordered* coalition structures, while we need to consider all permutations of them; b) do not allow empty coalitions in solutions—in SCSGA, an empty coalition corresponds to no agents choosing an alternative, while in CSG, empty coalitions have no clear purpose or practical interpretation; and c) evaluate coalition structures of any size (we are only interested in size-m ordered coalition structures, where m is the number of alternatives). These properties arguably renders it difficult (or impossible) to use them for SCSGA in a straightforward fashion without greatly sacrificing computational performance.

3   Basic Concepts and Notation

The SCSGA problem is defined as follows:

Input: a set of agents $A = \{a_1, ..., a_n\}$, a vector of alternatives $T = \langle t_1, ..., t_m \rangle$, and a function $v : 2^A \times T \mapsto \mathbb{R}$ that maps a value to every possible pairing of a coalition $C \subseteq A$ to an alternative $t \in T$.

Output: an *ordered coalition structure* (Definition 1) $\langle C_1, ..., C_m \rangle$ over A that maximizes $\sum_{i=1}^{m} v(C_i, t_i)$.

Definition 1. $\langle C_1, ..., C_m \rangle$ *is an ordered coalition structure over A if $C_i \cap C_j = \emptyset$ for all $i \neq j$, and $\bigcup_{i=1}^{m} C_i = A$. We omit the notion "over A" for brevity.*

As is common practice, we use:

$$V(S) = \sum_{i=1}^{m} v(C_i, t_i)$$

to denote the value of an ordered coalition structure $S = \langle C_1, ..., C_m \rangle$; the conventions $n = |A|$ and $m = |T|$ when it improves readability; and the terms *solution* and *ordered coalition structure* interchangeably. For a multiset X, we use $\mathcal{P}(X)$ to denote its powerset. We use Π_A for the set of all ordered coalition structures over A, and define:

$$\Pi_A^m = \{S \in \Pi_A : |S| = m\}.$$

Finally, we say that a solution S^* is *optimal* if and only if:

$$V(S^*) = \max_{S \in \Pi_A^m} V(S).$$

4   The Dynamic Programming Algorithm

The DP algorithm is straightforwardly based on computing the following recurrence:

$$w(U, k) = \begin{cases} v(U, t_k) & \text{if } k = 1 \\ \max_{C \in \mathcal{P}(U)} v(C, t_k) + w(U \setminus C, k - 1) & \text{if } k = 2, ..., m \end{cases} \tag{1}$$

where $U \subseteq A$. As shown in Theorem 1, this recurrence's value is equal to the value of the highest-valued k-sized ordered coalition structure over $U \subseteq A$.

Theorem 1. *If $U \subseteq A$ and $k \in \{1, ..., m\}$, then:*

$$w(U, k) = \max_{S \in \Pi_U^k} V(S).$$

Proof. By straightforward induction. This holds for $k = 1$, since $\langle U \rangle$ is the only 1-sized ordered coalition structure over U that exists, and consequently:

$$\max_{S \in \Pi_U^1} V(S) = V(\langle U \rangle) = v(U, t_1) = w(U, 1). \tag{2}$$

We now show for $j = 2, ..., m$, that if our theorem holds for $k = j - 1$, then it also holds for $k = j$. First, note that:

$$\max_{S \in \Pi_U^k} V(S) = \max_{C \in \mathcal{P}(U)} \left\{ v(C, t_k) + \max_{S \in \Pi_{U \setminus C}^{k-1}} V(S) \right\} \tag{3}$$

holds for $k = 2, ..., m$ and $U \subseteq A$. Now, for some $j \in \{2, ..., m\}$, let our inductive hypothesis be:

$$w(U, j - 1) = \max_{S \in \Pi_U^{j-1}} V(S)$$

for all $U \subseteq A$. This in conjunction with (1) gives:

$$w(U, j) = \max_{C \in \mathcal{P}(U)} \left\{ v(C, t_j) + \max_{S \in \Pi_{U \setminus C}^{j-1}} V(S) \right\}.$$

Consequently, together with (3), we have: $w(U, j) = \max_{S \in \Pi_U^j} V(S)$, which together with (2) proves the theorem. $\qquad\square$

Value	Prerequisite values
$w(\{a_1, a_2\}, 3)$	$w(\emptyset, 2)$, $w(\{a_1\}, 2)$, $w(\{a_2\}, 2)$, $w(\{a_1, a_2\}, 2)$
$w(\emptyset, 2)$	$w(\emptyset, 1)$
$w(\{a_1\}, 2)$	$w(\emptyset, 1)$, $w(\{a_1\}, 1)$
$w(\{a_2\}, 2)$	$w(\emptyset, 1)$, $w(\{a_2\}, 1)$
$w(\{a_1, a_2\}, 2)$	$w(\emptyset, 1)$, $w(\{a_1\}, 1)$, $w(\{a_2\}, 1)$, $w(\{a_1, a_2\}, 1)$
$w(\emptyset, 1)$	-
$w(\{a_1\}, 1)$	-
$w(\{a_2\}, 1)$	-
$w(\{a_1, a_2\}, 1)$	-

Fig. 1. The prerequisite values needed to compute $w(A, m)$ for $A = \{a_1, a_2\}$ and $m = 3$. The symbol "-" represents that no prerequisite values have to be computed.

Importantly for DP, the equality $w(A, m) = \max_{S \in \Pi_A^m} V(S)$ follows as a special case of Theorem 1. Consequently, a solution $S^* \in \Pi_A^m$ is optimal if and only if $V(S^*) = w(A, m)$. The DP algorithm works by computing $w(A, m)$, while simultaneously constructing two tables that are subsequently used to generate an optimal solution that corresponds to the process by which this value is computed. However, computing $w(A, m)$ recursively in a naïve fashion has the consequence that identical function calls have to be computed multiple times, as illustrated in Fig. 1.

In light of this, we introduce two different approaches for computing $w(A, m)$ that do not introduce such redundancy: Algorithm 1, which uses memoization to store intermediary results, so that a function call never has to be computed more than once; and Algorithm 2, which uses tabulation so that a value is only evaluated once all its prerequisite values have been computed.

Algorithm 1 : DPMemoization($U = A$, $k = m$)
Based on Theorem 1, this algorithm recursively computes $w(A, m)$, while simultaneously generating the two tables Γ_w and Γ_c.

1: **if** $\Gamma_w[U, k] \neq null$ **then**
2:     **return** $\Gamma_w[U, k]$
3: **if** $k = 1$ **then**
4:     $\Gamma_w[U, k] \leftarrow v(U, t_k)$; $\Gamma_c[U, k] \leftarrow U$ //Base case.
5:     **return** $v(U, t_k)$
6: **for all** $C \in \mathcal{P}(U)$ **do**
7:     $w \leftarrow v(C, t_k) + $ DPMemoization($U \setminus C, k - 1$)
8:     **if** $\Gamma_w[U, k] = null$, or $w > \Gamma_w[U, k]$ **then**
9:         $\Gamma_w[U, k] \leftarrow w$; $\Gamma_c[U, k] \leftarrow C$
10: **return** $\Gamma_w[U, k]$

Algorithm 2 : DPTabulation()

Based on Theorem 1, this algorithm iteratively computes $w(A, m)$, while simultaneously generating the two tables Γ_w and Γ_c.

1: **for all** $C \in \mathcal{P}(A)$ **do**
2:      $\Gamma_w[C, 1] \leftarrow v(C, t_1);\ \Gamma_c[C, 1] \leftarrow C$ //Base case.
3: **for** $k = 2, ..., m$ **do**
4:      **for all** $U \in \mathcal{P}(A)$ **do**
5:          **for all** $C \in \mathcal{P}(U)$ **do**
6:              $w \leftarrow v(C, t_k) + \Gamma_w[U \setminus C, k - 1]$
7:              **if** $\Gamma_w[U, k] = null$, or $w > \Gamma_w[U, k]$ **then**
8:                  $\Gamma_w[U, k] \leftarrow w;\ \Gamma_c[U, k] \leftarrow C$
9: **return** $\Gamma_w[A, m]$

For both approaches, the tables Γ_c and Γ_w are used to store the following coalitions and values:

- $\Gamma_c[U, k] \leftarrow U,$
- $\Gamma_w[U, k] \leftarrow v(U, t_k)$

for every $U \subseteq A$ and $k = 1$; and

- $\Gamma_c[U, k] \leftarrow \arg\max_{C \in \mathcal{P}(U)} v(C, t_k) + \Gamma_w[U \setminus C, k - 1],$
- $\Gamma_w[U, k] \leftarrow \max_{C \in \mathcal{P}(U)} v(C, t_k) + \Gamma_w[U \setminus C, k - 1]$

for every $U \subseteq A$ and $k = 2, ..., m$. If each coalition is represented in constant size using e.g., a fixed-size binary string defined by its *binary-coalition encoding* (Definition 2), these tables require $\mathcal{O}(m|\mathcal{P}(A)|) = \mathcal{O}(m2^n)$ space.

Definition 2. *The* binary coalition-encoding *of $C \subseteq A$ over $A = \langle a_1, ..., a_{|A|} \rangle$ is the binary string $j = b_{|A|}...b_1$ with:*

$$b_i = \begin{cases} 1 & if\ a_i \in C \\ 0 & otherwise \end{cases}$$

For example, the binary coalition-encoding of $\{a_1, a_3\}$ over $\langle a_1, a_2, a_3 \rangle$ is equal to 101.

To construct an optimal solution, DP uses Algorithm 3 together with the table Γ_c (that has been generated using either Algorithm 1 or Algorithm 2), with which DP's worst-case time complexity is $\mathcal{O}(m3^n)$, as shown in Theorem 2.

Algorithm 3 : DPConstruct()

Uses the table Γ_c (generated by e.g., Algorithm 1 or Algorithm 2) to construct an optimal ordered coalition structure.

1: $U \leftarrow A;\ S^* \leftarrow \emptyset_m$
2: **for** $i = m, ..., 1$ **do**
3:      $S^*[i] \leftarrow \Gamma_c[U, i];\ U \leftarrow U \setminus \Gamma_c[U, i]$
4: **return** S^*

Theorem 2. *DP's worst-case time complexity is $\mathcal{O}(m3^n)$.*

Proof. DPTabulation (Algorithm 2) makes $\mathcal{O}(2^n)$ elementary operations on lines 1–2, and then proceeds to perform a total of $\mathcal{O}(mQ_n)$ operations on lines 3–8 for some $Q_n \in \mathbb{N}^+$. DPConstruct runs in $\mathcal{O}(m)$. Therefore, DP's worst-case time complexity is equal to:

$$\mathcal{O}(2^n) + \mathcal{O}(mQ_n) + \mathcal{O}(m) = \mathcal{O}(2^n + mQ_n). \tag{4}$$

Now recall that, for a set with n elements, there exists exactly $\binom{n}{k}$ possible k-sized subsets. Consequently, we have:

$$Q_n = \sum_{i=0}^{n} \binom{n}{i} 2^i, \tag{5}$$

since we iterate over $(m-1)2^i$ i-sized subsets for $i = 0, ..., n$ on lines 4–5. Also, as a consequence of the *binomial theorem*, the following holds:

$$(1+2)^n = \sum_{i=0}^{n} \binom{n}{i} 1^{n-i} 2^i = \sum_{i=0}^{n} \binom{n}{i} 2^i.$$

From this and (5), it follows that $Q_n = (1+2)^n = 3^n$. This together with (4) proves the theorem.   □

5   The Hybrid Algorithm

Our hybrid algorithm (HY) is designed to combine the redundancy-eliminating capabilities of dynamic programming with the pruning abilities and anytime characteristics of branch-and-bound. In more detail, it incorporates these techniques with the search space presentation based on multiset permutations of integer partitions proposed by [6]. In their search space representation, each multiset permutation (ordered arrangement) of a size-m *zero-inclusive integer partition* of n (see Definition 3) corresponds to a set of solutions. More formally, if $P = \langle p_1, ..., p_m \rangle$ is such an ordered arrangement, it *represents* all solutions $\langle C_1, ..., C_m \rangle$ with $|C_i| = p_i$ for $i = 1, ..., m$.

Definition 3. *The multiset of non-negative integers $\{x_1, ..., x_k\}$ is a zero-inclusive integer partition of $y \in \mathbb{N}$ if:*

$$\sum_{i=1}^{k} x_i = y.$$

For example, the multiset $\{0, 1, 1, 2, 3\}$ is a zero-inclusive integer partition of 7, since $0 + 1 + 1 + 2 + 3 = 7$.

For brevity and convenience, we define the *subspace* $\mathcal{S}_P$ represented by P as the following set of solutions:

$$\mathcal{S}_P = \{\langle C_1, ..., C_m\rangle \in \Pi_A^m : |C_i| = p_i \text{ for } i = 1, ..., m\}.$$

For example, for a SCSGA problem instance with the set of agents $\{a_1, a_2, a_3\}$ and vector of alternatives $\langle t_1, t_2\rangle$ as input, $\langle 1, 2\rangle$ represents the following three solutions (and the subspace that constitutes them):

$$\langle\{a_1\}, \{a_2, a_3\}\rangle, \quad \langle\{a_2\}, \{a_1, a_3\}\rangle, \quad \langle\{a_3\}, \{a_1, a_2\}\rangle.$$

As shown by [6], it is possible to compute a lower and an upper bound for the value of the best solution in such a subspace without having to evaluate any ordered coalition structures. To accomplish this, first define:

$$\mathcal{K}_p = \{C \subseteq A : |C| = p\}.$$

Then, with the purpose to compute a lower bound, let:

$$\boldsymbol{A}(p, t) = \frac{1}{|\mathcal{K}_p|} \sum_{C \in \mathcal{K}_p} \boldsymbol{v}(C, t);$$

and to compute an upper bound, define:

$$\boldsymbol{M}(p, t) = \max_{C \in \mathcal{K}_p} \boldsymbol{v}(C, t).$$

A lower bound and an upper bound for all solutions represented by $P = \langle p_1, ..., p_m\rangle$ (if $\mathcal{S}_P \neq \emptyset$) can now be computed as $l_P = \sum_{i=1}^m \boldsymbol{A}(p_i, t_i)$ and $u_P = \sum_{i=1}^m \boldsymbol{M}(p_i, t_i)$, respectively. See [6] for proofs.

In light of these observations, we now propose a new algorithm (Algorithm 4) for searching such subspaces: *ADP* (for anytime DP). Technically, ADP uses depth-first branch-and-bound combined with an alteration of the dynamic programming techniques used in Algorithm 1. By using branch-and-bound, ADP only generates solutions that are better than the best solution that has already been found, and discards (prunes) branches of the recursion tree when they are deemed sufficiently bad. To accomplish this, ADP introduces the following variables:

- v^* : denotes the value of the best solution found so far; this is a globally kept variable initialized to $-\infty$, and it is not reinitialized when a subspace search is initiated.
- α : equals the sum of the values of all antecedent "fixed" coalition-to-alternative assignments (at shallower recursion depths).
- β : equals the most α can possibly increase at subsequent recursion steps deeper down in the recursion tree; it is initialized to u_P through a straightforward evaluation of the value function.

Algorithm 4 : $\mathrm{ADP}(P = \langle p_1, ..., p_m \rangle, \ U = A, \ k = m, \ \alpha = 0, \ \beta = u_P)$
Computes $\max_{S \in \mathcal{S}_P} \mathbf{V}(S)$ using dynamic programming together with depth-first branch-and-bound, while simultaneously generating entries for the tables Γ_c and Γ_w.

1: **if** $k = 1$ **then**   //Base case.
2:     **return** $\mathbf{v}(U, t_k)$
3: **if** $\alpha + \beta \leq v^*$ **then**
4:     **return** $-\infty$ //Cannot yield a better solution.
5: **if** $\Gamma_w[U, k]$ exists **then**   //Has this call been evaluated?
6:     **return** $\Gamma_w[U, k]$
7: $v \leftarrow -\infty; \ C \leftarrow \emptyset$
8: **for all** $C' \in \mathcal{P}(U) \cap \mathcal{K}_{p_k}$ **do**
9:     **if** computation budget is exhausted **then**
10:         **break**
11:         $\alpha' \leftarrow \alpha + \mathbf{v}(C', t_k); \ \ \beta' \leftarrow \beta - \mathbf{M}(p_k, t_k)$
12:         $v' \leftarrow \mathbf{v}(C', t_k) + \mathrm{ADP}(P, U \setminus C', k - 1, \alpha', \beta')$
13:     **if** $v' > v$ **then**
14:         $v \leftarrow v'; \ C \leftarrow C'$ //Found a better choice.
15: **if** $v \neq -\infty$ **then**
16:     $\Gamma_w[U, k] \leftarrow v; \ \Gamma_c[U, k] \leftarrow C$ //Cache best choice.
17:     **if** $\alpha + v > v^*$ **then**
18:         $v^* \leftarrow \alpha + v$ //We found a better solution.
19: **return** v

Consequently, since the sum $\alpha + \beta$ constitutes an upper bound on the recursion branch, the recursion can be discarded if $\alpha + \beta \leq v^*$ (see line 3 in Algorithm 4) without forfeiting optimality. Furthermore, ADP uses the tables Γ_c and Γ_w in the same fashion as DP uses them (i.e., to prevent evaluating the same function call again), with the difference that ADP only stores the values that are needed for generating the best solution for the subspace that is being investigated. The specific entries that are computed thus depends both on the subspace's representation, and the distribution of values—therefore, it is not clear beforehand how many entries that need to be computed (we investigate this further in Sect. 6.1). Finally, if Algorithm 4 returns a value larger than $-\infty$, then Γ_c can be used to construct a solution $\arg\max_{S \in \mathcal{S}_P} \mathbf{V}(S)$ in a similar fashion as DP does. If $-\infty$ is returned, then $\max_{S \in \mathcal{S}_P} \mathbf{V}(S) \leq v^*$.

To summarize, the complete hybrid algorithm (HY) works by continuously generating integer partitions, evaluating them, and then computing the aforementioned bounds of their multiset permutations with the aim to prune large portions of the search space. It thus generates the search space representation in a similar fashion as the state-of-the-art does. Then, when a subspace is to be searched, HY uses ADP to search it.

6   Benchmarks and Experiments

In accordance with the state-of-the-art for benchmarking SCSGA algorithms [6], we use *UPD*, *NPD* and *NDCS* for generating difficult problem instances:

- **UPD:** $v(C,t) \sim \mathcal{U}(0,1)$;
- **NPD:** $v(C,t) \sim \mathcal{N}(1,0.01)$; and
- **NDCS:** $v(C,t) \sim \mathcal{N}(|C|, \max(|C|, 10^{-9}))$;

for all $C \subseteq A$ and $t \in T$, where $\mathcal{U}(a,b)$ and $\mathcal{N}(\mu,\sigma^2)$ are the uniform and normal distributions, respectively. In our benchmarks, we store these values in an array, and we treat v as a black-box function that can be queried in $\mathcal{O}(1)$.

The result of each experiment was produced by calculating the average of the resulting values from 20 generated problem sets per experiment. Following best practice, we plot the 95% confidence interval in all graphs. All code was written in *C++11*, and all random numbers were generated with

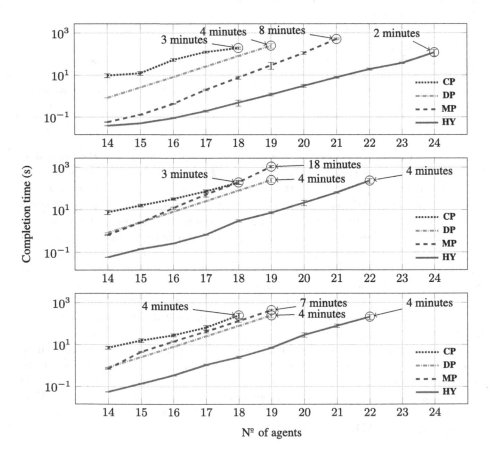

Fig. 2. The completion time (log-scale) for optimally solving problems with 8 alternatives and values generated with **UPD** (top), **NPD** (middle) and **NDCS** (bottom).

Algorithm	$t_{min}(s)$	$t_{max}(s)$	$t_{mean}(s)$	$t_{var}(s^2)$
MP (UPD)	0.02976	0.54829	0.10479	0.00572
HY (UPD)	0.02977	0.05833	0.03606	0.00003
DP (UPD)	0.85720	1.01132	0.86806	0.00017
MP (NPD)	0.04638	3.26065	0.77145	0.49433
HY (NPD)	0.03156	0.22626	0.06060	0.00092
DP (NPD)	0.85622	0.93133	0.86586	0.00013
MP (NDCS)	0.23562	2.11546	0.89745	0.00075
HY (NDCS)	0.04602	0.11447	0.06813	0.00009
DP (NDCS)	0.85946	0.89658	0.86906	0.00007

Fig. 3. Data from optimally solving problem sets with 14 agents and 8 alternatives.

`uniform_real_distribution` and `normal_distribution` from the *C++ Standard Library*. All tests were conducted with an Intel 7700K CPU and 16 GB memory.

6.1   Optimality Benchmarks

We plot the execution time to find optimum when solving problems with 8 alternatives and different numbers of agents in Fig. 2. The results show that HY is not as affected by the value distribution as the state-of-the-art algorithm (abbreviated MP) is, and that HY is considerably faster (by many orders of magnitude) compared to all other algorithms in these benchmarks. For example, for 18 agents and NPD, our algorithm finds optima in ≈1% of the time that CPLEX (abbreviated CP) and MP needs.

When we ran our optimality benchmarks, we noticed that MP sometimes spent a considerable amount of time searching. To investigate this further, we ran 100 experiments per problem instance and algorithm with $n = 14$ and $m = 8$. We then computed the minimum t_{min}, maximum t_{max}, mean t_{mean} and variance t_{var} for the algorithms' different completion times. The results of these experiments are shown in Fig. 3. As expected, they show that HY's execution time varies very little compared to MP's, and that MP's worst-case execution time is much worse than HY's.

Since HY requires additional memory due to using memorization, we investigate how its memoization table grows in the number of agents, and how it is affected by different value distributions. We tested this by keeping track of

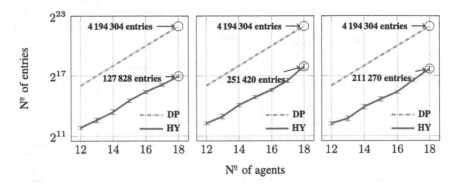

Fig. 4. The total number of entries (log-scale) stored in the memoization tables for problems with 8 alternatives and values generated with **UPD** (left), **NPD** (middle) and **NDCS** (right).

the aggregated number of entries ($= |\Gamma_w| = |\Gamma_c|$) in the algorithms' memoization tables during runtime. Our results from these experiments are plotted in Fig. 4, and show: i) that, at worst-case, HY approximately requires ≈10% of the number of entries that DP needs; and ii) that this number indeed depends on the distribution of values and not only on the problem instance's input size— for example, for UPD, HY typically only requires storing 5% of the number of entries that DP needs. These numbers are indicative to HY's ability to discard recursion branches.

6.2 Anytime Benchmarks

In our next benchmarks, we investigate the quality of the anytime solutions generated by HY (DP is not included, since it is not anytime). To this end, we also benchmark against two simple and easy-to-implement non-optimal algorithms, which results' we use as a worst-case baseline:

- A *random sampling* (RS) algorithm. RS works by randomly (uniformly) assigning every agent to an alternative. Then, when all agents have been assigned, it evaluates the resulting solution's value. It continuously runs this procedure until the time limit has been exceeded, at which point RS returns the best result it has found so far.
- A simple *greedy* (AG) algorithm. AG generates a solution by sequentially assigning agents to alternatives in a greedy fashion.

Moreover, we used 13 agents and 14 tasks for these benchmarks, resulting in a total number of $14^{13} \approx 8 \times 10^{14}$ possible solutions per problem instance. Our results from these experiments are presented in Fig. 5, with the execution time shown on the x-axis, and the *normalized ratio to optimal* on the y-axis. This ratio, for a feasible solution S', is defined as the following value:

$$\frac{V(S') - V(S_*)}{V(S^*) - V(S_*)}$$

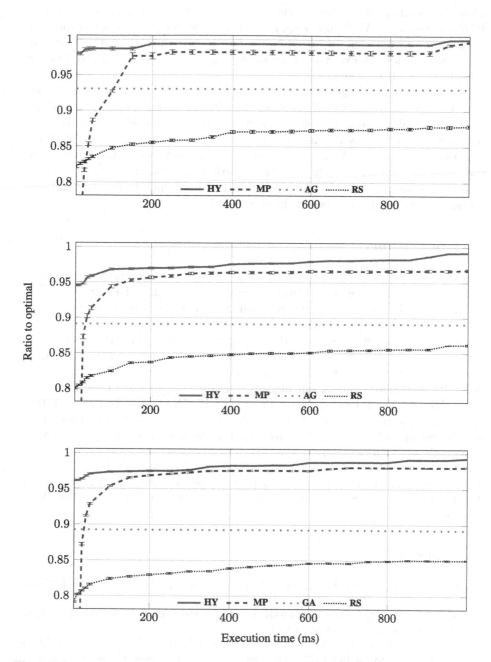

Fig. 5. The normalized ratio to optimal obtained by the different algorithms for problem sets generated using **UPD** (top), **NPD** (middle) and **NDCS** (bottom) with 13 agents and 14 tasks.

where S^* is an optimal solution, and S_* is a "worst" solution—in other words, $V(S^*) = \max_{S \in \Pi_A^m} V(S)$ and $V(S_*) = \min_{S \in \Pi_A^m} V(S)$. Also, note that in these tests, RS generated and evaluated approximately 4.4 million solutions per second; and that for the execution time in these graphs, CPLEX fails to find any feasible (interim) solutions.

As shown by the graphs in Fig. 5, HY generates at least 95%-efficient solutions in less than 10 ms for all problem sets with 13 agents and 14 tasks. Moreover, HY found near-optimal 99%-efficient solutions very rapidly for all distributions and benchmarks (e.g., at worst case for NPD, this takes roughly 900 ms). Moreover, compared to MP, it always finds better solutions for the same execution time. Our anytime benchmarks thus clearly show that HY is extremely fast at finding near-optimal solutions, and that it greatly outperforms the state-of-the-art in generating high-quality interim solutions.

7   Conclusions

We presented two different algorithms that use dynamic programming to optimally solve the simultaneous coalition structure generation and assignment problem: one based purely on dynamic programming, and a second hybrid approach that uses dynamic programming together with branch-and-bound. We benchmarked them against the state-of-the-art, and our results show that our hybrid approach greatly outperforms all other methods in all of our experiments (often by many orders of magnitude). For example, for 18 agents, 8 alternatives, and normally distributed values, our algorithm finds an optimum in roughly 3 3 s, while this takes both the industry-grade solver CPLEX and previous state-of-the-art approximately 3 min. For future work, we hope to investigate if metaheuristic algorithms, probabilistic search and/or machine learning can be applied to solve large-scale problems with many agents.

Acknowledgments. This work was partially supported by the Wallenberg AI, Autonomous Systems and Software Program (WASP) funded by the Knut and Alice Wallenberg Foundation.

References

1. Bolger, E.M.: A value for games with n players and r alternatives. Int. J. Game Theory **22**(4), 319–334 (1993)
2. Kuhn, H.W.: The Hungarian method for the assignment problem. Naval Res. Logist. (NRL) **2**(1–2), 83–97 (1955)
3. Michalak, T.P., Dowell, A.J., McBurney, P., Wooldridge, M.J.: Optimal coalition structure generation in partition function games. In: European Conference on Artificial Intelligence, pp. 388–392 (2008)
4. Pentico, D.W.: Assignment problems: a golden anniversary survey. Euro. J. Oper. Res. **176**(2), 774–793 (2007)
5. Präntare, F.: Simultaneous coalition formation and task assignment in a real-time strategy game. Master thesis (2017)

6. Präntare, F., Heintz, F.: An anytime algorithm for simultaneous coalition structure generation and assignment. In: Miller, T., Oren, N., Sakurai, Y., Noda, I., Savarimuthu, B.T.R., Cao Son, T. (eds.) PRIMA 2018. LNCS (LNAI), vol. 11224, pp. 158–174. Springer, Cham (2018). https://doi.org/10.1007/978-3-030-03098-8_10

7. Präntare, F., Heintz, F.: An anytime algorithm for optimal simultaneous coalition structure generation and assignment. Auton. Agents Multi-Agent Syst. **34**(1), 1–31 (2020)

8. Rahwan, T., Jennings, N.R.: An improved dynamic programming algorithm for coalition structure generation. In: Proceedings of the 7th International Joint Conference on Autonomous Agents and Multiagent Systems, pp. 1417–1420 (2008)

9. Rahwan, T., Jennings, N.: Coalition structure generation: dynamic programming meets anytime optimisation. In: Proceedings of the Twenty-Third AAAI Conference on Artificial Intelligence (2008)

10. Rahwan, T., Michalak, T.P., Jennings, N.R.: A hybrid algorithm for coalition structure generation. In: Twenty-Sixth AAAI Conference on Artificial Intelligence, pp. 1443–1449 (2012)

11. Rahwan, T., Michalak, T.P., Wooldridge, M., Jennings, N.R.: Coalition structure generation: a survey. Artif. Intell. **229**, 139–174 (2015)

12. Rahwan, T., Ramchurn, S.D., Jennings, N.R., Giovannucci, A.: An anytime algorithm for optimal coalition structure generation. J. Artif. Intell. Res. **34**, 521–567 (2009)

13. Sandholm, T., Larson, K., Andersson, M., Shehory, O., Tohmé, F.: Coalition structure generation with worst case guarantees. Artif. Intell. **111**(1–2), 209–238 (1999)

14. Yeh, D.Y.: A dynamic programming approach to the complete set partitioning problem. BIT Numer. Math. **26**(4), 467–474 (1986)

A Socio-psychological Approach to Simulate Trust and Reputation in Modal Choices

Khoa Nguyen[✉] and René Schumann

University of Applied Sciences Western Switzerland (HES-SO Valais Wallis) SiLab,
Rue de Technpole 3, 3960 Sierre, Switzerland
{khoa.nguyen,rene.schumann}@hevs.ch

Abstract. Trust and reputation are currently being researched broadly in multiple disciplines and often considered as main drivers for human's actions in many different scenarios. In the multiagent based simulation community, there are still concerns about qualifying and modelling them with sufficient details and adequateness in the context of decision-making. Besides, the diversity of application domains requires a method to combine trust and reputation with other determinants to provide a more complete picture for the deliberating process in complex systems. This paper presents a novel solution by applying subjective logic in conjunction with a modelling framework that utilises Triandis' Theory of Interpersonal Behaviour to simulate the modal choices of human individuals as an example. It uses the concept of opinion as a metric to measure the belief of an agent about the consequence(s) of an action, which can be updated through feedback. In addition, its consensus rule allows us to combine relevant opinions of the neighbours to evaluate the reputation of the target. By performing an experiment set up in the mobility domain, we demonstrate the framework ability to capture the ground truth of a service's reputation at different simulation scales and highlight the effects of these concepts on the figure of yearly rail-kilometres travelled.

Keywords: Trust and reputation · Social simulation · Agent-based modelling

1 Introduction

Creating autonomous agents capable of exhibiting human-like behaviours under uncertainty of complex environment is becoming increasingly relevant in the simulation research community [12,21]. One of the most popular methodologies for this purpose is to utilise trust and reputation to give an idea of the confidence one can have on the quality of potential cooperation or recommended systems [17]. However, one of the main concern for using these concepts is transparency [11], which includes human interpretability and explanations of ontologies in different application domains. Several models of trust and reputation have been

© Springer Nature Switzerland AG 2021
T. Uchiya et al. (Eds.): PRIMA 2020, LNAI 12568, pp. 34–50, 2021.
https://doi.org/10.1007/978-3-030-69322-0_3

proposed in the literature, such as those suggested in [10] and [17]. There is still, however, a lack of research efforts that emphasize on understanding the roles of them and their relationships with other determinants in human decision-making.

We aim to provide a framework that can address the matter of limited expressibility and linking highly abstract concepts with empirical data. It employs Triandis' Theory of Interpersonal Behaviour (TIB) [35] to provide a meaningful set of determinants that contribute to decision-making in socio-psychological research. TIB is a tri-level model that allows users to have the freedom of separating and highlighting the impacts of different psychological concepts to individuals and their society. To represent trust and reputation, we incorporate subjective logic to measure personal beliefs about available modal choices presented to the agent. Using feedback(s) from the environment, an agent has the capability to evolve its decision-making process over time depending on personal experiences and opinions from neighbours in its network.

The structure of this paper is as followed: We first consider some of the related projects that model trust and reputation at the individual level (Sect. 2). It is followed by a specification of our architecture, which contains the functions to calculate subjective probability and utility for each available options. Next, a case study of the implementation platform - BedDeM - is described in Sect. 4. Its main purpose is reproducing the collective ground truth of reputation for the rail services in both regional and national level and evaluating the impacts of it on the number of kilometres travelled. We then conclude our work and suggest further researching directions in Sect. 5.

2   Related Work

The state-of-the-art in agent's modal choice has been previously discussed in our papers [24,25]. This study focuses on the individual-level trust and reputation models for agent-based simulation purposes. One of the common approaches is for the agent to interact and study their behaviour patterns over a number of encounters, i.e *learning models*. In this case, the outcome of direct interaction is the measurement of trust. Another method involves the agent asking its network about their perceptions of the target(s), i.e *reputation models*. The final category is *socio-cognitive models*, which concerns with forming coherent beliefs about different characteristics of the partner(s) and reasoning about these beliefs to decide how much trust should one put in them.

2.1   Learning Models

The most common example to demonstrate the evolution of trust or cooperation over multiple interactions is Axelrod's tournaments around Prisoner's Dilemma [3]. By allowing agents to adapt and evolve their relationship using the cooperation strategy over multiple interactions, Wu et al. [38] showed that trust can actually emerge between them. Their model, however, does not take into account the fact that there might be some utility loss in short-term evaluation. Sen et al.

[31] demonstrated how reciprocity can emerge when the agent learns to predict the future benefits of cooperation. In case the number of interactions does not allow trust to be built, Mukhejee et al. [23] showed how trust can be acquired through mutually learning. In addition, Birk's learning method [6] allows agents to cooperate in a non-competitive environment. However, all of the models above assume complete information for the multi-agent learning algorithms to work and their results can only be obtained under very strict assumptions.

To become more realistic, the agent needs a way to evaluate how the target's action affect its goals using the data gathered through their interactions. Thus, many trust metrics have been derived. In the context of trading networks, Witkowski et al. [37] proposed a model; in which the trust for a partner is calculated through equations based on their past interactions and its update vary depending on the type of agent. Other models consider the quality of agents to be a bi-state value (good/bad), such as those of Scillo et al. [30], Mui et al. [22] and Sen and Sajja [32]. For open distributed systems that contain a richer set of outcomes, the REGRET model, which is developed by Sabater et al. [29], attributes some fuzziness to the notion of performance. Its evaluation of trust is not only based on an agent's direct perception of its partner's reliability but also their behaviours with others in the system. However, this can imply a number of problems if the information perceived by the agent is wrong or incomplete.

2.2   Reputation Models

In this subsection, we consider the reputation, which is mainly derived from an aggregation of opinions from members of a community about one individual. Yu et al. [40] use the concept of referrals, which are represented by pointers to other sources of information, similar to links on a Website. In this context, they show how the agent can explore a network using referrals gathered from their neighbours to gradually build up a model of its network. The representation of social networks was extended by the work of Schillo et al. [30]. They annotate the nodes with characteristics, such as honesty and altruism, which can then be used to deduce the trustworthiness of witnesses when calculating the reputation of potential partners. Higher-level concepts (e.g. group and neighbours) are utilised in [29,40] to related the closeness with the reliability of the witnesses. Nevertheless, all of the models above share the assumption that witness share information freely (i.e. without any cost or personal agenda).

Another popular methodology is aggregating ratings, whose applications come from mostly online communities. A typical example is eBay peer-to-peer rating system [33]. It can however, be unreliable when the users do not return any ratings or sellers try to manipulate the result to build their reputation. The model developed in [41] to deal with the absence of data using referrals and Dempster Shafter's Theory of evidence [39]. It treats the lack of belief as to the state of uncertainty and allows the combination of beliefs obtained from various sources. The models in [30,32] extended this work and demonstrated how agents cope with lying witness through learning rather than attributing subjective probability. Another method from Sabater et al. (i.e. REGRET system) [29] adopts the view from sociology to allow realism in term of ontological dimension. The reputation value in which is a weighted sum of subjective impressions from direct interactions, its group's impression of the target, its group's impression on the target's group and the agent's impression on the opponent's group. Despite that, REGRET does not handle the problem of a lying agent, i.e. ratings are not obtained in competitive environments but a more cooperative setup.

2.3   Socio-cognitive Models

The methods from previous sections are based on an assessment of the outcomes of interactions. At the same time, it is also important to consider the subjective perception of an individual on the indirect interaction to enable a more comprehensive analysis of characteristics of the potential partner [16]. The line of works in this respect was initialised by the work of Castelfranchi and Falcone [8,9,14], especially for the Belief-Desire-Intention agent architecture. It is strongly motived by human behaviours, which are not always rational. Another strategy of this type is from Brainov and Sandholm [7], which supports the need to model an opponent's trust with a rational approach.

Socio-cognitive modelling research is still in its early stage. Thus, these models mentioned above are often criticised for the lack of grounding in the rational mechanisms [28] which learning and reputation models provide. They could also exploit the assessment performed by the other model types by taking into account learning strategy over multiple interactions, the reputation of potential partners and their motivations and abilities regarding the interactions. However, it can be computationally expensive to allow social agents to reason about all the factors affecting their trust in others. Moreover, these agents are limited in their capacity to gather information from various sources that populate their environment [28].

3   Agent Decision-Making Architecture

In this paper, we propose a socio-cognitive agent architecture that can capture the roles of trust and reputation in decision-making. The first subsection illustrates how these concepts are being modeled using the subjective logic methodology. It is followed by the description of the decision-making mechanism, which implements the Triandis' Theory of Interpersonal Behavior to derive utility values for a set of alternatives options. Finally, we provide an overview of our agent architecture framework.

3.1   Modelling Trust and Reputation

A fundamental aspect of the human condition is that nobody can determine with absolute certainty whether a preposition about the world is true or false. Thus, whenever a statement is assessed, it should be done under the view of an individual and not to be represented in a general and objective belief [19]. Reviews from [5] and [18] provide good examples of how standard logic and probabilistic logic are designed for an idealised world, where these important aspects are often not considered and conclusions have to be drawn from insufficient evidence.

In this study, we follow framework proposed by Jøsang et al. [20] on subjective logic. It presents a specific calculus that uses a metric called *opinion* to express our subjective beliefs about the world. An opinion, denoted as $\omega_x^A = (b, d, u, a)$, indicates the party A's belief in the statement x. In this case, b, d and u represents *belief, disbelief* and *uncertainty* respectively, where $b + d + u = 1$ and $b, d, u \in [0, 1]$. All set of possible opinions can mapped into a point inside an equal-sided triangle in Fig. 1.

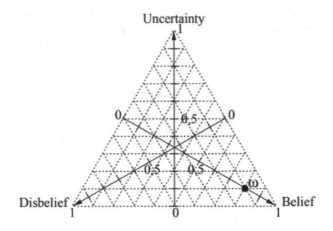

Fig. 1. The opinion-space trust model/opinion triangle [20]

The base rate parameter, $a \in [0, 1]$, determines how uncertainty shall contribute to the probability expectation value:

$$E(\omega_x^A) = b + au \tag{1}$$

In the binary event space (i.e. where there are only two possible outcomes - success or failure), subjective logic allows us to build an opinion from a set of evidences about x using the following equation:

$$\omega_x = \begin{cases} b_x = \frac{r}{r+s+W} \\ d_x = \frac{s}{r+s+W} \\ u_x = \frac{W}{r+s+W} \\ a_x = \text{base rate } x \end{cases} \tag{2}$$

where r is the number of positive evidences about x, s is the number of negative evidences about x, W is the non-informative prior weight, also called a unit of evidence, normally set to 2 and the default value of base rate a is usually set at $1/2$. In the case of no prior experience with the target, agent A's opinion of x is set as $\omega_x^A = (0, 0, 1, 1/2)$. Therefore, its probability expectation value is $E(\omega_x^A) = 1/2$.

We model reputation in this case using the consensus rule of independent opinions A and B:

$$\omega_x^{AB} = \omega_x^A \oplus \omega_x^B = \begin{cases} b_x^{AB} = \frac{b_x^A u_x^B + b_x^B u_x^A}{k} \\ d_x^{AB} = \frac{d_x^A u_x^B + d_x^B u_x^A}{k} \\ u_x^{AB} = \frac{u_x^A u_x^B}{k} \\ a_x^{AB} = \frac{a_x^A u_x^B + a_x^B u_x^A - (a_x^A + a_x^B) u_x^A u_x^B}{u_x^A + u_x^B - W u_x^A u_x^B} \end{cases} \quad (3)$$

where $k = u_x^A + u_x^B - u_x^A u_x^B$.

3.2 Utility Function

In order to create a system that can mimic the function of a human network, the first question to address is how to model our behaviours. In psychology, different theories in the school of cognitive model describe this process, e.g. Ajzen and Fishbein's Theory of Reasoned Action [15] and Ajzen's (1991) Theory of Planned Behaviour [1], etc. We decide to implement Triandis' Theory of Interpersonal Behaviour (TIB) [35] due to its inclusion of a more comprehensive set of determinants and the ability to combine these to form a complete picture of human decision-making. This set is also flexible enough to reflect other behaviour theories by exchanging the determinants and/or assigning weights to mark their contribution to the agent's reasoning process. Figure 2 shows a tree-structure representation of the main determinants in TIB.

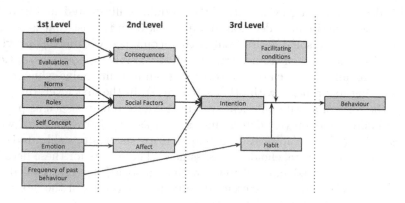

Fig. 2. Triandis' tri-level model [35]

Triandis suggests that one of the main factor to determine intention of an act is the value of perceived consequences, C, depending on the sum of the products of the subjective probability that a particular consequence will follow a behaviour (P_c) and the value of (or affect attached to) that consequence (V_c) (see page 16 [35]). Thus, the equation for expected utility of C is as followed:

$$EU_c = \sum_{i=1}^{n}(P_{c_i} V_{c_i})$$ (4)

where n is the number of consequences that a subject perceives as likely to follow a particular behaviour. The P_{c_i} value can be derived from the Eq. 1, i.e. $P_{c_i} = E(\omega_{c_i})$.

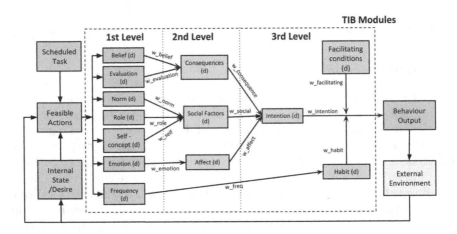

Fig. 3. Agent decision-making mechanism with TIB Module

A full decision-making cycle with TIB Module is illustrated in Fig. 3. An agent first selects an isolated decision-making task from the list that is sequentially executed. Its personal desire/goal is then combined with means provided by the external environment to generate a set of possible propositions/options. For all determinants (d), each option (opt) is given a utility value which comes from comparing its property with other's $(U_d(opt))$. In the first level, this value can be in the form of a real numerical system (for determinants such as price or time) or ranking function (for determinants such as emotion). Either of which can be calculated from empirical data (e.g. census, survey) or calibrated with expert's knowledge and stakeholders' assessment. The results for these determinants are then normalized and multiplied with an associated weight (called w_d); the sum of which becomes the referenced value for the option in the next level. This process is captured in the following equation:

$$EU_d(opt) = \sum_{a=1}^{A}(EU_a(opt) * w_a / (\sum_{o=1}^{O} EU_a(o)))$$ (5)

where $EU_d(opt)$ is the utility value of an option (opt) at determinant d. A is the set of all ancestors of d (i.e. determinants connects with d in the previous level). O is the set of all available options. $w(a)$ is the weight of ancestor a. In this case, the weight represents the importance of a decision-making determinant compare to others at the same level and emphasizes on the heterogeneity of individuals. It also allows the modeler to express a certain theory by cutting determinants (i.e. setting their values to 0) that are not relevant to a case study. The combination process then continues until it reaches the behavior output list; the utility value of which can be translated to the probabilities that an agent will perform that option. If the agent is assumed to be deterministic, it picks the option that is correlated to the highest or lowest utility depending on modeler's assumptions.

In our framework, the utility function of determinant *Consequences* is an exception case which follows Eq. 4. In addition, the expected value of determinant *Norm* can be derived from the probability expectation value of the collective opinion formed by the consensus rule (see Eq. 1 and Eq. 3). In Sect. 4, we focus on a simplified binary event space, i.e. an action has two outcomes - success or failure. More complex scenarios could be considered in the future by extending the result space to multiple dimensions (e.g. time, cost, satisfaction).

A running example in mobility domain can be seen in Fig. 4. *EU* in this case is a cost function, i.e. option that has smaller value is referred. We assume that an agent has access to 3 options: *walking*, using *car* or taking *train*. It expects a *car* journey would take around 0.2 h for good traffic, which is believed to be 80% chance. A late *car* drive would take up to 0.5 h. Using subjective logic Eq. 4, we have $EU_{Time}(\text{car}) = 0.2 * 80\% + 0.5 * 20\% \approx 0.26$. Similarly, $EU_{Time}(\text{train}) \approx 0.55$ and $EU_{Time}(\text{walking}) \approx 1$. Their total value, $\sum EU_{Time}$, is 1.81. For non-measurable value such as Norm, the agent uses the concept of reputation to rank the options: $EU_{Norm}(\text{train}) = 1$, $EU_{Norm}(\text{car}) = 2$, $EU_{Norm}(\text{walking}) = 3$ (best to worst); the sum of which is 6. If w_{Time} and w_{Norm} are 7 and 3 respectively, the new expected value in next level ($EU_{Attitude}$) of *walking* would be $1/1.81 * 7 + 3/6 * 3 \approx 5.37$, *train* would be $0.55/1.81 * 7 + 1/6 * 3 \approx 2{,}63$ and *car* would be $0.26/1.81 * 7 + 2/6 * 3 \approx 2.0$. Hence, according to determinant Attitude, *car* would have the highest chance to be picked for this agent, followed by *train* and *walking*.

3.3   An Overview

An agent's main components and their functions are illustrated in Fig. 5. When a task is assigned, the *Perception* observes the current state of the environment, other's opinions and combines them with the agent's internal state to produce a list of available options. They are given to the *Decision-making* unit to be evaluated using the functions (or preferences) from the *Memory*. Details of this process are described in Sect. 3.2. The *Communication* component then utilises this result to create a behaviour output and communicate this with the environment and others. A social agent can also have different objectives to achieve (e.g. influence others' decisions and/or promote a certain action), which might affect the outcome action and their opinions. The environment can then provide feedback(s) based on the numbers of demands and nature of the system

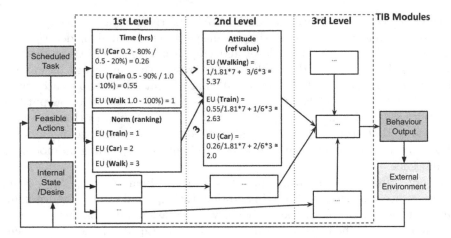

Fig. 4. An utility example in mobility domain

associated with the action. Agent remembers these past results in the *Memory*, which can then be used to modify the probability of expected values in future decision-making as described in Sect. 3.1.

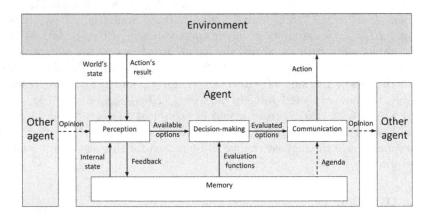

Fig. 5. Overview of agent's architecture

4 Experiment

This section focus on the usage of a platform called BedDeM to perform some experimentation regarding the effects of trust and reputation in mobility modal choices. It is being developed in Java based on the Repast library with the main purpose to generate yearly demands at the individual household level for the population of Switzerland. It is worth noticing that BedDeM is not a routing model and hence, agents only take feedback from the environment as the indication on whether a trip is either a success or a failure. More details of its main functions are described in the next subsection, which is followed by the current empirical mapping. We then consider some testing scenarios that highlight the effects of trust and reputation in mobility modal choices. The final subsection provides some discussion on the competency of BedDeM as a trust and reputation model and suggests some extensions for future development.

4.1   The Behaviour-Driven Demand Model (BedDeM)

As shown in Fig. 6, BedDeM consists of two processes. In the configuration phase, we applied cluster analysis on the Swiss Household Energy Demand Survey (SHEDS) [36] and the Mobility and Transport Micro-census (MTMC) [2] to generate the mobility profiles. This process is detailed in [4]. A number of random respondents from the surveys that matched these clusters are selected to generate a synthetic agent population for simulation.

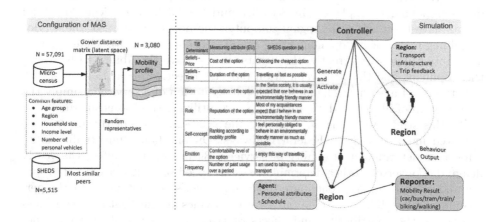

Fig. 6. Agent decision-making mechanism with TIB Module

These data are then passed to a controller in the simulation stage. Each agent contains a mapping of qualitative data in SHEDS to all TIB's determinants, which is calibrated to reproduce the traveling patterns for in MTMC of 2015. A sample of the first level determinants is included in Fig. 6. More details of the data mapping and agent's parameters calibration can be found in [25]. An agent represents a typical household in Switzerland and is assigned a weight-to-universe number so that the end results can be scaled back to the national level. Agents from the same cluster are considered neighbors when the reputation of a service needs to be calculated. Depend on the availability of transportation systems, the set of options in decision-making often consists of rail, bus, tram, car, walking, biking. The agents are then assigned to their respective regions, which contain information about the available public transportation and can be used to reflect the dynamic change in mobility infrastructure (e.g. traffic jams, available public transport) with regard to the simulating time. Each region also has a mechanism to provide feedback after receiving an action as the result of the agent's decision-making (see Sect. 4.2).

4.2 Setup

The purpose of this experiment is to investigate the effect of a public transportation's reputation to its demand, which is measured in yearly total kilometers travelled. The reputation in this case represented by a constant percentage, (ground truth value), i.e. punctuality. When the agent performs an action, a different percentage is randomly generated. If its value under the ground truth, the region will output a successful signal to the agent and vice versa. These consequences are connected with the duration of a trip for the agent. Successful feedback means the agent has performed the trip within its time estimation. In contrast, a failure message from the region means running time should be double for this trip. These information are taken into account in the next agent's decision-making as explained in Sect. 3.1 and Sect. 3.2. After decisions of all agents have been made, the region computes the new reputation of the service by joining its residents' opinions using consensus rule (see Eq. 3), while ignoring all empty opinions. Currently, the agents do not have the ability to lie about their opinions and thus, the reputation reflects collective perception about the punctuality of a service. The national level reputation of a service is simply the combination of all regional reputation by also utilizing the consensus rule.

In this study, we focus on changing the successful rate of the rail service operated mainly by Swiss Federal Railways. On one hand, punctuality is an important determinant of quality of service [13] and in turn, affect the yearly demand. Conversely, other determinants (e.g. speed of trains, average fare per km and safety) can also contribute to the customer's perception about the performance index [13]. Hence, the rail service provides an excellent testing ground to observe the contribution and effects of trust, reputation along with other socio-psychological determinants in the agent's decision-making process.

A summary of the setup for the experiment can also be found in Table 1. We can divide them into five main categories, whose details are as follow:

- *Perfect world scenario:* The successful rate of all trips is kept at 100%. This setup is similar to what has been done previously in [25]. Therefore, we expect that there's almost no uncertainty in the agent trust. This can act as a base to compare the effects of trust and reputation when they are implemented in later settings.
- *Real world scenario:* According to [27], around 87.8% of total trips were punctual in 2015, which is the year we calibrated our agents in [25]. We assign this number to all regional rail trips' successfully rate.

- *Agents starting with low or high expectation scenario:* The initial value of the probability expectation for an option x, $E(\omega_x)$, will be set at either 0 or 1, instead of 1/2 as suggested in Sect. 3.1. The punctuality of rail service is still kept at 87.8%.
- *Regional disruption scenarios:* The punctuality of rail service at a single region is set at 25%. Otherwise, it is similar to the real-world case, i.e. 87.8%. These structures can be used to test the effect of disruption at one single region to the figures of other regions and the national level.

Table 1. Collective ground truth/Punctuality (measured in percentage) of rail service in individual region for different testing scenarios

Scenario	Region 1	Region 2	...	Region 26
Perfect world	100	100	...	100
Real world	87.8	87.8	...	87.8
High expectation	87.8	87.8	...	87.8
Low expectation	87.8	87.8	...	87.8
Disrupt in region 1	*25*	87.8	...	87.8
Disrupt in region 2	87.8	*25*	...	87.8
...	...	...	...	...
Disrupt Region 26	87.8	87.8	...	*25*

4.3 Results

As the model contains an element of randomness, we perform 100 simulations for each scenario and compute the averages. Table 2 shows the reputation in the percentage of the rail service at the national level and three representative regions 1, 24 and 18. They are the highest, mid point and lowest in term of kilometres demand in the perfect world scenario. Other disruptive scenarios follow the same pattern as these representatives.

Reputation: In essence, reputation measures at the national level and regions that has large train usage (e.g. Region 1) are nearly the same as the ground truth. The lower overall kilometres travelled by agents, the less accurate cumulative reputation of the whole region. This can be seen in the figures of Region 18. When a disruption happens at a single region, the rail's reputation converse to the ground truth. Despite that, we observe no notable change in the national figures. Except for the disruptive regions, other regional figures also show no significant difference. This indicates the inter-connections between agents from separate regions are weak or limited; and therefore, the effects of interference cannot spread.

Table 2. Result of reputation (measured in percentage) and total demand (measured in kilometres travelled) of rail service at the national level and three representative regions

Scenario	Reputation (percentage)				Total demand (10^6km)			
	N	R 1	R 24	R 18	N	R 1	R 24	R 18
Perfect world	*99.6*	99.9	99.4	95.7	*9081.588*	3114.568	104.632	0.173
Real world	*86.3*	89.0	87.8	83.0	*8958.592*	3112.998	104.632	0.173
High expectation	*87.7*	87.6	82.5	84.8	*16000.392*	5002.029	142.432	97.759
Low expectation	*85.2*	87.3	86.5	74.5	*8878.993*	3105.089	104.632	0.173
Disrupt region 1	85.2	*25.7*	88.2	86.5	8865.848	*3105.089*	98.867	0.173
Disrupt region 24	87.4	88.5	*22.0*	95.7	8937.483	3112.998	*102.267*	0.173
Disrupt region 18	86.5	86.7	88.3	*12.8*	8947.010	3112.178	103.876	*0.173*

Total Rail-Kilometers: By implementing a lower percentage of trust and reputation in the real world setup, we observe a significant decrease in usage at the national level and major regions (e.g. Region 1). Having agents starting with high probability expectation affects the overall kilometres travelled, with the national figures almost doubled and high increases in all regions. Conversely, agents starting with low expectation cause a small drop in both national and Region 1's total kilometers. The demand at Region 24 and 18 however, do not exhibit any sizable changes in this scenario. As trust and reputation are only a subset of determinants in Triandis' Theory, these observations signify that agents have taken into account not only the probability expectation values but also other environmental difference.

There is no extensive impact on the national figures in the disruptive cases compare to the real world scenario. The reduction is noticeable when the disruption happens on the regions that have large demand where punctuation is the key issue there (e.g. Zurich, Geneva). In contrast, the interference does not make any substantial changes to the regions that originally have a small consumption number (i.e. Region 18) since the train is the only available option for these particular residents.

4.4 Discussion

The current preliminary results show that the reputation of the rail system in the agents' opinions can reflect the ground truth in the setup. As seen in the experiment result, the current mobility model is capable of showing the difference in reputation at two separate levels - regional and national. It suggests a throughout investigation at different angles is needed when a change happens (e.g. disruption, new services and policies). Realistic scenarios with more interference at a variety of scales can also be set up similarly. In addition, the experiment indicates that trust and reputation are two of the many determinants in the agent's decision-making; and thus, there are differences when comparing the change in total kilometres demands at the regional level in the high/low expectation and disruptive cases. By changing their weights in Utility Function (see Sect. 3.2), we also have the opportunity to further explore and compare their contribution to the agent's decision-making from a micro-level perspective.

There are some limitations in the model that needed to be considered in the future development stage. Firstly, it assumes that the punctuality of the rail service is static for the duration of the simulation. Using more up-to-date data from online sources such as [34], the traffic rate can be adapted dynamically based on the time of the simulation. Punctuality of other available options (e.g. car, bus, tram) is also an essential feature in order to reflect the transition in total demand more accurate. Another approach involves utilising subjective logic on groups of determinants in TIB to derive more sets of complex outcome scenarios for simulation purpose.

5   Conclusion

Our main contribution in this paper is the development and implementation of a novel concept using subjective logic to represent trust and reputation elements in a decision-making framework that utilises Triandis' Theory of Interpersonal Behaviour. Its main purpose is to provide a way to incorporate empirical data in the simulation process and make use of the variety in psychological ontologies to produce a more transparent explanation for social phenomena. Subsequently, this has the potential to facilitate the engagement of psychologists, sociologists, economists and the general public with multiagent modelling projects. We demonstrate the framework practicality by performing experiments aiming at replicating the punctuality of rail service and observing the effect of trust and reputation to the number of kilometres travelled. Although there are still some limitations, the initial results show that the model is fundamentally capable of archiving those targets.

This trust and reputation modelling framework can be further extended by allowing the usage of multinomial and hyper opinions in subjective logic [20]. In other words, the agent can consider the probabilities of the different possible outcomes that are formed by a set of independent determinants (e.g. price, time). Another direction would be to utilise fuzzy logic [26] to exam data in surveys and classify the quality of a trip as either success or failure, especially for qualitative determinants (e.g. emotion, self-concept). Using geographical statistics can also allow us to observe how physical proximity, the layout of regions and other environmental elements can hinder or facilitate interaction and interdependence among social groups. Since *Norm* is incorporated in the agent's decision-making (see Sect. 3.2), another potential direction is investigating on how to integrate moral preferences in the agent's reasoning. In addition, we also aim to use the framework to address the issues in trusted Artificial Intelligent and trust modelling as stated in [11], especially emphasis on creating support for interoperability and employ domain-specific ontologies in simulation research.

References

1. Ajzen, I.: The theory of planned behavior. Organ. Behav. Hum. Decis. Processes **50**(2), 179–211 (1991)
2. ARE/BfS: Verkehrsverhalten der Bevölkerung Ergebnisse des Mikrozensus Mobilität und Verkehr 2015. Federal Office for Spatial Development and Swiss Federal Statistical Office (2017)
3. Axelrod, R., Dion, D.: The further evolution of cooperation. Science **242**(4884), 1385–1390 (1988)
4. Bektas, A., Schumann, R.: How to optimize Gower distance weights for the k-medoids clustering algorithm to obtain mobility profiles of the swiss population (2019). To be published and represented in the Swiss Conference on Data Science (SDS) Conference - June 2019
5. Bhatnagar, R.K., Kanal, L.N.: Handling uncertain information: a review of numeric and non-numeric methods. In: Machine Intelligence and Pattern Recognition, vol. 4, pp. 3–26. Elsevier (1986)
6. Birk, A.: Learning to trust. In: Falcone, R., Singh, M., Tan, Y.-H. (eds.) Trust in Cyber-societies. LNCS (LNAI), vol. 2246, pp. 133–144. Springer, Heidelberg (2001). https://doi.org/10.1007/3-540-45547-7_8
7. Braynov, S., Sandholm, T.: Contracting with uncertain level of trust. Computational intelligence **18**(4), 501–514 (2002)
8. Castelfranchi, C., Falcone, R.: Principles of trust for MAS: cognitive anatomy, social importance, and quantification. In: Proceedings International Conference on Multi Agent Systems (Cat. No. 98EX160), pp. 72–79. IEEE (1998)
9. Castelfranchi, C., Falcone, R.: Trust is much more than subjective probability: mental components and sources of trust. In: Proceedings of the 33rd Annual Hawaii International Conference on System Sciences, p. 10. IEEE (2000)
10. Cho, J.H., Chan, K., Adali, S.: A survey on trust modeling. ACM Comput. Surv. (CSUR) **48**(2), 28 (2015)
11. Cohen, R., Schaekermann, M., Liu, S., Cormier, M.: Trusted AI and the contribution of trust modeling in multiagent systems. In: Proceedings of the 18th International Conference on Autonomous Agents and MultiAgent Systems, pp. 1644–1648. International Foundation for Autonomous Agents and Multiagent Systems (2019)
12. Dugdale, J.: Human behaviour modelling in complex socio-technical systems: an agent based approach. Ph.D. thesis (2013)
13. Duranton, S., Audier, A., Hazan, J., Langhorn, M.P., Gauche, V.: The 2017 European railway performance index. The Boston Consulting Group (2017)
14. Falcone, R., Castelfranchi, C.: Social trust: a cognitive approach. In: Castelfranchi, C., Tan, Y.H. (eds.) Trust and Deception in Virtual Societies, pp. 55–90. Springer, Dordrecht (2001). https://doi.org/10.1007/978-94-017-3614-5_3
15. Fishbein, M., Ajzen, I.: Belief, attitude, intention and behavior: an introduction to theory and research (1975)
16. Gambetta, D., et al.: Can we trust trust. In: Trust: Making and Breaking Cooperative Relations, vol. 13, pp. 213–237 (2000)
17. Granatyr, J., Botelho, V., Lessing, O.R., Scalabrin, E.E., Barthès, J.P., Enembreck, F.: Trust and reputation models for multiagent systems. ACM Comput. Surv. (CSUR) **48**(2), 27 (2015)
18. Henkind, S.J., Harrison, M.C.: An analysis of four uncertainty calculi. IEEE Trans. Syst. Man Cybern. **18**(5), 700–714 (1988)

19. Jøsang, A.: Artificial reasoning with subjective logic. In: Proceedings of the Second Australian Workshop on Commonsense Reasoning, vol. 48, p. 34. Citeseer (1997)
20. Jøsang, A.: Subjective Logic. Springer, Cham (2016). https://doi.org/10.1007/978-3-319-42337-1
21. Kambhampati, S.: Synthesizing explainable behavior for human-AI collaboration. In: Proceedings of the 18th International Conference on Autonomous Agents and MultiAgent Systems, pp. 1–2. International Foundation for Autonomous Agents and Multiagent Systems (2019)
22. Mui, L., Mohtashemi, M., Halberstadt, A.: A computational model of trust and reputation. In: Proceedings of the 35th Annual Hawaii International Conference on System Sciences, pp. 2431–2439. IEEE (2002)
23. Mukherjee, R., Banerjee, B., Sen, S.: Learning mutual trust. In: Falcone, R., Singh, M., Tan, Y.-H. (eds.) Trust in Cyber-societies. LNCS (LNAI), vol. 2246, pp. 145–158. Springer, Heidelberg (2001). https://doi.org/10.1007/3-540-45547-7_9
24. Nguyen, K., Schumann, R.: An exploratory comparison of behavioural determinants in mobility modal choices (2019)
25. Nguyen, K., Schumann, R.: On developing a more comprehensive decision-making architecture for empirical social research: lesson from agent-based simulation of mobility demands in Switzerland (2019)
26. Novák, V., Perfilieva, I., Mockor, J.: Mathematical Principles of Fuzzy Logic, vol. 517. Springer Science & Business Media, New York (2012)
27. Railways, S.F.: SBB: facts and figures 2018. Technical report (2018)
28. Ramchurn, S.D., Huynh, D., Jennings, N.R.: Trust in multi-agent systems. Knowl. Eng. Rev. 19(1), 1–25 (2004)
29. Sabater, J., Sierra, C.: REGRET: reputation in gregarious societies. Agents 1, 194–195 (2001)
30. Schillo, M., Funk, P., Rovatsos, M.: Using trust for detecting deceitful agents in artificial societies. Appl. Artif. Intell. 14(8), 825–848 (2000)
31. Sen, S., Dutta, P.S.: The evolution and stability of cooperative traits. In: Proceedings of the First International Joint Conference on Autonomous Agents and Multiagent Systems: Part 3, pp. 1114–1120. ACM (2002)
32. Sen, S., Sajja, N.: Robustness of reputation-based trust: boolean case. In: Proceedings of the First International Joint Conference on Autonomous Agents and Multiagent Systems: Part 1, pp. 288–293. ACM (2002)
33. Song, S., Hwang, K., Zhou, R., Kwok, Y.K.: Trusted P2P transactions with fuzzy reputation aggregation. IEEE Internet Comput. 9(6), 24–34 (2005)
34. Tool, O.: Analyzes on public transport in Switzerland. http://puenktlichkeit.ch (2019). Accessed 16 Oct 2019
35. Triandis, H.C.: Interpersonal Behavior. Brooks/Cole Pub. Co., Pacific Grove (1977)
36. Weber, S., et al.: Swiss household energy demand survey (SHEDS): objectives, design, and implementation. Technical report, IRENE Working Paper (2017)
37. Witkowski, M., Artikis, A., Pitt, J.: Experiments in building experiential trust in a society of objective-trust based agents. In: Falcone, R., Singh, M., Tan, Y.-H. (eds.) Trust in Cyber-societies. LNCS (LNAI), vol. 2246, pp. 111–132. Springer, Heidelberg (2001). https://doi.org/10.1007/3-540-45547-7_7
38. Wu, D., Sun, Y.: The emergence of trust in multi-agent bidding: a computational approach. In: Proceedings of the 34th Annual Hawaii International Conference on System Sciences, p. 8. IEEE (2001)
39. Yager, R., Fedrizzi, M., Kacprzyk, J.: Advances in the Dempster-Shafer theory of evidence (1994)

40. Yu, B., Singh, M.P.: Distributed reputation management for electronic commerce. Comput. Intell. **18**(4), 535–549 (2002)
41. Yu, B., Singh, M.P.: An evidential model of distributed reputation management. In: Proceedings of the First International Joint Conference on Autonomous Agents and Multiagent Systems: Part 1, pp. 294–301. ACM (2002)

Reasoning About Trustworthiness in Cyber-Physical Systems Using Ontology-Based Representation and ASP

Thanh Hai Nguyen[1]([✉]), Tran Cao Son[1], Matthew Bundas[1], Marcello Balduccini[2], Kathleen Campbell Garwood[2], and Edward R. Griffor[3]

[1] New Mexico State University, Las Cruces, USA
{thanhnh,stran,bundasma}@nmsu.edu
[2] St. Joseph's University, Philadelphia, USA
{mbalducc,kcampbel}@sju.edu
[3] National Institute of Standards and Technology, Gaithersburg, USA
edward.griffor@nist.gov

Abstract. This paper presents a framework for reasoning about trustworthiness in cyber-physical systems (CPS) that combines ontology-based reasoning and answer set programming (ASP). It introduces a formal definition of CPS and several problems related to trustworthiness of a CPS such as the problem of identification of the most vulnerable components of the system and of computing a strategy for mitigating an issue. It then shows how a combination of ontology based reasoning and ASP can be used to address the aforementioned problems. The paper concludes with a discussion of the potentials of the proposed methodologies.

Keywords: CPS · Ontology · ASP · Knowledge representation · Reasoning · Planning

1 Introduction

Cyber-physical systems (CPS) are sophisticated systems that include engineered interacting networks of physical and computational components. These highly interconnected and integrated systems provide new functionalities to improve quality of life and enable technological advances in critical areas, such as personalized health care, emergency response, traffic flow management, smart manufacturing, defense and homeland security, and energy supply and use. In addition to CPS, there are other terms (e.g., Industrial Internet, Internet of Things (IoT), machine-to-machine (M2M), smart cities) that describe similar or related systems and concepts. CPS and related systems (including the IoT and the Industrial Internet) are widely recognized as having great potential to enable innovative applications and impact multiple economic sectors in the worldwide economy. Evidence of the promise of CPS is evident in autonomous vehicles, intelligent buildings, smart energy systems, robots, and smart medical devices. Realizing the promise of CPS requires interoperability among heterogeneous components and

© Springer Nature Switzerland AG 2021
T. Uchiya et al. (Eds.): PRIMA 2020, LNAI 12568, pp. 51–67, 2021.
https://doi.org/10.1007/978-3-030-69322-0_4

systems, supported by new reference architectures using shared vocabularies and definitions. Addressing the challenges and opportunities of CPS requires broad consensus in foundational concepts, and a shared understanding of capabilities and technologies unique to CPS. The following example describes the Elevator Monitoring scenario, a simple concrete CPS with its concerns and requirements:

Example 1. Elevator Monitoring

The system consists of an elevator cabin (EC) *which is controlled by a control panel* (CP). *The panel communicates with the* elevator receiver *(ER), and calls the elevator to the required floor. The receiver communicates with the elevator's* pulley function *(PF), which releases/clenches and allows the elevator to move down/up along the rope and pulley to the designed floor. The* elevator sensor & camera *(ESCam) will detect the number of passengers in the cabin. If passenger number* >11, *the sensor* (ESCam) *will communicate to the receiver* (ER) *to stop the elevator from moving and flashes a warning light indicating an overload.*

The National Institute of Standards and Technology (NIST) has taken the first step towards addressing the aforementioned challenge. In the last few years, NIST has established the CPS Public Working Group (CPS PWG) to bring together a broad range of CPS experts in an open public forum to help define and shape key characteristics of CPS, which allows us to better manage development and implementation within, and across, multiple smart application domains. This resulted in the CPS Framework (CPSF) [11], which provides a principled design and analysis methodology for CPS that is intended to be applicable across all relevant domains of expertise. Preliminary research aimed at addressing questions related to the trustworthiness of a CPS utilizing the CPSF was presented in [2], which introduced a CPSF *ontology* capturing the keys elements of CPSF such as *facets* (modes of the system engineering process: conceptualization, realization and assurance), *concerns* (areas of concern) and *aspects* (clusters of concerns: functional, business, human, trustworthiness, timing, data, composition, boundaries, and lifecycle).

In this paper, we view a CPS as a dynamic system that consists of several components with various constraints and preferences which will be referred as *concerns* hereafter. Given a concrete state of the system, a concern might or might not be satisfied. This paper builds upon and extends the work from [2] in a number of important directions. First of all, it introduces precise mathematical formalization of CPS and of a variety of important questions related to the trustworthiness of the components of a CPS and of a CPS as a whole: (*i*) what are the most vulnerable (least trustworthy) components in a CPS? (*ii*) how to mitigate (or prevent) an attack on a component? (*iii*) what is the probability that a mitigation strategy will succeed? Of the above, (i) and (iii) have also not been addressed before in the context of CPSF. Additionally, the paper establishes a clear relationship between CPSF and the formalization of CPS. Finally, it demonstrates how the combination of ontology-based reasoning and ASP, together with a suitable extension of the CPS ontology from [2], can be leveraged for the development of solutions to the above questions. Hybrid reasoning aims at combining the best of both worlds, particularly for scalability in practical applications. Take for instance a large CPS such as an aircraft carrier. Answering the above questions requires sophisticated reasoning, which typically struggles with scalability. By combining the system scalability and describability of ontology-based reasoning with the flexibility of ASP, one can leverage the former to extract inference-rich information for the subsystems relevant to the task at hand, on which ASP-based reasoning can then carry out sophisticated reasoning in a more focused, efficient way.

2 Background

2.1 CPS Framework (CPSF), CPS Ontology, and Representation

CPSF defines a set of *concerns* related to a CPS such as *Trustworthiness, Functionality, Safety, etc.* These concerns are organized in a multi-rooted, tree-like structure (a "forest" in graph theory), where branching corresponds to the *decomposition of concerns*. Each tree is called a concern tree. The concerns at the roots of this structure, the highest level concerns, are called *aspects. Properties*[1] are features of a CPS that address a certain concern, e.g. encrypted traffic might address the privacy concern (see Table 1 for details). Specifically, the *Trustworthiness* aspect is related to the trustworthiness of CPS, including concerns such as *security*, *privacy*, *safety*, *reliability*, and *resilience*. In this paper, we adopt the definition of trustworthiness from the NIST CPSF, where the term is taken to denote *the demonstrable likelihood that the system performs according to designed behavior under any set of conditions as evidenced by its characteristics.*

The *CPS Ontology*, introduced in [2], defines concepts and individuals related to *Trustworthiness*, and the relationships between them (e.g., sub-class of, has-subconcern, etc.). Figure 1, excluding the nodes labeled CP, ER, PF, EC and ESCam and links labeled "relates", shows a fragment of the CPS ontology where circle nodes represent specific concerns and grey rectangle nodes represent properties. To facilitate information sharing, the CPS Ontology leverages standards such as the Resource Description Framework (RDF[2]) and the Web Ontology Language (OWL[3]) for describing the data, representing the entities and their relationships, formats for encoding the data and related metadata for sharing and fusing. An entity or relationship is defined in the ontology by a RDF-triple (*subject, predicate, object*). Table 1 lists the main classes and relationships in the CPS ontology. Most of the class names are self-describing. Intuitively, a relationship between a property and a concern indicates that the property positively (or negatively) affects the associated concern when it is true (or false). Specific concerns are represented as individuals: Trustworthiness as an individual of class *Aspect*, Security and Cybersecurity of class *Concern*. Edges linking aspects and concerns are represented by the relation has-subconcern. A relation has-subconcern is used to associate a concern with its sub-concerns. Thus, Trustworthiness aspect has-subconcern Security, which in turn has-subconcern Cybersecurity.

---

[1] There is an unfortunate clash of terminology between OWL properties and CPS properties. Throughout this paper, the intended meaning of the word 'property' can be identified from the context of its use.

[2] https://www.w3.org/TR/rdf-concepts/.

[3] https://www.w3.org/TR/owl-features/.

The notion of *satisfaction* of a concern is also introduced in [2]. In the simplest case, a concern is satisfied when all properties related to it, directly or indirectly (via the sub-concern relation) must be *true*. Inference can then be applied to propagate the satisfaction, or lack thereof, of concerns and properties throughout a concern tree. For example, given a concern that is not *satisfied*, one can leverage relations `has-subconcern` and/or `addressed-by` to identify the sub-concerns and/or properties that are not satisfied, either directly or indirectly.

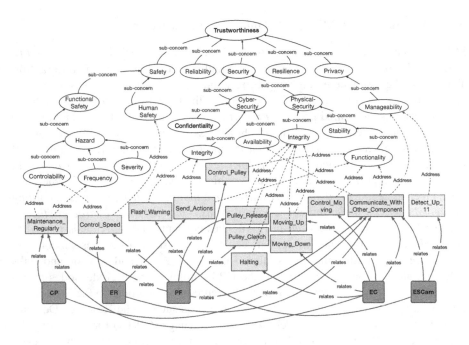

Fig. 1. A fragment of the trustworthiness concern ontology

2.2 Answer Set Programming

Answer set programming (ASP) [12, 16] is a declarative programming paradigm based on logic programming under the answer set semantics. A logic program Π is a set of rules of the form: $c \leftarrow a_1, \ldots, a_m, \text{not } b_1, \ldots, \text{not } b_n.$ where a_i's, and b_i's are atoms of a propositional language[4] and *not* represents (default) negation. Intuitively, a rule states that if a_i's are believed to be true and none of the b_i's is believed to be true then c must be true. For a rule r, r^+ and r^- denote the sets $\{a_1, \ldots, a_m\}$ and $\{b_1, \ldots, b_n\}$, respectively.

Let Π be a program. An interpretation I of Π is a set of ground atoms occurring in Π. The body of a rule r is satisfied by I if $r^+ \subseteq I$ and $r^- \cap I = \emptyset$. A rule r is satisfied by

---

[4] For simplicity, we often use first order logic atoms in the text which represent all of its ground instantiations.

Table 1. Main components of the CPS ontology

Class	Meaning
Concern	Concerns that stakeholders have w.r.t. to a system, such as *security*, *integrity*, etc. They are represented in the ontology as individuals. The link between a concern and its sub-concerns is represented by the `has-subconcern` relation
Aspect	High-level grouping of conceptually equivalent or related cross-cutting concerns (i.e. *human*, *trustworthiness*, etc.). In the ontology, *Aspect* is subclass of class *Concern*
Property	Class of the properties relevant to a given CPS. The fact that a property addresses a concern is formalized by relation `addressed-by`
Configuration	Features of a CPS that characterize its state, e.g. if a component is on or off. When property satisfaction can change at run-time, corresponding individuals will be included in this class
Action and Constraint	Actions are those within the control of an agent (e.g., an operator) and those that occur spontaneously. Constraints capture dependencies among properties (e.g., mutual exclusion)
Object property	Meaning
hasSubConcern	The object property represents the `has-subconcern` relationship between the concerns
addrConcern	The object property represents the `addressed-by` relation between a concern and a property

I if the body of r is satisfied by I implies $I \models c$. When c is absent, r is a constraint and is satisfied by I if its body is not satisfied by I. I is a model of Π if it satisfies all rules in Π. For an interpretation I and a program Π, the *reduct* of Π w.r.t. I (denoted by Π^I) is the program obtained from Π by deleting *(i)* each rule r such that $r^- \cap I \neq \emptyset$, and *(ii)* all atoms of the form *not b* in the bodies of the remaining rules. Given an interpretation I, observe that the program Π^I is a program with no occurrence of *not b*. An interpretation I is an *answer set* [8] of Π if I is the least model (wrt. $\subseteq$) of Π^I. Several extensions (e.g., *choice atoms*, *aggregates*, etc.) have been introduced to simplify the use of ASP. We will use and explain them whenever it is needed. Efficient and scalable ASP solvers are available[5].

3   OA4CPS: A Hybrid Reasoner for CPS

We now describe OA4CPS, a hybrid reasoning system for CPS, which combines ontology-based reasoning with ASP. As a prototypical system for reasoning about CPS, OA4CPS focuses on the trustworthiness aspect of CPS. The techniques developed in this paper can be easily extended to cover other aspects described in CPSF. Figure 2 depicts the overview of OA4CPS. The input of OA4CPS is a *CPS Theory Specification* $\Delta = (\mathscr{S}, I)$ (details follow shortly). The *translator* combines Δ with the relevant fragment Ω of the CPS Ontology obtained from a suitable query. The *translator* then

---

[5] See, e.g., https://potassco.org/clingo/.

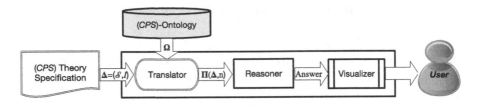

Fig. 2. Overall architecture of OA4CPS

produces an ASP program $\Pi(\Delta, n)$ where n is an integer, denoting the time horizon of interest for reasoning tasks over Δ. $\Pi(\Delta, n)$ is utilized by the *reasoner* to answer questions related to the trustworthiness of the system. The answers generated by the *reasoner* can be presented to the users in different formats (e.g., sunburst chart, hierarchy, etc.) by a *visualizer*. The focus of this section will be on the *reasoner* and how CPS specifications are translated to ASP programs for use with the *reasoner*. Details about the implementation of the translator and the visualizer are given in the next section.

3.1   From CPS Theory Specification to ASP Encoding

We view a CPS as consisting of *interacting cyber and physical components*, which affect properties defined in the CPS ontology, e.g. trustworthiness of the system. For this reason, we extend the CPS ontology with a `component` class, a `relates` relationship which represents the connection between components and properties in the CPS ontology, and an `action` class which allows for the representation and reasoning about actions in CPS. In this paper, we employ the action ontology described in [15] where the action profile (preconditions, effects, input, output, etc.) is described by an OWL ontology and reasoning about effects of actions is formalized via action language $\mathcal{B}$ [10]. From now on, "CPS ontology" refers to the CPS ontology in [2] with these features.

In the CPS ontology, a CPS is characterized by a set of concerns (represented as ontology individuals), a set of properties, and a relation linking properties to the concerns they address. Formally, a *CPS domain* $\mathcal{S}$ is a tuple (C, A, F, R) where C is a set of components; A is a set of actions that can be executed over $\mathcal{S}$; F is a finite set of fluents of $\mathcal{S}$; R is a set of relations that maps each $c \in C$ to a set of properties $R(c)$ defined in the CPS ontology. A *state* s of $\mathcal{S}$ is an interpretation[6] of F. A *CPS theory* is a pair $(\mathcal{S}, I)$ where $\mathcal{S}$ is a CPS domain and I is a state representing the *initial configuration* of $\mathcal{S}$. The execution of actions changes the states, e.g., the truth values of the properties, thereby affecting the trustworthiness of the system. As such, we can utilize the framework for reasoning about actions and changes to reason about the trustworthiness of a CPS. In this paper we adopt a hybrid approach to reasoning that leverages the power of ontology-based reasoning for drawing (time-independent) inferences about a CPS and its components and the flexibility of ASP for non-monotonic reasoning and reasoning about actions and change. For this reason, the translator takes in input a CPS theory $\Delta = (\mathcal{S}, I)$, queries the CPS ontology for relevant information, and produces the ASP

---

[6]   In the following, we will follow the convention to describe a state s as a subset of F and say that $f \in s$ is true in s and $f \notin s$ is false in s.

program $\Pi(\Delta, n)$ discussed earlier. We use ASP as it is well-known for working with ontologies (e.g., [4,7,14,15]). Due to the space limitation, we will illustrate the translation from Δ to $\Pi(\Delta, n)$ using a simplified CPS $\Delta_{Ele} = (\mathscr{S}_{Ele}, I_{Ele})$ for controlling an elevator in Example 1. We define $\Pi(\Delta_{Ele}, n) = \Pi(\Omega) \cup \Pi_d(\mathscr{S}_{Ele}) \cup \Pi(I_{Ele}) \cup \Pi_n(\mathscr{S}_{Ele})$. Each component of $\Pi(\Delta_{Ele})$ is defined next.

CPS Ontology. Let Ω be obtained by querying the CPS ontology for the task at hand. $\Pi(\Omega)$ is the ASP encoding of Ω and includes representations of the classes, individuals, and relationships as well as the supporting rules. Listing 1.1 depicts selected rules of $\Pi(\Omega)$.

Listing 1.1. $\Pi(\Omega)$ *(selected rules)*

```
1   class(concern). class(aspect). class(property). class(action).
2   subClass(aspect,concern). concern(X) :- aspect(X).
3   aspect(trustworthiness). isInstOf(trustworthiness,aspect).
4   concern(security). isInstOf(security,concern).
5   concern(cybersecurity). isInstOf(cybersecurity,concern).
6   concern(integrity). isInstOf(integrity,concern).
7   ...
8   subCo(cybersecurity,integrity). subCo(security,cybersecurity).
9   subCo(trustworthiness,security).
10  ...
11  prop(flash_warning). isInstOf(flash_warning,property).
12  addBy(integrity,flash_warning).
13  ...
14  subClass(X,Y):-subClass(Z,Y), subClass(X,Z).
15  ...
```

Components, Fluents, and Relations. The components of $\mathscr{S}_{Ele}$ are EC, CP, ER, PF, and ESCam. They are related to various properties defined in the CPS Ontology, e.g., CP is related to maintenance_regularly, communicate_with_other, etc. These components and relationships are depicted in the bottom part of Fig. 1, where squares (links labeled *relates*) represent components and (relationships). A component X is operating in different modes, each mode is a property P; this is denoted with a fluent $im(X, P)$ ('im' stands for 'in mode'). The *relates* relationship is translated into predicate of the form $rel(X, P)$. The sets of components, fluents, and relations of $\mathscr{S}_{Ele}$ are translated into a set of ASP facts, denoted by $\Pi_d(\mathscr{S}_{Ele})$, as follows:

Listing 1.2. $\Pi_d(\mathscr{S}_{Ele})$

```
1   comp(cp). comp(er). comp(pf). comp(ec). comp(escam).
2   fluent(im(escam,flash_warning)).fluent(im(er,control_speed)).
3   fluent(im(escam,detect_up_11)).fluent(im(ec,halting)).
4   ...
5   rel(cp,maintenance_regularly). rel(er,send_actions).
6   rel(er,communicate_with_other_comp). rel(er,control_speed).
7   rel(pf,control_speed). rel(ec,control_moving).
8   rel(escam,flash_warning). rel(escam,detect_up_11).
9   ...
```

Initial Configuration. Initially, properties associated with $\mathscr{S}_{Ele}$ can be *true* ($\top$) or *false* ($\bot$). The initial state is translated into a set of facts of the form $o(x, \top)$ or $o(x, \bot)$ for $x \in I$ or $x \notin I$ (Lines 1–5, Listing 1.3). An initial configuration I_{Ele} of the values of $\mathscr{S}_{Ele}$

is done by two rules that define the predicate h and ¬h at the time step 0 (Lines 6–7, Listing 1.3). Line 8 describes which properties having available patch.

Listing 1.3. $\Pi(I_{Ele})$

```
1   o(maintenance_regularly,T). o(control_speed,⊥).
2   o(flash_warning,T). o(send_actions,T). o(pulley_release,T).
3   o(pulley_clench,T). o(control_pulley,T). o(control_moving,T).
4   o(moving_up,T). o(moving_down,T). o(halting,T).
5   o(detect_up_11,⊥). o(communicate_with_other_comp,T).
6   h(P,0)  :- o(P,T), prop(P).
7   -h(P,0) :- o(P,⊥), prop(P).
8   availablePatch(control_speed).
```

Actions and Constraints. Actions change the status of the properties in $\mathscr{S}_{Ele}$ and constraints describe dependencies among CPS properties. For brevity, we focus on a few affecting the trustworthiness of the system. For simplicity of presentation, we assume that each property P can be changed by the action $tOn(P)$ or $tOff(P)$. In addition, there is an action $patch(P)$—a special action that could help restore P to the value *true* if the patch of P is available (availablePatch(P) holds). Furthermore, when escam detects more than 11 passengers, it sets the property *overloaded* to be true. Actions and constraints are translated to ASP rules accordingly following Table 2. In these rules, T is an integer ranging between 0 and n, $h^*(l,t)$ stands for $h(l,t)$ if l is a fluent and for $-h(f,t)$ if l is a negated fluent $\neg f$.

Table 2. Formulas of an action a

Statement type	ASP translation
(0) *Action declaration*	$\text{action}(a)$.
(1) *Executability condition*	$\text{exec}(a,T) :- \text{step}(T), h^*(p_1,T), \ldots, h^*(p_n,T)$.
(2) *Dynamic law*	$h^*(f,T+1) :- \text{step}(T), \text{occurs}(a,T), h^*(p_1,T), \ldots, h^*(p_n,T)$.
(3) *State constraint*	$h^*(f,T) :- \text{step}(T), h^*(p_1,T), \ldots, h^*(p_n,T)$.
(4) *Inertial axiom*	$h(f,T+1) :- \text{step}(T), h(f,T), \text{not } -h(f,T+1)$. $-h(f,T+1) :- \text{step}(T), -h(f,T), \text{not } h(f,T+1)$.

Listing 1.4. $\Pi_n(\mathscr{S}_{Ele})$

```
1    action(tOn(X))   :- prop(X).    action(tOff(X)) :- prop(X).
2    action(patch(X)) :- prop(X).
3    h(im(ec,halting),T) :- h(im(escam,overloaded),T), step(T).
4    exec(tOn(X),T)   :- -h(X,T), prop(X), step(T).
5    exec(tOff(X),T)  :- h(X,T), prop(X), step(T).
6    exec(patch(X),T):- prop(X), availablePatch(X),-h(X,T), step(T).
7    h(X,T+1)   :- occurs(tOn(X),T), step(T).
8    -h(X,T+1)  :- occurs(tOff(X),T), step(T).
9    h(X,T+1)   :- occurs(patch(X),T), step(T).
10   ...
```

3.2 Queries Related to Trustworthiness

Given a CPS theory $\Delta = (\mathscr{S}, I)$, [11] list several questions related to the trustworthiness of Δ and its components. We are interested in the following questions:

- *Question #1* ($\mathbf{Q_1}$): *What is the most/least trustworthy of component in Δ?* This is one of most important questions in CPSF, as discussed in [11].
- *Question #2* ($\mathbf{Q_2}$): *What can be done to mitigate an issue?*
- *Question #3* ($\mathbf{Q_3}$): *Which mitigation strategies have the best chance to succeed?* This question is a generalization of ($\mathbf{Q_2}$).

3.3 Queries Answering Using $\Pi(\Delta, n)$

In this section, we use $\Pi(\Delta, n)$ to answers $\mathbf{Q_1} - \mathbf{Q_3}$. For each query $\mathbf{Q_i}$, we develop a program $\Pi_i(\Delta)$ such that answer sets of $\Pi(\Delta, n) \cup \Pi_i(\Delta)$ are solutions of the query.

Most/Least Trustworthy Components. A component $c \in C$ might be related to many concerns through the properties in $R(c)$, whose truth values depend on the state s of the system. If a property $p \in R(c)$ is false in s, it might negatively affect a concern and affect the trustworthiness of the system. Likewise, if p is true in s, it will positively affect the concern and helps strengthen the trustworthiness of the system.

Assume that all concerns and properties are equally important, we could say that a component $c \in C$ is less trustworthy than a component $c' \in C$ if the number of concerns negatively associated to c is greater than the number of concerns negatively associated to c. Alternatively, we can characterize the trustworthiness of a component by the numbers of concerns that are positively or negatively affected by the component and use them in evaluating the components. In this paper, we adopt this second alternative. Since actions change the truth values of properties, we will define these numbers wrt. a state, i.e., for each $x \in C$ and a state s of $\mathscr{S}$, we define $twc^+(x,s)$ ($twc^-(x,s)$) as the number of concerns in Ω that are positively (negatively) impacted by component x in a state s.

Note that the direct relationship between a concern c and a property p in Ω is translated into $\mathrm{addBy}(c,p)$ in $\Pi(\Omega)$. We say that a property p addresses a concern c if (*i*) p directly addresses c; or (*ii*) there exists some subconcern c' of c that is addressed by p. As such, a concern c is positively (negatively) impacted by a component x at the step t if x is related to a property p that addresses c and p holds (does not hold) at t. Formally, for a state s of $\mathscr{S}$: $twc^+(x,s) = \Sigma_{p \in R(x), p \in s} |\{c \mid addBy(c,p)\}|$ and $twc^-(x,s) = \Sigma_{p \in R(x), p \notin s} |\{c \mid addBy(c,p)\}|$. Next, we propose an ordering among the components using the two numbers. Let $\delta(x,s) = twc^+(x,s) - twc^-(x,s)$.

Definition 1. *For a CPS $\mathscr{S} = (C, A, F, R)$, $c_1, c_2 \in C$, and state s of $\mathscr{S}$,*

- c_1 *is more trustworthy than c_2 in s, denoted by $c_1 \succ_s c_2$ (or c_2 is less trustworthy than c_1, denoted by $c_2 \prec_s c_1$), if $\delta(c_1,s) > \delta(c_2,s)$; and*
- c_1 *is as trustworthy as c_2 in s, denoted by $c_1 \sim_s c_2$, if $\delta(c_1,s) = \delta(c_2,s)$.*

$c_1 \succeq_s c_2$ *denotes that $c_1 \succ_s c_2$ or $c_1 \sim_s c_2$. c is the most (least) trustworthy component of $\mathscr{S}$ in s if $c \succeq_s c'$ ($c' \succeq_s c$) for every $c' \in C$.*

Proposition 1. *Let $\mathscr{S} = (C, A, F, R)$ be a CPS system and s be a state in $\mathscr{S}$. The relation $\succeq_s$ over the components of $\mathscr{S}$ is transitive, symmetric, and total.*

Proposition 1 shows that $\succeq_s$ has min/maximal elements, i.e., least/most trustworthy components of a system always exist. The program $\Pi_1(\mathscr{S})$ for computing these components is listed below.

Listing 1.5. $\Pi_1(\mathscr{S})$: Computing the most/least trustworthy component

```
1   addBy(C,P)  :- prop(P), addBy(O,P), subCo(C,O).
2   tw_p(P,N)   :- N=#count{C:addBy(C,P)}, prop(P).
3   pos(X,P,T)  :- comp(X), prop(P), step(T), rel(X,P), h(P,T).
4   neg(X,P,T)  :- comp(X), prop(P), step(T), rel(X,P),-h(P,T).
5   twcp(X,TW,T) :- TW=#sum{N,P:tw_p(P,N), prop(P), pos(X,P,T)},
6            comp(X), step(T).
7   twcn(X,TW,T) :- TW=#sum{N,P:tw_p(P,N), prop(P), neg(X,P,T)},
8            comp(X), step(T).
9   d(X,D,T) :- comp(X), step(T), twcp(X,TWp,T), twcn(X,TWn,T),
10           D=TWp-TWn.
11  most(X,T)  :- comp(X), step(T), d(X,M,T), M == #max{N:d(_,N,T)}.
12  least(X,T):- comp(X), step(T), d(X,M,T), M == #min{N:d(_,N,T)}.
```

In $\Pi_1(\mathscr{S})$, $tw\_p(p,n)$ says that p impacts n concerns. $pos(x,p,t)$ $(neg(x,p,t))$ states that x has a property p which positively (negatively) impacts the concerns related to it at the step t. $twcp(x,tw,t)$ $(twcn(x,tw,t))$ states that the number of concerns positively (negatively) impacted by x at step t is tw. $\#count\{C:addBy(C,P),prop(P)\}$ is an aggregate atom and encodes the cardinality of the set of all concerns addressed by P. Similarly, $\#sum\{...\}$, $\#max\{...\}$, and $\#min\{...\}$ are aggregate atoms and are self-explanatory.

Proposition 2. *For a CPS theory $\Delta = (\mathscr{S}, I)$ and an answer set S of $\Pi(\Delta, n) \cup \Pi_1(\mathscr{S})$, $twc^+(x, s_t) = k$ iff $twcp(x,k,t) \in S$ and $twc^-(x, s_t) = k$ iff $twcn(x,k,t) \in S$ where $s_t = \{h(f,t) \mid h(f,t) \in S\}$. Furthermore, x is a most (least) trustworthy component in s_t iff $most(x,t) \in S$ (least$(x,t) \in S$).*

The proposition confirms that the program correctly computes the values of $twc^+(x,s)$ and $twc^-(x,s)$ as well as the most (least) component of $\mathscr{S}$ in a state. Its proof follows immediately from the definition of the predicate *addBy* and the definition of aggregate functions in ASP. As such, to identify the most trustworthy component of $\mathscr{S}$, we only need to compute an answer set S of $\Pi(\Delta) \cup \Pi_1(\mathscr{S})$ and use Proposition 2.

Example 2. For Δ_{Ele}, we can easily see that (from Figure 1) $tw\_p(\text{control\_speed}, 6)$ and $tw\_p(\text{flash\_warning}, 4)$, etc. belong to any answer set of $\Pi(\Delta_{Ele}) \cup \Pi_1(\mathscr{S}_{Ele})$. Similar atoms are present to record the number of concerns affected by different properties. Furthermore, $twcp(cp, 15, 0)$, $twcn(cp, 0, 0)$, $twcp(er, 16, 0)$, $twcn(er, 6, 0)$, $twcp(pf, 28, 0)$, $twcn(pf, 6, 0)$, $twcp(ec, 32, 0)$, $twcn(ec, 0, 0)$, $twcp(escam, 13, 0)$, and $twcn(escam, 3, 0)$ belong to any answer set of $\Pi(\Delta_{Ele}) \cup \Pi_1(\mathscr{S}_{Ele})$: *EC* is the most trustworthy component; *ER* and *ESCam* are the least trustworthy components at step 0.

We conclude this part with a brief discussion on possible definitions of $\succeq$. The proposed definition assumes everything being equal. On the other hand, $twc^+(x,s)$ and $twc^-(x,s)$ can be used in different ways such as via the lexicographic order to define an ordering that prefers the number of positively impacted concerns over the negatively ones (or vise versa). Any ordering based on $twc^+(x,s)$ and $twc^-(x,s)$ could easily be implemented using ASP. Last but not least, in practice, the ordering $\succeq$ might be qualitative and user-dependent, e.g., an user might prefer confidentiality over integrity. $\succeq$ can be defined over a qualitative ordering and implemented in ASP in a similar fashion that preferences have been implemented (e.g., [9]).

Generating Mitigation Strategies. Let $\mathscr{S} = (C,A,F,R)$ be a CPS domain and s be a state of $\mathscr{S}$. A concern c is *satisfied* in a state s if all properties addressing c are true in s and all sub-concerns of c are *satisfied* in s; otherwise, it is unsatisfied. Mitigating an issue is therefore equivalent to identifying a plan that suitably changes the state of properties related to it. The mitigation problem can then be defined as follows:

Definition 2. *Let $\mathscr{S} = (C,A,F,R)$ be a CPS system and s be a state of $\mathscr{S}$. Let Σ be a set of concerns. A mitigation strategy addressing Σ is a plan $[a_1,\dots,a_k]$ whose execution in s results in a state s' such that for every $c \in \Sigma$, c is satisfied in s'.*

As planing can be done using ASP, the mitigation problem can be solved using the following code:

Listing 1.6. $\Pi_2(\mathscr{S})$: Computing Mitigation Strategy for concern c

```
1   -h(sat(C),T)  :-  addBy(C,P),-h(P,T).
2   -h(sat(X),T)  :-  subCo(X,Y),  not h(sat(Y),T).
3   -h(sat(X),T)  :-  subCo(X,Y),-h(sat(Y),T).
4   h(sat(C),T)   :-  not -h(sat(C),T),  concern(C).
5   1{occurs(A,T):action(A)}1  :-  step(T),  T<n.
6   :-  occurs(A,T),  not exec(A,T).
7   :-  not h(sat(c),n),  concern(c).
```

The first four rules are for reasoning about the satisfaction of concerns (see also [2]): $h(sat(C),T)$ states that concern C is satisfied at the time step T. The first rule states that C is not addressed if some of its properties is false. The next two rules propagate the unsatisfaction of a concern from its subconcern. Finally, a concern is satisfied if it cannot be proven that it is unsatisfied. In line 5, the rule containing the atom $1\{occurs(A,T) : action(A)\}1$ —a *choice atom*—is used to generate the action occurrences and says that at any step T, exactly one action must occur. The second to last rule states that an action can only occur if it is executable. The last rule helps enforce that $h(sat(c),n)$ must be true in the last state, at step n. For a set of concerns Σ, let $\Pi_2(\mathscr{S})[\Sigma]$ be the program obtained from $\Pi_2(\mathscr{S})$ by replacing its last rule with the set $\{:-not \ \ h(sat(c),n). \mid c \in \Sigma\}$. Based on the results in answer set planning, we have:

Proposition 3. *Let $\Delta = (\mathscr{S},I)$ be a CPS theory and Σ be a set of concerns. Then, $[a_0,\dots,a_{n-1}]$ is a mitigation strategy for Σ iff $\Pi(\Delta,n) \cup \Pi_2(\mathscr{S})[\Sigma]$ has an answer set S such that $occurs(a_i,i) \in S$ for every $i = 0,\dots,n-1$.*

We conclude the section with a brief discussion on possible changes to $\Pi_2(\mathscr{S})$ that might be useful in certain situations and can easily be implemented in ASP. Observe that the execution of an action might change the state of some properties between step 0 and n or might result in some concerns becoming unsatisfied. To prevent this, the following rule can be added to $\Pi_2(\mathscr{S}[\Sigma])$: :$-\mathtt{h}(\mathtt{sat}(\mathtt{C}),0), -\mathtt{h}(\mathtt{sat}(\mathtt{C}),\mathtt{T}), \mathtt{T} > 0$. which says that if C is satisfied at 0 then it should not be unsatisfied at any step > 0.

Example 3. Consider again Δ_{Ele}. Assume that `control_speed` and `detect_up_11` are initially false (Fig. 1), leading to many unsatisfied concerns (e.g., `Safety`, `Privacy`) and affecting the `Trustworthiness` of the system. In this situation, `tOn(control_speed)`, `patch(control_speed)` and `tOn(detect_up_11)` can be used to repair these properties (action `patch(detect_up_11)` is not executable). $\Pi_2(\mathscr{S})$ have four mitigation strategies of length 2:

- $\alpha_1 = \mathtt{tOn}(\mathtt{detect\_up\_11}) \cdot \mathtt{tOn}(\mathtt{control\_speed})$
- $\alpha_2 = \mathtt{tOn}(\mathtt{detect\_up\_11}) \cdot \mathtt{patch}(\mathtt{control\_speed})$
- $\alpha_3 = \mathtt{tOn}(\mathtt{control\_speed}) \cdot \mathtt{tOn}(\mathtt{detect\_up\_11})$
- $\alpha_4 = \mathtt{patch}(\mathtt{control\_speed}) \cdot \mathtt{tOn}(\mathtt{detect\_up\_11})$

Best Mitigation Strategies. Mitigation strategies computed in the previous subsection assumed that actions always succeeded. In practice, actions might not always succeed. In this case, it is preferable to identify strategies with the best chance of success. Assume that each action a is associated with a set of statements of the form: a **success_with** v **if** X where $v \in [0,1]$ and X is a consistent set of literals in $\mathscr{S}$. This statement says that if each $l \in X$ is true in a state s and a is executable in s then v is the probability of a's execution in s succeeds. We assume that if a occurs in two statements "a **success_with** v_1 **if** X_1" and "a **success_with** v_2 **if** X_2" with $X_1 \neq X_2$ then $v_1 = v_2$ or there exists $p \in F$ such that $\{p, \neg p\} \subseteq X_1 \cup X_2$. Furthermore, for a state s in which no statement associated with some action a is applicable, we assume that a succeeds with probability 1 in s if it is executable in s. It is easy to see that this set of statements defines a mapping $pr : A \times States \rightarrow [0,1]$ where $States$ denotes the set of all states of $\mathscr{S}$ and $pr(a,s)$ represents the probability that the execution of a in s succeeds. Such concepts can easily be added to the CPS ontology and information about the actions in the theory can easily be added to the theory specification.

In this setting, the execution of a sequence of actions (or a strategy) $[a_0, \ldots, a_{n-1}]$ in a state s succeeds with the probability $\Pi_{i=0}^{n-1} pr(a_i, s_i)$ where $s_0 = s$, and for $i > 0$, s_i is the result of the execution of a_{i-1} in s_{i-1}. Problem **Q3** focuses on identifying strategies with the maximal probability of success. Due to the space limitation, we will only briefly discuss how this problem can be addressed. Let $\Pi_3(\mathscr{S})$ be the program $\Pi_2(\mathscr{S})$ extended with the following rules:

- for each statement a **success_with** v **if** $p_1, \ldots, p_n$, the two rules:
  `pr(a,v,T) :- h*(p1,T),...,h*(pn,T).`
  `dpr(a,T) :- h*(p1,T),...,h*(pn,T).`
  which check for the satisfaction of the condition in a statement defining the probability of success in the step T and states that it is defined.
- the rule: `pr(A,1,T) :- exec(A,T), not dpr(A,T).`
  which says that by default, the probability of success of a at step T is 1.
- computing the probability of the state at step T:
  `prob(1,0).`
  `prob(U*V,T+1) :- prob(U,T),occurs(A,T),pr(A,V,T).` where the first rule says that the probability of the state at the time 0 is 1; $prob(v,t)$ states that the probability of reaching the state at the step t is v and is computed using the second rule.

We have that if $[a_0, \ldots, a_{n-1}]$ and S is an answer set of $\Pi(\Delta) \cup \Pi_3(\mathscr{S}) \cup \{occurs(a_i, i) \mid i = 0, \ldots, n-1\}$ then $prob(\Pi_{i=0}^{n-1} pr(a_i, s_i), n) \in S$. To compute the best strategy, we add the rule #maximize$\{$V : prob(V,n)$\}$. to $\Pi_3(\mathscr{S})$.

Example 4. Continue with Example 3. We assume that the probability of success of tOn(detect_up_11), tOn(control_speed), and patch(control_speed) are 0.8, 0.7, 0.3 in every state, respectively. In this case, the strategies α_1 and α_3 have the maximal probability to succeed.

4 Towards a Decision-Support System for CPSF

As a demonstration of the potential use of our approach, in this section we give a brief overview of a decision-support system that is being built for use by CPS designers, managers and operators. We also include preliminary considerations on performance aspects.

The decision-support system relies on an implementation of the translator and of the different modules for answering queries described in Sect. 3, and comprises a reasoning component and a visualization component. Figure 4 shows the reasoning component at work on two queries related to the elevator example. Notice how the user can ask the system to reason about satisfaction of concerns and to produce mitigation plans. The output of the reasoning component can then be fed to the visualization component, where advanced visualization techniques allow practitioners to get a birds-eye view of the CPS or dive into specific details. For instance, the sunburst visual from Fig. 3 provides a view of the CPS from Fig. 1 where the aspects are presented in the inner most ring. Moving outwards, the visualization shows concerns from increasingly deeper parts of the concern tree and properties. The left-hand side of the figure depicts the visualization in the case in which all concerns are satisfied (blue), while the right-hand side shows how the sunburst changes when certain concerns (highlighted as red) are not satisfied. Focusing on the right-hand side, the text box open over the visual reports that the trustworthiness aspect is currently not satisfied and the level at which this concern is not being met is the concern of privacy and the property of manageability. The visual allows for a pinpoint where within the CPS framework issues have arisen that when addressed can enable a working state.

To ensure flexibility and to allow for investigation on the scalability on larger CPS, the decision-support system is designed to support a variety of hybrid ontology-ASP reasoning engines. Currently, we consider four reasoning engines: the *naïve engine* is implemented by connecting, in a loosely-coupled manner[7], the SPARQL reasoner[8] and the Clingo ASP solver. This engine issues a single SPARQL query to the ontology reasoner at the beginning of the computation, fetching all necessary data. The *Clingo-Python engine* is another loosely-coupled engine, leveraging Clingo's ability to run

---

[7] By loosely-coupled, we mean that the components see each other as black-boxes and only exchange information, via simple interfaces, at the end of their respective computations. Compare this with a tightly-coupled architecture, where the components have a richer interfaces for exchange state information and controlling each other's execution flow while their computations are still running.

[8] https://www.w3.org/TR/rdf-sparql-query/.

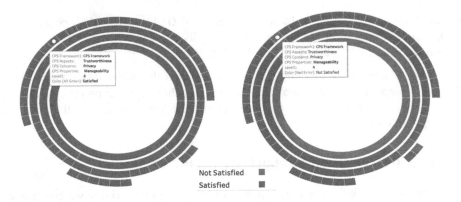

Fig. 3. Visualization component

Python code at the beginning of the computation. This engine issues multiple queries in correspondence to the occurrences of special "external predicates" in the ASP program, which in principle allows for a more focused selection of the content of the ontology. The *DLVHex2 engine* also uses a similar fragmentation of queries, but the underlying solver allows for the queries to be executed at run-time, which potentially results in more focused queries, executed only when strictly needed. Finally, the *Hexlite engine* leverages a similar approach, but was specifically designed as a smaller, more performant alternative to *DLVHex2*.

In this preliminary phase of our investigation on scalability, all reasoning engines have exhibited similar performance, as exemplified by Table 3. The table summarizes the results of question-answering experiments on the Lane Keeping/Assist System (LKAS) [2] domain and on the Elevator domain. The reasoning tasks considered are for answering questions $Q_1 - Q_3$ discussed earlier. While the results show that the naïve engine is marginally better than the others, the differences are quite negligible, all within 10%.

Table 3. CPS domains querying, extracting and reasoning summary

Query	LKAS				Elevator			
	Naïve	Clingo-Python	DLVHex2	Hexlite	Naïve	Clingo-Python	DLVHex2	Hexlite
Q_1	1.827s	2.013s	1.82s	1.831s	1.853s	2.03s	1.795s	1.88s
Q_2	1.91s	2.15s	1.913s	1.924s	1.933s	2.076s	1.941s	2.02s
Q_3	2.02s	2.33s	2.031s	2.027s	2.051s	2.253s	2.058s	2.181s

It is conceivable that larger-scale experiments will eventually exhibit similar patterns to those found in other research on the scalability of hybrid systems (e.g., [3]). We obtained positive indications on this from preliminary experiments we conducted

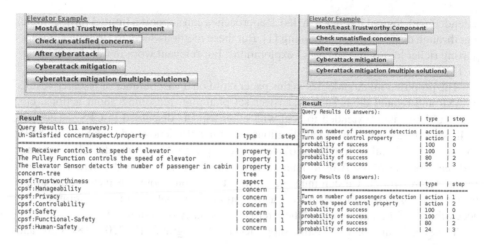

Fig. 4. Reasoning component

on ontologies featuring up to 150K triples, 85 classes, 61K individuals, 30 object properties, 40 data properties, and 45 subclass relations. In these experiments, running our system consistently took a minute or less. (We omit the details due to space considerations, since it is not the focus of this paper.) A thorough analysis will be the subject of a separate paper.

5 Conclusions, Related Work, and Discussion

This paper discusses three important problems related to the trustworthiness of CPS and their solutions using hybrid ontology-ASP reasoning. Specifically, for each problem, the paper presents a mechanism for answering it and proves relevant properties. To the best of our knowledge, this is the first attempt at a mathematically precise solution of issues in the CPSF, addressing the need for tools for evaluating the trustworthiness of CPS.

Due to space constraints, we limit our overview of related work to what we consider the most relevant approaches. The literature from the area of cybersecurity is often focused on the notion of graph-based attack models. Of particular relevance is the work on Attack-Countermeasure Trees (ACT) [18]. An ACT specifies how an attacker can achieve a specific goal on a IT system, even when mitigation or detection measures are in place. While ACT are focused on the Cybersecurity concern, our approach is rather generally applicable to the broader Trustworthiness aspect of CPS and can in principle be extended to arbitrary aspects of CPS and their dependencies. The underlying formalization methodology also allows for capturing sophisticated temporal models and ramified effects of actions. In principle, our approach can be extended to allow for quantitative reasoning, e.g. by leveraging recent work on Constraint ASP and probabilistic ASP [3,5,17]. As we showed above, one may then generate answers to queries that are *optimal* with respect to some metrics. It is worth pointing out that the combination of physical (non-linear) interaction and logical (discrete or Boolean) interaction of CPS can be modeled as a mixed-integer, non-linear optimization problem (MINLP) extended with logical inference. MINLP approaches can support a limited form of logic, e.g. through disjunctive programming [1]. But these methods seem to struggle with supporting richer logics and "what-if" explorations. For relevant work in this direction, see [6, 13].

The proposed methodologies in this paper build on a vast number of research results in ASP and related areas such as answer set planning, reasoning about actions, etc. and could be easily extended to deal with other aspects discussed in CPSF. They are well-positioned for real-world applications given the efficiency and scalability of ASP-solvers that can deal with millions of atoms, incomplete information, default reasoning, and features that allow ASP to interact with constraint solvers and external systems. In our future works, we continue monitoring to reason about the factors that affect to the *trustworthiness* of a CPS such as the probability that a component crashes, the accessibility of a component and the internal probability of system errors.

The second author is partially supported by NSF grants 1757207, 1812628, and 1914635.

Disclaimer. Official contribution of the National Institute of Standards and Technology; not subject to copyright in the United States. Certain commercial products are identified in order to adequately specify the procedure; this does not imply endorsement or recommendation by NIST, nor does it imply that such products are necessarily the best available for the purpose. Portions of this publication and research effort are made possible through the help and support of NIST via cooperative agreements 70NANB18H257 and 70NANB19H102.

References

1. Balas, E.: Disjunctive programming: Cutting planes from logical conditions. In: Nonlinear Programming, vol. 2, pp. 279–312. Elsevier (1975)
2. Balduccini, M., Griffor, E., Huth, M., Vishik, C., Burns, M., Wollman, D.A.: Ontology-based reasoning about the trustworthiness of cyber-physical systems. ArXiv abs/1803.07438 (2018)
3. Balduccini, M., Lierler, Y.: Constraint answer set solver EZCSP and why integration schemas matter. J. Theory Pract. Logic Program. (TPLP) **17**(4), 462–515 (2017)
4. Baral, C.: Knowledge Representation, Reasoning, and Declarative Problem Solving with Answer Sets. Cambridge University Press, Cambridge (2003)
5. Baral, C., Gelfond, M., Rushton, N.: Probabilistic reasoning with answer sets. Theory Pract. Logic Program. **9**(1), 57–144 (2009)
6. D'Iddio, A.C., Huth, M.: ManyOpt: an extensible tool for mixed, non-linear optimization through SMT solving. CoRR abs/1702.01332 (2017). http://arxiv.org/abs/1702.01332
7. Eiter, T.: Answer set programming for the semantic web. In: Dahl, V., Niemelä, I. (eds.) ICLP 2007. LNCS, vol. 4670, pp. 23–26. Springer, Heidelberg (2007). https://doi.org/10.1007/978-3-540-74610-2_3
8. Gelfond, M., Lifschitz, V.: Logic programs with classical negation. In: Warren, D., Szeredi, P. (eds.) Logic Programming: Proceedings of the Seventh International Conference, pp. 579–597 (1990)
9. Gelfond, M., Son, T.C.: Prioritized default theory. In: Selected Papers from the Workshop on Logic Programming and Knowledge Representation, LNAI, vol. 1471, pp. 164–223. Springer, Heidelberg (1998)

10. Gelfond, M., Lifschitz, V.: Action languages. Electron. Trans. Artif. Intell. **2**, 193–210 (1998)
11. Griffor, E., Greer, C., Wollman, D.A., Burns, M.J.: Framework for cyber-physical systems: volume 1, overview (2017)
12. Marek, V., Truszczyński, M.: Stable models and an alternative logic programming paradigm. In: The Logic Programming Paradigm: A 25-Year Perspective, pp. 375–398 (1999)
13. Mistr, M., D'Iddio, A.C., Huth, M., Misener, R.: Satisfiability modulo theories for process systems engineering. Eprints for the optimization community, 19 June 2017
14. Nguyen, T.H., Potelli, E., Son, T.C.: Phylotastic: an experiment in creating, manipulating, and evolving phylogenetic biology workflows using logic programming. TPLP **18**(3–4), 656–672 (2018). https://doi.org/10.1017/S1471068418000236
15. Nguyen, T.H., Son, T.C., Pontelli, E.: Automatic web services composition for phylotastic. In: PADL, pp. 186–202 (2018). https://doi.org/10.1007/978-3-319-73305-0_13
16. Niemelä, I.: Logic programming with stable model semantics as a constraint programming paradigm. Ann. Math. Artif. Intell. **25**(3,4), 241–273 (1999). https://doi.org/10.1023/A:1018930122475
17. Ostrowski, M., Schaub, T.: ASP modulo CSP: the clingcon system. J. Theory Pract. Logic Program. (TPLP) **12**(4–5), 485–503 (2012)
18. Roy, A., Kim, D.S., Trivedi, K.S.: Attack countermeasure trees (ACT): towards unifying the constructs of attack and defense trees. Secur. Commun. Netw. **5**(8), 929–943 (2012). https://doi.org/10.1002/sec.299

Optimal Deterministic Time-Based Policy in Automated Negotiation

Yasser Mohammad[1,2,3(✉)]

[1] NEC Corporation, Tokyo, Japan
y.mohammad@nec.com, yasserm@aun.edu.eg, y.mohammad@aist.go.jp
[2] Assiut University, Asyut, Egypt
[3] National Institute of Advanced Industrial Science and Technology (AIST), Tokyo, Japan

Abstract. Automated negotiation is gaining more attention as a possible mechanism for organizing self-interested intelligent agents in a distributed environment. The problem of designing effective negotiation strategies in such environments was studied extensively by researchers from economics, computer science, multiagent systems, and AI. This paper focuses on the problem of finding effective deterministic time-based offering strategies given an opponent acceptance model. This problem was studied earlier and optimal solutions are known for the simplest case of a static stationary acceptance model. This paper proposes an efficient approach for calculating the effect of different manipulations of the offering policy on expected utility and uses that to provide a faster implementation of the optimal algorithm for static stationary acceptance models and provide an approximate extension to more realistic acceptance models.

1 Introduction

Automated negotiation is a process for reaching agreements between automated agents. Recent applications of automatic negotiation include permission management in IoT systems, Wi-Fi channel assignment [4], agriculture supply chain support, supply chain management [11], and providing feedback for student negotiation skills [7].

One of the most commonly used automated negotiation protocols is the alternating offers protocol with its multilateral extension (the stacked alternating offers protocol) [1]. Several methods have been proposed for negotiation under this protocol [3]. These methods can be classified into exact solutions of simplified problems [2] and heuristic solutions to the most general case [8]. This paper falls within the first category.

Given a negotiation scenario (issues, utility function and opponent acceptance model), our goal is to find a deterministic time-based negotiation strategy the maximizes expected utility of the agent. The two simplifying assumptions in this case are the availability of a time-based acceptance model for the opponent (learned through past interactions), and the constraints that the policy

© Springer Nature Switzerland AG 2021
T. Uchiya et al. (Eds.): PRIMA 2020, LNAI 12568, pp. 68–83, 2021.
https://doi.org/10.1007/978-3-030-69322-0_5

to be found is deterministic and depends only on negotiation time (not on the opponent's past behavior during the negotiation).

The first simplification is justified in some real-world situations in which repeated negotiations with the same opponent are expected (as in the case of e-commerce). The second simplification is a constraint on the policy to be found an *not on the negotiation scenario itself*. This means that better policies that take into account the behavior of the opponent during the negotiation explicitly can lead to higher utilities for the agent. Our evaluation shows that despite this self-imposed handicap, the policies learned by the proposed method are on-bar with state-of-the-art methods that rely heavily on the behavior of the opponent during the negotiation.

The main idea behind the proposed method is to utilize fast $O(1)$ operations for evaluating the effect of different manipulations of a given policy on the expected utility to provide an efficient solution which is guaranteed to be optimal for *static* acceptance models and is an approximate solution for *general* acceptance models.

The reset of this paper is organized as follows: Section 2 provides the notation and defines the problem. Section 3 presents the GCA algorithm as the most related previous work. Section 4 introduces the proposed efficient operations for evaluating effects of different manipulations on the expected utility of a given policy and Sect. 5 builds upon this to provide a faster version of GCA for static acceptance models and an approximate solution for general acceptance models. Two evaluation experiments are reported in Sect. 6. Limitations and future directions are then discussed in Sect. 7. The paper is then concluded.

2 Notation and Problem Statement

A negotiation session is conducted between multiple agents representing self-interested actors over a set of issues. Issues can have discrete or continuous values. Every possible assignment of a value to each issue is called an *outcome* and during negotiation it may also be called an *offer*. Ω denotes the – possibly uncountable – set of all outcomes and ω indicates a member of this set (the ϕ value is a member of all outcome sets and represents disagreement).

If an agreement is reached, the agreed upon outcome is called a *contract* (ω_c). Each agent a is assumed to be self-interested with some internal *utility function* $u_a : \Omega \rightarrow [0, 1]$ that assigns a numeric value (assumed to be normalized to the range 0 to 1 in this work) to every possible outcome including the special *no-agreement* outcome.

Negotiation sessions are conducted in *rounds* in which different outcomes are offered/judged by the agents according to some negotiation *protocol*. Negotiation protocols can be moderated with a moderator-agent that have a special role or unmoderated with all agents having similar roles. Several negotiation protocols have been proposed over the years. They can either be mediated [6] or un-mediated [1]. This work utilizes the un-mediated Stacked Alternating Offers Protocol (SOAP) [1].

To provide an incentive for the agents to concede from the outcome with maximum utility, a time-limit is usually applied to the negotiation and the session is broken (times-out) automatically if no agreement is reached within a predefined real-time or number of rounds limit (T).

The SOAP protocol works as follows: An ordering of the agents is defined. The first agent starts the negotiation by *offering* an outcome ω^0 which is visible to all other agents. The next agent either *accepts* the offer (by offering it back), ends the negotiation (by offering the no-agreement outcome ϕ which is automatically accepted), or proposes a new offer. The process continues until an agent accepts an offer or ϕ is offered and is automatically accepted.

2.1 Policy

The behavior of an agent a is defined by its offering strategy acceptance strategy, and leaving strategy. For this work, we assume no discounting on utilities which means that ending a negotiation by leaving the table is never a rational choice. The optimal leaving strategy is simply never to end the negotiation.

For the acceptance strategy, two flavors will be discussed. The first approach is to follow the offering strategy and accept only an offer if it is the same as the next offer in the offering strategy. This is the approach taken in [2] and is called *strict-policy-adherence* hereafter. Another possibility is to accept an offer if its utility is higher than the expected utility from following the offering strategy. This is called *opportunistic-acceptance* hereafter as it enables the agent to take advantage of unexpected opportunities in the form of offers with high utility from the opponent.

An offering policy (abbreviated as just policy hereafter) is used by the agent to decide what to offer next during the negotiation. In this paper, we are interested in deterministic time-based policies. These policies are mappings from the negotiation relative time to an outcome where relative time is defined as the fraction of the time-limit that have already passed. Formally: $\pi : [0, 1] \leftarrow \Omega$. We focus on the case where the time-limit is given as a number of rounds T leading to a discrete policy of the form $\pi : [1, T] \leftarrow \Omega^1$. For this class of policies, we can refer to the outcome at index i of policy π as π_i.

2.2 Acceptance Models

In this paper we consider one agent engaged in a negotiation session. We assume that the agent has available to it an *acceptance model* (AM) representing the probability that the opponent would accept some outcome under certain conditions (a).

Figure 1 shows a hierarchy of AM types. The most *general* AMs have no constraints on how acceptance probabilities of different outcomes change during the negotiation. Formally: $a(\omega) = f(\omega, t, \pi, x)$, where x are external factors affecting

---

[1] Dealing with real-time deadlines will be discussed in Sect. 5.3.

the negotiation. If external influences can be ignored (e.g. the existence of outside options [9]), the acceptance model can be thought of as a function of the offers proposed by the negotiator: $a(\omega) = f(\omega, t, \pi)$. These are called *Dynamic* acceptance models.

In both of these cases, the probability that the opponent accepts an offer depends on the *policy* employed by the agent. This kind of acceptance model provides enough information for finding an optimal policy against that opponent but the interplay between the AM and the policy complicates the problem of finding an optimal solution considerably. Moreover, these types of models are the hardest to learn. We do not consider these two types of AMs in this paper.

If both external influences and past offers can be ignored, we have *time-dependent* AM (TDAM) that have the general form $a(\omega) = f(\omega, t)$. An important feature of these AMs is that the probability of acceptance does not depend on the policy given the offer which simplifies the problem of finding an optimal solution. Moreover, time-dependent AMs are easier to learn from negotiation records through counting.

The simplest form of TDAMs is the static AM (SAM) in which the probability of acceptance depends solely on the offer (i.e. no time dependence). This is the only type of AM for which an efficient optimal offering strategy learning algorithm is known [2].

2.3 Problem Statement

A negotiation scenario is defined – from the point of view of an agent engaged in it – by a tuple $(\Upsilon \equiv (T, \Omega, u, a)$) where:

$T \in \mathbf{I}$: The time-limit of the negotiation which can be specified as a number of rounds $a \in A$ or a real-time limit in a suitable time-unit[2].

$\Omega \equiv \{\omega\}$: Possible outcomes (assumed countable) where $|\Omega| \geq 2$. The special value ϕ represents the no-agreement outcome. For this rest of this paper we will let K be the cardinality of Ω.

$u: \Omega \to [0, 1]$ The utility function of the agent which maps every outcome to a real value representing the agent's utility of achieving this outcome. $u(\phi)$ is the *reservation-value* of the agent representing the utility of reaching no agreement.

$a: \Omega \times [0, T] \to [0, 1]$ The acceptance model. A TDAM is assumed. Static acceptance models are just a special case where $a(\omega, i) = a(\omega, j) \ \forall 0 \leq i, j \leq T$

The problem targeted in this paper (called Optimal Policy Learning [OPL]) can be stated as: *Given a negotiation scenario, find a deterministic time-based policy that maximizes the agent's expected utility.* Formally:

$$\pi^* = \arg \max_{\pi} \mathcal{EU}(\pi|\Upsilon)$$

---

[2] We start by assuming that the time-limit is specified as a number of rounds but will relax this requirement later.

3 Related Work: GCA

Algorithm 1. Greedy Concession Algorithm (GCA)[2]

1: $\pi \leftarrow <>$ ▷ Empty policy
2: **for** $k \leftarrow 1 : T$ **do**
3:      $\omega^* \leftarrow \arg\max_{\omega \in \Omega - \pi} \mathcal{EU}(sort_{\mathcal{EU}}(\pi \circ \omega))$
4:      $\pi \leftarrow sort_{\mathcal{EU}}(\pi \circ \omega^*)$ ▷ Operator o inserts an element in a set

---

Finding the optimal offering policy is one of the core problems of automated negotiation [3]. Several methods have been proposed over the years [8]. Most of these methods are heuristics try to find a good enough policy (evaluated empirically against a variety of opponents and in different domains).

In this work, we are more interested in finding an *optimal* or approximately optimal solution to the OPL problem which constraints the search space for policies enough to allow for theoretical advancement.

The most related work to the proposed method is the Greedy Concession Algorithm (GCA) proposed by Baarslag et al. which provides an optimal solution for the special case of static acceptance models (SAM) [2] and with the further constraints that outcomes cannot be repeated within the policy (i.e. $i \neq j \rightarrow \pi_i \neq \pi_j$).

The most important contribution of this work were two proofs showing that the optimal policy for such acceptance models are always conceding policies and they can be found by greedily building longer optimal policies given shorter ones.

A conceding policy π^c is defined as one satisfying the condition: $i < j \rightarrow u(\pi_i^c) \geq u(\pi_j^c)$. The greedy construction condition implies that the optimal policy of length T is included within the optimal policy of length $T + 1$ *up to a permutation of outcomes*.

Using these two properties (and the aforementioned two constraints on the problem: SAM and offer non-repetition) Baarslag et al. proposed GCA which incrementally builds the optimal policy starting by the optimal policy of length one known to be $\omega^* = \arg\max_\omega u(\omega)a(\omega)$. Algorithm 1 describes this approach. An efficient implementation of GCA will keep the policy in a sorted list by utility values allowing for insertion of new outcomes in $O(\log(K))$ operations. Nevertheless, the whole algorithm will still require $O(TK^2)$ steps because the calculation of expected utility for each outcome still requires $O(T)$ operations.

In this paper, we extend that work in two ways: Firstly, we provide a faster approach for finding optimal policies for SAMs. Secondly, we provide an approximate algorithm for finding optimal policies for TDAMs.

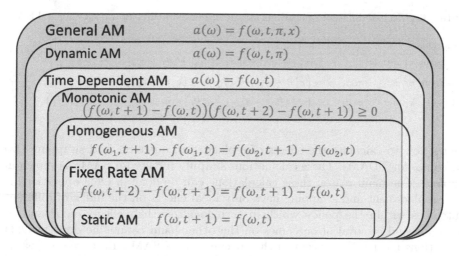

Fig. 1. Types of acceptance models studied in this work

4 Policy Operations

The *expected utility* for a policy π can easily be found as:

$$\mathcal{EU}(\pi) = \sum_{i=1}^{T} u(\pi_i)a(\pi_i) \prod_{j=1}^{i-1} 1 - a(\pi_j) \qquad (1)$$

We define the following components which will be used later in the proposed algorithm:

$P : [0, T] \to [0, 1]$ The aggregate multiplication of probability of rejection used in the evaluation of $\mathcal{EU}$.

$$P_i = \prod_{j=0}^{i-1} 1 - a(\pi_j) \qquad (2)$$

$S : [0, T] \to [0, 1]$ The cumulative sum of the expected utility value.

$$S_i = \sum_{j=0}^{i} u(\pi_j)a(\pi_j)P_j = S_{i-1} + u(\pi_i)a(\pi_i)P_i \qquad (3)$$

Using this notation, the expected utility $\mathcal{EU}(\pi)$ is simply S_T. Calculating the expected utility of a policy using Eq. 1 is an $O(|\pi|) = O(T)$ operation. To simplify the notation further we use a_i^j to mean $a(\pi_i, j)$ and u_i to mean $u(\pi_i)$ when the policy π is clear from the context. Moreover, the time superscript will be removed for SAMs to emphasize the fact that the acceptance probability does not depend on time.

Using P and S values, it is possible to find the change in expected utility for various manipulations of the policy π efficiently in $O(1)$ operations. Table 1

Table 1. Effect of different operations on the expected utility of a policy for a TDAM

Operation	Symbol	Effect on $\mathcal{EU}(\pi)$
Replacing π_i with ω	π_i^ω	$P_i(u(\omega)a(\omega,i) - u(\pi_i)a(\pi_i)) + (S_T - S_i)\frac{a(\omega,i)-a(\pi_i,i)}{1-a(\pi_i,i)}$
Swapping π_i, π_j	$\pi_{i\leftrightarrow j}$	$u_i\left(a_i^j P_j \frac{1-a_j^i}{1-a_i^j} - a_i^i P_i\right) + u_j\left(a_j^i P_i - a_j^j P_j\right) + (S_{j-1} - S_{i+1})\frac{a_i^i-a_j^i}{1-a_i^j}$
Swapping π_i, π_{i+1}	$\pi_{i\to 1}$	$u_i\left(a_i^{i+1}P_i(1-a_{i+1}^i) - a_i^i P_i\right) + u_{i+1}\left(a_{i+1}^i P_i - a_{i+1}^{i+1}P_{i+1}\right)$

shows how to calculate the effects of replacing an outcome, and swapping two outcomes for TDAMs. These calculations simplify further for SAMs as shown in Table 2. The main reason these calculations can be done in $O(1)$ operations is that replacement and swapping have only local effects on the index of different outcomes within the policy which in turn localizes their effects on P and S. Insertion and removal of outcomes on the other hand cannot be done in $O(1)$ operations for TADMs except in the special case of SAMs. Because our goal is to handle TADMs in general, we restrict our algorithms to use replacement and swapping only.

Table 2. Effect of different operations on the expected utility of a policy for a SAM

Replacing outcome at i with ω	π_i^ω	$P_i(u(\omega)a(\omega) - u(\pi_i)a(\pi_i)) + (S_T - S_i)\frac{a(\omega)-a(\pi_i)}{1-a(\pi_i)}$
Swapping outcomes at i, j	$\pi_{i\leftrightarrow j}$	$u_i a_i \left(P_j \frac{1-a_j}{1-a_i} - P_i\right) + u_j a_j (P_i - P_j) + (S_{j-1} - S_{i+1})\frac{a_i-a_j}{1-a_i}$
Swapping outcomes at i, $i+1$	$\pi_{i\to 1}$	$P_k a(\pi_i)a(\pi_{i+1})(u(\pi_{i+1}) - u(\pi_i))$
Inserting outcome ω at location t	$\pi_{\omega@i}$	$u(\omega)a(\omega)P_i - a(\omega)(S_T - S_{i-1})$

proof for π_i^ω Here we provide a simple proof for the results found in the first row of Table 1 and Table 2. The rest of the tables can be proved using similar manipulations and will not be detailed here.

$$\mathcal{EU}(\pi_k^\omega) = \sum_{i=1}^{k-1} u_i a_i^i P_i + u(\omega)a(\omega,k)P_k$$
$$+ \sum_{i=k+1}^{T} u_i a_i^i P_k (1 - a(\omega,k)) \prod_{j=k+1}^{i=1} 1 - a_j^j \tag{4}$$

$\mathcal{EU}(\pi)$ can be written as $\sum_{i=1}^{T} u_i a_i^i P_i = \sum_{i=1}^{k-1} u_i a_i^i P_i + u_k a_k^k P_k + \sum_{i=k+1}^{T} u_i a_i^i P_i$. Subtracting and after some manipulations we get:

$$\mathcal{EU}(\pi_k^\omega) - \mathcal{EU}(\pi) = P_k(u(\omega)a(\omega,k) - u_k a_k^k) - (S_T - S_k)$$
$$+ (S_T - S_k)\frac{1 - a(\omega,k)}{1 - a_k^k}$$
$$= P_k(u(\omega)a(\omega,k) - u(\pi_k)a(\pi_k)) + (S_T - S_k)\frac{a(\omega,k) - a(\pi_k,k)}{1 - a(\pi_k,k)} \tag{5}$$

$\square$

5   Proposed Algorithms

Based on policy manipulations with efficient $\mathcal{EU}$ calculations presented in Sect. 4, we provide two algorithms to deal with SAMs and general TDAMs in this section.

5.1   Static Acceptance Models: QGCA

A faster version of GCA (called Quick GCA hereafter) that employs the swapping operation defined in Table 2 (specifically the insertion operation) is shown in Algorithm 2. This algorithm is designed for static acceptance models.

Algorithm 2. Quick Greedy Concession Algorithm (QGCA)

1: $\pi \leftarrow <>$ ▷ Empty *linked* list
2: $\mathcal{L}_\omega = 0 \forall \omega \in \Omega$ ▷ Initialize location of all outcomes
3: $S_{-1}, P_{-1} \leftarrow 0, 1$
4: **for** $k \leftarrow 1 : T$ **do**
5:      $d^*, \omega^* \leftarrow -\infty, \phi$
6:      **for** $\omega \in \Omega$ **do**
7:          $i \leftarrow \mathcal{L}_\omega$ ▷ Lookup location of insertion
8:          $d_\omega \leftarrow S_{i-1} + (1 - a(\omega))(\mathcal{EU}(\pi) - S_{i-1}) + P_i \mathcal{EU}(\omega)a(\omega)$
9:          **if** $d_\omega \geq d^*$ **then**
10:             $d^*, \omega^* \leftarrow d_\omega, \omega$
11:         $\pi \leftarrow \pi \circ_{\mathcal{L}_{\omega^*}} \omega^*$ ▷ Insert best outcome in its correct place
12:         Update $S, P, \mathcal{L}$
13:         **if** no-repetition **then**
14:             $\Omega \leftarrow \Omega - \{\omega^*\}$

The main idea of QGCA is to use the S, P arrays and the fast evaluation of the effect of outcome insertion (Table 2) to speedup the process of finding the optimal outcome to insert when increasing the policy length. To achieve that we further keep track of the *optimal* insertion location of each outcome within the policy. From the fact that the optimal policy must be a conceding policy, it is directly inferred that – in order to keep optimality – an outcome ω can be inserted in an optimal policy π at location k only if the following condition is satisfied:

$$u(\pi_i) \geq u(\omega) \forall i < k$$

We keep the first of these locations in a map called $\mathcal{L} : \omega \leftarrow [0, T]$. Updating this map is straightforward after an outcome is inserted and can be done in $O(T)$ operations.

The first step (Lines $6 - 11$) is to find an outcome to add to the existing policy (remember that in the first step this policy is empty). For each outcome we get the location to insert that outcome in the list (Line 8) which is known and stored in $\mathcal{L}$ because outcomes with higher utility appear first in the policy

(Line 8). We then calculate the new expected expected utility ($\mathcal{EU}$) after this insertion (Line 9) using:

$$
\begin{aligned}
\mathcal{EU}(\pi \circ_i \omega) = S_{i-1} + (1 - a(\omega))(\mathcal{EU}(\pi) - S_{i-1}) \\
+ P_i \mathcal{EU}(\omega) a(\omega)
\end{aligned}
\tag{6}
$$

where $\pi \circ_i \omega$ is the policy that results from adding ω at location i, and $i \equiv \mathcal{L}_\omega$ is the correct location to insert ω in order to maximize $\mathcal{EU}$ according to the concession lemma [2].

We keep track of the outcome that leads to the maximum increase in $\mathcal{EU}$ (call it ω^*) (Line 10 − 11). Once we have the best outcome (ω^*), we simply insert it into the policy (Line 12) and update the $S, P, \mathcal{L}$ lists to reflect the new policy. Updating S and P is simple using the Eqs. 2, 3 respectively. $\mathcal{L}$ is updated by increasing $\mathcal{L}_\omega$ by one for all outcomes ω with a utility less than the utility of ω^* and keeping the rest of oc without change (this is an $O(K)$ operations).

Finally, we remove the just-added outcome (ω^*) from the list of outcomes to consider in the future (Ω) if the protocol does not allow repetition of offers.

The time complexity for finding the optimal *deterministic time-based policy* using QGCA is $O(KT)$ for static models compared with $O(K^2T)$ for GCA.

5.2   General Time Dependent Acceptance Models: PA

QGCA is only optimal for static acceptance models. Even the simplest opponents cannot be modeled by these acceptance models as explained in Sect. 2.2. In this section, we provide a method for approximating the optimal deterministic policy against an agent with a time-dependent acceptance model. Extension to dynamic acceptance models is not discussed in this paper.

The first step in our approach is to approximate the time-dependent acceptance model with a static acceptance model and apply QGCA to it. This approach is called QGCA$^+$ hereafter. Several approaches for carrying out this approximation. We simply use learn a SAM and a TDAM for each scenario (Sect. 5.3) and use the SAM for this step and the TDAM for the rest of the process. This step does not utilize the timing information. Call this initial policy π^c (for concession). As discussed earlier, the time-complexity of this step is $O(TK)$.

The second step is to improve this policy by finding the best permutation of π^c using a form of bubble sorting. Algorithm 3 gives the details of this process. The resulting policy is still not guaranteed to be optimal because it is restricted by the choices made by the QGCA$^+$ algorithm based on an approximation of the acceptance model. This policy is called π^b (for *bubble*). The time complexity of this step is $O(T^2)$. Note that this performance is only possible because we can find the change in expected utility for the swap in constant time and can also update the P and S matrices in constant time for this operation.

The final step is a form of simulated annealing starting from the result of PBS (π^b) resulting of the final policy π^a (for annealing). At every iteration r, A modification of the policy by changing one of its outcomes randomly is proposed π_s^ω. If the modification leads to a higher expected utility, the proposal is

---

Algorithm 3. Policy Bubble Sort (PBS)

1: $\pi \leftarrow \pi^c$ ▷ Start from the result of QGCA$^+$
2: **for** $r \leftarrow 1 : T$ **do**
3:      $\pi^- \leftarrow \pi$
4:      **for** $k \leftarrow 1 : T - 1$ **do**
5:          **if** $\mathcal{EU}(\pi_{k \rightarrow 1}) - \mathcal{EU}(\pi) > 0$ **then**
6:              $\pi \leftarrow \pi_{k \rightarrow 1}$
7:      **if** $\pi^- = \pi$ **then**
8:          **return** $\pi^b = \pi$
9: **return** $\pi^b = \pi$

---

accepted, otherwise the proposal is accepted only with the probability $\exp^{-\delta/\tau(r)}$ where δ is the decrease in expected utility due to the proposed operation and τ is a monotonically decreasing temperature term. This process is repeated a predefined number of iterations R. This algorithm is called *Policy Annealing* hereafter (PA) and is presented in Algorithm 4. The time complexity of this step is $O(RT)$ where R is the number of iterations.

The time-complexity of the complete system is $O(TK + T^2 + RT)$. By setting $R = KT$ which is what we used in our experiments, the total complexity becomes $O(T^2K)$ which is on the same order of magnitude as the original GCA algorithm – $O(K^2T)$ – but with the advantage of being usable for general TDAMs.

Algorithm 4. Policy Annealing

1: $\pi \leftarrow \pi^b$ ▷ Start from the result of PBS
2: **for** $r \leftarrow 1 : R$ **do**
3:      Randomly select a site s and an outcome $\omega \in \Omega - \{\pi_s\}$
4:      $\delta \leftarrow \mathcal{EU}(\pi_s^\omega) > \mathcal{EU}(\pi)$
5:      **if** $\delta > 0 \vee rand() > \exp^{-\delta/\tau(r)}$ **then**
6:          $\pi \leftarrow \pi_s^\omega$
7:      **for** $i \leftarrow 1 : T$ except s **do**   ▷ Find the best permutation
8:          **if** $\mathcal{EU}(\pi_{i \leftrightarrow s}) > \mathcal{EU}(\pi)$ **then**
9:              $\pi \leftarrow \pi_{i \leftrightarrow s}$
10: **return** $\pi^a = \pi$

5.3 Extensions

In this section, we discuss different extensions of the proposed methods to different negotiation scenarios.

Learning the Acceptance Model. In the real-world, acceptance models have to be learned from past experience. In this paper, we employ a simplistic method for learning the acceptance model to ensure that the performance reported is not just a side effect of an exceptionally good acceptance model.

During training, the agent acts randomly collecting all the negotiation logs. When an opponent accepts or proposes an offer, a counter for this outcome in the current negotiation round is incremented (current step for real-time scenarios). We then interpolate missing data linearly.

Handling Real-Time Deadlines. Up until now, we modeled the policy as a sequence mapping from round number to either an outcome or a utility value. This is an appropriate choice when the time-limit of the negotiation is defined in terms of round numbers. When the time-limit is defined in real-time (i.e. in seconds), the agent cannot know in advance the length of the policy to use.

A simple extension to such circumstance is to discretize time into a predefined number of steps (T) keeping the policy a discrete mapping. We still need to know the number of such steps to use for solving the optimization problem which depends on the number of steps that will actually be executed. To deal with this problem, while learning the acceptance model (Sect. 5.3) the agent can also learn a probability distribution over different time-lengths of the negotiation $(p(T))$. A policy can be generated for each length with a non-zero probability (for SAMs that requires no further calculations as these are already computed by QGCA). The agent can then use the policy corresponding to the length with the highest probability and switch dynamically to the more appropriate policy during the negotiation. This extension will be considered in future research.

6   Evaluation

The speed improvement of QGCA over GCA is algorithmic of order $O(K)$. The improvements brought by PBS and PA are on the other hand heuristic. In this section we report two experiments to evaluate these improvements.

All evaluations reported in this paper were conducted using the open-source NegMAS [12] negotiation library. State of art agents were run on the GENIUS [10] platform and connected to NegMAS through its Genius-bridge.

6.1   Probabilistic Opponents on Random Domains

The goal of this experiment was to evaluate the effectiveness of the PA algorithm and confirm the value added by each of its three stages (see Sect. 5) *when the assumptions of the OPL problem are satisfied*. To this end, we applied the proposed method to 100 domains with outcome space cardinality ranging between 10 and 100 with randomly selected utility functions for the evaluated agent each repeated 10 times to smooth out random effects. All negotiations were limited to a number of rounds equal to 50% of the number of outcomes. The opponent used a randomly generated TDAM acceptance model. Each configuration was repeated 100 times to smooth out random variations. The opponents did not offer and used a probabilistic acceptance strategy controlled by a randomly driven TDAM (a) with acceptance probability limited under $2/T$ leading to a total acceptance probability of no more then 0.5 for any outcome during the negotiation.

The evaluated agent received an acceptance model which is calculated as: $a(\omega, i) = \tilde{a}(\omega, i) + e(\omega, i)$ where e is sampled independently from a uniform distribution with a range of 20% the mean acceptance probability in a to simulate errors in learning the acceptance model.

The three stages of the proposed method (QGCA$^+$. PBS, PA) were evaluated against random offering, two baseline strategies (time-based boulware and naive tit-for-tat) and four state-of-the-art agents: PonPokoAgent (Winner of ANAC2017), Caudasaus (Winner of ANAC2016), ParsCat, and YXAgent (Second places in ANAC2016).

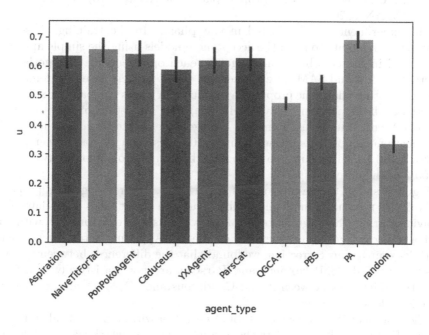

Fig. 2. Evaluation against probabilistic opponents.

Figure 2 shows the results of this analysis. As expected, PA outperforms PBS which outperforms QGCA$^+$ which supports the usefulness of every stage of the proposed algorithm. These differences were all statistically significant with a $p-$value less than 0.05 using a factorial t-test with Benferroni's multiple comparisons correction.

The differences that were *not* statistically significant were also suggestive. PA's performance was not different from the top state-of-the-art agents on statistical level even though it did not react in any way to the opponent's behavior. This is not as surprising as it sounds as the opponent did behave randomly in this experiment. Another finding from this experiment is that simple baseline agents behaved at the same level as state-of-the-art agents.

6.2 Realistic Domains and Opponents

For the rest of this section, we evaluate the proposed method using all negotiation domains with a cardinality between 10 and 100 in the GENIUS [10] package which contains all the domains used for the International Automated Negotiation Agents Competition (ANAC) since 2010 [5]. For multilateral scenarios of N agents, $N - 1$ different bilateral scenarios were constructed by selecting consecutive pairs of utility functions (leading to 62 different domains).

The opponents selected were state-of-the-art negotiation strategies. Namely: YXAgent, Caduceus, ParsCat (Top 3 places of ANAC2016), PonPokoAgent (Winner of ANAC2017).

The experiment was conducted in two phases. In the training phase, the agent acted randomly to learn the acceptance models using the simple approach highlighted in Sect. 5.3 by running against each opponent for 50 negotiations. Different TDAM and SAM were learned for each opponent at every domain.

In the testing phase, the proposed approach (PA), plus two baseline strategies (time-based boulware) and naive tit-for-tat) and four state of the art agents PonPokoAgent, Caudaseus, ParsCat, YXAgent negotiated against each of the aforementioned opponents in each domain 10 times. The number of rounds was limited to 10 which amounts to the agents being able to explore between 25% to 100% of the outcome space.

Figure 3 shows the results of this experiment. Even though the proposed method (PA) is run completely offline and the agent does not change its behavior during the negotiation in any way, its score is on bar with the most advanced negotiation heuristics evaluated. Applying factorial t-test with multiple-comparisons correction, we found that the differences between the proposed agent and PonPokoAgent and ParsCat are not statistically significant while the differences between it and Caudaseus and YXAgent are at a significance level less than 0.01.

The results of this experiment should be taken with a grain of salt for three reasons: Firstly, PA had access to the acceptance model which was not available to other agents. Secondly, the short negotiation time (10 rounds), made it harder for other agents to adapt their strategies to the behavior of the opponent. Finally, all agents except PA had access to the structure of the issue space (how many issues) and knew that the utility function was a linear combination of value functions. PA is incapable of exploiting this information in its current form.

The results are, nevertheless, instructive as they show that effective use of an empirically learned acceptance models can lead to improvements in the expected utility which is the main message of this paper.

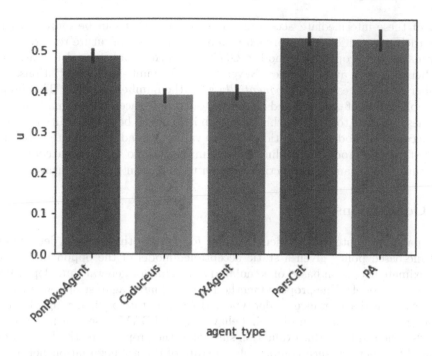

Fig. 3. Results of evaluation in GENIUS domains against state of the art opponents.

7   Limitations and Discussion

The main goal of this work is *not* to provide a new negotiation heuristic but
to extend existing foundational research on time-based strategies in negotiation.
One important result of this research is that concession – usually assumed to
be the default behavior during negotiation – is actually optimal only under the
assumption of a static acceptance model. This is clear from the fact that PA can
improve upon the *optimal* concession strategy found by QGCA$^+$. It is easy to
construct counter examples for both the concession lemma [2] and the optimality
of greedy policy construction for general time-dependent acceptance models.

A clear limitation of the proposed approach is that the policy is evaluated
based solely on past records. The opponent's behavior during the negotiation
does not affect the agent's choices. Baarlsag et al. suggested that GCA could be
effective in realistic negotiations by repeating the policy evaluation every iteration after updating the acceptance model based on the behavior of the agent
[2]. This same approach can be applied to the proposed method. Nevertheless, a
more founded approach is to develop an optimal procedure for dynamic acceptance models.

Even though we discussed a hierarchy of acceptance models in Sect. 2.2, existing methods including ours assumes either a SAM (GCA, QGCA) or the most
general TDAM (PBS, PA). Realistic acceptance models are expected to fall in
the range between these two extremes and designing optimal policy learners for

each of these intermediate acceptance model types that can be more efficient than the proposed TDAM approach is another direction of future research.

Finally, the proposed method is $O(K^2T)$ which is polynomial in both the number of rounds and outcomes. Nevertheless, for multi-issue negotiations, the number of outcomes grows *exponentially* with the number of issues. This limits the applicability of the proposed method to outcome-spaces with a small number of issues. One way to alleviate this limitation is to model both the utility function and acceptance models as functions of issue values instead of complete outcomes and extend the process of finding the optimal policy to take into account this structure. This is another direction we plan to pursue in the near future.

8 Conclusions

This paper presented an efficient method for finding the optimal deterministic time-based policy given a static acceptance model of the opponent and an approximate extension based on simulated annealing for general time-dependent acceptance models. The proposed method was evaluated against opponents that use the assumed acceptance model type and against state-of-the-art agents after learning an approximation of their behavior as a TDAM based on negotiation records. The results of this evaluation show that the proposed method is capable of providing performance comparable to state-of-the-art negotiation heuristics even though it does not react to the opponent's behavior during the negotiation.

References

1. Aydoğan, R., Festen, D., Hindriks, K.V., Jonker, C.M.: Alternating offers protocols for multilateral negotiation. In: Fujita, K., et al. (eds.) Modern Approaches to Agent-based Complex Automated Negotiation. SCI, vol. 674, pp. 153–167. Springer, Cham (2017). https://doi.org/10.1007/978-3-319-51563-2_10
2. Baarslag, T., Gerding, E.H., Aydogan, R., Schraefel, M.: Optimal negotiation decision functions in time-sensitive domains. In: 2015 IEEE/WIC/ACM International Conference on Web Intelligence and Intelligent Agent Technology (WI-IAT), vol. 2, pp. 190–197. IEEE (2015)
3. Baarslag, T., Hindriks, K., Hendrikx, M., Dirkzwager, A., Jonker, C.: Decoupling negotiating agents to explore the space of negotiation strategies. In: MarsaMaestre, I., Lopez-Carmona, M.A., Ito, T., Zhang, M., Bai, Q., Fujita, K. (eds.) Novel Insights in Agent-based Complex Automated Negotiation. SCI, vol. 535, pp. 61–83. Springer, Tokyo (2014). https://doi.org/10.1007/978-4-431-54758-7_4
4. De La Hoz, E., Marsa-Maestre, I., Gimenez-Guzman, J.M., Orden, D., Klein, M.: Multi-agent nonlinear negotiation for Wi-Fi channel assignment. In: Proceedings of the 16th Conference on Autonomous Agents and MultiAgent Systems, pp. 1035–1043. International Foundation for Autonomous Agents and Multiagent Systems (2017)
5. Fujita, K., Aydogan, R., Baarslag, T., Hindriks, K., Ito, T., Jonker, C.: Anac 2016 (2016). http://web.tuat.ac.jp/~katfuji/ANAC2016/
6. Ito, T., Hattori, H., Klein, M.: Multi-issue negotiation protocol for agents: exploring nonlinear utility spaces. IJCAI **7**, 1347–1352 (2007)

7. Johnson, E., Gratch, J., DeVault, D.: Towards an autonomous agent that provides automated feedback on students' negotiation skills. In: Proceedings of the 16th Conference on Autonomous Agents and MultiAgent Systems, pp. 410–418. International Foundation for Autonomous Agents and Multiagent Systems (2017)
8. Jonker, C.M., Aydogan, R., Baarslag, T., Fujita, K., Ito, T., Hindriks, K.V.: Automated negotiating agents competition (ANAC). In: AAAI, pp. 5070–5072 (2017)
9. Li, C., Giampapa, J., Sycara, K.: Bilateral negotiation decisions with uncertain dynamic outside options. IEEE Trans. Syst. Man Cybern. Part C (Appl. Rev.) **36**(1), 31–44 (2006)
10. Lin, R., Kraus, S., Baarslag, T., Tykhonov, D., Hindriks, K., Jonker, C.M.: Genius: an integrated environment for supporting the design of generic automated negotiators. Comput. Intell. **30**(1), 48–70(2014). https://doi.org/10.1111/j.1467-8640.2012.00463.x
11. Mohammad, Y., Fujita, K., Greenwald, A., Klein, M., Morinaga, S., Nakadai, S.: ANAC 2019 SCML (2019). http://tiny.cc/f8sv9y
12. Mohammad, Y., Greenwald, A., Nakadai, S.: Negmas: a platform for situated negotiations. In: Twelfth International Workshop on Agent-Based Complex Automated Negotiations (ACAN2019) in conjunction with IJCAI (2019)

Agent Simulation of Collision Avoidance Based on Meta-strategy Model

Norifumi Watanabe[1]([envelope]) [iD] and Kensuke Miyamoto[2]

[1] Research Center for Liberal Education, Musashino University,
1-1-20 Shinmachi, Nishitokyo-shi, Tokyo, Japan
noriwata@musashino-u.ac.jp
[2] Graduate School of Media and Governance, Keio University,
Fujisawa-shi, Kanagawa, Japan

Abstract. In our cooperative behavior, there are two strategies: a passive behavioral strategy based on others' behaviors and an active behavioral strategy based on the objective-first. However, it is not clear how to acquire a meta-strategy to switch those strategies. The purpose of the proposed study is to create agents with the meta-strategy and to enable complex behavioral choices with a high degree of coordination. In this study, we have experimented by using multi-agent collision avoidance simulations as an example of cooperative tasks. In the experiments, we have used reinforcement learning to obtain an active strategy and a passive strategy by rewarding the interaction with agents facing each other. Furthermore, we have examined and verified the meta-strategy in situations with opponent's strategy switched.

Keywords: Meta-strategy · Cooperative action · Collision avoidance · Reinforcement learning · Agent simulation

1 Introduction

As robots become more widespread in homes and other areas of daily life, the services provided by robots will improve and there will be more opportunities for them to work in cooperation with humans. We can switch between passive and active strategies, and sometimes we induce others to behave following our goals. However, it is not clear how to acquire the meta-strategies to switch those strategies. To realize a robot that communicates with people, the robot must acquire such a behavioral strategy.

A meta-strategy is the strategy behind the superficial behavioral decision-making process, and people decide their strategies and actions based on this meta-strategy. The meta-strategy model [1] defines a passive strategy and an active strategy. Passive strategies infer the intentions of others based on observations, determine their own intentions in light of them, and take action to achieve them. In active strategies, on the other hand, one first determines the goals one wants to achieve as intentions. We take the action that we judge to be

© Springer Nature Switzerland AG 2021
T. Uchiya et al. (Eds.): PRIMA 2020, LNAI 12568, pp. 84–99, 2021.
https://doi.org/10.1007/978-3-030-69322-0_6

shown to others from the point of how we should behave in order for others to infer our intentions, compared with our behavioral estimation model.

The intentions of others influenced by one's actions also influence the actions of others. It is possible to induce others to behave in a certain way. Furthermore, acting on one's own determined goals without estimating the intentions of others is also defined as a kind of strategy. The meta-strategy model assumes that people switch between these strategies themselves, and aims to build a more abstract model of behavioral decision-making by assuming a meta-strategy, which is a higher-level strategy for switching between strategies.

In order to investigate the behavior of a person in response to an agent taking active and passive strategies, we conducted a study in which two agents pass each other in turn in a virtual space and analyzed the trajectory of the person's movement in the virtual space [2]. From the results of the analysis, we were able to read the switching of strategies from the behavior of the robots in situations where human strategies switched significantly due to the differences in strategies of the two robots facing each other. We were also able to recognize that the agents had multiple behavioral strategies and that they switched between them on their part.

The purpose of this study is to get agents to have such a meta-strategy, to enable complex behavioral choices and a high degree of coordination. To investigate the effectiveness of a learning agent that switches between the two strategies, we first tested the effectiveness of a learning agent that simply responds to the surrounding state and a learning agent that gets similar rewards, but does not switch strategies. Next, we tested whether agents with meta-strategies can respond to changes in the strategies of others when the strategies of other agents with whom they collaborate change and the environment changes from one in which active strategies are effective to one in which passive strategies are effective and vice versa.

2 Background

In a study that aims to infer robot intentions, the robot does not engage in active activities, elicits interactions from humans, and also examines which actions are perceived as non-active activities [3,4]. Similarly, a robot is being developed that aims to elicit spontaneous communication from children [5]. These studies attempt to elicit active intention inference and action by having robots perform a limited number of actions. A study has also analyzed whether gestural communication can emerge as agents learn to pass each other [6].

If we think of collision avoidance as a problem of a robot avoiding an obstacle, a person, we can refer to research on path finding. Several algorithms have been reported to determine the direction of travel by representing the influence from the surroundings as a vector [7–9]. In these studies, the intentions of others who are autonomous in the environment are not considered important.

Then there is a study that pass each other the direction of travel of the pedestrian without assuming a straight line. In this study, pre-measuring and accumulating a gait data, such as a human movement path, it is possible to predict a traveling direction of a pedestrian [10,11]. However, this study is dependent on the environment, it cannot deal with unknown environment.

A study consider others to be part of the obstacles in the environment and use reinforcement learning to have agents perform competing coordination tasks. By varying the discount rate depending on the degree of renewal of the value function, it is believed that agents can adapt to an unstable environment, namely the behavior of others that changes as learning progresses, according to [12]. Previous study has provided additional rewards in agents' behavioral choices to differentiate behaviors that resolve conflicts. In this study, we also gave additional rewards for learning active and passive strategies.

3   Active and Passive Strategy Acquisition Experiments

3.1   Methods

As a first experiment, we conducted a cooperative behavior simulation experiment in which multiple agents share a path and avoid each other's path at a narrow place along the way.

In a real-time simulation, the behavior changes as time passes before the agent confirms and judges the behavior of the opponent. Therefore, in this study, we simulated in a grid environment. The corridor is a square space consisting of 17 corridors with a width of 2 and a side length of 17, with two narrow points on all side (Fig. 1). Agents rotate clockwise and counterclockwise. There are three agents in each direction. Black and white circles in the figure are initial placement of agents in two types of directions.

The agent can observe 2 squares in front, left, right and one square behind an agent (Fig. 2). There are four types of states for each square that an agent can distinguish: empty, wall, clockwise agent, and counterclockwise agent. In each state, the agent chooses to move forward or backward, turn left or right, or stop. The action decisions of agents at each step are made before all agents act, and the order of action is determined at random.

In a human-agent collision avoidance experiment [2] in a continuous space, it was suggested that the subject was reading the strategy that an agent was following from the difference in an agent action. However, since the interaction was only done once per trial per agent, it was not clear if the same opponent could respond to different strategies. Therefore, in this experiment, we prepared an environment in which agent can pass each other many times by going around the corridor in one trial and take cooperative action again with others whose strategy has changed. The field of view of an agent is set to a range of 2 squares in front, which can distinguish between the state where an agent in opposite direction is near and the state where there is no other person in the way.

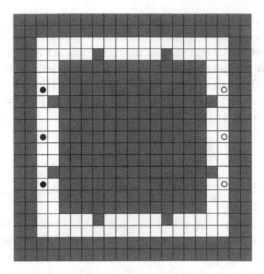

Fig. 1. Field and initial position of agents.

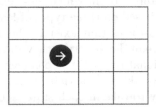

Fig. 2. Sight of agent when facing right.

In this experiment, we used Q-learning, a method of reinforcement learning, to learn the agent's behavior. In Q-learning, the state in which an agent is placed and the action value that the agent can act in that state are given as Q value. By updating Q value each time an action is taken, an agent that learns an effective action according to the state is realized. The value of an action is obtained from a reward r obtained by taking that action and the value of a transition destination state multiplied by a discount rate γ. The learning rate α is used to adjust how much the newly obtained value is reflected in Q value (Eq. 1).

$$\delta = r_{t+1} + \gamma \max_Q (s_{t+1}, a) - Q(s_t, a_t) \qquad (1)$$

The number of steps per episode was 500, and 3000 episodes were considered to be one trial. The number of steps per trial was 500 for 3000 episodes. The discount rate was set at 0.9 and the learning rate was set at 0.05. Five trials were conducted for each learning method. A temperature-parameterized softmax is used to determine the action from the value function (Eq. 2). The temperature parameter T decreases linearly from 5 to 0.1 during the first 500 episodes and is fixed at 0.1 and is fixed at 0.1 (Eq. 3).

$$\pi(s_t, a_t) = \frac{\exp\left(Q(s_t, a_t)/T\right)}{\Sigma_{a \in A} \exp\left(Q(s_t, a)/T\right)} \tag{2}$$

$$T = max(0.1 + 4.9 * \frac{500 - episode}{500}, 0.1) \tag{3}$$

Agents gain +1 if they can move forward in the direction they should move clockwise or counterclockwise in the corridor, −2 if they cannot move forward because of a wall or other agent in front of them, and −1 if they choose to go backward regardless of the direction. The correct direction in which an agent should go is updated when it reaches the square in the corner, according to the clock and counterclockwise direction in which an agent targets.

The agent was designed based on three types of learning strategies. The first agent considers others as obstacles that exist in the environment. Agents only get rewarded when they move in the direction they should go in the corridor. The second agent gets an additional reward if it passively gives way to the actions of others, or if it is given by taking an active action. The third agent considers what kind of action strategy to take in each state as one action, and learns the meta strategy, which is the upper strategy that switches between those lower strategies. In this experiment, there are two types of subordinate strategies: a strategy to give way and a strategy to give way. Using the meta strategy, select the sub strategy according to the situation (Eq. 4). Actions such as forward movement and change of direction are selected according to the probability of Eq. 2 using the Q value corresponding to the lower strategy selected by the meta strategy. The reward acquisition conditions for agents who learn meta strategies are the same as for agents who obtain cooperative rewards.

$$Q_t = \frac{\exp\left(metaQ(s_t, strategy_t)/T\right)}{\Sigma_{strategy \in S} \exp\left(metaQ(s_t, strategy)/T\right)} \tag{4}$$

In addition, to facilitate the acquisition of active and passive behaviors, agents also learn an additional reward of +2 for giving way to self and +1 for giving way to others, as a cooperative reward. We set more rewards for behaviors that could be returned to the laps more quickly, referring to previous study [12] that showed that they promoted behavioral differentiation.

The condition for obtaining the cooperative reward is that the player checks whether he and his agents are on the inner or outer perimeter of the field of view when an agent of the opposite direction is in the field of view at start of the step. If both agents are on the same side, they are considered to be in conflict with each other in terms of path. After agents' actions, we check the inner and outer perimeters again, and when the conflicts are resolved, we treat the outer agents as having been given the right of way and the inner agents as having given the right of way.

These rewards are given to agents who think in terms of cooperation with others and to agents who use meta-strategies. In order to acquire the two sub-strategies used by meta-strategy, giving and not giving way to others, we also trained clockwise and counterclockwise groups to be rewarded gave way or were given way, respectively.

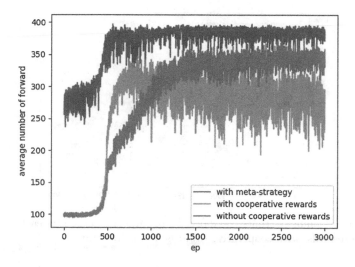

Fig. 3. Number of agents choosing forward with meta-strategy, with cooperative rewards, and without cooperative reward.

3.2 Results

Figure 3 shows the number of times the three types of learning agents chose to move forward in each episode. These graphs show the average number of forward moves of six agents per trial. In all learning methods, they have begun to actively take action to circumnavigate from around 500 episodes, when temperature parameters start to drop. Agents who did not provide cooperative rewards took more than 1,000 episodes before their learning converged.

There have been episodes where agents with cooperative rewards have chosen to make less forward action. The reason for this is that the rewards for coopera-tion were set too high, and this may have led to a value function that does not fit the original purpose of orbiting the corridor, preferring behavior that is judged to be cooperative (Fig. 4). In one example of the total and cooperative rewards earned by agent with cooperative rewards, the cooperative rewards accounted for most of the rewards earned as learning progressed (Fig. 5). Comparing the average number of forward in the last 1,000 episodes where the agents' behavior appeared to be stable, agents with cooperative rewards chose fewer forward than the other two learning methods (Table 1). Agents using the meta-strategy also had the smallest standard deviation and consistently had the highest number of forward. However, in common with all learning methods, there are episodes of low numbers of forward in places. The reason for this is that up to six agents are facing each other in a small space that only one agent can pass through, and the agents have to change directions before they can move to give way to others, therefore it takes longer to get out.

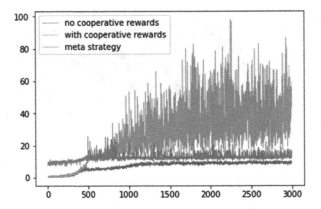

Fig. 4. Average number of times collaborative rewards are earned for each method (no cooperative rewards, with cooperative rewards and meta-strategy).

Table 1. Number of forward in the last 1000 episodes.

	Avg	Std
Without cooperative rewards	342.9	36.3
With cooperative rewards	280.7	89.1
Meta-strategy	384.6	24.5

In the case of multiple agents circling the corridor, the agents who introduced meta-strategy, which is the idea of gaining rewards when cooperating with others and switching multiple strategies, were able to achieve better learning results than those who simply chose their actions according to the surrounding conditions. On the other hand, meta-strategy agents and agents that earn rewards when cooperating under similar conditions have specialized in the acquisition of cooperative rewards. This suggests that the agent model is useful to switch sub-strategies depending on meta-strategy.

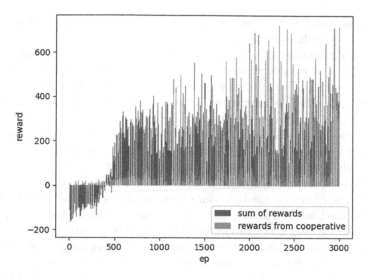

Fig. 5. Total and cooperative rewards earned by agent with cooperative rewards (1 trial).

4 Experiment of Cooperative Behavior Acquisition Using Meta-strategy

4.1 Methods

We then conducted experiments to further analyze the learning performance of agents with meta-strategies. We also changed some parameters, such as increasing the number of episodes, in response to the results of experiment Sect. 3.1.

In the second experiment, among six agents, only the first agent in the clockwise group's initial placement learns meta-strategy. The other five agents perform a minimal update of the value function. This is a situation in which five agents are used as teachers and one learning agent is being trained. A structure of the corridor and the initial placement of the agents in the experimental environment are the same as in experiment with Sect. 3.1. Agents learn two sub-strategies beforehand: the strategy to be taken when the clockwise/counterclockwise group to which they belong gives way passively, and the strategy to be taken when they go forward and ask for the path to be given actively. In experiment Sect. 3.1, we found that even in the later episodes where learning was considered to have progressed, there were cases where a number of forward in the episode was low because of an inability to get out of a situation that did not occur often, such as when multiple agents were gathered in one place. Therefore, we increased the overall number of episodes in this experiment and had the agents learn 100,000 episodes when learning the lower strategies. In the first 25,000 episodes, as in experiment Sect. 3.1, we induced learning by giving additional rewards during cooperation that were consistent with the strategy we wanted them to learn. Then, furthermore, we continued to study 75,000 episodes without any reward at the time of coordination and we reduced the impact on the value function of rewards given to induce learning.

At a certain number of episodes, the agents, who are the teachers, switch between active and passive strategies that allow the clockwise group to get their way and vice versa. The number of episodes until the change of behavior was set to 25,000 per set. The learning agent has two strategies at the same time, an active strategy and a passive strategy, and learns a meta-strategy to choose one of the strategies depending on a state. As the number of episodes increased, the number of episodes until the temperature parameter was lowered increased to 10,000. We also reduced the learning rate of sub-strategies to 0.01. To prevent the value function of sub-strategy from collapsing before the choice by meta-strategy changes, because the behavior of surroundings is substantially different from that at the time of learning, e.g., the opponents who would have given way at the time of learning sub-strategy prioritize their own path.

Because there were continued cases of passive giving strategies even when the learning agents changed to an environment where they could give way to others, when we checked the value function, we found that the value of active strategies did not change nearly as much before and after learning. We thought that this was because even though the learning agent was able to give way to an oncoming agent and the learning agent was able to circle the corridor and earn rewards more easily. It continued to choose passive strategy as a value function of the superiority of passive strategy before the change in environment, and continued to choose passive strategy without having the opportunity to confirm that the value of active strategy had increased.

Tentatively, this study incorporated the idea of ϵ-greedy method, which allows for random strategy selection and search to take place at a constant probability, regardless of temperature parameters. The value of ϵ was set to 0.1. In order to encourage the differentiation of learning agents' strategies, we gave them cooperative rewards under the same conditions as in experiment Sect. 3.1. The rewards were studied in three patterns: the same value as in experiment Sect. 3.1 (2 for active and 1 for passive), none (0, 0), and tenfold (20, 10). For each reward, we conducted three trials, one starting in an environment suitable for active strategies and one starting in an environment suitable for passive strategies for the learning agent. The number of sets was done until the learning agent had implemented one more set of environments for which active strategies were suitable after 100,000 episodes of learning. Thus, the number of sets is five if the active strategy starts in a suitable environment and six if passive strategy starts in a suitable environment.

4.2   Results

Table 2 shows average forward number and standard deviation of the learning agents for the latter 10,000 episodes of the 25,000 episodes per set, and Table 3 shows the data for each of 10 episodes immediately after the set, i.e., the teacher agent's strategy was switched.

Table 2. Selected number of forward in the last 10,000 episodes of set (pairs are the cooperative rewards given).

Rewards	Set 4 (passive suitable)		Set 5 (active suitable)	
	Avg	Std	Avg	Std
(0, 0)	389.1	20.9	389.4	15.5
(2, 1)	390.3	22.5	389.3	15.1
(20, 10)	387.2	19.2	372.7	31.0
Rewards	Set 5 (passive suitable)		Set 6 (active suitable)	
r(0, 0)	391.2	18.7	387.5	14.6
r(2, 1)	392.3	21.2	381.0	15.0
r(20, 10)	391.1	20.6	358.7	35.8

In particular, we tabulated the last set in which the learning agent's choice of an active strategy was effective, and one previous set in which a passive strategy was effective. The pairs of numbers on vertical axis are cooperative rewards given. Reward r is the result of trials that began in an environment where passive strategies suited to learning agents. All sets of patterns achieved about 350 to 400 forwards out of 500 steps in any set of patterns.

Table 3. Selected number of forward in the first 10 episodes after changing set (pairs are the cooperative rewards given).

Rewards	Set 4 (passive suitable)		Set 5 (active suitable)	
	Avg	Std	Avg	Std
(0, 0)	128.8	98.5	372.6	39.9
(2, 1)	92.8	111.9	362.7	41.1
(20, 10)	237.1	91.4	352.8	53.1
Rewards	Set 5 (passive suitable)		Set 6 (active suitable)	
r(0, 0)	249.2	103.5	344.6	62.1
r(2, 1)	295.6	94.8	353.9	54.2
r(20, 10)	355.0	63.9	354.2	47.6

Table 2 shows that in second half of the set, where learning is considered to have progressed sufficiently, the deviation is about 10% of the mean, and learning outcomes are almost the same for all reward patterns. Table 3 shows that learning agents are not able to respond immediately when the other agents' behavioral strategies suddenly switch and they need to give way to others, and they do not move forward in the corridor compared to a well-trained situation. However, the pattern of high cooperative rewards (20, 10) allowed them to move forward from the beginning by about 60%, compared to the end of set. On the other hand, when the environment changed to one in which the other agents passively gave way, they were able to proceed in all patterns more than 90% of the time when they had learned enough.

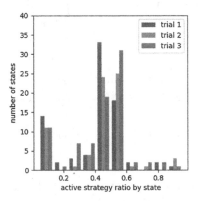

Fig. 6. Percentage of active strategies chosen by state (cooperative rewards (0, 0), after passive strategy is effective).

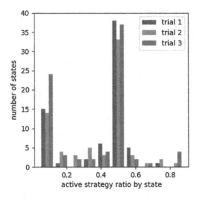

Fig. 7. Percentage of active strategies chosen by state (cooperative rewards (2, 1), after passive strategy is effective).

Figure 6, 7 and 8 show a histogram of number of states for each percentage that chose an active strategy in the fourth set for each cooperative reward. Figure 9, 10 and 11 show a similar histogram for the fifth set. For example, in Fig. 6, we computed the proportion of learning agents that chose an active strategy for each of the states encountered during the fourth set, i.e., between 7,501 episodes and 10,000 episodes, for each proportion, and made a histogram of number of states included. However, it does not include situations where less than 10,000

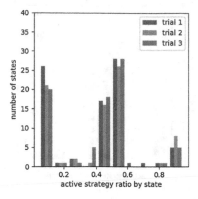

Fig. 8. Percentage of active strategies chosen by state (cooperative rewards (20, 10), after passive strategy is effective).

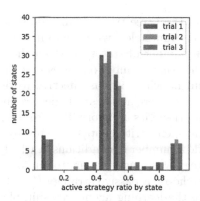

Fig. 9. Percentage of active strategies chosen by state (cooperative rewards (0, 0), after active strategy is effective).

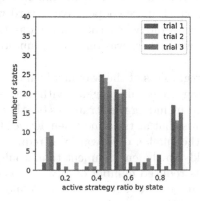

Fig. 10. Percentage of active strategies chosen by state (cooperative rewards (2, 1), after active strategy is effective).

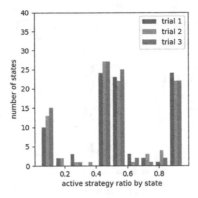

Fig. 11. Percentage of active strategies chosen by state (cooperative rewards (20, 10), after active strategy is effective).

times occur in any one of the three trials. It also does not include the absence of oncoming agents of the counterclockwise group in agent's sight.

From Fig. 6, 7 and 8, number of states in which the learning agent chose a passive strategy was higher than number of states in which it chose more active strategies in an environment where it was effective to take a passive strategy. Conversely, in environments where active strategies are more appropriate, number of states where active strategies are more likely to be chosen in learning from Fig. 10 and 11 for learning agents with cooperative rewards. For agents who were not cooperatively rewarded, number of conditions in which they were more likely to choose an active strategy was roughly equal to number of conditions in which they were more likely to choose a passive strategy (Fig. 9).

In the fifth set where the learning agent was suitable to be active, number of conditions in which an active strategy was actually selected in all three trials was one pattern in which no cooperative reward was given (0, 0), six patterns in which the cooperative reward was equal to that in experiment Sect. 3.1 (2, 1), and nine patterns in which more cooperative reward was given (20, 10). Of these conditions, there were four when the reward was (2, 1) and seven when the reward was (20, 10), when there was only one counterclockwise agent in the agent's sight.

Table 2 shows that, regardless of the way in which cooperative rewards were given, at the advanced stage of learning, agents with meta-strategies were able to adapt to the environment, including the strategies of others, and circumnavigate the corridor. Table 3 shows that at the time when active strategies were needed, only a small decrease in the number of forward was required and the participants were able to adapt quickly to the environment that would give way to self. On the other hand, all agents reduced number of forward to environmental changes that required passive strategies, but agents with much more cooperative rewards were able to respond faster than the other two rewards patterns. Together with an analysis of the histogram described below, the patterns that were not given the cooperative rewards were not switched strategies in the first place, and the patterns that were given the same values as in experiment Sect. 3.1 did not respond immediately, which is considered to be a similar situation to retraining.

The histogram for the fourth sets (Fig. 7 and 8) and fifth sets (Fig. 10 and 11) of agents who were given cooperative rewards shows that the learning agents' strategy choices also changed in response to the strategy changes of the other agents who served as teachers. In particular, the pattern that provided more cooperative rewards had a higher number of states that were able to choose equally effective strategies for the same state across trials. For agent who was not cooperatively rewarded, results showed that in environments where passive strategies were effective, they were able to choose passive strategies (Fig. 6), but in environments where active strategies were effective, they were not biased towards either strategy (Fig. 11).

Figure 12 shows an example of a situation in which the active strategy was selected on the fifth set in all three trials in two different patterns of cooperative rewards. We checked which strategy was selected more often in this situation going back through the sets, and found that the active strategy was appropriately selected in all three sets, even in the odd-numbered sets where it was appropriate for the learning agent to be active, as in the fifth set. In the even set where the other agents' strategies were reversed, there was a mix of passive strategy choices and half and half choices of both strategies. In the case of no cooperative reward, there was a mix of trials in all sets that chose more active strategies and trials that chose more passive strategies or were not biased toward either, with no consistent strategy choice in all three trials.

Based on the example of the situation in Fig. 12, an evaluation of whether the strategy worked or not is itself useful in the learning of agents who take cooperative behavior, since meta-strategy changed in response to environmental changes when cooperative rewards were given. However, the value of the reward need more consideration.

5   Discussion

We focused on the fact that cooperative behavior involves both active and passive strategies, and this was confirmed by cooperative behavior experiments between humans and agents. By applying this model to an agent model and using meta-strategies that switch between multiple strategies, we were able to select a strategy according to changes in the environment, namely the behavioral strategies

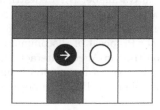

Fig. 12. Example of a classified state.

of the surrounding agents. However, as can be read from Figs. 6 to 11, a large number of conditions remain in which the selection rates of active and passive strategies are competitive. Although the value of the transition state in reinforcement learning is partly reflected by the discount rate, the state that the agent observes can be taken as either active or passive, and the agent's own strategy cannot be considered as correct one, because there are no obstacles around it.

A possible solution to this problem is to make one's strategy one of the continual internal states. In this case, it is expected that we need to make a distinction between uncoordinated states, where there are no others around, and coordinated states, where the internal state should be applied.

In this study, we used ϵ to keep exploration to correspond to environments with more or less rewards. In order to cope with complex state changes, it is necessary to construct a learning model in which agents can differentiate themselves. Additionally, meta-strategy itself is not limited to the use of two strategies, so it is necessary to deal with multiple strategies.

6 Conclusion

To clarify an effectiveness of learning agents that acquire meta-strategies that switch between two strategies, we first verified the effectiveness of learning agents that simply responded to the surrounding state, as well as learning agents that earned similar rewards but did not switch strategies. From the first experiment, we found that agents that acquired a meta-strategy were the most adaptable to their environment. Second, we conducted an experiment to see whether agents with a meta-strategy can respond to changes in the strategies of others when the strategies of the other agents with whom they collaborate change and the environment changes from one in which an active strategy is effective to one in which a passive strategy is effective and vice versa. Our experiments show that cooperative rewards can be designed to respond to changes in the environment, namely, the behavioral strategies of surrounding agents.

References

1. Yokoyama, A., Omori, T.: Modeling of human intention estimation process in social interaction scene. In: 2010 IEEE International Conference on Fuzzy Systems (FUZZ-IEEE), pp. 1–6 (2010)
2. Miyamoto, K., Takefuji, Y., Watanabe, N.: Pedestrian meta-strategy analysis of collision avoidance with two autonomous agents. In: 2015 IEEE 4th Global Conference on Consumer Electronics(GCCE 2015), pp. 467–469 (2016)
3. Sugahara, R., Katagami, D.: Proposal of discommunication robot. In: The First International Conference on Human-Agent Interaction, I-2-2 (2013)
4. Katagami, D., Tanaka, Y.: Change of impression resulting from voice in discommunication motion of baby robot. In: HAI Symposium 2015, pp. 171–176 (2015). (in Japanese)
5. Kozima, H., Michalowski, M.P., Nakagawa, C.: Keepon. Int. J. Soc. Robot. 1(1), 3–18 (2009). https://doi.org/10.1007/s12369-008-0009-8

6. Sato, T.: Emergence of robust cooperative states by Iterative internalizations of opponents' personalized values in minority game. J. Inf. Commun. Eng. (JICE) **3**(5), 157–166 (2017)
7. Kitamura, Y., Tanaka, T., Kishino, F., Yachida, M.: Real-time path planning in a dynamically changing 3-D environment. In: Proceedings of International Conference on Intelligent Robots and Systems, Osaka, pp. 925–931 (1996)
8. Kerr, W., Spears, D., Spears, W., Thayer, D.: Two formal gas models for multi-agent sweeping and obstacle avoidance. In: Hinchey, M.G., Rash, J.L., Truszkowski, W.F., Rouff, C.A. (eds.) FAABS 2004. LNCS (LNAI), vol. 3228, pp. 111–130. Springer, Heidelberg (2004). https://doi.org/10.1007/978-3-540-30960-4_8
9. Mastellone, S., Stipanović, D.M., Graunke, C.R., Intlekofer, K.A., Spong, M.W.: Formation control and collision avoidance for multi-agent non-holonomic systems: theory and experiments. Int. J. Robot. Res. **27**(1), 107–126 (2008)
10. Thompson, S., Horiuchi, T., Kagami, S.: A probabilistic model of human motion and navigation intent for mobile robot path planning. In: Proceedings of IEEE International Conference on Autonomous Robots and Agents, vol. 77, no. 775, pp. 1051–1061 (2009)
11. Hamasaki, S., Tamura, Y., Yamashita, A., Asama, H.: Prediction of human's movement for collision avoidance of mobile robot. In: Proceedings of the IEEE International Conference on Robotics and Biomimetics, pp. 1633–1638 (2011)
12. Yamada, K., Takano, S., Watanabe, S.: Reinforcement learning approaches for acquiring conflict avoidance behaviors in multi-agent systems. In: 2011 IEEE/SICE International Symposium on System Integration, pp. 679–684 (2011)

The Smart Appliance Scheduling Problem: A Bayesian Optimization Approach

Atena M. Tabakhi[1(✉)], William Yeoh[1], and Ferdinando Fioretto[2]

[1] Washington University in St. Louis, St. Louis, MO, USA
{amtabakhi,wyeoh}@wustl.edu
[2] Syracuse University, Syracuse, NY, USA
ffiorett@syr.edu

Abstract. Daily energy demand peaks induce high greenhouse gas emissions and are deleterious to the power grid operations. The autonomous and coordinated control of smart appliances in residential buildings represents an effective solution to reduce peak demands. This coordination problem is challenging as it involves, not only, scheduling devices to minimize energy peaks, but also to comply with user' preferences. Prior work assumed these preferences to be fully specified and known a priori, which is, however, unrealistic. To remedy this limitation, this paper introduces a Bayesian optimization approach for smart appliance scheduling when the users' satisfaction with a schedule must be elicited, and thus considered expensive to evaluate. The paper presents a set of ad-hoc energy-cost based acquisition functions to drive the Bayesian optimization problem to find schedules that maximize the user's satisfaction. The experimental results demonstrate the effectiveness of the proposed energy-cost based acquisition functions which improve the algorithm's performance up to 26%.

Keywords: Beyesian optimization · Smart appliance scheduling problem · User's preference elicitation · Constraint satisfaction problems

1 Introduction

Demand-side management (DSM) [14,19] in smart grids [6,7] consists of techniques and policies that allow customers to make informed decisions about their energy consumption while helping energy providers reducing peak load demand. DSM aims at encouraging customers to consume less energy during peak periods or shift their energy demand to off-peak periods [10]. To do so, a successful approach is to act on the schedule of shiftable loads, in which customers can shift the time of use for electrical appliances to off-peak hours [8,14].

Scheduling shiftable loads in residential buildings has become possible thanks to the advent of smart appliances (e.g., smart plugs, smart thermostats, smart

© Springer Nature Switzerland AG 2021
T. Uchiya et al. (Eds.): PRIMA 2020, LNAI 12568, pp. 100–115, 2021.
https://doi.org/10.1007/978-3-030-69322-0_7

washing machines, and smart dishwashers) [41]. These appliances enable users to automate their schedules and shift their executions during times when energy may cost less (e.g., under real-time electricity price [3,12]).

The *smart appliance scheduling* (SAS) problem in smart homes [8,25,41] is the problem of scheduling the operation of the appliances at any time of a day, subject to a set of user-defined constraints and preferences. Smart appliance scheduling aims at minimizing energy consumption and, consequently, reducing electricity costs [27]. Over the past few years, a large body of work has emerged to solve this problem. The majority of these works have focused on minimizing solely the energy consumption [1,3,42], ignoring users' *comfort/preferences* (see Sect. 2 for a thorough discussion). As a result, the solutions (i.e., appliances schedules) that these approaches provide may not be aligned with the users' preferences and, hence, may not be acceptable.

In response to this challenge, recent studies have formulated the appliance scheduling problem as a multi-objective optimization that minimizes users' discomfort and energy consumption [8,35,41]. To promote the users' comfort these studies assume perfect knowledge about the comfort information, which is not realistic in practice [2]. The work by Nguyen *et al.* contrasts this background and represents users' preferences as Normal distributions [20]. However, this approach requires the knowledge of a *satisfaction threshold* to represent the level of *users' satisfaction* with the proposed schedule. The common limitation of all these approaches is their assumption that the users' preferences are known (be it exactly or through the moments of their underlying distributions), which is unrealistic as these preferences are not only commonly unknown but must be elicited, which is considered to be an expensive process.

To contrast these limitations, this paper develops a scheduling system that minimizes energy consumption while modeling users' satisfaction with schedules as *expensive to evaluate* functions that can be approximately learned [12, 20,36,37,40]. These functions are expensive to evaluate in the sense that they require user interactions and feedback as part of the evaluations and users may not tolerate a large number of these interactions [9]. The paper adopts Bayesian optimization [15,18] to learn those users' satisfaction that are salient to optimization of the appliances' schedules. Bayesian optimization is an iterative process suitable for optimizing expensive to evaluate functions. It consists of two main components, a Bayesian statistical method to model the objective function and an acquisition function to determine the next location to sample.

The contributions of this paper are the following: (1) It develops a constraint-based model for scheduling appliances with an expensive to evaluate user's satisfaction; (2) It introduces a Bayesian optimization-based algorithm to find schedules that maximize the user's satisfaction while limiting the interactions between the system and the user; (3) It proposes a set of customized acquisition functions for the Bayesian optimization that are tailored to our formulation; and (4) It evaluates the effectiveness of the proposed Bayesian optimization algorithm over a variety of appliances scheduling problems. The proposed customized acquisition functions improve the algorithm's performance up to 26% compared to their baseline counterparts.

In Sect. 2, we discuss prior work that is related to the work presented in this paper. In Sect. 3, we provide a brief background before we explain our problem definition and solution approaches in Sects. 4 and 5, respectively. Finally, we experimentally evaluate our solution approaches in Sect. 6 and conclude in Sect. 7.

2   Related Work

Within the past decade, a wide variety of optimization approaches have emerged to model and solve the *smart appliance scheduling* (SAS) problems in residential buildings. For instance, integer linear programming [4,42], mixed integer programming [1,3], and convex optimization [26,31] techniques have been proposed to shift energy demand over a daily forecast price cycle in which the cost or energy consumption is minimized. Unlike most of these approaches that have solely focused on minimizing energy consumption or cost, our approach also considers users' comfort and preferences and proposes schedules that are more aligned with users' preferences while reducing energy cost.

Aside from our work, there also exist others who jointly optimized energy consumption and user preferences. For example, Fioretto *et al.* formulated the SAS problem as a distributed constraint optimization problem to minimize energy cost and peak load across a neighborhood of multiple smart homes, while allowing pre-defined users' constraints [8]. Zhu *et al.* used a variant of particle swarm optimization for the SAS problem to minimize energy cost and users' discomfort (opposite of users' preference/comfort) across a neighborhood of multiple smart homes, assuming a pre-defined users' comfort parameter [41]. Nguyen *et al.* formulated the SAS problem with probabilistic users' preferences–preferences for using appliances are uncertain, represented as Normal distributions. They proposed sample average approximation and depth-first search techniques to solve the SAS problem that aim at minimizing energy cost while ensuring that the user preference is within some acceptable threshold [20]. Finally, Tabakhi *et al.* used a distributed constraint optimization approach for the SAS problem to minimize energy cost and users' discomfort where constraints encode users' preferences that are represented as Normal distributions [34,35]. Different from these studies, we assume that the users' satisfaction with a schedule is unknown or expensive to evaluate, but could be approximately learned. Our proposed approach aims to find the schedule that maximizes user's satisfaction while reducing energy cost.

3   Background

This section reviews some basic notions about constraint satisfaction problems and Bayesian optimization.

3.1 Constraint Satisfaction Problems (CSPs)

The *Constraint Satisfaction Problem* (CSP) [23,24] is a powerful framework for formulating and solving combinatorial problems such as scheduling [30]. It is defined as a tuple $\mathcal{P} = \langle \mathcal{V}, \mathcal{T}, \mathcal{F} \rangle$, where $\mathcal{V} = \{v_1, \cdots, v_n\}$ is a set of n variables, $\mathcal{T} = \{T_1, \cdots, T_n\}$ is a set of domains, where each T_i is associated with variable V_i and expresses the possible values V_i can take, and $\mathcal{F} = \{f_1, \cdots, f_m\}$ is a set of m constraints, restricting the values that the variables can take simultaneously.

A constraint $f_j = \langle C(f_j), R(f_j) \rangle$ is a pair, where $C(f_j) \subseteq \mathcal{V}$ is the scope of f_j (i.e., a set of variables relevant to f_j) and $R(f_j)$ is a relation that consists of all the value combinations that the variables in $C(f_j)$ can take. The constraint f_j is *satisfied* if the variables take on one of the value combinations in $R(f_j)$ and is *unsatisfied* otherwise. The cardinality of $C(f_j)$ (i.e., the number of variables involved in f_j) is also called the constraint's arity.

A solution to a CSP is a value assignment to all variables such that all the constraints are satisfied. Solving a CSP is to find a solution of the CSP or to prove that no solution exists (i.e., no combination of value assignments satisfy all constraints).

3.2 Bayesian Optimization

Bayesian optimization [15,18] is a powerful method used to find a global maxima (or minima) of a function $u : X \to \mathbb{R}$

$$\max_{\mathbf{x}} u(\mathbf{x}), \tag{1}$$

where $\mathbf{x} \in X \subseteq \mathbb{R}^d$ [9]. The function $u(.)$ typically has the following properties:

- It is an "expensive to evaluate" function: In the context of this paper, evaluating u at a point $\mathbf{x}$ requires interacting with the user, who will not tolerate a large number of interactions.
- It is a "black-box" function: It is a continuous function but lacks known structures, like linearity or concavity or it is a "derivative-free" function when only $u(\mathbf{x})$ is observed and no first- or second-order derivatives exist [9].

Bayesian optimization is an iterative process consists of two main ingredients: A Bayesian statistical method for modeling the objective function, typically a *Gaussian Process* (GP) regression, and an *acquisition function* for deciding where to evaluate the objective function. A GP provides a posterior probability distribution of the function $u(\mathbf{x})$ at a candidate point $\mathbf{x}$. Then, the acquisition function measures the value that would be generated by evaluating u at a new point $\mathbf{x}'$, based on the current posterior distribution over u. Every time that the function is evaluated at a new point, the posterior distribution is updated [9]. We briefly discuss GPs regression and acquisition functions in the following.

Gaussian Process (GP) Regression [17,43] is a Bayesian statistical approach for modeling functions [9]. A GP provides a distribution over functions $u(\mathbf{x}) \sim$

$\mathcal{GP}(\mu(\mathbf{x}), \mathbf{k}(\mathbf{x}, \mathbf{x}'))$, specified by its mean function, μ and covariance (kernel) function k, for any pairs of input points x, and $\mathbf{x}'$ (where $\mathbf{x}, \mathbf{x}' \in \mathbf{X}$). Intuitively, a GP (i.e., $\mathcal{GP}(.,.)$) is similar to a function, except that instead of returning a scalar $\mathbf{u}(\mathbf{x})$, it returns the mean and standard deviation of a normal distribution over the possible values of u, at any arbitrary input point x. For convenience, we assume that the prior mean function is the zero mean function $\mu(\mathbf{x}) = 0$. The kernel function $\mathbf{k}(\mathbf{x}, \mathbf{x}')$ describes the covariance of a GP random variables. The mean function and the kernel function together define a GP. Some of the commonly used kernel functions are the radial basis function (RBF) [38], Matérn [38], and periodic [5] kernels. In the context of this paper, we choose the periodic kernel function as the default kernel function and show the behavior of the algorithm using Matérn and RBF kernels in Sect. 6.3.

Acquisition Functions use a GP model to guide the selection of a global maxima of the objective function u, by proposing sampling points in the search space. The acquisition function provides a trade-off between exploration and exploitation. Exploration means sampling (i.e., evaluating the objective function) at locations where the GP model has higher uncertainty and exploitation means that sampling at locations where the GP model has higher estimated values. Both exploration and exploitation correspond to high acquisition values. Determining where to evaluate next is achieved by maximizing the acquisition function.

More formally, the function u will be evaluated at $\mathbf{x}^+ = \mathrm{argmax}_{\tilde{\mathbf{x}}} \alpha(\tilde{\mathbf{x}})$ given a set of sampling points drawn from u, where α is the acquisition function. We will discuss standard acquisition functions in more detail in Sect. 5.

4 The Smart Appliance Scheduling (SAS) Problem with Users' Satisfaction

We describe the *Smart Appliances Scheduling* (SAS) problem and model it as a CSP, given the constraints imposed by users on the appliances. Our model is similar to the one defined in [20], except that we do not represent the users' preference as Normal distributions when we model the SAS problem. We first find all the SAS problem's feasible schedules using a CSP solver. Then, we assign a user's satisfaction to each schedule. Among all feasible schedules, our algorithm aims at finding the schedule that maximizes user's satisfaction.

Definition 1. *The* Smart Appliances Scheduling *problem P is a tuple* $\langle \mathcal{V}, \mathcal{T}, \mathcal{F} \rangle$, *where*

- $\mathcal{V} = \{v_1, \cdots, v_n\}$ *is a finite set of smart appliances.*
- $\mathcal{T} = \{T_1, \cdots, T_n\}$ *is a set of domains of smart appliances, where* $T_j = \{1, \cdots, \mathcal{H}\}$ *is a set of time slots for appliance* $v_j \in \mathcal{V}$, *and* $\mathcal{H}$ *is a finite time horizon. Each appliance* v_j *must choose a* start time $t_k \in T_j$ *to turn on.*
- $\mathcal{F} = \mathcal{F}_1 \cup \mathcal{F}_2$ *is a set of constraints, where*

$$\mathcal{F}_1 = \{\langle v_j, (\{Before, After, At\}, t_k) \rangle\} \tag{2}$$

is a set of unary constraints indicating that appliance v_j must be turned on either before, after, or at time $t_k \in T$; and

$$\mathcal{F}_2 = \{\langle (v_i, v_j), \{Before, After, Parallel\} \rangle\} \tag{3}$$

for some pairs of variables $v_i, v_j \in V$ (with $v_i \neq v_j$), is a set of binary constraints indicating that appliance v_i must be turned on either before, after, or at the same time that appliance v_j is turned on. We refer to these binary constraints as dependencies between appliances.

A candidate solution for P is a schedule $\mathbf{x} = \{(v_1, t_1), \cdots, (v_n, t_n)\}$ that consists of the set of all appliances v_j and their corresponding start times t_k. A solution for P is a schedule that satisfies all the unary and binary constraints. We also use the term *feasible schedules* to refer to solutions. The set of all feasible schedules is denoted by $\mathbf{X}$.

Given the set of feasible schedules $\mathbf{X}$, we are only interested in the schedules that maximize a user's satisfaction as the user can prefer one schedule over the other. The user's satisfaction with the schedule depends on various components. For example, temperature, the price of energy (electricity), the time of day, and personal concerns might affect the user's satisfaction [21, 29, 41].

4.1   The User's Satisfaction Function

We define a user's satisfaction function that is composed of two components similar to [29, 41] as follows:

$$\mathbf{u}_{v_j}^{t_k} = \left| \left(\frac{\alpha_c}{1 + e^{-c(\zeta,(v_j,t_k))}} - \frac{\alpha_e}{1 + e^{-\varepsilon(p,(v_j,t_k))}} \right) \right| \tag{4}$$

where:

- α_e and α_c are non-negative weights values such that $\alpha_e + \alpha_c = 1$.
- $c : \mathbb{R} \times V \times T \to \mathbb{R}$ is a *comfort function* (defined below) with $c(\zeta, (v_j, t_k))$ quantifying the comfort level of the users for appliance v_j to turn on at time t_k, given the user's comfort ζ.
- $\varepsilon : \mathbb{R} \times V \times T \to \mathbb{R}$ is an *energy cost function* (defined below) with $\varepsilon(p, (v_j, t_k))$ quantifying the cost of energy for appliance v_j to turn on at time t_k, given a real-time pricing schema p.

The comfort c is defined as:

$$c(\zeta, (v_j, t_k)) = \sum_{i=t_k}^{t_k + \delta_{v_j}} \varsigma_i \cdot \sigma \tag{5}$$

where $\varsigma_i \in \zeta$ is the user's comfort at time i, $\sigma \in [0, 1]$ is a parameter that determines user's sensitivity to any change in time, and δ_{v_j} is the duration of v_j (i.e., the period of time that v_j must run until it finishes its task without any interruption).

The cost of energy assumes that the energy provider of each smart home sets energy prices according to a real-time pricing schema p specified at regular intervals $t_k \in T$. The energy cost function is defined as:

$$\varepsilon(p, (v_j, t_k)) = \sum_{i=t_k}^{t_k + \delta_{v_j}} p_i \cdot \rho_{v_j} \tag{6}$$

where $p_i \in p$ is the price of energy at time i, ρ_{v_j} is the power consumption of appliance v_j at each time step, and δ_{v_j} is the duration of v_j.

Definition 2. *The user satisfaction on the dependency of variables v_i and v_j appearing in $\mathcal{F}_2$ is defined as*

$$\mathbf{u}_{(v_i, v_j)}^{(t_l, t_k)} = \mathbf{u}_{v_i}^{t_l} + \mathbf{u}_{v_j}^{t_k}$$

Definition 3. *The user's satisfaction of the schedule $\mathbf{x}$ is:*

$$\mathbf{u}(\mathbf{x}) = \frac{1}{|\mathcal{V}|} \left(\sum_{v_m \in \mathcal{F}_1} \mathbf{u}_{v_m}^{t_o} + 2 \sum_{(v_i, v_j) \in \mathcal{F}_2} \mathbf{u}_{(v_i, v_j)}^{(t_l, t_k)} \right) \tag{7}$$

The user's satisfaction with the suggested schedule is inherently subjective and varies from one individual to another. Due to a large number of feasible schedules for smart home appliances within a day, eliciting user's satisfaction for every schedule is cumbersome as users might not tolerate an unlimited number of queries. Thus, we presume that the user's satisfaction is an expensive to evaluate function and employ the Bayesian optimization strategy to optimize the function and find the best possible schedule $\mathbf{x}^*$:

$$\mathbf{x}^* = \underset{\mathbf{x}}{\operatorname{argmax}} \ \mathbf{u}(\mathbf{x}). \tag{8}$$

with only a limited number of queries to ask the user their satisfaction.

5   Bayesian Optimization for the SAS Problem

Recall that Bayesian optimization uses a Gaussian process to approximate the user's satisfaction function (defined in Definition 3) and an acquisition function to iteratively identify the next candidate schedule to evaluate given the observations (i.e., a set of candidate schedules and their corresponding users' satisfaction) thus far. Typically, an initial observation of at least two candidate schedules and their corresponding users' satisfaction is assumed to be available, denoted by $\mathcal{D}_0$ in Algorithm 1. Given the initial observation, the acquisition function is used to identify the next and subsequent candidate schedules to evaluate.

In this paper, we use an off-the-shelf CSP solver to find the set of all feasible schedules $\mathbf{X}$. Then, to generate the initial k observations, we randomly choose a set of k schedules from $\mathbf{X}$ and evaluate them using Eq. 7. After using the acquisition function to identify the next candidate schedule and evaluating it (i.e., eliciting the user's satisfaction with the candidate schedule), the prior is updated to produce a more informed posterior distribution over the user's satisfaction function. Algorithm 1 illustrates the above process.

Algorithm 1. Bayesian Optimization for the SAS problem

Input: The set of all feasible schedules $\mathbf{X}$, the number of initial observation k, an acquisition function α, and the number of queries Q

Output: The schedule with the highest user's satisfaction after Q queries

    Select k schedules from $\mathbf{X}$ randomly as the initial observation set $\mathcal{D}_0$

    Construct the GP model on $\mathcal{D}_0$

    for $n = 0, 1, 2, \cdots, Q$ **do**

        Find $\mathbf{x}_{n+1}$ by maximizing the acquisition function α: $\mathbf{x}_{n+1} = \text{argmax}_{\tilde{\mathbf{x}}}\, \alpha(\tilde{\mathbf{x}})$

        Elicit the user's satisfaction for schedule $\mathbf{x}_{n+1}$: $y_{n+1} \leftarrow \mathbf{u}(\mathbf{x}_{n+1})$

        Augment the observation set $\mathcal{D}_{n+1} = \mathcal{D}_n \cup \{(x_{n+1}, y_{n+1})\}$

        Re-construct the GP model of $\mathbf{u}$ on the augmented set $\mathcal{D}_{n+1}$

    end for

5.1 Existing Acquisition Functions

We briefly review some popular acquisition functions and adapt them to the SAS problem.

Expected Improvement (EI): Originally proposed by Mockus [16], the function tries to balance between exploration (evaluating at points with higher uncertainty) versus exploitation (evaluating at points with higher estimated values) and is defined as:

$$EI(\mathbf{x}) = \Delta(\mathbf{x}, \mathcal{F}_1, \mathcal{F}_2) \cdot \Big(\big(\mu(\mathbf{x}) - \mathbf{u}(\mathbf{x}^+) - \xi\big)\, \Phi(Z) + \sigma(\mathbf{x})\phi(Z)\Big), \qquad (9)$$

where $Z = \frac{\mu(\mathbf{x}) - \mathbf{u}(\mathbf{x}^+) - \xi}{\sigma(\mathbf{x})}$, $\mathbf{u}(\mathbf{x}^+)$ is the value of the best observation so far, $\mathbf{x}^+$ is the schedule with that observation, and finally:

$$\Delta(\mathbf{x}, \mathcal{F}_1, \mathcal{F}_2) = \begin{cases} 1 & \text{if } \mathbf{x} \text{ satisfies all constraints in } \mathcal{F}_1 \text{ and } \mathcal{F}_2 \\ 0 & \text{otherwise,} \end{cases} \qquad (10)$$

is the schedule satisfiability indicator function with $\mathcal{F}_1$ and $\mathcal{F}_2$ denoting the sets of constraints over the appliances of an individual' smart home. The above assigns zero improvement to all unsatisfiable schedules. The mean and standard deviation of the GP posterior, predicted at $\mathbf{x}$ are denoted as $\mu(\mathbf{x})$ and $\sigma(\mathbf{x})$, respectively. Additionally, Φ and ϕ denote the standard cumulative density function and probability density function, respectively. Finally, ξ is a parameter that trades exploration for exploitation, where higher ξ leads to more exploration.

Probability of Improvement (PI): An alternative function to EI [11,44], it is extended to be a constrained improvement function as follows:

$$PI(\mathbf{x}) = \Delta(\mathbf{x}, \mathcal{F}_1, \mathcal{F}_2) \cdot \Phi(Z) \qquad (11)$$

Upper Confidence Bound (UCB): Adopted for Bayesian optimization [32], it is extended to be a constrained acquisition function as follows:

$$UCB(\mathbf{x}) = \Delta(\mathbf{x}, \mathcal{F}_1, \mathcal{F}_2) \cdot (\mu(\mathbf{x}) + \kappa\sigma(\mathbf{x})) \qquad (12)$$

where κ is the parameter that trades off exploration and exploitation.

5.2   Acquisition Functions for the SAS Problem

We propose a set of acquisition functions that are extended from the existing functions above and are customized for our SAS problem. Specifically, These customized acquisition functions employ the energy cost function of the candidate schedule, defined below, as a contributing factor.

Definition 4. *The energy cost function of the candidate schedule* $\mathbf{x}$, *is the total energy cost of scheduling all the appliances involved in* $\mathbf{x}$:

$$\varepsilon(p, \mathbf{x}) = \sum_{(v_j, t_k) \in \mathbf{x}} \varepsilon(p, (v_j, t_k)) \tag{13}$$

and $\varepsilon(p, (v_j, t_k))$ *is the energy cost function defined in Eq. 6.*

In the following, we introduce the acquisition functions, where the energy cost function of the candidate schedule is used as a *trade-off parameter* to provide a better balance between exploration and exploitation during the optimization process.

EI with Energy Cost as a Trade-off Parameter (EI-ECT): The proposed acquisition function exploits the energy cost function $\varepsilon(p, \mathbf{x})$ of the candidate schedule $\mathbf{x}$ as the trade-off parameter in EI:

$$\text{EI-ECT}(\mathbf{x}) = \Delta(\mathbf{x}, \mathcal{F}_1, \mathcal{F}_2) \cdot \Big((\mu(\mathbf{x}) - \mathbf{u}(\mathbf{x}^+) - \varepsilon(p, \mathbf{x})) \Phi(Z_{ECT}) + \sigma(\mathbf{x}) \phi(Z_{ECT}) \Big) \tag{14}$$

where $Z_{ECT} = \frac{\mu(\mathbf{x}) - \mathbf{u}(\mathbf{x}^+) - \varepsilon(p, \mathbf{x})}{\sigma(\mathbf{x})}$, and $\mathbf{u}(\mathbf{x}^+)$ is the value of the best observation so far.

PI with Energy Cost as a Trade-off Parameter (PI-ECT): The proposed acquisition function exploits the energy cost function $\varepsilon(p, \mathbf{x})$ as a trade-off parameter in PI:

$$\text{PI-ECT}(\mathbf{x}) = \Delta(\mathbf{x}, \mathcal{F}_1, \mathcal{F}_2) \cdot \Phi(Z_{ECT}) \tag{15}$$

UCB with Energy Cost as a Trade-off Parameter (UCB-ECT): The proposed acquisition function exploits the energy cost function $\varepsilon(p, \mathbf{x})$ as a trade-off parameter in UCB:

$$\text{UCB-ECT}(\mathbf{x}) = \Delta(\mathbf{x}, \mathcal{F}_1, \mathcal{F}_2) \cdot \Big(\mu(\mathbf{x}) + \varepsilon(p, \mathbf{x}) \sigma(\mathbf{x}) \Big) \tag{16}$$

In the following, we introduce the acquisition functions, where the energy cost function of the candidate schedule is used as a *coefficient parameter* to improve the correlation between the acquisition function and the objective function $\mathbf{u}(\cdot)$ during the optimization process.

EI with Energy Cost as a Coefficient (EI-ECC): The proposed acquisition function exploits the energy cost function $\varepsilon(p, \mathbf{x})$ of the candidate schedule $\mathbf{x}$ as a coefficient in EI:

$$\text{EI-ECC}(\mathbf{x}) = \Delta(\mathbf{x}, \mathcal{F}_1, \mathcal{F}_2) \cdot \Big(\big(\mu(\mathbf{x}) - \mathbf{u}(\mathbf{x}^+) - \xi\big) \Phi(Z) + \sigma(\mathbf{x})\phi(Z) \Big) \cdot \varepsilon(p, \mathbf{x}) \tag{17}$$

PI with Energy Cost as a Coefficient (PI-ECC): The proposed acquisition function exploits the energy cost function $\varepsilon(p, \mathbf{x})$ as a coefficient in PI:

$$\text{PI-ECT}(\mathbf{x}) = \Delta(\mathbf{x}, \mathcal{F}_1, \mathcal{F}_2) \cdot \Phi(Z) \cdot \varepsilon(p, \mathbf{x}) \tag{18}$$

UCB with Energy Cost as a Coefficient (UCB-ECC): The proposed acquisition function exploits the energy cost function $\varepsilon(p, \mathbf{x})$ as a coefficient in UCB:

$$\text{UCB-ECC}(\mathbf{x}) = \Delta(\mathbf{x}, \mathcal{F}_1, \mathcal{F}_2) \cdot \big(\mu(\mathbf{x}) + \kappa\sigma(\mathbf{x})\big) \cdot \varepsilon(p, \mathbf{x}) \tag{19}$$

6 Empirical Evaluations

We empirically evaluate our new acquisition functions (i.e., EI-ECT, EI-ECC, PI-ECT, PI-ECC, UCB-ECT, and UCB-ECC) by comparing them against three popular acquisition functions (i.e., EI, PI, and UCB) that serve as baseline acquisition functions. Specifically, we compare their *loss*, defined as $\mathbf{u}_{max} - \mathbf{u}(\mathbf{x}^*)$, where $\mathbf{u}_{max}$ is the maximal value of the user's satisfaction, $\mathbf{x}^*$ is the best schedule elicited after a certain number of queries, and $\mathbf{u}(\mathbf{x}^*)$ is the user's satisfaction with that schedule [39]. To evaluate the performance of the Bayesian optimization algorithm with different acquisition functions, we report the loss averaged over 20 SAS problem instances with 10 runs per instance.

6.1 Experimental Setup

In all experiments, we set the time horizon $\mathcal{H} = 24$ with $|T| = 48$ time steps and vary the number of smart appliances $|\mathcal{V}| = [2, 5]$. Our focus is on scheduling the smart appliances that accept flexible schedules and are more likely to be available in typical homes. For instance, Tesla electric vehicle, Kenmore oven and dishwasher, GE clothes washer and dryer, iRobot vacuum cleaner, and LG air conditioner [8] can operate at any time step to finish their tasks. We randomly generated a set of unary constraints $\mathcal{F}_1$ enforced on appliances, a set of binary constraints $\mathcal{F}_2$ between appliances in each home and set the number of binary constraints $|\mathcal{F}_2| = p_1 \cdot \frac{(|\mathcal{V}|)(|\mathcal{V}|-1)}{2}$, where $p_1 = 0.4$.

We used MiniZinc [33], an off-the-shelf CSP solver, to solve the SAS problem instances and find the set of all feasible solutions $\mathbf{X}$. As defined earlier, the user's satisfaction is a function of energy cost and user's comfort given a schedule, which we describe below.

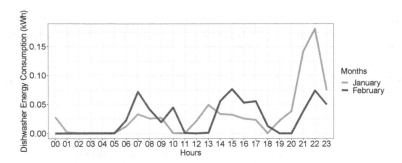

Fig. 1. Averaged hourly energy consumption in kWh for the dishwasher in January and February of 2018 for a single household in Texas. The data is collected by Pecan Street Inc.

Real-Time Pricing Schema: We adapted the pricing schema defined by California ISO (CAISO),[1] which includes the energy price (cents/kWh) at a granularity of 5-min intervals. To create the hourly real-time pricing schema p, we calculated the price by averaging over twelve data points in each hour and converting the price from cents to dollars. The duration of the task δ_{v_j} of each appliance v_j is set to 2 h.

User's Comfort: To create the user's comfort level ζ, we use the users load profile data collected by Pecan Street Inc [22].[2] The time-series energy datasets consist of energy consumption of multiple appliances in kWh that have been collected every 15 min for 25 homes in a region in Texas and 25 homes in California in 2018. For each of these 50 homes, we calculated each appliance's hourly energy consumption by summing up the four data points in each hour. For each of these appliances and hour of a day, we averaged the calculated hourly energy consumption over a one-month period, resulting in a total of 24 data points (per month per appliance). We assume that the user's comfort level corresponds to their daily load profile for each appliance.

Figure 1 illustrates the averaged energy consumption of the dishwasher at every hour of January and February in 2018 for one of the homes in Texas. From the figure, we can perceive, with a high probability, that the user preferred to turn on the dishwasher at night—the most preferred time was 10:00 p.m. in January 2018 as shown with the solid orange line in the figure. Then, we normalized these hourly values for each appliance and used them as the user's comfort ζ for that appliance. In all experiments, we set the number of schedules $k = 2$ in our initial observation and we vary the number of queries Q from 1 to 18.

---

[1] California ISO (CAISO). https://tinyurl.com/y8t4xa2r.
[2] Pecan Street Inc. https://www.pecanstreet.org/dataport/.

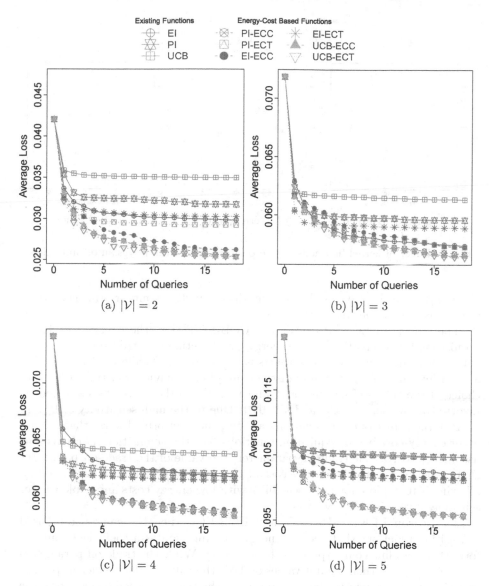

Fig. 2. The average loss of energy-cost based acquisition functions against the existing acquisition functions

6.2   Impact of Energy-Cost Based Acquisition Functions

Figure 2 shows the performance of different acquisition functions, where we report the average loss for each acquisition function. All acquisition functions were run with identical initial observations. As expected, for all acquisition functions, the losses decreased with increasing number of queries Q. In general, we

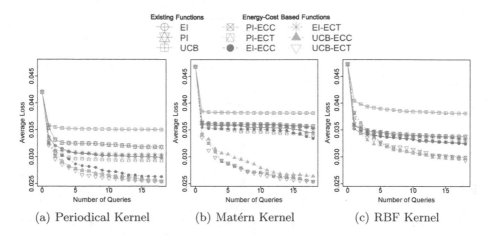

(a) Periodical Kernel   (b) Matérn Kernel   (c) RBF Kernel

Fig. 3. Effect of kernel functions on the performance of the Bayesian optimization

observe that our energy-cost based acquisition functions outperform their traditional baseline counterparts.

The reason EI-ECT, PI-ECT, and UCB-ECT (i.e., the energy-cost based acquisition functions that use the energy cost function as a trade-off parameter) outperform their baseline counterparts is the following: While EI, PI, and UCB acquisition functions give rise to distinct sampling behavior over time, the exact choice of the trade-off parameters ξ and κ is left to the users. As suggested by Lizotte [13], we set $\xi = 0.01$ and $\kappa = 0.01$. Due to the high sensitivity of PI and UCB to the choice of the trade-off parameter, they performed worse than EI and other energy-cost based acquisition functions. For the acquisition functions that use energy cost as the trade-off parameter, the value of the trade-off parameter changes according to the energy cost of the selected schedule ($\varepsilon(p, \mathbf{x}) > 0.01$), allowing it to explore for more schedules with low energy costs and exploit fewer schedules with high energy costs.

The reason EI-ECC, PI-ECC, and UCB-ECC (i.e., the energy-cost based acquisition functions that use the energy cost function as a coefficient) outperform their baseline counterparts is the following: While the trade-off parameters ξ and κ are set to their default values of 0.01, the value of the coefficient parameter changes according to the energy cost of the selected schedule, affecting the GP posterior's mean $\mu(\mathbf{x})$ and standard deviation $\sigma(\mathbf{x})$. It results in evaluations of the schedules in regions with: (i) Higher uncertainty when the standard deviation is larger than the mean, and (ii) Higher estimated values when the mean is larger than the standard deviation. The former explores schedules with lower energy costs more than those with higher energy costs, and the latter exploits schedules with lower energy costs more than those with higher energy costs.

These results demonstrate the energy-cost based functions that outperformed their baseline counterparts improve the Bayesian optimization algorithm's performance up to 26% by reducing the average loss.

6.3   Impact of Different Kernel Functions

In our next experiment, to evaluate the choice of kernel function, we employed three different commonly-used kernels (periodic [5], Matérn [38], and RBF [28, 38]), where we set the number of appliances $|\mathcal{V}| = 2$. Figure 3 shows the performance of the acquisition functions using different kernels, and the same trends from earlier experiments apply here as well.

7   Conclusions

The autonomous and coordinated control of smart appliances in residential buildings represents an effective solution to reduce peak demands. This paper, studied the associated *smart appliance scheduling* (SAS) problem that minimizes energy peaks while also complying with users' satisfaction about schedules. It focused on the realistic case when these users' satisfaction are unknown and, therefore, must be learned through an expensive elicitation process. To minimize the amount of elicitation requests, the proposed approach employs a *Bayesian optimization* (BO) framework, that is used to approximate a function of the user comfort and energy cost of the given schedule. The paper proposed a number of acquisition functions, which are a central component of BO as they drive the selection of desirable schedules to be evaluated (a.k.a. elicited). The proposed acquisition functions are SAS-specific and exploit the concept of *energy cost*, that encodes information about schedules cost. The experimental evaluations demonstrated the effectiveness of the proposed energy-cost based acquisition functions. Our model and solution approach thus extend the state of the art in Bayesian optimization to better formulate and solve agent-based applications with user preferences.

Acknowledgments. Tabakhi and Yeoh are partially supported by NSF grants 1550662 and 1812619, and Fioretto is partially supported by NSF grant 2007164. The views and conclusions contained in this document are those of the authors and should not be interpreted as representing the official policies, either expressed or implied, of the sponsoring organizations, agencies, or the U.S. government.

References

1. Amini, M.H., Frye, J., Ilić, M.D., Karabasoglu, O.: Smart residential energy scheduling utilizing two stage mixed integer linear programming. In: North American Power Symposium (2015)
2. Chen, L., Pu, P.: Survey of preference elicitation methods. Technical report, Swiss Federal Institute of Technology in Lausanne (EPFL) (2004)
3. Chen, Z., Wu, L., Fu, Y.: Real-time price-based demand response management for residential appliances via stochastic optimization and robust optimization. IEEE Trans. Smart Grid **3**(4), 1822–1831 (2012)
4. Du, P., Lu, N.: Appliance commitment for household load scheduling. IEEE Trans. Smart Grid **2**(2), 411–419 (2011)

5. Duvenaud, D.: The kernel cookbook. In: Advice on Covariance Functions, pp. 12–39 (2015)
6. Fang, X., Misra, S., Xue, G., Yang, D.: Smart grid-the new and improved power grid: a survey. IEEE Commun. Surv. Tutor. **14**(4), 944–980 (2011)
7. Farhangi, H.: The path of the smart grid. IEEE Power Energy Mag. **8**(1), 18–28 (2009)
8. Fioretto, F., Yeoh, W., Pontelli, E.: A multiagent system approach to scheduling devices in smart homes. In: Proceedings of AAMAS, pp. 981–989 (2017)
9. Frazier, P.I.: A tutorial on Bayesian optimization. CoRR abs/1807.02811 (2018)
10. Gelazanskas, L., Gamage, K.A.: Demand side management in smart grid: a review and proposals for future direction. Sustain. Cities Soc. **11**, 22–30 (2014)
11. Jones, D.R.: A taxonomy of global optimization methods based on response surfaces. J. Glob. Optim. **21**(4), 345–383 (2001)
12. Le, T., Tabakhi, A.M., Tran-Thanh, L., Yeoh, W., Son, T.C.: Preference elicitation with interdependency and user bother cost. In: Proceedings of AAMAS, pp. 1459–1467 (2018)
13. Lizotte, D.J.: Practical Bayesian optimization. University of Alberta (2008)
14. Logenthiran, T., Srinivasan, D., Shun, T.Z.: Demand side management in smart grid using heuristic optimization. IEEE Trans. Smart Grid **3**(3), 1244–1252 (2012)
15. Mockus, J., Mockus, L.: Bayesian approach to global optimization and application to multiobjective and constrained problems. J. Optim. Theory Appl. **70**(1), 157–172 (1991)
16. Mockus, J.: On Bayesian methods for seeking the extremum and their application. In: Proceedings of Information Processing, pp. 195–200 (1977)
17. Mockus, J.: Application of Bayesian approach to numerical methods of global and stochastic optimization. J. Global Optim. **4**(4), 347–365 (1994)
18. Mockus, J., Tiesis, V., Zilinskas, A.: The application of Bayesian methods for seeking the extremum. Towards Global Optim. **2**(117–129), 2 (1978)
19. Mohsenian-Rad, A.H., Wong, V.W., Jatskevich, J., Schober, R., Leon-Garcia, A.: Autonomous demand-side management based on game-theoretic energy consumption scheduling for the future smart grid. IEEE Trans. Smart Grid **1**(3), 320–331 (2010)
20. Nguyen, V., Yeoh, W., Son, T.C., Kreinovich, V., Le, T.: A scheduler for smart homes with probabilistic user preferences. In: Proceedings of PRIMA, pp. 138–152 (2019)
21. Peeters, L., De Dear, R., Hensen, J., D'haeseleer, W.: Thermal comfort in residential buildings: Comfort values and scales for building energy simulation. Applied energy 86(5), 772–780 (2009)
22. Rhodes, J.D., et al.: Experimental and data collection methods for a large-scale smart grid deployment: methods and first results. Energy **65**, 462–471 (2014)
23. Rossi, F., van Beek, P., Walsh, T. (eds.): Handbook of Constraint Programming. Elsevier, Amsterdam (2006)
24. Rossi, F., Petrie, C.J., Dhar, V.: On the equivalence of constraint satisfaction problems. In: European Conference on Artificial Intelligence, pp. 550–556 (1990)
25. Rust, P., Picard, G., Ramparany, F.: Using message-passing DCOP algorithms to solve energy-efficient smart environment configuration problems. In: Proceedings of IJCAI, pp. 468–474 (2016)
26. Samadi, P., Mohsenian-Rad, H., Schober, R., Wong, V.W.: Advanced demand side management for the future smart grid using mechanism design. IEEE Trans. Smart Grid **3**(3), 1170–1180 (2012)

27. Scott, P., Thiébaux, S., Van Den Briel, M., Van Hentenryck, P.: Residential demand response under uncertainty. In: International Conference on Principles and Practice of Constraint Programming, pp. 645–660 (2013)
28. Sedghi, M., Atia, G., Georgiopoulos, M.: Kernel coherence pursuit: a manifold learning-based outlier detection technique. In: Proceedings of ACSSC, pp. 2017–2021 (2018)
29. Shann, M., Seuken, S.: An active learning approach to home heating in the smart grid. In: Proceedings of IJCAI, pp. 2892–2899 (2013)
30. Song, W., Kang, D., Zhang, J., Cao, Z., Xi, H.: A sampling approach for proactive project scheduling under generalized time-dependent workability uncertainty. J. Artif. Intell. Res. 64, 385–427 (2019)
31. Sou, K.C., Weimer, J., Sandberg, H., Johansson, K.H.: Scheduling smart home appliances using mixed integer linear programming. In: Proceedings of CDC, pp. 5144–5149 (2011)
32. Srinivas, N., Krause, A., Kakade, S.M., Seeger, M.W.: Gaussian process optimization in the bandit setting: no regret and experimental design. In: Proceedings of ICML, pp. 1015–1022 (2010)
33. Stuckey, P.J., et al..: The evolving world of MiniZinc. In: Constraint Modelling and Reformulation, pp. 156–170 (2007)
34. Tabakhi, A.M.: Preference elicitation in DCOPs for scheduling devices in smart buildings. In: Proceedings of AAAI, pp. 4989–4990 (2017)
35. Tabakhi, A.M., Le, T., Fioretto, F., Yeoh, W.: Preference elicitation for DCOPs. In: Proceedings of CP, pp. 278–296 (2017)
36. Tabakhi, A.M., Yeoh, W., Yokoo, M.: Parameterized heuristics for incomplete weighted CSPs with elicitation costs. In: Proceedings of AAMAS, pp. 476–484 (2019)
37. Truong, N.C., Baarslag, T., Ramchurn, S.D., Tran-Thanh, L.: Interactive scheduling of appliance usage in the home. In: Proceedings of IJCAI, pp. 869–877 (2016)
38. Williams, C.K., Rasmussen, C.E.: Gaussian Processes for Machine Learning, vol. 2. MIT Press, Cambridge (2006)
39. Wilson, J., Hutter, F., Deisenroth, M.: Maximizing acquisition functions for Bayesian optimization. In: Advances in Neural Information Processing Systems (2018)
40. Xiao, Y., Tabakhi, A.M., Yeoh, W.: Embedding preference elicitation within the search for DCOP solutions. In: Proceedings of AAMAS, pp. 2044–2046 (2020)
41. Zhu, J., Lin, Y., Lei, W., Liu, Y., Tao, M.: Optimal household appliances scheduling of multiple smart homes using an improved cooperative algorithm. Energy 171, 944–955 (2019)
42. Zhu, Z., Tang, J., Lambotharan, S., Chin, W.H., Fan, Z.: An integer linear programming based optimization for home demand-side management in smart grid. In: IEEE PES Innovative Smart Grid Technologies Conference, pp. 1–5 (2012)
43. Žilinskas, A.: On the use of statistical models of multimodal functions for the construction of the optimization algorithms. In: Iracki, K., Malanowski, K., Walukiewicz, S. (eds.) Optimization Techniques, pp. 138–147. Springer, Heidelberg (1980). https://doi.org/10.1007/BFb0006597
44. Žilinskas, A.: A review of statistical models for global optimization. J. Global Optim. 2(2), 145–153 (1992)

Distance-Based Heuristic Solvers for Cooperative Path Planning with Heterogeneous Agents

Keisuke Otaki(✉) [iD], Satoshi Koide, Ayano Okoso, and Tomoki Nishi

Toyota Central R&D Labs., Inc., Bunkyo-ku 1-4-14, Tokyo 112-0011, Japan
{otaki,koide,okoso,nishi}@mosk.tytlabs.co.jp

Abstract. Cooperation among different vehicles is a promising concept for transportation services. For instance, vehicle platooning on highways with self-driving vehicles is known to decrease fuel consumption. This makes us construct paths on graphs, where many vehicles share sub-paths to form platoons. The platooning model has been recently generalized to model different types (e.g., trucks and UAVs) but existing exact solvers using Integer Programming (IP) are not experimentally evaluated on various settings and heuristic solvers are underdeveloped; hence solving large instances remains difficult. In this study, we propose heuristic solvers using a distance-based grouping of vehicles. Our solver first finds groups of vehicles and constructs paths in each group independently. We also experimentally investigate both exact and heuristic solvers. Experimental results suggest that IP-based solvers only solve small instances due to the overhead of compiling IP models. We observed that our solvers were almost fifth magnitude faster than the exact solver with at most 25% additional travel costs. Also, our method achieved roughly 15% additional costs if requests are clustered in terms of their locations, meaning that distance-based heuristic solvers could find moderate solutions within typically a few seconds.

Keywords: Path-planning · Cooperation · Heterogeneous agents

1 Introduction

Services provided by autonomous vehicles could solve transportation-related social problems by optimizing the way we use such a transportation system in Mobility as a Service (MaaS) [1,8,12,18]. An important part of the optimization is constructing routes of vehicles (a.k.a. *path-planning*). The optimized routes are important to utilize the cooperation among vehicles and to share resources used by services. In logistics, for example, providing meeting points among vehicles and customers is beneficial to construct efficient cross-docking operations for service providers [16,20]. For transportation services, designing routes for sharing a limited number of vehicles by users is a key perspective to reduce the total service cost [26]. Another example of cooperation by vehicles is known as

© Springer Nature Switzerland AG 2021
T. Uchiya et al. (Eds.): PRIMA 2020, LNAI 12568, pp. 116–132, 2021.
https://doi.org/10.1007/978-3-030-69322-0_8

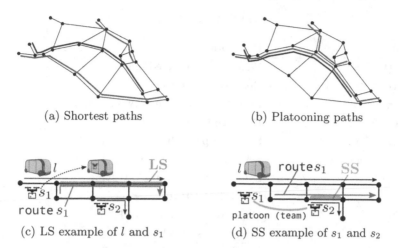

(a) Shortest paths   (b) Platooning paths

(c) LS example of l and s_1 (d) SS example of s_1 and s_2

Fig. 1. Concept of path-planning for multiple vehicles: (a) Shortest paths and (b) Cooperative paths (platooning). Conceptual examples of heterogeneous cooperation are displayed in (c) and (d): (c) a truck l and an UAV s_1 travel together (labeled as **LS**) and (d) two UAVs s_1 and s_2 travel together (labeled as **SS**).

platoons that consist of trucks; Forming platoons of trucks is beneficial to reduce fuel consumption because platoons decrease the air resistance [4,14].

The path-planning problem for multiple vehicles, named *cooperative path-planning* (CPP) problems, has been studied in various research areas: transportation [13,17], artificial intelligence [23,24,27], graph algorithms [3,9,28]. In the transportation domain, the problem assuming that one vehicle type such as trucks is named *vehicle platooning problem* [17]. Researchers have focused on optimizing the routes of fleet vehicles to reduce fuel consumption by forming platoons. Figure 1 shows examples when operating three trucks, where platooning paths illustrated in Fig. 1b could be more efficient than the shortest paths as shown in Fig. 1a. Note that researchers often deal with paths solely without taking time-synchronization into account in these contexts because the time could be encoded into the graph-structure (e.g., with time-extended graphs).

In previous work, the generalized problem of VPPs on heterogeneous vehicle types and cooperation has been studied [23,24]. Figures 1c and 1d illustrate examples. The heterogeneity enables us to consider different cooperation such as truck-truck or truck-UAV cooperation separately.

Contributions. The previous studies reported theoretical and computational aspects of the optimization problem of finding paths for multiple vehicles. Unfortunately, some scores for computational experiments with IP solvers (e.g., gaps and computational times) were not evaluated. Only small synthetic graphs are used to evaluate their solvers.

Table 1. Notations

Symbols	Descriptions
$G = (V, E, w)$	Weighted undirected graph
$r = (o, d) \in V \times V$	Request from o to d
$p_{o,d}, \pi_{o,d}$	Path/Shortest path between o and d on G
$dist(o, d) = |\pi_{o,d}|$	Distance between o and d in G
$\Pi(o, d), \Pi(r)$	Set of all paths from o to d ($r = (o, d)$)
$\mathcal{R} = \{r_n \mid n \in [N]\}$	Set of requests from N vehicles
$\mathcal{P} = \{p_n \in \Pi(r_n) \mid n \in [N]\}$	Solution: Set of paths satisfying $\mathcal{R}$
η	Factor in VPP ($0 < \eta < 1$)
$\mathbf{C}(\mathcal{P})$	Objective function in VPP
$\mathcal{T}$	Set of types of vehicles
$N_T, T \in \mathcal{T}$	Number of vehicles of type T
$\mathcal{C} \subseteq \mathcal{T} \times \mathcal{T}$	Cooperative relation
$\eta^{(T_1 T_2)}$	Factor between types T_1 and T_2 ($0 < \eta^{(T_1 T_2)} < 1$)
$\mathbf{C}^{(\mathrm{h})}(\mathcal{P}), \mathbf{C}^{(\mathrm{PPP})}(\mathcal{P})$	Objective function in 2MP^3 and PPP

We herein address two problems, which are not discussed enough in previous work[1]. First, there exists no sufficient evaluations via experiments using IP solvers about the difficulty arisen from vehicle types. Second, there exist no heuristic solvers as we mentioned.

We contribute the above problems by following results: First, we develop heuristic solvers for the optimization problem using shortest paths and graph matching in Sect. 3. Second, we experimentally analyze the difficulty of the problem with heterogeneous vehicle types using the modern solver Gurobi. In addition, we compare results by the heuristic solvers and those by Gurobi [10] for evaluation in Sect. 4.

2 Preliminary

For $n \in \mathbb{N}^+$, $[n] = \{1, 2, \cdots, n\}$, the symbol $\langle \cdot \rangle$ indicates a list of elements. Table 1 summarizes symbols and notations. The problem we address, named CPP problem, is to construct a set of paths for multiple vehicles simultaneously.

2.1 Graphs and Requests

Let $G = (V, E, w)$ be an underlying weighted undirected graph with the set V of vertices, the set $E \subseteq V \times V$ of edges, and the weight function $w : E \to \mathbb{R}$, which indicates the travel costs on G. We denote the value $w(u, v)$ by $w_{u,v}$

---

[1] Our previous extended abstract paper also discusses this topic [25].

for $(u, v) \in E$. More simply, we write w_e for $e = (u, v) \in E$. Without loss of generality, graphs in this paper are simple. A *path* $p_{o,d}$ connecting two vertices $o, d \in V$ is a list of vertices $p_{o,d} = \langle v_1, v_2, \dots, v_{k+1} \rangle$, where $v_1 = o$, $v_{k+1} = d$, and $(v_i, v_{i+1}) \in E$ for $1 \le i \le k$ and the value k is the length of path $p_{o,d}$, denoted by $|p_{o,d}| = k$. For a vertex $v \in V$ and a path p, we say $v \in p$ if $p_j = v$ for some $1 \le j \le |p| + 1$. Similarly, we say $(v_1, v_2) \in p$ if there exists j $(1 \le j \le |p|)$ satisfying $p_j = v_1, p_{j+1} = v_2$. For two vertices $o, d \in V$, the set of all paths connecting them is denoted by $\Pi(o, d)$ and a shortest path between them is denoted by $\pi_{o,d} \in \Pi(o, d)$. The *distance* between two vertices $o, d \in V$ is the sum of weights of all edges in $\pi_{o,d}$ and denoted by $dist(o, d)$ or $|\pi_{o,d}|$. Similarly, the distance along with a path $p_{o,d}$ is also denoted by $|p_{o,d}|$.

We assume that each vehicle has its transportation *request*. A request is a pair of vertices $r = (o, d) \in V \times V$. A path p *satisfies* the request $r = (o, d)$ if and only if $p \in \Pi(o, d)$. The term *route* denotes a path satisfying a request and *solution* denotes a set of paths satisfying all requests.

2.2 Vehicle Platooning Problem

We review the vehicle platooning problem (VPP) [17].

For a graph G, a set $\mathcal{R} = \{r_n = (o_n, d_n) \mid n \in [N]\}$ of requests for N vehicles, and a discount factor η $(0 < \eta < 1)$, the VPP is to compute a solution $\mathcal{P} = \{p_n \in \Pi(o_n, d_n) \mid n \in [N]\}$ that minimizes the objective function Eq. (1):

$$\mathbf{C}(\mathcal{P}) = \sum_{\substack{e \in E \\ \text{s.t. } N_{\mathcal{P}}(e) > 0}} w_e \left(1 + \eta \times (N_{\mathcal{P}}(e) - 1)\right), \tag{1}$$

where $N_{\mathcal{P}}(e) = |\{e \in p_i \mid p_i \in \mathcal{P}\}|$. Equation (1) encourages us to find $\mathcal{P}$ that contains edges, where many vehicles travel together to form platoons, and consequently the total cost $\mathbf{C}(\mathcal{P})$ is discounted as $N_{\mathcal{P}}(e)$ increases due to $\eta < 1$. In a platoon, a vehicle $n \in [N]$ can be regarded as a platooning parent (cost $1 \times w_{u,v}$) or a platooning child (cost $\eta \times w_e$) at each edge $e \in E$.

The VPP models cooperation among *homogeneous* vehicles to share subroutes since it is developed in the transportation domain. Figure 1a and 1b illustrate the difference between shortest paths and paths obtained by VPP. The VPP is proven to be NP-hard [17].

2.3 Cooperative Path Planning Problem

The CPP problem for heterogeneous vehicle types is named *two-modal palette platooning problem* (2MP^3) or *palette platooning problem* (PPP) as a generalization of VPP [23,24]. The idea is from Eq. (1); the platooning parent (whose cost is evaluated by $\times 1$) and child (done with $\times \eta$) are generalized when considering multiple vehicle types. The cooperation between vehicles is represented by a *(directed) binary relation* defined as follows:

Definition 1 (from [23]). *Suppose the set $\mathcal{T}$ consists of all vehicle types. The set $\mathcal{C} \subseteq \mathcal{T} \times \mathcal{T}$ represents of all combinations between vehicle types in $\mathcal{T}$, named cooperative relation. For $(T_1, T_2) \in \mathcal{C}$, we say that T_1 vehicles are parent and T_2 vehicles are children of (T_1, T_2). For $(T_1, T_2) \in \mathcal{C}$, we simply call it $\mathbf{T_1 T_2}$ cooperation (or effect). We say that the supposed cooperation in path-planning is heterogeneous if $|\mathcal{T}| > 1$.*

We could model cooperation among different types as follows.

Example 1. *Let us consider a logistic scenario, depicted in Figs. 1c and 1d, with two vehicle types L and S; L is a type corresponding to a large truck and S is that for a small UAV. We assume that large vehicles could carry items and another small UAVs (labeled by **LS** effect in Fig. 1c). A small UAV S can move as a solo distributor to locally distribute the items. Further, more than two UAVs could form a platoon to deliver large baggage (**SS** effect in Fig. 1d).*

In the CPP problem we optimize optimize both the routes of vehicles and the selection of effects allowed in $\mathcal{C}$ to construct a cost-minimum route for all vehicles. We assume that N_T vehicles of type $T \in \mathcal{T}$ could participate in our setting and identify a type T vehicle by $t \in [N_T]$. We also represent sets of requests for type T vehicles by $\mathcal{R}^{(T)}$. All vehicles could travel, have their own requests, and can cooperate with each other. The *two-modal palette platooning problem* (2MP³) is now formally defined below.

Definition 2. *Let $\mathcal{T} = \{L, S\}$ and $\mathcal{C} = \{(L, L), (L, S), (S, L), (S, S)\}$ with discount factors $\eta^{(TT')}$ for $(T, T') \in \mathcal{C}$. Two sets $\mathcal{R}^{(L)}$ and $\mathcal{R}^{(S)}$ of requests on a graph G for L and S vehicles are given. The 2MP³ is to compute solutions $\mathcal{P}$ that minimizes the objective function Eq. (2).*

$$\mathbf{C}^{(h)}(\mathcal{P}) = \sum_{T \in \{L, S\}} \sum_{e \in E} w_e g_e^{(h), T},$$

$$g_e^{(h), T} := \#(parent\ as\ T\ at\ e\ in\ \mathcal{P})$$
$$+ \sum_{T' \in \{L, S\}} \eta^{(TT')} \times \#(child\ of\ (T, T')\ at\ e\ in\ \mathcal{P}). \tag{2}$$

The value $g_e^{(h), T}$ in Eq. (2) indicates the evaluated number of vehicles when computing the cost with reduction effects. The capacity of stack-able UAVs (type S) in a truck (type L) should be considered in Example 1; hence we adopt *cooperation type-wise capacity constraint*, which is formally described below.

Definition 3. *For $(T, T') \in \mathcal{C}$ and a given capacity $Q^{(TT')}$, the cooperation between T and T' at $e \in E$ should satisfy*

$$Q^{(TT')} \geq \#(child\ of\ (T, T')\ at\ e). \tag{3}$$

It is straightforwardly possible to set different capacities for each vehicle $t \in [N_T]$ of type T. Note that the capacity in VPP is ∞.

Table 2. Decision variables in $\texttt{2MP}^3\texttt{-IP}$ (for $e \in E, l \in [N_L], s \in [N_S]$, and $T \in \mathcal{T} = \{L, S\}$)

Variables	Semantics
$f_{e,l}^{(L)}, f_{e,s}^{(S)}$	$= 1$ if and only if l, s moves on e
$L_{e,t}^{(T)}$	$= 1$ if vehicle t of type T is parent
$FL_{e,t}^{(T)}$	$= 1$ if vehicle t of type T is the L's child
$FS_{e,t}^{(T)}$	$= 1$ if vehicle t of type T is the S's child

2.4 Exact Solvers Using Integer Programming

This section summarizes an exact solver for our problem using integer programming (IP). We show an IP formulation for the $\texttt{2MP}^3$, named $\texttt{2MP}^3\texttt{-IP}$, based on [23]. Decision variables are explained in Table 2. We represent binary variables $f^{(L)}, f^{(S)}$ related to the routes and those $L^{(T)}, FL^{(T)}$, and $FS^{(T)}$ for representing the parent-child relation of vehicles given in $\mathcal{C}$. Using these variables, the value g_e in Eq. (2) is implemented as follows:

Definition 4. *For each $e \in E$, $f_{e,l}^{(L)}$ and $f_{e,s}^{(S)}$ are prepared with identifiers $l \in [N_L]$ or $s \in [N_S]$, and $L_{e,t}^{(T)}, FL_{e,t}^{(T)}, FS_{e,t}^{(T)}$ are used for $t \in [N_T]$ of type $T \in \mathcal{T}$. The 2MP^3 in Def. 2 can be formalized in IP, named 2MP^3-IP, as follows:*

$$\min \sum_{T \in \{L,S\}} \sum_{e \in E} \sum_{t \in [N_T]} g_{e,t}^{(h),T} \tag{4}$$

subject to

$$g_{e,t}^{(h),T} = L_{e,t}^{(T)} + \eta^{(LT)} FL_{e,t}^{(T)} + \eta^{(ST)} FS_{e,t}^{(T)} \qquad \text{for all } e \in E, t \in [N_T] \tag{5a}$$

$$L_{e,t}^{(T)} + FL_{e,t}^{(T)} + FS_{e,t}^{(T)} = f_{e,t}^{(T)} \qquad \text{for all } e \in E, t \in [N_T] \tag{5b}$$

$$\sum_{t_1 \in [N_T]} L_{e,t_1}^{(T)} \times Q^{(TT')} \geq \sum_{t_2 \in [N_{T'}]} FT'_{e,t_2} \qquad \text{for all } e \in E, (T, T') \in \mathcal{C} \tag{5c}$$

$$\sum_v \left(f_{u,v,t}^{(T)} - f_{v,u,t}^{(T)} \right) = \begin{cases} 1 & (u = o_t^{(T)}) \\ -1 & (u = d_t^{(T)}) \\ 0 & (o/w) \end{cases} \qquad \text{for all } u \in V, T \in \mathcal{T}, t \in [N_T]. \tag{5d}$$

Equation (4) with auxiliary variables defined in Eq. (5a) regulates the objective function in Eq. (2). Equation (5b) shows the exclusiveness of the parent-child relation. Equation (5c) corresponds to Eq. (3). Equation (5d) shows the flow-conservation constraints of solutions. To avoid self-loops arising from the discount effects, we additionally employ the *MTZ-constraint* [19] in addition to the above constraints.

Generalization. The model above can be generalized for $|\mathcal{T}| > 2$ and/or $\mathcal{C} \subset \mathcal{T} \times \mathcal{T}$ for PPP. Given $\mathcal{T}, \mathcal{C} \subseteq \mathcal{T} \times \mathcal{T}$, and $\eta^{(T\overline{T}')}$ for $(T, T') \in \mathcal{C}$. For a graph G, sets $\mathcal{R}^{(T)}$ of requests for $T \in \mathcal{T}$, the PPP is to compute a solution $\mathcal{P}$ that minimizes the objective function $\mathbf{C}^{(\mathrm{ppp})}(\mathcal{P}) := \sum_{T \in \mathcal{T}, e \in E} w_e g_e^{(\mathrm{ppp}), T}$, where $g_e^{(\mathrm{ppp}), T} :=$ #(parent of T at e in $\mathcal{P}$ + $\sum_{\substack{T' \in \mathcal{T} \\ \text{if } (T, T') \in \mathcal{C}}} \eta^{(TT')} \times$ #(child of (T, T') at e in $\mathcal{P}$).
That is, the combination of $\{L, S\} \times \{L, S\}$ in Eq. (2) is generalized using $\mathcal{T}$ and $\mathcal{C}$. The details of the IP formulation for PPP was provided in [23].

3   Distance-Based Heuristic Solver

CPP problem classes mentioned above (e.g., 2MP^3 and PPP) are computationally intractable since the simplest class VPP is NP-hard. We then expect that even modern IP solvers cannot solve large instances. We try to solve such instances by heuristics. However, such solvers for the classes (2MP^3 and PPP) are underdeveloped. We propose a simple heuristic solver as a first attempt.

3.1   High-Level Overview

We begin to divide the CPP problem into two sub-problems: (**P1**) routing problems of a small numbers of vehicles and (**P2**) (a kind of) assignment problems. We then have the following insights for them:

1. The routing problem (**P1**) could be computationally challenging because the obtained routes could contain detours due to $\eta^{(TT')}(<1)$ (e.g., [9]).
2. The assignment problem (**P2**) with the capacity constraint is also computationally challenging problem because it could relate to the knapsack problem.

Our idea is to focus on the assignment problem (**P2**) by assuming that vehicles *prefer* to follow shortest paths in many cases. That is, we first divide the given set of vehicles into small groups by (**P2**) and then optimize routes in the small groups independently by (**P1**). This procedure consists of the three steps.

Step 1. We evaluate *benefits* when two vehicles t, t' cooperate for $(T, T') \in \mathcal{C}$.
Step 2. Using the evaluated benefits, we construct a group of type T' vehicles for each type T vehicle to take care of the capacity constraints, where the group should be constructed to partition the set of type T' vehicles.
Step 3. Partitioned vehicles are selected in a some order and the routes for vehicles in the selected group are computed based on shortest paths.

In the following, when considering $(T, T') \in \mathcal{C}$ with factor $\eta^{(TT')}$, let us assume that T is the parent and the subscripts t and t' for T' are used, and the superscripts are omitted for the sake of simplicity. For example, (o_t, d_t) means an request of vehicle t of type T.

3.2   Step 1. Evaluating Benefits of Cooperation for Vehicle Pairs

We assume that the path p_t of type T parent vehicle is fixed a priori by some algorithms (e.g., shortest paths). We begin with the following lemma.

Lemma 1. Suppose a vehicle t travels on a route p_t. We define the *merge-split distance* as $d_{\mathrm{ms}}(o_{t'}, d_{t'} \mid p_t) := \min_{u,v \in p_t} dist(o_{t'}, v) + \eta^{(TT')} dist(v, u) + dist(u, d_{t'})$. If $d_{\mathrm{ms}}(o_{t'}, d_{t'} \mid p_t) > dist(o_{t'}, d_{t'})$, t' does not *gain benefit from cooperation*; hence the shortest path $\pi_{o_{t'}, d_{t'}}$ is the best for the vehicle t' when p_t is fixed. The gain is formally defined as $gain(t, t') := \frac{d_{\mathrm{ms}}(o_{t'}, d_{t'} \mid p_t)}{dist(o_{t'}, d_{t'})}$.

We denote the optimal meeting points by $v^\star$ and $u^\star$; the optimal path for t' is obtained as $p_{t'} = \pi_{o_{t'}, v^\star} + \pi_{v^\star, u^\star} + \pi_{u^\star, d_{t'}}$ by concatenating shortest paths. Note that $v^\star$ and $u^\star$ can be easily found by using the shortest paths from $(o_{t'}, d_{t'})$ to p_t and search for vertices on p_t. With this lemma, we can compute a set of pairs that possibly gain benefit from cooperation with respect to p_t.

3.3   Step 2. Finding Vehicle Groups by Assignments

We try to partition vehicles of type T' into some groups based on Lemma 1 to consider the capacity constraints and make the whole planning problem small. Formally, we assign a subset of vehicles of T' to each parent vehicle t of type T; the set Σ_t, is defined as $\Sigma_t := \{t' \in [N_{T'}] \mid gain(t, t') \leq 1\}$. In general, this does not give a (disjoint) partition of $[N_{T'}]$ when collecting all subsets for $t \in [N_T]$; hence we adopt the bipartite graph matching problem [15]. Figure 2 shows a way to build a bipartite graph on $(L, S) \in \mathcal{C}$ cooperation with $T = L$ and $T' = S$. The graph consists of nodes representing vehicles of type T and T', and the edge (t, t') of weight $w_{t,t'} = 1/gain(t, t')$ if and only if $gain(t, t') < 1$. If $gain(t, t') \geq 1$, we remove the edge (t, t') from the bipartite graph.

We choose a set of edges maximizing the total weight to obtain a partition. Since each parent vertex appears at most b times, where b is the capacity of (T, T') cooperation, we adopt two approaches. First one is to solve bipartite graph matching b times and construct a partition incrementally. Second method is directly selecting up to b edges on the constructed bipartite graph. This is actually formulated as the b-matching problem [15]. These two methods are compared in numerical experiments at Sect. 4.3.

3.4   Step 3. Constructing Routes

We first sort the pairs of cooperation from $\mathcal{C}$ in an ascending order of values $\eta^{(TT')}$. It is because the smaller η means that we could reduce more travel costs by cooperation. For $(T, T') \in \mathcal{C}$, (1) we fix the paths of parents using shortest paths, and (2) we construct the group of vehicles, and compute the paths of children based on the fixed paths at step (1). If paths of vehicles are already computed in certain previous step when processing the sorted list of $\mathcal{C}$, we ignore them and do not update the paths twice.

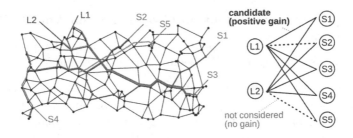

Fig. 2. Grouping based on $d_{\mathrm{ms}}(\cdot \mid p)$ in the cooperation $(L, S) \in \mathcal{C}$.

It is worthy noting that the step (1) could be easily improved by using graph algorithms. For example, the k-shortest paths using [5,29] can be applied to search for solutions in the manner of the local search algorithm. Although we ignore the update of paths if they are already computed as mentioned above, it is also possible to update paths twice in local search as well.

Pseudo Code. Collecting Step 1 to Step 3, our algorithm can be described as the pseudo code shown in Algorithm 1. Line 3–4 corresponds to Sect. 3.2 and Sect. 3.3. Any graph matching algorithm can be applied to construct a group of vehicles in Line 5. After finding such groups (corresponding to (**P2**)), we use Lemma 1 to solve (**P1**) in Line 6–8. Note that Algorithm 1 constructs CPP paths in one step in the current form; however, this could be improved by some standard techniques such as the local search as we mentioned.

Algorithm 1. Merge-Split and Matching-based Heuristic CPP Solver

---

Input: Graph G, Requests $\mathcal{R}^{(T)}$ from type T, Factors $\eta^{(TT')}$ for each $(T, T') \in \mathcal{C}$
Output: Solution $\mathcal{P}^{(T)}$ for type $T \in \mathcal{T}$
1: **for** each $(T, T') \in \mathcal{C}$ of the increasing order of $\eta^{(TT')}$ **do**
2:     Initialize $\mathcal{P}^{(T)}(t) = \pi_{o_t, d_t}$ using shortest paths if $\mathcal{P}^{(T)}(t)$ is not fixed before
        ▷ Other paths (e.g., k-shortest paths) are applicable as explained in Sec. 3.4
3:     Initialize the weight matrix $W \in \mathbb{R}^{N_T, N_{T'}}$
4:     Evaluate gains $W_{t,t'} \leftarrow gain(t, t')$
5:     Build Σ_t for $t \in [N_T]$ using a graph matching algorithm and W
6:     **for** each $t \in [N_T]$ with Σ_t **do**
7:         **for** each $t' \in \Sigma_t$ if $\mathcal{P}^{(T')}(t')$ is not fixed yet. **do**
8:             Construct $\mathcal{P}^{(T')}(t') \leftarrow p_{t'}$ of Lemma 1

---

4   Computational Experiments

We evaluate the IP formulation 2MP³-IP in Sect. 2.4 and heuristic solvers developed in Sect. 3. All numerical evaluations are conduced on a workstation with

Table 3. Road network in Kyoto (**K-**)

Label	$|V|$	E	Experiments (Sect.)
K-500	196	269	4.1, 4.2
K-750	501	1312	4.3
K-1000	972	1449	4.1, 4.3
K-1250	1624	4414	4.1, 4.3
K-1500	3344	5080	4.1, 4.3

Table 4. Random network (**R-**)

Label	$|V|$	E	Experiments (Sect.)
R-300	300	678	4.3
R-600	600	1400	4.3
R-900	900	2150	4.3

an Intel Xeon W-2145 CPU at 3.70 GHz with 64 GB of memory and Gurobi 8.1 as the IP solver. Python/Julia interfaces are used to implement scripts. All scripts run on a single thread.

Graphs and Requests Represented by Labels. We used two types of graphs in experiments. A type is graphs obtained from Kyoto in Japan via OpenStreetMap, represented by the prefix K. Another one is synthetic graphs that imitate road networks (generated by following [13]), represented by the prefix R. The size of graphs is regulated by the parameter d. For graphs obtained from Kyoto, d means the distance of the map considered. For synthetic graphs of prefix R, $d \in \{300, 600, 900\}$ means $|V|$. Graphs used in our experiments are summarized in Table 3 and Table 4.

To represent requests generated on graphs, we use labels: clustered (C) and random (R). Clustered requests start from vertices in the west part of G and travel to the east part. Random requests are generated by selecting two vertices on G randomly.

Parameters. For all instances, except for Sect. 4.1, we set $T = \{L, S\}$ and $C = \{(L, L), (L, S), (S, S)\}$. We set $\eta^{(LL)} = 0.8, \eta^{(LS)} = 0.2, \eta^{(SS)} = 0.9$ following the application scenario of logistics using large trucks and small UAVs, assumed in [24]. We generate random instances of $N_L = 10, N_S = 10$, and the capacities of each cooperation are $Q^{(LL)} = 3, Q^{(LS)} = 3$, and $Q^{(SS)} = 2$.

4.1 Evaluation of IP-Based Exact Solver

We examine the difficulty of the CPP problem itself based on the IP formulation for VPP developed in [17]. We evaluate the time for pre-processing (e.g., model build) and that for solving the given instance on graphs of different sizes to evaluate the performance of the solver-based approach. Here, graphs K-d with $d \in \{1000, 1250, 1500\}$ are used.

I/O and Model Building Overheads Evaluated on VPP. Table 5 shows the mean computational times for random requests (R) with $N_T \in \{10, 20\}$. We confirmed that all $|V|, |E|$, and N_T affect the times. The increment arisen from

Table 5. The mean computational times in [s] of VPP with $\eta = 0.8$; Build means the times to compile IP models and Solve means the times used by the IP solver.

(R)	Graph		$N_T = 10$		$N_T = 20$	
Name	$|V|$	$|E|$	Build	Solve	Build	Solve
K-1000	972	1312	19.15	10.15	35.91	17.04
K-1250	1624	2455	107.09	61.12	206.27	171.21
K-1500	3344	5080	258.47	91.43	501.52	238.11

Table 6. The mean computational times in [s] to see the capacity effects on VPP with $\eta = 0.7$ on a graph K-500 (R).

N_T	$Q^{(LL)} = 1$	2	4
10	12.23	7.85	3.77
15	103.25	71.64	63.14

the graph size is inevitable for IP solvers (see Build. columns). In our results, the bottleneck of the IP solver-based approach could be the increase of times used to build IP models. That is, the pre-processing times were as slow as the times for solving, and the pre-processing time is inevitable because it is essential for I/O in PCs.

Effects from Capacity. An important generalization from VPP to CPP (e.g, 2MP^3) is to consider the capacity of cooperation. To investigate the difficulty arisen from the capacity constraints, we use 2MP^3-IP with setting $\mathcal{T} = \{L\}$, $\mathcal{C} = \{(L, L)\}$, and a capacity parameter $Q^{(LL)}$. We then evaluate the mean computational times to solver VPP with the capacity constraints.

Table 6 shows our results measured on K-500 with $N_T \in \{10, 15\}$ and $Q^{(LL)} \in \{1, 2, 4\}$ using 10 random requests (R). The results indicate that the smaller $Q^{(LL)}$ requires the more times. We conjecture that the difficulty is arisen from the fact that the constraint is required to form a group of vehicles that minimizes the objective function. If $Q^{(LL)}$ gets large, we could make a large group. For smaller $Q^{(LL)}$, we need to try many combinations of parent-child relations.

Note that the heterogeneousness requires more computational times. We can confirm the result using IP formulation proposed (e.g., 2MP^3-LS-IP developed in [24]). For example, an instance on K-1000 with 20 vehicles in total requires $3\times$ Build time and the solver *cannot find any solution within 15 min*.

4.2 Evaluations of Gap Parameter in IP-Solver

The solver often stores not only a solution but also both upper and lower bounds of the objective value when the typical branch-and-bound procedure to explore (feasible) solutions. If the relative difference of the two bounds is bounded by

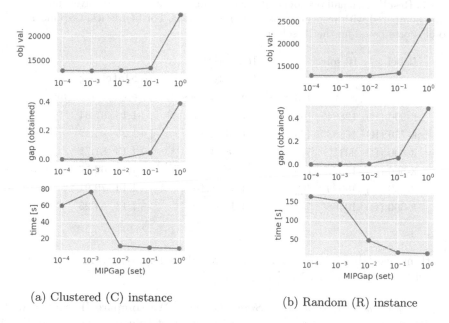

(a) Clustered (C) instance   (b) Random (R) instance

Fig. 3. Results with varying the `MIPGap` parameter: (above) objective values (middle) gap obtained after optimization and (bottom) computational times

`MIPGap`, the solver says the current solution is an optimal. The default value of `MIPGap` parameter in Gurobi is 10^{-4}. Thus, tuning this parameter is beneficial when we try to obtain some feasible solutions quickly. In other words, exact IP solvers with parameter tuning can be regarded as heuristic solvers. It is also valuable to investigate the problem deeply by tracing the values stored in the solver. We examine the effect of `MIPGap` parameter in Gurobi by experiments. To evaluate the effect of `MIPGap`, we use `2MP`^{3}`-IP` on the selected random (R) and clustered (C) requests on K-500. We set `MIPGap` to be in $\{10^{-4}, 10^{-3}, 10^{-2}, 10^{-1}, 10^{0}\}$ and observe (1) objective values, (2) obtained gaps by Gurobi, and (3) computational times measured in Gurobi. Figure 3 shows the measured three metrics above on random 10 instances. We can confirm that for relatively large gap (e.g., $10^{-1} = 10\%$ or $10^{-2} = 1\%$) the modern IP solver succeed to find feasible solutions efficiently. That is, less than 10 s for (C) and less than 50 s for (R) are enough to find feasible solutions. These results indicate that modern solvers can be used as a heuristic solver with a large gap parameter.

4.3   Experiments Using Heuristics

We examine the simple heuristic solver which we developed in Sect. 3. The process just using the *gain* values and constructs the group in a greedy manner is labeled as **Greedy**. If we incrementally build groups of vehicles using matching

Table 7. Results on small random and clustered instances, where IP solvers and heuristics are compared with respect to scores (S) and times. For heuristics, Gap means the ratio of scores based on the IP solver.

Label	IP solver		Heuristics			
			Greedy		b-**Matching**	
	S	Times [s]	Gap	Times [ms]	Gap	Times [ms]
K-500 (R)	12864*	168	+1.29	5.84	+1.16	67.54
K-750 (R)	16853*	465	+1.34	8.46	+1.25	95.47
R-300 (R)	9011*	503	+1.18	4.27	+1.13	81.71
K-500 (C)	13077	106	+1.38	5.78	+1.14	62.57
K-750 (C)	18029*	489	+1.38	8.16	+1.14	79.91
R-300 (C)	10568*	534	+1.47	3.49	+1.13	64.25

algorithms, we label it as **Matching**. If we adopt b-matching for this process, we label the method as b-**Matching**.

Comparing IP and Heuristics on Small Graphs. We compare IP solvers with these heuristic solvers on small graphs though exact solvers could find optimal solutions. We generate both random (R) and clustered requests (C) on three graphs (K-500, K-750, and R-300), wherein Gurobi could find solutions up to 10 min with the default `MIPGap`.

Table 7 summarizes the results. The superscript of ⋆ means that Gurobi stops with gaps and the times with underlines mean that the values include instances that cannot find the optimal values within the time limit. Note that the times by Gurobi include the `presolve`[2] or explorations at the root node of the branch-and-cut algorithm. We confirm that heuristics constantly construct the solution whose objective values are roughly 15–25% larger than the optimal values. Note that the results are comparable to the setting of `MIPGap` $\in [0.15, 0.25]$[3]. By comparing results, simple heuristics are faster than Gurobi with relaxed `MIPGap`.

Observing Heuristics on Larger Graphs. We evaluate solvers on large graphs, where IP solvers cannot find optimal solutions. Here we just compare the obtained heuristic solutions with shortest paths because on small graphs heuristics were faster with comparable objective values as we already confirmed above.

Table 8 shows the results on larger graphs (K-1000, K-1250, R-600, and R-900), where the IP solver cannot find any feasible solutions. We confirmed that our heuristics achieved the travel cost 20–25% less than the shortest paths. Note

---

[2] Typically, the modern IP solvers first try to transform the given problem instance into more convenient formulations for the strategy adopted in the solvers. This process (at least in Gurobi) is named `presolve`.

[3] More precisely, this parameter cannot be compared the resulted gaps directly since `MIPGap` is the gap between the upper and lower bounds. However, the value `MIPGap` is often related to the obtained gap as checked in Fig. 3.

Table 8. Results on large instances solved only by heuristics: (-Gap) means the gap based on the shortest paths and columns (times) means computational times.

Name	Greedy		Matching		b-Matching	
	(-Gap)	Times [ms]	(-Gap)	Times [ms]	(-Gap)	Times [ms]
K-1000 (R)	0.91	9.8	0.90	7.74	0.87	184.0
K-1250 (R)	0.92	12.2	0.89	8.03	0.85	406.3
R-600 (R)	0.94	4.9	0.94	5.58	0.89	160.3
R-900 (R)	0.93	3.5	0.95	5.72	0.90	210.4
K-1000 (C)	0.89	9.2	0.77	7.89	0.72	139.0
K-1250 (C)	0.88	7.8	0.76	9.52	0.71	282.3
R-600 (C)	0.91	5.7	0.78	8.18	0.74	113.8
R-900 (C)	0.89	4.5	0.78	6.90	0.74	140.3

that our heuristics run less than 1 s, although Gurobi cannot find any feasible solutions in the exact manner up to 10 min. Note that MIPGap $\in [10^{-2}, 10^{-1}]$ is a similar counterpart by the solver-based approach as examined in Sect. 4.2. In addition, our heuristics are still faster than the case where Gurobi is used as an heuristic solver by large MIPGap. Furthermore, from all the experimental results, we confirm that our solvers work more efficiently on clustered requests than the random requests. We conjecture that it arises from our algorithm based on the merge-split distance to define $gain(t, t')$.

4.4   Summary of Experiments

We experimentally evaluate IP formulations and our heuristic solver from Sect. 4.1 to Sect. 4.3. The results in Sect. 4.1 and Sect. 4.2 indicate that the CPP problem with heterogeneous vehicle types is a computationally challenging class even for modern IP solvers. Note that IP solvers are effective when we do proof-of-concepts or analyze problems deeply with additional constraints as used in [23]. When we focusing on computing routes approximately, modern IP solvers are less effective than simple heuristics using graph matching developed in Sect. 3.

5   Related Work

Our framework can be applicable to model various MaaS applications. Recently, concepts assuming cooperation among heterogeneous vehicles have attracted much attention. For example, EV trucks and UAVs cooperate for logistics[4].

---

[4] https://www.mercedes-benz.com/en/vehicles/transporter/vision-van/   (accessed 2020/11/4).

Futher, different functional self-driving vehicles are built and cooperate for services[5]. To mathematically model such complex MaaS services, it is essential that the vehicles are heterogeneous (i.e., modals, sizes, or functions). An application of cooperative path planning using heterogeneous agents for MaaS is seen in [21].

In the research literature, heterogeneousness is recently a key concept [2,7,21,22], where an mixed ILP (MILP) is used as a tool to discuss a new optimization concept. As a comparison with our study, [6,7] and [22] proposed MILP formulations that model cooperation among heterogeneous agents. Another search-based solver for such problems has been also studied [2]. We consider that the methods used for the solvers could be applicable to ours, though their objectives are entirely different from ours. Further, cooperating between large and small vehicles is also discussed as a multi-vehicle covering tour problem [11], which has a motivation similar to ours. We can highlight the difference between our study and theirs by considering the applicability of detours in the path as well, compared with shortest paths.

6   Conclusion

We study the cooperation among heterogeneous vehicle types in path-planning and experimentally evaluate the difficulty of the problem in various aspects. We develop heuristics for the CPP problems based on the partition of vehicles using the merge-split distance. From the experiments, we confirm that our assumptions are valid and heuristics work efficiently in real graph structures when we optimize the total travel cost that depends on the distance on graphs. Our future work will include theoretical discussions, and the integration with graph abstraction or indexing techniques to scale up heuristic solvers.

References

1. Agatz, N., Erera, A., Savelsbergh, M., Xign, W.: Opimization for dynamic ridesharing: a review. Eur. J. Oper. Res. **223**, 295–303 (2012)
2. Beck, Z., Teacy, L., Rogers, A., Jennings, N.R.: Online planning for collaborative search and rescue by heterogeneous robot teams. In: Proceedings of AAMAS2016, pp. 1024–1033 (2016)
3. Bit-Monnot, A., Artigues, C., Huguet, M.J., Killijian, M.O.: Carpooling: the 2 synchronization points shortest paths problem. In: Proceedings of ATMOS2013, pp. 150–163 (2013)
4. Bonnet, C., Fritz, H.: Fuel consumption reduction in a platoon: experimental results with two electronically coupled trucks at close spacing. Technical report, SAE Technical Paper (No. 2000–01-3056) (2000)
5. Eppstein, D.: Finding the k shortest paths. SIAM J. Comput. **28**(2), 652–673 (1998)
6. Flushing, E.F., Gambardella, L.M., Di Caro, G.A.: A mathematical programming approach to collaborative missions with heterogeneous teams. In: Proceedings of IROS2014, pp. 396–403 (2014)

---

[5] http://newsroom.toyota.co.jp/en/corporate/20546438.html (accessed 2020/11/4).

7. Flushing, E.F., Gambardella, L.M., Di Caro, G.A.: On decenteralized coordination for spatial task allocation and scheduling in heterogeneous teams. In: Proceedings of AAMAS2016, pp. 988–996 (2016)
8. Furuhata, M., Dessouky, M., Ordóñez, F., Brunet, M.E., Wang, X., Koenig, S.: Ridesharing: the state-of-the-art and future directions. Transp. Res. Part B **57**, 28–46 (2013)
9. Geisberger, R., Luxen, D., Neubauer, S., Sanders, P., Volker, L.: Fast detour computation for ride sharing. arXiv preprint arXiv:0907.5269 (2009)
10. Gurobi Optimization, LLC: Gurobi optimizer reference manual (2018). http://www.gurobi.com
11. Ha, M.H., Bostel, N., Lagngevin, A., Rousseau, L.M.: An exact algorithm and a metaheuristic for the multi-vehicle covering tour problem with a constraint on the number of vehicles. Eur. J. Oper. Res. **226**(2), 211–220 (2013)
12. Hietanen, S.: Mobility as a service, pp. 2–4 (2014)
13. van de Hoef, S., Johansson, K.H., Dimarogonas, D.V.: Coordinating truck platooning by clustering pairwise fuel-optimal plans. In: Proceedings of ITSC2015, pp. 408–415 (2015)
14. van de Hoef, S., Johansson, K.H., Dimarogonas, D.V.: Fuel-efficient en route formation of truck platoons. IEEE Trans. Intell. Transp. Syst. **19**(1), 102–112 (2017)
15. Korte, B., Vygen, J.: Combinatorial Optimization: Theory and Algorithms, 4th edn. Springer, Heidelberg (2007). https://doi.org/10.1007/978-3-540-71844-4
16. Ladier, A.L., Alpan, G.: Cross-docking operations: current research versus industry practice. Omega **62**, 145–162 (2016)
17. Larsson, E., Sennton, G., Larson, J.: The vehicle platooning problem: computational complexity and heuristics. Transp. Res. Part C Emerg. Technol. **60**, 258–277 (2015)
18. Ma, S., Zheng, Y., Wolfson, O.: Real-time city-scale taxi ridesharing. IEEE Trans. Knowl. Data Eng. **27**(7), 1782–1795 (2015)
19. Miller, C.E., Tucker, A.W., Zemlin, R.A.: Integer programming formulation of traveling salesman problems. J. ACM (JACM) **7**(4), 326–329 (1960)
20. Nikolopoulou, A.I., Repoussis, P.P., Tarantilis, C.D., Zachariadis, E.E.: Moving products between location pairs: cross-docking versus direct-shipping. Eur. J. Oper. Res. **256**(3), 803–819 (2017)
21. Nishi, T., Otaki, K., Okoso, A., Fukunaga, A.: Cooperative routing problem between customers and vehicles for on-demand mobile facility services. In: Proceedings of ITSC2020 (2020)
22. Ondráček, J., Vanek, O., Pěchouček, M.: Solving infrastracture monitoring problems with multiple heterogeneous unmanned aerial vehicles. In: Proceedings of AAMAS2015, pp. 1597–1605 (2015)
23. Otaki, K., Koide, S., Keiichiro, H., Okoso, A., Nishi, T.: Multi-agent path planning with heterogeneous cooperation. In: Proceedings of ICTAI2019, pp. 93–100 (2019)
24. Otaki, K., Koide, S., Okoso, A., Nishi, T.: Cooperative routing with heterogeneous vehicles. In: Proceedings of AAMAS2019, pp. 2150–2152 (2019)
25. Otaki, K., Koide, S., Okoso, A., Nishi, T.: Cooperative path planning for heterogeneous agents. In: Proceedings of SoCS2020, pp. 133–134 (2020)
26. Shang, S., Chen, L., Wei, Z., Jensen, C.S., Wen, J., Kalnis, P.: Collective travel planning in spatial networks. IEEE Trans. Knowl. Data Eng. **28**(5), 1132–1146 (2016)
27. Sharon, G., Stern, R., Felner, A., Sturtevant, N.R.: Conflict-based search for optimal multi-agent pathfinding. Artif. Intell. **219**, 40–66 (2015)

28. Takise, K., Asano, Y., Yoshikawa, M.: Multi-user routing to single destination with confluence. In: Proceedings of the 24th ACM SIGSPATIAL, pp. 72:1–72:4 (2016)
29. Yen, J.Y.: Finding the k shortest loopless paths in a network. Manage. Sci. **17**(11), 712–716 (1971)

Policy Advisory Module for Exploration Hindrance Problem in Multi-agent Deep Reinforcement Learning

Jiahao Peng$^{(\boxtimes)}$ and Toshiharu Sugawara

Computer Science and Engineering, Waseda University, Tokyo 1698555, Japan
{j.peng,sugawara}@isl.cs.waseda.ac.jp

Abstract. This paper proposes a method to improve the policies trained with multi-agent deep learning by adding a *policy advisory module* (PAM) in the testing phase to relax the *exploration hindrance problem*. Cooperation and coordination are central issues in the study of multi-agent systems, but agents' policies learned in slightly different contexts may lead to ineffective behavior that reduces the quality of cooperation. For example, in a disaster rescue scenario, agents with different functions must work cooperatively as well as avoid collision. In the early stages, all agents work effectively, but when only a few tasks remain with the passage of time, agents are likely to focus more on avoiding negative rewards brought about by collision, but this avoidance behavior may hinder cooperative actions. For this problem, we propose a PAM that navigates agents in the testing phase to improve performance. Using an example problem of disaster rescue, we investigated whether the PAM could improve the entire performance by comparing cases with and without it. Our experimental results show that the PAM could break the exploration hindrance problem and improve the entire performance by navigating the trained agents.

Keywords: Deep reinforcement learning · Multi-agent system · Cooperation · Sequential cooperative task · Social dilemma · Disaster rescue

1 Introduction

Cooperation and coordination are central issues in the study of multi-agent systems (MASs) because their appropriate behaviors markedly improve the efficiencies of individual efforts and have a profound effect on the overall performance. However, the design and implementation of coordinated behaviors are not apparent because these behaviors are diverse and their appropriateness is influenced by many factors, such as the capabilities of individual agents, environmental characteristics, and structures of tasks that agents must perform.

However, recent advances in multi-agent deep reinforcement learning have enabled agents to learn cooperative and coordinated behaviors to some degree.

© Springer Nature Switzerland AG 2021
T. Uchiya et al. (Eds.): PRIMA 2020, LNAI 12568, pp. 133–149, 2021.
https://doi.org/10.1007/978-3-030-69322-0_9

For example, for a cooperative-competitive game called *Predator-Prey*, where predators must cooperate to catch prey, Kim et al. [5] proposed a learning framework that enables agents to autonomously behave as a group in their cooperative behaviors. Lowe et al. [8] extended the *actor-critic* method to a new multi-agent deep learning (MADRL) algorithm called *multi-agent deep deterministic policy gradient* (MADDPG), where agents learn their behaviors using a centralized critic based on the observations and actions of all agents, and they achieved good learning efficiency in the same game. However, as the number of agents increases, efficient training of agents to learn cooperative strategies in a larger MAS becomes more difficult. Diallo et al. [2] proposed a learning framework in which agents share a centralized network during the training phase and copy the trained network to make decisions independently during the testing phase.

However, we have found that an agent's policy of cooperative behaviors drawn from a slightly different context may lead to inappropriate behaviors that may hinder others' cooperative behaviors, thus bringing down the overall performance. For example, let us consider a disaster rescue scenario in which rescue tasks require cooperation of multiple agents designed for specific functions as well as avoidance of collision that may significantly delay further operations. In this scenario, the task distribution in the environment may change over time: In early stages, all types of agents work cooperatively for densely distributed tasks. Subsequently, because the number of remaining tasks decreases and only a few tasks are left in the final stages, the agents have difficulty finding executable tasks and focus more on collision avoidance behaviors to prevent negative outcomes. This kind of problem does not occur frequently, but once it occurs, it takes a very long time to resolve. This situation seems to be exacerbated, for example, when coordination between heterogeneous agents is needed to complete sequential tasks, because almost all agents complete all their subtasks, but a few types of agents still have subtasks that are to be carried out. Hence, the majority of agents can become moving obstacles, and the remaining agents are likely to give up to explore the environment to find unfinished tasks; instead they choose action to avoid collision. Therefore, their relationship changes from cooperative to competing. This problematic situation is called the *exploration hindrance problem*. This situation appears similar to a sort of social dilemma in which performing no task is better than performing tasks. As a result, agents' cooperative behavior gradually disappears [7].

For the exploration hindrance problem, we propose a *policy advisory module* (PAM) that navigates agents' behaviors in the testing phase. The PAM gives agents reward biases for agents' movements to influence their policies learned with the MADRL in the testing phase and forces them to temporarily ignore possible collisions and move towards an executable unfinished subtask to resolve the problem. With navigation using the PAM, agents tend to take more efficient actions, which improves the global efficiency. We investigate whether the PAM can ease this problem and to what extent it may increase collisions using a *disaster rescue problem* as an example, in which a rescue task consists of two sequential subtasks that must be completed by two types of agents (rescue robots) designed for performing specific subtasks. Their goal is to perform tasks cooperatively and efficiently as well as avoid collision with other agents. When tasks become scarce in the final stages, the incentives to explore other tasks is reduced and agents are likely to choose conservative actions to avoid collision. The proposed PAM guides one type of agent to improve the efficiency for solving cooperative tasks. We experimentally demonstrate that the PAM can improve performance by easing the exploration hindrance problem, and evaluate it by performance comparison with and without the PAM in the testing phase. We also show that the increase of collision brought about by the PAM is relatively small because the other type of agent also learn to avoid collision.

2   Related Work

Many papers have discussed how different factors can affect the performance of *deep reinforcement learning* (DRL). For example, Henderson et al. [3] compared the performance of DRL algorithms by changing the reward scale, network structures, and other related parameters. They used different experimental results to demonstrate the sensibility of DRL and the difficulty and complexity required to train a good agent. Miyashita et al. [9] analyzed the coordination structures that agents learn with MADRL in the *pick up and floor laying problem*. They used different agents' views, which are an integration of observed local data with beliefs and history data that it memorizes, as input to *deep Q networks* (DQNs) to study how different types of input can influence the structure and performance of cooperative behavior.

Leibo et al. [7] analyzed the dynamics of policies in two sequential Markov games called *gathering apples* and *wolfpack hunting*. They studied how cooperation and competition emerge in environments with redundant/scarce resources. They introduced the concept of *sequential social dilemma* and showed that agents learn aggressive policies in environments with scarce resources, and less aggressive policies emerged in environments with redundant resources. One difficulty in training a robust policy in our scenario is that agents must deal with a similar social dilemma when tasks (or resources) do not respawn, so tasks gradually become scarce. Moreover, as the number of agents increases, social dilemma formed by agents with different policies becomes more intractable and difficult to break.

Thus, our problem can be considered a kind of social dilemma, and many studies have also focused on this topic [4,12,13]. For example, Yu et al. [13] studied the emergence of cooperation in social dilemmas by using emotional intrinsic rewards. They also investigated whether different structural relationships between emotions could lead to distinct behaviors of agents in cooperation. One drawback of this method is that it assumed other agents' emotions are available to adjust self-behavior, but building emotions as intrinsic rewards becomes extremely complicated if they are heterogeneous, and we cannot ignore the fact that different environmental contexts may also bring social dilemmas [7]. In contrast, our study discusses the hidden social dilemma among different types of agents in an environment whose characteristics gradually change over time as tasks are completed. Unlike the studies, in which social dilemma problems are solved in a complicated manner, such as altering weights of networks or adding communication protocols, our study assumes that the exploration hindrance problem can be solved by behavior navigation given by an outer module in the testing phase, leading to an overall performance improvement.

3   Problem Description

3.1   Dec-POMDP

We introduce discrete time t whose unit is *step*, where an agent can take one action every step. Given agent set $A = \{1, ..., n\}$, a *decentralized partially observable Markov decision process* (Dec-POMDP) [1,10] can be defined as a tuple $(S, J_A, P, \Omega_A, O_A, R)$, such that:

- S is a finite set of environmental states, where $s_t \in S$ represents the environmental state at time t;
- J_A is a set of joint actions $\langle a_t^1, ..., a_t^n \rangle$, where a_t^i represents the action chosen by agent $i \in A$ at time t;
- $P(s_t, \langle a_t^1, ..., a_t^n \rangle, s_{t+1})$ is the probabilistic transition function of environmental states;
- Ω_A is the set of joint states observed by all agents. For joint observation $\langle \omega_t^1, ...\omega_t^n \rangle = \Omega_t \in \Omega_A$, ω_t^i is i's observation of s_t at time t;
- O_A is the set of *observation probability functions* of agents $\langle O^1, ..., O^n \rangle$, where $O^i(\omega_t|s_t)$ is the probability that ω_t^i is observed by i when s_t; and
- R is the reward function. $r_t^i = R(\omega_t^i, a_t^i)$ represents the reward r_t^i that i receives by executing action a_t^i based on observed state ω_t^i at time t.

In state s_t at time t, agent $i \in A$ has the observation state ω_t^i with probability $O^i(\omega_t^i|s_t)$. Agent i chooses actions using its policy $a_t^i = \pi_i(\omega_t^i)$, where π_i represents the current policy of i. The environment transitions from s_t to s_{t+1} based on state transition function $P(s_t, \langle a_t^1, ..., a_t^n \rangle, s_{t+1}) = Pr(s_{t+1}|s_t, \langle a_t^1, ...a_t^n \rangle)$, and i receives reward $r_t^i = R(\omega_t^i, a_t^i)$. In Dec-POMDP, i learns policy $\pi_i(s)$ to maximize the expected cumulative reward $E_i[\sum_{t=0}^{T} r_t^i(\omega_t^i, a_t^i)]$. The final goal of all agents is to find a joint optimal policy $\pi^* = \langle \pi_1^*, ...\pi_n^* \rangle$ that maximizes the expected future reward of all agents in cooperative situations.

3.2   Agents and Sequential Tasks

We denote the set of tasks by $\mathcal{T} = \{T^1, ..., T^N\}$. Task $T^m \in \mathcal{T}$ consists of L different subtasks, $st_1^m, ..., st_L^m$, which must be completed sequentially, i.e., st_{l+1}^m becomes executable after st_l^m has been completed. We assume that subtasks $st_1^m, ..., st_{l-1}^m$ are completed when an agent tries to execute task st_l^m if there is no confusion. When task st_L^m is executed, task T^m disappears. There are L types of

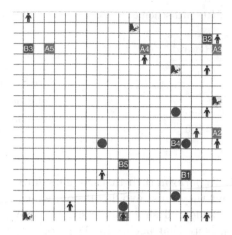

Fig. 1. Example environment of disaster rescue problem.

agents in A, and we denote A_l for $1 \le \forall l \le L$ as the set of *type-l agents* that can perform subtask st_l^m. Note that $A_1, \ldots, A_L$ are disjoint and $A = A_1 \cup \cdots \cup A_L$.

The environment where agents move around to explore and perform executable subtasks is a $G \times G$ square grid, and a number of tasks $\mathcal{T}$ are initially scattered there. Additionally, We place a number of traps on randomly selected cells where no task exists. A trap indicates a dangerous off-limit area caused by a disaster, and if an agent visits this area, it will be broken and cannot make any further movements. Our example problem is taken from the disaster rescue scenario illustrated in Fig. 1, where two type of agents move to execute their subtasks. In this figure, agents in A_1 and A_2 are denoted by symbols A and B, respectively, with ID numbers ($|A_1| = |A_2| = 5$), and a trap is represented by a blue circle. An agent has four movement actions, $M = \{up, down, left, right\}$, and one action *execute* to perform an executable subtask only when it stays at the cell with the subtask.

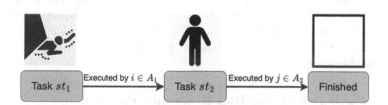

Fig. 2. Structure of sequential task.

The tasks in Fig. 1 consist of two sequential subtasks and are represented by the symbols in Fig. 2. The first subtask st_1 is "removing rocks" and can be performed by an agent in A_1; then, an agent in A_2 can perform subtask st_2, which is "saving a buried survivor". After st_2 is completed, the task disappears

Table 1. Reward scheme for disaster rescue problem.

Event	Reward
Move	−0.1
Execute	−1
Broken (by trap)	−250
Remove Rock	+100

Event	Reward
Save Survival	+100
Collision	−50
Time out	−100

from the environment. To perform their tasks, agents move around to explore the executable subtasks, but they must avoid collision, which is defined as multiple agents moving to the same cell simultaneously, because collision may hinder subsequent operations. Note that agents in A_2 ignore st_1 because they cannot save the survivor buried by rocks, and agents in A_1 ignore st_2 because they have no tools to save a survivor.

All agents have a limited view of radius k, where $k > 0$ is an integer, and can observe only local surrounding areas. This means that an agent can obtain all information in the square region whose side length is $2k + 1$ and center is itself. Additionally, we assume that all agents know their own coordinates in the environment by using a positioning system such as *global positioning system* (GPS). The agents' shared purpose is to save as many buried survivors as possible in cooperation with all types of agents, but they must avoid collisions and traps.

3.3   Rewards Setting

The reward scheme of the disaster rescue problem is defined in Table 1. An agent will receive negative reward −0.1 for each movement owing to energy consumption and receive −1 reward for meaningless execution at a cell with no executable subtask. When an agent falls into a trap, it never escapes and receives −250 reward as a punishment. Agents will receive −50 reward when they collide with one another. In contrast, an agent will receive +100 when it completes an executable subtask. We also introduce a time limit that if all survivors cannot be saved by the limit (which is defined as the maximal episode length, $U_{ep} > 0$), all agents will receive −100 as a punishment even if agents in A_1 have completed all of executable tasks.

3.4   Description of Exploration Hindrance Problem

In our disaster rescue scenario, both types of agents could usually complete tasks efficiently after sufficient learning, but we found that agents occasionally took an extremely long time to complete all tasks owing to the exploration hindrance problem. When tasks become scarce with the passage of time, agents are likely to take more conservative actions to avoid collision from other agents than explore requested subtasks, so their performance considerably decreases. We can observe a number of situations where the exploration hindrance problem occurs:

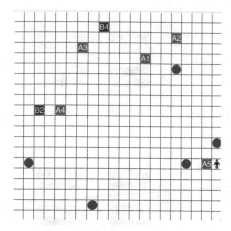

Fig. 3. Exploration hindrance situation in disaster rescue problem.

- When subtasks become scarce and only subtasks executable by type-2 agent $i \in A_2$ remain, i is occasionally surrounded by other types of agents (and traps), and thus, it chooses conservative actions to avoid collision. One example situation that illustrates the exploration hindrance problem in our experiment is shows in Fig. 3, where type-2 agents B2 and B4 were blocked by type-1 agents, so their exploration behaviors were hindered. As a result, they had to select actions that avoid possible collisions and could not approach the remaining task located at the lower right area of the environment.
- There is only one task observable only by two agents of the same type. When the distances from the task to both agents are the same, the agents will tend to choose actions to abandon the task; such an action may cause a small negative reward -0.1, but is better than taking more aggressive actions that may lead to the risk of receiving negative reward -50 due to collision. This situation might be similar to the famous social dilemma called the *Prisoner's Dilemma* [11], where an agent tends to choose less risky actions for itself, while ignoring the potential global benefits.

Because all agents are self-interested and are unconcerned regarding the subtasks that they cannot perform, when there are few tasks left, they tend to consider other agents as unpredictable moving obstacles, which hinder their exploration, rather than companions having shared beliefs and goals. Hence, although agent i can view an executable subtask in a distant position, when there are fewer nearby agents, the reward for performing a subtask no longer outweighs the risk of passing through those agents. In contrast, if there is only one agent near i, i will be able to through the agent and reach the executable subtask.

One simple method to break the exploration hindrance problem is to consider the probability of ε with which an agent takes a random action. However, as the number of agents increases, the severity of the exploration hindrance problem is increased. Therefore, agents' random actions are ineffective to resolve the

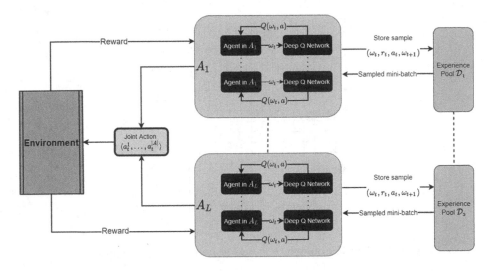

Fig. 4. Learning framework of multiple agents.

exploration hindrance problem formed by multiple agents. In our disaster rescue problem, the survivor's life cannot depend on such an extremely small probability of resolution, and hence, this problem must be eased or avoided using a more accurate method.

4   Proposed Method

4.1   Learning Architecture for Agents in Sequential Tasks

Individual agents have their own DQNs for DRL based on Dec-POMDP, and they receive rewards based on the results of joint actions of all agents. We assume that agents in A_l have the same observable area size, neural network structure, reward function R, and their state observation probability is O (see Sect. 3.3). The transition tuple of $(\omega_t^l, a_t^l, r_t^l, \omega_{t+1}^l)$ from one agent suits other agents with the same type and can be shared within agents of the same type. To speed up the learning process and make full use of valid tuples experienced by other agents, we propose a partly shared learning framework.

Figure 4 shows the learning framework in the disaster rescue problem when $L = 2$. Each agent has its own fixed target Q-network to make independent decision and is unaware of the next actions of other agents even if they have the same type. Meanwhile, agents in A_l store the training samples in the shared experience pool D_l whose elements are transition experienced tuples. Their networks will be trained every c steps made from the actions completed by the owner agent, where integer $c > 0$ is the *training interval*. At the end of each episode, the target networks of all agents will be updated according to their main DQNs.

4.2 Policy Advisory Module

Because agents can neither predict the location of the survivors nor the locations of traps until discovered in a disaster situation, the only information that an agent can know is its position and surroundings. We propose a global controller called a PAM, which stores the locations of tasks and their types reported from working agents in the environment. Subsequently, it gives reward biases to the requesting agents based on their current locations and the information stored in the PAM to break mutually restraining behaviors due to the exploration hindrance problem in the testing phase.

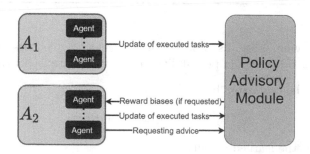

Fig. 5. Architecture of PAM for different types of agents.

The PAM consists of a global information map S_{map} which is the grid $G \times G$ identical to the environment. When agent $i \in A_l$ has executed task st_l^m, its location is reported to the PAM, and then the information of st_{l+1}^m is stored in S_{map}. This implies that the agent does not have the locations of task st_1^m. Additionally, agents report the location of a trap if they find it. This information flow from agents to the PAM in the testing phase is represented by right arrows in Fig. 5. Note that the current locations of all agents are not included in S_{map}.

When $i \in A \setminus A_1$ cannot find any executable subtasks in the final stages of the problem of each episode in the testing phase, it sends a message with its current position (cell), $c_i = (x_i, y_i)$, to the PAM to request advice on its next action to reach an executable subtask (see Fig. 5). More concretely, after the given timing of introduction of the PAM P_{th} (> 0), when i cannot find any executable subtask, it sends a message to request advice from the PAM. When the PAM receives the message, it gives the biases of $B(a)$ values for each movement action $a \in M$. The default value of $B(a)$ is 0, and if the PAM cannot find any subtasks executable by i, it sends this default value. If it finds an executable task at cell d in S_{map}, it generates the sequence of actions of i to move along a shortest path from c_i to d. Let a_0 be the first action in this sequence; the PAM sets $B(a_0) = V_{bias}$ and sends the bias to i, where $V_{bias} > 0$ is a predefined constant value of bias. The detailed algorithm is described in Algorithm 1, where the values of $B(a)$ for $a \in M$ are expressed in list format.

Algorithm 1: Algorithm of Policy Advisory Module

Given agent position c_i from agent i;
Initialize $B = \{0,0,0,0\}$ describing $B(a)$ for $\forall a \in M$;
$V_{bias} \geq 0$ is the reward bias;
if *there are executable tasks in S_{map}* **then**
  Generate the action sequence $Plan_i$ from c_i to the nearest task along with a
  shortest path ;
  Pop the first action a_0 from $Plan_i$;
  $B(a_0) = V_{bias}$;   // this is reflected in the list B.
end
return B;

After receiving the list of biases, agent i chooses the action $\arg\max_{a \in M} Q_i^{rev}(\omega_t^i, a)$ with the probability of $1 - \varepsilon$ in state ω_t^i at time t, where $Q_i^{rev}(\omega_t^i, a)$ can be calculated by

$$Q_i^{rev}(\omega_t^i, a) = Q_i(\omega_t^i, a) + B(a) \tag{1}$$

and $Q_i(\omega_t^i, a)$ is the learned Q-value so far.

We assume that the exploration hindrance problem in an MAS, in sequential cooperative tasks, can be solved by a few rather than all agents. In a disaster rescue environment, the number of finished tasks always satisfies the inequality $N(st_1) \geq N(st_2)$, where N represents the number of finished subtasks. Therefore, agents in A_2 suffer more from the exploration hindrance problem than agents in A_1. Although agent in A_1 have finished all executable tasks st_1, agents in A_2 are still concerned about both finishing subtasks and avoiding collision with surrounding agents, but the latter does not help in completing global tasks. Hence, we aim to use the PAM to provide reward bias to navigate agents in A_2 to escape from blocked areas and explore other locations. This may weaken the self-interest behaviors of collision avoidance, but we can partly respond to the behaviors of other agents because they have also learned their coordinated behaviors, including collision avoidance.

5   Experimental Evaluation

5.1   Experiment Settings

We conducted three experiments in a 20×20 environment with $|A_1| = |A_2| = 4$ and agents had three different sizes of view radius k of 3, 7 or 19 (global). In our experiments, agents used decayed ε-greedy strategy, i.e., $\varepsilon = \min(\varepsilon_{init}\varepsilon_d^n, \varepsilon_{min})$ in the n-th episode, to decide whether to explore the environment or exploit the learned policy, where ε_d is the decay rate and ε_{min} is the lower bound of ε. The detailed parameter settings are listed in Table 2. The experimental results shown below are the average values of 1000 independent experimental runs.

Table 2. List of parameters in the experiments.

Parameter	Value
Number of traps	5
Number of tasks	50
Number of episodes	30000
Batch size	64
Maximal episode length U_{ep}	500 steps
Initial ε value ε_{init}	0.995
ε decay rate ε_d	0.9985
Minimum ε value ε_{min}	0.05
Training interval c	5
Timing of PAM introduction P_{th}	0, 50, 80, 100

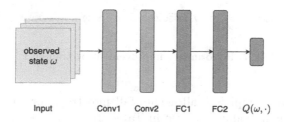

Fig. 6. Network structure of agent.

5.2 Network Structure in Agent

For convenience of analyzing the effect of the exploration hindrance problem and eliminating the difference in policies brought by network structure and other factors, we assume that all agents have the same network structure, training interval, and initial value/decay rate for the ε-greedy strategy. The network structure is shown in Fig. 6. The local states observed by an agent are divided into three matrices to feed to its network: the first one describes the relative positions of tasks and traps, the second one includes the locations of the same type of agents, and the third one includes the locations of different types of agents. Subsequently, the matrices are passed through two convolutional 2D layers whose filters are 32 and 64 with kernel size 3×3 and a padding of 1s. The outputs from convolutional 2D layers are further fed into a series of three fully connected layers with 32, 16, and 5 units. Activation function ReLU is used in the middle layers. An agent's network is optimized by Adam [6] with learning rate 0.0001.

5.3 Experiment 1—Training Results

First, we investigated the performance improvement over repeated episodes when the radius of agents' observable view was 3, 7 or 19. Note that an episode ends

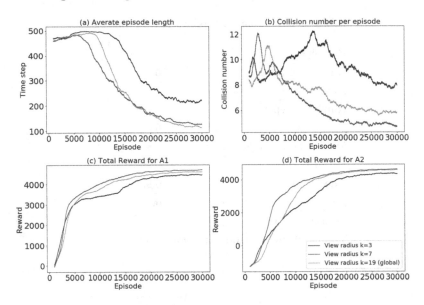

Fig. 7. Performance improvement by training.

when all tasks are completed, all agents fall into traps, or the episode length reaches its maximum value U_{ep} (see in Table 2). Therefore, when the episode length was 500, an agent could not complete all tasks. The experimental results in the training phase are shown in Fig. 7. From Fig. 7a and b, which show the average episode length and number of collisions per episode, respectively, their performance seems to be temporarily reduced in earlier episodes. Furthermore, if we compare Fig. 7c and d, the rewards received by A_2 agents were much lower than those by A_1 agents in the earlier training stages. Because the environment is initialized at every episode and the policies the agents learned in the earlier stage were not as effective as A_1, they required more time for learning to approach the executable subtasks that were found while avoiding traps and collisions.

Meanwhile, as the learning progressed, the performance, especially when $k = 7$, improved over time and agents could complete all tasks in the environment in shorter time and with less collisions (Fig. 7a and b). Figure 7c and d also indicate that agents eventually earned almost the same rewards regardless of their type. In addition, these graphs show that the learning speed of type-2 agents was lower than that of type-1 agents; this is because type-2 agents could perform tasks only after the type-1 agents' executions, so they had fewer chances to learn. All graphs in this figure indicate that the performance was the best and that the learning speed was the fastest when $k = 7$ in this experiment.

5.4   Ratio of Incompletion

Although Fig. 7 shows that agents could learn cooperative policies for their behaviors, if we consider the episode length, their dispersion was quite large; in

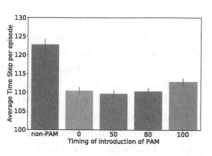

(a) Completion time (when completed)

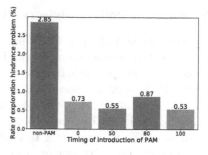

(b) Incompletion Ratio

Fig. 8. Completion time and incompletion ratio ($k = 7$).

fact, agents usually completed all tasks in approximately 135 steps, but occasionally, could not complete all tasks in less than the maximum episode length U_{ep}. To observe the agents' behaviors after learning, we investigated the average completion time when all the tasks were executed completely, and the incompletion ratio, that is, the ratio of the number of episodes in which all tasks could not be completed within U_{ep} to the number of episodes in the testing phase. These results when $k = 7$ are shown in Fig. 8.

Figure 8a indicates that agents took approximately 122.5 time steps when they completed all tasks (see the value of "non-PAM" in this figure, which means that the PAM was not used in the testing phase). The difference between this value and the completion time shown in Fig. 7 was caused by the fact that agents sometimes could not complete all tasks (approximately 2.8% of total episodes, as shown in Fig. 8b). Because $U_{ep} = 500$, which is much larger than 122.5, it can be observed that the effect of the exploration hindrance problem was significant.

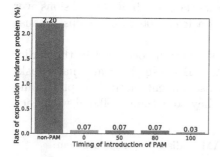

Fig. 9. Incompletion due to remaining st_2.

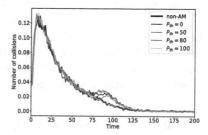

Fig. 10. Collision in episodes.

5.5   Effect of Policy Advisory Module

To investigate how the PAM can improve the performance of cooperative tasks, we examined the average completion time (only when agents completed all tasks) and the incompletion ratio. In this experiment, only agents in A_2 requested biases from the PAM as advice because the PAM has no information on st_1. The results when $P_{th} = 0, 50, 80,$, and 100 with $k = 7$ are shown in Fig. 8. First, we can observe from Fig. 8b that the incompletion ratio dropped to approximately 0.7% regardless of the value of P_{th}. In contrast, the average completion times were affected by P_{th} (when the agents started to request biases from the PAM); when $P_{th} = 0, 50$, and 80, the completion times were almost identical. In other cases, as P_{th} increased, the time required for completion slightly increased. This is because of the advice from the PAM; agents in A_2 quickly found executable subtasks, st_2, and advice in earlier stages could eliminate wandering movements by navigating type-2 agents. Meanwhile, because agents in A_1 did not ask the PAM for advice, there is a very small probability that agents in A_1 also suffer from the exploration hindrance problem, and thus, they could not complete all subtasks st_1; this probability was approximately 0.7%, as shown in Fig. 8b.

To understand the reason for task incompletion, we counted the number of experimental runs that did not complete all tasks and in which at least one st_2, which is executable by agents in A_2, remained; these results are shown in Fig. 9. This figure indicates that when agents in A_2 asked the PAM for biases as advice, they could almost always complete their executable tasks. Note that the difference between completion ratios in Figs. 9 and 8b indicates the number of episodes in which at least one st_1 was left but no st_2 remained.

5.6   Number of Collisions

Another concern related to the PAM is the increasing probability of collision because bias from the PAM may strongly affect the behaviors of agents and make them ignore potential collisions. Figure 10 shows the probability of collisions over time in an episode, where we omitted the data from 200 to 500 steps because the probability of collision was almost zero.

First, this graph indicates that almost all collisions occurred in the earlier stages with or without advice from the PAM. Because there are many tasks during this period, even if the PAM was not used, agents actively explored and approached executable subtasks, and thus, they sometimes collided with each

Table 3. Performance of agents with PAM in disaster rescue problem.

Time to start asking PAM	Finish time	Collision	Reward of agents in A_1	Reward of agents in A_2
non-PAM	133.57 (baseline)	5.34	4113.74	4118.48
$P_{th} = 0$	113.33 (-15.15%)	5.61	4252.22	4278.07
$P_{th} = 50$	111.81 (-16.29%)	5.72	4266.50	4282.92
$P_{th} = 80$	113.67 (-14.90%)	5.60	4250.38	4260.04
$P_{th} = 100$	114.91 (-13.97%)	5.42	4244.92	4241.29

other. As tasks decreased over time, type-2 agents scarcely found executable tasks, so they focused more on avoiding collision rather than exploring the environment. As a result, the number of collisions decreased. When type-2 agents could not find their tasks, they started to request advice from the PAM, and thus, collision may temporarily increase (after approximately $t = 75$, see Fig. 10). However, the increased number of collisions was quite small because agents in A_1 also learned to avoid collision. In summary, we list the average performance of agents with and without the PAM during the last 6000 episodes in Table 3.

6   Discussion

First, we confirmed that the proposed PAM could successfully navigate agents to preempt the exploration hindrance problem. When an agent cannot find any executable tasks, its policy based on the learned Q-function, $Q_i(s, a)$, in the training phase, concerns collision avoidance, and thus, actions of exploring other locations are rarely selected. This is based on analysis of our experiments that when tasks are scarce, an agent is likely to wander to avoid collision. Agents learned their policies mainly based on the experience in earlier stages of the problem, in which there were many tasks, so agents could receive many rewards. However, these are insufficient to break the wandering movements in the exploration hindrance problem. In contrast, the PAM can provide reward bias to an agent, so it is likely to break through barriers implicitly formed by other agents.

When we enlarged the size of environment to 30×30 and agents' observable view stays 7, the ability of exploration and exploitation for both agent groups drops and the average completion time without PAM increased to 239.21. When we introduced PAM in $P_{th} = 0, 50, 80$, and 100, the results of average completion time are respectively 191.19, 192.89, 191.93 and 194.87 which are decreased by almost 20% compared to the result without PAM. The exploration hindrance rate because of unfinished st_2 with PAM is about 0.13% while the result without PAM is 11.23%.

In our experiment, we set $U_{ep} = 500$. Clearly, if we set this parameter to a larger value, agents were more likely to escape the constrained state by chance without the PAM, but this will make the situation worse. In actual applications, agents must easily break such a state. Hence, we must appropriately decide/learn the value of P_{th} so as not to increase collisions and improve performance; we plan to study this topic as future work.

7   Conclusion and Future Work

We proposed the PAM to ease the exploration hindrance problem and evaluated it using a disaster rescue problem, where a task consisted of two sequential subtasks, each of which could be performed only by a certain type of agent. In earlier stages, there are many tasks, so both types of agents have a chance to learn to perform their tasks cooperatively and avoid collisions. When tasks become scarcer, the incentive for performing tasks decreases; the agents have greater chances to avoid collisions, but this behavior may hinder exploring actions. By comparing the performances of trained policies with and without the PAM in the testing phase, we experimentally demonstrated that when agents were trapped in the exploration hindrance problem, the ones without the PAM kept choosing actions to avoid collisions until an episode ends and left a few tasks unfinished. In contrast, agents with the PAM could ease the exploration hindrance problem by making more aggressive moves and were able to complete more tasks in a shorter time.

We would like to test the effects of PAM in other problem domains, such as the *pick up and floor laying problem* or in the environment with different size. We will also deepen the research of parameter learning so that PAM can generate V_{bias} based on a given reward scheme, as described in Sect. 6.

Acknowlegement. This work is partly supported by JSPS KAKENHI Grant number 20H04245.

References

1. Bernstein, D.S., Givan, R., Immerman, N., Zilberstein, S.: The complexity of decentralized control of Markov decision processes. Math. Oper. Res. **27**(4), 819–840 (2002). https://doi.org/10.1287/moor.27.4.819.297
2. Diallo, E.A.O., Sugawara, T.: Learning strategic group formation for coordinated behavior in adversarial multi-agent with double DQN. In: Miller, T., Oren, N., Sakurai, Y., Noda, I., Savarimuthu, B.T.R., Cao Son, T. (eds.) PRIMA 2018. LNCS (LNAI), vol. 11224, pp. 458–466. Springer, Cham (2018). https://doi.org/10.1007/978-3-030-03098-8_30
3. Henderson, P., Islam, R., Bachman, P., Pineau, J., Precup, D., Meger, D.: Deep reinforcement learning that matters. CoRR abs/1709.06560 (2017). http://arxiv.org/abs/1709.06560
4. Huang, K., Chen, X., Yu, Z., Yang, C., Gui, W.: Heterogeneous cooperative belief for social dilemma in multi-agent system. Appl. Math. Comput. **320**, 572–579 (2018)
5. Kim, D., et al.: Learning to schedule communication in multi-agent reinforcement learning. arXiv preprint arXiv:1902.01554 (2019)
6. Kingma, D.P., Ba, J.: Adam: a method for stochastic optimization. arXiv preprint arXiv:1412.6980 (2014)
7. Leibo, J.Z., Zambaldi, V.F., Lanctot, M., Marecki, J., Graepel, T.: Multi-agent reinforcement learning in sequential social dilemmas. CoRR abs/1702.03037 (2017). http://arxiv.org/abs/1702.03037
8. Lowe, R., Wu, Y.I., Tamar, A., Harb, J., Abbeel, O.P., Mordatch, I.: Multi-agent actor-critic for mixed cooperative-competitive environments. In: Advances in Neural Information Processing Systems, pp. 6379–6390 (2017)
9. Miyashita, Y., Sugawara, T.: Coordination in collaborative work by deep reinforcement learning with various state descriptions. In: Baldoni, M., Dastani, M., Liao, B., Sakurai, Y., Zalila Wenkstern, R. (eds.) PRIMA 2019. LNCS (LNAI), vol. 11873, pp. 550–558. Springer, Cham (2019). https://doi.org/10.1007/978-3-030-33792-6_40

10. Pynadath, D.V., Tambe, M.: The communicative multiagent team decision problem: analyzing teamwork theories and models. CoRR abs/1106.4569 (2011). http://arxiv.org/abs/1106.4569
11. Rapoport, A., Chammah, A.M., Orwant, C.J.: Prisoner's Dilemma: A Study in Conflict and Cooperation, vol. 165. University of Michigan Press, Ann Arbor (1965)
12. Stimpson, J.L., Goodrich, M.A.: Learning to cooperate in a social dilemma: a satisficing approach to bargaining. In: Proceedings of the 20th International Conference on Machine Learning (ICML 2003), pp. 728–735 (2003)
13. Yu, C., Zhang, M., Ren, F., Tan, G.: Emotional multiagent reinforcement learning in spatial social dilemmas. IEEE Trans. Neural Netw. Learn. Syst. **26**(12), 3083–3096 (2015)

Analysis of Coordination Structures of Partially Observing Cooperative Agents by Multi-agent Deep Q-Learning

Ken Smith[✉], Yuki Miyashita, and Toshiharu Sugawara[ID]

Computer Science and Communications Engineering, Waseda University,
Tokyo 169-8555, Japan
{k.smith,y.miyashita}@isl.cs.waseda.ac.jp, sugawara@waseda.jp
http://www.isl.cs.waseda.ac.jp/lab/index-e.html

Abstract. We compare the coordination structures of agents using different types of inputs for their deep Q-networks (DQNs) by having agents play a distributed task execution game. The efficiency and performance of many multi-agent systems can be significantly affected by the coordination structures formed by agents. One important factor that may affect these structures is the information provided to an agent's DQN. In this study, we analyze the differences in coordination structures in an environment involving walls to obstruct visibility and movement. Additionally, we introduce a new DQN input, which performs better than past inputs in a dynamic setting. Experimental results show that agents with their absolute locations in their DQN input indicate a granular level of labor division in some settings, and that the consistency of the starting locations of agents significantly affects the coordination structures and performances of agents.

1 Introduction

Although cooperation and coordination are crucial in many multi-agent systems for improving overall efficiency, designing the appropriate coordination and cooperation regime is challenging because many factors must be considered, such as the problem structure, environmental characteristics, and agent abilities. Recently, owing to the development of deep reinforcement learning (DRL), researchers have successfully acquired coordinated behaviors [1–3]. However, they usually focused only on improving the performance and how network architecture and parameter settings affected this performance and did not discuss the reason from the viewpoint of what kinds of coordination structures emerged in multi-agent environments. Therefore, we cannot predict the features of emerging coordination regimes, such as robustness, tolerance, and adaptability to changes in the environment and agents (such as the failure or upgradation of agents).

Because it is important to understand the features of the coordination regime, the coordinated/cooperative behaviors generated by DRL, and how these features are affected by the neural network and input structure, a few studies have

© Springer Nature Switzerland AG 2021
T. Uchiya et al. (Eds.): PRIMA 2020, LNAI 12568, pp. 150–164, 2021.
https://doi.org/10.1007/978-3-030-69322-0_10

attempted to identify the coordinated behaviors learned with DRL [4,5]. For example, Leibo et al. [5] discovered that agents may learn selfish or cooperative behaviors depending on the amount of resources. Miyashita & Sugawara [4] focused on the structures and information included in the input to networks and attempted to obtain a coordination regime in a task execution game within the multi-agent system context; subsequently, they analyzed coordination structures that emerged from agents by observing different aspects of the environment. They discovered that by allowing agents to observe their absolute locations within the environment, the agents can allocate their workload and improve the overall performance. However, the studies were conducted in a rudimentary environment. Consequently, there is not enough information to assess how agents with these observational methods would perform in more complex environments involving obstructions in movement and line of sight, which is critical for real world application; hence, further studies should be performed.

Our goal is to analyze the change in the coordinated behavior of agents generated by DRL based on input structures using a variant of a task execution game [4] in a more complex environment that is close to a real world setting to better clarify the relationship between the input structure and the generated coordination regime. Our experiments indicate that allowing agents to observe their absolute locations (e.g., information acquired using GPS) within their environments resulted in a high degree of divisional cooperation and improved performance. Furthermore, we discovered that under a less consistent environment, the agent's observational method must be reconfigured to maintain an improved performance level. However, the information provided to the agent remained nearly identical.

2   Related Studies

A significant amount of research has been conducted on DRL [6–13]; some studies have included coordination, cooperation, or communication between agents in a multi-agent setting [1–3,5,14]. For example, Gupta, Egorov, and Kochenderfer [2] compared the performances of several DRL algorithms in a cooperative multi-agent setting, where agents must coordinate with each other to succeed. The study indicated that one method outperformed the other methods, and that recurrent neural network architectures delivered better performances overall compared with feedforward networks. Lowe et al. [3] applied lenient learning to the deep Q-networks (DQNs) of agents in a multi-agent setting, which associates state–action pairs with decaying temperature values to avoid updating agent policies with outdated pairs. They discovered that by applying leniency to the learning process, cooperation was facilitated in a fully cooperative environment. Foerster, Assael, Freitas, and Whiteson [1] analyzed how multiple agents, each using their own recurrent DQN, attempted to solve riddles that required communication between agents to succeed. They discovered that agents successfully developed a communication protocol to solve these riddles, and that the communication protocols can be modeled in the form of a decision tree.

In general, these studies involved agent coordination but focused primarily on the performance of agents rather than the coordination regimes. Although the performance improvement of multi-agent systems is important, more research should be performed regarding the coordination structures of agents to acquire new information.

A few studies have focused on the analysis of coordination and cooperation regimes formed in a multi-agent setting. To illustrate, Diallo & Sugawara [14] analyzed strategic group formations developed using a combination of centralized and decentralized deep Q-learning in a nonstationary and adversarial multi-agent environment. The study used variants of the DQN and indicated that combining a double DQN and a DuelDQN generated strategies that delivered improved performances. Leibo et al. [5] investigated cooperative and selfish behaviors formed from multiple independently learning agents with DQNs playing two different games in a two-dimensional grid world environment. The researchers analyzed the agents' strategies in environments with varying degrees of resource scarcity and introduced the concept of sequential social dilemmas. Studies that focused on the coordination regimes of multi-agent systems, such as the aforementioned, are rare. Therefore, further research is required to investigate the coordination and cooperation structures of agents.

3   Problem Formulation

3.1   Problem and Environment

To analyze the coordinated behavior of multiple agents, we introduce a multi-agent problem called the *distributed task execution game*. The problem environment S can be represented as a two-dimensional grid comprising 35×20 cells. An example of this environment is shown in Fig. 1a. In this grid, three different types of objects can occupy the cells: agents, tasks, and walls. Each instance of an object occupies one cell. Walls are arranged in the environment to create a 35×2 corridor spanning the environment horizontally. Figure 1a shows the wall locations of the environment marked as gray boxes. From the corridor, agents can access four different rooms, each the size of 17×8 cells. Initially, a certain number of tasks were scattered in environment S. The corridor and cells between the corridor and each room did not have any task throughout the experiment.

Next, we introduce a time unit called a step. Let A be a set of agents; agent $i \in A$ randomly takes one action from $M = \{Up, Down, Left, Right\}$ in every step. If i moves on a cell that is occupied by a task, then it is assumed to be executed by i, and a new task is spawned at a randomly selected empty cell in room $s \in S$; therefore, the number of tasks in the environment is unchanged.

Once a task is executed, the agent that executed the task receives a positive reward. Each agent learns, using a DQN, to determine actions that maximize the reward earned by considering other agents' actions cooperatively. If i attempts to move to a cell containing a wall or outside of the environment, i remains in the same position for that step. We consider this event to be a wall collision. Likewise, if i attempts to move to a cell containing another agent, i does not change its position for that step; we consider this event to be an agent collision. After agents perform their actions and new tasks are spawned, the next step begins. At the end of step 300, the episode ends; the DQNs of all agents are updated independently with the rewards and observations of each agent. Subsequently, the environment is initialized for the next episode.

As shown in Fig. 2, certain areas in the environment are marked in blue or red. The areas marked in blue signify areas where tasks can spawn, whereas those marked in red signify areas where agents can spawn. The areas marked in red in Fig. 2a are numbered according to the ID of each agent, indicating that the same agent spawns in the exact same location whenever the environment is initialized.

Agents can only communicate with each other by observing each other's positions. They may use different types of views of the environment as inputs for their DQNs; therefore, they may view the environment differently. Regardless of the agent's view type, their visible area will be limited for tasks, walls, and other agents, which we refer to as the *agent's window* of observation. In this study, the agent's window of observation is a square of length N cells centered on the agent. For reference, Fig. 1a shows an example of the environment with the agent's window of observation when $N = 7$. The agent performing the observation is represented by the solid red square, and the agent's window of observation is represented by the red square outline surrounding the agent.

3.2   View Obstruction

We assumed that the agents could not view past walls in our environment and implemented a view obstruction feature for our agents. The view obstruction method employs a form of ray casting to determine the visibility region for each agent at every step.

To calculate the visibility region for an agent, we obtained the center point of the agent, selected a wall visible to the agent, and constructed two straight lines from the agent's center point to each end of the selected wall. These two lines serve as the agent's cone of vision for the selected wall. Any unit of space behind the wall and within the agent's cone of vision is marked as "not visible". The same procedure is repeated for every wall within the agent's window of observation. Because our environment is a grid, our visibility region calculations resulted in many cases of partially visible cells. We defined a cell to be visible to an agent if more than 50% of the area of the grid space is within the agent's visibility region.

4   Proposed Method

4.1   Agent View Methods

Depending on the experiment, different aspects of the environment will be included in the agents' DQN inputs to investigate the effect of the agents' views

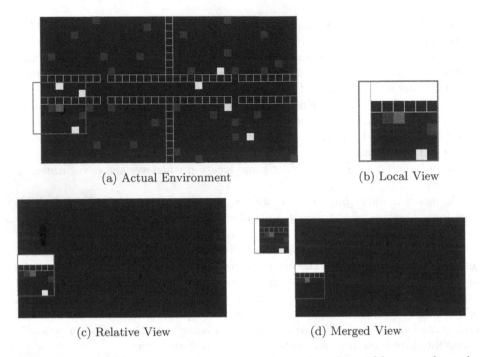

(a) Actual Environment   (b) Local View

(c) Relative View   (d) Merged View

Fig. 1. Comparison between actual environment and view observed by agent for each view method

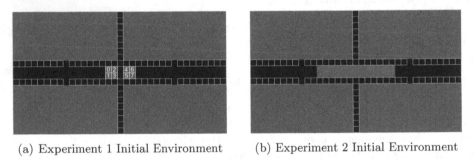

(a) Experiment 1 Initial Environment   (b) Experiment 2 Initial Environment

Fig. 2. Experimental environment

on their coordination structure learned with DRL. We adopted two view methods: *local view* and *relative view* [4]. In addition, we employed a new view method called the *merged view*. Figure 1 illustrates how an agent with each view type may view the environment. Red, blue, yellow, and white represent the observing agent, a task, another agent, and an invisible space, respectively.

The observations of the agents were encoded as a three-dimensional matrix containing values of either −1, 0, or 1. We call each slice of this matrix a channel. Each channel contains a specific aspect of the agent's observation, which can be the position of either the agent, other agents, tasks, or areas invisible to the agent because of a wall. Within these channels, an empty space is marked as 0, tasks and agents are marked as 1, and invisible areas or areas outside the environment are marked as −1.

4.2   Local View

The DQN input for agents with a local view is based solely on the details within the window of observation for each agent (Fig. 1b). The length and width of the DQN input are the same as those of each agent's window of observation. We divided the environment details within the agent's window of observation into three different channels for the DQN input. The first, second, and third channel encodes, respectively, the locations of other agents, tasks, and cells whose contents are invisible because the viewing agent's line of sight is blocked by walls. Furthermore, when an agent is near the edge of the environment, the agent's window of observation may overlap with a space that is outside the environment.

4.3   Relative View

The DQN input for agents with a relative view involves the window of observation for each agent as well as the outline of the entire environment (Fig. 1c). The length and width of the DQN input is the same as those of the entire environment. Within this DQN input, only the details of the environment within the viewing agent's window of observation are encoded. Areas outside of the viewing agent's window of observation are encoded as an empty space. The DQN input is separated into four channels. The first channel encodes the location of the viewing agent, the second channel encodes the locations of other agents within the viewing agent's window of observation, and the third channel encodes the locations of tasks within the viewing agent's window of observation. Finally, the fourth channel encodes the locations of cells whose contents are invisible because the viewing agent's line of sight is blocked by walls.

4.4   Merged View

The merged view involves two different DQN inputs for the same network. The size of one input is identical to that of the local view's DQN input, whereas that of the other input is identical to that of the relative view's DQN input. However, both inputs have two channels. For the local view input, the first and second channels contain information regarding the locations of other agents and tasks, respectively. For the relative view input, the first and second channels contain the agent's own position within the environment and the areas within the agent's view range that are invisible because of walls, respectively.

4.5   Neural Network Structure

We constructed our DQNs using the Keras library [15]. Tables 1, 2, and 3 show the layers and dimensions used for each model of the agent's view. We used

RMSprop [16] as the optimizer of the model; we employed experience replay with random sampling during training. The filter size was 2×2 for all convolutional and max pooling layers, and the stride was one and two for the convolutional and max pooling layers, respectively. The reward scheme for the agents was identical for all experiments; the agents began the episode with a reward value of 0; each agent's reward increased by 1 for each task executed during the episode.

Additionally, we adopted the ε-greedy strategy with decay, which attempts to obtain more rewarding behaviors that require investigating the environment through actions that initially appear to be not the most rewarding. The ε value decrease over time with a predetermined decay rate $\gamma_\epsilon > 0$, where at the end of each episode, the new ε value for the next episode is calculated to be $\varepsilon_{new} = \varepsilon_{old} * \gamma_\epsilon$.

Table 1. Network architecture (local view)

Layer	Input	Activation	Output
Convolutional	$7 \times 7 \times 3$		$7 \times 7 \times 32$
Max pooling	$7 \times 7 \times 32$		$3 \times 3 \times 32$
Convolutional	$3 \times 3 \times 32$		$3 \times 3 \times 64$
Max pooling	$3 \times 3 \times 64$		$1 \times 1 \times 64$
Flatten	$1 \times 1 \times 64$		64
FCN	64	ReLu	100
FCN	100	Linear	4

Table 2. Network architecture (relative view)

Layer	Input	Activation	Output
Convolutional	$35 \times 20 \times 4$		$35 \times 20 \times 32$
Max pooling	$35 \times 20 \times 32$		$17 \times 10 \times 32$
Convolutional	$17 \times 10 \times 32$		$17 \times 10 \times 64$
Max pooling	$17 \times 10 \times 64$		$8 \times 5 \times 64$
Flatten	$8 \times 5 \times 64$		2560
FCN	2560	ReLu	100
FCN	100	Linear	4

5 Experiment and Discussion

5.1 Experimental Setting

We conducted two experiments to analyze the performance and coordinated behaviors among agents using different DQN inputs in near identical simulations.

Each experiment involved one simulation per view method. Each simulation involved eight agents performing a distributed task execution game for several episodes. The parameters for each simulation within an experiment was identical except for the view method. The parameters for these experiments are listed in Table 4.

Table 3. Network architecture (merged view)

Input no.	Layer	Input.	Activation	Output
Input 1	Convolutional	$7 \times 7 \times 2$		$7 \times 7 \times 32$
	Max pooling	$7 \times 7 \times 32$		$3 \times 3 \times 32$
	Convolutional	$3 \times 3 \times 32$		$3 \times 3 \times 32$
	Max pooling	$3 \times 3 \times 32$		$1 \times 1 \times 32$
	Flatten	$1 \times 1 \times 32$		32
Input 2	Convolutional	$35 \times 20 \times 2$		$35 \times 20 \times 32$
	Max pooling	$35 \times 20 \times 32$		$17 \times 10 \times 32$
	Convolutional	$17 \times 10 \times 32$		$17 \times 10 \times 32$
	Max pooling	$17 \times 10 \times 32$		$8 \times 5 \times 32$
	Flatten	$8 \times 5 \times 32$		1280
Output	Concatenate	32, 1280		1312
	FCN	1312	ReLu	100
	FCN	100	Linear	4

Table 4. Parameters

(a) Learning parameters

Parameter	Value
Discount factor	0.90
Initial ε value	1
ε Decay rate	0.9998
RMSprop learning rate	0.0001
Memory capacity	20,000
Mini-batch size	32

(b) Experimental parameters

Parameter	Value
Environment width	35
Environment height	20
No. of agents	8
No. of tasks	30
Reward	1
Episode length (steps)	300
Simulation length (episodes)	25,000

5.2 Experiment 1: Static Spawn Location

In this experiment, we compared the behaviors and performances of agents using local and relative views. Each agent began at the same location for every episode, as shown in Fig. 2a. Each agent was assigned an ID number from 0 to 7. When the environment was initialized, agents spawn at the numbered location that matched with their ID. Consequently, each agent spawned in the exact same location at the start of each episode.

Figure 3a shows the moving mean average of the total number of tasks completed by all agents during each episode, where the margin represents the standard deviation. As shown in the figure, as the episodes increased, more tasks were completed on average in the relative view compared with the agents with the local view; this may be because agents with a relative view can possess more information regarding their absolute locations.

Figures 3b and 3c are similar to Fig. 3a, except that these figures display the numbers of times the agents collided with a wall and with each other, respectively. As shown, the average number of wall collisions converged to approximately the same value for both the local and relative views; furthermore, the relative view had a slightly higher rate of collisions compared with the local view, although the performance (the number of completed tasks) of the latter was better than that of the former. Particularly, in Fig. 3b, the number of wall collisions occasionally spiked (e.g., around episodes 10,000, 22,000, and 24,000 episodes), and during these spikes, the performance deteriorated significantly. In addition, the standard deviation of agent collision numbers for the relative view increased from around episode 17,500 onward, although the standard deviation of agent collision numbers for the local view decreased to a small value. These results indicate that the behaviors of agents with relative views were relatively less stable.

Additionally, we counted the number of tasks completed by each agent at each area of the map over episodes 24001 to 25000. Figures 4a and 4b show heatmaps of the tasks completed by each agent. As shown, for both the local and relative views, each agent completed tasks primarily in one room, i.e., the room closest to the agent at the start of the episode. It is noteworthy that two agents primarily completed the tasks in each room. Although there were two agents per room, the agents using the local view appeared to have completed tasks more evenly across the room compared with the agents using the relative view. Except for agents 1 and 3, agents using the relative view had one agent primarily complete tasks on one side of the room, while the other agent primarily completed tasks on the other side. This more detailed work division resulted in better performances when the agents used the relative view. Furthermore, we conducted the same experiment using the merged view; however, we discovered that the results were almost the same as those of the relative view.

5.3   Experiment 2: Dynamic Spawn Location

In this experiment, we compared the behaviors and performances of agents using local, relative, and merged views. Agents would begin each episode at a random position within a 10×2 window at the center of the environment, as shown in Fig. 2b. We began this experiment using only simulations from the local and relative views. However, we discovered a significant performance loss from relative view; therefore, we introduced another view method called the merged view, which provided a higher performance than the local view.

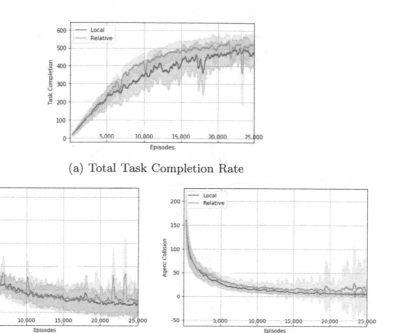

(a) Total Task Completion Rate

(b) Total Wall Collision Rate   (c) Total Agent Collision Rate

Fig. 3. Experiment 1: performance comparison

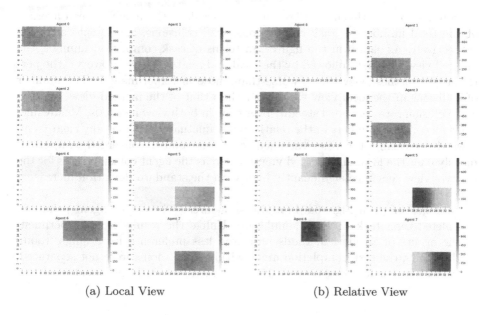

(a) Local View   (b) Relative View

Fig. 4. Experiment 1: task completion heatmap

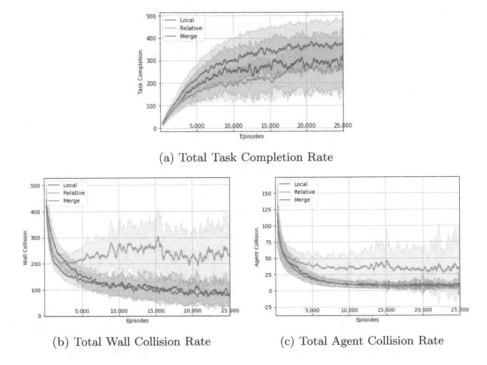

(a) Total Task Completion Rate

(b) Total Wall Collision Rate   (c) Total Agent Collision Rate

Fig. 5. Experiment 2: performance comparison

Similar to Experiment 1, Figs. 5a, b, and c show the moving mean average of the total numbers of task completions, wall collisions, and agent collisions, respectively. As shown in the figures, in terms of task completion number, the merged view was first, followed by the local and relative views. However, the performances of these views were worse than those in Experiment 1. The number of collisions in the local view was higher than that of the merged view, and the wall collision rate decreased steadily over time in both view methods. Meanwhile, the wall collision numbers in the relative view fluctuated without any clear trend toward decreasing. Likewise, the agent collision number converged to approximately 0 for the local and merged views, whereas the agent collision rates for the relative view remained significantly high with the standard deviation increasing over time.

The heatmaps in Figs. 6a, b, and c show areas where each agent primarily completed their tasks in each simulation. Unlike the results from Experiment 1, the agents of all view methods indicated less preference for a single room. Additionally, the task completion areas within some rooms were not separated, as evident by agents using the relative or merged view in Experiment 1.

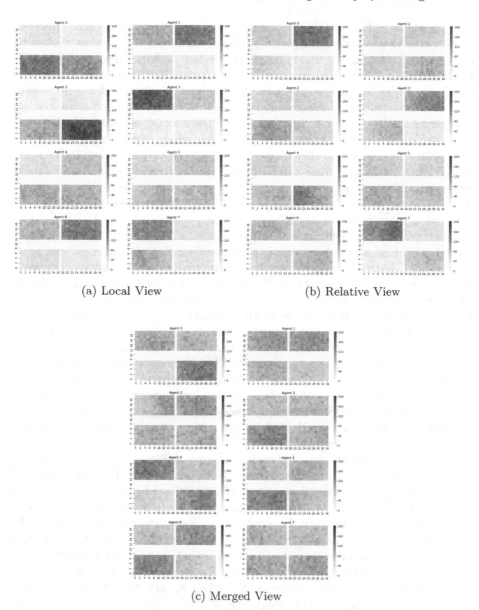

(a) Local View   (b) Relative View

(c) Merged View

Fig. 6. Experiment 2: task completion heatmap

5.4   Discussion

Several key insights can be inferred from the results regarding the behavior of
agents using different view methods. First, based on the heatmaps from Experiment 1, we observed a form of divisional cooperation occurring among agents
with local and relative views in terms of room selection. The agents would

allocate the workload evenly by having two agents visit each room. However, the relative view adds another level of divisional cooperation to the regime by having each pair of agents divide the room into halves. These findings are similar to those of Miyashita & Sugawara [4], where agents with a relative view would divide their 20×20 grid environment into different territories, but agents with a local view would not. When comparing our results with theirs, we can see that using local view or relative view affects the agents' learned behaviors, i.e., because their environment consisted of a single room, agents with local views worked in only one or two specific rooms but did not divide a room into a number of subareas. On the other hand, agents with relative views worked in a room separately. This implication is consistent in both results. In addition to room separation, the relative view offers a considerably better performance than the local view in terms of task completion.

Furthermore, the heatmaps of Experiments 1 and 2 (Figs. 4 and 6, respectively) show that agents can provide significantly different behavioral outcomes in terms of divisional cooperation and room preference when spawning occurs in the same location as opposed to a different location at the start of each episode. Moreover, the line graphs of Figs. 3a and Fig. 5a suggest that the relative view's task completion numbers can be hindered significantly by the variable spawn location and high number of collisions. However, the high task completion numbers of the merged view suggest that it is not caused by the agents observing their absolute location in the environment. This is because the agents using the merged and relative views observe the tasks, walls, and agents around themselves as well as their absolute locations in the environment. The only noticeable difference between the view methods is the method by which the observational information is input into the DQN, which may have contributed to the difference in the task completion number.

The difference in efficiency between these experiments can be explained partially using the heatmaps in Figs. 4 and 6. In Experiment 1, the same number of agents were in charge of each room, and a fairly adjusted coordination structure was obtained as a result of learning. Hence, the agents operated individually in the almost same-sized rooms. By contrast, in Experiment 2, the rooms to be visited were selected based on their initial locations; hence, the work became unbalanced. For example, three agents often operated in one room, while one or zero agents operated in another room, resulting in a decreased overall efficiency.

Finally, we conducted an experiment in which agents started from fixed locations until episode 25,000 and subsequently started at random locations to investigate whether the behavior learned in the first half is applicable in the latter half. The detailed graph is not provided herein; however, the overall performance and number of collisions were almost identical to those in Experiment 2. This suggests that the spawn locations significantly affected the agents' behaviors learned so far, and the agents reconstructed another coordination regime. In actual applications, both fixed and random spawn locations may be possible. Agents often have charging bases or storage locations. Thus, we think that fixed spawn locations are more likely to be present as the environmental setting.

By understanding the coordination structures that we focused on in this paper, we have the advantage of being able to easily infer the impact on changes in the system. For example, since agents in Experiment 1 consistently visited one room, one room will be neglected in the event of an agent malfunction allowing identification of the malfunctioning agent. It is also easy to predict which rooms will be neglected due to a failure of a certain agent, which is especially useful in security patrol contexts where identifying areas with loose security is critical. Furthermore, we can see that the different starting positions between Experiment 1 and Experiment 2 result in different coordination regimes. This difference suggests that the starting positions of agents can have a significant impact on how they will behave. For this reason, we believe careful consideration should be taken to the starting position when increasing the number of agents within an environment.

6   Conclusion

We analyzed the coordination structures observed in a multi-agent DRL setting, where agents learned to play a task execution game in a four-room environment. We observed the effects of allowing agents to view their absolute locations within their environments on the manner in which they coordinated with one another as well as the differences arising from a consistent or inconsistent starting location for each episode.

Our experimental results indicated that with a consistent starting location, agents that can view their absolute location had highest task execution rates and territory divisions among agents sharing the same room. Furthermore, compared with agents with a consistent starting location, we discovered that agents with an inconsistent starting location behaved considerably differently in terms of performance and coordination. Finally, we introduced a new method to observe an environment that mitigated the performance loss from an inconsistent starting location while maintaining the agent's ability to view their absolute location in the environment.

Future studies may involve performing similar experiments with modified environmental parameters, such as the agent's view range, task spawn frequency, environment size, and asymmetrical environmental conditions.

Acknowlegement. This work is partly supported by JSPS KAKENHI Grant number 17KT0044.

References

1. Foerster, J.N., Assael, Y.M., de Freitas, N., Whiteson, S.: Learning to communicate to solve riddles with deep distributed recurrent Q-networks. CoRR, vol. abs/1602.02672 (2016)

2. Gupta, J.K., Egorov, M., Kochenderfer, M.: Cooperative multi-agent control using deep reinforcement learning. In: Sukthankar, G., Rodriguez-Aguilar, J.A. (eds.) AAMAS 2017. LNCS (LNAI), vol. 10642, pp. 66–83. Springer, Cham (2017). https://doi.org/10.1007/978-3-319-71682-4_5

3. Lowe, R., Wu, Y., Tamar, A., Harb, J., Abbeel, P., Mordatch, I.: Multi-agent actor-critic for mixed cooperative-competitive environments. CoRR, vol. abs/1706.02275 (2017)

4. Miyashita, Y., Sugawara, T.: Cooperation and coordination regimes by deep Q-learning in multi-agent task executions. In: Tetko, I.V., Kurková, V., Karpov, P., Theis, F. (eds.) ICANN 2019. LNCS, vol. 11727, pp. 541–554. Springer, Cham (2019). https://doi.org/10.1007/978-3-030-30487-4_42

5. Leibo, J.Z., Zambaldi, V., Lanctot, M., Marecki, J., Graepel, T.: Multi-agent reinforcement learning in sequential social dilemmas. In: International Foundation for Autonomous Agents and Multiagent Systems, ser. AAMAS 2017, Richland, SC, pp. 464–473 (2017)

6. Lillicrap, T.P., et al.: Continuous control with deep reinforcement learning. CoRR, vol. abs/1509.02971 (2015)

7. van Hasselt, H., Guez, A., Silver, D.: Deep reinforcement learning with double Q-learning. CoRR, vol. abs/1509.06461 (2015)

8. Lample, G., Chaplot, D.S.: Playing FPS games with deep reinforcement learning. CoRR, vol. abs/1609.05521 (2016)

9. Mnih, V., et al.: Human-level control through deep reinforcement learning. Nature 518(7540), 529–533 (2015)

10. Mnih, V., et al.: Playing Atari with deep reinforcement learning. CoRR, vol. abs/1312.5602 (2013)

11. Wang, Z., Schaul, T., Hessel, M., Van Hasselt, H., Lanctot, M., De Freitas, N.: Dueling network architectures for deep reinforcement learning. In: Proceedings of the 33rd International Conference on International Conference on Machine Learning - Volume 48, ser. ICML 2016. JMLR.org, pp. 1995–2003 (2016)

12. Hausknecht, M., Stone, P.: Deep recurrent Q-learning for partially observable MDPs. CoRR, vol. abs/1507.06527 (2015)

13. Hessel, M., et al.: Rainbow: combining improvements in deep reinforcement learning. In: Proceedings of the Thirty-Second AAAI Conference on Artificial Intelligence, (AAAI 2018), New Orleans, Louisiana, USA, 2–7 February 2018, pp. 3215–3222. AAAI Press (2018)

14. Diallo, E.A.O., Sugawara, T.: Coordination in adversarial multi-agent with deep reinforcement learning under partial observability. In: 2019 IEEE 31st International Conference on Tools with Artificial Intelligence (ICTAI) (2019)

15. Chollet, F., et al.: Keras (2015). https://github.com/fchollet/keras

16. Tieleman, T., Hinton, G.: Neural Networks for Machine Learning - Lecture 6a - Overview of mini-batch gradient descent (2012)

Policy Adaptive Multi-agent Deep Deterministic Policy Gradient

Yixiang Wang and Feng Wu(✉)

School of Computer Science and Technology,
University of Science and Technology of China, Hefei, China
yixiangw@mail.ustc.edu.cn, wufeng02@ustc.edu.cn

Abstract. We propose a novel approach to address one aspect of the non-stationarity problem in multi-agent reinforcement learning (RL), where the other agents may alter their policies due to environment changes during execution. This violates the Markov assumption that governs most single-agent RL methods and is one of the key challenges in multi-agent RL. To tackle this, we propose to train multiple policies for each agent and postpone the selection of the best policy at execution time. Specifically, we model the environment non-stationarity with a finite set of scenarios and train policies fitting each scenario. In addition to multiple policies, each agent also learns a policy predictor to determine which policy is the best with its local information. By doing so, each agent is able to adapt its policy when the environment changes and consequentially the other agents alter their policies during execution. We empirically evaluated our method on a variety of common benchmark problems proposed for multi-agent deep RL in the literature. Our experimental results show that the agents trained by our algorithm have better adaptiveness in changing environments and outperform the state-of-the-art methods in all the tested environments.

Keywords: Reinforcement learning · Multi-agent reinforcement learning · Multi-agent deep deterministic policy gradient

1 Introduction

The development of modern deep learning has made reinforcement learning (RL) more powerful to solve complex decision problems. This leads to success in many real-world applications, such as Atari games [19], playing Go [22] and robotics control [12]. Recently, there is growing focus on applying deep RL techniques to multi-agent systems. Many promising approaches for multi-agent deep RL have been proposed to solve a variety of multi-agent problems, such as traffic control

This work was supported in part by the National Key R&D Program of China (Grant No. 2017YFB1002204), the National Natural Science Foundation of China (Grant No. U1613216, Grant No. 61603368), and the Guangdong Province Science and Technology Plan (Grant No. 2017B010110011).

© Springer Nature Switzerland AG 2021
T. Uchiya et al. (Eds.): PRIMA 2020, LNAI 12568, pp. 165–181, 2021.
https://doi.org/10.1007/978-3-030-69322-0_11

[18,27], multi-player games (e.g., StarCraft, Dota 2), and multi-robot systems [16].

Despite the recent success of deep RL in single-agent domains, there are additional challenges in multi-agent RL. One major challenge is the *non-stationarity* of multi-agent environment caused by agents that change their policies during the training and testing procedures. Specifically, at the training time, each agent's policy is changing simultaneously and therefore the environment becomes non-stationary from the perspective of any individual agent. To handle this issue, *multi-agent deep deterministic policy gradient* (MADDPG) [17] proposed to utilized a *centralized critic* with *decentralized actors* in the actor-critic learning framework. Since the centralized Q-function of each agent is conditioned on the actions of all the other agents, each agent can perceive the learning environment as stationary even when the other agents' policies change.

Although using a centralized critic stabilizes training, the learned policy of each agent can still be brittle and sensitive to its training environment and partners. It has been observed that the performance of the learned policies can be drastically worse when some agents alter their policies during execution [11]. To improve the robustness of the learned policies, *minimax multi-agent deep deterministic policy gradient* (M3DDPG) [13]—a *minimax* extension of MADDPG— proposed to update policies considering the worst-case situation by assuming that all the other agents acts adversarially. This minimax optimization is useful to learn robust policies in very competitive domains but can be too *pessimistic* in mixed competitive and cooperative or fully cooperative problems as shown later in our experiments.

In this paper, we consider one aspect of the non-stationarity issue in multi-agent RL, where the other agents may alter their policies as a result of changes in some environmental factors. This frequently happens in real-world activities. For example, in a soccer game, a heavy rain or high temperature usually causes the teams to change their strategies against each other. Take disaster response as another example. First responders often need to constantly adjust their plan in order to complete their tasks in the highly dynamic and danger environment. Therefore, it is often desirable for the agents to learn policies that can adapt with changes of the environment and others' policies.

Against this background, we propose *policy adaptive multi-agent deep deterministic policy gradient* (PAMADDPG)—a novel approach based on MADDPG—to learn adaptive policies for non-stationary environments. Specifically, it learns multiple policies for each agent and postpone the selection of the best policy at execution time. By doing so, each agent is able to adapt its policy when the environment changes. Specifically, we model the non-stationary environment by a finite set of known scenarios, where each scenario captures possible changing factors of the environment (e.g., weather, temperature, wind, etc. in soccer). For each scenario, a policy is learned by each agent to perform well in that specific scenario. Together with multiple policies for each agent, we also train a policy predictor to predict the best policy using the agent's local information. At execution time, each agent first selects a policy based on the policy predictor and then choose an action according to the selected policy. We evaluated our PAMADDPG algorithm on three common benchmark environments and compared it with MADDPG and M3DDPG. Our experimental results show that PAMADDPG outperforms both MADDPG and M3DDPG in all the tested environments.

The rest of the paper is organized as follows. We first briefly review the related work about handling non-stationary in multi-agent deep RL. Then, we describe the background on the Markov game and the MADDPG method, which are building blocks of our algorithm. Next, we propose our PAMADDPG algorithm to learn multiple policies and policy predictors. After that, we present the experiments with environments, setup, and results. Finally, we conclude the paper with possible future work.

2   Related Work

In recent years, various approaches [20] have been proposed to tackle different aspects of non-stationarity in multi-agent deep RL. We sample a few related work about multi-agent deep RL as listed below.

2.1   Centralized Critic

Using the centralized critic techniques, [17] proposed MADDPG for multi-agent RL using a centralized critic and a decentralized actor, where the training of each agent is conditioned on the observation and action of all the other agents so the agent can perceive the environment as stationary. [13] extended MADDPG and proposed M3DDPG using minimax Q-learning in the critic to exhibit robustness against different adversaries with altered policies. [8] proposed COMA using also a centralized critic with the counterfactual advantage estimation to address the credit assignment problem—another key challenge in multi-agent RL.

2.2   Decentralized Learning

A useful decentralized learning technique to handle non-stationarity is self-play. Recent self-play approaches store the neural network parameters at different points during learning. By doing so, self-play managed to train policies that can generalize well in environments like Go [23] and complex locomotion tasks [2]. Another technique [6] is by stabilizing experience replay using importance sampling corrections to adjust the weight of previous experience to the current environment dynamics.

2.3   Opponent Modeling

By modeling the opponent, [9] developed a second separate network to encode the opponent's behaviour. The combination of the two networks is done either by concatenating their hidden states or by the use of a mixture of experts.

In contrast, [21] proposed an actor-critic method using the same policy network for estimating the goals of the other agents. [5] proposed a modification of the optimization function to incorporate the learning procedure of the opponents in the training of agents.

2.4   Meta-learning

By extending meta-learning approaches for single-agent RL such as model agnostic meta-learning [3] to handle non-stationarity in multi-agent domains, [1] proposed an optimization method to search for initial neural network parameters that can quickly adapt to non-stationarity, by explicitly optimizing the initial model parameters based on their expected performance after learning. This was tested in *iterated adaptation games*, where an agent repeatedly play against the same opponent while only allowed to learn in between each game.

2.5   Communication

In this direction, [7] proposed the deep distributed recurrent Q-networks, where all the agents share the same hidden layers and learn to communicate to solve riddles. [26] proposed the CommNet architecture, where the input to each hidden layer is the previous layer and a communication message. [25] proposed the individualized controlled continuous communication model, which is an extension of CommNet in competitive setting. [4] proposed reinforced inter-agent learning with two Q-networks for each agents where the first network outputs an action and the second a communication message.

As briefly reviewed above, most of the existing work focus on handling non-stationarity mainly during training procedure. Although meta-learning approaches can learn to adapt agents' policies between different game, it requires to *repeatedly* play iterated adaptation games. In contrast, we build our algorithm on top of MADDPG to address the non-stationarity problem in general multi-agent RL at execution time. Besides, we do not assume explicit communication among the agents during execution as in MADDPG.

A complete survey about recent efforts of dealing non-stationarity in multi-agent RL can be found in [10, 20].

3   Background

In this section, we introduce our problem settings and some basic algorithms on which our approach is based.

3.1   Partially Observable Markov Games

In this work, we consider a *partially observable Markov games* [15] with N agents, defined by: a set of states S describing the possible configurations of all agents, a set of actions $A_1, \ldots, A_N$ and a set of observations $O_1, \ldots, O_N$ for each agent.

To choose actions, each agent i uses a stochastic policy $\mu_{\theta_i} : \mathcal{O}_i \times \mathcal{A}_i \mapsto [0, 1]$, which produces the next state according to the state transition function $\mathcal{T} : \mathcal{S} \times \mathcal{A}_1 \times \ldots \times \mathcal{A}_N \mapsto \mathcal{S}$.

At each time step, each agent i obtains rewards as a function of the state and agent's action $r_i : \mathcal{S} \times \mathcal{A}_i \mapsto \mathbb{R}$, and receives a local observation correlated with the state $\mathbf{o}_i : \mathcal{S} \mapsto \mathcal{O}_i$. The initial states are determined by a state distribution $\rho : \mathcal{S} \mapsto [0, 1]$. Each agent i aims to maximize its own total expected return: $R_i = \sum_{t=0}^{T} \gamma^t r_i^t$, where $\gamma \in (0, 1]$ is a discount factor and T is the time horizon.

Here, we assume that the state transition function $\mathcal{T}$ is unknown and therefore consider to learn the policies μ_{θ_i} for each agent i using multi-agent *reinforcement learning* (RL) methods. Note that each agent must choose an action based on its own policy and local observation during execution.

3.2   Multi-agent Deep Deterministic Policy Gradient

Policy gradient methods are a popular choice for a variety of RL tasks. The main idea is to directly adjust the parameters θ of the policy in order to maximize the objective $J(\theta) = \mathbb{E}_{s \sim p^\mu, a \sim \mu_\theta}[R(s, a)]$ by taking steps in the direction of $\nabla_\theta J(\theta)$, i.e., the gradient of the policy written as:

$$\nabla_\theta J(\theta) = \mathbb{E}_{s \sim p^\mu, a \sim \mu_\theta} \left[\nabla_\theta \log \mu_\theta(a|s) Q^\mu(s, a) \right] \tag{1}$$

where p^μ is the state distribution and Q^μ is the Q-function.

The policy gradient framework has been extended to deterministic policies $\mu_\theta : \mathcal{S} \mapsto \mathcal{A}$. In particular, under certain conditions the gradient of the objective $J(\theta) = \mathbb{E}_{s \sim p^\mu}[R(s, a)]$ can be written as:

$$\nabla_\theta J(\theta) = \mathbb{E}_{s \sim \mathcal{D}} \left[\nabla_\theta \mu_\theta(a|s) \nabla_a Q^\mu(s, a) \big|_{a = \mu_\theta(s)} \right] \tag{2}$$

Since the *deterministic policy gradient* (DPG) [24] relies on $\nabla_a Q^\mu(s, a)$, it requires that the action space $\mathcal{A}$ (and thus the policy μ) be continuous. *Deep deterministic policy gradient* (DDPG) [14] is a variant of DPG where the policy μ and critic Q^μ are approximated with deep neural networks. DDPG is an off-policy algorithm, and samples trajectories from a replay buffer of experiences that are stored throughout training. It also makes use of a target network, as in DQN [19].

Multi-agent DDPG (MADDPG) [17] extends the DDPG method to multi-agent domains. The main idea behind MADDPG is to consider action policies of other agents. The environment is stationary even as the policies change, since $P(s'|s, a_1, \ldots, a_N, \pi_1, \ldots, \pi_N) = P(s'|s, a_1, \ldots, a_N) = P(s'|s, a_1, \ldots, a_N, \pi_1', \ldots, \pi_N')$ for any $\pi_i \neq \pi_i'$. The gradient can be written as:

$$\nabla_{\theta_i} J(\mu_i) = \mathbb{E}_{\mathbf{x}, a \sim \mathcal{D}} \left[\nabla_{\theta_i} \mu_i(a_i|o_i) \nabla_{a_i} Q_i^\mu(\mathbf{x}, a_1, \ldots, a_N) \big|_{a_i = \mu_i(o_i)} \right] \tag{3}$$

where $Q_i^\mu(\mathbf{x}, a_1, \ldots, a_N)$ is a *centralized action-value function* that takes as input the actions of all agents, $a_1, \ldots, a_N$, in addition to the state information $\mathbf{x}$, and outputs the Q-value for agent i. Here, Q_i^μ can be updated as:

$$\mathcal{L}(\theta_i) = \mathbb{E}_{\mathbf{x},a,r,\mathbf{x}'}\left[(Q_i^\mu(\mathbf{x},a_1,\ldots,a_N) - y)^2\right],$$
$$y = r_i + \gamma Q_i^{\mu'}(\mathbf{x}',a_1',\ldots,a_N')\big|_{a_j'=\mu_j'(o_j)} \tag{4}$$

where $(\mathbf{x}, a, r, \mathbf{x}')$ is sampled from the experience replay buffer $\mathcal{D}$, recoding experiences of all agents.

3.3   Dealing Non-stationarity in MADDPG

As aforementioned, one of the key challenges in multi-agent RL is the environment non-stationarity. This non-stationarity stems from breaking the Markov assumption that governs most single-agent RL algorithms. Since the transitions and rewards depend on actions of all agents, whose decision policies keep changing in the learning process, each agent can enter an endless cycle of adapting to other agents. Although using a centralized critic stabilizes training in MADDPG, the learned policies can still be brittle and sensitive to changes of the other agents's policies.

To obtain policies that are more robust to changes in the policy of other agents, MADDPG proposes to first train a collection of K different sub-policies and then maximizing the ensemble objective $\max_{\theta_i} J(\theta_i)$ as:

$$J(\theta_i) = \mathbb{E}_{k\sim\text{uniform}(1,K),s\sim p^\mu,a\sim\mu^{(k)}}\left[R_i(s,a)\right]$$
$$= \mathbb{E}_{k,s}\left[\sum_{t=0}^{T}\gamma^t r_i(s^t,a_1^t,\ldots,a_N^t)\Big|_{a_i^t=\mu_i^{(k)}(o_i^t)}\right] \tag{5}$$
$$= \mathbb{E}_s\left[\frac{1}{K}\sum_{k=1}^{K}Q_i^\mu(s,a_1,\ldots,a_N)\Big|_{a_i=\mu_i^{(k)}(o_i)}\right]$$

where $\mu_i^{(k)}$ is the k-th sub-policies of agent i. By training agents with an ensemble of policies, the agents require interaction with a variety of the other agents' policies. Intuitively, this is useful to avoid converging to local optima of the agents' policies. However, the ensemble objective only considers the *average* performance of agents' policies training by *uniformly* sampling the policies of the other agents.

Alternatively, M3DDPG [13]—a variation of MADDPG—proposes to update policies considering the worst situation for the purpose of learning robust policies. During training, it optimizes the policy of each agent i under the

---

Algorithm 1: Training and execution for PAMADDPG

---

1 # At training time:
2 $\forall i : \Pi_i \leftarrow \emptyset, \phi_i \leftarrow$ initialize the predictor parameters
3 **foreach** *scenario* $c \in C$ **do**
4      $\forall i : \Pi_i \leftarrow$ learn and add a set of policies for agent i
5      $\forall i : \phi_i \leftarrow$ learn and update the predictor for agent i

6 # At execution time:
7 $\forall i : h_i^0 \leftarrow \emptyset$
8 **for** *time step* $t = 1$ **to** T **do**
9   **for** *agent* $i = 1$ **to** N **do**
10          $o_i^t \leftarrow$ receive a local observation for agent i
11          $\mu_i \leftarrow$ select a policy from Π_i by $\phi_i(o_i^t, h_i^{t-1})$
12          $a_i^t \leftarrow$ select an action by $\mu_{\theta_i}(o_i^t)$
13          $h_i^t \leftarrow$ append o_i^t to h_i^{t-1}

14   Execute actions $\langle a_1^t, \ldots, a_N^t \rangle$ to the environment
15   Collect rewards $\langle r_1^t, \ldots, r_N^t \rangle$ from the environment
16 **return** $\forall i : R_i = \sum_{t=0}^{T} \gamma^t r_i^t$

---

assumption that all other agents acts adversarially, which yields the minimax objective $\max_{\theta_i} J(\theta_i)$ as:

$$J(\theta_i) = \min_{a_{j \neq i}} \mathbb{E}_{s \sim p^\mu, a_i \sim \mu_i} [R_i(s, a)]$$

$$= \min_{a_{j \neq i}^t} \mathbb{E}_s \left[\sum_{t=0}^{T} \gamma^t r_i(s^t, a_1^t, \ldots, a_N^t) \Big|_{a_i^t = \mu_i(o_i^t)} \right] \qquad (6)$$

$$= \mathbb{E}_s \left[\min_{a_{j \neq i}} Q_{M,i}^\mu(s, a_1, \ldots, a_N) \Big|_{a_i = \mu_i(o_i)} \right]$$

where $Q_{M,i}^\mu(s, a_1, \ldots, a_N)$ is the modified Q function representing the current reward of executing $a_1, \ldots, a_N$ in s plus the discounted worst case future return starting from s. With the minimax objective, the training environment of each agent becomes stationary because the behavior of all the other agents only depends on $-r_i$, i.e., the negative reward of agent i itself. However, this adversarial assumption could be too *pessimistic* if the game among the agents is not zero-sum or even is cooperative.

Ideally, the well trained agents should be able to *adapt* their policies with the changes in the environment. This motivated the development of our algorithm that will be introduced in details next.

4   Policy Adaptive MADDPG

In this section, we propose *policy adaptive multi-agent deep deterministic policy gradient* (PAMADDPG), which is based on MADDPG, to deal with environment non-stationarity in multi-agent RL. As in MADDPG, our algorithm operate under the framework of *centralized training* with *decentralized execution*. Thus, we allow the agents to share extra information for training, as long as this information is not used at execution time. We assume that the learned policies can only use local information and there is no explicit communication among agents during execution. Specifically, our algorithm is an extension of actor-critic policy gradient methods with multiple decentralized actors and one centralized critic, where the critic is augmented with extra information on the policies of the other agents.

In this work, we consider a setting where agents are trained and executed in an environment that can categorized into a finite set of scenarios. These scenarios are known during training. However, at execution time, agents have no prior knowledge about which scenario they will locate in. Therefore, the agents must act adaptively during execution. Note that the scenarios cannot be modeled as state variables because we make no assumption about the initial distribution and transition probabilities of scenarios, which can be any probabilities in our setting. Intuitively, a scenario in our setting models a collection of environmental factors that can cause the agents to alter their policies.

Let $\mathcal{C}$ denote a finite set of scenarios for the agents. Here, each scenario $c \in \mathcal{C}$ can be modeled by a partially observable Markov game as aforementioned. We assume that all the scenarios in $\mathcal{C}$ have identical state space and the same action and observation space for all the agents. Particularly, each scenario $c \in \mathcal{C}$ may have different state transition function $\mathcal{T}^c$ and different reward function r_i^c for each agent i, so that agents in different scenarios may require different policies. Formally, we define a scenario $c \in \mathcal{C}$ as a tuple: $\langle \mathcal{S}, \{\mathcal{A}_i\}, \{\mathcal{O}_i\}, \mathcal{T}^c, \{r_i^c\} \rangle$ with notations in Markov games.

As aforementioned, to be able to adapt in different scenarios, we propose to train multiple policies for each agent and postpone the selection of its policy at execution time. In addition to multiple policies for each agent, we also train a policy predictor that can be used by the agent to determine the best policy during execution. Given this, the agent is able to adapt its policy when the environment changes. As summarized in Algorithm 1, PAMADDPG consists of two main procedures: 1) learning multiple policies and 2) learning policy predictors, which will be described in details next.

4.1 Learning Multiple Policies

We can extend the actor-critic policy gradient method as described in MADDPG to work with each scenario. Specifically, given a scenario $c \in \mathcal{C}$, the gradient for policy μ_i^c with respect to parameters θ_i^c can be written as:

$$\nabla_{\theta_i^c} J(\mu_i^c) = \mathbb{E}_{\mathbf{x}, a \sim \mathcal{D}^c} \left[\nabla_{\theta_i^c} \mu_i^c(a_i|o_i) \nabla_{a_i} Q_i^{\mu,c}(\mathbf{x}, a_1, \dots, a_N) \big|_{a_i = \mu_i^c(o_i)} \right] \quad (7)$$

where $\mathcal{D}^c$ is the experience replay buffer recording experiences with tuples $(\mathbf{x}, a_1, \dots, a_N, r_1^c, \dots, r_N^c, \mathbf{x}')$ of all agents at the scenario c and $\mathbf{x} = (o_1, \dots, o_N)$.

Here, the centralized action-value function $Q_i^{\mu,c}$ is updated as:

$$\mathcal{L}(\theta_i^c) = \mathbb{E}_{\mathbf{x},a,r,\mathbf{x}'}[(Q_i^{\mu,c}(\mathbf{x}, a_1, \ldots, a_N) - y)^2]$$
$$y = r_i + \gamma \, Q_i^{\mu',c}(\mathbf{x}', a_1', \ldots, a_N')\big|_{a_j' = \mu_j'^c(o_j)} \tag{8}$$

where $\mu'^c = \{\mu_{\theta_1'^c}, \ldots, \mu_{\theta_N'^c}\}$ is the set of target policies with delayed parameters $\theta_i'^c$.

Here, the key challenge is that policies trained by MADDPG may converge to different local optima. Therefore, the other agents may choose policies that are different from the ones learned by MADDPG. To address this, we propose to train a collection of K different policies for each agent in a single scenario. Each policy can have different initial parameters and selection of the partners' policies. This will grow the populations in the policy set of each agent and further improve the robustness during testing. Unlike MADDPG, we do not ensemble the K policies to a single policy but keep all the individual policies as candidates for execution.

4.2   Learning Policy Predictors

We denote $\phi_i : \mathcal{H}_i \rightarrow \Delta(\Pi_i)$ the policy predictor that uses agent i's local observation history $h_i^t = (o_i^1, \ldots, o_i^t)$ to compute the distribution over agent i's policy set Π_i. Our goal is to determine at execution time which policy should be used by agent i in order to achieve the best performance. Here, we use a recurrent neural network to train a policy predictor ϕ_i, containing a layer of LSTM and some other layers. This structure allows the agent to reason about the current scenario using its observation sequence.

Here, $\phi_i(o_i^t, h_i^{t-1})$ is a function that takes the input of the current observation o_i^t and the last-step history h_i^{t-1} at the time step t, and outputs the policy distribution $p_i^t(\cdot) \in [0,1]$ over agent i's policy set Π_i. Now, the action selection process of agent i at time step t can be written as:

$$p_i^t = \phi_i(o_i^t, h_i^{t-1})$$
$$\mu_i = \arg\max_{\mu_i' \in \Pi_i} p_i^t(\mu_i') \tag{9}$$
$$a_i^t = \mu_{\theta_i}(o_i^t)$$

Together with training the policy, we use replay buffer to train ϕ_i in order to avoid the early instability and adverse effects during training process. Specifically, we create a dedicated replay buffer $\mathcal{B}_i$ for ϕ_i during training. It stores (h_i, μ_i) at the end of each episode, where $h_i = (o_i^1, \ldots, o_i^T)$ is agent i's observation sequence at this episode and μ_i is the currently trained policy. The main training procedure of ϕ_i is to sample a random minibatch of samples (h_i, μ_i) from $\mathcal{B}_i$ and update the parameters of ϕ_i by minimizing the cross-entropy loss function as follow:

$$\nabla_{p_i} J(\phi_i) = \mathbb{E}_{(h_i, \mu_i) \sim \mathcal{B}_i} \left[\sum_{t=1}^{T} \text{CE} \left(\phi_i(o_i^t, h_i^{t-1}), t \right) \right]$$

$$= \mathbb{E}_{(h_i, \mu_i)} \left[\sum_{t=1}^{T} \sum_{\mu_i' \in \Pi_i} -y^{\mu_i'} \log \left(p_i^t(\mu_i') \right) \right] \quad (10)$$

$$\text{where } y^{\mu_i'} = \begin{cases} 1, & \mu_i' = \mu_i \\ 0, & \mu_i' \neq \mu_i \end{cases} \text{ and } p_i^t = \phi_i(o_i^t, h_i^{t-1}).$$

The overall learning procedures of PAMADDPG are outlined in Algorithm 2.

5 Experiments

We empirically evaluate our algorithm on three domains built on top of the particle-world environments[1] originally used by the MADDPG paper [17]. To create various scenarios, we modify some of the physical properties of the environments so that the agents must alter their policies in order to success in different scenarios. By doing so, we expect to examine the adaptiveness of our PAMADDPG algorithm when testing in different scenarios.

5.1 Environments

The particle world environment consists of N cooperative agents, M adversarial agents and L landmarks in a two-dimensional world with continuous space. In the experiments, we consider two mixed cooperative and competitive domains (i.e., Keep-away and Predator-prey) and one fully cooperative domain (i.e., Cooperative navigation), as shown in Fig. 1, and modify these domains to generate different scenarios as below.

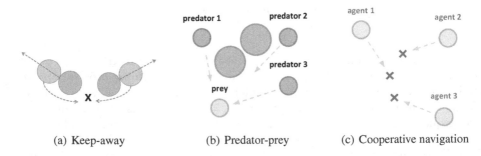

(a) Keep-away   (b) Predator-prey   (c) Cooperative navigation

Fig. 1. Illustrations of the three environments.

---

[1] Code from: https://github.com/openai/multiagent-particle-envs.

Algorithm 2: Learning agents' policies and predictors

---

1 **foreach** *episode* **do**

2   Initialize a random process $\mathcal{N}$ for action exploration

3   Receive initial observations $\mathbf{x} = (o_1, \ldots, o_N)$

4   **for** *time step $t = 1$* **to** T **do**

5   For each agent i, select $a_i = \mu_{\theta_i}(o_i) + \mathcal{N}_t$ w.r.t the current policy and exploration noise

6   Execute action $a = (a_1, \ldots, a_N)$ and observe reward $r = (r_1, \ldots, r_N)$ and new state $\mathbf{x}'$

7   Store $(\mathbf{x}, a, r, \mathbf{x}')$ in $\mathcal{D}$ and set $\mathbf{x} \leftarrow \mathbf{x}'$

8   **for** *agent $i = 1$* to N **do**

9   Sample a random minibatch of M samples $(\mathbf{x}^m, a^m, r^m, \mathbf{x}'^m)$ from replay buffer $\mathcal{D}$

10   Set $y^m = r_i^m + \gamma\, Q_i^{\mu'}(\mathbf{x}', a')\big|_{a_j' = \mu_j'(o_j^m)}$

11   Update critic by minimizing the loss:

$$\mathcal{L}(\theta_i) = \frac{1}{M}\sum_{m=1}^{M}(y^m - Q_i^{\mu}(\mathbf{x}^m, a^m))^2$$

12   Update actor using the sampled gradient:

$$\nabla_{\theta_i} J(\mu_i) \approx \frac{1}{M}\sum_{m=1}^{M}\nabla_{\theta_i}\mu_i(o_i^m)$$

$$\nabla_{a_i} Q_i^{\mu}(\mathbf{x}^m, a^m)\big|_{a_i = \mu_i(o_i^m)}$$

13   Sample a random minibatch of K samples (h_i^k, μ_i^k) from replay buffer $\mathcal{B}_i$

14   Update predictor ϕ_i by minimizing the loss:

$$\nabla_{p_i} J(\phi_i) \approx \frac{1}{K}\sum_{k=1}^{K}\sum_{t=1}^{T}\sum_{\mu_i'} -y^{\mu_i'}\log(p_i^t(\mu_i'))$$

15   Update target network parameters θ_i for each agent i as:
$\theta_i' \leftarrow \tau\theta_i + (1 - \tau)\theta_i'$

16   Collect history $h_i = (o_i^1, \ldots, o_i^T)$ and store (h_i, μ_i) in replay buffer $\mathcal{B}_i$ for each agent i

---

Keep-Away. This environment consists of L landmarks including a target landmark, $N = 2$ cooperating agents who know the target landmark and are rewarded based on their distance to the target, and $M = 2$ agents who must prevent the cooperating agents from reaching the target. Adversaries accomplish this by physically pushing the agents away from the landmark, temporarily occupying it. While the adversaries are also rewarded based on their distance to the target landmark, they do not know the correct target.

We create $K = 3$ scenarios that require agents to learn to adapt with. In each scenario, we simulate different "wind" conditions in the environment. The wind will affect the moving speed of the agents in a certain direction computed as: $v_i' = v_i + w * \beta_i$, where v_i is the original speed, $w = [w_N, w_W, w_S, w_E]$ is the wind force for four directions, and $\beta_i = 5$ is the acceleration rate. In the experiments, we consider no wind (i.e., $w = 0$) in Scenario 1, southwest wind (i.e., $w_S = w_W = 0.5$ and 0 otherwise) in Scenario 2, and northeast wind (i.e., $w_N = w_E = 0.5$ and 0 otherwise) in Scenario 3 respectively.

Predator-Prey. In this environment, $N = 4$ slower cooperating agents must chase $M = 2$ faster adversary around a randomly generated environment with $L = 2$ large landmarks impeding the way. Each time the cooperative agents collide with an adversary, the agents are rewarded while the adversary is penalized. Agents observe the relative positions and velocities of the agents, and the landmark positions.

We create $K = 3$ scenarios to simulate different body conditions for the good and bad agents. This is done by using different maximum speeds $\bar{v}$ and accelerations β for the agents in the environment, i.e., $(\bar{v}_{good}, \beta_{good}, \bar{v}_{bad}, \beta_{bad})$. We set the parameters so that the agents will compete in different levels, i.e., weak, medium, and strong. Specifically, we set $(3.0, 3.0, 3.9, 4.0)$ in Scenario 1, $(2.0, 4.0, 2.6, 5.0)$ in Scenario 2, and $(3.0, 5.0, 3.9, 6.0)$ in Scenario 3.

Cooperative Navigation. In this environment, agents must cooperate through physical actions to reach a set of L landmarks. Agents observe the relative positions of other agents and landmarks, and are collectively rewarded based on the proximity of any agent to each landmark. In other words, the agents have to "cover" all of the landmarks. Furthermore, the agents occupy significant physical space and are penalized when colliding with each other.

Similar to the Keep-away environment described above, we created $K = 3$ scenarios in this environment also with three wind conditions, i.e., no wind for Scenario 1, southeast wind for Scenario 2, and northwest wind for Scenario 3.

5.2   Setup

We compared our PAMADDPG algorithm with MADDPG[2] and M3DDPG[3], which are currently the leading algorithms for multi-agent deep RL, on the environments as described above. In our implementation, the agents' policies are represented by a two-layer ReLU MLP with 64 units per layer, which is the same as MADDPG and M3DDPG, and the policy predictors are represented by a two-layer ReLU MLP and a layer of LSTM on top of them.

We used the same training configurations as MADDPG and M3DDPG, and ran all the algorithms until convergence. Then, we tested the policies computed

---

[2] Code from: https://github.com/openai/maddpg.
[3] Code from: https://github.com/dadadidodi/m3ddpg.

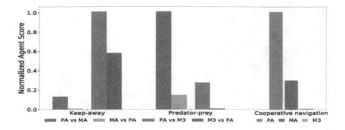

Fig. 2. Overall performance of PAMADDPG (PA), MADDPG (MA), and M3DDPG (M3) on the environments.

by the algorithms on each environment with 10,000 further episodes and report the averaged results. For fair comparison, all algorithms were tested on a fixed set of environment configurations. Each testing environment is generated by randomizing the basic configurations and randomly selecting a scenario. As aforementioned, the agents do not know which scenario is selected for the environment during testing procedure.

Note that MADDPG and M3DDPG do not consider different scenarios in their original implementations. For fair comparison, we try to train their policies in a way that their performance is improved when working with different scenarios. Specifically, in our experiments, MADDPG trained policies with all scenarios and optimized the objective as:

$$J(\theta_i) = \mathbb{E}_{c\sim\text{uniform}(\mathcal{C}),s\sim p^c,a\sim\mu}[R_i(s,a)] \tag{11}$$

As aforementioned, we do not know the true distribution before testing so MADDPG was trained with the uniformly distributed scenarios. Following the min-max idea of the standard version, M3DDPG maximized the objective in the worst-case scenario in the experiments as:

$$J(\theta_i) = \min_{c\in\mathcal{C},a_{j\neq i}} \mathbb{E}_{s\sim p^c,a_i\sim\mu_i}[R_i(s,a)] \tag{12}$$

By doing so, we can evaluate the effectiveness of our algorithm with multiple policies comparing with MADDPG and M3DDPG using only a single policy for each agent when the environment changes.

5.3   Results

We measure the performance of agents with policies learned by our PAMADDPG and agents with policies learned by MADDPG and M3DDPG in each environment. In the first two mixed cooperative and competitive domains, we switch the roles of both normal agent and adversary as in the MADDPG and M3DDPG papers to evaluate the quality of learned policies trained by different algorithms.

The results on the three environments are demonstrated in Fig. 2. As shown in the figure, each group of bar shows the 0−1 normalized score for the environment,

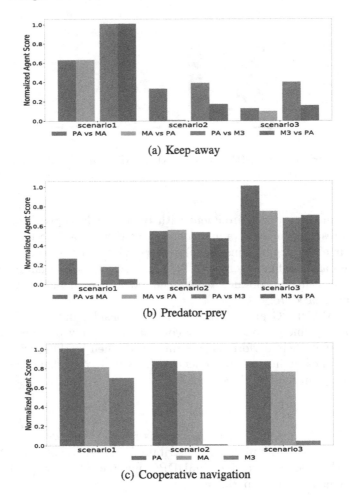

Fig. 3. Performance of PAMADDPG (PA), MADDPG (MA), and M3DDPG (M3) on different scenarios.

where a higher score shows better performance for the algorithm. In the first two environments, PAMADDPG outperforms M3DDPG and MADDPG because PAMADDPG achieves higher scores when playing normal agents (i.e., PA vs MA, PA vs M3) than the ones as adversaries (i.e., MA vs PA, M3 vs PA). Interestingly, PAMADDPG performs better when playing against MADDPG (i.e., PA vs MA, MA vs PA) than the case against M3DDPG (i.e., PA vs M3, M3 vs PA) in the Keep-away environment, while PAMADDPG shows better performance against M3DDPG than the case against MADDPG in the Predator-prey environment. Intuitively, this is because the Predator-prey environment is more competitive than the Keep-away environment so that M3DDPG who considers the worst-case situation works better than MADDPG when paired with our algorithm. In the Cooperative navigation environment, PAMADDPG consistently outperforms

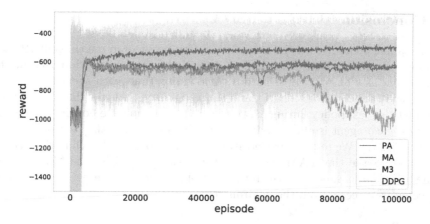

Fig. 4. Learning reward of PAMADDPG (PA), MADDPG (MA), M3DDPG (M3), and DDPG on the Cooperative navigation environment after 10,000 episodes.

MADDPG and M3DDPG. M3DDPG has the worst performance in terms of scores because this environment is a fully cooperative domain while M3DDPG makes unrealistic assumption that all the other agents act adversarially.

Figure 3 shows the results of our PAMADDPG comparing with MADDPG and M3DDPG when testing on different scenarios in each environment. In the Keep-away environment, PAMADDPG outperforms MADDPG and M3DDPG on Scenarios 2 and 3 while performs similarly on Scenario 1. This is because MADDPG and M3DDPG tends to converge to the policies fitting Scenario 1, which is expected to work poorly in Scenarios 2 and 3. In contrast, our PAMADDPG can adapt its policies to fit different scenarios during testing. In the Predator-prey environment, PAMADDPG outperforms MADDPG on Scenarios 1 and 3 but not Scenario 2, and M3DDPG on Scenarios 1 and 2 but not Scenario 3. Similar to the Keep-away environment, this is because MADDPG converges to the policies fitting Scenario 2 while M3DDPG converges to the policies fitting Scenario 3. As we can see from the figure, PAMADDPG achieves slightly less scores than MADDPG and M3DDPG on Scenarios 2 and 3 respectively. This is because the Predator-prey environment is very competitive and the policy predictors in PAMADDPG take time to form correct predictions. In the Cooperative navigation environment, our PAMADDPG outperforms MADDPG and M3DDPG for all the scenarios. Again, M3DDPG has the worst performance because this is a fully cooperative environment.

Figure 4 shows the average reward of different approaches on the Cooperative navigation environment during the training process. As we can see from the figure, our PAMADDPG algorithm converges to better reward than all the other methods. As expected, the reward of DDPG decreases after 80,000 episodes due to non-stationarity in multi-agent RL. As shown in the figure, the reward of MADDPG fluctuates about 60,000 episodes while the reward of PAMADDPG becomes stable after convergence.

6   Conclusion

In this paper, we addressed the non-stationarity problem in multi-agent RL and proposed the PAMADDPG algorithm. We model the non-stationarity in the environment as a finite set of scenarios. At training time, each agent learns multiple policies, one for each scenario, and trains a policy predictor that can be used to predict the best policy during execution. With the multiple policies and policy predictor, each agent is able to adapt its policy and choose the best one for the current scenario. We tested our algorithm on three common benchmark environments and showed that PAMADDPG outperforms MADDPG and M3DDPG in all the tested environment. In the future, we plan to conduct research on learning the scenarios directly from the environment.

References

1. Al-Shedivat, M., Bansal, T., Burda, Y., Sutskever, I., Mordatch, I., Abbeel, P.: Continuous adaptation via meta-learning in nonstationary and competitive environments. arXiv preprint arXiv:1710.03641 (2017)
2. Bansal, T., Pachocki, J., Sidor, S., Sutskever, I., Mordatch, I.: Emergent complexity via multi-agent competition. arXiv preprint arXiv:1710.03748 (2017)
3. Finn, C., Abbeel, P., Levine, S.: Model-agnostic meta-learning for fast adaptation of deep networks. In: Proceedings of the 34th International Conference on Machine Learning, pp. 1126–1135 (2017)
4. Foerster, J., Assael, I.A., de Freitas, N., Whiteson, S.: Learning to communicate with deep multi-agent reinforcement learning. In: Proceedings of the Advances in Neural Information Processing Systems, pp. 2137–2145 (2016)
5. Foerster, J., Chen, R.Y., Al-Shedivat, M., Whiteson, S., Abbeel, P., Mordatch, I.: Learning with opponent-learning awareness. In: Proceedings of the 17th International Conference on Autonomous Agents and MultiAgent Systems, pp. 122–130 (2018)
6. Foerster, J., et al.: Stabilising experience replay for deep multi-agent reinforcement learning. In: Proceedings of the 34th International Conference on Machine Learning, pp. 1146–1155 (2017)
7. Foerster, J.N., Assael, Y.M., de Freitas, N., Whiteson, S.: Learning to communicate to solve riddles with deep distributed recurrent q-networks. arXiv preprint arXiv:1602.02672 (2016)
8. Foerster, J.N., Farquhar, G., Afouras, T., Nardelli, N., Whiteson, S.: Counterfactual multi-agent policy gradients. In: Proceedings of the 32nd AAAI Conference on Artificial Intelligence (2018)
9. He, H., Boyd-Graber, J., Kwok, K., Daumé III, H.: Opponent modeling in deep reinforcement learning. In: Proceedings of the International Conference on Machine Learning, pp. 1804–1813 (2016)
10. Hernandez-Leal, P., Kaisers, M., Baarslag, T., de Cote, E.M.: A survey of learning in multiagent environments: dealing with non-stationarity. arXiv preprint arXiv:1707.09183 (2017)
11. Lazaridou, A., Peysakhovich, A., Baroni, M.: Multi-agent cooperation and the emergence of (natural) language. arXiv preprint arXiv:1612.07182 (2016)
12. Levine, S., Finn, C., Darrell, T., Abbeel, P.: End-to-end training of deep visuomotor policies. J. Mach. Learn. Res. 17(1), 1334–1373 (2016)

13. Li, S., Wu, Y., Cui, X., Dong, H., Fang, F., Russell, S.: Robust multi-agent rein-
    forcement learning via minimax deep deterministic policy gradient. In: Proceedings
    of the AAAI Conference on Artificial Intelligence (2019)
14. Lillicrap, T.P., et al.: Continuous control with deep reinforcement learning. arXiv
    preprint arXiv:1509.02971 (2015)
15. Littman, M.L.: Markov games as a framework for multi-agent reinforcement learn-
    ing. In: Proceedings of the 11th International Conference on Machine Learning,
    pp. 157–163 (1994)
16. Long, P., Fanl, T., Liao, X., Liu, W., Zhang, H., Pan, J.: Towards optimally decen-
    tralized multi-robot collision avoidance via deep reinforcement learning. In: Pro-
    ceedings of the 2018 IEEE International Conference on Robotics and Automation,
    pp. 6252–6259 (2018)
17. Lowe, R., Wu, Y., Tamar, A., Harb, J., Abbeel, O.P., Mordatch, I.: Multi-agent
    actor-critic for mixed cooperative-competitive environments. In: Proceedings of the
    Advances in Neural Information Processing Systems, pp. 6379–6390 (2017)
18. Ma, J., Wu, F.: Feudal multi-agent deep reinforcement learning for traffic sig-
    nal control. In: Proceedings of the 19th International Conference on Autonomous
    Agents and Multiagent Systems (AAMAS), Auckland, New Zealand, pp. 816–824,
    May 2020
19. Mnih, V., et al.: Human-level control through deep reinforcement learning. Nature
    518(7540), 529 (2015)
20. Papoudakis, G., Christianos, F., Rahman, A., Albrecht, S.V.: Dealing with
    non-stationarity in multi-agent deep reinforcement learning. arXiv preprint
    arXiv:1906.04737 (2019)
21. Raileanu, R., Denton, E., Szlam, A., Fergus, R.: Modeling others using oneself in
    multi-agent reinforcement learning. arXiv preprint arXiv:1802.09640 (2018)
22. Silver, D., et al.: Mastering the game of go with deep neural networks and tree
    search. Nature **529**(7587), 484 (2016)
23. Silver, D., et al.: Mastering chess and shogi by self-play with a general reinforcement
    learning algorithm. arXiv preprint arXiv:1712.01815 (2017)
24. Silver, D., Lever, G., Heess, N., Degris, T., Wierstra, D., Riedmiller, M.: Determin-
    istic policy gradient algorithms. In: Proceeding of the 31st International Conference
    on Machine Learning, pp. 387–395 (2014)
25. Singh, A., Jain, T., Sukhbaatar, S.: Learning when to communicate at scale in
    multiagent cooperative and competitive tasks. arXiv preprint arXiv:1812.09755
    (2018)
26. Sukhbaatar, S., Fergus, R., et al.: Learning multiagent communication with back-
    propagation. In: Proceedings of the Advances in Neural Information Processing
    Systems, pp. 2244–2252 (2016)
27. Wu, C., Kreidieh, A., Parvate, K., Vinitsky, E., Bayen, A.M.: Flow: architecture
    and benchmarking for reinforcement learning in traffic control. arXiv preprint
    arXiv:1710.05465 (2017)

Multi-agent Planning with High-Level Human Guidance

Feng Wu[1]([✉])[iD], Shlomo Zilberstein[2], and Nicholas R. Jennings[3]

[1] School of Computer Science and Technology, University of Science and Technology of China, Hefei, China
wufeng02@ustc.edu.cn
[2] College of Information and Computer Sciences, University of Massachusetts Amherst, Amherst, USA
shlomo@cs.umass.edu
[3] Department of Computing, Imperial College London, London, UK
n.jennings@imperial.ac.uk

Abstract. Planning and coordination of multiple agents in the presence of uncertainty and noisy sensors is extremely hard. A human operator who observes a multi-agent team can provide valuable guidance to the team based on her superior ability to interpret observations and assess the overall situation. We propose an extension of decentralized POMDPs that allows such human guidance to be factored into the planning and execution processes. Human guidance in our framework consists of intuitive high-level commands that the agents must translate into a suitable joint plan that is sensitive to what they know from local observations. The result is a framework that allows multi-agent systems to benefit from the complex strategic thinking of a human supervising them. We evaluate this approach on several common benchmark problems and show that it can lead to dramatic improvement in performance.

Keywords: Multi-agent planning · Decentralized POMDP · Human guidance

1 Introduction

Planning under uncertainty for multi-agent systems is an important and growing area of AI. A common model used to handle such team planning problems is the *Decentralized Partially Observable Markov Decision Process* (DEC-POMDP) [4]. While optimal and approximate algorithms have been developed for DEC-POMDPs [15,21,23–25], they assume that the agents' plans remain fixed while they are being executed. Specifically, when a plan computed by these

This work was supported in part by the National Key R&D Program of China (Grant No. 2017YFB1002204), the National Natural Science Foundation of China (Grant No. U1613216, Grant No. 61603368), and the Guangdong Province Science and Technology Plan (Grant No. 2017B010110011).

T. Uchiya et al. (Eds.): PRIMA 2020, LNAI 12568, pp. 182–198, 2021.
https://doi.org/10.1007/978-3-030-69322-0_12

solvers is executed by the agents, it cannot be changed or modified by human operator who may supervise the agents' activities. In real-world problems, this lack of responsiveness and flexibility may increase the likelihood of failure or that the agents damage their workspace or injure people around.

The multi-agent systems community has long been exploring ways to allow agents to get help from humans using various forms of *adjustable autonomy* [5,8,10,14,19]. Human help could come in different forms such as teleoperation [9] or advice in the form of goal bias [6]. Tools to facilitate human supervision of robots have been developed. Examples include a single human operator supervising a team of robots that can operate with different levels of autonomy [3], or robots that operate in hazardous environments under human supervision, requiring teleoperation in difficult situations [11]. However, none of these methods explores these questions with respect to the DEC-POMDP model, with the added challenge that several agents must coordinate based on their partial local information.

In this paper, we focus on a specific setting of DEC-POMDPs in which agents are guided by *runtime high-level commands* from their human operator who supervises the agents' activities. There are several advantages to using high-level commands for guiding agents compared with teleoperation. First, high-level commands are more intuitive and require a lower learning curve for operators. For example, the high-level command "returning home" is much easier for humans to understand and use than the detailed procedure of teleoperating a mobile robot back to its initial location. Second, with high-level commands, operators can focus on the strategic level of thinking while agents take care of the massive low-level sensing and control work (e.g., perception, manipulation, and navigation). By doing so, humans and agents can contribute to the tasks best suited for them. Third, communication between humans and agents usually involves delays and humans need some lead time to respond. Therefore, it is very challenging to teleoperate a system when instant response by the robots to the dynamically changing environment is required, or when there are fewer operators than agents. In contrast, high-level commands such as "searching a building", "cleaning a house", or "pushing a box together", require lower rate of synchronization than teleoperation and can be used to guide the team.

However, planning with high-level human commands for DEC-POMDPs also introduces several challenges. To start, we must allow operators to define useful commands that they will use in the specific domain. The meaning of each command must be encoded in the model so that the solver can interpret it and compute plans for the agents. Furthermore, plans must be represented so that the agents can select actions based on not only their local information but also the command from the operator. In our settings, computing those plans is challenging because we do not know how the operator will command the agents when running the plan. During execution time, similar to teleoperation, we must handle communication delays (although it is less demanding than teleoperation) and help the operators avoid mistakes or unexpected operations.

To this end, we extend the standard finite-horizon DEC-POMDP model and propose HL-DEC-POMDPs, which include humans in the loop of the agents' decision making process. More specifically, we provide a new model that allows operators to define a set of high-level commands. Each command has a specific context that can be easily understood by human operators. These commands are designed for situations where the operator can provide useful guidance. We present planning algorithms for this new model to compute plans conditioned on both the local information of an agent and the command initiated by the operator. In the execution phase, the operator interacts with the agents with the high-level command similar to teleoperation: the operator observing the agents' activities initiates commands and the agents follow a plan based on the command from the operator. In fact, teleoperation can be viewed as a special case of our approach where each low-level control operation is mapping to a high-level command. We also provide a mechanism for handling delays and an algorithm to suggest feasible commands to the operator. This is helpful for the operator to select the best command and avoid mistakes. This is the first work to bring humans in the loop of multi-agent planning under the framework of DEC-POMDPs. We contribute a novel model to consider human supervision of autonomous agents and an efficient algorithm to compute human-in-the-loop plans.

2   Related Work

In terms of guiding agents with high-level commands, our work is similar to the coaching system in RoboCup soccer simulation where a coach who gets an overview of the whole game sends commands to the players of its own team. However, the coach is also a software agent (there is no human in the loop) and its decision is mainly on recognizing and selecting the opponent model [12,17]. For planning with human guidance, MAPGEN [1], the planning system for Mars rover missions, allows operators to define constraints and rules for a plan, which are subsequently enforced by automated planners to produce the plan. However, this approach is only for single-agent problems and does not consider the uncertainty in the environment. It is not clear how this can be done for DEC-POMDPs.

For human-robot interaction, there has also been research on mobile robots that can proactively seek help from people in their environment to overcome their limitations [18,26]. Researchers have started to develop robots that can autonomously identify situations in which a human operator must perform a subtask [22] and design suitable interaction mechanisms for the collaboration [26].

3   The HL-DEC-POMDP Model

Our model is an extension of the standard DEC-POMDP. Before presenting our model, we first briefly review the DEC-POMDP model. Formally, a *Decentralized Partially Observable Markov Decision Process* (DEC-POMDP) is defined as a tuple $\langle I, S, \{A_i\}, \{\Omega_i\}, P, O, R \rangle$, where:

- I is a set of n agents where $|I| = n$ and each agent has a unique ID number $i \in I$.
- S is a set of states and $b^0 \in \Delta(S)$ is the initial state distribution where $b^0(s)$ is the probability of $s \in S$.
- A_i is a set of actions for agent i. Here, we denote $\boldsymbol{a} = \langle a_1, a_2, \cdots, a_n \rangle$ a joint action where $a_i \in A_i$ and $\boldsymbol{A} = \times_{i \in I} A_i$ the set of joint actions where $\boldsymbol{a} \in \boldsymbol{A}$.
- Ω_i is a set of observations for agent i. Similarly, we denote $\boldsymbol{o} = \langle o_1, o_2, \cdots, o_n \rangle$ a joint observation where $o_i \in \Omega_i$ and $\boldsymbol{\Omega} = \times_{i \in I} \Omega_i$ the joint set where $\boldsymbol{o} \in \boldsymbol{\Omega}$.
- $P : S \times \boldsymbol{A} \times S \rightarrow [0, 1]$ is the Markovian transition function and $P(s'|s, \boldsymbol{a})$ denotes the probability distribution of the next state s' when agents take $\boldsymbol{a}$ in s.
- $O : S \times \boldsymbol{A} \times \boldsymbol{\Omega} \rightarrow [0, 1]$ is the observation function and $O(\boldsymbol{o}|s', \boldsymbol{a})$ denotes the probability distribution of observing $\boldsymbol{o}$ after taking $\boldsymbol{a}$ with outcome state s'.
- $R : S \times \boldsymbol{A} \rightarrow \Re$ is the reward function and $R(s, \boldsymbol{a})$ is the immediate reward of the team when all the agents take joint action $\boldsymbol{a}$ in state s.

Now, we turn to our model. A *Decentralized Partially Observable Markov Decision Process with Humans in the Loop* (HL-DEC-POMDP) is defined as a tuple $\mathcal{M} = \langle I, S, C, \{A_i\}, \{\Omega_i\}, P, O, R \rangle$, with the following additional component C and modification of the reward function R:

- C is a set of high-level commands for human operators. We assume that when a command $c \in C$ is initiated by the operator it can be received by all the agents.
- $R : S \times C \times \boldsymbol{A} \rightarrow \Re$ is the reward function and $R(s, c, \boldsymbol{a})$ is the immediate reward of the team when all the agents take $\boldsymbol{a}$ in state s with command c.

In the execution phase of HL-DEC-POMDPs, the operator can initiate a command $c \in C$ to the agents. Thus, each agent i can make its decision based on both its local observation o_i from the environment and the command c from the operator. Intuitively, HL-DEC-POMDP is at least as hard as the standard DEC-POMDP (i.e., NEXP-hard) since DEC-POMDP is a special case of our model with only one command (i.e., $|C| = 1$). In this model, the operator can observe the agents' activities and guide them with predefined commands $c \in C$.

To intuitively explain what the high-level commands are and how they work in HL-DEC-POMDPs, we use the cooperative box-pushing problem [20] as example. This is a common DEC-POMDP benchmark problem where two agents in a grid world must coordinate to independently push small boxes or cooperatively push the large box. In this problem, a possible set of commands for the operator could be $C = \{$ *"pushing a large box"*, *"pushing small boxes"*, *"automatic"*$\}$. Each command has a specific meaning, which is intuitive for people familiar with the problem. Moreover, they all focus on the high-level decisions that can be used straightforwardly by the operator to guide the agents. The design of commands depends on the requirements of the operator on her supervision tasks. For example, if the operator wants the agents to push the two small boxes separately, the command *"pushing small boxes"* can be split into two commands as *"pushing the left small box"* and *"pushing the right small box"*.

In our model, the meaning of each command $c \in C$ is specified in the reward function R. Given a command, we can generate a reward function to achieve the desirable behavior of the agents similar to building the reward model for standard DEC-POMDPs. For example, when $c = $ "pushing small boxes", R with c is defined so that only pushing small boxes has positive rewards. Planning with this reward function will output a plan that lets all the agents go for the small boxes. Similarly, if $c = $ "pushing a large box", only pushing a large box is rewarded in R. If the operator sets the command $c = $ "automatic", the agents will push boxes as the original box-pushing problem (i.e., the large box has higher reward than the small boxes). In this example, each command is defined for all the agents. Indeed, the command set can be augmented to include more complex commands so that each agent gets a specific instruction. For example, a command can be $c = $ "agent A pushing a small box and agent B, C pushing the large box". Similarly, the reward function R can be specified for this command.

Notice that the command initiated by operators does not affect the transition model of the states but only the reward received by the agents (i.e., the reward function R in the model). By so doing, we assume that the operator cannot directly interact with the environment using the commands. Instead, the operator can guide the agents with the commands to achieve expected behaviors of the agents. Typical scenarios of our setting include operators situated in a base station remotely supervising the agents in some workspace. It is worth pointing out that each command can be efficiently transferred to the agents with its index because C is predefined and known for all the agents.

In HL-DEC-POMDP, a local policy q_i for agent i is a conditional rule mapping from its observation-action history $h_i \in H_i$ and the command $c \in C$ to an action $a_i \in A_i$, i.e., $q_i : H_i \times C \to A_i$. A joint policy $\boldsymbol{q} = \langle q_1, q_2, \cdots, q_n \rangle$ is a collection of local policies, one for each agent. The goal of solving a HL-DEC-POMDP is to find a joint policy $\boldsymbol{q}^*$ for the agents that maximizes the expected value:

$$V(b^0, c^0, \boldsymbol{q}^*) = \mathbb{E}\left[\sum_{t=0}^{T-1} R^t \middle| b^0, c^0, \boldsymbol{q}^*\right] \tag{1}$$

where c^0 is the initial command initiated by the operator.

4   Solving HL-DEC-POMDPs

In the HL-DEC-POMDP model, we represent our policies by stochastic policy trees where the nodes and branches are parameterized by probability distributions. Specifically, a stochastic policy for agent i is defined recursively as: $q_i = \langle \pi_i, \lambda_i \rangle$, where:

- π_i is an action selection function that specifies a distribution over the actions. $\pi_i(a_i | q_i, c)$ denotes the probability of selecting action a_i in node $q_i \in Q_i$ with command c.
- λ_i is a node transition function that defines a distribution over the sub-trees. $\lambda_i(q_i' | q_i, o_i, c)$ denotes the probability of selecting node q_i' (a sub-tree with q_i' as its root) when o_i is observed and command c is given by the operator.

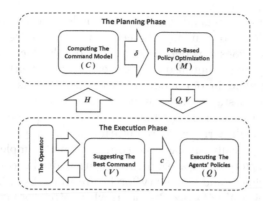

Fig. 1. Overview of our framework

Note that the action selection function is defined at the root node of q_i and the node transition function is defined for the branches of the root node where q'_i is a sub-policy of q_i after observing o_i with c. Here, c is the command for selecting the policy q'_i. Indeed, a (deterministic) policy tree is a special case of our stochastic policy. At each node q_i, the agent executes an action a_i sampled from $\pi_i(\cdot|q_i, c)$. Based on its observation o_i and the command c, it will transition to a new node q'_i sampled from the function $\lambda_i(\cdot|q_i, o_i, c)$.

Given a state s and a command c, the expected value of a joint policy $\boldsymbol{q}$ represented by our stochastic policy trees can be computed recursively by the Bellman equation:

$$
V^t(s, c, \boldsymbol{q}) = \sum_{\boldsymbol{a} \in A} \prod_{i \in I} \pi_i(a_i|q_i, c) \Bigg[R(s, c, \boldsymbol{a}) + \sum_{s' \in S} P(s'|s, \boldsymbol{a}) \sum_{o \in \Omega} O(\boldsymbol{o}|s', \boldsymbol{a})
$$
$$
\sum_{\boldsymbol{q}'} \prod_{i \in I} \lambda_i(q'_i|q_i, o_i, c) \sum_{c' \in C} \delta^t(c'|\cdot) \cdot V^{t+1}(s', c', \boldsymbol{q}') \Bigg] \tag{2}
$$

where $\delta^t(c'|\cdot)$ is the distribution of choosing command c'.

The basic framework of our approach is shown in Fig. 1. In the planning phase, we first generate a command model δ^t and then compute the policies and values. In the execution phase, we take the command input of the operator and compare it with the command computed by our algorithm. If they are different, we suggest our command to the operator and ask her to confirm or amend her choice. Next, her choice is sent to the agents who will execute the policies based on the command from the operator. The following sections will given more detail on our algorithms.

4.1   The Command Model

As shown in Eq. 2, the command model is a rule of selecting commands. However, commands in our approach are actually selected by the operator at runtime.

Thus, a model of how command decisions are made by the operator is needed for the planning phase so that our planner can optimize the agents' policies. Although human decisions may depend on many complex factors (not only their perspective of the problem but also their expertise and experience), we assume that the next command in our model is selected only based on the current command and the next state at a single point in time. Other inputs such as the history of the previous commands and indications of the operator's attentiveness are not used. Although a richer representation might improve the predictive quality, it will dramatically increase the computational complexity of learning and planning. Therefore, we leave an investigation of the correct balance of representational richness and simplicity for future work. Specifically, we define the command model as $\delta^t : C \times S \times C \to [0, 1]$ where $\delta^t(c'|c, s')$ is a probability of selecting command c' for the next step given the current command c and the next state s'. Here, we use probability distributions to model human decisions because whether a command is selected and its likelihood appears to be highly stochastic in our problems. Note that the command model is only used in the planning phase. The operator does not need to know the state to select her commands during execution time. There are several methods to specify δ^t, depending on the characteristic of the problem domain and the role of the operator.

A Fixed Command Model. In a *fixed command model* the command is assumed that any command issued by an operator will remain the same for the rest of the decision steps, resulting in the following simple command model:

$$\delta^t(c'|c, s') = \begin{cases} 1 \ c' = c \\ 0 \ c' \neq c \end{cases} \tag{3}$$

The policies computed with this command model allow the operator to switch among different reward models (i.e., objectives) during execution time. Once a command is selected by the operator, the agents will stick to that "mode" until a different command is issued. For example, in the cooperative box-pushing problem, if a command is set for the agents to push small boxes, they will repeatedly push small boxes until they are allowed to push the large box. If the policies for each reward model are independently computed, it is nontrivial for the agents to switch to other policies in the execution phase given the partial observability of the agents in DEC-POMDPs. Therefore, our approach is more sophisticated given that our policies straightforwardly allow the agents to transition to other "mode" without re-coordination.

A Learned Command Model. Another option is to learn the command model from a log of data collected in previous trial executions. The data log records the joint action-observation history of the agents, the obtained rewards, and the commands initiated by the operators: $H = (c^0, a^0, r^0, o^1, c^1, a^1, r^1, o^2, \cdots, c^{T-1}, a^{T-1}, r^{T-1})$. Given this, the operators do offline analysis of the data and evaluate the agents' performance. In this process, additional rewards could be specified by the operators, which may include some of the operators' evaluation on the agents' behaviors that is not captured by the model. For example, if a robot injured people in the environment when doing a task, a penalty should be given to it by the operators. At the end of the analysis, the rewards in H are replaced by mixtures of the original rewards and the rewards specified by the operators.

Given the data evaluated by the operators, we can learn a new command model δ^t that maximizes the expected value. Because the model and joint policies $\boldsymbol{q}$ are known for the previous executions, the parameters of δ^t can be optimized by a gradient ascent method similar to [16] using the agents' history data. Specifically, Eq. 1 can be rewritten with the histories in H as follow:

$$V(b^0, c^0, \boldsymbol{q}) = \sum_{t=0}^{T-1} \sum_{h^t \in H^t} Pr(h^t|b^0, c^0, \boldsymbol{q}) r^t(h^t) \tag{4}$$

where $H^t {\subseteq} H$ is the histories up to time t, $r^t(h^t)$ is the reward given by the end of h^t, and $Pr(h^t|b^0, c^0, \boldsymbol{q})$ is the probability for h^t that can be computed given the model and policies. Then, we can calculate the derivative of V for each δ^t and do a gradient ascent on V by making updates $\Delta\delta^t = \beta\partial V(b^0, c^0, \boldsymbol{q})/\partial\delta^t$ with step size β.

4.2   Point-Based Policy Optimization

As aforementioned, our HL-DEC-POMDP model is as hard as the DEC-POMDP (i.e., NEXP-hard). Therefore, optimal algorithms are mostly of theoretical significance. To date, state-of-the-art optimal approaches can only solve DEC-POMDP benchmark problems with very short horizons [7,15]. To solve large problems, one of the popular techniques in the DEC-POMDP literature is using Memory-Bounded DP (MBDP) [21]—a variation of the DP algorithm. At each iteration, it first backups the policies of the previous iteration as the standard DP. Then it generates a set of belief points and only retains the polices that have the highest value on those points for the next iteration. By doing so, the number of possible policies at each iteration does not blow up with the horizon. Several successors of MBDP have improved significantly the performance of the approach, particularly the point-based DP technique [13], which we build on to compute policies for our extended problem representation.

The main process is outlined in Algorithm 1. Similar to DP, the policy is optimized backwards from the last step to the first one. At each iteration (Lines 1–8), we first sample N pairs of (b, d) from the first step down to the current step (Line 5) where $b \in \Delta(S)$ is a probability distribution over the state space S and $d \in \Delta(C)$ is a probability distribution over the command set C. Then, we compute a joint policy for each sampled (b, d) pair (Line 6). Sampling can be performed efficiently by running simulations on heuristic policies. The heuristic policy can be either the policy obtained by solving the underlying MDP or just a random policy where agent i's action is uniformly selected from its action set

---

Algorithm 1: Point-Based DP for HL-DEC-POMDPs

Input: the HL-DEC-POMDP model $\mathcal{M}$.
Output: the best joint policy $\boldsymbol{Q}^0$.
for $t = T - 1$ **to** 0 **do**
    $Q^t \leftarrow \emptyset$
    for $k = 1$ **to** N **do**
        $(b, d) \leftarrow$ sample a joint belief state b and a command distribution d up
           to the current step t
        `// Equation 5`
        $q \leftarrow$ compute the best policy with (b, d)
        $Q^t \leftarrow Q^t \cup \{q\}$
    `// Equation 6`
    $V^t \leftarrow$ evaluate $\boldsymbol{Q}^t$ for $\forall s \in S, c \in C, \boldsymbol{q} \in \boldsymbol{Q}^t$
return $\boldsymbol{Q}^0$

A_i. In the underlying MDP, the command is treated as a state variable. Hence the state space of the underlying MDP is $\mathbb{S} = S \times C$ and its transition function is $\mathbb{P}(s', c'|s, c, \boldsymbol{a}) = \delta^t(c'|c, s')P(s'|s, \boldsymbol{a})$. This is a standard MDP that can be solved by dynamic programming. A simple technique to improve sampling efficiency is to use a *portfolio* of different heuristics [21].

In each simulation of the t-th DP iteration, we first select an initial command c and draw a state $s \sim b^0(\cdot)$ from the initial state distribution. Next, we compute a joint action $\boldsymbol{a}$ using the heuristic. Then, we sample the next state $s' \sim P(\cdot|s, \boldsymbol{a})$ based on the transition function and draw the next command $c' \sim \delta^t(\cdot|c, s')$ from the command model. This process continues with the state $s \leftarrow s'$ and the command $c \leftarrow c'$ until the sampling horizon is reached. Here, for the t-th DP iteration, the sampling horizon is $(T-t-1)$. In the last step of the simulation, the state s and command c are recorded with $b(s) \leftarrow b(s)+1$ and $d(c) \leftarrow d(c)+1$. We repeat the simulation K times and produce the distributions (b, d) by averaging the samples: $b(s) \leftarrow b(s)/K$ and $d(c) \leftarrow d(c)/K$. According to the central limit theorem, the averaged values (b, d) will converge to the true distributions of states and commands as long as K is sufficiently large.

Give each sampled pair (b, d), the best joint policy $\boldsymbol{q}$ can be computed by solving the following optimization problem:

$$\max_{\pi_i, \lambda_i} \sum_{s \in S} b(s) \sum_{c \in C} d(c) \sum_{\boldsymbol{a} \in A} \prod_{i \in I} \pi_i(a_i|q_i, c) \Big[R(s, c, \boldsymbol{a}) + \sum_{s' \in S} P(s'|s, \boldsymbol{a})$$
$$\sum_{o \in \Omega} O(\boldsymbol{o}|s', \boldsymbol{a}) \sum_{\boldsymbol{q}'} \prod_{i \in I} \lambda_i(q_i'|q_i, o_i, c) \sum_{c' \in C} \delta^t(c'|c, s') V^{t+1}(s', c', \boldsymbol{q}') \Big]$$
$$\text{s.t.} \quad \forall i, c, a_i, \; \pi_i(a_i|q_i, c) \geq 0, \forall i, c, \sum_{a_i \in A_i} \pi_i(a_i|q_i, c) = 1$$
$$\forall i, c, o_i, q_i', \; \lambda_i(q_i'|q_i, o_i, c) \geq 0, \forall i, c, o_i, \sum_{q_i' \in Q_i'} \lambda_i(q_i'|q_i, o_i, c) = 1$$
$$(5)$$

where the variables π_i and λ_i are the parameters of agent i's policy and the objective is to maximizes the expected value $V^t(b, d, \boldsymbol{q}) = \sum_{s \in S} b(s) \sum_{c \in C} d(c) V^t(s, c, \boldsymbol{q})$. The constraints in Eq. 5 guarantee that the opti-

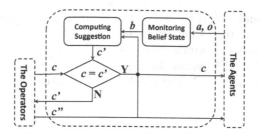

Fig. 2. The command suggestion system

mized policy parameters π_i and λ_i are probability distributions (i.e., all distributions are non-negative and sum to 1).

After a set of policies are generated, we evaluate each joint policy $q \in Q^t$. Specifically, we compute the expected values as defined in Eq. 2 for every state $s \in S$ and command $c \in C$ (Line 8) as follow:

$$V^t(s, c, q) = \sum_{a \in A} \prod_{i \in I} \pi_i(a_i|q_i, c) \left[R(s, c, a) + \sum_{s' \in S} P(s'|s, a) \sum_{o \in \Omega} O(o|s', a) \right.$$
$$\left. \sum_{q'} \prod_{i \in I} \lambda_i(q_i'|q_i, o_i, c) \sum_{c' \in C} \delta^t(c'|c, s') V^{t+1}(s', c', q') \right] \tag{6}$$

where V^{t+1} is the value obtained in the previous iteration.

All the above computations assume that the operator can make decisions and initiate commands at the same rate as the agents (i.e., at each step, the operator initiates a command and then each agent selects an action). This might be unrealistic in practice for two reasons: First, the decision cycle of autonomous agents could be much faster. For example, a mobile robot can move very quickly and response to the environment in a fraction of a second. However, depending on the problem, the operator usually takes a few seconds or even minutes to response (she may need to scan the environment and understand the current situation and then issues a command by pressing a button). Second, the communication between operators and agents could introduce a delay. When a operator is situated at a distant base station, it may take some time for the state information to be transferred and displayed on the operator's screen. Similarly, it may also take time for the operator's command to be transferred to the agents. Depending on the distance between the operator and agents, the communication delay may range from a few seconds to several hours (e.g., when communicating with space exploration rovers). Thus, it is more realistic to assume that the operator's decisions are made at a lower rate.

Specifically, we assume that the operator's decision is made at every interval of τ steps (i.e., $0, \tau, 2\tau, 3\tau, \cdots$) up to the horizon T. Within an interval, the command is initiated by the operator at the beginning and remains fixed until the end. To compute the policies, our sampling algorithm must be adapted to only draw a new command $c' \sim \delta^t(\cdot|c, s')$ at the beginning of an interval. Similarly, in Eqs. 5 and 6, if the time step t is at the beginning of an interval, we use the same command model to optimize and evaluate the policies. Otherwise, we use the fixed command model defined by Eq. 3 to keep the command fixed within the interval. Indeed, if $\tau = T$, the fixed model is actually used for the whole planning process.

4.3   Suggesting Commands to the Operators

In the execution phase, the operator guides the agents by selecting commands. We assume she takes the full responsibility for every command initiated by her. Nevertheless, it will be useful if our system can verify her choice and give her suggestions when necessary. The operator may make mistakes, especially when she becomes distracted or tired after long shift. She may also neglect some key factors of the current situation that may affect her decision (e.g., low battery level of some robots). Therefore, it will be helpful if our system can remind her or provide an alternative choice that might be better than the operator's original command. Given the suggestion computed by our system, the operator can evaluate the suggested command and her original command and make the final decision.

Figure 2 illustrates our suggestion mechanism for the operator. As we can see, the operator first makes her decision and initiate command c. Then, our system computes a command c' based on its current information about the agents b. If this command c' is different from the operator's choice c, our system will present its suggestion c' to the operator and ask her to confirm or amend her choice. The operator can insist on her original command if she feels confident about it or selects another command. Her final decision c'' is sent to the agents. We deliberately postpone our suggestions to the operator so that her decisions are not biased by the suggestions. Our system does not intend to replace the operator and make decisions for her. Instead, it is designed to provide a chance for her to correct mistakes (if any) or improve her decision (if possible). Notice that the suggestions are computed by a software agent running on the operator's system (e.g., computers at her base station) where an overview of the whole agent team is available as for the operator.

To give suggestions, we compute in the planning phase the values of selecting every command $c' \in C$ as follows:

$$V^t(s, c, \boldsymbol{q}; c') = \sum_{\boldsymbol{a} \in \boldsymbol{A}} \prod_{i \in I} \pi_i(a_i|q_i, c) \left[R(s, c, \boldsymbol{a}) + \sum_{s' \in S} P(s'|s, \boldsymbol{a}) \sum_{o \in \Omega} O(o|s', \boldsymbol{a}) \right.$$
$$\left. \sum_{\boldsymbol{q}'} \prod_{i \in I} \lambda_i(q_i'|q_i, o_i, c) V^{t+1}(s', c', \boldsymbol{q}') \right]$$
(7)

where V^{t+1} is the expected value computed by Eq. 6 in Algorithm 1. Then, in the execution phase, our system computes the best next command c' (from the system's perspective) that maximizes this value as:

$$c' = \arg\max_{c \in C} \sum_{s \in S} b^t(s) V^t(s, c^t, \boldsymbol{q}; c) \tag{8}$$

This command c' will be compared with the operator's original choice c. If they are different, c' will be suggested to the operator. We can also present to the operator the difference in value between these two commands for reference:

$$D(c||c') = \sum_{s \in S} b^t(s)[V^t(s, c^t, \boldsymbol{q}; c') - V^t(s, c^t, \boldsymbol{q}; c)] \tag{9}$$

Notice that both Eqs. 8 and 9 require knowledge of the current joint belief state $b^t(s)$. As shown in Fig. 2, this joint belief state is monitored and updated in our suggestion system during execution time. Here, the joint belief state is computed recursively by the Bayesian rule:

$$b^{t+1}(s') = \alpha \, O(o^{t+1}|s', \boldsymbol{a}^t) \sum_{s \in S} b^t(s) P(s'|s, \boldsymbol{a}^t) \tag{10}$$

where b^t is the previous belief state (b^0 is the initial state distribution), o^{t+1} is the agents' latest joint observation, $\boldsymbol{a}^t$ is a joint action taken by the agents at the previous step, and $\alpha = 1/\sum_{s' \in S} b^{t+1}(s')$ is the normalization factor. Once the up-to-date information is transferred back from the agents to the operator, the joint belief state can be updated by Eq. 10. Indeed, our suggestion system is a POMDP agent that takes the same input as the operator (i.e., the agents' $\boldsymbol{a}$ and $\boldsymbol{o}$), maintains a belief b^t over the current state, and makes suggestions to the operator based on the expected value V^t of the agents' policies.

5 Experiments

We implemented our algorithm and tested it on two common benchmark problems previously used for DEC-POMDPs: Meeting in a 3×3 Grid [2] and Cooperative Box-Pushing [20]. For each problem, we first designed a set of high-level commands C and the corresponding reward function R as in our HL-DEC-POMDP model. Then, we ran our planning algorithm to compute policies for the agents. During execution time, we let a person (the operator) guide the agents with the commands in C while the agents execute the computed policies accordingly. The suggestions for the operator are computed during the process.

We invited 30 people to participate in our tests as operators. Before the tests, they were given tutorials on the domains, what they should do for each domain, and how they can command the simulated robots using our interface. Then, we divided them into two groups. The first 5 people were asked to guide the agents given the policies computed using the fixed command model. We recorded their operations and learned a new command model from the logged data. After that, we asked the second group to command the agents with the

Table 1. Results for two benchmark problems

τ	Learned	Fixed	MBDP	Learned	Fixed	MBDP
	Meeting in a 3×3 grid ($T=20$)			Cooperative box-pushing ($T=20$)		
1	189.69, 1.87	133.70, 1.32	24.95, 0.23	45.10, 0.7%	43.48, 0.9%	−11.34, 87.1%
3	175.28, 1.73	114.88, 1.13	–	26.31, 4.2%	18.17, 4.9%	–
7	154.34, 1.51	94.12, 0.92	–	11.82, 35.5%	9.75, 42.7%	–

policies computed using the learned model. Each person guided the agents with different intervals ($\tau = 1$, 3, 7) and repeated each individual test 10 times. The averaged performance of the two groups was reported for each test. To show how agents benefit from high-level human guidance, we also present the results of the flat MBDP policies on our domains where no human decisions are involved.

The results were summarized in Table 1. For the first problem, the first value in a cell is the overall reward and the second value shows how many times on average the robots met at the highly rewarded corners in a test. For the second problem, the first value is also the overall reward while the second value shows the percentage of the total tests when the animal got injured by the robots. From the table, we can see that in both domains human guidance can produce dramatic improvements in performance over the flat MBDP policies and the learned command model does produce significant additional performance gains. For example, in the second domain, the animals were very likely to be injured without human guidance (87.1%) while the chance with our high-level commands reduced to less than 1%. Note that the robots' actions in our first domain are very stochastic (with only the success rate of 0.6). Our values are also significantly better than the MBDP policies in this domain. Without human guidance, we observed that the robots met equally at one of the 4 corners. Overall, our results confirmed the advantage of human guidance in agents' plans.

Additionally, communication delays (τ) were well handled by our high-level commands. With $\tau = 7$, the operators only allowed to command the agents 2 times within the total 20 steps. However, our values with guidance are still significantly better than the results without guidance. In contrast, we observed that tele-operation with the same delays made no difference to the results due to the problem uncertainty. In the tests, we observed that our suggested mechanisms were useful to the operators especially when the problem was reset (once agents meet at a corner in the first problem or a box is pushed to the goal location in the second). Most of the operators were not aware of the change until they were asked to confirm their commands. We also observed that the commands were more frequently modified after the participants repeated their test 6 to 7 times and they did become more likely to make mistakes when felt tired.

6   Conclusions

We introduce the HL-DEC-POMDP model—a novel extension of DEC-POMDPs to incorporate high-level human guidance in the agents' plans. Specifically, our model allows the operators of the agents to define a set of high-level commands that are intuitive to them and useful for their daily supervision. We also presented algorithms that can compute the plans for the operators to guide the agents with those commands during execution time. This enables the agents to take advantage of the operators' superior situation awareness. This is nontrivial because the agents' policies do not only depend on the operators' commands but also on their local information and how this will affect the decision of the other agents. Moreover, our model is more robust to communication delays than simple teleoperation because commands need only provide high-level guidance. In our planning algorithms, the quality of agents' plans can be improved by learning from the operators' experience. In our experiments, whenever the operators have information or knowledge that is not captured in the agents' plans, significant improvements in agents' performance have been observed with high-level human guidance. In the future, we plan to test our model and algorithm on larger domains where high-level human guidance could play a crucial role.

A   The Benchmark Problems

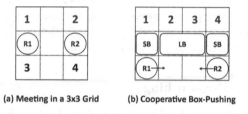

(a) Meeting in a 3x3 Grid   (b) Cooperative Box-Pushing

Fig. 3. The benchmark problems

A.1   Meeting in a 3 × 3 Grid

In this problem, as shown in Fig. 3(a), two robots R1 and R2 situated in a 3×3 grid try to stay in the same cell together as fast as possible. There are 81 states in total since each robot can be in any of the 9 cells. They can move *up, down, left, right,* or *stay* so each robot has 5 actions. Their moving actions (i.e., the actions except *stay*) are stochastic. With probability 0.6, they can move in the desired direction. With probability 0.1, they may move in another direction or just stay in the same cell. There are 9 observations per robot. Each robot can observe if it is near one of the corners or walls. The robots may meet at any of the 4 corners. Once they meet there, a reward of 1 is received by the agents. To make the problem more challenging, the agents are reset to their initial locations when they meet at the corners.

We design the high-level commands so that the robots are asked to meet at a specific corner. In more detail, the command set for this problem is $C =$

$\{c_0, c_1, c_2, c_3, c_4\}$ where c_0 allows the agents to meet at any corner and $c_i (i \neq 0)$ is the command for the robots to meeting in the corner labeled with i in Fig. 3(a). Depending on what we want to achieve in the problem, the commands can be more general (e.g., meeting at any of the top corners) or specific (e.g., meeting at the top-left corner without going through the center). The reward function is implemented so that they are rewarded only when they meet at the specific corner (for c_0, the original reward function is used). For example, $R(c_1, \cdot, \cdot) = 1$ only when they meet at the top-left corner and 0 otherwise.

During execution time, we simulate a random event to determine whether meeting at one of the corners has a much higher reward (i.e., 100) and which corner. It is a *finite state machine* (FSM) with 5 states where state 0 means there is no highly rewarded corner and state i ($1 \leq i \leq 4$) means the corner labeled with i has the highest reward. The transition function of this FSM is predetermined and fixed for all the tests, but it is not captured by the model and not known during planning time. Therefore, they are not considered in the agents' policies. The event can only be observed by the operator at runtime. This kind of a stochastic event can be used to simulate a disaster response scenario, where a group of robots with pre-computed plans are sent to search and rescue victims at several locations (i.e., the corners). For each location, the robots must cooperate and work together (i.e., meeting at the corner). As more information (e.g., messages reported by the people nearby) is collected at the base station, one of the locations may becomes more likely to have victims. Thus, the operators should guide the robots to search that location and rescue the victims there.

A.2   Cooperative Box-Pushing

In this problem, as shown in Fig. 3(b), there are two robots R1 and R2 in a 3×3 grid trying to push the large box (LB) together or independently push the small boxes (SB). Each robot can *turn left, turn right, move forward,* or *stay* so there are 5 actions per robot. For each action, with probability 0.9, they can turn to the desired direction or move forward and with probability 0.1 they just stay in the same position and orientation. Each robot has 5 observations to identify the object in front, which can be either *an empty field, a wall, the other robot, a small box,* or *the large box.* For each robot, executing an action has a cost of 0.1 for energy consumption. If a robot bumps into a wall, the other robot, or a box without pushing it, it gets a penalty of 5. The standard reward function is designed to encourage cooperation. Specifically, the reward for cooperatively pushing the large box is 100, while the reward of pushing a small box is just 10. Each run includes 100 steps. Once a box is pushed to its goal location, the robots are reset to an initial state.

The high-level commands $C = \{c_0, c_1, c_2, c_3\}$ are designed as follow: (c_0) the robots should push any box; (c_1) the robots should only push the small box on the left side; (c_2) the robots should only push the small box on the right side; (c_3) the robots should only push the large box in the middle. Specifying the corresponding reward function is straightforward. For c_0, we use the original reward function. For c_i ($1 \leq i \leq 3$), we reward the agents ($+100$) for pushing the right box and penalize them for pushing other boxes (-100).

Similar to the previous domain, we also simulate a random event representing a trapped animal in one of the cells labeled with numbers in Fig. 3(b). The animal is hidden behind a box so the robots cannot see it with their cameras. However, if the robots push a box while an animal is on the other side of that box, it will get injured and the robots get a high penalty of 100. The random event is modeled by a FSM with 5 states where state 0 represents no animal and state i ($1 \leq i \leq 4$) means an animal is trapped in the cell labeled i. If the animal gets injured, the FSM transitions to another state based on a predefined transition function. Again, this event is neither captured by the agents' model nor their policies. The animal can only be observed by the operators during execution time with an additional camera attached behind the boxes. This setting allows us to simulate a scenario where the operators supervise robots performing risk-sensitive tasks. For example, robots doing construction work on a crowded street.

References

1. Ai-Chang, M., et al.: MAPGEN: mixed-initiative planning and scheduling for the mars exploration rover mission. IEEE Intell. Syst. 19(1), 8–12 (2004)
2. Amato, C., Dibangoye, J.S., Zilberstein, S.: Incremental policy generation for finite-horizon DEC-POMDPs. In: Proceedings of the 19th International Conference on Automated Planning and Scheduling, pp. 2–9 (2009)
3. Bechar, A., Edan, Y.: Human-robot collaboration for improved target recognition of agricultural robots. Ind. Robot Int. J. 30(5), 432–436 (2003)
4. Bernstein, D.S., Givan, R., Immerman, N., Zilberstein, S.: The complexity of decentralized control of Markov decision processes. Math. Oper. Res. 27(4), 819–840 (2002)
5. Bradshaw, J.M., et al.: Kaa: policy-based explorations of a richer model for adjustable autonomy. In: Proceedings of the 4th International Conference on Autonomous Agents and Multiagent Systems, pp. 214–221 (2005)
6. Côté, N., Canu, A., Bouzid, M., Mouaddib, A.I.: Humans-robots sliding collaboration control in complex environments with adjustable autonomy. In: Proceedings of Intelligent Agent Technology (2013)
7. Dibangoye, J.S., Amato, C., Buffet, O., Charpillet, F.: Optimally solving Dec-POMDPs as continuous-state MDPs. In: Proceedings of the Twenty-Third International Joint Conference on Artificial Intelligence (2013)
8. Dorais, G., Bonasso, R.P., Kortenkamp, D., Pell, B., Schreckenghost, D.: Adjustable autonomy for human-centered autonomous systems. In: IJCAI Workshop on Adjustable Autonomy Systems, pp. 16–35 (1999)
9. Goldberg, K., et al.: Collaborative teleoperation via the internet. In: Proceedings of the 2000 IEEE International Conference on Robotics and Automation, vol. 2, pp. 2019–2024 (2000)
10. Goodrich, M.A., Olsen, D.R., Crandall, J.W., Palmer, T.J.: Experiments in adjustable autonomy. In: Proceedings of IJCAI Workshop on Autonomy, Delegation and Control: Interacting with Intelligent Agents, pp. 1624–1629 (2001)
11. Ishikawa, N., Suzuki, K.: Development of a human and robot collaborative system for inspecting patrol of nuclear power plants. In: Proceedings 6th IEEE International Workshop on Robot and Human Communication, pp. 118–123 (1997)

12. Kuhlmann, G., Knox, W.B., Stone, P.: Know thine enemy: a champion RoboCup coach agent. In: Proceedings of the 21st National Conference on Artificial Intelligence, pp. 1463–1468 (2006)
13. Kumar, A., Zilberstein, S.: Point-based backup for decentralized POMDPs: complexity and new algorithms. In: Proceedings of the 9th International Conference on Autonomous Agents and Multiagent Systems, pp. 1315–1322 (2010)
14. Mouaddib, A.I., Zilberstein, S., Beynier, A., Jeanpierre, L.: A decision-theoretic approach to cooperative control and adjustable autonomy. In: Proceedings of the 19th European Conference on Artificial Intelligence, pp. 971–972 (2010)
15. Oliehoek, F.A., Spaan, M.T., Amato, C., Whiteson, S.: Incremental clustering and expansion for faster optimal planning in decentralized POMDPs. J. Artif. Intell. Res. **46**, 449–509 (2013)
16. Peshkin, L., Kim, K.E., Meuleau, N., Kaelbling, L.P.: Learning to cooperate via policy search. In: Proceedings of the 16th Conference on Uncertainty in Artificial Intelligence, pp. 489–496 (2000)
17. Riley, P.F., Veloso, M.M.: Coach planning with opponent models for distributed execution. Auton. Agents Multi-Agent Syst. **13**(3), 293–325 (2006). https://doi.org/10.1007/s10458-006-7449-z
18. Rosenthal, S., Veloso, M.M.: Mobile robot planning to seek help with spatially-situated tasks. In: Proceedings of the 26th AAAI Conference on Artificial Intelligence (2012)
19. Scerri, P., Pynadath, D., Tambe, M.: Adjustable autonomy in real-world multi-agent environments. In: Proceedings of the 5th International Conference on Autonomous Agents, pp. 300–307 (2001)
20. Seuken, S., Zilberstein, S.: Improved memory-bounded dynamic programming for decentralized POMDPs. In: Proceedings of the 23rd Conference Conference on Uncertainty in Artificial Intelligence, pp. 344–351 (2007)
21. Seuken, S., Zilberstein, S.: Memory-bounded dynamic programming for DEC-POMDPs. In: Proceedings of the 20th International Joint Conference on Artificial Intelligence, pp. 2009–2015 (2007)
22. Shiomi, M., Sakamoto, D., Kanda, T., Ishi, C.T., Ishiguro, H., Hagita, N.: A semi-autonomous communication robot: a field trial at a train station. In: Proceedings of the 3rd ACM/IEEE International Conference on Human Robot Interaction, pp. 303–310. ACM, New York (2008)
23. Szer, D., Charpillet, F.: Point-based dynamic programming for DEC-POMDPs. In: Proceedings of the 21st National Conference on Artificial Intelligence, pp. 1233–1238 (2006)
24. Wu, F., Jennings, N.R., Chen, X.: Sample-based policy iteration for constrained DEC-POMDPs. In: Proceedings of the 20th European Conference on Artificial Intelligence (ECAI), pp. 858–863 (2012)
25. Wu, F., Zilberstein, S., Chen, X.: Trial-based dynamic programming for multi-agent planning. In: Proceedings of the 24th AAAI Conference on Artificial Intelligence, pp. 908–914 (2010)
26. Yanco, H.A., Drury, J.L., Scholtz, J.: Beyond usability evaluation: analysis of human-robot interaction at a major robotics competition. Hum.-Comput. Interact. **19**(1–2), 117–149 (2004)

Preference Elicitation in Assumption-Based Argumentation

Quratul-ain Mahesar[1]([✉]), Nir Oren[2], and Wamberto W. Vasconcelos[2]

[1] Department of Informatics, King's College London, London, UK
quratul-ain.mahesar@kcl.ac.uk
[2] Department of Computing Science, University of Aberdeen, Aberdeen, UK
{n.oren,w.w.vasconcelos}@abdn.ac.uk

Abstract. Various structured argumentation frameworks utilize preferences as part of their inference procedure. In this paper, we consider an inverse of the standard reasoning problem, seeking to identify what preferences could lead to a given set of conclusions being drawn. We ground our work in the Assumption-Based Argumentation (ABA) framework, and present an algorithm which computes and enumerates all possible sets of preferences (restricted to three identified cases) over the assumptions in the system from which a desired conflict-free set of conclusions can be obtained under a given semantics. After describing our algorithm, we establish its soundness, completeness and complexity.

1 Introduction

Assumption-based argumentation (ABA) [10,17] is a structured argumentation formalism where knowledge is represented through a deductive system comprising of a formal language and inference rules. Defeasible information is represented in the form of special entities in the language called *assumptions*. Attacks are then constructively defined over sets of assumptions whenever one set of assumptions supports the deduction of the contrary of some assumption in a different set of assumptions. ABA is equipped with different semantics for determining 'winning' sets of assumptions. In turn, sets of 'winning' (aka acceptable) arguments can be determined from the 'winning' sets of assumptions, since the assumption-level and argument-level views are fully equivalent in ABA.

ABA$^+$ [9] extends ABA with preferences to assist with discrimination among conflicting alternatives. Assumptions are the only defeasible component in ABA and therefore preferences are defined over assumptions rather than arguments as is the case in preference-based argumentation frameworks (PAFs) [2]. Unlike PAFs—that use attack reversal with preferences given over arguments—ABA$^+$ uses attack reversal with preferences given over assumptions (at the object level), that form the support of arguments. Preferences are integrated directly into the attack relation, without lifting preferences from the object level to either the argument or the extension levels (as is done in systems such as ASPIC$^+$ [14]).

ABA semantics allows one to compute an acceptable or winning set of arguments, and the semantics of ABA$^+$ extend ABA semantics to take preferences

© Springer Nature Switzerland AG 2021
T. Uchiya et al. (Eds.): PRIMA 2020, LNAI 12568, pp. 199–214, 2021.
https://doi.org/10.1007/978-3-030-69322-0_13

over assumptions into account. In this paper we focus on the problem of eliciting the preferences which unify an ABA framework with its ABA$^+$ counterpart, seeking to answer the following questions.

1. What are the possible preferences over assumptions for a given conflict-free extension in an ABA framework that ensure the acceptability of the extension using ABA$^+$ semantics?
2. How do we find all possible sets of such preferences?
3. What are the unique and common preferences for a given extension compared to all other extensions (under a multi-extension semantics)?

The following example suggests one scenario applying these ideas.

Example 1. (Journey Recommendation) Alice uses an online journey recommendation system to find options for travelling between two cities. The system suggests travelling either by ground or air. If Alice chooses to travel by ground, then the system can infer that Alice likes to travel by train and not by plane. The system can *learn* Alice's preferences from this interaction and suggest the right recommendation next time. In the future, the system can *justify* its recommendation to Alice by arguing that travelling by ground is the best option for her since she prefers to travel by train. Furthermore, if the train company states that their trains are "air-conditioned vehicles", then the system could learn an additional preference, namely that Alice prefers to travel on an "air-conditioned vehicle".

Preferences not only help in finding the best solutions (via winning arguments) suitable for a particular user but also in justifying such solutions. In turn, computing all possible sets of preferences helps in finding all justifications. Previous work on the topic [12]—which we build on—considered only abstract argumentation frameworks (namely Dung's AAFs and PAFs), and this paper extends the state of the art by considering a structured setting, building on ABA and ABA$^+$ frameworks. Moving to a structured setting is non-trivial and requires additional issues to be addressed that do not arise in the abstract cases.

The remainder of this paper is structured as follows. In Sect. 2, we present the background on ABA and ABA$^+$ frameworks. In Sect. 3, we present our approach and algorithm for preference elicitation in an ABA framework, and we establish the soundness, completeness and complexity of the algorithm. In Sect. 4, we present the demonstration of the algorithm. In Sect. 5, we present the related work. Finally, we conclude and suggest future work in Sect. 6.

2   Background

We begin by introducing ABA and ABA$^+$, with the following material taken from [9,10,17]. An ABA framework is a tuple $(\mathcal{L}, \mathcal{R}, \mathcal{A}, ^-)$, where:

1. $(\mathcal{L}, \mathcal{R})$ is a deductive system with $\mathcal{L}$ a language (a set of sentences) and $\mathcal{R}$ a set of rules of the form $\varphi_0 \leftarrow \varphi_1, ..., \varphi_m$ with $m \geq 0$ and $\varphi_i \in \mathcal{L}$ for $i \in \{0, ..., m\}$.

φ_0 is referred to as the *head* of the rule, and $\varphi_1, ..., \varphi_m$ is referred to as the *body* of the rule. If $m = 0$, then the rule $\varphi_0 \leftarrow \varphi_1, ..., \varphi_m$ is said to have an *empty body*, and is written as $\varphi_0 \leftarrow \top$, where $\top \notin \mathcal{L}$.

2. $\mathcal{A} \subseteq \mathcal{L}$ is a non-empty set, whose elements are referred to as *assumptions*;
3. $^- : \mathcal{A} \rightarrow \mathcal{L}$ is a total map where for $a \in \mathcal{A}$, the $\mathcal{L}$-sentence $\bar{a}$ is referred to as the *contrary* of a.

A *deduction*[1] for $\varphi \in \mathcal{L}$ supported by $S \subseteq \mathcal{L}$ and $R \subseteq \mathcal{R}$, denoted by $S \vdash_R \varphi$, is a finite tree with:

(i) the root labelled by φ,
(ii) leaves labelled by $\top$ or elements from S,
(iii) the children of non-leaf nodes ψ labelled by the elements of the body of some rule from $\mathcal{R}$ with head ψ, and R being the set of all such rules.

For $E \subseteq \mathcal{L}$, the *conclusions* $Cn(E)$ of E is the set of sentences for which deductions supported by subsets of E exist, i.e., $Cn(E) = \{\phi \in \mathcal{L} : \exists S \vdash_R \phi, S \subseteq E, R \subseteq \mathcal{R}\}$.

The semantics of ABA frameworks are defined in terms of sets of assumptions meeting desirable requirements, and are given in terms of a notion of *attack* between sets of assumptions. A set of assumptions $A \subseteq \mathcal{A}$ *attacks* a set of assumptions $B \subseteq \mathcal{A}$, denoted by $A \rightsquigarrow B$ iff there is a deduction $A' \vdash_R \bar{b}$, for some $b \in B$, supported by some $A' \subseteq A$ and $R \subseteq \mathcal{R}$. If it is not the case that A attacks B, then we denote this by $A \not\rightsquigarrow B$.

For some $E \subseteq \mathcal{A}$, E is *conflict-free* iff $E \not\rightsquigarrow E$; E *defends* $A \subseteq \mathcal{A}$ iff for all $B \subseteq \mathcal{A}$ with $B \rightsquigarrow A$ it holds that $E \rightsquigarrow B$. A set $E \subseteq \mathcal{A}$ of assumptions (also called an *extension*) is *admissible* iff E is conflict-free and defends itself; *preferred* iff E is $\subseteq$-maximally admissible; *stable* iff E is conflict-free and $E \rightsquigarrow \{b\}$ for every $b \in \mathcal{A} \backslash E$; *complete* iff E is admissible and contains every set of assumptions it defends; *grounded* iff E is a subset-minimal complete extension.

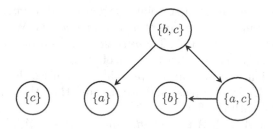

Fig. 1. Example assumption graph $\mathcal{G}_1$

Example 2. A variant of Example 1, where both vehicles are air-conditioned, can be represented in ABA as follows. Let there be an ABA framework $\mathcal{F} = (\mathcal{L}, \mathcal{R}, \mathcal{A}, ^-)$ with:

---

[1] We only consider *flat* ABA frameworks, where assumptions cannot be deduced from other assumptions.

(i) language $\mathcal{L} = \{a, b, c, d, e, f\}$;
(ii) set of rules $\mathcal{R} = \{d \leftarrow a, c;\ e \leftarrow b, c\}$;
(iii) set of assumptions $\mathcal{A} = \{a, b, c\}$;
(iv) contraries are then given by: $\bar{a} = e, \bar{b} = d, \bar{c} = f$.

Here a and b stand for "plane" and "train" respectively, and c stands for "air-conditioned vehicle". The contraries of a and b, namely e and d stand for "ground" and "air", and the contrary of c, namely f stands for "hot".

$\mathcal{F}$ is illustrated in Fig. 1. Here, nodes represent sets of assumptions and directed edges denote attacks. $\{b, c\}$ attacks $\{a\}$, $\{a, c\}$ attacks $\{b\}$, $\{a, c\}$ and $\{b, c\}$ attack each other and $\{c\}$ is un-attacked and does not attack anyone.

$\mathcal{F}$ has two preferred and stable extensions $\{a, c\}$ and $\{b, c\}$, with conclusions $Cn(\{a, c\}) = \{a, c, d\}$ and $Cn(\{b, c\}) = \{b, c, e\}$, respectively. $\mathcal{F}$ has a unique grounded extension $\{c\}$, with conclusions $Cn(\{c\}) = \{c\}$. Furthermore, all of $\{c\}$, $\{a, c\}$ and $\{b, c\}$ are complete extensions.

ABA$^+$ is an extension of the ABA framework with a preference ordering $\leq$ over the set $\mathcal{A}$ of assumptions, defined as follows.

Definition 1. *An ABA$^+$ framework is a tuple $(\mathcal{L}, \mathcal{R}, \mathcal{A},^-, \leq)$, where $(\mathcal{L}, \mathcal{R}, \mathcal{A},^-)$ is an ABA framework and $\leq$ is a pre-ordering defined on $\mathcal{A}$.*

$<$ is the strict counterpart of $\leq$, and is defined as $a < b$ iff $a \leq b$ and $b \not\leq a$, for any $a \in \mathcal{A}$ and $b \in \mathcal{A}$. The attack relation in ABA$^+$ is then defined as follows.

Definition 2. *Let $A, B \subseteq \mathcal{A}$, A $<$-attacks B, denoted by $A \rightsquigarrow_< B$ iff either:*

(i) there is a deduction $A' \vdash_R \bar{b}$, for some $b \in B$, supported by $A' \subseteq A$, and $\not\exists a' \in A'$ with $a' < b$; or
(ii) there is a deduction $B' \vdash_R \bar{a}$, for some $a \in A$, supported by $B' \subseteq B$, and $\exists b' \in B'$ with $b' < a$.

The $<$-attack formed in the first point above is called a *normal attack*, while the $<$-attack formed in the second point is a *reverse attack*. We write $A \not\rightsquigarrow B$ to denote that A does not $<$-attack B. The *reverse attack* ensures that the original conflict is preserved and that conflict-freeness of the extensions is attained, which is the basic condition imposed on acceptability semantics. Flatness is defined as for standard ABA frameworks, and we assume that the ABA and ABA$^+$ frameworks we deal with are flat.

Furthermore, for $A \subseteq \mathcal{A}$, A is *$<$-conflict-free* iff $A \not\rightsquigarrow_< A$; also, A *$<$-defends* $A' \subseteq \mathcal{A}$ iff for all $B \subseteq \mathcal{A}$ with $B \rightsquigarrow_< A'$ it holds that $A \rightsquigarrow_< B$. In ABA$^+$, an extension $E \subseteq \mathcal{A}$ is *$<$-admissible* iff E is *$<$-conflict-free* and *$<$-defends* itself; *$<$-preferred* iff E is $\subseteq$-maximally *$<$-admissible*. *$<$-stable* iff E is *$<$-conflict-free* and $E \rightsquigarrow_< \{b\}$ for every $b \in \mathcal{A} \backslash E$; *$<$-complete* iff E is *$<$-admissible* and contains every set of assumptions it *$<$-defends*; *$<$-grounded* iff E is a $\subseteq$-minimal *$<$-complete* set of assumptions.

Example 3. We extend the ABA framework of Example 2 to ABA$^+$ by including preferences over assumptions. Let there be an ABA$^+$ framework $\mathcal{F}^+ = (\mathcal{L}, \mathcal{R}, \mathcal{A},^-, \leq)$ with:

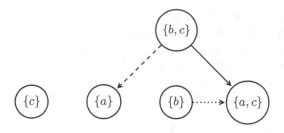

Fig. 2. Example assumption graph $\mathcal{G}_2$

(i) $\mathcal{L} = \{a, b, c, d, e, f\}$;
(ii) $\mathcal{R} = \{d \leftarrow a, c;\ e \leftarrow b, c\}$;
(iii) $\mathcal{A} = \{a, b, c\}$;
(iv) $\bar{a} = e, \bar{b} = d, \bar{c} = f$.
(v) $a < b$ (i.e., $<$ is a pre-order with $a \leq b, b \not\leq a$).

Here $a < b$ represents the preference that Alice prefers to travel by train compared to plane. $\mathcal{F}^+$ is graphically represented in Fig. 2 where the nodes contain sets of assumptions and directed edges denote attacks. Dashed arrows indicate normal attacks, dotted arrows indicate reverse attacks and solid arrows indicate $<$-attacks that are both normal and reverse.

In $\mathcal{F}^+$, $\{b, c\}$ supports an argument for the contrary e of a, and no assumption in $\{b, c\}$ is strictly less preferred than a. Thus, $\{b, c\}$ $<$-attacks $\{a\}$, as well as any set containing a via normal attack. On the other hand, $\{a, c\}$ (supporting an argument for the contrary d of b) is prevented from $<$-attacking $\{b\}$, due to the preference $a < b$. Instead $\{b\}$, as well as any set containing b, $<$-attacks $\{a, c\}$ via reverse attack. Overall, $\mathcal{F}^+$ has a unique $<$-σ extension (where $\sigma \in \{grounded, preferred, stable, complete\}$), namely $E = \{b, c\}$, with conclusions $Cn(E) = \{b, c, e\}$.

3   Approach for Preference Elicitation in ABA

In this section, we present an extension-based approach for preference elicitation in an ABA framework. The core idea is that by observing what conclusions a reasoner draws based on their knowledge base, we can reason about what preferences over assumptions they must hold. Thus, given an ABA framework, and a conflict-free extension (under a given semantics σ), we identify the preferences necessary to obtain this set of assumptions within an ABA$^+$ $<$-σ extension.

For any two assumptions a and b in an ABA framework, we use the strict preference relation $a < b$ to denote that a is strictly less preferred to b, i.e., a is of lesser strength than b, and we use the preference relation $a = b$ to denote that a and b are of equal strength or preference. There are then three possible cases for which the preferences between assumptions are computed for a given conflict-free extension E in an ABA framework.

Case 1: Suppose $a \in \mathcal{A}$, $\beta \subseteq \mathcal{A}$, $a \in E$, $\beta \not\subseteq E$, and a is attacked by β, i.e., $\beta \vdash_R \bar{a}$, where $R \subseteq \mathcal{R}$ and a is not defended by any unattacked assumptions other than a in the extension. Then $\forall b \in \beta$, it is the case that $b \leq a$ (i.e., $b < a$ or $b = a$, and $a \not< b$) and $\exists b' \in \beta$ such that $b' < a$. This ensures that there is at least one assumption in β that is strictly less preferred than the assumption a whose contrary β supports deductively, and a is not strictly less preferred than any assumption in β.

For example, let $\beta = \{b_1, b_2\}$ and $\beta \vdash_R \bar{a}$ be given, then we have the following set of sets of all possible preferences: $\{\{b_1 < a, b_2 = a\}, \{b_1 = a, b_2 < a\}, \{b_1 < a, b_2 < a\}\}$.

Case 2: Suppose $\alpha \subseteq \mathcal{A}$, $b \in \mathcal{A}$, $\alpha \subseteq E$, $b \notin E$, and α attack b, i.e., $\alpha \vdash_R \bar{b}$, where $R \subseteq \mathcal{R}$ and b does not attack α. Then $\forall a \in \alpha$, it is the case that $b \leq a$ (i.e., $b < a$ or $b = a$, and $a \not< b$). This ensures that any assumption a is not strictly less preferred than the assumption b.

For example, let $\alpha = \{a_1, a_2\}$ and $\alpha \vdash_R \bar{b}$ be given, then we have the following set of sets of all possible preferences: $\{\{b < a_1, b = a_2\}, \{b = a_1, b < a_2\}, \{b < a_1, b < a_2\}, \{b = a_1, b = a_2\}\}$.

Case 3: Suppose $a \in \mathcal{A}$, $\beta, \gamma \subseteq \mathcal{A}$, $a \in E$, $\gamma \subseteq E$, $\beta \not\subseteq E$, and a is attacked by β, i.e., $\beta \vdash_R \bar{a}$ but defended by any unattacked set of assumptions γ, i.e., $\gamma \vdash_R \bar{b}$, where $b \in \beta$. Then $\forall b \in \beta$, it is the case that $b \leq a$ and $a \leq b$ (i.e., $b < a$ or $b = a$ or $a < b$).

For example, let $\beta = \{b_1, b_2\}$ and $\beta \vdash_R \bar{a}$ be given, and assume $\gamma \vdash_R \bar{b}$ for some $b \in \beta$. Then we have three possible set of sets of preferences:

1. $\{\{b_1 < a, b_2 = a\}, \{b_1 = a, b_2 < a\}, \{b_1 < a, b_2 < a\}\}$, i.e., there is at least one assumption in β that is strictly less preferred than the assumption a whose contrary β supports deductively.
2. $\{\{b_1 = a, b_2 = a\}\}$, i.e., all assumptions in β are equal to the assumption a whose contrary β supports deductively.
3. $\{\{a < b_1, a = b_2\}, \{a = b_1, a < b_2\}, \{a < b_1, a < b_2\}\}$, i.e., assumption a whose contrary β supports deductively is strictly less preferred than at least one assumption in β.

The final set of sets of preferences is the union of the above three set of sets of preferences given by $\{\{b_1 < a, b_2 = a\}, \{b_1 = a, b_2 < a\}, \{b_1 < a, b_2 < a\}, \{b_1 = a, b_2 = a\}, \{a < b_1, a = b_2\}, \{a = b_1, a < b_2\}, \{a < b_1, a < b_2\}\}$

We now present Algorithm 1 that exhaustively computes all possible sets of preferences over assumptions for a given input extension (a conflict-free set of assumptions) in an ABA framework using the above three cases. The input of Algorithm 1 consists of:

(i) An ABA framework.
(ii) An extension E which is a conflict-free set of assumptions such that $E \subseteq \mathcal{A}$, where $\mathcal{A}$ is the set of assumptions in an ABA framework.

The algorithm computes and outputs a set consisting of finite sets of possible preferences between assumptions, where each set of preferences is represented as $Prefs = \{a < b, b = c, ...\}$ such that $\{a, b, c\} \subseteq \mathcal{A}$.

Algorithm 1. Compute all preferences

Require: ABA, an ABA framework
Require: E, an extension (conflict-free set of assumptions)
Ensure: $PSet$, the set of sets of all possible preferences
 1: **function** ComputeAllPreferences(ABA, E)
 2:     $PSet \leftarrow$ ComputePreferences₁(ABA, E)
 3:     $PSet \leftarrow$ ComputePreferences₂($ABA, E, PSet$)
 4:     $PSet \leftarrow$ ComputePreferences₃($ABA, E, PSet$)
 5:     **return** $PSet$
 6: **end function**

Algorithms $2, 3, 4$ compute case 1, case 2 and case 3 preferences respectively. The following are the main steps in Algorithm 2:

(i) Line 3: Iteratively pick a single assumption a from the extension E.
(ii) Line 4: Find all attacking assumptions B that support contrary of assumption a deductively.
(iii) Lines 5–33: For each B, if there is no unattacked assumption C (where $C \neq a$ and $C \in E$) that attacks B, then compute all possibilities where at least a single $b \in B$ is less preferred to a.

The following are the main steps in Algorithm 3:

(i) Line 3: Iteratively pick a single assumption a from the extension E.
(ii) Line 4: Find assumption b whose contrary A supports deductively, where $a \in A$.
(iii) Lines 5–13: For all assumptions b attacked by a, compute all possibilities where b is either less preferred to a or equal to a.

The following are the main steps in Algorithm 4:

(i) Line 3: Iteratively pick a single assumption a from the extension E.
(ii) Line 4: Find all attacking assumptions B that support contrary of the assumption a deductively.
(iii) Lines 6–30: For each B, if there is an unattacked assumption C (where $C \neq a$ and $C \in E$) that attacks B, then compute all possibilities (different sets) where:
   (a) At least a single $b \in B$ is less preferred to a and ensure that a cannot be less preferred to b in these sets of preferences.
   (b) a is less preferred to at least a single $b \in B$ and ensure that b cannot be less preferred to a in these sets of preferences.
   (c) For all $b \in B$, b is equal to a.

We establish that our approach is sound (i.e., all its outputs are correct) and complete (i.e., it outputs all possible solutions with the three cases).

Algorithm 2. Compute preferences (Case 1)

Require: ABA, an ABA framework
Require: E, an extension (conflict-free set of assumptions)
Ensure: $PSet''$, a set of sets of preferences
 1: **function** ComputePreferences$_1$(ABA, E)
 2:     $PSet \leftarrow \{\{\}\}$, $PSet' \leftarrow \emptyset$, $PSet'' \leftarrow \emptyset$, $PSet''' \leftarrow \emptyset$
 3:     **for all** $a \in E$ **do**
 4:        $Attackers \leftarrow \{B \mid \exists y \in Y : B \in y, B \notin E, Y \vdash_R \bar{a}, R \subseteq \mathcal{R}\}$
 5:        **for all** $B \in Attackers$ **do**
 6:           $Defenders \leftarrow \{C \mid \exists x \in X : C \in x, C \neq a, C \in E,\ X \vdash_R \bar{b},\ b \in B,$
             $\nexists z \in Z : D \in z,\ D \notin E$ s.t. $Z \vdash_R \bar{C},\ R \subseteq \mathcal{R}\}$
 7:           **if** $Defenders = \emptyset$ **then**
 8:             **for all** $b \in B$ **do**
 9:                **if** $(a \neq b)$ and $(\nexists Prefs'' \in PSet''$ s.t. $(b < a) \in Prefs''$ or
      $(b = a) \in Prefs''$ or $(a < b) \in Prefs'')$ **then**
10:                   **for all** $Prefs \in PSet$ **do**
11:                     $PSet' \leftarrow PSet' \cup \{Prefs \cup \{b < a\}\}$
12:                     $PSet' \leftarrow PSet' \cup \{Prefs \cup \{b = a\}\}$
13:                   **end for**
14:                   $PSet \leftarrow PSet'$
15:                   $PSet' \leftarrow \emptyset$
16:                **end if**
17:             **end for**
18:             **if** $\exists Prefs \in PSet$ s.t. $Prefs$ has all equal relations **then**
19:                $PSet \leftarrow PSet \setminus \{Prefs\}$
20:             **end if**
21:             **if** $PSet'' = \emptyset$ **then**
22:                $PSet''' \leftarrow PSet$
23:             **else**
24:                **for all** $Prefs \in PSet$ **do**
25:                   **for all** $Prefs'' \in PSet''$ **do**
26:                     $PSet''' \leftarrow PSet''' \cup \{Prefs \cup Prefs''\}$
27:                   **end for**
28:                **end for**
29:             **end if**
30:             $PSet'' \leftarrow PSet'''$
31:             $PSet''' \leftarrow \emptyset$, $PSet \leftarrow \{\{\}\}$
32:           **end if**
33:        **end for**
34:     **end for**
35:     **return** $PSet''$
36: **end function**

Theorem 1. *Algorithm 1 is sound in that given an ABA framework and an extension E (under a given semantics σ) as input, every output preference set $Prefs \in PSet$ when used with the ABA framework, i.e., ABA^+ framework, results in the input E (under a given $<$-σ semantics).*

Algorithm 3. Compute preferences (Case 2)

Require: ABA, an ABA framework
Require: E, an extension (conflict-free set of assumptions)
Require: $PSet$, a set of sets of preferences
Ensure: $PSet$, an updated set of sets of preferences
 1: **function** ComputePreferences$_2(ABA, E, PSet)$
 2:      $PSet' \leftarrow \emptyset$
 3:      **for all** $a \in E$ **do**
 4:          $Attacked \leftarrow \{b \mid b \in \mathcal{A},\ a \in A\ s.t.\ A \vdash_R \bar{b},\ b \in B\ s.t.\ B \nvdash_R \bar{a},\ R \subseteq \mathcal{R}\}$
 5:          **for all** $b \in Attacked$ **do**
 6:              **if** $(a \neq b)$ and $(\nexists Prefs \in PSet\ s.t.\ (b < a) \in Prefs$ or
               $(b = a) \in Prefs$ or $(a < b) \in Prefs)$ **then**
 7:                  **for all** $Prefs \in PSet$ **do**
 8:                      $PSet' \leftarrow PSet' \cup \{Prefs \cup \{b < a\}\}$
 9:                      $PSet' \leftarrow PSet' \cup \{Prefs \cup \{b = a\}\}$
10:                  **end for**
11:                  $PSet \leftarrow PSet',\ PSet' \leftarrow \emptyset$
12:              **end if**
13:          **end for**
14:      **end for**
15:      **return** $PSet$
16: **end function**

Proof. We prove this by exploring all cases and how these are handled by Algorithms 2–4. Each set of preferences computed for each subset of assumptions $\alpha, \beta, \gamma \subseteq \mathcal{A}$ is such that $\alpha, \gamma \subseteq E, \beta \cap E = \emptyset$. We proceed to show how each of the auxiliary Algorithms 2–4 help us achieve this.

$\forall b \in B$ where $B \subseteq \beta$, Algorithm 2 computing each case 1 preference set with at least one preference of the form $b < a$, where $a \in A, A \subseteq \alpha, B \vdash_R \bar{a}$ ensures that the following holds:

1. There is no unattacked $C \in \gamma$ such that $\exists c \in C, c \neq a, C \vdash_R \bar{b}$ where $b \in B$ (lines 6–7).
2. $a \in E$, since a is preferred to at least one of its attacking assumption b in B, which invalidates the attack $B \vdash_R \bar{a}$.
3. Since the input extension E consists of conflict-free assumptions, if $a \in E$ then its attacking assumption $b \notin E$ where $b \in B$. This supports that $\beta \cap E = \emptyset$.

$\forall a \in A$ where $A \subseteq \alpha$, Algorithm 3 computing each case 2 preferences of the form $b < a, b = a$, where $b \in B, B \subseteq \beta, A \vdash_R \bar{b}, B \nvdash_R \bar{a}$ ensures the following holds:

1. Since A attacks B and B does not attack A, we have two different preferences between a and b, namely, $b < a, b = a$. Therefore $a \in E$ with respect to each of these preferences.
2. Preferences $b < a, b = a$ will be in different preference sets, as per lines 8 and 9. We will have $Prefs_1 \leftarrow Prefs \cup \{b < a\}$ and $Prefs_2 \leftarrow Prefs \cup \{b = a\}$, where $Prefs$ consists of preferences of case 1.

Algorithm 4. Compute preferences (Case 3)

Require: ABA, an ABA framework
Require: E, an extension (conflict-free set of assumptions)
Require: $PSet$, a set of sets of preferences
Ensure: $PSet$, an updated set of sets of preferences
1: **function** ComputePreferences$_3$($ABA, E, PSet$)
2:    $PSet_1 \leftarrow \emptyset$, $PSet_2 \leftarrow \emptyset$
3:    $PSet_1' \leftarrow \emptyset$, $PSet_2' \leftarrow \emptyset$
4:    **for all** $a \in E$ **do**
5:        $Attackers \leftarrow \{B \mid \exists y \in Y : B \in y, B \notin E, Y \vdash_R \bar{a}, R \subseteq \mathcal{R}\}$
6:        **for all** $B \in Attackers$ **do**
7:            $Defenders \leftarrow \{C \mid \exists x \in X : C \in x, C \neq a, C \in E, X \vdash_R \bar{b}, b \in B,$
            $\nexists z \in Z : D \in z, D \notin E \text{ s.t. } Z \vdash_R \bar{C}, R \subseteq \mathcal{R}\}$
8:            **if** $Defenders \neq \emptyset$ **then**
9:                $PSet_1 \leftarrow PSet$, $PSet_2 \leftarrow PSet$
10:                **for all** $b \in B$ **do**
11:                    **if** $(a \neq b)$ and $(\nexists Prefs \in PSet_1 \text{ s.t. } (b < a) \in Prefs$ or
                    $(b = a) \in Prefs$ or $(a < b) \in Prefs)$ **then**
12:                        **for all** $Prefs \in PSet_1$ **do**
13:                            $PSet_1' \leftarrow PSet_1' \cup \{Prefs \cup \{b < a\}\}$
14:                            $PSet_1' \leftarrow PSet_1' \cup \{Prefs \cup \{b = a\}\}$
15:                        **end for**
16:                        $PSet_1 \leftarrow PSet_1'$, $PSet_1' \leftarrow \emptyset$
17:                    **end if**
18:                **end for**
19:                **for all** $b \in B$ **do**
20:                    **if** $(a \neq b)$ and $(\nexists Prefs \in PSet_2 \text{ s.t. } (b < a) \in Prefs$ or
                    $(b = a) \in Prefs$ or $(a < b) \in Prefs)$ **then**
21:                        **for all** $Prefs \in PSet_2$ **do**
22:                            $PSet_2' \leftarrow PSet_2' \cup \{Prefs \cup \{a < b\}\}$
23:                            $PSet_2' \leftarrow PSet_2' \cup \{Prefs \cup \{b = a\}\}$
24:                        **end for**
25:                        $PSet_2 \leftarrow PSet_2'$, $PSet_2' \leftarrow \emptyset$
26:                    **end if**
27:                **end for**
28:                $PSet \leftarrow PSet_1 \cup PSet_2$
29:            **end if**
30:        **end for**
31:    **end for**
32:    **return** $PSet$
33: **end function**

$\forall b \in B$ where $B \subseteq \beta$, Algorithm 4 computing each case 3 preferences of the form $b < a, b = a, a < b$, where $a \in A, A \subseteq \alpha, C \subseteq \gamma$ such that C is unattacked, $B \vdash_R \bar{a}, C \vdash_R \bar{b}$ ensures the following holds:

1. Since C defends A from the attack of B, we have three different preferences between a and b, namely, $b < a$, $b = a$ and $a < b$. Therefore $a \in E$ with respect to each of these preferences.

2. Preferences $b < a, b = a, a < b$ will be in different preference sets, as per lines 10–27. We will have $Prefs_1 \leftarrow Prefs \cup \{b < a\}$, $Prefs_2 \leftarrow Prefs \cup \{b = a\}$ and $Prefs_3 \leftarrow Prefs \cup \{a < b\}$, where $Prefs$ consists of preferences of cases 1 and 2.

Theorem 2. *Algorithm 1 is complete in that given an ABA framework and an extension E (under a given semantics σ) as input, if there is a preference set $Prefs \in PSet$ (restricted to three identified cases stated earlier) which when used with the ABA framework, i.e., ABA^+ framework, results in the input E (under a given $<$-σ semantics), then Algorithm 1 will find it.*

Proof. Similar to above, we prove this by exploring all cases and how these are handled by algorithms 2–4. We find all sets of preferences computed for each subset of assumptions $\alpha, \beta, \gamma \subseteq \mathcal{A}$ such that $\alpha, \gamma \subseteq E, \beta \cap E = \emptyset$. We proceed to show how each of the auxiliary Algorithms 2–4 help us achieve this.

$\forall b \in B$ where $B \subseteq \beta$, Algorithm 2 computes all case 1 preference sets with at least one preference of the form $b < a$, where $a \in A$, $A \subseteq \alpha$, $B \vdash_R \bar{a}$. Lines 3–34 exhaustively search for $a \in E$ for which there is an attacker B (not attacked by any unattacked C). If there are such $a, b \in \mathcal{A}$ where $b \in B$, the algorithm will find them and add at least one preference of the form $b < a$ to a set of preferences.

$\forall a \in A$ where $A \subseteq \alpha$, Algorithm 3 computes all case 2 preferences of the form $b < a, b = a$, where $b \in B$, $B \subseteq \beta$, $A \vdash_R \bar{b}$, $B \nvdash_R \bar{a}$. Lines 3–14 exhaustively search for $a \in E$ for which there is an attacked set of assumptions B and B does not attack A where $a \in A$. If there are such $a, b \in \mathcal{A}$ where $b \in B$, the algorithm will find them and add each $b < a, b = a$ to a different set of preferences.

$\forall b \in B$ where $B \subseteq \beta$, Algorithm 4 computes all case 3 preferences of the form $b < a$, $b = a$, $a < b$, where $a \in A$, $A \subseteq \alpha$, $C \subseteq \gamma$ such that C is unattacked, $B \vdash_R \bar{a}$, $C \vdash_R \bar{b}$. Lines 4–31 exhaustively search for $a \in E$ for which there is an attacker B and there is a defender C that attacks B. If there are such $a, b \in \mathcal{A}$ where $b \in B$, the algorithm will find them and add each $b < a, b = a, a < b$ to a different set of preferences.

For a given conflict-free extension E (under a given semantics σ) in an ABA framework, the complexity (worst-case) of finding all possible sets of preferences (using the three cases stated earlier) between the assumptions that ensure the acceptability of extension E under the corresponding $<$-σ semantics in ABA^+ is exponential due to the exponential complexity of the constituent functions of Algorithm 1.

4 Demonstration (Example)

In this section, we present an illustrative example to demonstrate Algorithm 1 given the ABA framework $\mathcal{F}$ of Example 2 and its corresponding assumption graph $\mathcal{G}_1$ shown in Fig. 1. $\mathcal{F}$ has two preferred extensions $E_1 = \{a, c\}$, $E_2 = \{b, c\}$. To demonstrate Algorithm 1 we consider the preferred extension $E_1 = $

$\{a, c\}$ for computing preferences[2]. Table 1 shows the preferences computed as follows:

- At line 2, Algorithm 2 is called, which returns the sets of case 1 preferences.
- At line 3, Algorithm 3 is called, which returns the sets of preferences with cases 1 and 2 combined together.
- Finally at line 4, Algorithm 4 is called, which returns the sets of preferences with cases 1, 2 and 3 combined together.

Table 1. Computing preferences for extension $E_1 = \{a, c\}$

Line no.	Preference sets
2	$\{b < a, c = a\}$
	$\{b = a, c < a\}$
	$\{b < a, c < a\}$
3	$\{b < a, c = a, b < c\}$
	$\{b < a, c = a, b = c\}$
	$\{b = a, c < a, b < c\}$
	$\{b = a, c < a, b = c\}$
	$\{b < a, c < a, b < c\}$
	$\{b < a, c < a, b = c\}$
4	$\{b < a, c = a, b < c\}$
	$\{b < a, c = a, b = c\}$
	$\{b = a, c < a, b < c\}$
	$\{b = a, c < a, b = c\}$
	$\{b < a, c < a, b < c\}$
	$\{b < a, c < a, b = c\}$

Table 2 presents the sets of preferences for the two preferred extensions $\{a, c\}$ and $\{b, c\}$, and the unique and common preferences for an extension in comparison to another extension. The unique preferences for an extension in comparison to all other extensions for a given multi-extension semantic can be computed by Algorithm 5. Furthermore, the common preferences for an extension in comparison to all other extensions can be computed by Algorithm 6.

An important reason for finding all possible preferences is that, in a multi-extension semantic, if there are more than two extensions, e.g., E_1, E_2, E_3, then there might be a preference $Pref_1$ that is unique for E_1 in comparison to the preferences of E_2, and a preference $Pref_2$ that is unique for E_1 in comparison to the preferences of E_3, and the set of preferences $\{Pref_1, Pref_2\}$ would still result in the extension E_1 and not E_2 or E_3.

---

[2] Due to space restrictions we only demonstrate this on preferred extensions, but the approach works on all conflict-free extensions.

Table 2. Preferences for the preferred extensions $\{a,c\}$ and $\{b,c\}$

Preferred extensions	Preference sets	Unique preferences	Common preferences
$\{a,c\}$	$\{b < a, c = a, b < c\}$	$b < a$	$b = a$
	$\{b < a, c = a, b = c\}$	$c < a$	$b = c$
	$\{b = a, c < a, b < c\}$	$b < c$	$c = a$
	$\{b = a, c < a, b = c\}$		
	$\{b < a, c < a, b < c\}$		
	$\{b < a, c < a, b = c\}$		
$\{b,c\}$	$\{a < b, c = b, a < c\}$	$a < b$	
	$\{a < b, c = b, a = c\}$	$c < b$	
	$\{a = b, c < b, a < c\}$	$a < c$	
	$\{a = b, c < b, a = c\}$		
	$\{a < b, c < b, a < c\}$		
	$\{a < b, c < b, a = c\}$		

Algorithm 5. Algorithm for Computing Unique Preferences

Require: *PrefSet₁*, set of preference sets for extension E_1.
Require: *PrefSets*, set consisting of the set of preference sets for all other given extensions except E_1.
Ensure: *UniquePrefs*, unique preferences for E_1.
1: **function** ComputeUniquePreferences(*PrefSet₁*, *PrefSets*)
2:     **for all** *Prefs₁* ∈ *PrefSet₁* **do**
3:         **for all** p ∈ *Prefs₁* **do**
4:             **if** ∀*PrefSet* ∈ *PrefSets* ∄*Prefs* ∈ *PrefSet* s.t. p ∈ *Prefs* **then**
5:                 *UniquePrefs* ← *UniquePrefs* ∪ p
6:             **end if**
7:         **end for**
8:     **end forreturn** *UniquePrefs*
9: **end function**

---

5 Related Work

A preference-based argumentation framework (PAF) [2] has been previously studied to represent an abstract argumentation framework [11]. Following this, [12] proposed an extension-based approach for computing preferences for a given set of conflict-free arguments in an abstract argumentation framework. However, the preferences are computed over abstract arguments which are atomic and the algorithms do no not take into account structural components of arguments such as assumptions, contraries and inference rules in the context of structured argumentation formalisms in particular ABA and ABA$^+$.

Algorithm 6. Algorithm for Computing Common Preferences

Require: $PrefSet_1$, set of preference sets for extension E_1.
Require: $PrefSets$, set consisting of the set of preference sets for all other given extensions except E_1.
Ensure: $CommonPrefs$, common preferences for E_1.
1: **function** ComputeCommonPreferences($PrefSet_1$, $PrefSets$)
2:      **for all** $Prefs_1 \in PrefSet_1$ **do**
3:          **for all** $p \in Prefs_1$ **do**
4:              **if** $\forall PrefSet \in PrefSets \; \exists Prefs \in PrefSet \; s.t. \; p \in Prefs$ **then**
5:                  $CommonPrefs \leftarrow CommonPrefs \cup p$
6:              **end if**
7:          **end for**
8:      **end for**
        return $CommonPrefs$
9: **end function**

Value-based argumentation framework (VAF) [1,4,5] extends a standard argumentation framework to take into account values and aspirations to allow divergent opinions for different audiences. Furthermore, value-based argumentation frameworks (VAFs) have been extended to take into account the possibility that arguments may support multiple values, and therefore, various types of preferences over values could be considered in order to deal with real world situations [11]. Another variation is an extended argumentation framework (EAF) [13] that considers the case where arguments can express preferences between other arguments.

ABA$^+$ [9] generalises preference-based argumentation framework (PAF) [2] that introduced the concept of attack reversal from less preferred arguments. Another extension of the ABA framework with preferences is (p_ABA) [18] that employs preferences on the extension level to discriminate among extensions. ASPIC$^+$ [14] encompasses many key elements of structured argumentation such as strict and defeasible rules, general contrariness mapping and various forms of attacks as well as preferences. DeLP [39], an early version of preference-based argumentation framework [2], and Deductive Argumentation [7], use preferences to discard attacks from arguments less preferred than the attacked arguments. While the above structured argumentation frameworks allow handling of preferences over argument components, the main limitation is that preferences need to be stated in advance.

6 Conclusions and Future Work

In this paper, we presented a novel solution for an important problem of preference elicitation in structured argumentation which to the best of the authors' knowledge has never been attempted before. The main contribution and novelty of our work compared to previous research is given as follows:

1. Whilst previous work considered eliciting preferences in abstract argumentation, in this work, we focused on eliciting preferences in structured argumentation, i.e., ABA. Hence, the preferences are computed over assumptions rather than abstract arguments.
2. We presented a novel algorithm for the structured setting in ABA. We established, its soundness, completeness and complexity (worst-case).
3. We presented algorithms for finding unique and common preferences of an extension in comparison to the preferences of all other extensions for a given multi-extension semantics.

As future work, we plan to do an empirical evaluation of our proposed work on concrete examples. At present, we provide a mechanism for filtering preferences via Algorithms 5– 6 by finding unique and common preferences, we aim to extend this in the future to identify useful patterns or combinations of preferences such as the ones specified in Sect. 4. Moreover, it will be interesting to find out what case of preferences are more likely to be unique or common for a multi-extension semantics.

In this work, we were interested in eliciting preferences at the assumption level, however in the future, we aim to go beyond this by exploring other structured argumentation frameworks [6,14], in particular ASPIC$^+$ [14]. We intend to investigate the relationship between extension enforcement [3,8] and our work. As one application, our work could be used in dialogue strategies [15,16] where an agent may have the capability of inferring preferences and reach her goal if she enforces at least one of several desired sets of arguments with the application of preferences. Moreover, she may figure out which set of desired arguments is the closest one to being accepted, i.e, the one that requires minimum number of unique preferences, i.e., minimal change in the argumentation framework.

Acknowledgements. This work was supported by EPSRC grant (EP/P011829/1), *Supporting Security Policy with Effective Digital Intervention (SSPEDI).*

References

1. Airiau, S., Bonzon, E., Endriss, U., Maudet, N., Rossit, J.: Rationalisation of profiles of abstract argumentation frameworks: characterisation and complexity. J. Artif. Intell. Res. **60**, 149–177 (2017)
2. Amgoud, L., Vesic, S.: Rich preference-based argumentation frameworks. Int. J. Approximate Reasoning **55**(2), 585–606 (2014)
3. Baumann, R.: What does it take to enforce an argument? minimal change in abstract argumentation. In: Proceedings of the 20th European Conference on Artificial Intelligence, pp. 127–132 (2012)
4. Bench-Capon, T.J.M.: Persuasion in practical argument using value-based argumentation frameworks. J. Logic Comput. **13**(3), 429–448 (2003)
5. Bench-Capon, T.J.M., Doutre, S., Dunne, P.E.: Audiences in argumentation frameworks. Artif. Intell. **171**(1), 42–71 (2007)
6. Besnard, P., et al.: Introduction to structured argumentation. Argum. Comput. **5**(1), 1–4 (2014)

7. Besnard, P., Hunter, A.: Constructing argument graphs with deductive arguments: a tutorial. Argum. Comput. **5**(1), 5–30 (2014)
8. Coste-Marquis, S., Konieczny, S., Mailly, J.G., Marquis, P.: Extension enforcement in abstract argumentation as an optimization problem. In: Proceedings of the Twenty-Fourth International Joint Conference on Artificial Intelligence, pp. 2876–2882 (2015)
9. Cyras, K., Toni, F.: ABA+: assumption-based argumentation with preferences. In: Principles of Knowledge Representation and Reasoning: Proceedings of the Fifteenth International Conference, KR, pp. 553–556 (2016)
10. Dung, P.M., Kowalski, R.A., Toni, F.: Assumption-based argumentation. In: Simari, G., Rahwan, I. (eds.) Argumentation in Artificial Intelligence. Springer, Boston (2009). https://doi.org/10.1007/978-0-387-98197-0_10
11. Kaci, S., van der Torre, L.: Preference-based argumentation: arguments supporting multiple values. Int. J. Approx. Reasoning **48**(3), 730–751 (2008)
12. Mahesar, Q., Oren, N., Vasconcelos, W.W.: Computing preferences in abstract argumentation. In: Miller, T., Oren, N., Sakurai, Y., Noda, I., Savarimuthu, B.T.R., Cao Son, T. (eds.) PRIMA 2018. LNCS (LNAI), vol. 11224, pp. 387–402. Springer, Cham (2018). https://doi.org/10.1007/978-3-030-03098-8_24
13. Modgil, S.: Reasoning about preferences in argumentation frameworks. Artif. Intell. **173**(9), 901–934 (2009)
14. Modgil, S., Prakken, H.: The ASPIC$^+$ framework for structured argumentation: a tutorial. Argum. Comput. **5**(1), 31–62 (2014)
15. Rienstra, T., Thimm, M., Oren, N.: Opponent models with uncertainty for strategic argumentation. In: Proceedings of the Twenty-Third International Joint Conference on Artificial Intelligence, pp. 332–338. IJCAI/AAAI (2013)
16. Thimm, M.: Strategic argumentation in multi-agent systems. KI **28**(3), 159–168 (2014)
17. Toni, F.: A tutorial on assumption-based argumentation. Argum. Comput. **5**(1), 89–117 (2014)
18. Wakaki, T.: Assumption-based argumentation equipped with preferences and its application to decision making, practical reasoning, and epistemic reasoning. Comput. Intell. **33**(4), 706–736 (2017)

Declarative Preferences in Reactive BDI Agents

Mostafa Mohajeri Parizi(✉), Giovanni Sileno, and Tom van Engers

Complex Cyber Infrastructure, Informatics Institute, University of Amsterdam,
Amsterdam, The Netherlands
{m.mohajeriparizi,g.sileno,vanengers}@uva.nl

Abstract. Current agent architectures implementing the *belief-desire-intention*
(BDI) model consider agents which respond reactively to internal and external
events by selecting the first-available plan. Priority between plans is hard-coded
in the program, and so the reasons why a certain plan is preferred remain in the
programmer's mind. Recent works that attempt to include explicit preferences in
BDI agents treat preferences essentially as a rationale for planning tasks to be
performed at run-time, thus disrupting the reactive nature of agents. In this paper
we propose a method to include declarative preferences (i.e. concerning states of
affairs) in the agent program, and to use them in a manner that preserves reactivity. To achieve this, the plan prioritization step is performed offline, by (a) generating all possible outcomes of situated plan executions, (b) selecting a relevant
subset of situation/outcomes couplings as representative summary for each plan,
(c) sorting the plans by evaluating summaries through the agent's preferences.
The task of generating outcomes in several conditions is performed by translating the agent's procedural knowledge to an ASP program using discrete-event
calculus.

Keywords: BDI agents · CP-nets · Preferences · Belief-desire-intention ·
Answer set programming

1 Introduction

In the last decades several attempts have been made to move from machine-oriented
views of programming towards concepts and abstractions that more closely reflect
the way in which humans conceive the world. In particular, the *belief-desire-intention*
framework (BDI) [30], building upon a theory of mind [5], has been introduced to
provide a basis for the implementation of computational agents that exhibit rational
behaviour, using the same representations that we typically use to address human
behaviour. In the decision-making literature, instead, particular attention is given to
the role of preferences: any model of agency involving decision-making is deemed to
abide the agent's preferences [28]. This does not imply that any model of agency will
rely on explicit preferences, rather it affirms the general principle that when there are
multiple goals that should be achieved (or multiple ways to achieve a certain goal or
even multiple sets of states that can be reached) the best course of action is the one that
abides the most to the agent's preferences [28]. In practice, preferences can vary from

© Springer Nature Switzerland AG 2021
T. Uchiya et al. (Eds.): PRIMA 2020, LNAI 12568, pp. 215–230, 2021.
https://doi.org/10.1007/978-3-030-69322-0_14

the implicit "maximize utility" of optimizing agents [27] to explicit preferences specified in a preference representation language [7,34]. Unexpectedly, none of the main BDI languages presented in the literature support explicit preferences.

The present work proposes an approach for adding explicit declarative preferences (i.e. preferences about states of affairs possibly holding in the world) into BDI agent scripts. The novel contribution consists in presenting an offline method aiming to preserve the reactive executable nature of BDI agents. Declarative preferences are *compiled* together with the procedural knowledge and knowledge about primitive actions specified in the program into prioritized procedural knowledge. The resulting script is usable by any (AgentSpeak(L)-like) BDI interpreter such as Jason [3] or AgentScriptCC [25] without any modification to the reasoning cycle. The compilation approach has been selected to provide programmers with a higher abstraction model without compromising performance in execution. Indeed, our target use case is to embed purpose and constraints to programs—using intentional agents as controllers of given programs—for applications running on data-sharing infrastructures.

The paper is structured as follows. Section 2 provides an overview on related literature. Section 3 contains the proposed approach as the core of our contribution. Section 4 presents an illustrative example of application. Finally Sect. 5 contains the discussion and a note on future developments.

2   Background

BDI Agents. Agents specified following a BDI framework are represented by three mental attitudes. Beliefs are facts that the agent believes to be true. Desires capture the motivational dimension of the agent, typically conflated with the more concrete form of *goals*, representing procedures/states that the agent wants to perform/achieve. Intentions are selected conducts (or *plans*) that the agent commits to (in order to advance its desires).

Since their origin [30], the essential feature associated to BDI architectures is the ability to instantiate abstract plans that can (a) react to specific situations, and (b) be invoked based on their purpose. Consequently, the BDI execution model naturally relies on a *reactive* model of computation, usually in the form of some type of *event-condition-action* (ECA) rules often referred to as *goal-plan rules*. Goal-plan rules are uninstantiated specifications of the *means* (in terms of course of actions, or plan) for achieving a certain *goal* [30]. These constructs represent essentially the procedural knowledge (*how-to*) of the agent.

In current BDI implementations, preferences between these optional conducts are specified through a static ordering assigned by the programmer, typically via the ordering of rules in the code: the higher a rule is in the script, the more priority the associated plan has. This explains why most current frameworks including Jason [3], 2APL [8], AgentScriptCC [25], etc. are genuinely *reactive*: the scripts are interpreted without the need for any additional introspection/deliberation steps. However, these frameworks also expose functions that can be modified to implement alternative mechanism for goal-plan rule selection during the deliberation cycle. The latter option has been taken by almost all works adding explicit preferences to BDI agents [7,27,34]: the selection of the most preferred alternative is taken as a *reflective* process, where preferences provide a *rationale* to be applied online during the agent's deliberation cycle. The idea of relying on an offline step is instead proposed also in [24], but they only focused on *procedural preferences* ("I prefer to be doing a_i rather than doing a_j"), which have a different level of abstraction w.r.t. to declarative preferences ("I prefer being in state s_i rather than being in state s_j").

Preference Languages. Several models of preferences have been presented in the decision-making and planning literature, with various levels of granularity and expressiveness (see e.g. [11]). The most straightforward *quantitative* approaches are based upon *utility theory* and related forms of decision theory. In [6] one can find some examples of integration of these types of preferences in a BDI architecture.

Although quantitative approaches bring clear computational advantages, they also suffer from the non-trivial issue of translating users' preferences into utility functions. This explains the existence of a family of *qualitative* or hybrid solutions, as LPP [1] and PDDL3 [16]. Proposals exist for integrating LPP in BDI agents [34]. Other preference models, as CP-nets (qualitative) [4] and GAI networks (quantitative) [17], have been specifically introduced for taking into account dependencies and conditions between preferences via *compact representations* [28], highly relevant in domains with a large number of features. In the present work we will focus on CP-Nets because they rely on weaker assumptions, and exhibit primarily a qualitative nature. To our knowledge, [24] was the first attempt to introduce this type of representational models in a BDI architecture, although focusing only on procedural preferences.

More in detail, conditional *ceteris paribus* preferences networks (CP-nets) are a compact representation of preferences in domains with finite *attributes of interest* [4]. An attribute of interest is an attribute in the world (e.g. *weather*) that the agent has some sort of preference over its possible values (e.g. *sunny* and *rainy*). CP-nets build upon the idea that most of the preferences people make explicit are expressed jointly with an implicit *ceteris paribus* ("all things being equal") assumption. For instance, when players say "I prefer victory over loss", they do not mean at all costs and situations, but that they prefer victory, all other things being equal. An example of conditional preference could be "If I'm losing a game, I prefer to enjoy myself".

From Agent Scripts to Logic Programs. Reasoning about the effects of actions/plans in different contexts is a step necessary to decide their conditional, relative preferability. To implement a proof of concept for the proposed off-line approach, we relied here on the translation of agent scripts to ASP programs, but other choices would have also been possible. In the literature there are a few works that link BDI programs to logic programs [2], but, for the present work, we take inspiration from [10], which presents a formal method for translating a HTN planning domain to logic programs. This choice was motivated by the close connection between BDI programs and HTN planning domains, which has been explored extensively in the literature [23,33].

Answer set programming (ASP) is a knowledge representation and reasoning (KRR) paradigm, based on the *stable-model semantics* [15], oriented towards difficult (NP-hard) search problems. ASP is used successfully in a variety of applications in both academia and industry. In ASP, similarly to Prolog, the programmer models a problem in terms of rules and facts, rather than specifying an algorithm. The resulting code is given as input to a solver, which returns multiple *answer sets* or stable models that satisfy the problem.

Discrete Event Calculus. Modeling and reasoning with effects of actions efficiently is still an open question in AI and logic; however, focusing on logic programming, most solutions build upon *situation calculus* [22] and *event calculus* [18,32]. For our proof of concept we will consider *discrete event calculus* (DEC) [26]. By translating the agent script into a DEC compatible ASP program and solving this program with DEC axioms we are able to evaluate the execution outcome of the translated program.

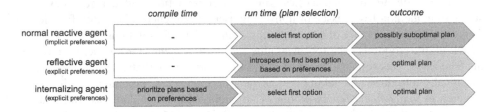

Fig. 1. Comparison of different approaches towards preferences in BDI agents.

3   Method

The approach proposed here aims to integrate (embed or *internalize*) preferences into BDI scripts without modifying the BDI deliberation cycle as it is normally implemented in current BDI agent platforms. For doing so, we extend agent programs with two additional knowledge components: (1) *declarative preferences* (i.e. about states of affairs), and (2) expectations about the effects of *primitive actions*. Such enriched script is not directly used for execution (i.e. fed to the BDI interpreter). We proceed instead with an off-line method that compiles this script into a new one:

(a) by using the expectations about primitive actions, we create a set of contextualized outcomes for each goal-plan rule;
(b) for each possible context condition, goal-plan rules are ordered from best to worst, based on their outcome according to the preference specifications;
(c) the script is rewritten but this time the placement of each goal-plan rule follows its position in the ordering obtained at step (b).

Note that both preferences and primitive actions specifications are omitted from the newly generated script, which is now executable by BDI interpreters/compilers such as Jason [3] or AgentScriptCC [25]. This contrasts other approaches that extend BDI frameworks with preference checking at run-time as a rationale for plan selection (e.g. [34]). Figure 1 schematizes the differences between approaches.

3.1   Components of Extended Agent Programs

Our approach requires three components for specifying agent programs: goal-plan rules, expectations about primitive actions, and preferential structures based on CP-nets.

Goal-Plan Rules. A goal-plan rule pr is a tuple $\langle e, c, p \rangle$, where: e is a *triggering event*, addressing an *invocation condition* e.g., adoption/failure of an unistantiated goal, assertion/retraction of a belief; c, the *context condition*, is a first-order formula over the agent's belief base, that, if true, makes the rule *applicable*; p, the *plan body*, consists of a finite sequence of steps $[a_1, a_2, ..., a_n]$ where each a_i is either a *goal* (i.e. an invocation attempting to trigger a goal-plan rule), or a *primitive action*. A goal-plan rule pr_i is then an *option* or a *possibility* for achieving a goal g, if the invocation condition of pr_i matches with g, and the context condition of pr_i matches the current state of the world, as perceived or encoded in the agent's beliefs.

We will refer here to a syntax close to that of AgentSpeak(L) [29], although with slightly different semantics. Unlike AgentSpeak(L), which does not primarily support declarative goals [8], ! g will denote here an *achievement goal*. This means that g is a state or condition in the world that can hold or not hold (cases denoted respectively as g or ~g). Positive and negative achievement goals, e.g. concerning the production and removal of a condition g, will be denoted respectively as ! g and ! ~g. A primitive action named a will be denoted as #a. Then, for any condition g, + ! g denotes a *goal-invocation* (possible triggering event of goal-plan rule). As an example of a script, consider:

```
+!g : c <= !a.
+!g <= !~b.
```

This code means that if the triggering event + ! g occurs, if c holds, the agent commits to *achieve* a, otherwise (that is, c does not hold) the agent commits to *achieve* ~b, or equivalently, to *escape* b. The backward sense of the arrow "<=" highlights the derivation due to instrumental reasoning (plans as a mean to reach the goal).

The standard AgentSpeak(L) syntax provides no unique identifier to distinguish goal-plan rules (although Jason offers some *labeling* construct). There is also no standard way to have direct access to the plan of a rule. A possible solution to identify a specific plan without explicit labeling is to refer to the invocation condition of the associated rule alongside its position, e.g. with respect to other rules with the same invocation condition. Thus, the two plans in the code excerpt above about achieving g via achieving a and escaping b will be respectively denoted as ! g [0] and ! g [1].

Primitive Actions. Primitive actions are the lowest-level actions that can be used in the procedural knowledge of an agent; they are the actual means for the agent to change the environment (or itself). As a matter of fact, BDI agents rely on goal-plan rules as an abstract task decomposition tool, mapping high-level recipes to an appropriate sequence of primitive actions to be performed in the environment.

Several approaches to specify expectations about primitive actions are available in the literature, especially in the AI planning field (e.g. *operators* for works derived from

STRIPS [13], *primitive tasks* for works based on HTNs [12]), but they are not common in the BDI literature. This is because, in contrast to a common assumption in planning, BDI agents are deemed to interact with a non-deterministic environment; even more, as it is stated in [8], the effects of external (primitive) actions are "actually" determined by the environment and might be not known or incorrectly known by the agents beforehand. While this is true at run-time, it is also reasonable to consider that an agent can have some expectations about the effects of its (primitive) actions beforehand. For instance, when an agent buys a train ticket it may encounter many problems and not receive a ticket, but it is fair to assume that the agent knows that "if I buy a train ticket, then I will have a ticket".

Because the preference compilation method proposed here occurs off-line, our work can be associated to a certain extent to the planning domain–although here agents do not create new plans but deal only with the given procedural knowledge. In STRIPS primitive actions are specified with the description of their effects, and of the conditions under which they are applicable, while in HTN primitive actions are only specified by their effects (delegating the precondition to methods). To take advantage of the complementary aspects of STRIPS and HTN approaches to primitive actions (more expressiveness and more control for the designer), we consider the hybrid solution proposed in [20]: "omitting strict action preconditions, assuming instead that actions leave the state unchanged if their preconditions are not met". This means that, although preconditions are part of action specification, they do not determine the applicability of the action, but they merely put conditions over the effects. A very similar approach is taken in the agent language 2APL [8] for *belief update actions*.

More formally, a primitive action a is specified as a tuple $\langle h, \Delta \rangle$, where h is the head or name of the action and Δ is the set of conditional effects of the action. Each $\delta \in \Delta$ is a combination of effects, captured as $\langle c, e \rangle$, in which c is a logical expression modeling the condition necessary for that combination to occur, and e is a list of effects each having a modifier + or – and a propositional atom t. If the expression c is true when the action occurs, then, after action completion, atoms with the + modifier are expected to hold and atoms with the – are expected to not hold. In case multiple more that one condition holds, all applicable effects are expected to happen and if there are conflicts the precedence goes to the effect described later. A simple syntax is used to represent the primitive action effects in the forms of #h{LCE}, where h is the head of action, and LCE is a dot separated list of condition-effects CE in the form of c => e and where c is the is a propositional expression representing the condition e is a comma (,) separated list of positive (initialization) or negative (termination) effects. Consider for instance the following statement:

```
#a { c1 => +p,-q. c2 => +q. }
```

The forward sense of the arrow "=>" highlights the production nature of CE components (action in conditions produces effects). The previous formula means that (the agent expects that) if the primitive action a occurs, if c1 holds, then p will become true, if c2 holds, then q will become true. It can also happen that both c1 and c2 hold which results in a contradiction between +q and -q in the post-condition. As this approach utilises an ASP solver (Sect. 3.2) a contradiction stops the answer branch. We introduce specific axioms to raise a warning in this case.

CP-Nets for Declarative Preferences. Constraining our attention on declarative goals, the preferences we target are about the presence or absence of certain conditions, here captured respectively by positive or negative literals. In this frame, the attributes of interests for the CP-net concern possible conditions that might *occur* in the world.

In behavioural terms, each attribute has two possible values: (1) achieving or maintaining the condition g, here denoted with the goal name !g, (2) avoiding or escaping the condition g, denoted as !~g. Following a syntax similar to the one used for procedural preferences in [24], we denote the preference for achieving/maintaining the condition g over avoiding/escaping it in condition c as:

!g > !~g : c.

In general, c might be an higher priority preferential attribute, a contextual condition or a logical true in the case of an unconditional preference.

3.2 Transformation to Logic Program

In order to evaluate plans in terms of their preferability, we need to infer the contextualized outcomes associated to each goal-plan rule. A possible solution for this task is to translate the initial BDI script with the added knowledge of primitive action specifications to a discrete event calculus (DEC)-based ASP program, so that each answer set of the program is a contextualized outcome for a goal-plan rule. The following section describes the translation method we followed. Other discrete simulation techniques (possibly more efficient) are indeed possible, but such difference in implementation would not functionally change the present proposal.

An agent program is a tuple $\langle S, A, P, G \rangle$, where S is a set of propositions representing all possible beliefs about the world that can be true or false at each time; A is a set of primitive actions, each formalized as $\langle h, \Delta \rangle$; P is a set of goal-plan rules, each formalized as $\langle e, c, p \rangle$; G is a set of (achievement) goals derived from the goal-plan rule heads. The following properties and relations can be identified:

1. For each goal $g \in G$, $g \in S$.
2. For each goal-plan rule $pr = \langle e, c, p \rangle \in P$, the atoms used in the expression c are propositions in S.
3. The effects of each primitive action $\alpha \in P$ is denoted as $\langle c, add, del \rangle$. The atoms of the expression c and the atoms present in add and del are all propositions in S.
4. Each step of the plan body of each goal-plan rule is either a primitive action #a or a sub-goal !g. In the former case there is a primitive action $\alpha \in A$ that $\alpha = \langle a, \Delta \rangle$ and in the latter case there is a $g \in G$.
5. All proposition $s \in S$ falls at least under one of the sets relevant for properties 1, 2, and 3.

Thus, for each *proposition* $s \in S$, a predicate *fluent*(s) is added to the logic program, expressing that s is a *fluent* of DEC. The state of a proposition s at each time t is captured by the predicate *holdsAt*(s, t). For each *primitive action* $\alpha_i = \langle a_i, \Delta_i \rangle$ a predicate *event*(a_i). is added to the logic program expressing that a_i is an *event* of DEC. For each goal $g \in G$ a predicate *goal*(g) and for each goal-plan rule $g_i = \langle g, c, p \rangle \in P$, a predicate *plan*$(g_i, g)$ is added to the program. Note that only primitive actions and propositions are translated into DEC predicates, whereas goal-plans and goals are only means to guide primitive actions.

Following DEC axioms, the execution of an action (event) a at time t is represented with the predicate $happens(a,t)$. In our translation we use a predicate $doAction/3$ that contains also the goal-plan rule of which this action is part of. Their relationship is captured as follows:

$$happens(A, T) \leftarrow doAction(A, P, T), event(A), time(T). \tag{1}$$

The conditional effects of primitive actions to the program are expressed by the DEC predicates $initiates/3$ and $terminates/3$. For each the primitive action $\alpha = \langle a, \Delta \rangle$, for each effect $\delta = \langle c, e \rangle \in \Delta$, for each conditional effect of initiating a proposition s with modifiers + or − under condition c, a logical rule in form of respectively rules (2) and (3) is added to the program. In the most general case, the condition expression c is a logical formula $\mathcal{C}(T)$, translated respectively by the predicates $holdsAt(c_i, T)$ and $not\ holdsAt(c_i, T)$.

$$initiates(a, s, T) \leftarrow time(T), \mathcal{C}(T). \tag{2}$$
$$terminates(a, s, T) \leftarrow time(T), \mathcal{C}(T). \tag{3}$$

To represent the adoption, completion and selection of goals or sub-goals by the agent, we introduce the predicates $adoptGoal/4$, $complGoalAt/3$, $selPlan/3$. An instantiation $adoptGoal(g, p, t', t)$ states that goal $g \in G$ is adopted by the agent at time t, as a sub-goal of plan p that started at t'; $complGoalAt(g, t, t')$ conveys that the goal g–adopted at time t–is completed at time t'; $selPlan(g_i, g, t)$ means that the plan g_i is instantiated to achieve goal g at time t.

The first step for mapping the goal-plan rules concerns the context condition. We introduce the predicate $applPlan(P, T)$, meaning that goal-plan rule P is *applicable* at time T. For each goal-plan rule $g_i = \langle g, c, p \rangle$ we add the following rule (c is again translated to $\mathcal{C}(T)$ by using predicate $holdsAt/2$):

$$applPlan(g_i, T) \leftarrow time(T), plan(g_i, G), \mathcal{C}(T). \tag{4}$$

Next, we connect triggering events to plan bodies while also taking into account the applicability of the goal-plan rules. Axiom (5) makes sure that when a goal is adopted, for each answer set exactly one of its applicable plans are selected:

$$\{selPlan(P', G, T) : applPlan(P', T), plan(P', G)\} = 1 \leftarrow adoptGoal(G, P, T', T). \tag{5}$$

Mapping the sequence of actions (steps) specified in a plan is less direct. Following the method presented in [10], we consider that the selection of the plan at a time t only triggers the first step of the plan at time $t + 1$, and from then on the completion of each step at a time t triggers the next step at time $t + 1$, save for the final step of the plan that triggers the completion of the plan at time $t + 1$. The reason behind this method is that each step of a plan can be either a sub-goal or a primitive action; if we can fairly assume a primitive action takes exactly one time-step to execute, the same can not be said for sub-goals (as, depending on their refinements, they can take several time-steps to complete).

The first step ($k = 0$) of the plan g_i associated to a goal g is encoded in rule (6) or (7) if the first step respectively is a primitive action a or adoption of a sub-goal g'.

$$doAction(a, g_i, T + 1) \leftarrow selPlan(g_i, g, T). \tag{6}$$

$$adoptGoal(g', g_i, T, T + 1) \leftarrow selPlan(g_i, g, T). \tag{7}$$

From the second step on ($k \geq 1$), the kth step is encoded to happen at time $t' + 1$ if t' is the time of completion of $k - 1^{\text{th}}$ step, as shown in rule (8) if the kth step is the execution of a primitive action a, rule (9) if the kth step is the adoption of a sub-goal g' or rule (10) if $k - 1^{\text{th}}$ is the final step of plan g_i:

$$doAction(a, g_i, T' + 1) \leftarrow *. \tag{8}$$

$$adoptGoal(g', g_i, T, T' + 1) \leftarrow *. \tag{9}$$

$$complGoal(g, T, T' + 1) \leftarrow *. \tag{10}$$

The right side of these rules ($*$) has to be replaced with right side of rules (11) or (12) if $k - 1^{\text{th}}$ step is respectively a primitive action a' or the adoption of sub-goal g''.

$$** \leftarrow selPlan(g_i, g, T), doAction(a', g_i, T'), T' > T. \tag{11}$$

$$* \leftarrow selPlan(g_i, g, T), adoptGoal(g'', g_i, T, T''),$$
$$complGoal(g'', T'', T'), T' > T'' \tag{12}$$

The following axiom is added to reflect the achievement nature of goals. When a goal $!g$ completes at time T', then g is a state in the world that holds at time T':

$$holdsAt(G, T') \leftarrow goal(G), complGoal(G, T, T') \tag{13}$$

We use the following axiom to let the ASP grounder create time-steps as it goes; i.e. $t + 1$ is a time step if t is a time-step and there is a step scheduled for t:

$$time(T + 1) \leftarrow time(T),$$
$$(selPlan(..., T); doAction(..., T);$$
$$adoptGoal(..., T); complGoal(..., T)). \tag{14}$$

After translating the script into an ASP program we need to find all the *traces* (i.e. outcomes of execution paths) of the script for all possible entry points (i.e. context conditions). Here, there is no assumption of a single entry point for the script and, based on internal or external events, any goal could in principle be adopted in any condition. Axiom (15) is used to force the solver to adopt exactly one goal as entry point in each answer set:

$$\{adoptGoal(G, init, 0, 1) : goal(G)\} = 1. \tag{15}$$

The answer sets of this program, denoted as R, will contain all the hypothetical paths that the agent script can start and run, including all the different refinements, i.e. all different initial states that may be at the starting point.

3.3 Plan Priority Extraction and Script Rewriting

Prioritizing plans is needed only if there is more than one plan for achieving a goal; therefore, for the rest of this section when we refer to all goals, we refer to all goals that have more than one plan associated to them.

As a first step we need to find all the conditions for which a plan g_i can be instantiated, here denoted as a multi-set $C(g_i)$. To do this, for each trace $r \in R$, for each k-th occurrence of predicate $selPlan(g_i, g, t) \in r$, we create a set $c(g_i, r)[k]$ (for simplicity denoted as $c(g_i, r)$, assuming there is only one occurrence). Then $c(g_i, r)$ is representative of a state for which plan g_i is instantiated in the trace. Using the trace r, and assuming $selPlan(g_i, g, t) \in r$, $c(g_i, r)$ is constructed by the following elements:

1. **Motivational Context**: all the goals g' whose decomposition in r contain the plan g_i, i.e. all the goals that are adopted before but not completed at t; formally, all g' such that $(adoptGoal(g', P, T, t') \wedge complGoalAt(g', t', t'')) \in r$ with $t' \le t \le t''$;
2. **Propositions**: all positive (resp. negative) fluent f of the program which is in the trace r as $holdsAt(f, t)$ (resp. $not\ holdsAt(f, t)$);
3. **Achieved Goals**: all the goals g'' that are *achieved* as part a motivational context of the plan g_i prior to t; based on axiom (13), a completed goal g is present in the trace as $holdsAt(g, t)$.

An outcome of a trace r is a propositional state of the final time-step of the trace, denoted as $\Gamma(r)$, and includes all the (declarative) goals achieved in r plus the state of all the fluents at the final time-step.

Under the condition of consistency of the preferential structure and the *preferential comparison algorithm* presented in [4], there is a (possibly strict) order between outcomes, and we say an outcome $\Gamma(r)$ is preferred to outcome $\Gamma(r')$ and denote it as $\Gamma(r) \succeq \Gamma(r')$. Each $C(g_i)$ is a multi-set, meaning that for different traces $r, r' \in R$, we often have $c(g_i, r) = c(g_i, r')$ but $\Gamma(r) \ne \Gamma(r')$. This informally means that, in the same conditions, selecting a plan can have multiple different *reachable* outcomes. An outcome is called reachable for a plan g_i if *all* refinements of g_i will result in that outcome . However, as observed in [21], this approach starts from a very pessimistic view, ignoring the fact that the agent itself (not an adversary) chooses which refinements to make in the future, so instead of thinking what it might bring about in all refinements, we are interested in what is the *best* outcome that can happen under some refinement (the best outcome here indicates the optimal outcome according to the preferences specified in the CP-net).

The next step of the algorithm is *summarizing* the outcomes of plans, which means generating an optimal outcome for each plan g_i of each goal g, under each different unique condition. The optimal outcome is dependent on the conditions in which the plan was selected. More formally, an outcome $\Gamma(r)$ is optimal for the condition plan g_i under condition $c(g_i, r)$, if, for all other traces r' such that $c(g_i, r) = c(g_i, r')$, we have $\Gamma(r) \succeq \Gamma(r')$ or $\Gamma(r') \not\succeq \Gamma(r)$. This optimal outcome of plan g_i under condition of $c = c(g_i, r)$ is referred to as $\gamma(g_i, c)$.

At this point, we need to find a best-to-worst ordering between the optimal outcomes of plans of each goal g for each condition that g may be adopted. The conditions for which a plan g_i is instantiated are a subset of the conditions for which the goal g can be adopted, which means $C(g_i) \subseteq C(g)$. Similarly, the conditions for which a goal may be adopted is the union of the conditions for which all plans g_i may be instantiated.

We say that a plan $g_i \succeq g_j$ under condition $c \in C(g)$ if one of the following is true:

1. we have $c \in C(g_i)$ but $c \notin C(g_j)$
2. we have both $c \in C(g_i)$ and $c \in C(g_j)$ and also $\gamma(g_i, c) \succeq \gamma(g_j, c)$

The first rule is trivial and means that under a certain condition a plan that can be instantiated and has an outcome is preferred to one that even hypothetically does not have any outcomes. The second rule means that under similar conditions, between two plans, one that has the preferred optimistic outcome is always preferred. By running this procedure on all goals we can produce an ordering between plans.

4 Application

Suppose that a player agent has three ways to play a match: playing for fun, do whatever needed to win, or play conservative to avoid to lose. Suppose now that the player might want e.g. to enjoy its game as much as winning, but it might also prefer to gain support from observers, unless its position in the ranking (captured by propositions `first` and `last`—that can not be true at the same time) is really low. Let us start from the following procedural knowledge:

```
+!match <= !enjoy. // match[0]
        <= !win.   // match[1]
        <= !~lose. // match[2]
+!enjoy <= #funny_playing.
+!~lose <= #robust_playing.
+!win <= #opportunistic_playing.
```

And the following expectations about primitive actions:

```
#funny_playing { => +support, -win. }
#robust_playing { => +support, -enjoy. }
#opportunistic_playing { => -support, -lose }
```

We then specify our agent by the following preferences

```
!win > !~win : last.
!support > !~support : ~last.
!win > !~win : support, ~last.
!enjoy > !~enjoy : first.
```

By applying the method presented in 3.2 we obtain a logic program[1]. As an indicative excerpt, we report the goal-plan rule for `match[0]`:

```
adopts_goal(enjoy, match_0, T, T+1)
    :- selects_plan(match_0, match, T).
finished(match, match_0, T, T2+1) :-
    selects_plan(match_0, match, T),
    adopts_goal(enjoy, match_0, T, T2),
    finished(enjoy, P, T2, T3), T3 > T2.
```

---

[1] Source available at https://gitlab.com/Mohajeri/as2asp.

By solving the program with `clingo` [14], we obtain 192 answer sets ($|R| = 192$). The only goal in the program with alternative plans is `!match` and so only the answer sets containing this goal are needed. Focusing on its three goal-plan rules we consider 36 answer sets from which we extract 6 unique outcomes for each plan. An example of condition and outcome extracted from a trace r for plan $g_i = $ `match[0]` is:

```
condition c1: ~win,~support,~enjoy,~lose,first,~last
outcome o1: ~win,support,enjoy,~lose,first,~last
```

Relating to the formalization of previous part we can say that $c($`match[0]`$, r) = $ c1 and $\Gamma(r) = $ o1.

Each answer set is evaluated in terms of the given preferential structure, resulting in a partial ordering between different outcomes of traces. For instance, the answer sets with outcome o2 are preferred over the answer sets with outcome o3. The *dominance checking* is done with the tool CRISNER [31]:

```
outcome o2: ~win,support,enjoy,~lose,first,~last
outcome o3: win,~support,~enjoy,~lose,first,~last
```

Following our formalization, if we take two answer sets (traces) r and r' such that $\Gamma(r) = $ o2 and $\Gamma(r') = $ o3, according to the preferential structure we infer that $\Gamma(r) \succeq \Gamma(r')$. Then, following the ranking, we can give contextualized priorities to plans, observing that e.g. if we have a condition:

```
condition c2: ~win,~support,~enjoy,~lose,first,~last
```

the plan `match[0]` is preferred over plan `match[1]`, whereas plan `match[1]` is preferred over `match[2]`. Formally this means that, under condition c2, we have

$$\text{match[0]} \succeq \text{match[1]} \succeq \text{match[2]}$$

Considering all existing plans, the initial procedural knowledge can be then prioritized. For the 3 plans associated to `+!match` there are 6 possible orderings. The following code provides an example of conditional ordering obtained via our method (including a *boolean simplification* step for the pre-conditions):

```
+!match : (last | ~enjoy) & ~first
          <= !~lose.
          <= !win.
          <= !enjoy.
+!match : (~last | lose) & (last | enjoy) & ~win
          <= !enjoy.
          <= !win.
          <= !~lose.
```

5 Discussion and Further Developments

The strong support in the decision-making literature for *compact representations* of verbalized preferences—as for instance those captured e.g. by CP-nets [4]—motivates their use in computational agents, especially in applications in which agents are deemed to reproduce human behaviour. Indeed, our more general research effort aims to capture intentional characterizations of (computational) behaviour of computational agents in data-sharing infrastructures in support of policy-making and regulation activities. Regulating data-sharing requires to reproduce to a certain extent constructs similar to those observed in human institutions (e.g. For which purpose the agent is asking access to the resource? On which basis the infrastructure is granting access?). For *traceability* and *explainability* reasons, decisions concerning actions need to be processed by the infrastructure as much as other relevant operational aspects.

Introducing explicit preferences in BDI scripts brings three advantages: (1) It increases the *representational depth*, capturing what is the rationale behind the priority in plan selection; (2) It makes agent models more readable and *explainable*, as choices are in principle transparently derived from the preferential structure; (3) It makes the programs more *reusable*: it is plausible that agents (e.g. representatives of organizations) in a certain domain might share the same procedural knowledge even when having different preferences, as much as that agents might change their policy without changing their procedural knowledge.

The connections between desires, preferences and goals requires further clarification. In the current work we started from the AgentSpeak(L) view of desires, for which "goals are viewed as adopted desires" and while this is mostly accepted by the BDI community, it hints to a gap between goals and desires pointed out already almost twenty years ago [9]. In this work we used preferences essentially to specify desires (in the sense of *soft goals*) (e.g. "I want to enjoy the game" as "I prefer to enjoy the game more than not enjoying the game") and relative strength between desires (if not losing, "I want to gain support more than winning" as "I prefer to gain support more than winning"). The priority between plans is then selected so as to satisfy at best the desires of the agent. Note that in general the literature suggests that preferences are derived from desires [19]; for our purposes, however, we discovered that two could be seen as functionally equivalent. Further investigation is needed to see the consequences of this reduction.

The proposed method here is indeed a contribution towards enhancing BDI agent-programming languages with syntactic and semantic facilities to support explicit preferences, but, in contrast to other works, it also fulfills the aim of maintaining *reactivity*, one of the core properties of BDI agents (see [35], or [3], referring to AgentSpeak(L) agents as "reactive planning systems"). BDI agents are theoretically developed to act in dynamic environments and an offline view on preferences may seem too limiting at first, as preferences of a dynamic agent can change in a highly dynamic environment. This might explain why so few authors chose this path. However, we will put forward two reasons why this is still a relevant issue. First, agent programs, today, are static in nature; any modification at run-time relies on implicit forms of meta-programming whose general effects are difficult to be anticipated. For instance, preferences might be incomplete and/or conflicting. By adding an additional compilation step, these issues might be captured while rewriting the script, so the user can be required to take action to settle them. Second, reactivity is a valuable property to enable computationally scalable implementations (cf. modern reactive programming). Indeed, the uses we are aiming to (simulations in support of policy-making, applications running on data-sharing infrastructures) would greatly benefit of this choice. If each agent had to repeat online the full derivation from preferences to preferred plan, the computational overhead would strongly negatively affect performance. Besides this, with our method, we can still allow agents to re-adapt periodically: i.e. update their preferences based on some criteria (e.g. mimicking more successful agents), then update and reload their run-time script. This approach is also cognitively more realistic: we, as humans, do not deliberate upon our preferences for each action we perform.

However, we also acknowledge that the exploration of all context conditions and possible outcomes is in general an intractable problem, even if we rely on optimized solvers. The proposal presented here has to be seen merely as a functional proof of concept; for actual use additional heuristics need to be added to reduce the search space to most relevant nodes, for instance exploiting weights in ASP resolution.

In general, preferences might be not only concerning desired states of affairs, but also possible states of affairs, or expectations about primitive actions, thus determining that certain contexts are more relevant than others. This part of the problem has also connections with probabilistic logic programming and reasoning with uncertainties.

In terms of priority for future developments, however, we recognize the work presented in this paper has been limited to propositional logic; clearly, extending it to consider first-order logic (FOL) descriptions of both agent scripts and preferences is an important objective for actual applicability. Additionally, while plan selection is the only component of the BDI execution model studied in this work, a similar approach could also be taken for other components of the deliberation cycle, for which other authors resorted to reflective methods, like intent selection and event selection [36].

Finally, although the logic of CP-nets is widely accepted in the literature, the presence in our research of sequential choices and different types of goals adds complexities that the CP-net syntax is not adequate to address in its default form; we acknowledge the need for a more principled extension or an exploration of other representational models for preferences.

Acknowledgments. This paper results from work done within the NWO-funded project *Data Logistics for Logistics Data* (DL4LD, https://www.dl4ld.net) in the Commit2Data program (grant no: 628.001.001).

References

1. Bienvenu, M., Fritz, C., McIlraith, S.A.: Planning with qualitative temporal preferences. In: Proceedings of the 10th International Conference on the Principles of Knowledge Representation and Reasoning (KR2006), pp. 134–144 (2006)
2. Blount, J., Gelfond, M., Balduccini, M.: A theory of intentions for intelligent agents. In: Calimeri, F., Ianni, G., Truszczynski, M. (eds.) LPNMR 2015. LNCS (LNAI), vol. 9345, pp. 134–142. Springer, Cham (2015). https://doi.org/10.1007/978-3-319-23264-5_12
3. Bordini, R.H., Hübner, J.F., Vieira, R.: *Jason* and the golden fleece of agent-oriented programming. In: Bordini, R.H., Dastani, M., Dix, J., El Fallah Seghrouchni, A. (eds.) Multi-Agent Programming. MSASSO, vol. 15, pp. 3–37. Springer, Boston, MA (2005). https://doi.org/10.1007/0-387-26350-0_1

4. Boutilier, C., Brafman, R.I., Domshlak, C., Hoos, H.H., Poole, D.: CP-nets: a tool for representing and reasoning with conditional ceteris paribus preference statements. J. Artif. Intell. Res. **21**, 135–191 (2004)
5. Bratman, M.E.: Intention, Plans, and Practical Reason, vol. 10. Harvard University Press, Cambridge (1987)
6. Cranefield, S., Winikoff, M., Dignum, V., Dignum, F.: No pizza for you: value-based plan selection in BDI agents. In: Proceedings of the 26th International Joint Conference on Artificial Intelligence (IJCAI2017), pp. 178–184 (2017)
7. Dasgupta, A., Ghose, A.K.: Implementing reactive BDI agents with user-given constraints and objectives. Int. J. Agent-Oriented Softw. Eng. **4**(2), 141 (2010)
8. Dastani, M.: 2APL: a practical agent programming language. Auton. Agent. Multi-Agent Syst. **16**(3), 214–248 (2008). https://doi.org/10.1007/s10458-008-9036-y
9. Dignum, F., Kinny, D., Sonenberg, L.: From desires, obligations and norms to goals. Cogn. Sci. Q. **2**, 405–427 (2002)
10. Dix, J., Kuter, U., Nau, D.: Planning in answer set programming using ordered task decomposition. In: Günter, A., Kruse, R., Neumann, B. (eds.) KI 2003. LNCS (LNAI), vol. 2821, pp. 490–504. Springer, Heidelberg (2003). https://doi.org/10.1007/978-3-540-39451-8_36
11. Domshlak, C., Hüllermeier, E., Kaci, S., Prade, H.: Preferences in AI: an overview. Artif. Intell. **175**(7–8), 1037–1052 (2011)
12. Erol, K., Hendler, J., Nau, D.S.: HTN planning: complexity and expressivity. In: Proceedings of the 12th AAAI Conference on Artificial Intelligence, pp. 1123–1129 (1994)
13. Fikes, R.E., Nilsson, N.J.: STRIPS: a new approach to the application of theorem proving to problem solving. Artif. Intell. **2**(3–4), 189–208 (1971)
14. Gebser, M., Kaminski, R., Kaufmann, B., Schaub, T.: Clingo = ASP + control: Preliminary report. CoRR abs/1405.3694 (2014)
15. Gelfond, M., Lifschitz, V.: The stable model semantics for logic programming. In: Proceedings of International Logic Programming Conference and Symposium, pp. 1070–1080 (1988)
16. Gerevini, A., Long, D.: Plan constraints and preferences in PDDL3. Technical report (2005)
17. Gonzales, C., Perny, P.: GAI networks for utility elicitation. In: Proceedings of the 9th International Conference on the Principles of Knowledge Representation and Reasoning (KR2004), pp. 224–233 (2004)
18. Kowalski, R., Sergot, M.: A logic-based calculus of events. N. Gener. Comput. **4**(1), 67–95 (1986)
19. Lorini, E.: Logics for games, emotions and institutions. IfCoLog J. Log. Appli. **4**(9), 3075–3113 (2017)
20. Marthi, B., Russell, S., Wolfe, J.: Angelic Hierarchical Planning: Optimal and Online Algorithms (Revised). Technical Report UCB/EECS-2008-150, pp. 1–22 (2008)
21. Marthi, B., Russell, S.J., Wolfe, J.: Angelic semantics for high-level actions. In: Proceedings of the 17th International Conference on Automated Planning and Scheduling, pp. 232–239 (2007)
22. McCarthy, J., Hayes, P.J.: Some philosophical problems from the standpoint of artificial intelligence. In: Machine Intelligence, pp. 1–51. Edinburgh University Press (1969)
23. Meneguzzi, F., De Silva, L.: Planning in BDI agents: a survey of the integration of planning algorithms and agent reasoning. Knowl. Eng. Rev. **30**(1), 1–44 (2013)
24. Mohajeri Parizi, M., Sileno, G., van Engers, T.: Integrating CP-nets in reactive BDI agents. In: Baldoni, M., Dastani, M., Liao, B., Sakurai, Y., Zalila Wenkstern, R. (eds.) PRIMA 2019. LNCS (LNAI), vol. 11873, pp. 305–320. Springer, Cham (2019). https://doi.org/10.1007/978-3-030-33792-6_19

25. Mohajeri Parizi, M., Sileno, G., van Engers, T., Klous, S.: Run, agent, run! architecture and benchmark of actor-based agents. In: Proceedings of Programming Based on Actors, Agents, and Decentralized Control (AGERE20). ACM (2020)
26. Mueller, E.T.: Event calculus reasoning through satisfiability. J. Log. Comput. **14**(5), 703–730 (2004)
27. Nunes, I., Luck, M.: Softgoal-based plan selection in model-driven BDI agents. In: 13th International Conference on Autonomous Agents and Multiagent Systems, AAMAS 2014, pp. 749–756 (2014)
28. Pigozzi, G., Tsoukiàs, A., Viappiani, P.: Preferences in artificial intelligence. Ann. Math. Artif. Intell. **77**(3–4), 361–401 (2016). https://doi.org/10.1007/s10472-015-9475-5
29. Rao, A.S.: AgentSpeak(L): BDI agents speak out in a logical computable language. In: Van de Velde, W., Perram, J.W. (eds.) MAAMAW 1996. LNCS, vol. 1038, pp. 42–55. Springer, Heidelberg (1996). https://doi.org/10.1007/BFb0031845
30. Rao, A.S., Georgeff, M.P.: BDI agents: from theory to practice. In: Proceedings of the First International Conference on Multi-Agent Systems (ICMAS1995), pp. 312–319 (1995)
31. Santhanam, G.R., Basu, S., Honavar, V.: Dominance testing via model checking. Proc. Natl. Conf. Artif. Intell. **1**, 357–362 (2010)
32. Shanahan, M.: The event calculus explained. In: Wooldridge, M.J., Veloso, M. (eds.) Artificial Intelligence Today. LNCS (LNAI), vol. 1600, pp. 409–430. Springer, Heidelberg (1999). https://doi.org/10.1007/3-540-48317-9_17
33. de Silva, L., Padgham, L., Sardina, S.: HTN-like solutions for classical planning problems: an application to BDI agent systems. Theoret. Comput. Sci. **763**, 12–37 (2019)
34. Visser, S., Thangarajah, J., Harland, J.: Reasoning about preferences in intelligent agent systems. In: Proceedings of the International Joint Conference on Artificial Intelligence (IJCAI2011), pp. 426–431 (2011)
35. Wooldridge, M.J., Jennings, N.R.: Intelligent agents: theory and practice. Knowl. Eng. Rev. **10**(2), 115–152 (1995)
36. Yao, Y., Logan, B.: Action-level intention selection for BDI agents. In: Proceedings of the 15th International Conference on Autonomous Agents and Multiagent Systems (AAMAS2016), pp. 1227–1236 (2016)

Predicting the Priority of Social Situations for Personal Assistant Agents

Ilir Kola[1]([⊠])[iD], Myrthe L. Tielman[1][iD], Catholijn M. Jonker[1,2][iD],
and M. Birna van Riemsdijk[3][iD]

[1] Delft University of Technology, Delft, The Netherlands
{i.kola,m.l.tielman,c.m.jonker}@tudelft.nl
[2] Leiden Institute of Advanced Computer Science, Leiden, The Netherlands
[3] University of Twente, Enschede, The Netherlands
m.b.vanriemsdijk@utwente.nl

Abstract. Personal assistant agents have been developed to help people
in their daily lives with tasks such as agenda management. In order to
provide better support, they should not only model the user's internal
aspects, but also their social situation. Current research on social context tackles this by modelling the social aspects of a situation from an
objective perspective. In our approach, we model these social aspects of
the situation from the user's subjective perspective. We do so by using
concepts from social science, and in turn apply machine learning techniques to predict the priority that the user would assign to these situations. Furthermore, we show that using these techniques allows agents
to determine which features influenced these predictions. Results based
on a crowd-sourcing user study suggest that our proposed model would
enable personal assistant agents to differentiate between situations with
high and low priority. We believe this to be a first step towards agents
that better understand the user's social situation, and adapt their support accordingly.

Keywords: Social situations modelling · Adaptive personal
assistants · Machine learning techniques · Explainable AI

1 Introduction

Artificial agents that play the role of personal assistants are increasingly becoming part of everyday life (e.g. [14]). These agents have focused on representing
internal aspects of the user, such as their values, goals, or emotions [25]. However, research in social science suggests that human behaviour is shaped both by
these internal aspects, as well as by the situation someone is in [16]. Situations
have a physical aspect (e.g., where it takes place) and a social one (e.g., who

This work is part of the research programme CoreSAEP, with project number
639.022.416, which is financed by the Netherlands Organisation for Scientific Research
(NWO).

T. Uchiya et al. (Eds.): PRIMA 2020, LNAI 12568, pp. 231–247, 2021.
https://doi.org/10.1007/978-3-030-69322-0_15

is involved). We focus on the latter: our goal is to build methods which allow personal assistant agents to model the social situation of a user, and use that information to reason about how to provide socially-aware support.

The need for enabling intelligent support agents (such as personal assistants) to understand the social situation of the user has been acknowledged as one of the main open questions in agent research [12,32]. Existing work on modelling social context focuses on modelling the social practices of a situation (e.g. [7]), or the place where the interaction is taking place (e.g. [20]). In our approach, we model situations from the perspective of the user of the personal assistant agent by modelling how the user relates to the people in that situation on a number of relevant dimensions. This complements [7], which models the social practices *of a situation*, while we focus on modelling the perspective of an individual *on that situation*. This requires additional social features to describe social relations between people that go beyond their roles in the situation. Based on information about how the user relates to the social situation, we investigate how an agent can interpret that situation in order to determine desired actions that can support the user. Regarding our technical approach, we combine the strengths of existing work: we propose an explicit model of a social situation (similar to [7]), and combine it with learning techniques to derive new information (similar to [20]).

To illustrate our approach, we take the example of a personal assistant agent which helps busy users manage their agenda automatically (e.g. [21]). We consider each meeting to be a social situation. The agent takes as input situation cues (e.g. the setting of the meeting, such as a work meeting) and relationship features (e.g. the quality of the relationship, such as a very positive relationship) [15]. Based on this the agent determines which meeting the user would likely want to attend when two meetings overlap. If the user is too busy to respond to meeting requests themselves, the agent can take this decision for the user. The agent may then inform the user about this choice while noting which aspects of the situation led to this choice. This is a first step towards enabling the agent to explain its decisions to the user.

In this paper we investigate the building blocks that would be needed to create such a personal assistant agent. First of all, we need a way to determine which meeting is considered to be more important to the user. To facilitate this process, we quantify the importance of each meeting by assigning it a numerical value to which we refer as the *priority* score of the meeting. Our assumption is that people implicitly follow this priority score when deciding about conflicting meetings by choosing the one with the highest priority. This will be evaluated via our research hypothesis:

RH - When choosing between two meetings, people select the one with higher priority in the majority of the cases.

The task of the agent now becomes to learn a model which predicts the numerical priority of meetings. We explore whether we can tackle this task by using machine learning techniques on a data set containing information on hypothetical meeting scenarios collected from multiple people. This leads to our first research question:

RQ1 - Can we use machine learning techniques to predict the priority of social situations based on situation cues and relationship features?

In our view for human-centered personal assistants, the ability of the agent to explain its decisions to the user is a fundamental requirement. This is because in such a system, it is important for the user to trust the suggestions of the agent. Lim et al. [17] suggest that in socio-technical applications, users trust the agent more when they understand why the agent has selected attending a specific meaning. Making the decisions of the agent explainable consists of three parts: the agent should be able to determine the internal processes that led to a certain suggestion, to generate an explanation based on them, and to present this explanation to the user [22]. Our focus is on the first part: we explore methods that allow the agent to determine which features of a social situation contribute to the prediction of priority. The other parts will be explored in future work.

Our predictive model is built using information from multiple people, however people can have differing preferences. To achieve more personalization, we extend the model by including personal values as input features for our predictive model. Values are considered to be a driving factor in human behaviour [8], so we explore their role in helping better predict the priority of social situations:

RQ2 - Does adding information about the personal values of users as input features to the predictive model increase that model's accuracy of prediction of the priority of social situations?

The rest of this paper is structured as follows: In Sect. 2 we present our approach for tackling the research questions and hypothesis. In Sect. 3 we introduce background knowledge related to the concepts we use. Sect. 4 presents a crowd-sourcing user study conducted to collect data for building and evaluating our models, which is done in Sect. 5. Section 6 concludes this paper.

2 Proposed Approach

We propose an architecture that allows personal assistants agents to model the user's social situation, and use this information to predict the priority of this social situation, or, in other words, predict how important this specific situation is. A high-level depiction of the architecture is presented in Fig. 1[1]).

Overall, the framework works as follows: In the offline stage, a supervised learning algorithm takes as input multiple social situations from different users, described in terms of their social relationship features and situational features. The learning target is the priority of these situations. This forms our prediction model. During run time, the personal assistant agent is provided with the features of two different meetings which overlap. Using the priority prediction model, it determines the priority score of each meeting, it keeps on the schedule the meeting with the highest priority, and informs the user. At this point, the agent also determines the features that have the highest impact on this prediction, which will in future work lead to generating explanations.

---

[1] Icons used in Fig. 1 were made by Freepik and retrieved from www.flaticon.com.

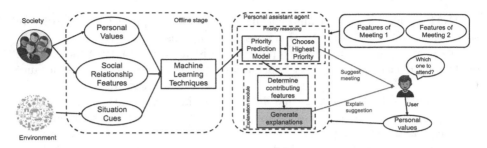

Fig. 1. High level representation of the proposed architecture. Circles represent the modelled concepts, whereas boxes represent learning/reasoning steps. Items marked in blue are concepts that we do not explicitly tackle in this work. (Color figure online)

In order to provide more personalized support, we add to the model information about the personal values of the user. The assumption is that people with similar value preferences will also assign more similar priorities to specific situations. For instance, users who value achievement and success might give a higher priority to work meetings. Therefore, having the value information as an input in our model can potentially lead to better predictions.

A key concept that we use in this work is assigning a numerical score to the priority of social situations. Using this approach, as opposed to directly choosing between two conflicting meetings from a set of input features, has several advantages. First of all, using priority can facilitate the explanations given to the user by the personal assistant agent: the agent first tells the user which meeting has the highest priority, and secondly it explains why. Furthermore, having a numerical representation of priority comes with technical benefits, since the task of learning preference rankings from pairwise choices can be computationally intractable [5].

3   Concepts and Methods

In our vision, personal assistant agents should be able to provide human-centred support. This means the support actions should be transparent and intelligible. This guides our choices from two points of view: concepts (Sect. 3.1) and techniques (Sect. 3.2) used for modelling. This means we should use techniques that allow insight into their decision making process, combined with concepts that are understandable to the users. For this reason, we combine explainable machine learning techniques with concepts from social sciences. Using explainable machine learning techniques means that, when given a set of features which model a social situation, the model is able to output both a prediction as well as which features contributed to this prediction. Lim et al. [17] show that such a procedure improves the intelligibility of context-aware intelligent systems. The set of features that we use to model social situations is borrowed from social science literature. Since these are concepts that we use in everyday life, they should be understandable to the user. In this section, we present the rationale behind the concepts and techniques that we use.

3.1 Social Science Concepts

Our focus in this work is on modelling social situations - situations involving our user and people from their social circle. Kola et al. [15] propose modelling social situations involving two people as a combination of social relationship features, which represent how the two people are related to one another, and situation cues, which represent the circumstances in which the situation takes place. In this approach, the set of features that describes a social situation is based on social science literature that aims at modelling the relevant aspects of social relationships and situations. These concepts can be both concrete and objective (e.g., geographical distance between the user and the other person, for how long they know each-other), as well as subjective (e.g., quality of the relationship between the user and the other person).

Personal values represent key drivers of human decision making [27,29]. Friedman and colleagues [8] define values as "what a person or group of people consider important in life". People hold various values (e.g. wealth, health, independence) with different degrees of importance. The most prominent models of human values were proposed by Rokeach [27] and Schwartz [29]. In our work, we use the model proposed by Schwartz since it offers validated measurement instruments with fewer items than Rokeach, which makes them more suited to online surveys. Furthermore, Schwartz builds on the work of Rokeach and other researchers, so there is overlap in their proposed value lists.

3.2 Machine Learning Methods

A predictive model for a personal assistant has to fulfil two main requirements. Firstly, it should be able to achieve satisfying accuracy for smaller data sets, since acquiring large amounts of data from human subjects can be challenging. Secondly, in order to provide human-centred support, the algorithms should provide insights on which features influence a specific prediction. Ensemble methods [6] are a family of machine learning techniques which fit these requirements. These techniques combine predictions from multiple learning algorithms in order to increase accuracy. The idea is to combine accurate and diverse weaker learners, in order to exploit the strength of each learner. Ensemble methods are shown to perform better than the individual learners they consist of [6]. Furthermore, they are shown to perform well and generalize better for smaller data sets [26]. When the base learners are decision trees, it is also possible to have insights into the features that led to a certain decision, as we will show further on. Another advantage is their accuracy when dealing with structured data. A recent survey [28] shows that ensemble methods have won different machine learning competitions, thus demonstrating high predictive power.

Some of the more successful methods are random forests [3] and gradient boosting machines [9]. Random forests are a specific example of bagging methods

[2]. In bagging, each learner is built independently over a random sub-sample of the data, and the decision is made by aggregating the outputs. The sub-sampling procedure reduces the variance of the method, which is usually a problem for decision trees. In addition, in random forests, for each split of the tree only a subset of the features is considered, this way we avoids the possibility of all the trees selecting the same features and ignoring others. Gradient boosting machines are an example of boosting methods [9]. In boosting, weaker learners are trained sequentially (and not in parallel like in bagging), and each new learner tries to correct its predecessor. Gradient boosting achieves this by fitting the new predictor to the residual errors of the previous ones.

Understanding why a model makes certain predictions is a general goal in machine learning, especially when it comes to providing human-centred support. Lundberg and Lee [18] propose a unified framework for interpreting predictions, called Shapley Additive Explanations (SHAP). The benefits of using this framework are that it provides both global interpretability for the model (i.e. which are generally the most important predictors), as well as local interpretability (i.e. which are the most influential predictors for each individual observation). We use this framework in order to gain insight into the predictions of our model.

4   Crowd-Sourcing User Study

In this user study we gather data for constructing and evaluating our models. The study was approved by the ethics committee of Delft University of Technology.

4.1   Choice of Concepts

Features of Social Situations. In order to set up the user study, we need to define a set of features that will be used to model social situations. Our starting point is the feature set proposed in [15], where social situations are described through a set of relationship features and a set of situation cues. Since their feature set is based on a limited number of social science models, we start by conducting a more extensive literature review. Then, we conduct an exploratory pre-study in order to investigate what aspects of a social situation people take into account when determining how important that situation is. Thus, our feature set is evaluated both from a theoretical and practical perspective.

In our literature review, we found five comprehensive models which aim at describing aspects of dyadic social relationships, three of which were not taken into consideration in [15]. The results are presented in Table 1.

Next, in the exploratory pre-study, we collect answers from 33 participants through Amazon Mechanical Turk[1]. Our goal was to explore which features do participants find important when thinking about the priority of social situations. First, participants were asked to describe five social situations in which they participated in the past week. They were instructed to provide at least the

---

[1] https://www.mturk.com/.

time, location, activity and role of the other person, in order to ensure they were thinking about concrete situations. Furthermore, these suggested activities provide the basis for the formation of the hypothetical scenarios in our main user study (Sect. 4.2). Then, they were asked to consider which aspects of the situation play a role in determining the priority they would assign to a social situation, and the relative importance of these aspects towards determining priority. This question was asked separately for the relationship features and the situation cues. In both questions, participants were free to add answer options, and for each feature they ranked its importance (i.e., how much is it taken into account) in determining the priority of the situation on a 5-point Likert scale ranging from 'Not at all important' to 'Extremely important'. The set of relationship features that had an importance of 3 or higher and were mentioned by at least 20% of the participants, are marked with a + in the last column of Table 1.

The relationship features that we use to model social situations are marked in bold in Table 1. We select the aspects which appear in at least two columns of the table. To that set, we add two more features, namely the age difference between the user and the other person, and whether the two have the same or different genders. Despite not being directly relationship features, age and gender appear as relevant aspects of social relationships in most research from social sciences [4, 24], so we believe this warrants their addition to our model. These features are not included in Table 1, since it exclusively contains relationship features.

Table 1. Different aspects of social relationships present in the literature as well as in the exploratory pre-study. The items written in bold text form our set of social relationship features. Items marked with an asterisk are the features proposed in [15].

Relationship feature	[24]	[4]	[1]	[11]	[23]	Pre study
Role*	+	+	+	−	+	+
Contact Frequency*	+	+	+	−	+	+
Geo-distance*	+	−	+	−	−	+
Years known*	+	+	+	−	+	+
Hierarchy*	−	−	−	+	+	−
Relationship quality*	−	−	+	−	−	+
Depth of acquaintance*	+	+	−	+	−	+
Formality level*	−	−	−	+	+	−
Trust level*	−	−	−	−	−	−
Shared interests	+	+	−	−	+	+
Communication aspects	−	−	−	−	+	−
Reciprocity	−	−	−	+	−	−
Complexity	−	−	−	+	−	−

When it comes to situation cues, we use the ones proposed by Kola et al. [15], since the literature review and exploratory pre-study did not reveal new elements that warrant addition. Thus, our set of situation cues consists of: setting (work, family, sports, casual), event frequency (regular, occasional), initiator (user, other person, neither) and help dynamic (giving, receiving, neither).

Personal Values. For a list of personal values to elicit from participants, we turn to the European Social Survey [30]. It consists of a list of 18 statements (two for each universal value group - Self-direction, Stimulation, Hedonism, Achievement, Power, Security, Conformity, Benevolence and Universalism) that describe features/qualities of a person (e.g., "Thinking up new ideas and being creative is important to him/her/them. He/She/They like(s) to do things in his/her/their own original way."), where each statement represents a personal value (e.g., creativity). The subjects were asked to assess how similar they believe this person is to them, on a scale from 1 (Not like me at all) to 6 (Very much like me). The original survey consists of 21 values, however, we removed the statements of the value group "Tradition" since its values (devotion, religion) do not fit with the type of scenarios that participants were presented with. Furthermore, in the category "Security" we replaced the statement for the value National Security with the statement for the value Health for the same reason. The statement for the value Health was taken from an extended version of this survey which consists of 40 items [30].

4.2   Method

Participants. We recruited 302 subjects on the online crowd-sourcing platform Prolific Academic. Using a crowd-sourcing platform allowed us to efficiently obtain a large sample size in a short amount of time. Respondents received monetary compensation for the time they spent, as per the platform policies. After eliminating the ones who did not pass at least two of our three attention checks, our data consists of answers from 278 subjects. 149 of them are female, 127 are male, and two participants selected the option "other" when asked about their gender. The average age of the subjects is 36.2 years old (SD = 12.3).

Procedure. Subjects answered an online survey[2]. After being briefed about the purpose of the study, they were presented with its four parts. In the *first part*, subjects were asked about their relationship with five people from their social circle. The questions were the relationship features that are marked in bold in Table 1. Ideally, we wanted the subjects to select people with whom they have different types of relationships. Kola et al. [15] suggest that when left without guidance, subjects tend to select people closer to them. This, in turn, leads to less variety and a more imbalanced data set. To avoid this, we pre-determined

---

[2] The survey questions and the data can be found in the supplementary materials in https://doi.org/10.4121/13176923.

some of the features as follows: the first person the subject selects had to be a family member. The second person had to be one of their (current or past) direct supervisors or managers. The third person had to be someone with whom they have a negative or very negative relationship. The fourth person had to be one of their friends. The last person had to be someone that the subject does not know very well. Subjects were instructed to simply provide us with the initials of these people. This way, on one hand anonymity is preserved, and on the other hand, we could refer back to these people in the next parts of the experiment.

In the *second part*, subjects were presented with eight hypothetical social situations, which were meeting scenarios involving one of the people from the first part (selected randomly). We used hypothetical situations, since this gives us control over the types of situations subjects are presented with, ensuring a wide variety. To make the situations seem realistic, we presented subjects with activities that are common for people in their daily lives. Meeting situations were formed by combining situation cues: setting, activity within setting, event frequency, initiator, and help dynamic, as described in Sect. 4.1 (E.g. "You have a weekly work meeting with your team leader where you expect to get feedback on a project that you are working on."). Activities are not part of our situation cues, however, we included them in the description of the scenarios in order to make them more concrete. These activities were collected in the exploratory pre-study described in Sect. 4.1. The activities were grouped into settings, and for each setting, we selected the ones that were suggested more often: four for the casual setting, three for the work setting, three for the family setting, and two from the sports setting, for a total of twelve activities. We selected more activities for the casual setting and less for sports, to reflect the proportions of activities mentioned by the participants of the exploratory user study. Each subject was presented with eight of these twelve activities. Subjects were asked what priority they would assign to each situation on a 7-point Likert scale (ranging from Very Low to Very High). Furthermore, they were asked how likely they are to encounter a similar situation in their daily life on a 5-point Likert scale (ranging from Very Unlikely to Very Likely). This information is used to assess whether the hypothetical scenarios seem realistic to the subjects.

In the *third part*, subjects were presented with five pairs of situations (from the second part), and for each pair, they were asked the following question: "Suppose that in a certain week you are very busy due to some other unexpected commitment, so you can attend only some meetings and cancel some others. Which of these two meetings would you attend?". Lastly, in the *fourth part* subjects answered the survey about personal values described in Sect. 4.1.

4.3   Description of Data

In order to be able to build a model that generalizes better, it is important to have a wide variety of data. Overall, we notice that this is the case for most of the social features. The roles were represented as follows: friends - 29.5%, family members - 26,31%, supervisors/managers - 21.3%, co-workers - 8.71%, neighbours - 5.53%, members of the same group - 3.02%. Features such as geographical distance (64.8% living less than 1 h away), depth of acquaintance (mean = 3.28, SD = 1.33), frequency of contact (mean = 2.91, SD = 1.4) and formality level (mean = 2.27, SD = 1.45) follow a similar distribution to the ones reported in Kola et al. [15], so we do not report them fully for space purposes. Relationship quality was on average slightly positive (mean = 0.55, SD = 1.26, on a scale where −2 = very negative, −1 = negative, 0 = neutral, 1 = positive, 2 = very positive). Fixing its value for one of the selected people led to more balanced answers for relationship quality as compared to the ones reported in [15].

When it comes to the priority of the scenarios, subjects assigned relatively high priorities. The average priority was 5.12 (on a 7-point Likert scale), with a standard deviation of 1.96. Participants found the scenarios on average to be relatively realistic (mean = 3.02, SD = 1.5, on a 5-points Likert scale), with 47.9% of the scenarios being 'Likely' or 'Very Likely'.

In the third part of the user study, we asked subjects to specify which meeting they would attend if they had to select between two meetings. We use this data to test whether subjects mostly select meetings which have a higher priority. In 25% of the cases, subjects were presented with two meetings which have the same priority, so we cannot use this fraction of the data to test our hypothesis. This is an unintended result of the experimental setup, and in future experiments this can be controlled beforehand. For the data in which it is possible to make a distinction, subjects select the meeting with a higher priority in 58% of the cases, and the one with lower priority in 42% of the cases. This result marginally supports our research hypothesis, however, 42% remains a large figure. One potential reason can be the noise in the data caused by the fact that we present subjects with hypothetical scenarios, since some of these scenarios are situations that subjects do not normally encounter in their lives. To test this assumption, we remove the meetings which subjects consider to be 'somewhat unlikely' or 'very unlikely' in part 2 of the experiment. In the remaining data, in 68% of the cases subjects select the meeting with the higher priority. This is significantly higher than 58% (Two-Proportions Z-Test, $p < 0.05$), which suggests unlikely meetings can be a source of noise. Further reasons why some subjects select the meeting with a lower priority will be explored in future work.

When asked about personal values, subjects reported on average the following scores (on a 6-points scale): Benevolence - 4.81 (SD = 0.93), Self-direction - 4.75 (SD = 0.93), Universalism - 4.7 (SD = 1), Security - 4.49 (SD = 1), Hedonism - 4.03 (SD = 1.09), Conformity - 3.96 (SD = 1.22), Stimulation - 3.87 (SD = 1.26), Achievement - 3.78 (SD = 1.28), and Power - 3.22 (SD = 1.36).

5   Predicting Priority of Social Situations

In the following subsections, we use the data from the crowd sourcing user study to explore our research questions.

5.1 Predictive Models and Results

In this section, we present the models that we use to predict the priority of social situations, and compare their performance. Models take as input the full list of social relationship features and situation cues. Subjects could assign priorities on a scale from 1 to 7, so we model this task as a regression task, since there would be too many classes to model it as a classification task for the amount of data that we have. This means, given a set of features, the model predicts a continuous score between 1 and 7. We believe this should not pose an issue although subjects were presented with discrete answer choices, since these choices were ordinal, and the concept of priority is in itself continuous.

As mentioned in Sect. 3, we use a random forest model as well as a gradient boosting machine model. Specifically, we use the RandomForestRegressor and XGBRegressor implementations from the Scikit-learn package in Python[3]. We split the data and randomly assign 80% to the training set and 20% to the test set. We perform parameter tuning by using cross validation on the training set. We report the performance of these models on the test set. For comparison we include a decision tree model, since this approach was previously used to predict the priorities of social situations [15]. Furthermore, we include three baseline predictors based on heuristics, namely: an algorithm which always predicts the mean priority score, an algorithm which predicts a random score between 1 and 7, and an algorithm which always predicts the most chosen class (in this case, a priority of 7). Including such baseline predictors is common practice for new machine learning tasks with no predetermined benchmarks (e.g. [10]).

We start by reporting the Mean Absolute Errors, as well as the Mean Squared Errors for predictions on the test set. Results are reported in Table 2.

Table 2. Model errors in predicting the priorities of situations. Differences between predictions are statistically significant ($p < 0.05$). In bold, the best performing model.

Model	Mean absolute error	Mean Squared error
Random prediction	2.53 (SD = 1.76)	9.17
Predict most chosen class	1.84 (SD = 1.93)	7.1
Predict mean	1.56 (SD = 1.15)	3.72
Decision tree	1.81 (SD = 1.79)	6.21
Random Forest	**1.35 (SD = 1.02)**	**3.25**
XGBoost	1.43 (SD = 1.12)	3.34

As we can see from the results, the best performing model is the Random Forest model, followed by XGBoost. They outperform the Decision Tree model, as well as the baseline heuristic predictors that we used as a comparison.

---

[3] The code can be accessed under: https://github.com/ilir-kola/priority-social-situations.git.

In practical terms, it means our best model on average makes a prediction error of 1.35, on our 7 point scale. However, this number is just an average, so it gives limited insight into individual predictions. For this reason, we look more in detail into what does this error mean for the three best performing models from Table 2.

In general, our data set is to some extent unbalanced, since there are more situations which receive a high priority (i.e. 5, 6 or 7) compared to the ones receiving a low priority (i.e. 1, 2 or 3). In our specific domain - a personal assistant that manages the user's agenda - it is often more important to be able to distinguish a situation with a low priority from one with a high priority (or vice versa), rather than to be able to differentiate between two meetings with different degrees of high (or low) priority. This is a well-known controversy (e.g. [31]) arising from interpreting Likert scales as numeric intervals: a prediction error of 2 which confuses 'Slightly high' with 'Very high' does not have the same nuance as a prediction error of 2 which confuses 'Slightly high' with 'Slightly low', because of the change of category (from high to low) involved in the latter example. By dichotomizing our data into situations with high priority (i.e. with a priority higher than 4) and low priority (i.e. with a priority lower than 4), we can evaluate how often do the predictors assign a high priority to a situation with a low priority, as well as the other way around (similar to Type 1 and Type 2 errors). The algorithm which always predicts the mean (i.e., 5.12) always predicts a high priority, so it is always right for situations with a high priority, and always wrong for situations with a low priority. The Random Forest model and XGBoost perform equally well for high priority situations: none of them is classified to have a low priority by Random Forest, and only 2.17% of them by XGBoost. When it comes to situations with low priority, these models clearly outperform the heuristic predictor: Random Forest wrongly classifies only 30% of situations to have high priority, whereas for XGBoost the value is 29.5%.

Our results suggest that Random Forest and XGBoost outperform heuristic predictors both in absolute errors as well as when considered in the context of our application domain. Random Forest has a slight edge on XGBoost, however, the difference is not high enough so as to declare a clear winner.

5.2 Determining Important Features for Predictions

A key advantage of the machine learning models is the fact that it is possible to get insight into their decision process. This allows for the possibility to explain to the users which features led to a certain prediction, and adapt the model if needed. We use the TreeExplainer method of the SHAP package, which is based on the work of Lundberg and Lee [18].

From a global perspective, the most informative features are setting, relationship quality, age difference, and role. This means these are the features that mostly contribute to the predictions. However, when running the predictive model without the least important features (i.e., hierarchy, geographical distance, other person's gender), we notice a drop in accuracy. This suggests that all the features are to some extent important in predicting specific situations.

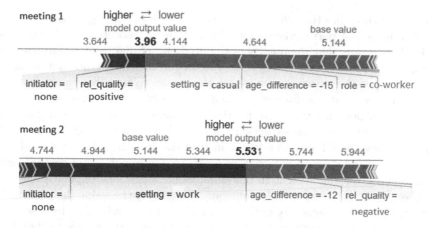

Fig. 2. Explaining the features that led to specific predictions. Larger bars have more impact on the decision. Features marked in red contributed to making the priority prediction higher, whereas the ones in blue lower. The text under the bar indicates the values of each feature for the specific situations. (Color figure online)

To illustrate the interpretations of individual predictions we use two specific social situations which our model had to predict (Fig. 2). In both situations, setting is the feature with the highest influence. We notice in this example that the work setting causes the meeting to have a higher priority, whereas the casual setting contributes to a lower one. As expected, a positive relationship quality makes the priority of the meeting higher, as opposed to the negative relationship quality. In both cases, meeting a younger person contributes to a lower priority.

This method allows for insight into the decision process of the agent, and can form a basis towards explaining the suggestion to the user. Miller [19] proposes that explanations in AI should be contrastive: people want to know why the agent suggested a certain action rather than another one. This is inherently part of our method, since the agent can explain to the user why one meeting was selected instead of another. Furthermore, people prefer an explanation that consists of a few causes rather than many. Using the SHAP package allows this, since it identifies the features with the highest impact.

5.3 Role of Personal Values in Predicting Priorities

We start our work by building a predictive model using data from multiple people, however, we want to explore whether it is possible to have some degree of personalization for the user. To achieve this, we explore whether adding information on the personal values of the users helps to increase the accuracy of the model. The underlying assumption is that users with similar value preferences will assign similar priorities to situations. This is based on the definition of values, which are considered to be drivers of behaviour. First, we train our Random Forest model with the original set of features, as well as 9 new features representing the score that the user assigned to each of value groups (Sect. 4.1), collected in the last part of the user study. The mean absolute error, in this case, is 1.38. This means that the quality of the predictions slightly deteriorates when adding information about values. One reason for this might be that adding 9 new features to the existing ones causes the model to have too many features, which can deteriorate performance. Another possible reason can be related to the salience of personal values in different situations. Schwartz [29] argues that in order for values to influence action not only should they be important to the actor, but they should also be relevant in that specific context. Kayal et al. also propose the use of domain values in order to reason about social commitments [13]. We check for this insight in our data. Some situations explicitly mention that the user is expected to help someone. Therefore, the value 'helpfulness' is salient in these situations. We notice that subjects who value helpfulness more, on average assign a significantly higher priority to situations where they have to help someone, as compared to subjects who value helpfulness less (6 vs. 5.09, $p < 0.01$ when performing the Mann-Whitney test). For meetings that do not involve giving help, the differences in the priorities assigned by these subjects are not significant. This suggests that certain values which are salient to the domain can potentially help predictions.

6   Conclusions

6.1   Contributions

In this work, we propose an approach which enables personal assistant agents to predict the priority of a user's social situation. The approach relies on concepts from social sciences which are used to model social situations, as well as machine learning techniques which are used to learn the priority scores from data from multiple people. First, we review literature from social sciences and propose a set of features which we use to model the social situations of a user. Then, we conduct a crowd-sourcing user study in order to gather the data needed to build our predictive models and evaluate our approach. The subjects' answers suggest that having a numerical representation of priority can in principle be used to help deciding which meeting to attend in cases of overlapping meetings. The results marginally supports our hypothesis (RH): 58% of the subjects select the meeting with a higher priority. This can form the basis for allowing a personal assistant agent to use its priority predictions to choose between the meetings.

Next, we show that ensemble models such as Random Forests outperform baseline models in predicting the priorities of social situations, especially when it comes to differentiating between situations with high and low priorities (RQ1). Furthermore, we present a procedure which enables the personal assistant agent to determine the features that contributed to the predictions, which in future work will be presented as explanations to the user. We envision that this, together with the fact that features are taken from social science literature and are there-fore more understandable for people, can help achieving the vision for more transparent and intelligible personal assistant agents. Lastly, we test whether adding information about the personal values of the user can help us lower the prediction error (RQ2). Results show that in our setting this is not the case, since the mean absolute error of the model suffers a slight increase. However, insights from the data suggest that using personal values which are salient in the specific situation has the potential to be a more successful approach.

6.2 Limitations and Future Work

First of all, our experimental setup presented subjects with hypothetical scenarios. This was done to ensure variety in the data, however, this comes at the cost of the data being noisier, since some of the scenarios might be unlikely to actually occur, so the subjects might not answer consistently. It would be useful to conduct a user study in which subjects report all their social situations from a fixed period of time, in order to evaluate our models with more realistic data. Furthermore, asking subjects which meeting they would attend when two meetings overlap (part 3 of the user study) presented them with a binary choice, which does not inform us how certain they were about their selection. An alternative would be to provide participants with a slider, where they can state how inclined they would be to attend one of the meetings [13]. In future work, we aim to enable personal assistant agents to provide full explanations regarding their decisions to the user. This is based on our assumption that presenting the user with the social features that contributed to a prediction makes the work of the personal assistant agent more transparent. This has to be tested in practice. Next, we will investigate the possibility of a feedback loop between the user and the agent based on the explanations, in order to further personalize support. This would be important especially for cases where the subjects disagree with the agent's decisions. Lastly, we will explore whether our models can be used to predict other aspects of social situations other than priority.

References

1. Antonucci, T.C., Akiyama, H.: Social networks in adult life and a preliminary examination of the convoy model. J. Gerontol. **42**(5), 519–527 (1987)
2. Breiman, L.: Bagging predictors. Mach. Learn. **24**(2), 123–140 (1996)
3. Breiman, L.: Random forests. Mach. Learn. **45**(1), 5–32 (2001)
4. Burt, R.S.: Network items and the general social survey. Soc. Networks **6**(4), 293–339 (1984)
5. Chevaleyre, Y., Koriche, F., Lang, J., Mengin, J., Zanuttini, B.: Learning ordinal preferences on multiattribute domains: The case of CP-NETs. In: Fürnkranz, J., Hüllermeier, E. (eds.) Preference Learning, pp. 273–296. Springer, Heidelberg (2010). https://doi.org/10.1007/978-3-642-14125-6_13
6. Dietterich, T.G.: Ensemble methods in machine learning. In: Kittler, J., Roli, F. (eds.) MCS 2000. LNCS, vol. 1857, pp. 1–15. Springer, Heidelberg (2000). https://doi.org/10.1007/3-540-45014-9_1
7. Dignum, F.: Interactions as social practices: towards a formalization. arXiv preprint arXiv:1809.08751 (2018)

8. Friedman, B., Kahn, P.H., Borning, A., Huldtgren, A.: Value sensitive design and information systems. In: Doorn, N., Schuurbiers, D., van de Poel, I., Gorman, M.E. (eds.) Early engagement and new technologies: Opening up the laboratory. PET, vol. 16, pp. 55–95. Springer, Dordrecht (2013). https://doi.org/10.1007/978-94-007-7844-3_4

9. Friedman, J.H.: Greedy function approximation: a gradient boosting machine. Annals of statistics, pp. 1189–1232 (2001)

10. Gu, S., Kelly, B., Xiu, D.: Empirical asset pricing via machine learning. Technical report, National Bureau of Economic Research (2018)

11. Heaney, C.A., Israel, B.A.: Social networks and social support. Health Behav. Health Educ. Theory Res. Pract. **4**, 189–210 (2008)

12. Kaminka, G.A.: Curing robot autism: a challenge. In: Proceedings of the 2013 International Conference on AAMAS, pp. 801–804. IFAMAAS (2013)

13. Kayal, A., Brinkman, W.P., Neerincx, M.A., Riemsdijk, M.B.V.: Automatic resolution of normative conflicts in supportive technology based on user values. ACM Trans. Internet Technol. (TOIT) **18**(4), 1–21 (2018)

14. Kepuska, V., Bohouta, G.: Next-generation of virtual personal assistants (microsoft cortana, apple siri, amazon alexa and google home). In: 2018 IEEE 8th Annual Computing and Communication Workshop and Conference, pp. 99–103. IEEE (2018)

15. Kola, I., Jonker, C.M., van Riemsdijk, M.B.: Who's that? - social situation awareness for behaviour support agents. In: Dennis, L.A., Bordini, R.H., Lespérance, Y. (eds.) EMAS 2019. LNCS (LNAI), vol. 12058, pp. 127–151. Springer, Cham (2020). https://doi.org/10.1007/978-3-030-51417-4_7

16. Lewin, K.: Field theory and experiment in social psychology: concepts and methods. Am. J. Sociol. **44**(6), 868–896 (1939)

17. Lim, B.Y., Dey, A.K., Avrahami, D.: Why and why not explanations improve the intelligibility of context-aware intelligent systems. In: Proceedings of the SIGCHI Conference on Human Factors in Computing Systems, pp. 2119–2128 (2009)

18. Lundberg, S.M., Lee, S.I.: A unified approach to interpreting model predictions. In: Advances in Neural Information Processing Systems, pp. 4765–4774 (2017)

19. Miller, T.: Explanation in artificial intelligence: insights from the social sciences. Artif. Intell. **267**, 1–38 (2019)

20. Murukannaiah, P.K., Singh, M.P.: Platys social: relating shared places and private social circles. IEEE Internet Comput. **16**(3), 53–59 (2012)

21. Myers, K., Berry, P., Blythe, J., Conley, K., Gervasio, M., McGuinness, D.L., Morley, D., Pfeffer, A., Pollack, M., Tambe, M.: An intelligent personal assistant for task and time management. AI Mag. **28**(2), 47–47 (2007)

22. Neerincx, M.A., van der Waa, J., Kaptein, F., van Diggelen, J.: Using perceptual and cognitive explanations for enhanced human-agent team performance. In: Harris, D. (ed.) EPCE 2018. LNCS (LNAI), vol. 10906, pp. 204–214. Springer, Cham (2018). https://doi.org/10.1007/978-3-319-91122-9_18

23. Pabjan, B.: Measuring the social relations: social distance in social structure - a study of prison community. Acta Physica Polonica Series B **36**(8), 2559 (2005)

24. Phillips, S.L., Fischer, C.S.: Measuring social support networks in general populations. Stressful life events and their contexts, pp. 223–233 (1981)

25. Pinder, C., Vermeulen, J., Cowan, B.R., Beale, R.: Digital behaviour change interventions to break and form habits. ACM Trans. Comput. Hum. Inter. (TOCHI) **25**(3), 15 (2018)

26. Polikar, R.: Ensemble based systems in decision making. IEEE Circuits Syst. Mag. **6**(3), 21–45 (2006)

27. Rokeach, M.: The Nature of Human Values. Free Press, New York (1973)
28. Sagi, O., Rokach, L.: Ensemble learning: a survey. Wiley Interdisc. Rev. Data Mining Knowl. Discov. **8**(4), e1249 (2018)
29. Schwartz, S.H.: Universals in the content and structure of values: theoretical advances and empirical tests in 20 countries. Adv. Exp. Soc. Psychol. **25**(1), 1–65 (1992)
30. Schwartz, S.H.: Human values. European Social Survey Education Net (2005)
31. Sullivan, G.M., Artino Jr., A.R.: Analyzing and interpreting data from likert-type scales. J. Graduate Med. Educ. **5**(4), 541–542 (2013)
32. Van Riemsdijk, M.B., Jonker, C.M., Lesser, V.: Creating socially adaptive electronic partners: interaction, reasoning and ethical challenges. In: Proceedings of the 2015 International Conference on AAMAS, pp. 1201–1206. IFAMAAS (2015)

Mutex Propagation for SAT-based Multi-agent Path Finding

Pavel Surynek[1]([✉])[iD], Jiaoyang Li[2], Han Zhang[2], T. K. Satish Kumar[2],
and Sven Koenig[3]

[1] Faculty of Information Technology, Czech Technical University in Prague,
Thákurova 9, 160 00 Praha 6, Czechia
pavel.surynek@fit.cvut.cz

[2] Henry Salvatori Computer Science Center, University of Southern California,
941 Bloom Walk, Los Angeles, USA
{jiaoyanl, zhan645}@usc.edu, tkskwork@gmail.com

[3] Information Sciences Institute, University of Southern California,
4676 Admiralty Way, Marina del Rey, USA
skoenig@usc.edu

Abstract. Multi-agent path finding (MAPF) is the problem of planning a set of non-colliding paths for a set of agents so that each agent reaches its individual goal location following its path. A mutex from classical planning is a constraint forbidding a pair of facts to be both true or a pair of actions to be executed simultaneously. In the context of MAPF, mutexes are used to rule out the simultaneous occurrence of a pair of agents in a pair of locations, which can prune the search space. Previously mutex propagation had been integrated into conflict-based search (CBS), a major search-based approach for solving MAPF optimally. In this paper, we introduce mutex propagation into the compilation-based (SAT-based) solver MDD-SAT, an alternative to search-based solvers. Our experiments show that, despite mutex propagation being computationally expensive, it prunes the search space significantly so that the overall performance of MDD-SAT is improved.

Keywords: Multi-agent path finding · Mutex propagation · Satisfiability solving (SAT)

1 Introduction

Multi-agent path finding (MAPF) instance is specified by a graph $G = (V, E)$ and a set of k agents $\{a_1 \dots a_k\}$, where agent a_i has start location $s_i \in V$ and goal location $g_i \in V$. Time is discretized into time steps. Between successive timesteps, each agent can either *move* to an adjacent empty location or *wait* in its current location. Both move and wait actions incur a cost of one, unless the agent terminally waits at its goal location, which does not incur any costs. A *path* for agent a_i is a sequence of move and wait actions that lead agent a_i from location s_i to location g_i. A *conflict* happens when two agents are at the same location at the same timestep (called *a vertex conflict*) or traverse the

© Springer Nature Switzerland AG 2021
T. Uchiya et al. (Eds.): PRIMA 2020, LNAI 12568, pp. 248–258, 2021.
https://doi.org/10.1007/978-3-030-69322-0_16

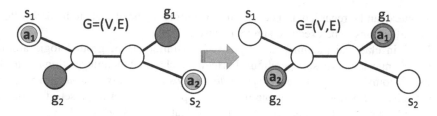

Fig. 1. A MAPF instance with two agents.

same edge in opposite directions at the same timestep (called *an edge conflict*). The objective is to find a set of conflict-free paths for all agents while minimizing the sum of the costs of these paths (called *sum-of-costs*). Although MAPF is NP-hard to solve optimally [19], it has many real-world applications, such as warehouse robots [18] and quadrotor swarms [7].

A MAPF instance is illustrated in Fig. 1. One of the agents (say a_1) has to wait until the other agent (a_2) reaches its goal location since the agents would otherwise collide in the middle section of G.

Zhang et al. [20] introduced *mutex propagation*, a technique originally from artificial intelligence planning, to MAPF and used it to identify and efficiently resolve symmetric conflicts occurred in *conflict-based search* (CBS) [11], a popular search-based algorithm that solves MAPF optimally. They used mutex propagation to capture reachability information for agent pairs and automatically generate symmetry-breaking constraints, resulting in a branching rule for CBS that is capable of outperforming both CBS [6] and CBS with handcrafted symmetry-breaking constraints [9].

In this paper, we demonstrate the power of mutex propagation in the framework of MDD-SAT [16], a popular SAT-based algorithm that can also solve MAPF optimally. MDD-SAT expands the underlying graph G in time resulting in a structure analogous *planning graph* [4]. A Boolean formula whose satisfying assignments represents MAPF solutions up to the certain sum-of-costs is then built using the expansion and consulted to the SAT solver [2].

2   Background

We first introduce mutex propagation in classical planning and in MAPF as well as CBS with mutex propagation.

Mutex propagation has its origin in classical planning. It is a form of constraint propagation that corresponds to directed 3-consistency, which in turn is a truncated form of path consistency [17]. Like all constraint propagation techniques, it makes implicit constraints explicit, and it does so efficiently. Applied to the planning graph [4], mutex propagation tightly approximates the set of all states reachable from a given start state in polynomial time [17]. Therefore, it has been successfully used to design reachability heuristics for plan-space and state-space planners [10] and to improve SAT-based planners [8].

A mutex can be regarded as a constraint forbidding a pair of facts to be both *TRUE* or a pair of actions to be executed simultaneously.

States in classical planning are expressed as finite sets of ground logic atoms. Actions change states via set operations. Formally, a classical planning action is a triple of sets of atoms (p, e^+, e^-), called *precondition, positive effects*, and *negative effects* respectively. The action is applicable in state S represented as a finite set of atoms iff $p \subseteq S$, and the result of the application is the new state $S' = (S \setminus e^-) \cup e^+$.

We say that actions (p_1, e_1^+, e_1^-) and (p_2, e_2^+, e_2^-) applicable in state S are *dependent*, a basic form of mutex, iff $(p_1 \cup e_1^+) \cap e_2^- \neq \emptyset$ or $(p_2 \cup e_2^+) \cap e_1^- \neq \emptyset$. In other words, actions conflict in their precondition and effects. The mutex relation can be inductively propagated further to atoms: We say that atoms q_1 and q_2 are mutex iff all pairs of actions producing them are pair wise mutex and there is no action that produces both q_1 and q_2 [1]. Similarly, two actions $(p_1', e_1'^+, e_1'^-)$ and $(p_2', e_2'^+, e_2'^-)$ in the next timestep are mutex iff **(i)** they are dependent or **(ii)** there are atoms $r_1 \in p_1'$ and $r_2 \in p_2'$ that are mutex.

We show one possible representation of MAPF instance, with the *move-to-unoccupied* rule using classical planning actions. Action $move(a, u, v)$ with $a \in A$ and $u, v \in V$, that moves agent a from location u to location v can be defined as $(p_{move}, e_{move}^+, e_{move}^-)$ (a, u, v) and action $wait(a, u)$, that makes agent a wait in location u, can be defined as $(p_{wait}, \emptyset, \emptyset)$ (a, u) where:

$$p_{move}(a, u, v) = \{empty(v), at(a, u)\},$$
$$e_{move}^+(a, u, v) = \{empty(u), at(a, v)\},$$
$$e_{move}^-(a, u, v) = \{empty(v), at(a, u)\},$$
$$p_{wait}(a, u) = \{at(a, u)\}.$$

This representation of MAPF actions naturally rules out vertex conflicts through the dependence of actions (a pair of agents can collide in a vertex only through a pair of dependent/mutex actions). This first level of mutexes is covered in the compilation-based MAPF formulations by a constraint permitting at most one agent per vertex. However, the next levels of mutexes obtained through propagation were omitted in previous compilation-based approaches, such as MDD-SAT and others [15].

2.1 Mutex Propagation in MAPF

Multi-valued decision diagrams (MDDs) for MAPF were introduced in [12]. An MDD of $l + 1$ levels for agent a_i (denoted MDD_i) is a directed acyclic graph that consists of all paths of cost at most l for agent a_i. The nodes at level t in the MDD correspond to all locations at timestep t on these paths. A node v^t in MDD_i represents a copy of location v at level t, while a directed edge (u^t, v^{t+1}) in MDD_i represents a copy of edge $\{u, v\} \in E$ between level t and $t + 1$. There are only one node at level 0 and one node at level $l + 1$, which correspond to the start location s_i and the goal location g_i, respectively, of agent a_i.

---

[1] No operation actions (noops) are usually assumed for each atom q where $noop(q) = (\{q\}, \{q\}, \emptyset)$.

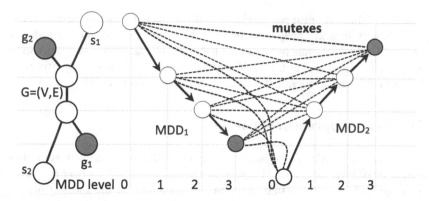

Fig. 2. MDDs for a_1 and a_2 from Fig. 1 for sum-of-costs = 3. Mutexes form a biclique between nodes of MDD_1 and MDD_2.

MDDs are constructed for single agents and essentially capture reachability information similar to planning graphs in classical planning. Therefore, mutex propagation is used on MDDs in [20] to capture reachability information for agent pairs. Two MDD nodes n_i and n_j at the same level t of the MDDs of two different agents a_i and a_j are *mutex* iff any path that moves agent a_i from its start location s_i at timestep 0 to the location of n_i at timestep t has at least one conflict with any path that moves agent a_j from its start location s_j at timestep 0 to the location of n_j at timestep t. The definition of MDD edges being mutex is similar. Any pair of MDD nodes (edges) that corresponds to a vertex (edge) conflict is mutex (called *initial mutex*), and any pair of MDD nodes (edges) whose incoming edges (source nodes) are pairwise mutex is also mutex (called *propagated mutex*) (Fig. 2).

2.2 Conflict-Based Search with Mutex Propagation

Conflict-based search (CBS) is an optimal two-level search-based MAPF algorithm. The low level plans shortest paths for all agents (each one ignoring the path of other agents) that satisfy the spatio-temporal constraints introduced by the high level, while the high level searches in a *constraint tree* (CT) and resolves the conflicts between agents by adding constraints. The root CT node contains no constraints and a shortest path on graph G for each agent. When expanding a CT node N, CBS first checks for conflicts among the paths of N. If the paths are conflict-free, CBS terminates and returns the paths. Otherwise, CBS chooses a conflict and resolves it by generating two child CT nodes that inherit the constraints and the paths of N. For each child CT node, CBS first adds a new constraint that prohibits one of the agents from using the conflicting vertex/edge at the conflicting timestep and then calls the low-level search to replan a path for this agent. CBS guarantees optimality by performing best-first searches on both its high and low levels.

CBS was improved by using MDDs with mutex propagation in [20] to identify and efficiently resolve *cardinal conflicts*, a type of conflict where all pairs of shortest paths of the two conflicting agents have at least one vertex or edge conflict. CBS can try many combinations of these shortest paths, which results in many CT nodes expansions. CBS using MDDs with mutex propagation, on the other hand, immediately identifies such cardinal conflicts and generate two sets of constraints (instead of two single constraints) to resolve them with a single CT node expansion. It significantly outperforms both CBS [6] and CBS with handcrafted symmetry-breaking constraints [9].

3   SAT-Based Approach: MDD-SAT

MDD-SAT first builds MDDs for individual agents with regard to given sum-of-costs ξ. The number of levels μ for the MDDs is $\mu = \mu_0 + (\xi - \xi_0)$ [16], where μ_0 is a lower bound on the *makespan* calculated as the maximum length of the shortest individual paths of the agents from their start locations to their goal locations and ξ_0 is a lower bound on the sum-of-costs calculated as the sum of lengths of the shortest individual paths.

A propositional variable is introduced for each node and edge in the MDDs. We use $\mathcal{X}_v^t(a_i)$ to denote the variables corresponding to nodes and $\mathcal{E}_{u,v}^t(a_i)$ to denote the variables corresponding to edges. The meaning of the variables reflects the correspondence between the existence of directed paths connecting from the start nodes to the goal nodes in the MDDs and the existence of a solution to the MAPF instance. $\mathcal{X}_v^t(a_i)$ is *TRUE* iff agent a_i is in location $v \in G$ at timestep t and $\mathcal{E}_{u,v}^t(a_i)$ is *TRUE* iff agent a_i moves from location u to location v at timestep t.

The MAPF movement rules are encoded as clauses using these variables. Satisfying assignments correspond to directed paths in MDDs due to the following constraints for all agents $a \in A$ and locations $u, v \in V$ and timestep $t \in \{0, 1, ..., \mu - 1\}$. Intuitively, the constrains express that, if an agent is in a location at timestep t, it must leave via exactly one directed edge and appear in the target location of the edge at timestep $t + 1$:

$$\mathcal{X}_u^t(a_i) \Rightarrow \bigvee_{v^{t+1} \mid (u^t, v^{t+1}) \in MDD_i} \mathcal{E}_{u,v}^t(a_i) \tag{1}$$

$$\sum_{v^{t+1} \mid (u^t, v^{t+1}) \in MDD_i} \mathcal{E}_{u,v}^t(a_i) \leq 1 \tag{2}$$

$$\mathcal{X}_v^{t+1}(a_i) \Rightarrow \bigvee_{u^t \mid (u^t, v^{t+1}) \in MDD_i} \mathcal{E}_{u,v}^t(a_i) \tag{3}$$

$$\sum_{u^t \mid (u^t, v^{t+1}) \in MDD_i} \mathcal{E}_{u,v}^t(a_i) \leq 1 \tag{4}$$

$$\mathcal{E}_{u,v}^t(a_i) \Rightarrow \mathcal{X}_u^t(a_i) \wedge \mathcal{X}_v^{t+1}(a_i) \tag{5}$$

The following constraint is defined for all locations $v \in V$ and all timesteps $t \in \{0, 1, ..., \mu\}$:

$$\sum_{a_i \in A \mid v^t \in MDD_i} \mathcal{X}_v^t(a_i) \leq 1 \tag{6}$$

Constraints (1–5) ensure that paths in the MDDs are represented. Constraints (1) and 2 state that if an agent is in a location it must leave it via exactly one outgoing edge.

Similarly, constraints (3) and (4) state that, if an agent is in a location then it must arrive there via exactly one incoming edge. Constraints (6) encode conflict avoidance. It states that at most one agent is in a location v at a timestep t.

All pseudo-Boolean *at-most-one* constraints are expressed as clauses. One possible representation of this constraint is a clique of binary clauses that forbid agents a_i and a_j to be in location v at timestep t: $\neg \mathcal{X}_v^t(a_i) \vee \neg \mathcal{X}_v^t(a_i)$.

Finally, the bound on the number of edge variables set to *TRUE* can be represented by a *cardinality constraint* [3, 13] that ensures that the sum-of-costs of the represented solutions is at most ξ (see [16] for details). Altogether, we construct a Boolean formula $\mathcal{F}(\xi)$ that is satisfiable iff the MAPF has a solution with sum-of-costs ξ. Due to the construction of $\mathcal{F}(\xi)$, a MAPF solution can be read off from a satisfying truth-value assignment of $\mathcal{F}(\xi)$, which can be found by an off-the-shelf SAT solver [2].

Solution to the MAPF instance with minimal sum-of-costs corresponds to the first satisfiable Boolean formula in $\mathcal{F}(\xi_0)$, $\mathcal{F}(\xi_0 + 1)$, ... since the satisfiability of $\mathcal{F}(\xi)$ is monotonic in ξ.

3.1 Mutexes in SAT-Based Solver

Mutex propagation can be integrated into the MDD-SAT solver at the stage of construction of the MDDs. The knowledge of which nodes are mutex in MDDs can be reflected in the construction of $\mathcal{F}(\xi)$ via binary clauses.

Assume that nodes n_i and n_j the MDDs for agents a_i and a_j respectively are mutex at timestep t. Then, we add clause $\neg \mathcal{X}_{n_i}^t(a_i) \vee \neg \mathcal{X}_{n_j}^t(a_j)$ to $\mathcal{F}(\xi)$, which directly follows the definition of two nodes being mutex by stating that a_i and a_j cannot be in the locations of nodes n_i and n_j respectively at timestep t.

To understand the role of mutexes in Boolean formulae, we study them in relation to *unit propagation* (UP) [5], a standard technique implemented in SAT solvers. UP is a form of resolution inference that extends the partial consistent assignment of truth values to Boolean variables. In a clause, in which all literals but one are *FALSE* by the partial assignment, the last literal must be *TRUE* for the clause to be *TRUE*.

When mutexes are expressed as binary clauses, setting $\mathcal{X}_u^t(a_i)$ to *TRUE* enables UP to infer that $\mathcal{X}_v^t(a_j)$ is *FALSE* due to clause $\neg \mathcal{X}_u^t(a_i) \vee \neg \mathcal{X}_v^t(a_j)$. Sometimes the same inference can be made without having the mutex clause.

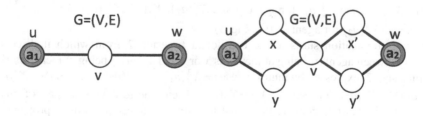

Fig. 3. Unit propagation cannot simulate mutex propagation due to branching.

Consider a corridor consisting of three locations u, v, and w. Agents a_1 and a_2 are trying to move through the corridor from opposite directions (Fig. 3 left). After constructing the MDDs for 2 timesteps we have the Boolean variables $\mathcal{X}_u^0(a_1)$, $\mathcal{X}_v^1(a_1)$, $\mathcal{X}_w^2(a_1)$, $\mathcal{X}_w^0(a_2)$, $\mathcal{X}_v^1(a_2)$, and $\mathcal{X}_u^2(a_2)$ as well as the corresponding variables for the edges (omitted) (Fig. 4). There is a conflict at timestep 1 since the agents would collide in location v. Mutex propagation hence discovers that agent a_1 cannot be in location w at timestep 2 if agent a_2 is in location u (timestep 2) resulting in the mutex clause $\neg\mathcal{X}_w^2(a_1) \vee \neg\mathcal{X}_u^2(a_2)$. Setting $\mathcal{X}_w^2(a_1)$ to *TRUE* propagates to setting $\mathcal{X}_u^2(a_2)$ to *FALSE* via UP. However, the same effect can be achieved without having the mutex clause.

Assume again that $\mathcal{X}_w^2(a_1)$ is set to *TRUE*. Through $\neg\mathcal{X}_w^2(a_1) \vee \mathcal{E}_{v,w}^1(a_1)$ (3) via UP, $\mathcal{E}_{v,w}^1(a_1)$ is set to *TRUE*. Then, through $\neg\mathcal{E}_{v,w}^1(a_1) \vee \mathcal{X}_v^1(a_1)$ (5) via UP, $\mathcal{X}_v^1(a_1)$ is set to *TRUE*. Through $\neg\mathcal{X}_v^1(a_1) \vee \mathcal{X}_v^1(a_2)$ (6) via UP, $\mathcal{X}_v^1(a_2)$ is set to *FALSE*. Through $\neg\mathcal{E}_{v,u}^1(a_2) \vee \mathcal{X}_v^1(a_2)$ (5) $\mathcal{E}_{v,u}^1(a_2)$ is set to *FALSE*. Finally, through $\neg\mathcal{X}_u^2(a_2) \vee \mathcal{E}_{v,u}^1(a_2)$ (3) via UP, $\mathcal{X}_u^2(a_2)$ is set to *FALSE* (we note that different propagation chains can be used to obtain the same outcome).

We were quite fortunate in the above example because all relevant clauses were binary, and UP propagates very well through them. In general, however, UP is less powerful than mutex propagation, as formalized in the following proposition:

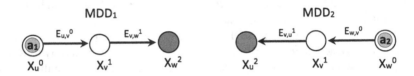

Fig. 4. Mutex propagation simulated by unit propagation.

Proposition 1. *Formula $\mathcal{F}(\xi)$ built using MDDs with mutex propagation allows for strictly stronger Boolean constraint propagation than the formula without mutexes.*

Proof. Consider a corridor with branching (Fig. 3 right) consisting of locations u, x, y, (x and y form the first branch) v, x', y', (x' and y' form the second branch), and w. Two agents a_1 and a_2 start to move in opposite directions from u and w respectively leading to a conflict at location v at timestep 2. After building MDDs, we obtain the Boolean variables representing agents' locations $\mathcal{X}_u^0(a_1)$, $\mathcal{X}_x^1(a_1)$, $\mathcal{X}_y^1(a_1)$, $\mathcal{X}_v^2(a_1)$, $\mathcal{X}_{x'}^3(a_1)$, $\mathcal{X}_{y'}^3(a_1)$, and $\mathcal{X}_w^4(a_1)$ for agent a_1 and $\mathcal{X}_w^0(a_2)$, $\mathcal{X}_{x'}^1(a_2)$, $\mathcal{X}_{y'}^1(a_2)$, $\mathcal{X}_v^2(a_2)$, $\mathcal{X}_x^3(a_2)$, $\mathcal{X}_y^3(a_2)$, and $\mathcal{X}_u^4(a_2)$ for agent a_2 (see Fig. 5).

Mutex propagation starts at the conflict at timestep 2 from which it discovers mutexes between agent a_1 being at locations x or y and agent a_2 being at locations x' or y' at time step 3, expressed by mutex clauses $\neg\mathcal{X}_x^3(a_1) \vee \neg\mathcal{X}_{x'}^3(a_2)$, $\neg\mathcal{X}_x^3(a_1) \vee \neg\mathcal{X}_{y'}^3(a_2)$, $\neg\mathcal{X}_y^3(a_1) \vee \neg\mathcal{X}_{x'}^3(a_2)$, and $\neg\mathcal{X}_y^3(a_1) \vee \neg\mathcal{X}_{y'}^3(a_2)$. Then, due to having no pair of mutex free actions delivering agents to their goal locations at timestep 4, mutex propagation infers a mutex between agent a_1 being at location w and agent a_2 being at location u at timestep 4, expressed by a mutex clause $\neg\mathcal{X}_w^4(a_1) \vee \neg\mathcal{X}_u^4(a_2)$.

If $\mathcal{X}_w^4(a_1)$ is set to *TRUE*, then UP sets $\mathcal{X}_u^4(a_2)$ to *FALSE* due to the last mutex clause. Now assume again that $\mathcal{X}_w^4(a_1)$ is set to *TRUE* without having mutex clauses.

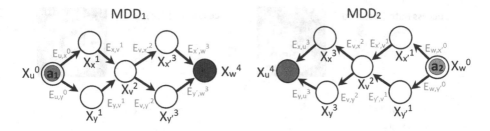

Fig. 5. MDDs consisting of 4 timesteps for agents a_1 and a_2 from Fig. 3.

$\mathcal{X}_w^4(a_1)$ occurs in clauses: $\neg\mathcal{X}_w^4(a_1) \vee \mathcal{E}_{x',w}^3(a_1) \vee \mathcal{E}_{y',w}^3(a_1)$ (3), $\neg\mathcal{E}_{x',w}^3(a_1) \vee \mathcal{X}_w^4(a_1)$ (5), and $\neg\mathcal{E}_{y',w}^3(a_1) \vee \mathcal{X}_w^4(a_1)$ (5). UP however does not propagate from this point towards timestep 3 since none of the affected clauses becomes unit. ∎

3.2 Experimental Evaluation

We integrated mutex propagation into the existing C++ implementation of MDD-SAT, which uses the Glucose 3.0 SAT solver [1]. MDD-SAT with and without mutex propagation (denoted MDD-SAT-MTX and MDD-SAT respectively) were compared with respect to their runtime on a number of MAPF scenarios from movingai.com [14].

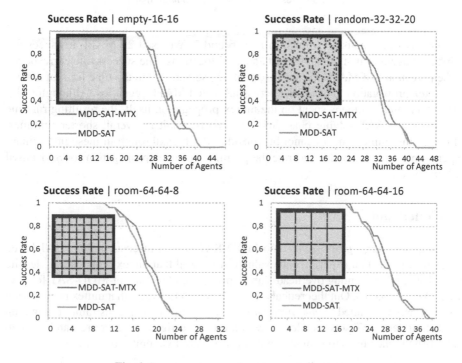

Fig. 6. Success rate experiments on small maps.

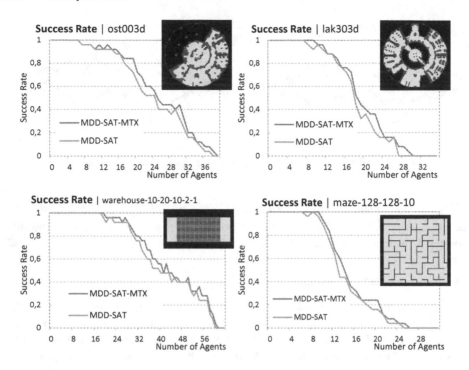

Fig. 7. Success rate experiments on large maps.

Success rate results are shown in Figs. 6 and 7. We used 25 MAPF instances per number of agents having random start and goal locations. The success rate corresponds to the percentage of MAPF instances (out of 25) solved within the time limit of 300 s.

Mutex propagation is beneficial across all tested MAPF scenarios. Although a significant amount of time is spent on the mutex propagation itself, the resulting runtime savings during SAT solving phase will eventually result in overall shorter runtimes. Although the improvement cannot be considered a breakthrough in these preliminary experiments, our results demonstrate the promise of mutex propagation for SAT-based MAPF solvers.

4   Conclusion

We integrated *mutex propagation* into MDD-SAT, a sum-of-costs optimal SAT-based solver for MAPF. Our experimental evaluation showed that mutex propagation, despite it is substantial computing overhead, can improve the efficiency of MDD-SAT for several MAPF scenarios. Out theoretical analysis showed however, that mutex propagation in some cases is entailed by *unit propagation*, a built in Boolean constraint propagation in most modern SAT solvers. Hence, we plan to investigate in future research how to adapt MAPF encodings to simulate mutex propagation via unit propagation.

Acknowledgements. The research at the Czech Technical University in Prague was supported by GAČR - the Czech Science Foundation, under grant number 19-17966S. The research at the University of Southern California was supported by National Science Foundation (NSF) under grant numbers 1409987, 1724392, 1817189, 1837779, and 1935712 as well as a gift from Amazon. The views and conclusions contained in this document are those of the authors and should not be interpreted as representing official policies, either expressed or implied, of the sponsoring organizations, agencies, or the U.S. government.

We would like to thank anonymous reviewers for their valuable comments.

References

1. Audemard, G., Lagniez, J.-M., Simon, L.: Improving glucose for incremental SAT solving with assumptions: application to MUS extraction. In: Järvisalo, M., Van Gelder, A. (eds.) SAT 2013. LNCS, vol. 7962, pp. 309–317. Springer, Heidelberg (2013). https://doi.org/10.1007/978-3-642-39071-5_23

2. Audemard, G., Simon, L.: Predicting learnt clauses quality in modern SAT solvers. In: IJCAI 2009, Proceedings of the 21st International Joint Conference on Artificial Intelligence, Pasadena, California, USA, July 11–17, 2009, pp. 399–404 (2009)

3. Bailleux, O., Boufkhad, Y.: Efficient CNF encoding of boolean cardinality constraints. In: Rossi, F. (ed.) CP 2003. LNCS, vol. 2833, pp. 108–122. Springer, Heidelberg (2003). https://doi.org/10.1007/978-3-540-45193-8_8

4. Blum, A., Furst, M.L.: Fast planning through planning graph analysis. Artif. Intell. **90**(1–2), 281–300 (1997)

5. Dowling, W.F., Gallier, J.H.: Linear-time algorithms for testing the satisfiability of propositional horn formulae. J. Logic Program. **1**(3), 267–284 (1984)

6. Felner, A., Li, J., Boyarski, E., Ma, H., Cohen, L., Kumar, T.K.S., Koenig, S.: Adding heuristics to conflict-based search for multi-agent path finding. In: Proceedings of the Twenty-Eighth International Conference on Automated Planning and Scheduling, ICAPS 2018, Delft, The Netherlands, 24–29 June, 2018, pp. 83–87. AAAI Press (2018)

7. Hönig, W., Preiss, J.A., Kumar, T.K.S., Sukhatme, G.S., Ayanian, N.: Trajectory planning for quadrotor swarms. IEEE Trans. Robotics **34**(4), 856–869 (2018)

8. Kautz, H.A., Selman, B.: Pushing the envelope: Planning, propositional logic and stochastic search. In: Proceedings of the Thirteenth National Conference on Artificial Intelligence and Eighth Innovative Applications of Artificial Intelligence Conference, AAAI 96, IAAI 96, Portland, Oregon, USA, 4–8 August, 1996, vol. 2, pp. 1194–1201. AAAI Press/The MIT Press (1996)

9. Li, J., Surynek, P., Felner, A., Ma, H., Kumar, T.K.S., Koenig, S.: Multi-agent path finding for large agents. In: The Thirty-Third AAAI Conference on Artificial Intelligence, AAAI 2019, The Thirty-First Innovative Applications of Artificial Intelligence Conference, IAAI 2019, The Ninth AAAI Symposium on Educational Advances in Artificial Intelligence, EAAI 2019, Honolulu, Hawaii, USA, 27 January–1 February, 2019, pp. 7627–7634. AAAI Press (2019)

10. Nguyen, X., Kambhampati, S.: Extracting effective and admissible state space heuristics from the planning graph. In: Proceedings of the Seventeenth National Conference on Artificial Intelligence and Twelfth Conference on on Innovative Applications of Artificial Intelligence, 30 July–2 August, 2000, Austin, Texas, USA, pp. 798–805. AAAI Press/The MIT Press (2000)

11. Sharon, G., Stern, R., Felner, A., Sturtevant, N.R.: Conflict-based search for optimal multi-agent pathfinding. Artif. Intell. **219**, 40–66 (2015)

12. Sharon, G., Stern, R., Goldenberg, M., Felner, A.: The increasing cost tree search for optimal multi-agent pathfinding. Artif. Intell. **195**, 470–495 (2013)
13. Sinz, C.: Towards an optimal CNF encoding of boolean cardinality constraints. In: van Beek, P. (ed.) CP 2005. LNCS, vol. 3709, pp. 827–831. Springer, Heidelberg (2005). https://doi.org/10.1007/11564751_73
14. Sturtevant, N.R.: Benchmarks for grid-based pathfinding. Trans. Comput. Intell. AI Games **4**(2), 144–148 (2012). http://www.movingai.com
15. Surynek, P.: Time-expanded graph-based propositional encodings for makespan-optimal solving of cooperative path finding problems. Ann. Math. Artif. Intell. **81**(3–4), 329–375 (2017)
16. Surynek, P., Felner, A., Stern, R., Boyarski, E.: Efficient SAT approach to multi-agent path finding under the sum of costs objective. In: ECAI 2016–22nd European Conference on Artificial Intelligence, 29 August–2 September 2016, The Hague, The Netherlands - Including Prestigious Applications of Artificial Intelligence (PAIS 2016). Frontiers in Artificial Intelligence and Applications, vol. 285, pp. 810–818. IOS Press (2016)
17. Weld, D.S.: Recent advances in AI planning. AI Mag. **20**(2), 93–123 (1999)
18. Wurman, P.R., D'Andrea, R., Mountz, M.: Coordinating hundreds of cooperative, autonomous vehicles in warehouses. AI Mag. **29**(1), 9–20 (2008)
19. Yu, J.: Intractability of optimal multirobot path planning on planar graphs. IEEE Robot. Autom. Lett. **1**(1), 33–40 (2016)
20. Zhang, H., Li, J., Surynek, P., Koenig, S., Kumar, T.K.S.: Multi-agent path finding with mutex propagation. In: Proceedings of the Thirtieth International Conference on Automated Planning and Scheduling, Nancy, France, 26–30 October, 2020, pp. 323–332. AAAI Press (2020)

A SMT-based Implementation for Safety Checking of Parameterized Multi-Agent Systems

Paolo Felli, Alessandro Gianola$^{(\boxtimes)}$, and Marco Montali

Free University of Bozen-Bolzano, Bolzano, Italy
{pfelli,gianola,montali}@inf.unibz.it

Abstract. We address the problem of verifying whether unwanted states, characterized as a given state formula, are reachable in a given parameterized multi-agent system (PMAS), i.e., whether the PMAS is unsafe. As the multi-agent system is parameterized, it only describes the finite set of possible agent templates, while the actual number of concrete agent instances for each template is unbounded and cannot be foreseen. However, as safety depends in general on the number of agent instances, the verification result must be correct irrespective of such a number. After having defined two distinct execution semantics of PMASs, in this paper we focus on an implemented approach for checking safety, which is composed of two steps. First, we have implemented a modeling tool, called *SAFE*, that allows to specify the agent templates in the PMAS and their possible interactions, and to automatically translate this model into a textual encoding of an array-based system (ABS). Second, we check safety via infinite-state model checking based on satisfiability modulo theories (SMT), by using the general purpose SMT-based model checker MCMT, which accepts ABS specifications as input. We show the correctness guarantees of this approach by relying on the theory of ABSs. Finally we discuss how this approach lends itself to richer parameterized and data-aware MAS settings beyond the state-of-the-art solutions in the literature, using SMT-based results now available thanks to this work.

Keywords: Multi-Agent Systems · Safety · Parameterized verification · Satisfiability modulo theories

1 Introduction

Multi-agent systems (MASs) are commonly used in many complex, real-life domains, so it has become crucial to be able to verify such systems against given specifications. This typically amounts to check the existence of execution strategies for the achievement of given goals or to compute counterexamples as evidence of points of potential failure. Model checking [14] is one of the most common approaches to verification of MASs, often with a focus on strategic abilities [9]. However, a common limitation in this literature is the assumption

© Springer Nature Switzerland AG 2021
T. Uchiya et al. (Eds.): PRIMA 2020, LNAI 12568, pp. 259–280, 2021.
https://doi.org/10.1007/978-3-030-69322-0_17

that the system is finite-state and fully specified, which in many applications requires to propositionalize crucial system features. Other approaches have thus tackled the verification of MASs in settings that are intrinsically infinite-state [20], for which explicit model-checking techniques cannot be used off-the-shelf. These are the settings in which either some sort of *data component* is present or where the concrete component instances of the MAS are not explicitly listed beforehand. Our work falls into the latter category, that is the one of verification of parameterized MASs (PMASs), recognized as a key reasoning task and addressed by a growing literature [8,16,20,28]. In PMASs, the number of agents is *unbounded* and *unknown*, so that possibly infinite concrete MASs need to be considered: the task is to check whether the specification is met by any (or all) concrete MASs that adhere to some behavioral structure (typically a set of agent *templates*), without fixing the number of actual agents a priori. Here, we focus on checking *safety*, namely that no state satisfying a state formula (existentially quantifying on agent instances) is reachable for any number of agent instances. E.g., checking that there will never be two agents in the restricted area. Note that this differs from checking that a strategy (for some agent) exists to prevent unsafe states. Safety checking (and reachability) is a crucial property of MASs as well as finite and infinite dynamic systems, with a long-standing tradition (e.g., [3]). Applications are numerous, from the verification of properties of swarms to industry 4.0 [6], where one wants to check that instances of a product family will be manufacturable by robots from a fixed model catalogue.

In this paper we present our verification technique based on an SMT [7] approach for array-based systems (ABSs) [4,5,11,13,23,24]. We provide a formal model of PMASs with two different execution semantics and we discuss how the safety problem for these systems can be correctly handled in the ABS framework. We detail our solution and comment on its implementation based on the well-established SMT-based model-checker MCMT [25]: we develop a tool called *SAFE*, an intuitive user interface that allows to directly encode PMASs. *SAFE* returns a textual representation of ABS that can be used as input specification file for MCMT. This implementation makes available the third-party model checker MCMT for checking the safety of PMASs. The remainder of this paper is organized as follows. In Sect. 2, we state the contributions of this work and relate our results to the previous literature on parameterized verification and, in particular, verification of parameterized multi-agent systems. Then, in Sect. 3 we provide the definition of Parameterized MAS (PMAS) and we present two different semantics for PMASs, i.e. the concurrent and the interleaved ones: this distinction gives rise to two corresponding classes of PMASs. In Sect. 3.2 the (un)safety checking problem for PMASs is introduced. In Sect. 4 we present our user-interface tool, called SAFE, illustrating the implementation of our approach, based on the state-of-the-art MCMT model checker. We conclude and discuss future work in Sect. 6, where we comment on how this framework lends itself to accommodate a further source of infinity, i.e. the *data* dimension. We now introduce our running example.

Example Scenario. Imagine a robotic swarm attacking a defence position, protected by a robot cannon. There are only two possible paths to reach the position: an attacker must first move to waypoint A or B, then move again to reach the target. Attackers can only move to either waypoint if the paths to A or B are not covered in snow, and similarly for reaching the target. The snow condition is not known in advance. The defensive cannon can target either waypoint with a blast or with an EMP pulse. The cannon program is so that a blast can only be fired if there are robots in that waypoint, and at least one robot under fire is hit. If instead the EMP pulse is directed towards A or B, no robot can move there. The cannon can use either the blast or activate the pulse at the same time but, while the EMP is active, the cannon can continue firing blasts. The EMP can cover either A or B, not both. The number of attackers is not known.

It appears that, even if all paths are free of snow, an effective defensive plan exists: at the beginning, use the pulse (say against A); let the enemy robots make their moves to B (the pulse remains active on A), then use the blast against B to destroy robots there. Whenever further attackers move to B, use again the blast, otherwise wait. If one path is not viable the plan is even simpler. Question: does this strategy work? Answer: only if the blast destroys all robots in the waypoint against which it is fired. Q: if blasts do not hit all robots under fire, how many attackers may have a chance of reaching the target? A: at least two, if they move to the waypoint B together, since blasts always hit at least one robot. Q: is any attack plan for at least two robots guaranteed to work? A: no. This scenario is trivial, however a complex network of waypoints or cannons capable of targeting multiple waypoints can make this arbitrarily complex, also given that the snow conditions cannot be foreseen, requiring to reason by cases. If "playing" as attackers, computing an attack plan that has chances against any number of cannons is even more complex.

In this paper we tackle this type of scenarios, showing how they can be modeled and solved, but also that our solution technique is powerful enough to be used to account for a number of features that cannot be included in this preliminary work, e.g., the inclusion of full fledged relational database storing public and private agent data information with read and write access.

2 Related Work and Contribution

The related work is constituted by the literature on parameterized verification [8] and more specifically verification of PMASs.

The literature on parameterized verification is related but nonetheless distinct from our approach. The problem has been studied in the context of verification of reactive systems, e.g., for the analysis of broadcast protocols. The problem of checking whether a specification is true in a parameterized system is, e.g., shown to be decidable for forms of regular specifications [20] but undecidable even for stuttering-insensitive properties such as LTL\X formulae [18] if asynchronous rendezvous is allowed. As summarized in [8], decidability results for these systems are based on reduction to finite-state model checking via abstraction [27,32], *cutoff* computations (i.e. a bound on the number of instances that need to be verified [17,19]) or by proving that they can be represented as well-structured transition systems [3,21]. Similarly to these settings, we are tackling verification of parameterized PMASs by relating our decidability results with the assumed MAS execution semantics and shape of the allowed guards, relating our modeling choices to a MAS setting. However, we here focus on safety and our technique is not based on (predicate and counter) abstractions, cutoffs or reductions to finite-state model checking. Also, the multi-agent systems we consider do not assume a particular topology, and the conjunctive and disjunctive guards considered in [18] are here extended toward a FO setting by also allowing relation symbols. Our theoretical results are based on the model-theoretic framework of ABS [13,24] and can be seen as a declarative, first-order counterpart of theories of well-structured transition systems for which compatible results are known in the community (see, e.g., [3,8]). Indeed, our focus is not on providing a characterization of the decidability boundaries for safety checking of PMASs, but to demonstrate the effectiveness of employing backward reachability with soundness, completeness, and termination guarantees (thus decidability). Finally, as argued below, the application of our results is novel, effective and yields decidability results of direct and immediate applicability to a clear class of PMASs.

Regarding specifically the verification of PMASs, the closest model is that of [28,29] and open MASs [16,30]. In [16,30], the authors study MASs where agents can join and leave dynamically. As in our work, agents are characterized by a type and their number is not bounded. They employ synchronous composition operations over automata on infinite words and their procedure can verify strategic abilities for LTL goals by reduction to synthesis. Notwithstanding the fact that we only look at safety, a mechanism for joining/leaving the system can be captured natively in our formalization of PMASs. A similar framework is in [30], sharing the same model of [28] and related papers, with agent templates similar to those considered here. Compared with that work, we restrict to the key task of checking safety (reachability), instead of tackling model checking of arbitrary specifications. Safety checking (and, conversely, reachability analysis) is a crucial task with a long tradition in AI and in the field of reasoning about actions. Although not included here, we can capture many variants of execution semantics considered in [28]. As in our case, the results in that work depend on the chosen execution semantics, hence on the combinations of possible action types that are allowed. In the general case, their procedure requires to check the existence of a cutoff; if it exists, the verification result is correct, otherwise the procedure halts with no result. The existence of a cutoff depends on the existence of a simulation property (between the agent templates and the environment) to be checked on the abstract system, which has to be computed first. Conversely, our technique does not require cutoffs nor any notion alike: we directly obtain a complete procedure in general and we get a full decision procedure for interleaved PMASs.

By departing from the literature mentioned above, we present here a verification technique based on an SMT-based [7] approach for ABSs [5,13,23,24]. This is a very well-understood SMT-based formalism for which a number of results of practical applicability already exist [10,12,22]. Our approach is the first to establish a formal connection between the verification of PMASs and the long-standing tradition of SMT-based model checking for ABSs. Also, leveraging SMT-techniques makes the framework directly extendible in multiple directions: for example, we can easily introduce theories constraining agent data, i.e. elements can be retrieved by agents from relational databases (both shared or private) with constraints such as key dependencies, in the line with [10,11,13]. On this, it is our aim to combine this framework with the RAS formalism in [11,13]. Adding theories, data-aware extensions, restricted arithmetics, cardinality constraints, are all now concretely viable directions for checking safety of PMASs.

Finally, we exploit *operationally* the connection between the PMAS and the SMT tradition, encoding safety checks of PMASs into the general-purpose model checker MCMT [25]. Since both the modeling of PMASs and their translation into input files for MCMT is particularly laborious, we have realized the intuitive web tool (*SAFE* [2]) for modeling and encoding PMASs into MCMT.

3   PMASs: Parameterized MAS

In this section we give our definition of PMASs and of two alternative execution semantics. This model, although novel, shares many similarities with known parametric systems in the literature.

We consider a set Θ of (semantic) data types, used for variables. Each type $\theta \in \Theta$ comes with a (possibly infinite) domain Δ_θ, and a type-wise equality operator $=_\theta$. For instance, types are reals, integers, booleans, etc. We simply write $=$ when the type is clear. We also consider a set $\mathcal{R}$ of relations over types in Θ, which we treat as *uninterpreted* relations (i.e. simple relation symbols). These are used to model background information in the MAS but *are never updated during its execution*, constituting a *read-only* component. E.g., the snow condition in the scenario can be modeled via these relations, as we will show. We consider the usual notion of FO interpretations $\mathcal{I} = (\Delta^{\mathcal{I}}, \cdot^{\mathcal{I}})$ with $\Delta^{\mathcal{I}} = \bigcup_{\Theta} \Delta_\theta$ and $\cdot^{\mathcal{I}}$ is an FOL interpretation function for symbols in $\mathcal{R}$.

Definition 1. *An **agent template** is a tuple* $T = \langle ID, L, l^0, V, type, val, \mathcal{A}^{loc}, \mathcal{A}^{syn}, P, \delta \rangle$ *having:*

- *an infinite set ID of unique agent identifiers of sort* ID*;*
- *a finite set L of local states, with initial state* $l^0 \in L$*;*
- *a finite set V of local (i.e., internal) agent state variables;*
- *a variable-type assignment* $type : V \mapsto \Theta$*;*
- *a variable assignment* $val : L \times V \mapsto \bigcup_\Theta \Delta_\theta$*, with* $val(l, v) \in \Delta_\theta$ *for* $\theta = type(v)$*;*
- *a non-empty, finite set of action symbols* $\mathcal{A} \doteq \mathcal{A}^{loc} \cup \mathcal{A}^{syn}$ *(described later), s.t.* $\mathcal{A}^{loc} \cap \mathcal{A}^{syn} = \emptyset$*;*

- a *protocol function* specifying the conditions under which each action is executable. *It is a function* $P : \mathcal{A} \mapsto \Psi$, *where* Ψ *are agent formulae, defined in the next section, that allow to "query" the current state of the whole PMAS;*
- a *transition function* $\delta : L \times \mathcal{A} \mapsto L$, *describing how the local state is affected by the execution of an action* α: *the template moves from a state* l *to a state* l' *when executing an action* α *iff* $\delta(l, \alpha) = l'$, *also denoted* $l \xrightarrow{\alpha} l'$. *We assume* δ *to be total.*

An **environment template** is a special agent template T_e with fixed identifier (i.e., $ID = \{e\}$): there is exactly one environment. Intuitively, a **(concrete) agent** is a triple composed of an agent ID, its template and its current local state. Analogously, a **(concrete) environment** is a pair consisting of the template T_e and its current state (again, e is a constant).

Example 1. We use a template T_{att} for robots, with variables loc (enumeration [init,A, B,target]) and destroyed (boolean). The former variable is used for storing an agent's location, whereas the latter is for specifying whether the agent is destroyed. The actions are gotoA, gotoB and gotoT for moving to waypoints (from the initial location) and to the target (from either waypoint), plus additional actions blastA, blastB representing the action of "being destroyed" by a shot fired at position A or B, respectively. For instance, a transition $l \xrightarrow{\text{gotoA}} l'$ exists in δ for this template when $val(l, \text{loc}) = \text{init}$ and $val(l, \text{destroyed}) = \text{false}$, and the resulting local state l' is such that $val(l', \text{loc}) = \text{A}$ (plus further assignments for inertia). Other actions are defined in a similar manner. Figure 1 depicts this template, represented as a labeled finite-state transition system. The cannon is modeled as (part of) the environment, whose template T_e has actions pulseA, pulseB, blastA, blastB and variables pulse-loc (enumeration [A, B, nil]). The former is used to store the location (waypoint A or B) toward which the pulse is currently directed. The snow is captured by a binary relation over locations (e.g. $Snow(\text{init,A})$), whose interpretation is unbounded. Protocols are given later. □

Let $\{T_1, \ldots, T_n, T_e\}$ be a set of agent (and environment) templates, with $T_t = \langle ID_t, L_t, l_t^0, V_t, type_t, val_t, \mathcal{A}_t^{loc}, \mathcal{A}^{syn}, P_t, \delta_t \rangle$ for $t \in \{1, \ldots, n, e\}$. We denote a concrete agent of type T_t, $t \in [1, n]$, and ID j by writing $\langle j, l_j \rangle_t$, and similarly we denote the concrete environment by $\langle e, l_e \rangle_e$. We also denote a vector of k such concrete agents of type T_t as $\langle \boldsymbol{I}, \boldsymbol{L} \rangle_t$, where $\boldsymbol{I} \in ID_t^k$ and $\boldsymbol{L} \in L_t^k$ are vectors of IDs and local states, respectively. Importantly, we assume that agent IDs are unique and template variables disjoint, i.e., $ID_t \cap ID_{t'} = \emptyset$ and $V_t \cap V_{t'} = \emptyset$ for $t, t' \in \{1, \ldots, n, e\}$, $t \neq t'$.

A **PMAS** is a tuple $\mathcal{M} = \langle \{T_1, \ldots, T_n\}, T_e, \mathcal{R} \rangle$ consisting of n agent templates, one environment template and the relations. Note that a PMAS specifies the initial local state of all agents for each template, but *does not specify how many concrete agents exist for each template*. A **configuration** is a tuple $g = \langle \{\langle \boldsymbol{I}_1, \boldsymbol{L}_1 \rangle_1, \ldots, \langle \boldsymbol{I}_n, \boldsymbol{L}_n \rangle_n \}, \langle e, l_e \rangle_e \rangle$, which thus identifies the number of agent instances (the size of each $\boldsymbol{I}_t$, $t \in [1, n]$, may differ). A configuration is *initial* iff all agents are in their initial local state. Clearly, *infinite possible initial*

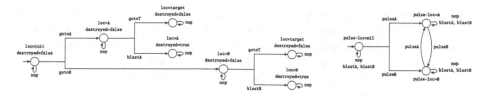

Fig. 1. A depiction of the templates T_{att} (left) and T_e (right). The label next to each local state l specifies the value $val(l, v)$ of each $v \in V$.

configurations exist, since the number of concrete agents for each template is unbounded and not known a priori. As shorthand, we denote the local state l_j of agent $\langle j, l_j \rangle_t$ in configuration g as $g.j$, thus writing $\langle j, g.j \rangle_t$.

3.1 Agent Formulae

Here we define the agent formulae used for protocols in Definition 1 as quantifier-free formulae $\psi(\underline{j}, self, e, \underline{v})$ where $\underline{j}$ are the free variables of sort ID, $self$ is a special constant used to denote the current agent, e is the special ID (constant) of the concrete environment, $\underline{v}$ are template variables (for any template). These follow the grammar:

$$\psi \doteq (v^{[j]} = k) \mid R(x_1, \cdots, x_m) \mid j_1 = j_2 \mid \neg\psi \mid \psi_1 \vee \psi_2$$

where $v \in V$, k is a constant in Δ_θ for $\theta = type(v)$, R is a relation symbol in $\mathcal{R}$ of arity $m \geq 1$ (defined over types $\theta_1, \ldots, \theta_m$), each x_i is either a variable $v_i^{[j]}$ or a constant $k_i \in \Delta_{\theta_i}$, and j, j_1, j_2 are the variables of sort ID in $\underline{j}$ or the constant $self$ or the ID constant e for the environment (with a little abuse of notation, in this paper we use symbols j to denote variables of sort ID or, as in the previous section, concrete IDs). Note that in a relation term we are restricted to use only one variable j of sort ID. The usual logical abbreviations apply. Intuitively, these formulas are implicitly quantified existentially over agent IDs. As we will formalize next, they allow to test (dis)equality of agent variables with respect to agent constants (IDs), and to check whether a tuple is in a relation (whose elements are agent variables). For instance, $(v^{[j]} = k)$ informally means that there exists an agent ID j so that $v = k$ for the such agent.

An **ID grounding** of a formula $\psi(\underline{j}, self, e, \underline{v})$ in g is an assignment σ which assigns each variable j of sort ID in $\underline{j}$, as well as the constant $self$, to a concrete agent ID in g (denoted $\sigma(j)$ and $\sigma(self)$, respectively). It also assigns the constant e to itself, i.e. we impose $\sigma(e) = e$. Intuitively, for a formula to be true in g, one needs to find a suitable σ that makes the formula true.

Definition 2. *Given an interpretation $\mathcal{I}_0$, a configuration g satisfies a formula ψ under $\mathcal{I}_0$, denoted $g \models_{\mathcal{I}_0} \psi$, iff there exists an ID grounding σ of ψ in g such that $g, \sigma \models_{\mathcal{I}_0} \psi$, with:*

- *$g, \sigma \models_{\mathcal{I}_0} (v^{[j]} = k)$ iff $val_t(g.\sigma(j), v) = k$, where $v \in V_t$; i.e. the concrete agent $\langle \sigma(j), g.\sigma(j) \rangle_t$, i.e. with ID $\sigma(j)$ and template T_t, is so that $v = k$;*

– $g, \sigma \models_{\mathcal{I}_0} R(x_1, \cdots, x_m)$ *iff* $R^{\mathcal{I}_0}(y_i, \ldots, y_m)$, *where* y_i *is as follows for each* $i \in [1, m]$. *If* x_i *is a constant* k, *then* y_i *is* k; *if instead* x_i *is a variable* $v^{[j]}$ *with* $v_i \in V_t$ *for some template* $t \in \{1, \ldots, n, e\}$ *then* y_i *is* $val_t(g.\sigma(j), v)$. *Intuitively, R holds under* $\mathcal{I}_0$ *for the constants and values of variables, where the value of* $v^{[j]}$ *is taken from the local state of agent with* ID $\sigma(j)$;
– $g, \sigma \models_{\mathcal{I}_0} (j_1 = j_2)$ *iff* $\sigma(j_1) = \sigma(j_2)$;
– $g, \sigma \models_{\mathcal{I}_0} \neg\psi$ *iff* $g, \sigma \not\models_{\mathcal{I}_0} \psi$;
– $g, \sigma \models_{\mathcal{I}_0} \psi_1 \vee \psi_2$ *iff* $g, \sigma \models_{\mathcal{I}_0} \psi_1$ *or* $g, \sigma \models_{\mathcal{I}_0} \psi_2$.

Note that *self* is freely assigned to an agent ID: if g satisfies a formula with *self*, then an agent exists that can be taken as *self*. We write $g \models_{\mathcal{I}_0}^j \psi$, if needed, to denote that there exists σ with $\sigma(self) = j$ so that $g, \sigma \models_{\mathcal{I}_0} \psi$. This informally reads as ψ *is true in* g *for agent with* ID j. E.g., assuming g is s.t. $v_1 = 6$ for agent with ID 3, and $v_1 = 5$ for agent with ID 7, then $g \models_{\mathcal{I}_0}^3 (v_1^{[self]} = 6) \wedge (v_1^{[j]} = 5)$.

Example 2. (cont.d) In the running example, the program of the cannon is so that the cannon can fire on a waypoints only if there is at least one attacker (not already destroyed) in that location. Hence, we have $P_e(\texttt{blastA}) = (\texttt{loc}^{[j]} = \texttt{A}) \wedge (\texttt{destroyed}^{[j]} = \texttt{false})$ (recall that $V_t \cap V_{t'} = \emptyset$ for $t \neq t'$, hence given a variable we know to which template it belongs). Similarly for $\texttt{blastB}$. Moreover, only positions that are not targeted by the pulse and are clear of snow can be accessed: $P_{att}(\texttt{gotoA}) = (\texttt{pulse-loc}^{[e]} \neq \texttt{A}) \wedge \neg Snow(\texttt{init}, \texttt{A})$ (similarly for $\texttt{gotoB}$). Note that we are assuming that the interpretation $\mathcal{I}_0$ is fixed, hence the snow condition (the relation $Snow$) is fixed and is not affected by the execution. As we are going to show in Sect. 3.2, however, we define our safety check so as to check that a condition cannot be reached irrespective of the initial interpretation, so as to consider any possible snow condition (we do so by checking whether there exists an interpretation so that the condition can be reached).

3.2   Concurrent and Interleaved PMASs

In this section we introduce the two main execution semantics, hence defining two distinct types of PMASs, called concurrent and interleaved. These are distinguished by how the (single-step) transitions of the system are defined, which has to do with the types of interactions that are allowed between the agents and the environment.

A **(global) transition** of a PMAS describes its evolution when a vector of actions $\boldsymbol{\alpha}$ (one for each concrete agent in g and one for the environment) are executed from a configuration $g = \langle\{\langle \boldsymbol{I}_1, \boldsymbol{L}_1\rangle_1, \ldots, \langle \boldsymbol{I}_n, \boldsymbol{L}_n\rangle_n\}, \langle e, l_e\rangle\rangle$, so that a new configuration of the form $g' = \langle\{\langle \boldsymbol{I}_1, \boldsymbol{L}_1'\rangle_1, \ldots, \langle \boldsymbol{I}_n, \boldsymbol{L}_n'\rangle_n\}, \langle e, l_e'\rangle\rangle$ is reached. This is denoted by simply writing $g \xrightarrow{\boldsymbol{\alpha}} g'$.

Since each concrete agent and the environment may either perform an action (in $\mathcal{A}_t^{loc} \cup \mathcal{A}^{syn}$) or remain idle, multiple executions semantics can be defined, depending on the constraints we impose on $\boldsymbol{\alpha}$. We now describe more in detail the sets $\mathcal{A}_t^{loc}$ and $\mathcal{A}^{syn}$ introduced in Definition 1.

Symbols in $\mathcal{A}_t^{loc}$, for each t, are called **local actions**, and those in $\mathcal{A}^{syn}$ **synchronization** actions. Actions in $\mathcal{A}_t^{loc}$ can only affect the local state of the concrete agent which executes them, whereas actions in $\mathcal{A}^{syn}$ represent the synchronization between one or more agents and the environment and thus can affect the local state of each agent involved. Intuitively, the synchronization actions are used to model explicit communication actions or any action with effects that are not private to the single agent or to the environment.

As a consequence, not every vector α is meaningful: synchronization actions in $\mathcal{A}^{syn}$ are shared across all templates and are used to model global events that are (potentially) observable by any agent, whereas local actions in $\mathcal{A}^{loc}$ are private and can be freely executed. We constrain the possible evolutions so that synchronization actions and local actions do not happen at the same time, so that we can distinguish those steps in which the PMAS evolves in response to public actions, events or messages from those steps in which agents update their local state.

Concurrent PMASs. First, we focus on those PMASs in which either all agents perform local actions if possible or, whenever a synchronization action is executed, then all agents and the environment are forced to synchronize (whenever this is possible), as formalized below. Intuitively, synchronization actions are seen as public events, affecting the local state of each concrete agent. For capturing this execution semantics, we adopt the following definition to characterize the global transitions that are said to be *legal*.

Definition 3. *Given $\mathcal{I}_0$, a global transition $g \xrightarrow{\alpha} g'$ is said to be **legal** iff:*

- $g'.j = \delta_t(g.j, \alpha.j)$ *for every $\langle j, g.j \rangle_t$, $t \in \{1, \ldots, n, e\}$, i.e., all the agents and the environment evolve as per their template;*
- $g \models_{\mathcal{I}_0}^j P_t(\alpha.j)$ *for every $\langle j, g.j \rangle_t$, i.e., each action is executable and the constant self is substituted by j when evaluating the protocol of the chosen action;*
- *either only local actions are executed (by all agents and environment), or the environment and at least one agent synchronize with action $\alpha \in \mathcal{A}^{syn}$. In the former case, however, agents are allowed to remain idle iff they cannot execute any local action, and in the latter iff they cannot execute the synchronization action α. Formally, either:*

  - *no j exists so that $\alpha.j \in \mathcal{A}^{syn}$, and for every $\langle j, g.j \rangle_t$ if $\alpha.j = nop$ then no $\alpha \in \mathcal{A}_t^{loc}$ exists with $g \models_{\mathcal{I}_0}^j P_t(\alpha)$;*
  - *$\alpha.e = \alpha \in \mathcal{A}^{syn}$ and at least one $j \neq e$ exists so that $\alpha.j = \alpha$. Moreover, for every agent $\langle j, g.j \rangle_t$ either (i) $g \models_{\mathcal{I}_0}^j P_t(\alpha)$ and $\alpha.j = \alpha$ or (ii) $g \not\models_{\mathcal{I}_0}^j P_t(\alpha)$ and $\alpha.j = nop$.*

Interleaved PMASs. In these systems, at each step either *(i)* a subset of concrete agents (and the environment) perform a (non *nop*) action in $\mathcal{A}_t^{loc}$ on their local state or *(ii)* the environment and a *subset* of the agents synchronize by executing the same action in $\mathcal{A}^{syn}$. *nop* is a special no-op action: $\delta_t(l, nop) = l$ for all t, l. Local and synchronization actions cannot be mixed. We denote by $\alpha.j$ the action of the agent with ID j, or of the environment if $j = e$.

Definition 4. *Given an interpretation* $\mathcal{I}_0$, $g \xrightarrow{\alpha} g'$ *is* **legal** *iff:*

- $g'.j = \delta_t(g.j, \alpha.j)$ *for every* $\langle j, g.j \rangle_t$, $t \in \{1, \ldots, n, e\}$, *i.e., agents and environment evolve as per their template;*
- $g \models^j_{\mathcal{I}_0} P_t(\alpha.j)$ *for every* $\langle j, g.j \rangle_t$, *i.e., each action is executable and self is replaced by j for evaluating protocols;*
- *either only local actions are executed (by some agents and environment) or the environment and at least one agent synchronize via* $\alpha \in \mathcal{A}^{syn}$. *Other agents perform nop. Formally, either:*

  - *no j exists so that* $\alpha.j \in \mathcal{A}^{syn}$, *that is, no synchronization action is executed; or*
  - *the environment and at least one agent synchronize, while other agents can either synchronize as well or freely decide to remain idle. Formally,* $\alpha.e = \alpha \in \mathcal{A}^{syn}$ *and* $i \neq e$ *exists with* $\alpha.i = \alpha$, *while* $\alpha.j \in \{\alpha, nop\}$ *and* $g \models^j_{\mathcal{I}_0} P_t(\alpha.j)$ *for every* $\langle j, g.j \rangle_t$.

Example 3. (cont.d) The actions blastA/B are synchronization actions (modeling the firing action and the 'being hit' action of robots). According to the definition above, when the example is modeled as an interleaved PMAS, then blastA is not guaranteed to destroy all targets because not all agents in location A are forced to synchronize with such action. In fact, the two cases in which a blast destroys all agents in the location, or just a subset, are elegantly captured by simply assuming a concurrent or interleaved semantics. In the former, a global transition including blastA (by the environment) is legal iff all agents execute blastA as well if this action is executable, that is, if they can be hit because they are in the location at which the cannon is firing.

Runs of PMASs and the Reachability Problem. Based on the one-step definition of (legal) global transition, we now define the notion of runs for concurrent and interleaved PMASs. Given a PMAS $\mathcal{M} = \langle \{T_1, \ldots, T_n\}, T_e, \mathcal{R} \rangle$, a **(global) run** is a pair $\langle \rho, \mathcal{I}_0 \rangle$ where ρ is a sequence $\rho = g^0 \xrightarrow{\alpha^1} g^1 \xrightarrow{\alpha^2} \cdots$ and $\mathcal{I}_0$ is an interpretation for relation symbols as before. We restrict to runs that *(i)* are legal and *(ii)* start from an initial configuration, i.e., with all concrete agents in their initial local state. A global transition as above specifies how each concrete agent $g.j$ evolves depending on the nature of the action $\alpha.j$. As already stated, once fixed at the start of ρ, $\mathcal{I}_0$ *does not change* and is used at each step for evaluating formulae.

Definition 5. *An agent formula* ψ_{goal} *is* **reachable** *in* $\mathcal{M}$ *iff there exists* $\mathcal{I}_0$ *and an initial configuration* g^0 *of* $\mathcal{M}$ *s.t. a configuration g with* $g \models_{\mathcal{I}_0} \psi_{goal}$ *is reachable through a run* $\langle \rho, \mathcal{I}_0 \rangle$ *from* g^0.

The verification task at hand is to assess whether ψ_{goal} is reachable, i.e. $\mathcal{M}$ is **unsafe** w.r.t. ψ_{goal}. If a formula is unreachable then it is so for any number of agents and all possible interpretations. In such a cases, $\mathcal{M}$ is said to be **safe** w.r.t. ψ_{goal}.

4   A Practical Solution to the Reachability Problem for PMASs

In this section, we illustrate our implementation approach and the tool called *SAFE*, which makes available the model checker MCMT [25] for checking the safety of PMASs. Through this tool-chain, one can (*i*) specify a PMAS $\mathcal{M}$ with *SAFE* and then (*ii*) check its safety with MCMT.

Theorem 1. *Given a PMAS $\mathcal{M}$ and a formula ψ_{goal} (expressing the unsafe condition):*

- *If $\mathcal{M}$ is interleaved then MCMT always terminates with the correct answer (i.e., MCMT provides a full decision procedure);*
- *If $\mathcal{M}$ is concurrent, if MCMT terminates reporting that the PMAS is safe, then the answer is correct. If the PMAS is unsafe, then MCMT will terminate with the correct answer.*

The results stated in the previous theorem follow from the fact that MCMT implements the formal framework of array-based systems [13,24]: this formalism allows us to encode PMASs into suitable state and transition formulae conforming the format required by MCMT and respecting the desired execution semantics. The proof should be adapted following the line of reasoning from [13] (for interleaved PMASs) and [26] (for concurrent PMASs). Note that, if a concurrentPMAS is safe, MCMT may still report an incorrect answer.

These results are consistent with results in the literature (see Sect. 2). For example, the model checking solution in [28] guarantees a correct verification outcome when a cutoff exists, otherwise the procedure halts with no result. The existence of a cutoff depends on the existence of a simulation property (between the agent templates and the environment) to be checked on the abstracted system, which has to be computed first. In our approach, the theorem above provides guarantees based only on the assumptions on the type of PMAS (whether it is interleaved or concurrent).

4.1   MCMT: Model Checker Modulo Theories

MCMT [25] is a declarative and deductive symbolic model checker for safety properties of infinite-state systems, based on backward reachability and fixpoints computations (with calls to an SMT solver). The input to the software is a textual representation of an *Array-based System* (ABS), briefly introduced below, which essentially are a symbolic representation for infinite-state systems. Given an ABS and an existential formula (as the agent formulae in Sect. 3.1), MCMT is able to check whether a state satisfying the formula is reachable or not, which exactly matches our verification task (Definition 5). If the system is unsafe, a *witness* is provided.

ABSs. "Array-based Systems" [24] is a generic term used to refer to *infinite state transition systems* implicitly specified using a declarative, logic-based formalism

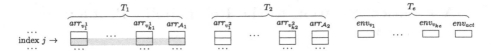

Fig. 2. A depiction of the encoding of agent templates and environment. (Color figure online)

in which arrays are manipulated via logical formulae. Intuitively, they describe a system that, starting from an initial configuration (specified by an initial formula), is progressed through transitions (specified by transition formulae). The precise definition depends on the specific application, and it makes use of a multi-sorted theory with one kind of sorts for the indexes of arrays and another for the elements stored therein. The content of an array is unbounded and updated during the evolution. We exploit this to capture the possible evolutions of a PMAS through suitable transition formulae so that we can use MCMT for verification, as it supports both forms of existential and universal quantification needed for expressing interleaved and concurrent execution semantics of PMASs. If universal quantification is used, a warning is issued, as this may generate spurious runs (see Theorem 1).

For lack of space, in this paper we do not provide a thorough formal treatment of ABS nor of how a PMAS can be encoded into an ABS, but we directly show and comment the resulting textual encoding, in the next section. Consistently with this, ABSs are only used as the internal representation of our implementation, and we do not require users of our implementation to know how these work nor how to manually encode a PMAS into an ABS.

In Fig. 2 we depict the main intuition behind the overall encoding approach: an ABS features array variables and simple variables (called global variables). The variables in each agent template are encoded by array variables, so that the value of each variable v for an agent with ID j can be written in the position j of that array arr_v (the length and content of arrays is unbounded). An additional array arr_{A_t}, one for each template T_t, stores the action currently "declared" by agents. So the local state l of a concrete agent $\langle j, l \rangle_t$ is encoded by the values written for index j for the arrays for template T_t (e.g., the red area in Fig. 2). The environment variables are instead encoded via global variables, because only one concrete environment exists.

4.2   MCMT Input Files for Interleaved and Concurrent PMASs

We now exemplify the textual encoding by listing the salient portions of the input file for our running example. An input file for MCMT is a textual representation of an ABS that includes *(i)* the declaration of individual and array variables, *(ii)* the initial state formula, *(iii)* the goal state formula, *(iv)* the list of transition formulae that specify how the system evolves. As stated in the previous section, these files are only used as the internal representation of our implementation, but we do not require users to know how these work nor how to manually encode a PMAS.

With the exception of minor syntactic details, the textual encoding is the same for the interleaved and concurrent cases, hence in this paper we focus on the former case only.

First, we define the sorts that are used in the ABS, which intuitively represent the variables types that we are going to use. For the running example, we have actions, booleans, strings used for locations (init,A,B,target), one turn type used to implement the alternation between the cannon and the robots, and finally an internal book-keeping type Phase that we need for the encoding. The encoding captures all possible evolutions of the PMAS by restricting how global and array variables are be updated at each step, using a flag of type PhaseSort to guide the progression.

```
:smt (define-type Action)          :smt (define-type turnSort)     :smt (define-type BOOLE)
:smt (define-type StringLoc)       :smt (define-type PhaseSort)
```

Then, constants and relations are declared with their corresponding sort:

```
:smt (define Snow ::(-> StringLoc StringLoc ))  :smt (define blastA ::Action)   :smt (define target ::StringLoc)
:smt (define pulseA ::Action)      :smt (define blastB ::Action)   :smt (define P0 ::PhaseSort)
:smt (define pulseB ::Action)      :smt (define TRUE ::BOOLE)      :smt (define PL ::PhaseSort)
:smt (define gotoA ::Action)       :smt (define FALSE ::BOOLE}     :smt (define PS ::PhaseSort)
:smt (define gotoB ::Action)       :smt (define A ::StringLoc)     :smt (define turnTEMPS ::turnSort)
:smt (define goTargetA ::Action)   :smt (define B ::StringLoc)     :smt (define turnREST ::turnSort)
:smt (define goTargetB ::Action)   :smt (define init ::StringLoc)
```

Then, local and global variables are declared (see Fig. 2 and its description):

```
:local locATT StringLoc            :local actATT Action            :global actEnv Action
:local destroyedATT BOOLE          :global pulseLoc StringLoc      :global phase PhaseSort
```

The three arrays (the local variables) are used, respectively, to hold the location of robots, their destroyed (boolean) state, the actions they currently selected for execution (array actAtt). The remaining three (global) variables are used to hold the location toward which the pulse is currently directed, the action selected for execution by the environment, the phase value needed for encoding the transitions (i.e., a variable phase of type PhaseSort).

Further, the initial states are represented by means of a conjunctive formula, where x is a variable of sort *array index*, implicitly quantified universally:

```
:initial
:var x
:cnj (= pulselocE NULL_StringLoc) (= actE NULL_Action) (= locATT[x] init) (= destroyedATT[x] FALSE)
    (= actATT[x] NULL_Action) (= turn turnTEMPS) (= phase P0)
```

The conditions above require that: the EMP pulse is not directed towards any waypoint, the environment has declared no action, all robots are in their initial state, no robot is destroyed, no robot declared yet an action, the turn is of the cannon (and the book-keeping variable phase is equal to 0). Note that nothing is said about the *Snow* relation, as we want to check that the system is safe irrespective of the snow conditions.

Further, we specify the safety formula to verify. For our example, this formula requires that at least one robot exists (we use an index z1, implicitly quantified existentially) so that the cell of array locATT has value equal to target, namely the robot is in the target location:

```
:u_cnj (= locATT[z1] target)
```

The remaining portion of the file is constituted by a list of transition formulae, which essentially encode the possible ways in which the ABS can evolve. These are constituted by a *guard* condition and a sequence of *if-then-else* updates.

For instance, the transition formula below specifies the conditions (guard) for allowing a robot to declare an action (in this case, action gotoB). The effect of this transition is to write gotoB in a suitable cell of the array actAtt. The guard is composed of six conjuncts: action gotoB can be declared by a robot (identified by the existentially quantified index variable x – i.e., agent *self* in Sect. 3.1) when the robot in the initial location, no action was already declared by the robot, the robot is not destroyed, the EMP pulse is not directed at waypoint B and there is no snow on the path between the initial location and B. The two cases in the second and third column, capturing an *if-then-else* update, make sure that only the cell corresponding to index x (i.e., *self*) is updated, while all other cells in the arrays remain unchanged (namely, the first case is applied for the array index j = x and the second to all array indexes j ≠ x). By simply repeating a variable name, we specify that the variable is unchanged: in the second column, the value of array actATT (that holds the actions declared by all attacking robots for the current round) is updated to gotoB for the array index j=x, whereas in the third column we repeat actATT[j].

```
:transition                    :numcases 2
:var j
:var x                         :case (= x j)              :case
:guard (= phase 0)               :val locATT[j]             :val locATT[j]
       (= actATT[x] NULL_Action)  :val destroyedATT[j]       :val destroyedATT[j]
       (= locATT[x] init)         :val gotoB                 :val actATT[j]
       (= destroyedATT[x] FALSE)  :val pulseLoc              :val pulseLoc
       (not (= pulseLoc B))       :val actEnv                :val actEnv
       (= Snow (start B) FALSE)   :val L                     :val L
```

The following is an example of transition in which a synchronization action (blastA) is declared by the environment together with one robot (see Definition 4), capturing the fact that that robot will be hit by the blast when the effects of the action will be applied in a subsequent transition (before that, more robots will be allowed to participate in the synchronization, i.e., to declare the same action). The guard makes sure that an agent index exists (variable x) so that the agent is in waypoint A and it has not yet declared an action (this will be the robot that will be hit), and that a further index exists (variable y, with value possibly equal to the value of x) that is in A (this is the robot that satisfies the protocol function of the action blastA, requiring the existence of a possible target). In the first case (second column), the value of actAtt[x] is updated to blastA.

```
:transition                          :numcases 2
:var x
:var y                               :case (= x j)              :case
:var j                                 :val locATT[j]             :val locATT[j]
:guard (= phase 0)                     :val destroyedATT[j]       :val destroyedATT[j]
       (= actATT[x] NULL_Action)       :val blastA                :val actATT[j]    .
       (= locATT[x] A)                 :val pulselocE             :val pulselocE
       (= locATT[y] A)                 :val actE                  :val actE
       (= destroyedATT[y] FALSE)       :val S                     :val S
```

The encoding of the rest of the transitions follows the same approach, although one has to manually write all the transitions, which is a delicate and cumbersome task, prone to error (the running example, for the interleaved execution semantics, requires 26 transitions). This justifies the need of a user-oriented approach, which we comment in Sect. 4.3.

Executing MCMT. Once the textual encoding is done, MCMT can be simply executed via command line, specifying as argument the textual file: ./mcmt file.txt. For more details and options, please refer to the MCMT manual [1].

4.3   *SAFE*: the Swarm Safety Detector

Here we present and illustrate *SAFE* [2], i.e., our own implementation of a user interface that allows to directly employ in practice the results presented in this paper. The tool automatizes the textual encoding of the PMAS into MCMT input files (i.e., ABS files), by relying on a *MAS-oriented* modeling framework. This allows the user to focus on modeling the PMAS, i.e., the agent templates and the environment template, without worrying about how their constructs can be encoded for MCMT under the distinct execution semantics. The tool also allows to convert the witnesses for unsafety that MCMT returns (when the input ABS is unsafe) back into executions of the original PMAS. *SAFE* is a user-friendly, effective, implemented approach for modeling and verifying the safety of PMASs. Some preliminary experimental evaluation is discussed in Sect. 5.

The *SAFE* Modeling Interface. The interface of *SAFE*: the Swarm Safety Detector is available at [2] in its *Base* version, which allows to model and interleavedPMASs and encode them into ABSs. Further versions, called *SAFE For all* and *SAFE Data*, allow to model concurrentPMASs and their *data-aware* extensions, and are currently in development. Figure 3 shows the running example of this paper as it appears in the *SAFE* GUI.

SAFE **Templates.** In its present version, the representation of agent and environment templates used by *SAFE* differs slightly from the one used here, although it is equivalent. Indeed, Definition 1 defines an agent templates as a labeled, finite-state transition system, whereas *SAFE* assumes a more succinct representation, where instead of listing explicitly the local states and transitions of the templates, we assume a STRIPS-like approach. Therefore, instead of an explicit finite-state machine labeled by actions, actions are specified by means of pre- and post- conditions;

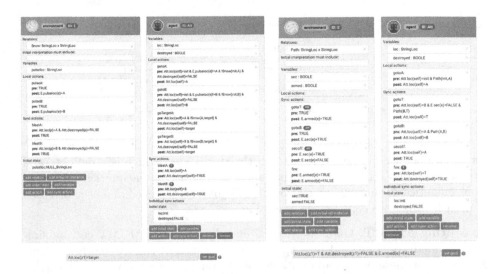

Fig. 3. The main part of the *SAFE Base* interface, showing (on the left) the PMAS model for the running example and (on the right) the example in Sect. 5.1. The GUI provides intuitive buttons to either add or remove any component from the templates, so that there is no manual coding required.

SAFE Base includes some minor features that were not included in the formal model discussed here, as these are primarily implementation details:

- Apart from local actions and synchronization actions, the tool allows a further type of actions, called *individual* synchronization actions, that can only be executed by the environment and by exactly another agent at the same time;
- The *turn-based* mechanics, which allows to alternate the actions of two distinct subsets of the templates (as in our running example), is a core-feature of the tool and can be easily enabled or disabled without the need of manually implementing the alternation logic. In order to make this compatible with the execution semantics for synchronization actions, *SAFE* Base allows an additional annotation of these actions, by which it is possible to specify the *initiator* template of each synchronization action.

5   Execution of *SAFE*-MCMT

The textual encoding of the ABS corresponding to the PMAS in the running example is solved by MCMT v.3.0, on a machine with Ubuntu 18.04, 3.60 GHz Intel Core i7-7700 CPU, in 1.67 s using Z3 (version 4.8.9.0) as background SMT solver. MCMT correctly reports that the system is unsafe. The input file, of which some parts are listed and commented in the previous section, has 3 local variables for the robot template *att*, 3 global variables and 26 transitions. MCMT gives in output this sequence as witness of unsafety:

[t2][t17][t3_1][t15][t1][t16][t5_1][t15], where each tn represents the execution of the n-th transition in the input file, following the order in which they appear. In this case, they correspond to the following sequence of actions: pulseB, gotoA, pulseA, goTarget. Trivially, the robots reach the target while avoiding the EMP pulse used by the cannon, which in this instance does not even attempt to use the blasts to destroy robots.

When a PMAS is determined to be unsafe, *SAFE* does not provide support for embedding into the model the witness provided by MCMT, so it is the responsibility of the user to update their MAS by taking insights from the witness and then check the new model again.

By increasing the number of agent templates and number of waypoints required to reach the target on either of the two paths (i.e., by having waypoints $A_1, \ldots, A_n$ and $B_1, \ldots, B_n$), we can test the scalability of our approach (i.e., the use of *SAFE* and MCMT for checking safety of PMASs) with respect to the minimum *length* of possible runs of the PMAS that achieve the goal formula. In these versions of the running example, cannon blasts hit all locations on the same path simultaneously, the EMP pulse can block all robots on the entire path at which it is directed, and the protocol of the cannon is so that it can freely fire at either path without checking that there are available robot targets. This is achieved by adding a further path variable to robot templates. The number of transitions in the encoding also increases.[1]

As it can be seen from the experiments, the number of transitions and execution time increase slightly. The length of the shortest unsafe runs also increases. There is of course a direct relationship between the length of the PMAS runs that must be checked and the *depth* of the state-space exploration of MCMT, although the number of possible combinations of actions, for the agents and environment, remains the same at each step.

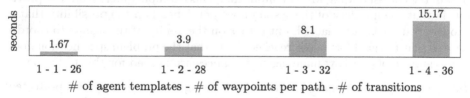

# of agent templates - # of waypoints per path - # of transitions

If instead we increase the number of templates, by introducing further *copies* of the robot template from the original problem instance (preserving only waypoints A and B), then both the number of transitions and variables increase substantially, leading to much longer execution times. This was expected, as the possible global states of the PMAS, as well as the number of possible combinations of actions, grow exponentially. We report below (in red color) on the average execution times for the case of 1–3 robot templates (in addition to the

---

[1] These examples are available at: http://safeswarms.club/page/mcmt/exZb with **Z**=1..4.

environment template).[2] This shows how the cost of the verification is greatly affected by the number of templates. Interestingly, if we remove the assumption that the agents and the environment alternate their moves (thus also removing the global variable turn that is automatically added by *SAFE*), determining the unsafety of the PMAS becomes much faster (times shown in blue).[3]

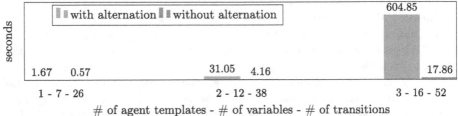

# of agent templates - # of variables - # of transitions

Contrary to intuition, the verification becomes more challenging as the PMAS becomes more specified (that is, with more detailed pre- and post-conditions of actions, turn alternation flags, goal conjuncts). This may constitute a limitation to the use of *SAFE* and MCMT for larger examples, although the examples in the literature involve typically at most two agent templates. Moreover, we should keep in mind that these problem instances are intrinsically computationally demanding. For example, for the case of 3 agent templates, more than 3M calls are made to Z3, and more than 2.5k nodes were explored.

5.1   A Further Example

We present in this subsection a second example, which we encode in *SAFE* to obtain the corresponding MCMT input file. This example differs from the previous in that the unsafety of the system does not depend on the possibility that a proper strategy is not enacted, but rather on the ability of the agents to coordinate so that the goal formula is reached. Note that the problem specification does not contain hints on how many agent instances are needed for this to happen.

Description of the Example. A swarm of robotic agents wants to reach a protected room denoted as C. To do so, they have to first move to a room A, then to a room B, then to C. The corridors between these locations are either open or closed, and this is not known nor controllable. Moreover, a security system prohibits to move from B to C unless the system is first switched off in room A. However, by moving from A to B, the security system automatically turns on again. Moreover, in room C a further security system, when armed, activates an EMP pulse to disable robots in the room, and it is armed whenever C is entered. The pulse becomes unarmed after use, but always disables at least one robot. We want to

---

[2] These examples are available at: http://safeswarms.club/page/mcmt/exZ with **Z**=1..3.

[3] To replicate these experiments, it is sufficient to disable the template alternation through the GUI.

check whether it is possible, after the EMP is activated, that there can be robots in C which are not disabled. By careful analysis, we can see that the answer is positive if all corridors are open: at least two robots need to move to A, then B. At least one further robot can then disable the security system after moving to A, so that the others can enter C. Then, after the EMP is activated, there are chances that one robot will not be disabled. Note how this relies on the ability of considering that more robots are in C.

We use a template T_{att} for robots, with variables room (enumeration [init,A,B,C]) and disabled (boolean). For the environment template T_e, secON and armed are used for specifying whether the security system is on, and whether the pulse is armed. Template T_{att} has actions goA, goB and goC, plus additional actions off, pulse representing the action of switching off the security system and of "being disabled" by the pulse. The environment has actions goB, goC, off, as T_{att} has, because these are synchronization actions which have an impact on the environment: the security system is re-activated, the EMP is armed, the security system is disabled. The fact that corridors between rooms are either open or closed is captured by elements in a binary relation over rooms (e.g. Corr(A,B)), as we quantify over its interpretation.

For example, given a global state in which an agent instance of T_{att} is in local state l and T_e is in local state l_e, the agent can execute a transition $l \xrightarrow{\text{goC}} l'$ only if Corr(B,C) is in $\mathcal{I}_0$, $val_{att}(l, \text{room}) = $ B and $val_e(l_e, \text{secON}) = $ false in T_e, and the resulting local state l' of the agent is such that $val_{att}(l', \text{room}) = $ C while the environment reaches a local state l'_e so that $val_e(l'_e, \text{armed}) = $ true (plus further assignments for inertia). Other actions are defined in a similar manner. For instance, the protocol of off in T_{att} is $\text{room}^{self} = $ A.

Execution in MCMT. Figure 3 shows this example modeled in *SAFE*. The resulting MCMT input file (i.e., the textual encoding of the ABS corresponding to the PMAS) is solved by MCMT v.3.0, on the same machine as before, in 2 min and 22 s and in 56 s respectively using Yices (version 1.0.40) and Z3 (version 4.8.9.0) as background SMT solvers. MCMT correctly reports that the system is unsafe.[4] The generated input file ("download MCMT input") contains 501 lines of code and has 3 local variables for T_{att}, 4 global variables and 15 transitions formulae. MCMT returns this witness for unsafety: [t1_3][t2_2][t2_1][t3][t5_2][t9_1][t13][t6_3][t14] [t4_2][t8_1][t12][t7_2][t15], where each tn represents the execution of the n-th transition in the input file, following the order in which they appear (subscripts refer to the number of instantiated index variables). In this case, they correspond to the following sequence of actions, where each action is executed by one agent (or by the environment): goA,goA,goA,goB,goB,off,goC,goC,pulse.

---

[4] The example, modeled via *SAFE*, is publicly available at: http://safeswarms.club/ page/mcmt/rooms.

6   Conclusions and Future Work

In this paper, we have presented a model of parameterized multi-agent systems, defined the verification task of checking whether the model is safe, and provided a custom, MAS-oriented tool that allows to make use of a generic SMT-model checker off-the-shelf.

Our technique is based on a very well-understood SMT-based theory for which a number of results of practical applicability already exist, and research is active. To the best of our knowledge, the usage of SMT techniques in the context of multi-agent systems is novel: for the first time in order to verify safety of parameterized MASs we exploit a state-of-the-art model checker (MCMT) that discharges safety tests via proof obligations to an efficient SMT-solver. The advantages of using the SMT technology are several: *(i)* first of all, it allows us to exploit a full-fledged *declarative* and symbolic framework where all system specifications can be entirely given with only logical formulae; *(ii)* a plethora of effective techniques for symbolic reasoning are available, like decision procedures for combined theories or quantifier handling through instantiation and quantifier elimination; *(iii)* the theories underlying the SMT-solvers guarantee a large expressivity and flexibility, as well as the possibility of integrating techniques like acceleration, predicate abstraction and invariant synthesis; *(iv)* one of the most important features of an SMT-based approach is the generality, since there is a large spectrum of other classes of systems (distributed, timed, fault tolerant, sequential systems etc.) which this framework can be integrated with.

Finally, note that the background theories employed by the SMT-solver in this paper are only the empty theory or EUF (although, these theories are customary and very significant in the SMT literature): more involved theories are not used because the empty theory or EUF suffices to formalize the uninterpreted symbols characterizing FO interpretations we deal with. Nevertheless, the possibility of extensions is readily available thanks to our work. We can easily introduce theories with axioms for constraining array elements: e.g., elements can be retrieved from full-fledged relational databases with constraints (e.g. key dependencies), as studied in [10,13,31]. This proves beneficial both foundationally and practically, and opens up a number of interesting continuations of our work. From the foundational perspective, thanks to the connection between PMASs and ABSs, *data-aware* extensions of our framework can be directly incorporated, along the line studied in [13]. This supports finite action signatures with infinite number of possible parameter values, and also to store and inspect infinite data values. In addition, there are several other already available extensions of ABS, like the use of restricted arithmetics, cardinality constraints, that are all now concretely usable directions for checking safety of PMASs.

From the applied perspective, as argued before, any advancements for SMT on array-based systems can in principle have a direct application: the effective techniques provided by SMT technology can be exploited for performing symbolic reasoning in these natural extensions. At the same time, the existence of advanced heuristics and approximation techniques triggers a natural continuation of our tool-chain, tailored to efficiency issues. In fact, it is well-known that the performance of symbolic verification techniques can be improved by orders of magnitude if such techniques are suitably developed for the domain at hand [15]. A thorough experimental evaluation of this approach is left as future work.

Acknowledgements. This work was partially supported by the Unibz RTD project SMARTEST.

References

1. MCMT: Model Checker Modulo Theories. http://users.mat.unimi.it/users/ghilardi/mcmt. Accessed 1 Sep 2020
2. SAFE: the swarm safety detector. http://www.safeswarms.club. Accessed 1 Sep 2020
3. Abdulla, P.A., Cerans, K., Jonsson, B., Tsay, Y.K.: General decidability theorems for infinite-state systems. In: Proceedings of LICS, pp. 313–321. IEEE (1996)
4. Alberti, F., Bruttomesso, R., Ghilardi, S., Ranise, S., Sharygina, N.: An extension of lazy abstraction with interpolation for programs with arrays. Formal Methods Syst. Des. **45**(1), 63–109 (2014). https://doi.org/10.1007/s10703-014-0209-9
5. Alberti, F., Ghilardi, S., Sharygina, N.: A framework for the verification of parameterized infinite-state systems. Fund. Inform. **150**(1), 1–24 (2017)
6. Alechina, N., Brázdil, T., De Giacomo, G., Felli, P., Logan, B., Vardi, M.Y.: Unbounded orchestrations of transducers for manufacturing. In: Proceedings of AAAI, pp. 2646–2653 (2019)
7. Barrett, C.W., Tinelli, C.: Satisfiability modulo theories. In: Handbook of Model Checking, pp. 305–343 (2018)
8. Bloem, R., Jacobs, S., Khalimov, A.: Decidability of Parameterized Verification. Morgan & Claypool Publishers, San Rafael (2015)
9. Bulling, N., Goranko, V., Jamroga, W.: Logics for reasoning about strategic abilities in multi-player games. In: Models of Strategic Reasoning - Logics, Games, and Communities, pp. 93–136 (2015)
10. Calvanese, D., Ghilardi, S., Gianola, A., Montali, M., Rivkin, A.: Formal modeling and SMT-based parameterized verification of data-aware BPMN. In: Hildebrandt, T., van Dongen, B.F., Röglinger, M., Mendling, J. (eds.) BPM 2019. LNCS, vol. 11675, pp. 157–175. Springer, Cham (2019). https://doi.org/10.1007/978-3-030-26619-6_12
11. Calvanese, D., Ghilardi, S., Gianola, A., Montali, M., Rivkin, A.: From model completeness to verification of data aware processes. In: Lutz, C., Sattler, U., Tinelli, C., Turhan, A.-Y., Wolter, F. (eds.) Description Logic, Theory Combination, and All That. LNCS, vol. 11560, pp. 212–239. Springer, Cham (2019). https://doi.org/10.1007/978-3-030-22102-7_10
12. Calvanese, D., Ghilardi, S., Gianola, A., Montali, M., Rivkin, A.: Model completeness, covers and superposition. In: Fontaine, P. (ed.) CADE 2019. LNCS (LNAI), vol. 11716, pp. 142–160. Springer, Cham (2019). https://doi.org/10.1007/978-3-030-29436-6_9
13. Calvanese, D., Ghilardi, S., Gianola, A., Montali, M., Rivkin, A.: SMT-based verification of data-aware processes: a model-theoretic approach. Math. Struct. Comp. Sci. **30**(3), 271–313 (2020)
14. Bloem, R., Chatterjee, K., Jobstmann, B.: Graph games and reactive synthesis. Handbook of Model Checking, pp. 921–962. Springer, Cham (2018). https://doi.org/10.1007/978-3-319-10575-8_27

15. Conchon, S., Goel, A., Krstic, S., Mebsout, A., Zaïdi, F.: Invariants for finite instances and beyond. In: Proceedings of FMCAD, pp. 61–68. IEEE (2013)
16. Condurache, R., De Masellis, R., Goranko, V.: Dynamic multi-agent systems: conceptual framework, automata-based modelling and verification. In: Baldoni, M., Dastani, M., Liao, B., Sakurai, Y., Zalila Wenkstern, R. (eds.) PRIMA 2019. LNCS (LNAI), vol. 11873, pp. 106–122. Springer, Cham (2019). https://doi.org/10.1007/978-3-030-33792-6_7
17. Emerson, E.A., Kahlon, V.: Reducing model checking of the many to the few. In: McAllester, D. (ed.) CADE 2000. LNCS (LNAI), vol. 1831, pp. 236–254. Springer, Heidelberg (2000). https://doi.org/10.1007/10721959_19
18. Emerson, E.A., Kahlon, V.: Model checking guarded protocols. In: Proceedings of LICS, pp. 361–370. IEEE (2003)
19. Emerson, E.A., Namjoshi, K.S.: On reasoning about rings. Int. J. Found. Comput. Sci. 14(4), 527–550 (2003)
20. Esparza, J., Ganty, P., Leroux, J., Majumdar, R.: Verification of population protocols. Acta Inf. 54(2), 191–215 (2017)
21. Finkel, A., Schnoebelen, P.: Well-structured transition systems everywhere!. Theoret. Comput. Sci. 256(1), 63–92 (2001)
22. Ghilardi, S., Gianola, A., Montali, M., Rivkin, A.: Petri nets with parameterised data. In: Fahland, D., Ghidini, C., Becker, J., Dumas, M. (eds.) BPM 2020. LNCS, vol. 12168, pp. 55–74. Springer, Cham (2020). https://doi.org/10.1007/978-3-030-58666-9_4
23. Ghilardi, S., Nicolini, E., Ranise, S., Zucchelli, D.: Towards SMT model checking of array-based systems. In: Proceedings of IJCAR, pp. 67–82 (2008)
24. Ghilardi, S., Ranise, S.: Backward reachability of array-based systems by SMT solving: termination and invariant synthesis. Log. Methods Comput. Sci. 6(4), 1–48 (2010)
25. Ghilardi, S., Ranise, S.: MCMT: a model checker modulo theories. In: Giesl, J., Hähnle, R. (eds.) IJCAR 2010. LNCS (LNAI), vol. 6173, pp. 22–29. Springer, Heidelberg (2010). https://doi.org/10.1007/978-3-642-14203-1_3
26. Ghilardi, S., Ranise, S., Valsecchi, T.: Light-weight SMT-based model checking. Electron. Notes Theor. Comput. Sci. 250(2), 85–102 (2009)
27. John, A., Konnov, I., Schmid, U., Veith, H., Widder, J.: Parameterized model checking of fault-tolerant distributed algorithms by abstraction. In: Proceedings of FMCAD, pp. 201–209. IEEE (2013)
28. Kouvaros, P., Lomuscio, A.: Parameterised verification for multi-agent systems. Artif. Intell. 234, 152–189 (2016)
29. Kouvaros, P., Lomuscio, A.: Parameterised verification of infinite state multi-agent systems via predicate abstraction. In: Proceedings of AAAI, pp. 3013–3020 (2017)
30. Kouvaros, P., Lomuscio, A., Pirovano, E., Punchihewa, H.: Formal verification of open multi-agent systems. In: Proceedings of AAMAS, pp. 179–187 (2019)
31. Li, Y., Deutsch, A., Vianu, V.: VERIFAS: a practical verifier for artifact systems. In: Proceedings of VLDB, pp. 283–296 (2017)
32. Pnueli, A., Xu, J., Zuck, L.: Liveness with (0,1, infty)- counter abstraction. In: Brinksma, E., Larsen, K.G. (eds.) CAV 2002. LNCS, vol. 2404, pp. 107–122. Springer, Heidelberg (2002). https://doi.org/10.1007/3-540-45657-0_9

A Goal-Based Framework for Supporting Medical Assistance: The Case of Chronic Diseases

Milene Santos Teixeira[1], Célia da Costa Pereira[2], and Mauro Dragoni[3(✉)]

[1] University of Trento, Trento, Italy
m.santosteixeira@unitn.it
[2] Université de Nice Sophia Antipolis, Nice, France
celia.pereira@unice.fr
[3] Fondazione Bruno Kessler, Povo, Italy
dragoni@fbk.eu

Abstract. Chronic diseases cause many deaths worldwide each year. The most common action to manage this type of disease is to conduct expensive pathological tests whose goal is to assess risks and identify early complications to patients' health or to prevent the patient from developing other diseases. The choice of which action/test to perform is therefore important. There are in the literature some guideline-based decision-support systems which help to assist practitioners to choose the appropriate therapeutic action for their patients. The idea of such systems is to structure a guideline as a set of choices to be made by the clinician. However, such a set of actions/tests/decisions can change according to new information obtained concerning the patient state (direct answers from the patient, blood test results, etc.). Because the time factor may be crucial and because executing tests is expensive, it is then important for the practitioners to ask for or to quickly obtain useful information helping take the good decision in order to achieve the goals of excluding the risks as soon as possible, which means with a minor quantity of information/tests required. In this paper, we address the challenges introduced above by proposing an agent-based framework that supports the development of an intelligent goal-driven agent to help practitioners in choosing the most useful action to perform (question to ask a patient, test, etc.) in the case of a chronic disease. The framework supports the selection of the next dialogue action by measuring the usefulness, with respect to a goal, of a piece of information to be obtained. We introduce our framework through the use of a running example, showing how an agent can drive the interaction based on both its background knowledge and the new information it acquires. Experiments performed concerning two chronic diseases, namely asthma and type-2 diabetes, validate our approach. Finally, we discuss further possible scenarios where our framework can be applied in different ways.

© Springer Nature Switzerland AG 2021
T. Uchiya et al. (Eds.): PRIMA 2020, LNAI 12568, pp. 281–298, 2021.
https://doi.org/10.1007/978-3-030-69322-0_18

1   Introduction and Motivations

Chronic diseases cause many deaths worldwide each year [1]. Many works in the literature propose solutions to help decreasing this number. Most of them propose solutions to assist health care practitioners, thus helping them to take *good decisions* according to the patient health conditions [2,3] and other works aim at assisting the patients managing themselves – *Self-monitoring of health* [4–9]. However, as it has been underlined in [10], medical assistance combine medical actions performed by health care professionals who *observe* signs and symptoms and decide on questions, interventions, prescriptions or tests to treat the health problem of a particular patient. A recent study by [11] proposes a review of monitoring strategies in current United kingdom guidelines for patients with type 2 diabetes, chronic kidney disease, and hypertension. This study highlighted the uncertainties in the guidelines and the need for further research. Manning, who studied several publishers of clinical guideline resources for practitioners [12], suggested that primary care Information Technology providers should develop Artificial Intelligence (AI) engines that would *interact* with the data acquired by the physician *during the consultation* (free text, reading codes, etc.) and to link such data to the National Institute for Health and Care Excellence guidelines on specific conditions (background knowledge).

The agent-based framework we are proposing here which supports the development of an intelligent goal-driven agent to help practitioners in choosing the most useful action to perform in the case of a chronic disease, is in this line. Indeed, because the most common action to manage chronic diseases is to conduct expensive pathological tests whose goal is to assess risks and identify early complications to patients' health or to prevent the patient from developing other diseases, the choice of which action/test to perform is therefore important: the time factor may be crucial and executing tests is expensive. It is then important for the practitioners to ask for or to quickly obtain useful information helping take the good decision in order to achieve the *goals* of excluding the risks as soon as possible, which means with a minor quantity of information/tests required. This is the main aim of our framework: to be used by practitioners during a consultation and support her in the process of selecting the next dialogue action by measuring the usefulness, with respect to a risky situation (goal), of a piece of information to be obtained. Here, as *dialogue*, we mean the whole interaction process between an agent and the environment (practitioners, sensors, services, etc.) and not limited to a conversation between the agent and the human actor.

We start from the framework proposed in [13] whose aim is to characterize how useful a piece of information is for a cognitive agent which has some beliefs and goals. Here, we adapt and extend it by introducing several elements, enabling its application into a complex real-world problem: helping managing chronic diseases in the healthcare domain.

We consider different types of information which are stored by categories (set of slots): (i) S_a: information acquired directly by asking the patient, (ii) S_b: information acquired directly through sensors, (iii) S_c: information acquired from the patient's electronic file, (iv) S_d: information acquired from the history of data provided by the patient, (v) S_e: information acquired through external services. Depending on the domain, each set of slots can be instantiated with the information needed. For example, in the case of diabetes, type S_a slots corresponds to the categories of foods consumed, type S_b slots to the measured blood sugar levels, type S_d slots to what the patient ate during the week. In the case of asthma, those of type S_a correspond to the symptoms that the patient reports, those of type S_b to the breathing measured by a device, those of type S_e to the data of the pollen controllers. In a real-time monitoring system for crisis prevention and/or compliance with treatment plans, all goals are coded starting from the guidelines and the system must prevent the patient from going to put himself in situations at risk—the different goals are to save the patient from the risky situations identified in the guidelines. Our work is in line with the framework used in [3]. However, in addition to what is proposed in that work, which is based on the measurement of *all* values (obtained from sensors), our framework give us also the possibility to (i) choose the most useful measurement to do, (ii) obtain information from the patient and use it when making a decisions, and to (iii) use background knowledge.

The overall result is the generation of a multi-turn interactions that uses as few questions as possible to retrieve the usefull information, seeking for a fast, but also cautious advises to the patient. As we can see from the experiment results, the approach is domain-configurable, that is, it can be applied to different domains within healthcare by modeling the domain knowledge properly.

2   Preliminaries

In this section, we will present some definitions composing our framework.

Definition 1. *An agent a is a discrete entity aiming to classify a patient with respect to a set of classes. An agent a has its own belief base B_a and a set of goals G_a.*

In this paper, we will often appoint our agent as a *dialogue agent*. However, we would like to stress again that, here, the word *dialogue* means the whole process of interaction between the agent and the environment (practitioners, sensors, services, etc.), it is not limited to a conversation between the agent and the human actor.

Definition 2. *The agent belief base B_a contains the collection of the truth values (true, false, or unknown) associated with each information unit s, as well as a set of rules R_a supporting the patient classification task by stating which information units are required to achieve each goal.*

B_a is updated after the arrival of a new piece of information that is relevant for changing the truth value of an information unit s contained in B_a.

Definition 3. *An information unit s (called hereafter "slot") is a relevant information, increasing the knowledge of the belief base B_a necessary for achieving a goal g.*

We consider different types of information: (i) information acquired directly by asking the patient (slots of type S_a), (ii) information acquired directly through sensors (slots of type S_b), (iii) information acquired from the patient's electronic file (slots of type S_c) (iv) information acquired from the history of data provided by the patient (slots of type S_d) and (v) information acquired through external services (slots of type S_e). The types of information required correspond to the ones presented in the guidelines.

The default value of a slot s is *unknown* if no information concerning it is acquired. During the information acquisition process, the value of a slot s can change to *true* or *false* depending on the input.

Definition 4. *A goal $g \in G_a$ is a class for which an agent a has to know if a patient is classified with it or not. The classification task is performed by applying the rules defined in R_a.*

A goal can be characterized thanks to two values: (i) a confidence degree $C(g)$ representing the amount of true information (i.e., the truth value of a slot s is *true*) that the agent a collected about the goal g, and (ii) $M(g)$ representing the amount of information that the agent a still have to collect for having a complete knowledge concerning the goal g, i.e., missing information. Let τ be a threshold given by an expert. A goal g can be considered achieved (the patient may be considered as belonging or not to the class) if: (i) $C(g) \geq \tau$ or if (ii) $C(g) + M(g) < \tau$. The former means that the information collected by the agent a is enough for classifying the patient as belonging to the class g. The latter means that even if all missing information would be set to *true*, the value of $C(g)$ will not pass the threshold τ. Hence, the agent a can classify the patient as not belonging to the class g. In both cases, the agent a achieves the goal. This is one of the peculiarities of the healthcare domain, since a physician should be supported by intelligent agents able to both detect and exclude undesired situations.

Another aspect is the possibility of giving an importance degree to each goal g, hereafter called "priority".

Definition 5. *The priority o of a goal g is a real value in the interval $[0, 1]$ representing the importance degree that the goal g has within the belief base B_a. The set of all priority values is given by O_{G_a}*

Definition 6. *A rule $r \in R_a$ allows to classify a patient into a class g based on the information collected by an agent a. A rule can be represented as follows: $s_1 \oplus s_2 \oplus \ldots \oplus s_{n_g} \Rightarrow g$, where s_i represents the ith slot related to g and n_g is the number of slots related to g.*

Definition 7. *The premise set $P(g)$ is the set of all the slots that help classifying goal g, i.e., $P(g) = \{s \mid s \in lhs(g)\}$, where "lhs" is the left hand side of a rule $r \in R_a$.*

Definition 8. *Let g_j be a goal and s_i be a slot. The association between g_j and s_i is represented through a real value $w_{ij} \in [0, 1]$, called "weight". The weight* *represents how relevant the information contained in the slot s_i is for achieving the goal g_j. We will also note the assotiation between goal g with Slot s as $w(s, g)$.*

The same slot can appear in more than one rule r since some information units can be shared by more than one goal. Each value w_{ij} is directly provided by domain experts (guidelines) or inferred from background knowledge and its computation is out of scope of this paper. The only constraint is that, given the jth goal, it holds the hypothesis $\sum_{i=0}^{n_{g_j}} w_{ij} = 1$, where n_{g_j} is the number of slots associated with the goal g_j. Even if this constraint holds, these values are not probabilities. The rationales behind this constraint are the following. First, we require that if all the slots associated with a specific goal are set to *true*, the agent is "sure" that the patient will be considered as belonging to the risky situation specified by the goal. Second, the classification of a patient with respect to a goal is performed by comparing the confidence that an agent has with respect to the possibility that a patient belongs to that goal, with a threshold τ. Hence, in order to perform this comparison fairly, the numerical boundaries of the confidence has to be the same for all goals.

We introduce in Sect. 3 a working example that will be used throughout the paper and that will show how these elements can be instantiated into a real-world case.

3   Working Example

In this section, we present an illustrative example to facilitate understanding of the proposed framework and to show how the framework can be instantiated in a real-world scenario. In this example, whose aim is to help the reader understand our framework, we only consider the slots of type S_a, i.e. the slots concerning information obtained from the patient during a consultation with a practitioner.

Let us define a scenario in which, through dialogue, an agent aims to obtain the symptoms experienced by a patient in order to diagnose the possibility that the patient is in one or more risky situations which can occur in case of the chronic disease α.

Here, we assume to have a finite set $G_a = \{g_1, g_2, g_3, g_4\}$ of goals expressing risky situations related to α and a finite set $S = \{s_1, ..., s_d\}$ of symptoms related to the different risky situations; d corresponds to the number of slots (pieces of information) related to the different risky situations. We also have the assumptions that (i) each symptom s (represented by a slot) can be a premise for more than one risky situation and (ii) the truth value of each slot s can be 0 (i.e., the symptom has not been experienced) or 1 (i.e., the symptom has been experienced). For the continuous values, like "fever measures", etc., 1 and 0 means respectively that the value exceeds or is below the threshold according to the guidelines.

Table 1 shows the list of risky situations related to the chronic disease α, the list of symptoms, and the weight values w represent the associations between

Table 1. Chronic disease α/Symptoms domain knowledge/Weights

Risky situations		Symptoms											
		Abdominal pain	Pruritus	Respiratory distress	Fever	Early awakening	Nausea	Incontinence	Shortness of breath	Pain	Diarrhea	Asthenia	Yellow sputum
		(s_1)	(s_2)	(s_3)	(s_4)	(s_5)	(s_6)	(s_7)	(s_8)	(s_9)	(s_{10})	(s_{11})	(s_{12})
Acute liver failure	(g_1)	0.36	0.28	0.20	0.16	–	–	–	–	–	–	–	–
Pseudo-membranous colitis (colitis)	(g_2)	0.09	–	–	0.30	0.26	0.22	0.13	–	–	–	–	–
Tricuspid insufficiency	(g_3)	0.11	–	–	0.05	–	0.16	–	0.42	0.26	–	–	–
Kidney failure	(g_4)	–	–	–	0.13	–	–	–	0.35	–	0.26	0.22	0.04

symptoms and the risky situation. These information compose the belief base B_a that an agent a has during the interaction with a patient. The aim of the agent is to achieve all the set of goals G_a by classify the patient with respect to each risky situation, i.e., to know if the patient is in one or more risky situations or not.

The classification task is performed by applying the rules R_a that allow to classify the patient with respect to each risky situation.

$$s_1 \oplus s_2 \oplus s_3 \oplus s_4 \Rightarrow g_1$$
$$s_1 \oplus s_4 \oplus s_5 \oplus s_6 \oplus s_7 \Rightarrow g_2$$
$$s_1 \oplus s_4 \oplus s_6 \oplus s_8 \oplus s_9 \Rightarrow g_3$$
$$s_4 \oplus s_8 \oplus s_{10} \oplus s_{11} \oplus s_{12} \Rightarrow g_4$$

Finally, we consider that the domain knowledge includes also information concerning entailments about co-occurrence of symptoms, for example a patient with high fever also has "just" fever. This knowledge is also provided by the experts. In our example, we assume to have the following three entailments:

$$s_6 \rightarrow s_1;\ s_1 \rightarrow s_9; s_{10} \wedge s_{11} \rightarrow s_4$$

We rely on this example in Sect. 4 when our framework is presented.

4   Proposed Framework

We propose a new agent-based framework for supporting the management of risky situations in the case of chronic diseases, thanks to (i) a slot filling interaction that is conducted with a patient (we will name such slots S_a), (ii) information acquired directly through sensors (we will name such slots S_b), (iii) information acquired from the patient's electronic file (we will name such slots S_c), (iv) information acquired from the history of data provided by the patient (we will name such slots S_d) (v) information acquired through external services (we will name such slots S_e). Not all the slots must be filled, i.e., depending on the risky situation, each set of slots can be instantiated with the information needed or not.

It is important to highlight that both, the conversion of a dialogue action into a natural language utterance and the natural language processing of the answer given by the patient are out of scope of this work.

4.1 The Proposed Extension

To address the challenge of effectively selecting the next dialogue action that most contributes for the classification (risky or not), we extend the framework proposed in [13] that models information usefulness for goal-driven agents. The rationales behind this choice are the following: (i) here, the main aim of the dialogue agent is to understand which is (or which are) the class to which the patient belongs to according to the values given to the slots (through the answers that he/she gives to the questions); (ii) such values can be viewed as the components in the left-hand side (lhs) of a rule, allowing to associate possible slots (e.g., symptoms) to a particular class (e.g., disease); and (iii) the dialogue agent aims to mimic the reasoning task of a physician, who can be considered as a cognitive agent, i.e., someone with a background knowledge (beliefs) about the patient and about other subjects (e.g., the possible relations or the probability of co-occurrence between the symptoms, etc.).

We consider a propositional language L of which a subset, L_G, is the language used to represent the rules associated with the goals. We will consider a *dialogue agent* which is aware of both all the beliefs/knowledge (in addition to information concerning entailments, this includes the pieces of information obtained thanks to Slots of types S_b, S_c, S_d and S_e), and the goals of the physician, as well as the patient's answers (slots of type S_a). The dialogue agent a has a goal set G_a (classes or risky situations) which corresponds then to the physician goals from the language of possible goals L_G. For example, in the context of managing chronic diseases, the goal of the agent is to understand from the different symptoms (s_1, s_2, ...), if the patient is in a risky situations or not. We would like to notice that, unlike in [13] where the goal achievement is binary, here we consider a gradual definition to compute the extent to which a given situation is considered as risky and we consider a threshold (τ) which allows us to decide if the result is positive (the patient is in a risky situation) or not (the patient is not in a risky situation).

Moreover, the dialogue agent a has a belief base B_a composed of two subsets B_a^m and B_a^g. B_a^m is the set of formulas from $L \backslash L_G$ which represents a's beliefs about the slot-values, e.g., the patient has *pruritus* (s_2), the patient has *fever* (s_4), *nausea* (s_6), *incontinence* (s_7), etc. B_a^m may also contain other physician background knowledge like the co-occurrence between the slots, e.g., *Pain Abdominal* implies *Pain* ($s_1 \rightarrow s_9$). This means that, if *Pain Abdominal* is reported during the dialogue as one of the experienced symptoms by the patient, B_a is automatically updated with both the values concerning the slots *Pain Abdominal* and *Pain*. B_a^g instead, contains as many rules of the form $s_1 \oplus s_2 \oplus \ldots \oplus s_{n_g} \Rightarrow g$ (as stated in Definition 6), where each s_i is a literal of $L \backslash L_G$, representing a slot that influences the achievement of goal g, as there are

$g \in G_a$. Such rules represent the beliefs of a about which information is needed to determine a class, achieving then a given goal. These pieces of information are indeed the slot-values of the different types presented at the begining of this section. For example, to understand if the patient risks an *Acute liver failure* (g_1), the physician needs to know if the patient has *Pain Abdominal* (s_1), *Pruritus* (s_2), *Distress respiratory* (s_3), and *Fever* (s_4), i.e., $s_1 \oplus s_2 \oplus s_3 \oplus s_4 \Rightarrow g$. The set of the elements in the left-hand-side of this rule is the premise of g (Definition 7), i.e., $P(g) = \{s_1, \ldots, s_4\}$.

Let us suppose that the agent acquires more and more information about the patient's actual state, approaching the classification into one or more risky situations. The units of information that are still missing can be represented as follows.

Definition 9 (Missing Information). *Let a be a dialogue agent with its belief base B_a and its goal set G_a. Let $g \in G_a$ be such that $B_a \not\models g$ [1]. The missing information for goal g, $Missing(B_a, g)$, is defined as follows:*

$$Missing(B_a, g) = \{l : l \in P(g) \text{ and } B_a \not\models l\} \tag{1}$$

$Missing(B_a, g)$ is the set of all the slots in the premise of g which cannot be deduced from B_a (i.e., which are not yet believed by the agent and therefore the dialogue agent should acquire them).

Remark 1. In the particular case in which $B_a^m = \emptyset$, $Missing(B_a, g) = P(g)$, i.e., the missing piece of information to achieve g is $P(g)$.

Because different goals can have missing information in common, we need to introduce the notion of *multiset of missing information*.

Definition 10 (Multiset of missing information). *Let a be a dialogue agent whose belief base is B_a and whose goal set is G_a. The multiset[2] of missing information to achieve the goals in G_a is:*

$$Missing(B_a, G_a) = \bigcup_{k=1}^{|G_a|} Missing(B_a, g_k) \tag{2}$$

with $\bigcup$ representing the union on multisets, $\| $ representing the cardinality of a set.

Let us consider the following definitions:

Definition 11. *Let $G(s)$ be the set of goals related to slot s. We define $G(s) = \{g \in G_a \mid s \in P(g)\}$.*

---

[1] In propositional logic, $\phi \models \psi$ means that ψ is a logical consequence of ϕ. Here, it means that we can classify the patient as having disease g from what we already know/believe ($B_a \models g$, see Definition 15).

[2] Reminder: a multiset is a set whose elements can have several occurrences, such as $\{p, q, p\}$.

Definition 12. *Let $W(g)$ be the set of all the weights related to the symptoms associated to goal g. $W(g) = \{w(s, g) \mid s \in P(g)\}$.*

We can now define the overall importance of requiring an answer concerning slot s, $N_1(s)$, (which represents the extent to which s would help getting closer to a classification), with respect to all the goals $g \in G_a$ as follows:

$$N_1(s) = \begin{cases} \sum_{g \in G(s)} w(s, g) + \sum_{s' \mid B_a \cup s \models s' \wedge B_a \not\models s'} w(s', g) & \text{if } s = true, \\ \sum_{g \in G(s)} w(s, g) + \sum_{s' \mid B_a \cup s' \models s \wedge B_a \not\models s} w(s', g) & \text{if } s = false. \end{cases} \tag{3}$$

where $w(s', g) = 0$ if $s' \notin P(g)$ and s comes from the multiset of missing information (Definition 10). We can notice that $N_1(s)$ is the gradual definition (and therefore an extension) of the N_1 component proposed in [13].

We can also compute the overall weight, $N_2(s)$, that concerns the slots which are still missing after receiving the value of slot s as follows:

$$N_2(s) = \left(\sum_{g \in G_a} \sum_{k \in W(g)} k \right) - N_1(s). \tag{4}$$

We can notice that our definition of $N_2(s)$ is a generalization (a gradual counterpart) of the one proposed in [13].

To characterize a goal as being achieved or not, we need to know the amount of already known information about the slots related to it and the amount of information which is still missing.

Definition 13. *The amount of information that the agent a collected about the goal g, is given by the following two measures:*

$$\mathcal{C}(g) = \sum_{(s \mid B_a \models s) \wedge (s \in P(g))} w(s, g) \tag{5}$$

representing the information slot set to true, and:

$$\mathcal{C}(\neg g) = \sum_{(s \mid B_a \models \neg s) \wedge (s \in P(g))} w(s, g) \tag{6}$$

representing the information slot set to false.

Definition 14. *The amount of information that the agent a still has to collect for having a complete knowledge concerning goal g, $\mathcal{M}(g)$ is given by:*

$$\mathcal{M}(g) = \sum_{s' \in Missing(B_a, g)} w(s', g) \tag{7}$$

Let τ be a threshold which allows to characterize a goal as being achieved or not, according to the guidelines.

Definition 15. *A goal g is achieved, i.e., we can assert that the patient is in a risky situation, noted $B_a \models g$, if and only if:*

- $\mathcal{C}(g) \geq \tau$: *the amount of information already available is* sufficient *to make a positive diagnosis, i.e., the patient's life is in danger, Or*
- $\mathcal{C}(g) + \mathcal{M}(g) < \tau$: *the amount of information already available is* sufficient *to make a negative diagnosis, i.e., the patient's life is not in danger.*

The value of τ obviously influences the capability of an agent concerning the achievement of goals. High values of τ reduces the possibility of classifying a patient as belonging to a specific goal, but increases the possibility that a patient would not belong to any goal. The opposite occurs for low values of τ.

Remark 2. We can notice that if there are not missing slots, i.e., $\mathcal{M}(g) = 0$, we have: $\mathcal{C}(g) + \mathcal{C}(\neg g) = 1$.

This remark shows how the total amount of information is preserved when all slots are filled.

Definition 16. *The set of goals that a slot s allows the dialogue agent to achieve is:*

$$E(s) = \{g \in G_a | B_a \cup s \models g \land B_a \not\models g\}. \tag{8}$$

4.2   Next Question Selection

This work provides a function that measures the usefulness of a (not-yet-filled) slot[3] By comparing the usefulness value of the different slots, it is possible to select the *best candidate question/test/check* for the next information acquisition, i.e., the one that allows us to achieve/get closer to a classification.

The usefulness measure takes into account several factors:

- Class' priority: a priority can be set to each class. Therefore, whenever priority values are available, slots related to classes with higher priority have their usefulness value increased. Our working example does not present priorities among the classes, therefore the neutral value 1.0 is assigned.
- Information filled by the slot: some slots are capable of filling more information than others, since they are related to more than one class or the domain knowledge reports some co-occurrence or entailement.
- Slot's weight: as previously stated, according to the domain, not all pieces of information (slots) have the same relevance with respect to a class. For example, a physician may inform that *abdominal pain* (s_1) is more relevant than *fever* (s_4) for determining that the patient has *Acute liver failure* (g_1) and, therefore, the latter would present a higher usefulness value to this class. The usefulness measure also takes into account that a slot can be present in different classes with different weights.

---

[3] Of course, here we are interested in knowing the utility of the slots which are not a logical consequence of the belief base B_a, i.e., which cannot be deduced from previous beliefs/knowledge.

Due to the different requirements of health domains, when we compute the usefulness value of a slot s, we need to consider what happens in both cases, i.e. if the slots s is set to 1 (the symptom occurred) or to 0 (the symptom did not occur). The resulting equation for computing the usefulness of a slot s is the following:

$$U(s) = \left[\left(|E(s)| + \frac{N_1(s)}{N_1(s) + N_2(s)}\right)^{s=0} + \left(|E(s)| + \frac{N_1(s)}{N_1(s) + N_2(s)}\right)^{s=1}\right]\frac{O_{G_a}^s}{G_a^s} \quad (9)$$

where:

- $|E(s)|$ is the number of goals that are satisfied thanks to the information about slot s, i.e., the number of classes (risky situations) for which we can conclude if the patient belongs to them or not after checking the slot s;
- $N_1(s)$ and $N_2(s)$ are computed by taking into account the weights associated with s in all goals;
- $O_{G_a}^s$ is the sum of the priorities associated with the goals having the slot s in their premise.
- $|G_a^s|$ is the number of goals having the slot s in their premise.

The coefficient $\frac{O_{G_a}^s}{|G_a^s|}$ allows to increase the usefulness value of slots that are premise of *more important* goals.

The proposed approach follows the principle of **coverage**, i.e., it aims to explore the domain as much as possible in order to investigate different possibilities that may lead to a classification. As defined in the proposed function, this is achieved by increasing the usefulness value of slots that, besides enabling the achievement of as many goals as possible, also cover more information from a single *action for information acquisition* (question/test/check), such those that are common to more than one cluster or that co-occur. For example, obtaining the value for the symptom *Abdominal pain* (s_1) will cover not only one, but some risky situations (g_1, g_2, g_3) and also the symptom *Pain* (s_9), due to the entailment stated in Sect. 3; therefore, its usefulness value is increased (because $N_1(s)$ increases). The main advantage of this approach is to empower the cautiousness of the practitioner within sensitive scenarios. As a disadvantage, this approach may be slow to reach the classification when G_a is a large set.

5   The Framework in Action

We discuss here the application of the proposed framework to the working example described in Sect. 3. For demonstration purposes, we set the value of τ to 0.75. Let us suppose to have a dialogue started by a patient in which he/she reported a general illness and the *fever* and *nausea* symptoms.

Step 1: the agent acquires these two information and set the truth values for the slots s_4 and s_6 to 1.

Step 2: by analyzing the co-occurrence knowledge, the agent sets also the slots s_1 and s_9 to 1 from the application of both the $s_6 \rightarrow s_1$ and $s_1 \rightarrow s_9$

entailments. C_{G_a} values change in: $C_{g_1} = 0.52$, $C_{g_2} = 0.61$, $C_{g_3} = 0.58$, $C_{g_4} = 0.13$.

Step 3: the agent computes $U(s)$ for the remaining slots. The three most useful slots resulted: $U(s_8) = 4.05$, $U(s_2) = 2.19$, $U(s_5) = 2.18$.

Step 4: the agent asks for the symptom associated with s_8 (i.e. *Shortness of breath*) and the patient replies that he/she does not experiences this. The slot s_8 is set to 0, and the different values of $\mathcal{C}(g)$ remain unchanged. However, by checking the values of $\mathcal{C}(g) + \mathcal{M}(g)$ for the goals g_3 and g_4, we can observe the values of 0.58 and 0.65 respectively. This means that the agent can already exclude two possible risky situations since even if all missing information would be set to 1, both $\mathcal{C}(g_3)$ and $\mathcal{C}(g_4)$ will be lower than τ.

Step 5: the agent computes $U(s)$ for the remaining slots. The two most useful slots resulted: $U(s_2) = 2.40$, $U(s_5) = 2.37$, while the others have values lower than 0.5.

Step 6: the agent asks for the symptom associated with s_2 (i.e. *Pruritus*) and the patient replies that he/she does experiences this. The slot s_2 is set to 1 and the different values change in: $\mathcal{C}(g_1) = 0.80$, $\mathcal{C}(g_2) = 0.61$, $\mathcal{C}(g_3) = 0.58$, and $\mathcal{C}(g_4) = 0.13$. This answer allows the agent to conclude that the patient is in the risky situation g_1.

Here, based on the decision policy applied by the domain expert, we can obtain different behaviors. For example, the adoption of a *cautious* approach can bring the agent to perform other steps as shown below.

Step 7: the agent computes $U(s)$ for the remaining slots. The most useful slot resulted $U(s_5) = 2.47$, while the others continue to have values lower than 0.5.

Step 8: the agent asks for the symptom associated with s_5 (i.e. *Early awakening*) and the patient replies that he/she does not experiences this. The slot s_5 is set to 0, and the different values of $\mathcal{C}(g)$ remain unchanged. Hence, the goal (class) g_1 remains the only goal which the patient belongs to. Indeed, by checking the values of $\mathcal{C}(g) + \mathcal{M}(g)$ for the different goals, we can observe a value of 0.74 for the goals g_2. This means that the agent excludes also this risky situation since it becomes impossible for $\mathcal{C}(g_2)$ to reach the threshold τ.

Differently, in case of a positive answer for the slot s_5, the different values of $\mathcal{C}(g)$ would change in: $\mathcal{C}(g_1) = 0.80$, $\mathcal{C}(g_2) = 0.87$, $\mathcal{C}(g_3) = 0.58$, $\mathcal{C}(g_4) = 0.13$. Hence, the agent would conclude that the patient is in two possible risky situations. Even if this situation somehow introduces uncertainty in the analysis of patient's conditions because there are more than one risky situation, it is a duty of the domain expert to decide which actions to take. This practice is commonly accepted within the healthcare domain as intelligent systems aim to support domain experts and not to replace them.

6   Evaluation

The previous section discusses a small running example showing in practice which are the execution steps performed by using the proposed framework. The evaluation of the proposed framework has been performed on two real-world scenarios concerning the management of risky situations in two chronic diseases, namely type-2 diabetes (this scenario is hereafter referred as *SM1*) and of asthma (this scenario is hereafter referred as *SM2*).

SM1 requires the monitoring of food intake and physical activities performed by a patient during specific time-spans with respect to a set of guidelines. In this scenario, we encoded the guidelines provided by the American Diabetes Association (ADA).[4] The encoding of such guidelines corresponded to a set of 87 goals and 174 information slots grouped as follows:

- 79 slots of type S_a corresponding to food categories that are relevant for the ADA guidelines and that a patient can explicitly provide;
- 4 slots of type S_b corresponding to values acquired from the glucometer before and after a meal or a physical activity session;
- 12 slots of type S_c corresponding to information acquired from personal health records of patients concerning past hospitalizations, upsets, etc.;
- 79 slots of type S_d corresponding to the last-week intake concerning food categories that are relevant for the ADA guidelines and that are acquired from an external knowledge repository.

While, *SM2* requires the monitoring of respiratory issues from two perspectives: (i) by processing the symptoms provided by a patient; and, (ii) by providing recommendations based on the analysis of patient profile and data acquired from external services. In this scenario, we encoded the guidelines provided by the American Lung Association (ALA).[5] The encoding of such guidelines corresponded to a set of 7 goals and 69 information slots grouped as follows:

- 22 slots of type S_a corresponding to the symptoms that are relevant for the ALA guidelines and that a patient can explicitly report;
- 11 slots of type S_b corresponding to the type of parameters that are acquired from inhalers and other medication devices;
- 8 slots of type S_c corresponding to information acquired from personal health records of patients concerning past hospitalizations, upsets, etc.;
- 16 slots of type S_d corresponding to patient's habits that are relevant for the ALA guidelines and that are acquired from an external knowledge repository (e.g. if a patient uses to go running on a specific day of the week);
- 12 slots of type S_e corresponding to information that are relevant for the ALA guidelines and that are acquired from external services (e.g. weather forecast, pollen forecast, etc.).

We validated the effectiveness of the proposed framework with respect to three baselines:

- Baseline 1 (BS1): at each iteration, the selected slot is the most popular one. This means that the agent will check in its knowledge which is the information slot valued as "unknown" and having the highest number of occurrences.

---

[4] https://www.diabetes.org/.
[5] https://www.lung.org/.

- Baseline 2 (BS2): at each iteration, the selected slot is the one with the highest overall weight within the knowledge base. The overall weight of a slot s is computed by summing all the weights $w(s, g)$ associated with the slot s in the entire set of goals G_a.
- Baseline 3 (BS3): this baseline is a variation of BS1 where at each iteration, the selected slot is the one having the highest normalized frequency. The normalized frequency of a slot s is computed by dividing the number of occurrences of s by the number of slots valued as "unknown" within the knowledge base.

We analyzed three metrics: precision, recall, and the average number of steps required by the agent for classifying the patient. In our setting, the algorithm stopped when for at least one goal the expression $\mathcal{C}(g) \geq \tau$ is *true*. Precision and recall are computed by checking if the set of goals for which the expression above is *true* contains the correct one. While, the average number of steps is computed by considering the number of information request performed by the agent before reaching a conclusion.

The evaluation has been performed by simulating the interactions between the agent and a set of patients. The simulations have been though in order to cover all goals defined in each scenario. Since in this work we did not take into account the analysis of how the value of τ can be set, we run a simulation for each possible value of τ within the interval $[0.00, 1.00]$ with an incremental step of 0.01 between two consecutive simulations. Finally, each simulation starts with a fixed number of slots already set. These slots represent the information provided by the patient when she starts the interaction with the system. For each value of τ, we performed three simulations with 1, 2, or 3 slots set on startup, respectively. This parameter made it possible to observe how the effectiveness of our approach changes according to the amount of information provided at startup.

Figures 1, 2, and 3 show the results observed on SM1, while Fig. 4, 5, and 6 show the results observed for SM2. Within all figures, the x-axis reports the

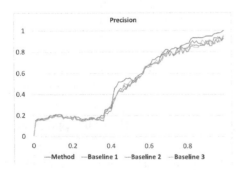

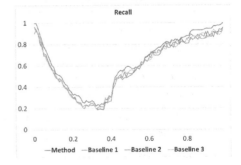

Fig. 1. Diabetes use case: graph of the precision metric observed for all values of the threshold τ within the interval $[0.0, 1.0]$.

Fig. 2. Diabetes use case: graph of the precision metric observed for all values of the threshold τ within the interval $[0.0, 1.0]$.

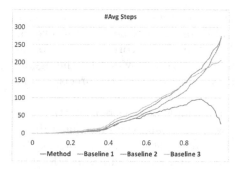

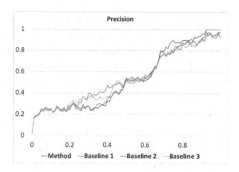

Fig. 3. Diabetes use case: graph of the number of steps required by the agent to reach a conclusion observed for all values of the threshold τ within the interval $[0.0, 1.0]$.

Fig. 4. Asthma use case: graph of the precision metric observed for all values of the threshold τ within the interval $[0.0, 1.0]$.

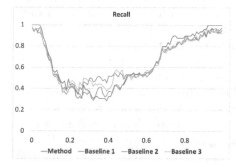

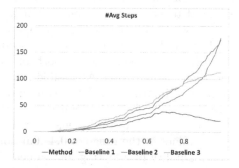

Fig. 5. Asthma use case: graph of the precision metric observed for all values of the threshold τ within the interval $[0.0, 1.0]$.

Fig. 6. Asthma use case: graph of the number of steps required by the agent to reach a conclusion observed for all values of the threshold τ within the interval $[0.0, 1.0]$.

different values of τ, while the y-axis reports the precision and recall observed at each step or the average number of steps.

The analysis of the obtained results highlighted four main points of interest.

By observing the graphs shown in Fig. 3 and 6, we can notice how at a certain point the number of steps decreases. This behavior is quite strange by considering that by increasing the value of τ the expected number of steps needed for passing the threshold should increase as well. A more deep analysis revealed that by adopting our framework for selecting the next slot to fill, the agent increases the capability of detecting unreachable goals. Hence, it is possible for the agent to reduce the number of steps for classifying the patient with respect to the correct goal.

Together with the reduction of the number of steps required by the agent for reaching a conclusion, we can observe also an improvement of the overall effectiveness of our framework. Indeed, for high values of τ, corresponding to the need of having a high confidence about the conclusion provided by the agent, the proposed framework outperforms all the baselines for both the precision and recall values.

By focusing on the recall graph, there are a couple of aspects that attracted our attention: the high recall observed for low τ values and the subsequent drop. The former is justified by the fact that the patient starts the interaction by providing some information, i.e. some slots are filled on startup. Thus, for low values of τ, the possibility that the correct goal is contained within the set of goals passed the threshold is high. On the contrary, the precision values are low since, especially if the filled slots are very popular, many goals can be satisfied by considering only the information provided on startup. The latter is given by considering that, medium values of τ means that the agent is in the middle of acquiring information and it seems that in many cases there are goals, then resulted to be the wrong ones, that are satisfied with this partial knowledge. Future work will consider to investigate more on this behavior.

Finally, by comparing the two scenarios, even if the proposed framework outperforms the baselines in both of them, it resulted to be more effective in the most complex one. A possible reason is that within scenarios having a low number of information slots, strategies relies on frequencies can be more effective, especially for lower values of τ. However, it is important to remark two aspects. First, real-world scenarios within the healthcare domain considers precision values in the range of $0.4-0.6$ not acceptable by domain experts. Hence, the possibility of adopting low values of τ in practice is very low. Second, the proposed framework demonstrated to be more effective with respect to the baselines by exploiting a dramatically lower number of interactions. The latter is a very important aspect within the healthcare domain since it allows to understand which is the current healthy status of a patient and, at the same time, to reduce the effort for providing the knowledge required for reaching a conclusion.

7 Final Remarks

We presented a goal-based framework to support the management and control of risk situations for chronic diseases. We discussed the concept of information usefulness in a health dialogue and we formalized the metrics that allow to compute the usefulness value of a missing slot. A running example about diagnosis has been used for showing how the framework can be instantiated.

As previously mentioned, the proposed usefulness measure has as one of its main benefits the generation of a "short" information acquisition process due to the careful selection of the slot that most contributes with usefull information. As further benefits, this approach avoids the need of large historical databases and the costs of supporting costly information acquisition to obtain a reliable output.

By proposing this approach, we do not claim to cover the state transition of the information acquisition process, which is also a role of the practitioner. Instead, we intend to contribute as a heuristic measure that covers the needs of the health domain to support the choice of the next dialogue action. This heuristic can be applied together with some of the strategies, for example, those currently used for dialogue management, such as automated planning [14] or finite state machines [15], which can also benefit from the content of the belief base B_a to determine the dialogue state.

To increase the elicitation of information, some other strategies can also be integrated in a dialogue system, such as the use of a mixed-initiative design associated to the manipulation of open answers, which would allow the spontaneous input of information by the patient.

This work opens several research directions to be accomplished in the future. First, in this work we considered binary values for setting the slots. The use of fuzzy sets, allowing to confirm a slot to a certain degree, would be an interesting extension of the proposed framework. Second, we will focus on designing an evaluation protocol for validating agents instantiating our framework. Finally, we plan to integrate and deploy our framework into existing architectures in order to start its application into real-world scenarios.

Acknowledgement. Célia da Costa Pereira acknowledges support of the PEPS AIR-INFO project funded by the CNRS. This work has been carried out during her visit at Process & Data Intelligence research unit at Fondazione Bruno Kessler of Trento.

References

1. Dennis, S., et al.: Chronic disease management in primary care: from evidence to policy. Med. J. Aust. **188**(05), S53–S56 (2008)
2. Johnson, P., Tu, S., Booth, N., Sugden, B., Purves, I.: Using scenarios in chronic disease management guidelines for primary care. In: Proceedings/AMIA Annual Symposium, pp. 389–393 (2000)
3. Hernández, D., Villarrubia, G., Barriuso, A.L., Lozano, Á., Revuelta, J., De Paz, J.F.: Multi agent application for chronic patients: monitoring and detection of remote anomalous situations. In: Bajo, J., et al. (eds.) PAAMS 2016. CCIS, vol. 616, pp. 27–36. Springer, Cham (2016). https://doi.org/10.1007/978-3-319-39387-2_3
4. Park, H.S., Cho, H., Kim, H.S.: Development of a multi-agent m-health application based on various protocols for chronic disease self-management. J. Med. Syst. **40**(1), 36 (2015)
5. Kraus, S.: Intelligent agents for rehabilitation and care of disabled and chronic patients. In: AAAI. AAAI Press, pp. 4032–4036 (2015)
6. Huygens, M.W.J., et al.: Self-monitoring of health data by patients with a chronic disease: does disease controllability matter? BMC Fam. Pract. **18**(1), 40 (2017)
7. Croatti, A., Montagna, S., Ricci, A., Gamberini, E., Albarello, V., Agnoletti, V.: BDI personal medical assistant agents: the case of trauma tracking and alerting. Artif. Intell. Med. **96**, 187–197 (2019)

8. Abdel-Basset, M., Manogaran, G., Gamal, A., Chang, V.: A novel intelligent medical decision support model based on soft computing and IoT. IEEE Internet Things J. **7**(5), 4160–4170 (2020)
9. Moreira, M.W.L., Rodrigues, J.J.P.C., Korotaev, V., Al-Muhtadi, J., Kumar, N.: A comprehensive review on smart decision support systems for health care. IEEE Syst. J. **13**(3), 3536–3545 (2019)
10. Kamišalić, A., Riaño, D., Kert, S., Welzer, T., Zlatolas, L.N.: Multi-level medical knowledge formalization to support medical practice for chronic diseases. Data Knowl. Eng. **119**, 36–57 (2019)
11. Elwenspoek, M.M.C., Patel, R., Watson, J.C., Whiting, P.: Are guidelines for monitoring chronic disease in primary care evidence based? BMJ **365** (2019)
12. Manning, C.L.: Artificial intelligence could bring relevant guidelines into every consultation. BMJ **366** (2019)
13. Cholvy, L., da Costa Pereira, C.: Usefulness of information for goal achievement. In: Baldoni, M., Dastani, M., Liao, B., Sakurai, Y., Zalila Wenkstern, R. (eds.) PRIMA 2019. LNCS (LNAI), vol. 11873, pp. 123–137. Springer, Cham (2019). https://doi.org/10.1007/978-3-030-33792-6_8
14. Behnke, G., et al.: To plan for the user is to plan with the user: integrating user interaction into the planning process. In: Biundo, S., Wendemuth, A. (eds.) Companion Technology. CT, pp. 123–144. Springer, Cham (2017). https://doi.org/10.1007/978-3-319-43665-4_7
15. Lee, K., Lee, Y.S., Nam, Y.: A model of FSM-based planner and dialogue supporting system for emergency call services. J. Supercomput. **74**(9), 4603–4612 (2018). https://doi.org/10.1007/s11227-018-2432-4

Optimal Control of Pedestrian Flows by Congestion Forecasts Satisfying User Equilibrium Conditions

Hiroaki Yamada[1]([✉]) and Naoyuki Kamiyama[2,3]

[1] Fujitsu Laboratories Ltd., Kawasaki, Japan
yamadah@fujitsu.com
[2] Institute of Mathematics for Industry, Kyushu University, Fukuoka, Japan
kamiyama@imi.kyushu-u.ac.jp
[3] JST, PRESTO, Kawaguchi, Japan

Abstract. Reducing congestion is one of the most important issues in theme park management. Optimization algorithms for reducing congestion in theme parks using simulation optimization methods have been proposed. In many existing methods, theme park managers directly regulate the movement of visitors. However, restricting the freedom to wander considerably reduces the visitor satisfaction. Thus, when controlling congestion in theme parks, we must consider the trade-off between reducing congestion and restricting freedom. In this paper, we propose an indirect control method for pedestrian flows using congestion forecasts and information distribution. Specifically, we propose a simulation-based heuristic algorithm for the problem of finding an optimal information distribution policy for congestion forecasts satisfying user equilibrium conditions.

1 Introduction

Congestion is ubiquitous in theme parks, and is chiefly caused by popular rides and attractions. Reducing congestion can reduce the waiting time of visitors, thus improving visitor satisfaction. Furthermore, because congestion can cause accidents, it is one of the most important issues in theme park management. Of course, it is not difficult to observe that we can easily reduce congestion by regulating the movement of visitors. However, restricting the freedom to wander considerably reduces visitor satisfaction. Thus, when controlling congestion in theme parks, we must consider the trade-off between reducing congestion and restricting freedom. This is one of the characteristic problems in the optimal control of pedestrian flows.

Recently, some theme parks have introduced information distribution systems to reduce congestion without restricting the freedom to wander and reducing visitor satisfaction. For example, some theme parks disseminate the current waiting times of attractions through smartphone apps to reduce huge congestion at popular attractions. However, distributing the current congestion information

© Springer Nature Switzerland AG 2021
T. Uchiya et al. (Eds.): PRIMA 2020, LNAI 12568, pp. 299–314, 2021.
https://doi.org/10.1007/978-3-030-69322-0_19

causes visitors to react to the information and avoid crowded attractions. Consequently, although congestion is reduced at the places that were expected to be crowded, new congestion occurs in the places that were not expected to be crowded. Furthermore, such a situation may repeat during a day. This situation is called the *hunting phenomenon* (see [1]). This implies that the conventional information distribution policy may not optimize the entire system.

Yamada and Kamiyama [2] proposed a framework for an information distribution method for avoiding the hunting phenomenon. This method supplies congestion forecasts, which satisfy user equilibrium conditions for a part of the visitors (see Fig. 1). A *user equilibrium* is a situation where no one can improve her/his utility by changing only her/his decision (i.e., it is a Nash equilibrium). In [2], a user equilibrium is specifically defined as the situation where the future predicted by the forecast will materialize if the visitors follow the congestion information. Because the future that the forecast predicts will materialize, the visitors will have no regrets if they decide their actions following her/his utility and the given information. Therefore, if we can supply a user equilibrium as the congestion forecast, we can facilitate the materialization of the forecast. Yamada and Kamiyama [2] call this reproducible congestion forecast a *congestion forecast satisfying the user equilibrium conditions*. The algorithm proposed in [2] finds a congestion forecast that approximately satisfies the user equilibrium conditions by focusing on the state after people have visited a place infinitely times.

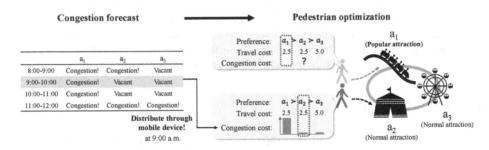

Fig. 1. Illustration of pedestrian flow control by congestion information. We attempt to optimize pedestrian flows by distributing congestion information to some of the visitors. A visitor who does not have any information about the current congestion condition selects the most preferred attraction. On the other hand, a visitor who has information about the current congestion condition considers the congestion and selects the second-best attraction.

The aim of this study is to formalize and evaluate the information distribution method proposed in [2] based on simulation optimization [3]. Simulation optimization is a methodology for optimizing complex systems by mapping the target system to a simulation and optimizing the simulation by methods such as black-box optimization algorithms [4]. Following a review of the related work, we explain our agent-based simulation model of a theme park and define our problem in Sect. 2. In Sect. 3, we explain our algorithm. In Sect. 4, we discuss the results of the computational experiments. Finally, Sect. 5 concludes this paper.

We summarize the highlights of our algorithm. First, our algorithm is inspired by the algorithms for computing an equilibrium traffic assignment in road networks [5]. Second, the algorithm can solve a large-scale instance by decomposing the original problem into sub-problems and sequentially solving the sub-problems. Especially, we focus on the time structure of the simulation. Because the actions of agents at the later time steps do not affect their decisions at the earlier time step, we can consider the policy from the earlier time steps to the later time steps sequentially. We believe that our algorithm is a good example of decomposing a large simulation optimization problem by using the structure of the agent model.

1.1 Related Work

One of the most popular simulation optimization approaches is to enumerate a small number of alternatives and evaluate all policies by using simulation. Then, we select the best policy based on the results of the simulation (see [6–8]). Because we have to select a small number of policies in advance, we cannot analyze all possibilities with this approach. In order to deal with this issue, black-box optimization approaches have been recently studied (see, e.g., [4]). Black-box optimization approaches can be used without knowledge and analysis of the simulation model. However, in agent-based simulation (ABS), because agents react to policies and change their behavior or interact with each other, the direct use of black-box optimization cannot provide a solution or may require extensive calculation time to obtain a solution. Another popular approach is the analytical approach. Masuda and Tsuji [9] studied the effect of priority tickets (i.e., fast passes) on a congestion equilibrium. By using models based on game theory, they obtained optimal control methods in the situation where people behave strategically. This kind of method can treat well-formalized policies such as priority tickets and pricing of attractions. However, this kind of approach is not flexible because it needs strict assumptions. To the best of our knowledge, no one has studied an algorithm for finding an optimal information distribution policy in a pedestrian (agent) situation using an analytical approach.

In the field of simulation excluding ABS, many researchers have developed algorithms by focusing on various properties/problems of simulations (see [10]). However, excepting those using black box optimization directly in ABS, few optimization algorithms are available. The main contribution of this paper is that it develops a new optimization algorithm by focusing on the properties/problems of ABS, especially the time structures of the agents' decisions and the collective property of user equilibrium.

2 Simulation Model and Problem Formulation

In this section, we first explain the simulation model and the parameters used in this model. Then, we formulate the problem.

For each positive integer x, we define $[[x]] := \{1, 2, \ldots, x\}$, i.e., $[[x]]$ denotes the set $\{1, 2, \ldots, x\}$. We denote by $[0, 1]$ the set of real numbers from 0 to 1. Furthermore, we denote by $\mathbb{N}$ the set of positive integers.

2.1 Simulation Model

In this study, we consider the following simulation model of a theme park. Each attraction has a capacity, which is the maximum number of visitors who can use this attraction simultaneously. Notice that the visitors who cannot use an attraction have to wait in line for this attraction. Furthermore, each attraction has a fixed processing time (i.e., the time required to ride this attraction once). In this paper, *congestion* is defined as queues of visitors waiting to enjoy an attraction (e.g., rides), and *reducing congestion* means reducing the maximum length of queues for an attraction. A fixed number of visitors randomly arrives at and leaves the theme park. The arrival time and departure time of each visitor obey a probability distribution (e.g., the normal distribution). In the theme park, each visitor i repeats the following sequence of actions. First, the visitor i selects an attraction a that she/he wishes to visit next. Then, the visitor i moves to the attraction a. If no one is (or a sufficiently small number of visitors are) waiting in the queue for the attraction a, the visitor i can immediately ride the attraction a. Otherwise, the visitor i waits at the end of the line. After riding the attraction a, the visitor i selects the next attraction again. This sequence of actions is repeated until the visitor leaves the theme park.

2.2 Parameters

The parameters in the model are described as follows.

- $T \in \mathbb{N}$, which represents the number of time slots.
- $\ell \in \mathbb{N}$, which represents the number of time steps in one time slot.
- $m \in \mathbb{N}$, which represents the number of agents.
- A finite set $A = \{a_1, a_2, \ldots, a_n\}$ of n attractions.
- A finite set P of locations where the agents can exist. We assume that $A \subseteq P$.
- A travel cost function $d \colon P^2 \to [0, 1]$. For each pair $(p_1, p_2) \in P^2$, $d(p_1, p_2)$ represents the travel cost between p_1 and p_2. Here, $d(p_1, p_2)$ is a normalized travel time.
- $q \in \{0, 0.1, \ldots, 1\}$, which represents the proportion of visitors who receive the congestion information.
- Q, which represents the set of visitors who receive the congestion information. We assume that $|Q| = qm$ and Q is chosen uniformly at random.

For example, if we consider the simulation from 8:00 a.m. to 6:00 p.m. and each slot is one hour, then $T = 10$. Furthermore, if one slot is one hour and one time step is one minute, then $\ell = 60$. For each integer $t \in [[T]]$, we define

$$I_t := \{(t-1)\ell + 1, 1(t-1)\ell + 2, \ldots (t-1)\ell + \ell\}.$$

That is, I_t represents the set of time steps in the tth slot.

Furthermore, for each agent i, we are given the following parameters.

- The arrival time at_i and the departure time dt_i of i. We assume that $at_i, dt_i \in [[T\ell]]$ and $at_i \leq dt_i$. We assume that the set of arrival times $\{at_i \mid i \in A\}$ and the set of departure times $\{dt_i \mid i \in A\}$ are randomly decided according to a fixed probability distribution.
- The preference function $\alpha_i \colon A \to [0, 1]$ of i. For each attraction $a \in A$, $\alpha_i(a)$ represents the preference of the visitor i for the attraction a.

The current status of an agent $i \in N$ is described using a pair (p, c_i) of the current position $p \in A$ of i and the current congestion information $c_i \in [0, 1]^A$ of i such that $\max_{a \in A} c_i(a) = 1$. For each attraction $a \in A$, $c_i(a)$ represents the current congestion information about a that i has. If a visitor does not receive the congestion forecast, then $c_i(a)$ is same value for every attraction $a \in A$ (e.g., $c_i(a) = 1$). This represents the visitor expects all of congestion levels are same due to no information.

In theme parks, visitors select the next attraction to visit based on the distance from the current position to that attraction. Furthermore, if a visitor has some information about congestion, then she/he selects an attraction with short waiting time based on the information. That is, she/he tries to avoid congested attractions. In this study, we use the agent model proposed in [6], as it can consider information gathering and decision making. In [6], the multinomial logit model is used to model people's behavior and reproduce the congestion in theme parks. More specifically, the utility $U_i(a, p)$ of a visitor i at a position p for each attraction a is defined by

$$U_i(a, p) := \alpha_i(a) + \beta_1 d(a, p) + \beta_2 c_i(a), \tag{1}$$

where β_1, β_2 are the parameters for balancing the travel cost and congestion cost. In this model, once a visitor rides on an attraction, she/he will remove it from a list her/his want to ride. Notice that the congestion cost may change when the visitor i obtains a new congestion forecast. As mentioned above, if a visitor i does not receive a congestion forecast, then $c_i(a) = 1$ for every attraction $a \in A$. In the simulation, visitors sequentially decide the attraction to visit by maximizing their utility function (1). The visitors always decide sequentially and do not plan route in advance.

2.3   Problem Formulation

Here, we define our problem. The simulation has two elements of randomness. The first is the set of visitors who receive the distributed congestion information (i.e., the set Q), and the second is the arrival time and departure time of each visitor. We denote by ξ the realization of this randomness of the system. A *congestion forecast* is a function $F \colon [[T]] \times A \to [0, 1]$ such that for every integer $t \in [[T]]$, $\max_{a \in A} F(t, a) = 1$.

Assume that we are given a congestion forecast F. For each integer $\theta \in [[T\ell]]$ and each attraction $a \in A$, we define $w_F(\theta, a; \xi)$ as the length of the waiting queue for the attraction a at the time step θ when we use F as the input of the simulation with a realization ξ of the randomness of the system. Furthermore, for each integer $t \in [[T]]$ and each attraction $a \in A$, we define $\overline{w}_F(t, a; \xi)$ by

$$\overline{w}_F(t, a; \xi) := \frac{1}{\ell} \sum_{\theta \in I_t} w_F(\theta, a; \xi).$$

That is, $\overline{w}_F(t, a; \xi)$ is the average length of the waiting queue for the attraction a during the tth slot. For each integer $t \in [[T]]$, we define

$$m_F(t; \xi) := \max_{a \in A} \overline{w}_F(t, a; \xi).$$

Thus, $m_F(t; \xi)$ is the maximum average length of the waiting queue among all the attractions during the tth slot. $\mathsf{max\_len}(F; \xi)$ is defined by

$$\mathsf{max\_len}(F; \xi) := \max\{m_F(t; \xi) \mid t \in [[T]]\}.$$

For each pair $(t, a) \in [[T]] \times A$, we define the real number $\mathbf{Sim}_F(t, a; \xi)$ by

$$\mathbf{Sim}_F(t, a; \xi) := \frac{\overline{w}_F(t, a; \xi)}{m_F(t; \xi)}.$$

Notice that $\mathbf{Sim}_F(t, a; \xi)$ is the normalized congestion by the simulation for the congestion forecast F. For each integer $t \in [[T]]$, we define

$$\mathbf{Err}_t(F; \xi) := \frac{1}{n} \sum_{a \in A} \left| \mathbf{Sim}_F(t, a; \xi) - F(t, a) \right|.$$

In other words, $\mathbf{Err}_t(F; \xi)$ represents the average of the absolute errors between the forecast and the result of the simulation at the tth slot. Lastly, we define

$$\mathbf{Err}(F; \xi) := \sum_{t \in [[T]]} \mathbf{Err}_t(F; \xi).$$

That is, $\mathbf{Err}(F; \xi)$ is the sum of the absolute errors between the forecast and the result of the simulation.

We are now ready to formulate the problem of finding a congestion forecast F. In the problem, the congestion forecast F has to approximately satisfy user equilibrium conditions. The problem can be formulated as follows. In (2), ε is a small real number given in advance.

$$
\begin{aligned}
\text{Minimize} \quad & \mathsf{max\_len}(F; \xi) \\
\text{subject to} \quad & \mathbf{Err}(F; \xi) \leq \varepsilon \\
& F \colon [[T]] \times A \to [0, 1].
\end{aligned}
\tag{2}
$$

Notice that the constraint of the problem of (2) means that F approximately satisfies the user equilibrium conditions.

3   Algorithm

In this section, we explain our algorithm for finding an appropriate congestion forecast. The algorithm comprises two parts. In the first part, we try to find a congestion forecast satisfying the user equilibrium conditions (see Algorithm 1). In the second part, we optimize the proportion of visitors who receive the congestion information.

3.1   Finding Congestion Forecast

In Algorithm 1, we are given a positive real number ε' and a positive integer Δ, where ε' is the stopping accuracy of the algorithm and Δ is the upper bound of the number of iterations for determining the forecast of each slot. Recall that ξ is a realization of the randomness of the system.

Algorithm 1: Algorithm for finding congestion forecast

---

1 Define an initial forecast $F_0 \colon [[T]] \times A \to [0,1]$ by $F_0(t,a) := 1$ for each pair $(t,a) \in [[T]] \times A$.

2 **for** $t = 1, 2, \ldots, T$ **do**

3 $\quad$ Define $G_{t,0} := F_{t-1}$ and $\gamma_{t,0} := 1$. Set $\delta := 0$.

4 $\quad$ **while** $\mathbf{Err}_t(G_{t,\delta}; \xi) > \varepsilon'$, $\gamma_{t,\delta} \neq 0$, and $\delta \leq \Delta$ **do**

5 $\quad\quad$ Define the function $h_{t,\delta} \colon [[T]] \times A \to [0,1]$ by

$$h_{t,\delta}(t',a) := \begin{cases} \mathbf{Sim}_{G_{t,\delta}}(t,a;\xi) & \text{if } t' = t \\ G_{t,\delta}(t',a) & \text{if } t' \neq t. \end{cases}$$

6 $\quad\quad$ For each real number $x \in \{0, 0.1, \ldots, 1\}$ and each pair $(t',a) \in [[T]] \times A$, we define

$$H_{t,\delta}^x(t',a) := (1 - x) \cdot G_{t,\delta}(t',a) + x \cdot h_{t,\delta}(t',a).$$

7 $\quad\quad$ For each real number $x \in \{0, 0.1, \ldots, 1\}$, we define the function $E_{t,\delta}^x \colon [[T]] \times A \to [0,1]$ by

$$E_{t,\delta}^x(t',a) := \frac{H_{t,\delta}^x(t',a)}{\max_{a' \in A} H_{t,\delta}^x(t',a')}.$$

8 $\quad\quad$ Define $\gamma_{i,\delta+1}$ as a minimizer of

$$\min_{x \in \{0, 0.1, \ldots, 1\}} \mathbf{Err}_t(E_{t,\delta}^x; \xi).$$

9 $\quad\quad$ Define $G_{t,\delta+1} := E_{t,\delta}^{\gamma_{t,\delta+1}}$. Set $\delta := \delta + 1$.

10 $\quad$ **end**

11 $\quad$ Define $F_t := G_{t,\delta}$.

12 **end**

13 Output F_T, and halt.

In Algorithm 1, we first set the initial forecast as F_0. Then, we sequentially determine the forecast of each slot from the first slot to the Tth slot. In the tth iteration of the main loop (i.e., Steps 2–12), we determine the forecast of the tth slot. If the error of the current forecast $G_{t,\delta}$ is sufficiently small (i.e., $\mathbf{Err}_t(G_{t,\delta};\xi) \leq \varepsilon'$), then we stop this iteration. Furthermore, if the current forecast $G_{t,\delta}$ is not improved or the number of iterations for this slot is sufficient, then we stop this iteration. Otherwise, we try to improve the current forecast $G_{t,\delta}$. First, we construct the function $h_{t,\delta}$ from $G_{t,\delta}$ by replacing the forecast of the tth slot with the result of the simulation for $G_{t,\delta}$. Then, we update $G_{t,\delta}$ by using $h_{t,\delta}$. We also optimize the degree of the update (i.e., $\gamma_{t,\delta}$). We repeat this from the first slot to the Tth slot.

3.2 Optimizing the Proportion of Visitors Receiving Congestion Information

Here, we consider the problem of optimizing the proportion of visitors who receive the congestion information. If q is fixed, then we can use Algorithm 1. Therefore, in order to optimize the proportion of visitors who receive the congestion information, we set the candidate sets of the proportion of visitors receiving the congestion information as $\{0, 0.1, \ldots, 1\}$, and evaluate each candidate. More precisely, for each real number $q \in \{0, 0.1, \ldots, 1\}$, we compute the output F^q of Algorithm 1 under the assumption that q is given as an input. Then, we find a minimizer q^* of

$$\min_{q \in \{0, 0.1, \ldots, 1\}} \mathsf{max\_len}(F^q; \xi).$$

Finally, we output F^{q^*}, and halt the processing.

4 Computational Experiments

In this section, we explain the experimental settings and compare our algorithm with black-box optimization methods. Then, we apply our algorithm to a large-scale instance, and analyze the scalability of our algorithm. Finally, we consider the convergence of our algorithm.

4.1 Experimental Settings

The simulation used in the computational experiments represents a theme park, which is modeled using a queueing network. The geography of the theme park is represented by using a directed graph (see Fig. 2). The nodes represent the attractions, and edges represent the roads, which have travel times. An attraction consists of one queue lane and several service units. The service units represent, for example, rides of the roller coaster. If visitors are waiting in the queue lane for an attraction, a new visitor lines up at the end of the line. Otherwise, the new visitor can ride on a vacant service unit. Each unit has a capacity and time identified as parameters.

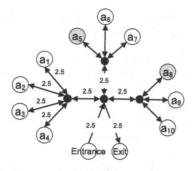

Fig. 2. An example of the geography of a large-scale instance. Gray nodes represent popular attractions.

In the computational experiments, we prepare two parameter sets called the large-scale instance and small-scale instance. First, the large-scale instance is a real scale setting, which models a single day in the entire theme park. Second, the small-scale instance is a downsized setting for the comparison experiments. In both the instances, there exist a few popular attractions, and the others are normal attractions. The goal of optimization is leveling the usage between the popular attractions and the normal attractions.

Large-Scale Instance. In the large-scale instance, there are 50,000 visitors and 10 attractions $A = \{a_1, a_2, \ldots, a_{10}\}$. The attractions a_5, a_8 are popular attractions. The others a_1, a_2, a_3, a_4, a_6, a_7, a_9, and a_{10} are normal attractions. The simulation is performed from 8:00 a.m. to 6:00 p.m. (i.e., $T = 10$), and each time step corresponds to a minute (i.e., $\ell = 60$). The preferences $(\alpha_i(a_1), \alpha_i(a_2), \ldots, \alpha_i(a_{10}))$ of the visitors can be grouped into two types based on the attractions. The first type prefers the popular attractions, i.e., $\alpha_i(a_5)$ and $\alpha_i(a_8)$ are 1. In the second type, the visitor does not prefer the popular attractions, i.e., $\alpha_i(a_1)$, $\ldots$, $\alpha_i(a_4)$, $\alpha_i(a_6)$, $\alpha_i(a_7)$, $\alpha_i(a_9)$, and $\alpha_i(a_{10})$ are 1. Half of the agents have the first type of preference, and the others have the second type of preference. The arrival time of an agent is stochastic, and it obeys the normal distribution with the expected value of 8:30 a.m. and standard deviation of 60 min. Similarly, the departure time of an agent obeys the normal distribution with expected value of 4:30 p.m. and standard deviation of 60 min. The geography of the theme park is described in Fig. 2. There exist three zones and each zone consists of three or four attractions. The travel time of each edge is 2.5 min, and $d(a, p)$ is the normalized sum of the travel time of the shortest path from the current position p to the attraction a (e.g., if a visitor i is at Entrance and evaluates the travel cost to a_5, $d(a_5, \text{Entrance})$ is $7.5/10.0 = 0.75$, where 7.5 is the sum of the travel times of the shortest path and 10.0 is the sum of the travel times of the longest path of the network). If the visitor i does not receive the congestion information, then $c_i(a) = 1$ for each attraction a. If the visitor i receives the congestion information F, then $c_i(a) = F(t, a)$ for each attraction a at the time step in I_t. We define $\beta_1 := -1$ and $\beta_2 := -1$. Each agent deterministically selects an attraction that maximizes her/his utility. Each attraction has 100 units, the capacity of each unit is 6, and the running time is 10 min.

Small-Scale Instance. The small-scale instance is similar to the large-scale instance. However, the number of visitors is 500, and the number of attractions is 3 with only 1 unit. The simulation is performed from 8:00 a.m. to 12:00 p.m. (i.e., $T = 4$). The geography simply comprises one zone with one popular attraction a_1 and two normal attractions a_2, a_3. There exist 3×4 parameters for optimization. For simplicity, we assume that $d(a, p) = 0$ for every attraction a and every position p.

In the following experiments, we set the parameters of Algorithm 1 by $\varepsilon' :=$ 0.01 and $\Delta := 10$.

4.2   Comparison with Black-Box Optimization Methods

In this subsection, we compare our algorithm with the Nelder–Mead method (NM method) [11] and Bayesian optimization (BO) [12]. The NM method and BO, which are called derivative-free optimization methods or black-box optimization methods, are frequently used for simulation optimization because they do not need derivatives of the system. The experiments were conducted for the small-scale instance, and we attempted to find an optimal congestion forecast for the case where $q = 0.5$. Because the NM method and BO cannot optimize a discrete variable, we only treat continuous variables (a congestion forecast). We compared the number of iterations in each case. The NM method was implemented in Scikit-learn [13] and BO was implemented in the Bayesian optimization module [14]. It should be remarked that both hyper-parameters were not tuned. We compared our algorithm with the black-box optimization method in terms of the maximum queue length $\mathsf{max\_len}(F; \xi)$ and forecasting error $\mathbf{Err}(F; \xi)$. Because the NM method and BO can treat a single objective function, we define a new objective function

$$g(F; \xi) := z \cdot \frac{\mathbf{Err}(F; \xi)}{N_1} + (1 - z) \cdot \frac{\mathsf{max\_len}(F; \xi)}{N_2}.$$

That is, $g(F; \xi)$ is the weighted sum of two objectives $\mathsf{max\_len}(F; \xi)$ and $\mathbf{Err}(F; \xi)$. We use the weight $z = 0.5$ and the normalization factors $N_1 = 1$, $N_2 = 100$. Figure 3 shows the transitions of $g(F; \xi)$, the maximum queue length $\mathsf{max\_len}(F; \xi)$, and the forecasting error $\mathbf{Err}(F; \xi)$. The NM method and BO need greater number of iterations to reach the algorithm result. Especially, because the forecasting error is not at all reduced, we expect that they require a huge number of iterations. It may be possible to reduce the number of iterations by using appropriate hyper parameters. However, to identify the appropriate hyper parameters, we need domain knowledge about simulation models or tuning algorithms requiring numerous iterations.

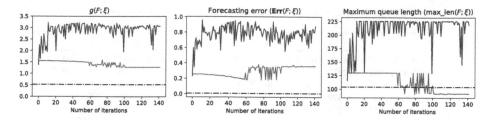

Fig. 3. Comparison of the algorithms. The red and blue lines denote the NM method and BO, respectively, and the black lines denote the result after 142 iterations of our algorithm (the solution converged). (Color figure online)

4.3   Optimization in Large-Scale Simulation

In this subsection, we evaluate our algorithm for the large-scale instance. From the change in queue lengths (Fig. 4), we can see that the congestion at the popular attractions a_5, a_8 can be reduced by the forecast. Moreover, the obtained congestion forecast (Table 1) matches the forecast obtained from the algorithm (the right graph in Fig. 4). This is the same for any q when the calculation converges (i.e., $\delta \leq \Delta$ for all t). The number of total iterations is 3638, and the calculation time is 3 d, 9 h, and 5 min. Actually, we parallelized the code, and thus the calculation time was shortened from 81 h to 10.5 h. The main reason of the increase in the calculation time is the increase in the simulation time. In the small-scale instance, a single execution of the simulation requires merely 1 to 2 s. On the other hand, the corresponding duration for the large-scale instance is 80 to 90 s. The other reason is the increase in the number of iterations. Strangely, the number of iterations increases by just 3 times (from 1190 to 3086) even though the number of optimization variables is increased by approximately 10 times (from 12 to 100).

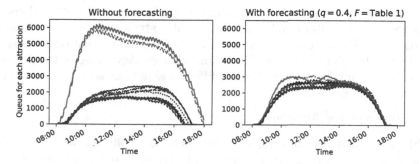

Fig. 4. Lengths of the waiting queues. The red lines are the popular attractions a_5, a_8. In the right figure, we use the information distribution obtained by our algorithm ($q = 0.4$, $F =$ Table 1). (Color figure online)

Table 1. Congestion forecast obtained by our algorithm.

T	a_1	a_2	a_3	a_4	a_5	a_6	a_7	a_8	a_9	a_{10}
1	0.720418	0.675817	0.696171	0.692837	1.	0.670981	0.762788	0.995877	0.685597	0.696621
2	0.808647	0.811263	0.812272	0.79651	1.	0.718593	0.736128	0.997293	0.713978	0.717667
3	0.841241	0.803143	0.823742	0.835404	0.991737	0.737548	0.745148	1.	0.73498	0.741999
4	0.899661	0.863094	0.894522	0.889992	1.	0.784652	0.770107	0.984395	0.799494	0.785912
5	0.902241	0.924524	0.893276	0.862496	0.933075	0.807642	0.818644	1.	0.809866	0.790043
6	0.870545	0.888406	0.906036	0.844671	1.	0.784408	0.799651	0.94668	0.805791	0.824702
7	0.926221	0.955718	0.937145	0.917229	1.	0.893041	0.89844	0.993736	0.899123	0.884014
8	0.935964	1.	0.961879	0.920934	0.986462	0.867541	0.866823	0.97186	0.870089	0.911179
9	0.922942	1.	0.911364	0.87543	0.91263	0.811624	0.780999	0.878249	0.827324	0.791795
10	0.829386	1.	0.763565	0.722922	0.9501	0.622605	0.497716	0.961467	0.529893	0.450597

Our algorithm sequentially solves a sub-problem for each time slot. Thus, the number of iterations linearly increases with regard to the number of time slots. In this case, the number of time slots is increased by 2.5 times (from 4 to 10), and thus the number of iterations is increased by approximately 2.5 times. This implies that our algorithm is scalable with regard to the number of time slots (i.e., T). However, the scalability with regard to the number of forecasting variables (i.e., the number of attractions in A) is unclear. We analyze this point in the next subsection.

4.4 Scalability Analysis

In this subsection, we investigate the scalability of our algorithm. First, we apply our algorithm to various combinations of the number of time slots (i.e., T) and the number of forecasting variables (i.e., the number of attractions $|A|$). Figure 5 shows that the number of iterations increases approximately linearly with regard to the number of time slots and the number of forecasting variables. Second, we apply our algorithm to a variety of congestion situations. It is possible to create various degrees of congestion by changing the number of popular attractions and the proportion of visitors preferring the popular attractions. The result shows that our algorithm can reduce congestion in any congestion situation (see Fig. 6). Moreover, although the number of iterations changes depending on the degree of congestion, the number of iterations in different situations is at most two times.

4.5 Convergence Analysis

In this subsection, we numerically investigate the convergence of our algorithm. Figure 7 is a congestion forecast calculated by our algorithm on error distribution. The graphs show that the algorithm can find a set of values mostly corresponding to the minimum error in three error distribution structures ($q = 0.2, 0.5, 0.7$). The graphs imply that there are situations with no forecast satisfying the user equilibrium conditions (i.e., $\min \mathbf{Err}_t(F; \xi) > \varepsilon'$). Even in such situations, the algorithm can find values that mostly minimize the error.

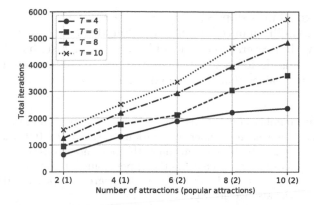

Fig. 5. Relation between the total number of iterations of our algorithm, number of attractions (horizontal axis), and the number of time slots (series). The experiments were conducted for a small-scale instance.

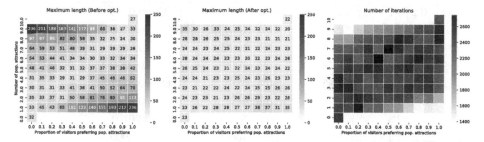

Fig. 6. Maximum length of the waiting queue for various combinations of the number of popular attractions and proportion of visitors preferring the popular attractions (left graph). The center graph is the result of distributing the optimal congestion forecast after optimization. The right graph shows the number of iterations for the small-scale instance, $T = 4$ and $|A| = 10$. Heavy congestion is observed on the bottom right of each graph, as many visitors gather at some popular attractions. Heavy congestion is also observed on the upper left of each graph, as many visitors gather at some "normal" attractions. For example, in the situation where 10% of the visitors prefer 9 popular attractions (upper left), the remaining visitors (90%) prefer the remaining attraction (1 normal attraction). The closer the situation is to the diagonal from the upper right to the lower left, the greater is the decrease in congestion.

Figure 8 shows the congestion forecasts calculated by the algorithm from various initial forecasts (F_0). The graphs show that the algorithm can find a forecast that mostly realizes the minimum error regardless of the initial forecasts. Table 2 shows the average number of iterations and the reason for stopping in 100 different initial forecast trials. In every trial, the algorithm stops before reaching the upper bound $\Delta = 10$. If the minimum error can be smaller than ε', the algorithm is stopped because $\min \mathbf{Err}_t(F; \xi) \le \varepsilon'$ and a forecast satisfying the user equilibrium conditions can be found. If there is no minimum error smaller than ε', the algorithm is stopped because $\gamma = 0$ and naturally, no forecast satisfying the user equilibrium condition can be found. In summary, our algorithm can converge within several iterations of various error distribution structures. Even when there is no forecast satisfying the user equilibrium conditions, the algorithm can find values that mostly minimize the error.

Table 2. Average number of iterations, the reason for stopping, and the average error of the 100 trials. The average number of iterations is shown for 100 trials for various initial forecasts. The 2nd to 4th column shows the percentage of the three reasons for stopping: the number of iterations reaches the upper bound (Iterations $> \Delta$), the error is below the stopping accuracy (Error $\leq \varepsilon'$), or the degree of update is 0 ($\gamma = 0$). The 5th column shows the average error of 100 trials.

q	Time slot	Average number of iterations	Reasons for stopping		Iterations $> \Delta$
			Error $\leq \varepsilon'$	$\gamma = 0$	Average error
0.2	T1	3.21	0% 0%	100%	0.0446
	T2	2.07	0% 100%	0%	0.0000
	T3	2.01	0% 100%	0%	0.0000
	T4	1.73	0% 100%	0%	0.0000
0.5	T1	3.83	0% 0%	100%	0.0357
	T2	1.73	0% 95%	5%	0.0008
	T3	3.77	0% 5%	95%	0.0101
	T4	1.84	0% 100%	0%	0.0000
0.7	T1	3.36	0% 0%	100%	0.0882
	T2	1.87	0% 94%	6%	0.0011
	T3	3.63	0% 2%	98%	0.0110
	T4	1.79	0% 100%	0%	0.0000

5   Conclusion

In this paper, we formalized and evaluated the pedestrian flow control method by using congestion forecasts satisfying the user equilibrium conditions proposed in [2]. More precisely, we proposed a simulation optimization algorithm for finding appropriate congestion forecasts and information distribution policy. Then, we evaluated the usefulness of our algorithm through computational experiments. As shown in Sect. 4.2, even though the number of variables is small, it is not easy for existing black-box algorithms to solve the problem with a small number of iterations. On the other hand, our algorithm can approximately solve a large-scale simulation having many optimization variables in a reasonable time (see Sect. 4.3). Moreover, the efficiency of our algorithm may not be limited to certain conditions (see Sect. 4.5), and the convergence of the algorithm is satisfactory (see Sect. 4.4).

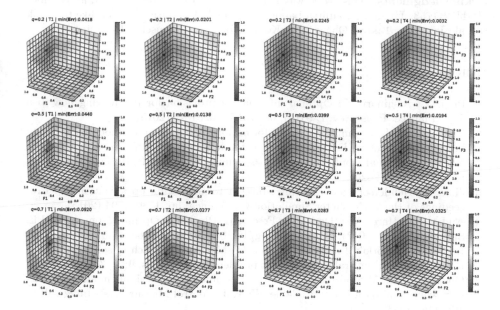

Fig. 7. Error distribution for the various proportion of visitors receiving congestion information ($q = 0.2, 0.5, 0.7$). Each grid represents a situation where a certain congestion forecast (corresponding to the $F1$ axis, $F2$ axis, $F3$ axis) is provided. If the congestion forecast is normalized, then one of the values ($F1$, $F2$, $F3$) is always 1. The color of each grid represents a forecasting error ($\mathbf{Err}_t(F; \xi)$) in each situation. The errors are calculated using a grid search. The circle represents the congestion forecast calculated by our algorithm. The triangle is the initial forecast (F_0) of our algorithm. F_0 is chosen randomly.

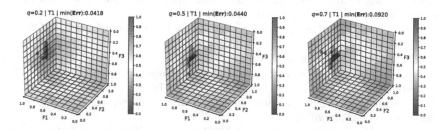

Fig. 8. Congestion forecast calculated by our algorithm from various initial forecasts (F_0). We conducted 100 trials with different initial forecasts. The circle represents the congestion forecast calculated for each trial. The error distribution of $T1$ is the same for all trials, but the error distributions of $T2, T3, and\ T4$ are different among for each trial. Therefore, only $T1$ is shown.

Acknowledgments. This work was supported by JST, PRESTO Grant Number JPMJPR1753, Japan, and Fujitsu Laboratories, Ltd. The authors would like to thank Hiroaki Iwashita, Takuya Ohawa, and Kotaro Ohori for the useful discussions.

References

1. Imai, T., Nishinari, K.: Optimal information provision for maximizing flow in a forked lattice. Phys. Rev. E **91**(6), 062818-1–062818-7 (2015)
2. Yamada, H., Kamiyama, N.: An information distribution method for avoiding hunting phenomenon in theme parks (extended abstract). In: Proceedings of the 19th International Conference on Autonomous Agents and Multiagent Systems, pp. 2050–2052 (2020)
3. Jian, N., Henderson, S.G.: An introduction to simulation optimization. In: Proceedings of the 2015 Winter Simulation Conference, pp. 1780–1794 (2015)
4. Audet, C., Hare, W.: Derivative-Free and Blackbox Optimization. SSORFE. Springer, Cham (2017). https://doi.org/10.1007/978-3-319-68913-5
5. LeBlanc, L., Morlok, E., Pierskalla, W.: An efficient approach to solving the road network equilibrium traffic assignment problem. Transp. Res. **9**(5), 309–318 (1975)
6. Ohori, K., Iida, M., Takahashi, S.: Virtual grounding for facsimile model construction where real data is not available. SICE J. Control Measur. Syst. Integr. **6**(2), 108–116 (2013)
7. Bufala, N.D., Kant, J.: An evolutionary approach to find optimal policies with an agent-based simulation. In: Proceedings of the 18th International Conference on Autonomous Agents and Multiagent Systems, pp. 610–618 (2019)
8. Shigenaka, S., Takami, S., Ozaki, Y., Onishi, M., Yamashita, T., Noda, I.: Evaluation of optimization for pedestrian route guidance in real-world crowded scene (extended abstract). In: Proceedings of the 18th International Conference on Autonomous Agents and Multiagent Systems, pp. 2192–2194 (2019)
9. Masuda, Y., Tsuji, A.: Congestion control for a system with parallel stations and homogeneous customers using priority passes. Netw. Spat. Econ. **19**(1), 293–318 (2019)
10. Amaran, S., Sahinidis, N.V., Sharda, B., Bury, S.J.: Simulation optimization: a review of algorithms and applications. Ann. Oper. Res. **240**(1), 351–380 (2015). https://doi.org/10.1007/s10479-015-2019-x
11. Nelder, J.A., Mead, R.A.: A simplex method for function minimization. Comput. J. **7**, 308–313 (1965)
12. Mockus, J.: On Bayesian methods for seeking the extremum. In: Proceedings of Optimization Techniques IFIP Technical Conference Novosibirsk. Volume 27 of Lecture Notes in Computer Science, pp. 400–404 (1974)
13. Pedregosa, F., et al.: Scikit-learn: machine learning in Python. J. Mach. Learn. Res. **12**, 2825–2830 (2011)
14. Fernando, N.: Bayesianoptimization (2019). https://github.com/fmfn/Bayesian Optimization

Short Papers

Automated Negotiation Mechanism and Strategy for Compensational Vehicular Platooning

Sînziana-Maria Sebe[1]([envelope])[iD], Tim Baarslag[2][iD], and Jörg P. Müller[1][iD]

[1] Institute of Informatics, Clausthal University of Technology, Clausthal-Zellerfeld, Germany
sinziana-maria.sebe@tu-clausthal.de
[2] Centrum Wiskunde and Informatica, Science Park 123, 1098 XG Amsterdam, Netherlands

Abstract. Our research is developing flexible strategies for forming and routing future platoons of automated urban logistics vehicles. We propose the notion of compensational platooning using automated negotiation between agents representing vehicles. After the vehicles reach the end of a common route, an agent can propose part of its route along with a monetary value to platoon partners for further together-travel. If negotiation is successful, a new platoon is formed and follows the proposed route. If the compensation is too small or the route proposed oversteps the agent's limitations, the offer is rejected and the vehicles continue their travel separately. A contribution of this paper is a negotiation strategy that proposes compensation based on beliefs of what the opponent's payment threshold would be. In doing so, the bid with the highest acceptance likelihood is calculated, keeping negotiations short and effective. Our model is tested on a synthetic network and a real urban example. We show that by using negotiation, vehicles can identify mutually beneficial new routes that a centralised/distributed approach would not find, with utility improvements of up to 8%.

Keywords: Automated negotiation · Opponent modelling · Platoon matching · Decentralised agent coordination

1 Introduction

With the steady growth of e-commerce, logistic providers are expanding and accelerating the way they conduct their shipments to same-day deliveries. To reduce emissions, road occupancy and the costs of logistics companies, small electric autonomous delivery vehicles could take over deliveries. However, having multiple such vehicles in an already congested network could further impede traffic and ultimately prove to be chaotic and counterproductive.

As a solution we investigate platoons, a formation where vehicles travel with small inter-vehicular distances, behaving as one unit. Platooning has been shown

© Springer Nature Switzerland AG 2021
T. Uchiya et al. (Eds.): PRIMA 2020, LNAI 12568, pp. 317–324, 2021.
https://doi.org/10.1007/978-3-030-69322-0_20

to positively affect traffic through better usage of road-space [1], and decongestion of intersections in urban environments [8]. To increase the probability of platoons forming, we require technology that allows vehicles from different logistic service providers to cooperate. Encouraging such competitive formations will be done by monetarily incentivising vehicles, along the lines of the fuel savings sharing presented in [4]. The authors found that optimal individual utility is reached with an even distribution of profits between competing vehicles.

While optimisation methods can create mutually beneficial routes for all vehicles considered, agent negotiation can be leveraged on top of existing centralised and distributed solutions to further improve utility. Therefore, compensational platooning is offering payment for vehicles to travel together in a platoon after the end of an optimiser-found route. The compensation needs to be high enough to convince the opponent to participate, while also being low enough for the ego-vehicle to prefer cooperation over the status quo solution. To increase the likelihood of an agreement being reached, vehicles should be equipped with an opponent modelling module. Our work presents a general model of turning knowledge collected about the opponent into a bid acceptance probability. By having an approximate insight of the opponent's reservation value, we can calculate agreeable bids, ensuring that at every round, only the best offer is being made. We show that negotiation provides a benefit when added to a distributed solution (presented in [10]), by allowing vehicles to form platoons on routes that may not necessarily be beneficial for all vehicles, but can be made more attractive through payments.

2   Related Work

A distributed approach to platoon formation is presented in [10], which uses an optimisation algorithm to find the longest common route between vehicles while respecting their limitations. Road-side units (RSU) equipped with the algorithm are distributed at every node in the network and get triggered when two or more vehicles are at the same place at the same time. The algorithm dynamically groups and routes the vehicles according to traffic density, the vehicles' current position, destinations and restrictions.

In the context of traffic and platooning, negotiation is used mainly as a conflict resolution mechanism; either merging [7], vehicle ordering [6], or intersection crossing [9]. None of these works employ negotiation as a platoon formation method.

Ensuring that the strategy used during negotiation will lead to win-win, as well as non-exploitative solutions, we turned to opponent modelling techniques. Previous works focused on estimating reservation value [13] or strategy [3]. Acceptance probability research [5] considered the case where the two negotiation parties have interacted before and can use previous knowledge to model the bids their opponent is more likely to accept. In this work, however, we tackle the problem of opponent modelling by creating an acceptance probability of bids based on estimations of the opponent's reservation value without prior knowledge.

3   Model

Routes. Each vehicle has a route, which is given to it by its logistics provider or the RSU situated in the environment. The latter is responsible for the initial creation and routing of the platoon with an optimiser approach. For our scope we consider a route to be a sequence of edges defined as $R = ((Split, V_i), (V_i, V_{i+1}),$ $...(V_n, Destination))$ for all vehicles, where $Split$ is the split point (end of the common route given by the RSU) and V_i intermediary nodes.

Pricing. To incentivise platoon travel, traffic management authorities can use congestion pricing, represented by traffic density d_e (the number of vehicles per time unit in a specific space). Alone travel incurs full payment, whereas platoons receive preferential prices due to their proven decongestion abilities [8]. The congestion price of an edge increases with the platoon size, which is then shared among the vehicles comprising it [4]. The price function is defined as

$$p_e = \begin{cases} d_e/nvp + d_e/\omega, & \text{if } nvp > 1 \\ d_e, & \text{otherwise} \end{cases} \tag{1}$$

where nvp is the number of vehicles in a platoon and ω the increase coefficient imposed by traffic management (based on the congestion in the immediate area).

Utility Function. Traditionally, the goal of routing problems is to either minimise cost, travel distance or travel duration [12]. With these three aspects, we can represent the vehicle's preferences using an additive utility function depending on route length (l) and pricing (p). The latter encompasses costs and time spent in traffic due to their dependence on traffic density. Therefore, the utility function is defined as

$$U_{veh} = -\sum_{e \in R} (\pi \cdot l_e + \rho \cdot p_e) \tag{2}$$

with the purpose of maximising, π, ρ representing the vehicle's preferences and $\pi + \rho = 1; \pi, \rho \geq 0$.

Agents. Vehicles are represented by agents that have a set of preferences and limitations. They seek to improve their utility through platoon formation by communicating with nearby agents and making offers about alternative routes they can travel on together.

Offers. An offer consists of a route and a monetary compensation $(R, comp)$. The route will contain a subsequence of the initiating agent's best route and be noted as R'_i. The compensation is an amount of money offered by the initiator to convince a potential accepting agent to agree to travel together on the proposed route. A viable compensation lies at the intersection of both agents' acceptable offer spaces.

Compensation Offer Space. This is defined by the aspiration and reservation values. For the initiating agent i, the compensation offered is financed through the savings generated from platooning. The maximum compensation offered will be denoted as the reservation value $comp_i = [0; RV_i]$. For the accepting agent a, the compensation offered has to be high enough to get it to change its route. The minimum compensation it will accept, also noted as reservation value, is the one that provides the same utility as its original best route $comp_a = [RV_a; \infty)$.

Protocol. We consider bilateral negotiations with the protocols used being either a *Take it or Leave it (ToL)* or an *Alternating Offers* protocol. Allowing for feedback from the opponent, an agent can adjust their bids to increase the likelihood of the negotiation ending in an agreement. We included *ToL* as a baseline approach to negotiation for comparison with our more advanced bidding strategy.

Deadline. A deadline is the upper limit on negotiation rounds and is set by the traffic management authority based on how congested the immediate area is.

3.1   Problem Solution

The initiator selects a subset of edges from its ideal route, computes a compensation based on its reservation value and sends it out to possible accepting agents. The reservation value is calculated as $RV_i = \sum_{e \in R'_i} d_e - p_e$. For an accepting agent to be able to fully assess the viability of an offer, it needs to receive a complete route, from the split point to their destination. This is done by the RSU, supplementing the route offered by the initiator and having it finish at the acceptor's destination. The acceptor knows the compensation $comp$ offered and the d_e and l_e for all the edges in the new route R'_a. However, it does not know the price it is expected to pay and by extension the platoon savings; since it could then extrapolate the initiator's ideal route and reservation value. This is covered by the RSU, which supplements the value of the offer with the corresponding platoon savings. The acceptor ensures the proposed route does not exceed its limitations by calculating the utility.

$$U'_a = -\pi \cdot \sum_{e \in R'_a} (l_e) - \rho \cdot [\sum_{e \in R'_a} (d_e) - comp] \tag{3}$$

If any limitations are met, the utility returned is 0. Afterwards, it computes its reservation value for the proposed route.

$$RV_a = (U_a + \sum_{e \in R'_a} \pi \cdot l_e)/\rho \tag{4}$$

If the compensation offered by the initiator is below the previously calculated reservation value, the accepting vehicle can send a counter-offer with higher compensation to increase its utility. The agents engage in making alternative offers within their defined offer space until an agreement is reached or the deadline expires.

4 Negotiation Strategy

To increase the likelihood of bids being accepted, they are chosen based on the knowledge agents can extrapolate about their opponent. Agents keep track of a probability distribution of their opponent's reservation value which they update with every new bid received. Based on this they calculate which of their bids can be accepted. However, the bid that has the highest likelihood of being accepted does not necessarily translate to better utility, since the concession made could be too large. Determining how much to concede at every step, is done by Baarslag et al. [2] with the Greedy Concession Algorithm. Given our setting, we assume that the opponents follow a time-based strategy, making concessions based on the time available until the deadline.

Estimating the Reservation Value. The agent's offer space is bound by their aspiration and reservation values, but during negotiation, the aspiration value will change to reflect the possible payment interval at a specific time. Therefore, we consider a fixed interval when calculating bids, which will be $[X(0)_i, RV_i]$ for an initiator and $[RV_a, X(0)_a]$ for an accepting opponent, where $X(0)$ represents their first offer/counteroffer. The opponent's bids follow a concession curve [3], dependent on time and strategy, encompassed in the α coefficient, which can follow either a polynomial or exponential curve.

$$X(n) = \begin{cases} RV + (1 - \alpha(n)) \cdot (X(0) - RV), & \text{if agent is initiator} \\ X(0) + \alpha(n) \cdot (RV - X(0)), & \text{if agent is acceptor} \end{cases} \tag{5}$$

While a correct estimate of the reservation value can be obtained by studying the opponent's strategy, our approach is to transform a probability distribution of the reservation value to an acceptance probability of bids. An agent starts negotiations with an uninformed prior and with every round updates its beliefs about the opponent, thus skewing the reservation value distribution.

RV to Acceptance Probability. As mentioned before, bids follow a concession curve as time progresses based on the agent's strategy, which ends at the deadline in their reservation value. By having a distribution of the potential reservation value, we can create multiple such curves, with a higher density at its peak (the black lines in Fig. 1). The acceptance probability of any of our bids depends on the values on these curves for the specific time-step considered. Our bid has a higher acceptance probability if it is higher than the projected values for an initiator opponent, and lower for an acceptor opponent. Therefore, the probability of a bid $Y(s)$ being accepted is:

$$P(Y(s))^{accepted} = \begin{cases} P(X(s) \leq Y(s)), & \text{if opponent is acceptor} \\ P(X(s) \geq Y(s)), & \text{if opponent is initiator} \end{cases} \tag{6}$$

where $X(s)$ is defined in Eq. 5. With the resulting tuples of bid and acceptance probability, the agents calculate their ideal bids and their sequence using the Greedy Concession Algorithm [2].

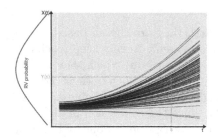

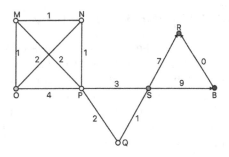

Fig. 1. Bid Y(s) with respect to the concession curves of a normal RV distribution for an initiator opponent.

Fig. 2. Example network.

5   Experiments

To validate our approach, we used a simulation framework that incorporated vehicular movement and platooning, as well as a negotiation component containing the bidding module. As a benchmark for comparison, we are using the distributed platooning approach presented in [10]. This current paper studies strictly the effect negotiation has on platoons when they reach the end of the distributed-found route. As an illustration, we present the network in Fig. 2 where the notations on the edges represent their respective traffic density. We currently consider just a two-vehicle platoon (Blue and Red) starting at node O, trying to get as "cheaply" as possible to their destinations B and R. For generalisability, an alternative network was modelled, depicting the Tiergarten neighbourhood in Berlin paired with a realistic traffic demand model derived from [11]. For the experiments we considered greedy agents that seek to maximise their profit, hence the coefficients of the utility function were: $\pi = 0.2, \rho = 0.8$.

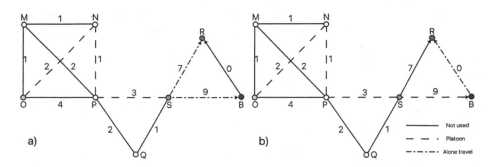

Fig. 3. Vehicle platooning with optimisation (a) and negotiation (b) approach.

Illustration. With the optimiser approach presented in Fig. 3a, the platooning stops at node S, with each vehicle travelling individually to their destination from there. When we introduced negotiation Blue made an offer for edge S-B, and with the *ToL* protocol the compensation offered lead to rejection and thus, the same results as the optimiser solution. When using the *Alternating Offers* protocol paired with the bidding strategy, Red accepted the offer and the vehicles continued travelling in a platoon until node B (Fig. 3b)), where Red continued alone to its destination R. The costs accrued by the vehicles were improved using negotiation and by extension, so did the utility (see Table 1). For the cost, we have a saving of 1.88% for Blue and 12% for Red. As for the utility, we measured a 1.83% and 8.13% improvement for Blue and Red respectively.

Berlin Tiergarten. We also investigated the applicability of our approach on a realistic example, namely the Tiergarten neighbourhood of Berlin. For the sake of continuity, we consider Blue to be the initiating agent and Red to be the accepting agent. They split after platooning for two edges, Blue offers one extra edge, which leads to Red travelling an extra three edges alone. Much like the previous example, the compensation of the offer made with the *ToL* protocol is not sufficient and leads to rejection. This is attributed to the length of the detour route, whose influence can be more clearly seen in Table 2. Using the *Alternating Offers* protocol an agreement is reached and the agents continue platooning. The savings that negotiation offers, in this case, are rather small. We do note that the example provided as the illustration is also based on the Berlin network. Therefore, we claim that more notable improvements are realistic, in the case of shorter and less crowded streets.

Table 1. Numerical results for Illustration network.

Vehicle	Cost	Distance	Utility
Optimiser			
Blue	9	1	−7.4
Red	7	1	−5.8
Negotiation			
Blue	8.83	1	−7.264
Red	6.16	2	−5.328

Table 2. Numerical results for Berlin Tiergarten.

Vehicle	Cost	Distance	Utility
Optimiser			
Blue	324	0.466	−259.2932
Red	1191	0.094	−952.8188
Negotiation			
Blue	318.11	0.466	−254.5812
Red	1155.89	3.2	−925.325

6   Conclusion and Outlook

With this paper, we incorporate negotiation between vehicles as a way of decentralised platoon building while addressing the specific requirements related to negotiation in urban traffic (effective bids and quick agreements). To ensure that the offers made will lead to a win-win conclusion, vehicles are equipped with an opponent modelling module. We present a negotiation strategy that models the acceptance probability of an agent's bids based on ever-updating knowledge about the opponent. This allows the vehicle agents to reach an agreement quickly and effectively by offering bids with a high likelihood of being accepted. The experiments show an improvement in both cost and utility. Testing on a real urban network with realistic traffic demand proved that this approach is effective, but would be best suited on short and non-traffic heavy streets, where there is a higher number of alternative routes that the vehicles can follow. This model can support platoon-to-vehicle and platoon-to-platoon negotiation as well, since a platoon would act as a singular agent, aggregating the utility functions of its vehicles and then negotiating on their behalf. Further research can address those scenarios, as well as multilateral negotiations.

References

1. Amoozadeh, M., Deng, H., Chuah, C.N., Zhang, H.M., Ghosal, D.: Platoon management with cooperative adaptive cruise control enabled by vanet. Veh. Commun. **2**(2), 110–123 (2015)
2. Baarslag, T., Gerding, E.H., Aydogan, R., Schraefel, M.: Optimal negotiation decision functions in time-sensitive domains. In: 2015 IEEE/WIC/ACM International Conference on Web Intelligence and Intelligent Agent Technology (WI-IAT), vol. 2, pp. 190–197. IEEE, Piscataway, New Jersey, US (2015)
3. Hou, C.: Predicting agents tactics in automated negotiation. In: Proceedings. IEEE/WIC/ACM International Conference on Intelligent Agent Technology (IAT 2004), pp. 127–133. IEEE, Piscataway, New Jersey, US (2004)
4. Johansson, A., Mårtensson, J.: Game theoretic models for profit-sharing in multi-fleet platoons. In: 2019 IEEE Intelligent Transportation Systems Conference (ITSC), pp. 3019–3024. IEEE (2019)
5. Lau, R.Y., Li, Y., Song, D., Kwok, R.C.W.: Knowledge discovery for adaptive negotiation agents in e-marketplaces. Decis. Support Syst. **45**(2), 310–323 (2008)
6. Lesher, M., Miller, T.S., et al.: Self-ordering of fleet vehicles in a platoon (Jul 5 2018), uS Patent App. 15/395, 219
7. Lind, H., Ekmark, J.: Control system for travel in a platoon (Aug 23 2016), uS Patent 9,423,794
8. Lioris, J., Pedarsani, R., Tascikaraoglu, F.Y., Varaiya, P.: Platoons of connected vehicles can double throughput in urban roads. Transp. Res. Part C: Emerg. Technol. **77**, 292–305 (2017)
9. Medina, A.I.M., Van de Wouw, N., Nijmeijer, H.: Automation of a t-intersection using virtual platoons of cooperative autonomous vehicles. In: 2015 IEEE 18th International Conference on Intelligent Transportation Systems, pp. 1696–1701. IEEE, Piscataway, New Jersey, US (2015)
10. Sebe, S.M., Müller, J.P.: Pfara: a platoon forming and routing algorithm for same-day deliveries. arXiv preprint arXiv:1912.08929 (2019)
11. Stabler, B., Bar-Gera, H., Sall, E.: Transportation networks for research (2018). https://github.com/bstabler/TransportationNetworks
12. Toth, P., Vigo, D.: The vehicle routing problem. SIAM (2002)
13. Zeng, D., Sycara, K.: Bayesian learning in negotiation. Int. J. Hum.-Comput. Stud. **48**(1), 125–141 (1998)

A Cognitive Agent Framework in Information Retrieval: Using User Beliefs to Customize Results

Dima El Zein[(⊠)] and Célia da Costa Pereira

Université Côte d'Azur, CNRS, I3S, UMR 7271, Nice, France
elzein@i3s.unice.fr, Celia.DA-COSTA-PEREIRA@univ-cotedazur.fr

Abstract. This paper presents a framework for a cognitive agent in information retrieval that customizes the list of returned documents based on what the agent believes about the user knowledge. Throughout the interactions between the agent and the user, the agent builds its beliefs by extracting the content of the documents examined by the user. The agent's belief base consists of "simple beliefs" represented by the document's keywords as well as "contextual rules" that allow the agent to derive new beliefs about the user knowledge. The agent is therefore able to compare its own beliefs about the user knowledge with the knowledge conveyed by a given document, and thus understand if the document really contains useful information for the user or not. Finally, in case of inconsistency, the agent revises its belief base to restore consistency.

Keywords: Cognitive agent · Information retrieval · Knowledge extraction · Belief revision

1 Introduction and Motivation

The aim of Information Retrieval (IR) systems is to provide the user with *relevant* information for a given query. While in the traditional information retrieval approaches, relevance consists of matching the documents with the topics of the user query, more recent systems consider personalizing the returned results according to the user's interests. To this aim, they use, for example, information about *query logs, click-through, time spent examining the document*, or the explicit and/or implicit feedback from the users. In recent decades, relevance has also been viewed as a multi-faceted concept and several criteria or dimensions have been considered to assess its value [1,2].

We believe that users can be considered as cognitive agents [3] having their own beliefs and knowledge about the world. They try to fulfill needs for information by requesting queries and acquire new information by examining the results. Taking into account the cognitive components of the user in information search engines has recently been set as one of the "major challenges" by the IR community [4]. However, many years ago, Maron already stressed in [5], that

© Springer Nature Switzerland AG 2021
T. Uchiya et al. (Eds.): PRIMA 2020, LNAI 12568, pp. 325–333, 2021.
https://doi.org/10.1007/978-3-030-69322-0_21

a document relevance should consider the user's prior knowledge or "cognitive map". He defined the value of a retrieved document as the extent to which its content helps the user fill a gap in his/her cognitive map.

More recently, Cholvy *et al.* [6] proposed 3 definitions for measuring the *usefulness* of information for a cognitive agent. The definitions are based on the fact that a user requesting information needs it to achieve a goal. Therefore, they consider as useful, any piece of information allowing to decrease the information gap to achieve the goal. However, their proposal is adapted to a static situation in which the agent's beliefs do not need to be updated after the arrival of new information.

In this paper, when returning results to the users, we are aiming to consider the cognitive attitudes of the users, in particular their knowledge. We propose a framework for Information Retrieval systems which is run by cognitive rule-based agent. The agent has some beliefs about the user knowledge that are extracted from the content of the documents examined by the user. The content extraction is done using the Rapid Extraction Keyword Extraction (RAKE) [7] method. A belief revision operator is incorporated into the model to ensure that the agent's beliefs about the user are consistent and not contradictory.

2   Rule-Based Agents

A Rule-based agent consists of facts (ground literals) and rules (Horn clauses). Here, rules and facts are "treated" as beliefs. The facts represent information that the agent has currently obtained about its environment. They might change over time as a result of the addition/deletion of other facts from the agent's beliefs due to: (i) new information (dynamic environment) (ii) the rule's reasoning process itself. The rules are relationships between facts, and will be used to derive new beliefs (*derived beliefs*) from the agent's existing beliefs.

The agent's beliefs are then represented in predicate logic, in the form of literals and Horn clause rules. The rules have the form $\alpha_1 \& \alpha_2 \ldots \& \alpha_n \rightarrow \beta$ where $\alpha_1, \alpha_2, \ldots, \alpha_n (n \geq 1), \beta$ are literals. β is called the derived belief, and each α_i is a premise of the rule. The & represents the logical *and* operator.

3   Belief Revision

3.1   AGM Belief Revision

Belief revision is the process of modifying the belief base to maintain its consistency whenever new information becomes available. The AGM belief revision theory [8] defines postulates that a rational agent should satisfy when performing belief revision. In such theory, a belief base is closed under logical consequence. We consider a belief base K and a new piece of information α. K is inconsistent, when both α and $\neg\alpha$ are in $Cn(K)$, or $Cn(K) = \bot$, or both α and $\neg\alpha$ are logical consequences of K. Three operators are considered: *Expansion* $K + \alpha$: adds a new belief α that does not contradict with the existing beliefs. *Contraction* $K \div$

α: removes a belief α and all other beliefs that logically imply/entail it. *Revision* $K * \alpha$: adds a belief α as long as it does not cause contradiction in K. If the addition will cause inconsistencies in K, the revision operation starts by minimal changes in K to make it consistent with α, then adds α. In particular, if the agent has to contract a belief α, it does not contract other beliefs that derived α, as long they are consistent with the remaining beliefs (*minimal change*) – *coherence approach* [9].

The AGM framework comprises sets of postulates to be respected by these operators to ensure consistent and minimal belief revision.

On another side, the Reason-maintenance belief revision approach considers tracking dependencies between beliefs, so that the reason(s) for believing in a belief α can be traced. When α should be given up, the agent must ensure that α is no longer derivable and give up believing the things that derived it.

3.2   Partial Entrenchment Ranking

A belief is gradual and an agent might have beliefs more entrenched (or accepted) than others. Williams [10] have proposed a quantitative approach for the AGM framework, by developing finite partial entrenchment rankings to represent epistemic entrenchment – a piece of information is labelled by a degree of confidence denoting how strongly we believe it. The epistemic entrenchment [11] captures the notions of significance, firmness, or defeasibility of beliefs.

Epistemic entrenchment relations induce preference orderings of beliefs according to the importance of these beliefs in the face of change. If inconsistency arises during a belief revision operation, the least significant beliefs (i.e., beliefs with the lowest entrenchment degree) are given up in order to restore consistency.

3.3   Tracking Beliefs and Preferences

We present in this section the approach proposed by Alechina *et al.* [12] to track beliefs and calculate their preference for rule-based agents. The core of their work was a proposition for belief revision and contraction for such agents which are a synthesis of AGM and reason maintenance styles. The details of their algorithms will not be described here as they do not fit the purpose of the paper. The authors considered preferences on beliefs, assuming that a user might prefer some beliefs over others. Those preferences are used to decide which belief(s) should be removed to restore consistency.

The dependency between beliefs is considered as follows. For every fired rule instance, a Justification J will record: (i) a belief α, which corresponds to the derived belief and (ii) a *support list*, s, which contains the premises of the rules (contextual beliefs of a plan used to derive α). The dependency information of a belief had the form of two lists: *dependencies* and *justifications*. A *dependencies list* records the justifications of a belief, and a *justifications list* contains all the Justifications where the belief is a member of a support.

They define preferences using a notion of quality associated with justifications, assuming the quality of a justification is represented by non-negative integers in the range 0, ..., m, where the value of 0 means lowest quality and m means the highest quality. The lower the value, the least the quality.

Definition 1. *The preference value of a belief α, $p(\alpha)$, is equal to that of its highest quality justification.*

$$p(\alpha) = \max\{qual(J_0), \ldots, qual(J_n)\} \tag{1}$$

Definition 2. *The quality of justification J, $qual(J)$, is equal to the preference of the least preferred belief in its support list.*

$$qual(J) = \min\{p(\alpha) : \alpha \in \text{support of } J\} \tag{2}$$

Literals with no supports (or empty support) are assigned the lowest quality. An *a priori* quality is assigned to each justification with empty support.

4   Knowledge Extraction from Documents - RAKE

The RAKE (Rapid Automatic Keyword Extraction) [7] is an unsupervised, domain-independent, and language-independent method used for extracting keywords from documents.

RAKE starts its extraction on a document by parsing the text into a set of candidate keywords. First, the document text is split into an array of words by specified word delimiters. This array is then split into sequences of contiguous words at phrase delimiters and stop word positions. Words within a sequence are assigned the same position in the text and together are considered a candidate keyword. After every candidate keyword is identified and the graph of word co-occurrences is complete, a score is calculated for each candidate keyword. The method evaluates several metrics for calculating word scores, based on the degree and frequency of word vertices in the graph: (1) word frequency *freq(w)*, (2) word degree *deg(w)*, and (3) ratio of degree to frequency *deg(w)/freq(w)*.

RAKE also identifies keywords that contain interior stop words such as *axis of evil*. To find these, it looks for pairs of keywords that adjoin one another at least twice in the same document and in the same order. A new candidate keyword is then created as a combination of those keywords and their interior stop words. The score for the new keyword is the sum of its member keyword scores. After candidate keywords are scored, the top one-third scoring candidates are selected as keywords for the document.

5   Proposed Framework

Our framework proposes a rule-based agent for Information Retrieval systems that uses its cognitive abilities to acquire beliefs about its user's knowledge to customise the returned results. When the IR agent has α in its belief base, it believes that the user knows that α is true. If the belief base contains $\neg\alpha$, then the agent believes the user knows that α is not true. When neither α nor $\neg\alpha$ is in the belief base, the agent believes neither the user knows α is true nor the user knows that α is false.

The user knowledge is extracted from the documents he/she has examined and the rules are acquired through the integration with external entities like semantic entities, ontology or knowledge mining tools. We represent the contextual rules by Horn clause rules and consider them static. The origin of the rules is not discussed in this paper; this is left for future work.

As belief is gradual, we adopt the partial entrenchment approach briefly discussed in Sect. 3.2 to represent the degrees of the derived beliefs. The entrenchment degree for a derived belief will be calculated based on the premises of the rule that derived it. The degrees of the extracted beliefs instead, will be calculated based on the score of the corresponding keywords in the document. The beliefs can be revised and the relations between them are tracked as proposed by the Alechina's approach and discussed in Sect. 3.3, i.e. by using the concept of *beliefs* and *justifications* with their related *preference degree value* and *quality of justification*.

Finally, we employ the agent beliefs to return filtered results to the user.

5.1   Model Architecture

In this section, we present a client-side web search agent implementing the methods discussed in the previous sections to personalize search while learning about the user knowledge. The agent can be a browser plugin acting as a proxy for web search engines or a filter built on top of existing search applications.

By running the agent on the client-side, no information about the user behaviour and activity is released to the outside as they all reside on his/her computer. Also, in terms of server scalability and efficiency, the model distributes computation and storage among its users rather than centralising them.

The framework has 3 main modules: (1) rule-based module, modeling the beliefs and rules. It performs inference reasoning about the user's knowledge and revise its beliefs if needed, to maintain consistency. (2) Knowledge extractor module, extracting knowledge from the documents examined by the user. (3) Result filtering module; selecting the "useful" documents to be proposed to the user. These modules work together, as follows, for every submitted query: (i) the system sends the query to the search engine/application, (ii) receives the result from the search engine, and (iii) filters them by excluding those that are not useful to the user, according to the user knowledge. After the user has clicked on the results, the agent updates its beliefs about the knowledge supposed to be acquired by the user. Finally, a reasoning cycle is performed to run the applicable rules and revise the beliefs as needed.

5.2   Extracting Knowledge and Belief Entrenchment

The agent belief base is composed of the beliefs it learns about its user and of the contextual rules it owns. When the user reads a document d, the agent learns the user has acquired some knowledge about its content; so it uses some knowledge extraction/NLP tool to extract the representation of the document content. We use the RAKE method [7] as an easy and understandable method, to extract the keywords representing the document and calculate their related scores. The beliefs resulting from this process are referred to as *extracted beliefs*. As the keywords are associated to the agent beliefs, their related scores are associated to degrees of beliefs. We define the degree of a belief as follows:

Definition 3. *The degree of a belief α is the degree to which the agent believes the user is knowledgeable about α. It is represented by a decimal ranging between 0 and 1, where 0 means the lowest degree –the agent believes the user has absolutely no knowledge about α, and 1 means the highest degree –the agent believes the user has the maximum knowledge about α.*

Let us consider document $d = \{k_1, \ldots, k_n\}$. We suppose that a keyword k_i is associated with an extracted belief b_j whose degree is calculated as follows:

$$degree(b_j) = \lambda \cdot \frac{Rakescore(k_i)}{\max_{k_j \in d} Rakescore(k_j)}. \tag{3}$$

In Eq. 3 the score of an extracted RAKE keyword is first divided by the highest keyword score of the document: the score is hence normalized. It is then multiplied by an adjustment factor $\lambda \in [0, 1]$. The adjustment factor is used to weaken the magnitude of the scores: when λ is equal to 1, the "top score" keyword of all examined documents will be assumed to have the maximal degree 1, which means that the agent assumes the user has the maximal knowledge about this keyword. The adjustment factor may vary based on different characteristics such as the source of the document, for example.

A *derived belief* is the belief resulting from firing the agent's rules. The dependency between the beliefs is tracked by the concept of justification and dependencies lists as per Alechina's approach presented in Sect. 3.3. Our definition of degree of derived beliefs is inspired by their notion of preference. Indeed, we use Eq. 1 to calculate the degree of a derived belief, and Eq. 2 to calculate the quality of a justification.

5.3   Revising Beliefs

While the agent is acquiring more information about the user, it is adding beliefs to its belief base. The beliefs might be new, already existing, or contradicting with the existing ones; that calls for the need of revising beliefs to ensure the belief base is consistent. The belief revision approach we have adopted here combines the AGM and reason-maintenance styles while tracking the beliefs.

In case of contradiction between a pair of beliefs, we give preference to the more entrenched one, i.e. the belief with the highest degree. Our model does not contract a belief α unless a more preferred contradictory belief $\neg\alpha$ was added. When contracting a belief α, we don't see a need to contract beliefs that derived α: when the rule deriving α tries to add it again, the addition will be discarded because it will be faced by $\neg\alpha$ that is more preferred. In other terms, we contract the belief in question with its related justification(s), without contracting neither the rule's premises nor the rule itself. For example, consider an agent's belief base:

$$B = \{astronomy[0.8], astronomy \rightarrow planet(pluto)\}.$$

The agent reasoning will result in the execution of the rule and therefore adding *planet(pluto)* with an entrenchment degree of 0.8. Suppose the agent was later informed that the agent believes pluto is not a planet, assuming the degree of entrenchment of the related belief is 0.9. The agent attempts to add $\neg planet(pluto)[0.9]$ in its belief base. Upon revising the beliefs, *planet(pluto)* is contracted and $\neg planet(pluto)$ is added, since the belief with the higher degree is given priority. However, when *planet(pluto)* is removed, the fact that the user knows about astronomy does not change: the belief *astronomy* is not contracted. The related rule remains in the belief base as well.

5.4 Document Similarity and Result Filtering

The filtering process will be dependent on the similarity between the agent's current beliefs and the documents to be proposed to the user.

We propose a similarity function, $Sim(B, d)$, that calculates this similarity measure based on the degrees of the intersected beliefs and the document knowledge. The formula is inspired by the similarity function proposed by Lau *et al.* in [13]. We consider a set of beliefs $B = \{b_1, b_2, \ldots, b_m\}$ and a document $d = \{k_1, k_2, \ldots, k_n\}$ characterized by a set of keywords representing the content. Let us consider S, the set of keywords appearing both in d and in B defined by $S = \{k_i \in d : extent(B, k_i) > 0 \vee extent(B, \neg k_i) > 0\}$.

$$Sim(B, d) = \begin{cases} \dfrac{\max\{\sum_{k_i \in d}[extent(B, k_i)) - extent(B, \neg k_i)], 0\}}{|S|} & \text{if } |S| \neq 0 \\ 0 \text{ otherwise.} \end{cases} \quad (4)$$

The $extent(B, k) = degree(k)$, if $k \in B$; and 0 otherwise. The $degree(k)$ is calculated as discussed in Sect. 5.2. The similarity formula "rewards" the documents containing keywords that are in the set B.

We set a cutoff value γ that allows to decide whether the knowledge inside a document is similar to a set of beliefs or not. The filter is used according to the intended application: when the purpose of framework is to reinforce the user knowledge, then documents that are "near" the agent beliefs will be returned returned. The documents having a similarity score greater than the cutoff will be returned as the final results to the user. Contrarily, when the framework is employed for novelty purposes, the documents having similarity below the cutoff will be returned.

6   Conclusion and Future Work

In this paper, we proposed an innovative framework for a rule-based information retrieval agent which relies on its cognitive abilities to learn about the user's knowledge, and propose new/relevant documents accordingly.

The components of the framework are: (1) rule-based module, modeling the agent's beliefs and rules. It performs inference reasoning about the user's knowledge and revise its beliefs if needed, to maintain consistency. (2) Knowledge extractor module, extracting knowledge from the documents examined by the user. (3) Result filtering module, selecting the "useful" documents to be proposed to the user.

The process of acquisition of information is session and time independent. Another advantage of the proposed framework is that it can be built on top of existing non-cognitive search engines, applications, or open-source libraries.

As for future work, we plan to take into account the confidence in the sources of the documents, which will probably affect the degree of entrenchment of a belief. Another possible extension could be to integrate some semantic analysis in order to deal with synonyms.

References

1. Pasi, G., Bordogna, G., Villa, R.: A multi-criteria content-based filtering system, pp. 775–776, January 2007
2. da Costa Pereira, C., Dragoni, M., Pasi, G.: Multidimensional relevance: A new aggregation criterion, pp. 264–275, April 2009
3. Móra, M., Lopes, G., Maria Vicari, R., Coelho, H.: BDI models and systems: Bridging the gap, pp. 11–27, January 1998
4. Culpepper, J.S., Diaz, F., Smucker, M.D.: Research frontiers in information retrieval: Report from the third strategic workshop on information retrieval in Lorne (SWIRL 2018). In: SIGIR Forum, vol. 52, issue no 1, pp. 34–90 (2018)
5. Maron.: Mechanized documentation: The logic behind a probabilistic interpretation. National Bureau of Standards Miscellaneous Publications (1964)
6. Cholvy, L., da Costa Pereira, C.: Usefulness of information for goal achievement. In: Baldoni, M., Dastani, M., Liao, B., Sakurai, Y., Zalila Wenkstern, R. (eds.) PRIMA 2019. LNCS (LNAI), vol. 11873, pp. 123–137. Springer, Cham (2019). https://doi.org/10.1007/978-3-030-33792-6_8
7. Rose, S., Engel, D., Cramer, N., Cowley, W.: Automatic Keyword Extraction from Individual Documents, pp. 1–20, March 2010
8. Alchourrón, C.E., Gärdenfors, P., Makinson, D.: On the logic of theory change: partial meet contraction and revision functions. J. Symb. Log. **50**(2), 510–530 (1985)
9. Gärdenfors, P.: Belief revision: An introduction, Series. Cambridge Tracts in Theoretical Computer Science. Cambridge University Press, pp. 1–28 (1992)
10. Williams, M.-A.: Iterated theory base change: A computational model, pp. 1541–1549, Januaray 1995

11. Gärenfors, P., Makinson, D.: Revisions of knowledge systems using epistemic entrenchment, pp. 83–95, March 1988
12. Alechina, N., Jago, M., Logan, B.: Preference-based belief revision for rule-based agents. Synthese **165**, 159–177 (2008). https://doi.org/10.1007/s11229-008-9364-0
13. Lau, R., Bruza, P., Song, D.: Belief revision for adaptive information retrieval, July 2004

Deep Reinforcement Learning
for Pedestrian Guidance

Hitoshi Shimizu[1,2](✉), Takanori Hara[2], and Tomoharu Iwata[1]

[1] NTT Communication Science Laboratories, Kyoto, Japan
{hitoshi.shimizu.kg,tomoharu.iwata.gy}@hco.ntt.co.jp
[2] Nara Institute of Science and Technology, Nara, Japan
hara.takanori.hm8@is.naist.jp

Abstract. In large-scale events where many people gather, providing them with appropriate, efficient, and safe guidance about where to proceed is critical to ease congestion. We can evaluate guidance candidates using a pedestrian flow simulator to find appropriate guidance. However, evaluating many candidates by simulation requires high computational cost, which prohibits real-time guidance. We propose a method that finds appropriate guidance in real-time for observed situations based on deep reinforcement learning. Our proposed method learns a function that outputs appropriate guidance given the observed situation to minimize the average travel time of pedestrians. The difficulty here is that the real-world measurements of pedestrian travel time are limited due to privacy issues since it tracks individuals. Though our method uses only the observation obtained without locating specific individuals: the number of pedestrians who are moving on roads, it is guaranteed by Little's law to be equivalent to minimizing the average travel time. Our experimental results for unknown pedestrian flow show that our proposed method outperforms rule-based controls, and its guidance is as effective as one selected from many candidates by repeated simulations with massive computational cost.

Keywords: Crowd simulation · Reinforcement learning · Pedestrian guidance

1 Introduction

At large-scale events where thousands of people gather, appropriate, safe, and efficient guidance must be provided to ease congestion. To find appropriate guidance, we can evaluate guidance candidates on a pedestrian flow simulator. Yamashita et al. [9] developed a technique that simulated all candidates exhaustively. To search for better guidance with fewer simulations, Otsuka et al. [5] proposed to use Bayesian optimization (BO), and Shigenaka et al. [6] proposed to use Covariance Matrix Adaptation Evolution Strategy (CMA-ES). Although both BO and CMA-ES methods require fewer simulations than an exhaustive

© Springer Nature Switzerland AG 2021
T. Uchiya et al. (Eds.): PRIMA 2020, LNAI 12568, pp. 334–342, 2021.
https://doi.org/10.1007/978-3-030-69322-0_22

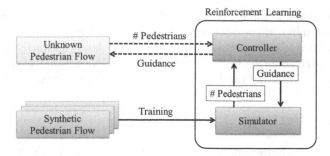

Fig. 1. Our proposed scheme achieves pedestrian flow control using deep reinforcement learning and simulator. Using the observed number of pedestrians on the roads as a reward and observations, the Controller learns with various kinds of simulated pedestrian flow data. After training, it can output appropriate guidance for unknown pedestrian flows.

search, many evaluations with simulators are unavoidable and prohibit real-time guidance for unknown pedestrian flow.

Therefore we proposed a new scheme shown in Fig. 1. Our method uses a crowd simulation and reinforcement learning [7], which maximizes the *reward* obtained by selecting the *action* based on the *state* observed by the agent. By learning with various kinds of simulated pedestrian flow data (shown as *Synthetic Pedestrian Flow* in the Fig. 1), our proposed method outputs guidance for unknown pedestrian flows (shown as *Unknown Pedestrian Flow* in the Fig. 1). We experimentally demonstrate the effectiveness of our proposed method using a pedestrian flow simulator and consider an example problem that identifies which roads to block and encourages detours when the number of pedestrians on each road is observed as input.

We evaluate the guidance by the average travel time of pedestrians, where shorter average travel time is better guidance. However, since pedestrian travel times must track individuals, such measurements are often not provided due to privacy concerns. Aggregated data are more readily available because it does not locate specific individuals. As shown in the Fig. 1 as $\boxed{\text{\# Pedestrians}}$ between *Controller* and *Simulator*, our method uses the observed number of pedestrians on the roads as a reward and a state, which is one type of aggregated data. Minimizing the number of pedestrians is guaranteed by Little's law to be equivalent to minimizing the average travel times.

Kato et al. [2] proposed a method to guide pedestrians from the fireworks event venue to the station. Their method also uses a crowd simulation and reinforcement learning. However, their proposed method depends on the road network, which makes it difficult to adjust the parameters. Because the reward of our proposed scheme is normalized, it has the advantage of being independent of the road network.

Our contributions are the followings: (1) To handle such congestion situations in real-time, we propose a method that learns a function with a deep RL that outputs appropriate guidance based on observations. (2) The proposed reward based on the number of pedestrians has no privacy issues, and is guaranteed to be equivalent to the average travel time by Little's law. (3) Experiment results show that its performance exceeds a rule-based guidance policy and comes close to one selected from many candidates by repeated simulations.

2   Problem Settings

We consider a situation where many people start walking at different times from different beginning points to different end points by roads. The controller agent selects a guidance (action) from a set of actions at each time step. The task is to find the sequence of guidance that minimizes the average travel times of people $\frac{1}{I}\sum_{i=1}^{I}\tau_i$, where τ_i is the travel time of pedestrian i and I is the number of pedestrians. The definitions of each symbol in the paper are summarized in Table 1.

3   Proposed Method

The total travel time of pedestrians is equivalent to the time integral of the number of them moving at each time. This relationship, which is called Little's law [3], is shown in Fig. 2. Gray area S enclosed by the red line that indicates the cumulative number of departures and the blue line that indicates the cumulative number of arrivals at each time can be expressed by two types of expressions: $S = \sum_{i=1}^{I}\tau_i = \int_{t=0}^{T} N_t dt \approx \sum_{t=1}^{T} N_t \Delta$, where N_t is the number of moving pedestrians at time t and Δ is the interval between adjacent time steps. $\sum_{t=1}^{T} N_t \Delta$ is the summation for the time direction, and $\sum_{i=1}^{I}\tau_i$ is the summation for each pedestrian. Approximation is acceptable when Δ is small enough for fluctuation in N_t. Therefore, average travel time $\frac{1}{I}\sum_{i=1}^{I}\tau_i = \frac{S}{I}$ can be minimized by taking actions that minimize the total number of pedestrians traveling at each time $\sum_{t=1}^{T} N_t = \frac{S}{\Delta}$ because I and Δ are constants.

   Little's law holds even for a single pedestrian. The tasks of minimizing the time for a moving object to reach its goal have frequently been addressed in the history of reinforcement learning [7]. The Little's law discussed here clarifies that a small negative reward to each step usually leads to the shortest travel time[1]. Our proposed method will be useful for tasks where a moving object must reach its goal in the shortest time.

   In addition, if the absolute values of the rewards widely vary, adjusting the other RL parameters is difficult. Therefore, the rewards must be normalized, for example, into a range of -1 to 1 (see Footnote 1). It is very difficult to assess how effective the currently selected strategy is without any evaluation criteria. Therefore, we propose a method to evaluate the relative effectiveness of the currently selected strategy by comparing it with the strategy that does

---

[1] https://github.com/Unity-Technologies/ml-agents/blob/master/docs/Learning-Environment-Best-Practices.md.

not do anything (no strategy). Thus we propose the reward EDGE/OPEN shown in Table 4. This reward satisfies $-1 \leq r_t \leq 1$, and $r_t = 1$ when $N_t = 0$, and it satisfies $r_t = 0$ when $N_t = N_t^o$ if $N_t^o > 0$.

In the case that the number of pedestrians is observed for the reward, using the observation as the state is more convenient and efficient. To measure the number of pedestrians, just measuring their total does not identify where the congestion is occurring. Also, observing the number of people only at one time step does not tell whether their number is increasing or decreasing. For example, we can use the number of pedestrians on each road of multiple time steps as the state.

4 Experiments

We evaluated our proposed method on a task as an example that finds guidance to ease congestion around the entrance at the start of a big event. We used an in-house crowd simulator [5], where pedestrians move on the road network. Figure 3 shows the road network around Japan National Stadium in Tokyo, which is the stage of the simulation. Pedestrians start to walk from six stations to the stadium's six gates, and are crowded on the roads in front of the gates. Pedestrians pass through 317 roads. For a state, we used the number of pedestrians on these roads for the past four steps, which give a 1268-dimensional vector.

The number of pedestrians in one scenario ranged from 10,000 to 90,000 in 10,000 increments. In each scenario, the proportion of stations where pedestrians appear was varied using random numbers from a Dirichlet distribution. The expected value was set as the ratio of Table 2 by referring to the actual number

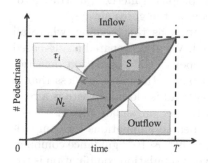

Fig. 2. Little's law: red line represents cumulative number of departures, and blue line represents cumulative number of arrivals. Red and blue lines eventually meet at (T, I), where let T be the time when the last person arrives. S is the gray area surrounded by red and blue lines. (Color figure online)

Table 1. Notation

Symbol	Description
I	number of pedestrians in system: $i \in \{1, \cdots, I\}$
J	number of roads: $j \in \{1, \cdots, J\}$
T	number of time steps: $t \in \{1, \cdots, T\}$
Δ	intervals between adjacent time steps
N_t	number of moving pedestrians at time t
N_t^o	the total number of pedestrians on the roads with the strategy that does not do anything
v_t^i	velocity of pedestrian i at time t
ρ_t^i	density of a road in front of pedestrian i at time t
ρ_t^j	averaged density of a road j at time t
x_t^j	number of pedestrians on road j at time t
τ_i	travel time of pedestrian i

Fig. 3. Ratio of pedestrians emerging from each station.

Table 2. Ratio of pedestrians emerging from each station.

Station ID	Usage ratio of pedestrians
1	29%
2	11%
3	6%
4	11%
5	20%
6	22%

Table 3. Maximum number of people who pass each second at each gate.

Gate ID	Throughput [person/sec]
A	3
B	8
C	3
D	3
E	5
F	3

of station users. The timing of the pedestrians emerging from the station was distributed, so that they peaked 30 min after the start of simulation. At its entrance, assuming that the number of security staff varies depending on the gate, the maximum number of people who pass through it per second were set (Table 3).

We consider a guidance that temporarily closes the gate to avoid congestion at it. When a gate is closed, we assumed that pedestrians head to the nearest open gate. Since there are six gates, there are $2^6 = 64$ open and closed combinations. However, we added a constraint that no more than two adjacent gates can be closed simultaneously to avoid long detours. Then we have 39 guidance candidates. Guidance lasts at least ten minutes, and a different guidance can be selected every ten minutes. The simulation time is set to 250 min to allow all pedestrians to enter the stadium regardless of which guidance to choose. Guidances are selected 25 times per episode. In the proposed method, a strategy of doing nothing (no strategy) corresponds to open all the gates always.

We compared the proposed method with OPEN as the baseline, where all gates are always open and no guidance is applied. We also prepared a rule-based guidance shown as RULE, where all gates are open if the population densities (number of people/road area) of all roads in front of the gates are less than a threshold, and the gate with the highest density road is closed if there is a road above the threshold. The threshold was set to 1.0 person/square meter.

GREEDY shows the guidance obtained by repeated simulations for comparison. With 25 time steps and 39 actions, there are $39^{25} \sim 10^{40}$ guidance combinations. Since the computation time to execute every simulation combination is too long, GREEDY starts from OPEN and tries all the actions at each time step, and then adopts the best action sequentially in chronological order. FIX randomly selects the guidance policy obtained by GREEDY for test scenarios, regardless of the actual scenario. We also prepared the comparing methods with various rewards shown in Table 4, referring to the study of RL in traffic signal control. Note that there is privacy issues if its expression contains τ_i.

As a learning model, we used a state-of-the-art RL method called Advantage Actor-Critic (A2C) [4,8], which learns based on the experiences gained after every episode is completed. The value function $(V(x))$ and the action-value function $(Q(x, a))$ were approximated by a common neural network with two hidden layers, each of which has 100 units. We used the ReLU function [1] to make each layer output nonlinear, and actions were sampled by softmax function of Q-value during training.

5   Results

Figure 4 shows the average travel time for each episode when training with the rewards in Table 4. We used 16 training scenarios, which consist of eight different amounts of pedestrians ranging from 10,000 to 80,000, each with two different station use ratios. We performed 200 episodes × 16 simulations scenarios for training: 3,200 times for each deep RL. Within 200 episodes, the average travel time of EDGE/OPEN, SPEED, TIME/OPEN, and TIMEONCE/OPEN converge stably to smaller values than others.

We created 90 test scenarios, consisting of nine groups whose number of pedestrians ranged from 10,000 to 90,000 in 10,000 increments, which is not included in the training data. Table 5 shows the result of applying the guidances to the test scenarios. Figure 5 shows the breakdown of the average travel time by the number of pedestrians. Both Table 5 and Fig. 5 are evaluated as a ratio of OPEN. Although the average travel time of FIX resembled that of RULE, its effect was less effective than GREEDY. Note that the GREEDY and FIX methods need iterative evaluations ($39 \times 25 = 975$ times of simulations) for the target scenario. These results required about 25 min to execute 39 parallel simulations 25 times.

Although TIME/OPEN was the best RL results in Table 5, it is problematic due to privacy issues. SPEED also gives good results when I is large; its performance

Table 4. (left) Rewards for deep RL. Rewards with /OPEN use the result of OPEN for normalizing.

Name	Reward
EDGE/OPEN (proposed method)	$\max\left(-1, \frac{N_t^o - N_t}{N_t^o}\right)$ if $N_t^o > 0$ 0 if $N_t^o = 0$ and $N_t = 0$ -1 if $N_t^o = 0$ and $N_t > 0$
EDGE	$(I - N_t)/I$
TIMEONCE/OPEN	$(\sum_i \tau_i^o - \tau_i)/\sum_i \tau_i^o$ if $t = T$ 0 if $t \neq T$
TIMEONCE	$-\sum_i \tau_i / TI$ if $t = T$ 0 if $t \neq T$
TIME/OPEN	$\sum_i \frac{\tau_i^o - \tau_i}{\tau_i^o} \mathbb{1}((t-1)\Delta < \tau_i \leq t\Delta)$
GOAL	$\frac{1}{I}\sum_i^I \mathbb{1}((t-1)\Delta < \tau_i \leq t\Delta)$
GOALCUM	$\frac{1}{I}\sum_i^I \mathbb{1}(\tau_i \leq t\Delta)$
SPEED	$(\bar{v}^{\max} - v_t)/\bar{v}^{\max}$, where $\bar{v}^{\max} = \frac{1}{I}\sum_i^I v_i^{\max}$ and $v_t = \frac{1}{N_t}\sum_j x_t^j \times v(\rho_j)$

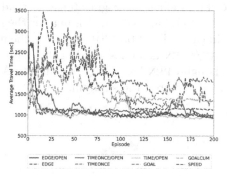

Fig. 4. (right) Evaluation values in episodes during training of reinforcement learning. Horizontal axis is number of episodes. Vertical axis is average travel time.

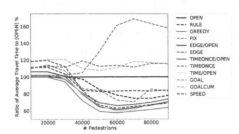

Table 5. (right) Average ratio of travel time to OPEN for each method for 90 scenarios. Ref. represents reference methods for comparison. OPEN took 1493.2 [s] on average. Bold indicates results that are not significantly different from best result (TIME/OPEN) except for GREEDY in paired t-test ($p < 0.05$).

Fig. 5. (left) Evaluation of each method against test data. Horizontal axis is number of pedestrians. Vertical axis is ratio of average travel time to OPEN. Each point is the average of the results of 10 test data.

	Method	Ratio to OPEN %
Ref.	RULE	87.5
	GREEDY	74.1
	FIX	90.4
RL: reward	EDGE/OPEN	**79.8**
	EDGE	91.9
	TIMEONCE/OPEN	80.8
	TIMEONCE	113.7
	TIME/OPEN	**79.0**
	GOAL	132.5
	GOALCUM	115.5
	SPEED	85.0

is poor when I is small (Fig. 5). This method increases the moving speed by increasing users of the detours, which may cause extra travel time. Therefore, our proposed EDGE/OPEN yields the best result as the RL reward. The time required for the method to make a decision was about 5 ms each time, which was much smaller than GREEDY (25 min), and satisfies the demand for real-time use.

In Figs. 4 and 5, we can compare the solid line (with /OPEN) and dashed lines (without /OPEN) of the same color. These results show that normalization with /OPEN is effective. Figure 6 shows road conditions in the same simulations of EDGE/OPEN and OPEN. 40 min after the start, the pedestrians did not select gate D in OPEN, but EDGE/OPEN guides them to it by closing other gates. At 80 min, EDGE/OPEN has lines at five gates with better balance than OPEN. At 120 min, although OPEN has a long line at gate A, most pedestrians of EDGE/OPEN have already entered the stadium.

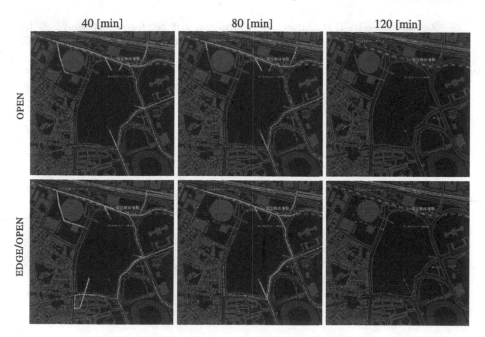

Fig. 6. $I = 80000$. Average travel times of OPEN and EDGE/OPEN were 2481.0 and 1658.3 [s], respectively. Dot colors represent pedestrian speeds: blue is fast and red is slow. Red lines in front of gates are pedestrian lines for entry. (Color figure online)

References

1. Glorot, X., Bordes, A., Bengio, Y.: Deep sparse rectifier neural networks. In: Proceedings of the Fourteenth International Conference on Artificial Intelligence and Statistics (AISTATS), pp. 315–323 (2011)
2. Kato, Y., Shigenaka, S., Nishida, R., Onishi, M.: Real-time pedestrian control by reinforcement learning. In: Proceedings of the 64th Annual Conference of the Institute of Systems, Control and Information Engineers (ISCIE), pp. 312–316 (2020)
3. Little, J.D., Graves, S.C.: Little's law. In: Building Intuition, pp. 81–100. Springer (2008)
4. Mnih, V., et al.: Asynchronous methods for deep reinforcement learning. In: Proceedings of International Conference on Machine Learning (ICML), pp. 1928–1937 (2016)
5. Otsuka, T., Shimizu, H., Iwata, T., Naya, F., Sawada, H., Ueda, N.: Bayesian optimization for crowd traffic control using multi-agent simulation. In: Proceedings of the 22st International Conference on Intelligent Transportation Systems (ITSC), IEEE (2019)
6. Shigenaka, S., Takami, S., Ozaki, Y., Onishi, M., Yamashita, T., Noda, I.: Evaluation of optimization for pedestrian route guidance in real-world crowded scene. In: Proceedings of the 18th International Conference on Autonomous Agents and MultiAgent Systems (AAMAS), pp. 2192–2194. IFAAMAS (2019)
7. Sutton, R.S., Barto, A.G.: Reinforcement Learning: An Introduction. MIT press, Cambridge (2018)

8. Xu, Z., van Hasselt, H.P., Silver, D.: Meta-gradient reinforcement learning. In: Advances in Neural Information Processing Systems (NeurIPS), pp. 2396–2407 (2018)
9. Yamashita, T., Okada, T., Noda, I.: Implementation of simulation environment for exhaustive analysis of huge-scale pedestrian flow. SICE J. Control Meas. Syst. Integr. **6**(2), 137–146 (2013). https://doi.org/10.9746/jcmsi.6.137

NegMAS: A Platform for Automated Negotiations

Yasser Mohammad[1,2,3]($\boxtimes$), Shinji Nakadai[1,2], and Amy Greenwald[4]

[1] NEC Corporation, Tokyo, Japan
{y.mohammad,nakadai}@nec.com
[2] National Institute of Advanced Industrial Science and Technology (AIST),
Tokyo, Japan
[3] Assiut University, Asyut, Egypt
[4] Brown University, Providence, USA
amy_greenwald@brown.edu

Abstract. Alongside the widespread adoption of AI technology throughout the business world, automated negotiation is similarly gaining more interest within the multiagent system (MAS) research community. This interest has prompted the development of research-oriented automated negotiation platforms like GENIUS. This paper introduces NegMAS, Negotiations Managed by Agent Simulations/Negotiation MultiAgent System, which was developed to facilitate research and development of agents that negotiate in dynamic situations characterized by interrelated utility functions with all negotiation related decisions managed by agents.

1 Introduction

Negotiation is one of the most prevalent methods for reaching agreements between self-interested parties. In automated negotiation, autonomous (software) agents negotiate among themselves, or with human negotiators, on behalf of their users. Negotiation research can be traced back to the seminal work of Nash on bargaining theory [17], and Rubinstein's analysis of the alternating offers protocol in the perfect-information case [18], both major game-theoretic advances. More recently, research in automated negotiations has attracted researchers in multi-agent systems (e.g., [6]) and machine learning (e.g., [20]).

Few platforms have been designed to support research in automated negotiations. The de-facto standard platform is the General Environment for Negotiation with Intelligent multi-purpose Usage Simulation (GENIUS) [14]. GENIUS was designed to facilitate research in automated negotiation by providing an extensive analytic toolkit for developers. Since 2010, it has since been the official platform for the Automated Negotiating Agents Competition (ANAC). By serving in this capacity, it has accrued a large number of negotiation strategies and domains, making it an indispensable tool for researchers in automated

© Springer Nature Switzerland AG 2021
T. Uchiya et al. (Eds.): PRIMA 2020, LNAI 12568, pp. 343–351, 2021.
https://doi.org/10.1007/978-3-030-69322-0_23

negotiation. The platform has been available as an open-source project since 2018[1].

A related open-source project that was released in 2019 is the GeniusWeb [2] platform, which provides an open architecture for negotiation over the internet. Based on GENIUS, it shares most of its core strengths (i.e., availability of an extensive analytic toolbox, multiple built-in negotiation strategies and domains, etc.), but it further provides flexibility in the way agents can be implemented and deployed.

Yet another negotiation related platform is the *Invite* platform, developed for research and training purposes by Concordia University [12]. Like the pocket negotiator project [11], the main focus of this platform is supporting human-human negotiations.

Commercial platforms in the form of negotiation support systems are also being developed. One such example is ContractRoom [1]. This platform provides easy-to-use tools that enable human negotiators to reach agreements faster, such as a mechanism that facilitates online collaboration. This mechanism is augmented with artificial intelligence, but is still mostly a human-human negotiation support system; it does not venture into the realm of automated negotiations.

All of these platforms assume a static negotiation situation in that the set of issues and the utility functions are fixed throughout the negotiation session. Moreover, they provide little support for interdependent negotiation sessions, which are required to model situations that involve concurrent negotiations and dynamic utility functions. We believe that the primary missing feature that can help overcome most, if not all, of the limitations of existing platforms is the ability to embody negotiations within a rich simulation environment, where utility functions arise endogenously and interdepend across concurrent negotiations. Such *situated negotiations* are closer to reality, so a platform that supports them can provide a bridge between state-of-the-art automated negotiation research and real-world applications.

The main contribution of this paper is the introduction of the Negotiations Managed by Agent Simulations/Negotiation MultiAgent System (NegMAS) platform, which was designed to model situated negotiations, thereby handling most of the aforementioned shortcomings with existing automated negotiation platforms.

NegMAS is intended to complement existing automated negotiation platforms (e.g., GENIUS) by addressing the structural issues stemming from the specific nature of situated negotiations. Moreover, NegMAS is developed as an open-source public project; as such, it is open to contributions from the whole research community. It provides a common API that supports multiple programming language (currently python and Java). Finally, it is designed to work either as a stand-alone system or as a client to a distributed system, implementing the same API, thus providing a scalable solution.

The rest of this paper is organized as follows: Sect. 2 presents details of the design philosophy and design decisions made in NegMAS to support situated negotiations. Section 3 summarizes the analytic tools available in NegMAS. Section 4 describes an example application developed using NegMAS.

---

[1] NegMAS is available at https://www.github.com/yasserfarouk/negmas.

2 System Design

This section presents an overview of NegMAS' key components and their interactions. As a general design principle, NegMAS is intended to make common cases easy to implement, with less common cases still possible, but assuming common default settings for most parameters of its components.

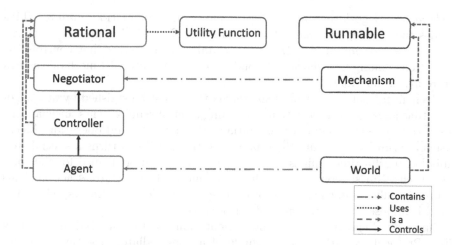

Fig. 1. Main entities in NegMAS and their relationships.

Rational and Runnable. The two main entities in NegMAS are *Rational* and *Runnable*. Rational entities have a form of self interest, represented by a utility function, which in turns, represents preferences. These include *Negotiators* for carrying out automated negotiations; *Controllers* for orchestrating multiple negotiations; and *Agents* for representing simulated entities (e.g., companies, individuals, etc).

Runnable entities represent processes in the environment. They control the flow of control. Currently NegMAS has two kinds of Runnable entities: *Mechanisms* to represent negotiations (or other agreement-seeking mechanisms like auctions; and *Worlds* to represent simulated worlds within which negotiations take place.

Worlds. The simulation environments within which agents operate in NegMAS are called *worlds*. As all worlds use the same interface, some common functionality is provided. These include a public bulletin board on which common information available to all agents in the world is posted, and summary statistics calculations. The world also provides contract persistence (i.e., saving contracts even after a simulation ends), name resolution services, logging, and statistics calculation.

Each world contains a simulator that is responsible for running the environment. Moreover, the world simulator executes all mechanisms within it. Agents can affect the simulation through actions that the world defines.

New world types can be created by inheriting the abstract *World* class and implementing its abstract methods. At a minimum, a single simulation step method needs to be implemented. The designer can also customize the speed of negotiations relative to the simulation speed, and the order of simulation operations (e.g., do negotiations happen throughout a step, only at its start, or only at its end?), among other things.

Mechanisms. Negotiations are conducted based on a negotiation *protocol*, which encodes the *rules of engagement* for negotiators. Negotiation protocols are the primary *mechanisms* in NegMAS. A mechanism is an entity that controls the interactions among negotiators. Beyond negotiation protocols, mechanisms can also represent auctions.

Mechanisms define a set of *requirements* that must be satisfied by any negotiator that joins them. In addition to defining a set of requirements, mechanisms also have to define two operations: initialization and a round operation. Mechanisms are run by executing the round operation until it returns a special stop symbol or until a time limit is reached. Time limits can be defined for the complete mechanism session or for each round and each negotiator's action. This feature simplifies implementation of *bounded rationality* negotiators, where the bound is imposed by computational considerations.

Currently, NegMAS includes implementations of the Stacked Alternating Offers Protocol (SAOP), as an example of a non-mediated negotiation protocol [3], the Single Text Negotiation Protocol as an example of a mediated protocol [10], the first-price and second-price auctions, as examples of one-shot mechanisms, and an English auction, as an example of a dynamic auction [19]. Adding new mechanisms to NegMAS involves implementing only a single method.

Agents. The main actor in NegMAS is the agent. An agent represents an autonomous entity that has well defined objectives (which can, but need not, be explicitly encoded in a utility function). Figure 1 shows an example of an agent, which, using a controller and two independent negotiators, is engaged in four simultaneous negotiations.

Agents in NegMAS interact within a simulation that is part of a *world*. Within a world, agents can access public information as well as their own private state, and can execute actions as well as engage in negotiations. Agents are responsible for deciding what negotiations to engage in, which utility functions to use, and how to change their utility functions based on changes in the world simulation, their internal state, or outcomes of other negotiations. Moreover, agents may have other activities not directly related to negotiation that are crucial to achieving their objectives. For example, an agent representing a factory manager needs to control the production lines in that factory based on results of its negotiations.

Negotiators. Negotiations occur between *negotiators*. All negotiator types define capabilities that are matched with the requirements of the negotiation protocol before agents are allowed to join negotiation mechanisms. This makes it possible to define negotiation strategies that are applicable across multiple negotiation protocols.

All negotiators define a set of callbacks that can be used to update the negotiator's internal state or behavior based on salient events during the negotiation, including the negotiation's start and end, a round's start and end, errors, and utility function updates.

It is not possible to define general purpose negotiators in NegMAS independent of a negotiation protocol. NegMAS provides implementations of simple negotiation strategies for the SAOP in the bilateral [5] and multilateral cases [3], including the time-based aspiration level strategy with exponential and polynomial aspiration functions [6], and the Naive version of the tit-for-tat strategy described in Baarslag, *et al.* [4].

Beyond these built-in negotiators, NegMAS can also access most negotiation agents defined in the GENIUS platform [14] through a GeniusNegotiator class that allows these agents to participate in negotiation sessions running on NegMAS. Note, however, that since NegMAS supports richer simulation environments than GENIUS, GENIUS negotiators are not always applicable: e.g., they assume static utility functions.

Controllers. Negotiators can participate in but one negotiation at a time. This means that they cannot support concurrent negotiations, which are characteristic of real-world negotiations. NegMAS thus provides a *controller* entity capable of orchestrating the behavior of multiple negotiators (its children). Any method that is implemented by the controller takes precedence over the same method implemented by any of its negotiators. This way, controllers can decide to delegate some of their activities to negotiators, while still maintaining centralized control.

Utility Functions. NegMAS provides the basic components necessary to model a wide swath of negotiation scenarios, including *Issues* and *Outcomes*, as well as a variety of utility functions. In contrast to existing negotiation environments, utility functions in NegMAS are active entities that evolve over time. They are implemented as objects in the standalone version, and as processes in the distributed version.

NegMAS supports three kinds of utility function interfaces: cardinal, comparative, and ranking. *Cardinal* utility functions need to implement a mapping from any possible outcome (or a partial outcome) to a utility value. Utility values can be real numbers or a probability distribution over real numbers (e.g. uniform, Gaussian, etc.). *Comparative* utility functions need to implement only a comparison operator between any two outcomes, allowing for indifference. *Ranking* utility functions need to implement a ranking function that returns, for any list of outcomes, a partial ordering over them.

Currently NegMAS supports the following types of cardinal utility functions (among others): linear utility functions, generalized additive independence models [7], hyperrectangle utility functions [9] and non-linear combinations thereof, and, more generally, any nonlinear mapping from the outcome space to utilities, implemented, for example, as an arbitrary neural network.

Each of these special cases of cardinal utility functions is represented in Neg-MAS as its own type, making it possible to implement case-specific algorithms. For example, finding the range of a linear utility function can be done exactly and more efficiently than finding the range of a non-linear utility function. Defining new types of cardinal utility functions involves overriding a single method.

General support for time-discounted cardinal utility functions, with both linear and exponential discounting, is also available. Moreover, NegMAS supports partial outcome specification for multi-dimensional outcome spaces, meaning specification of values for only a partial set of the outcomes, which is used in some mediated protocols [13].

3   Tools and Common Components

To develop effective negotiation algorithms, it is beneficial to designers to have at their disposal a variety of analytic tools for modeling the negotiation scenario and understanding the results of negotiations. NegMAS comes with a growing set of analytic tools that supports developers in this quest. Some of the most important tools available in NegMAS include: Pareto-front evaluation; methods for evaluating the Nash-bargaining, maximum-welfare, and other salient points in the outcome space. Moreover, NegMAS provides tools for outcome space modeling and parameterized generation of utility functions and simulation conditions.

Several visualization primitives are provided in NegMAS for visualizing world simulations, including negotiation requests, negotiation results, and contract signing and execution. Figure 2 shows the default visualization of a sample negotiation conducted between a seller and a buyer.

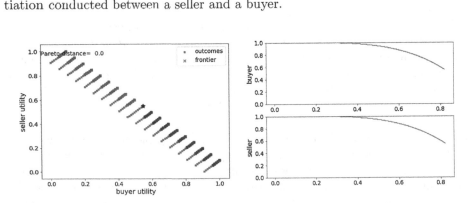

Fig. 2. An example of a negotiation showing the offers exchanged and the final agreement.

Additionally, several visualization options pertaining to the negotiation context are available to the developer. Figure 3 depicts one such example, where all negotiation-related events between different agents are shown as edges between vertices, the latter of which represent agents within a simulated world.

NegMAS provides a common tournament management interface which can be used to run tournaments among agents in any world by implementing just four components: a configuration generator to generate different world configurations, an assigner that assigns competitors to these worlds, a world generator that builds world simulations given configurations together with complete assignments, and a score calculator that calculates the scores of agents based on related world simulations.

4 Applications

NegMAS is still young, yet it is already being used actively for research and development of negotiation agents. It was used in both 2019 [16] and 2020 as the platform for the Supply Chain Management League conducted as part of the Automated Negotiation Agents Competition held in conjunction with IJCAI. In this application, NegMAS was used to implement a genuine situated negotiations situation in which autonomous agents decide when to negotiate, about what, and with whom, using dynamic utility functions that emerge endogenously from the supply chain simulation dynamics rather than being dictated from outside the system.

NegMAS has also been used as a platform for preference elicitation research [15], where the ability to model uncertainties in utility functions is especially important, and in path planning for self-interested robots [8], where it is useful to be able to handle a large number of concurrent negotiations efficiently.

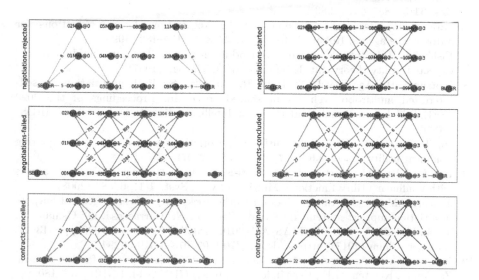

Fig. 3. A visualization of a simulated world in NegMAS. Depicted here are some negotiation and contract-related events. The developer has full control over what events to visualize.

5   Conclusions

This paper presents NegMAS, a new platform for automated negotiations that provides tools for developing negotiation protocols and automated negotiation agents. The proposed system is designed to model realistic negotiation scenarios with dynamic utility functions that are endogenous to the environment within which agents are embedded. Representing dynamic utility functions is essential in real-world applications of automated negotiation. The new platform is being developed as an open-source project with the goal of engaging the automated negotiation research community.

Acknowledgments. Amy Greenwald is supported in part by NSF Award CMMI-1761546.

References

1. Contract room platform (2019). https://www.contractroom.com/
2. Geniusweb platform (2019). https://ii.tudelft.nl/GeniusWeb/technicians.html
3. Aydoğan, R., Festen, D., Hindriks, K.V., Jonker, C.M.: Alternating offers protocols for multilateral negotiation. In: Fujita, K., et al. (eds.) Modern Approaches to Agent-based Complex Automated Negotiation. SCI, vol. 674, pp. 153–167. Springer, Cham (2017). https://doi.org/10.1007/978-3-319-51563-2_10
4. Baarslag, T., Hindriks, K., Jonker, C.: A tit for tat negotiation strategy for real-time bilateral negotiations. In: Complex Automated Negotiations: Theories, Models, and Software Competitions, pp. 229–233. Springer (2013)
5. Chatterjee, K., Samuelson, W.: Bargaining under incomplete information. Oper. Res. **31**(5), 835–851 (1983)
6. Faratin, P., Sierra, C., Jennings, N.R.: Negotiation decision functions for autonomous agents. Robot. Auton. Syst. **24**(3–4), 159–182 (1998)
7. Fishburn, P.C.: Interdependence and additivity in multivariate, unidimensional expected utility theory. Int. Econ. Rev. **8**(3), 335–342 (1967)
8. Inotsume, H., Aggarewal, A., Higa, R., Nakadai, S.: Path negotiation for self-interested multirobot vehicles in shared space. In: Proceedings of the 2020 IEEE/RSJ International Conference on Intelligent Robots and Systems (IROS) (2020)
9. Ito, T., Hattori, H., Klein, M.: Multi-issue negotiation protocol for agents: exploring nonlinear utility spaces. IJCAI **7**, 1347–1352 (2007)
10. Ito, T., Klein, M., Hattori, H.: A multi-issue negotiation protocol among agents with nonlinear utility functions. Multiagent Grid Syst. **4**(1), 67–83 (2008)
11. Jonker, C.M., et al.: An introduction to the pocket negotiator: a general purpose negotiation support system. In: Criado Pacheco, N., Carrascosa, C., Osman, N., Julián Inglada, V. (eds.) EUMAS/AT -2016. LNCS (LNAI), vol. 10207, pp. 13–27. Springer, Cham (2017). https://doi.org/10.1007/978-3-319-59294-7_2
12. Kersten, G.E.: Are procurement auctions good for society and for buyers? In: Zaraté, P., Kersten, G.E., Hernández, J.E. (eds.) GDN 2014. LNBIP, vol. 180, pp. 30–40. Springer, Cham (2014). https://doi.org/10.1007/978-3-319-07179-4_4
13. Klein, M., Faratin, P., Sayama, H., Bar-Yam, Y.: Protocols for negotiating complex contracts. IEEE Intell. Syst. **18**(6), 32–38 (2003)

14. Lin, R., Kraus, S., Baarslag, T., Tykhonov, D., Hindriks, K., Jonker, C.M.: Genius: an integrated environment for supporting the design of generic automated negotiators. Comput. Intell. **30**(1), 48–70 (2014). https://doi.org/10.1111/j.1467-8640.2012.00463.x
15. Mohammad, Y., Nakadai, S.: Optimal value of information based elicitation during negotiation. In: Proceedings of the 18th International Conference on Autonomous Agents and MultiAgent Systems. AAMAS 2019, pp. 242–250. International Foundation for Autonomous Agents and Multiagent Systems (2019)
16. Mohammad, Y., Viqueira, E.A., Ayerza, N.A., Greenwald, A., Nakadai, S., Morinaga, S.: Supply chain management world. In: Baldoni, M., Dastani, M., Liao, B., Sakurai, Y., Zalila Wenkstern, R. (eds.) PRIMA 2019. LNCS (LNAI), vol. 11873, pp. 153–169. Springer, Cham (2019). https://doi.org/10.1007/978-3-030-33792-6_10
17. Nash Jr., J.F.: The bargaining problem. Econometrica J. Econometric Soc. **18**, 155–162 (1950)
18. Rubinstein, A.: Perfect equilibrium in a bargaining model. Econometrica J. Econometric Soc. **50**, 97–109 (1982)
19. Wurman, P.R., Wellman, M.P., Walsh, W.E.: A parametrization of the auction design space. Games Econ. Behav. **35**(1–2), 304–338 (2001)
20. Zeng, D., Sycara, K.: Bayesian learning in negotiation. Int. J. Hum. Comput. Stud. **48**(1), 125–141 (1998)

Simulation of Unintentional Collusion Caused by Auto Pricing in Supply Chain Markets

Masanori Hirano[1]($\boxtimes$)(iD), Hiroyasu Matsushima[2](iD), Kiyoshi Izumi[1],
and Taisei Mukai[3](iD)

[1] School of Engineering, The University of Tokyo, Tokyo, Japan
`hirano@g.ecc.u-tokyo.ac.jp`, `izumi@sys.t.u-tokyo.ac.jp`
`https://mhirano.jp/`
[2] Center for Data Science Education and Research, Shiga University, Shiga, Japan
`hiroyasu-matsushima@biwako.shiga-u.ac.jp`
[3] Comprehensive Research Organization, Waseda University, Tokyo, Japan
`t.mukai@kurenai.waseda.jp`

Abstract. In this paper, we address the problem of unintentional price collusion, which happens due to auto pricing, such as systems using reinforcement learning. Firstly, Q-learning, sarsa, and deep Q-Learning models were used for auto pricing to test whether they cause collusion. To test them, we performed multi-agent simulations of a competitive market with a pre-defined demand function. In each simulation, the agents learn their pricing strategies using reinforcement learning. And we defined and calculated the new collusion metric representing how agents collude. Secondly, we tested cases with open and shield bidding with multiple numbers of agents. In our result, we observe that deep Q-Learning demonstrates the highest collusion metric. Also, contrary to expectations, we found that shield bidding has no significant effect on collusion levels when agents employ outperforming reinforcement learning, such as deep Q-learning. Moreover, the number of agents also contribute to less collusion levels.

Keywords: Auto pricing · Unintentional collusion · Reinforcement learning · Deep learning · Market

1 Introduction

Generally, many automated processes are being introduced today. In some shops, the prices are changed based on automatic algorithms using supply-demand and sales information. These auto pricing systems are favorable to sellers. However, the current systems are a rule-based system whose performance is limited. Moreover, recently, there has been a trial to automate the negotiations in buying and selling among products' supply chains such as [1].

© Springer Nature Switzerland AG 2021
T. Uchiya et al. (Eds.): PRIMA 2020, LNAI 12568, pp. 352–359, 2021.
https://doi.org/10.1007/978-3-030-69322-0_24

On the other hand, recently, many works relating to reinforcement learning, game theory, and mechanism design have been proposed with some implemented in real-life scenarios [5]. In terms of the auto pricing system, reinforcement learning can be applied to it. Moreover, for making the best of the auto pricing strategy, it is crucial to think of pricing competition in game theoretic terms. Although applying these technologies to the auto pricing system makes it more beneficial and efficient, the new technologies poss some risks. The risks of auto pricing were pointed out in [4]. This indicates that the auto pricing system using Q-learning can learn unintentional price collusion without direct interaction between competitors. Moreover, the risks seem to be increasing using cutting-edge technologies. The performances of Q-Learning are limited compared with other recent technologies such as deep Q-Learning. Used more outperforming reinforcement learning, the risks of unintentional collusion is assumed to be more increasing. It is because we could assume that a more outperforming learning method can learn strategies more efficiently.

In this paper, we test the risk of some reinforcement learning models for unintentional price collusion using our new collusion metric.

2   Related Works

As a supply chain model, Yasser *et al.* showed their supply chain management world model [8]. Yasser also released his platform for supply chain management called *"negmas"* [7]. This platform was also used for the supply chain management league (SCML) in the 10th International Automated Negotiating Agents Competition (ANAC2019) [1].

There are a lot of works trying to apply game theory to real-world tasks. The old and well-known models for pricing competition are Bertrand's duopoly model [3] and the Cournot competition model. Both models tried to analyze the duopoly market using game theory. Hence, we adopt the former as the basis of our paper. As another work applying game theory to the real-world task, Tambe showed the application of the Stackelberg competition for aviation security [11].

In the context of reinforcement learning, many works and developments have been made throughout a long history. The Q-learning is a famous reinforcement learning, which is an off-policy reinforcement learning based on Q-table [12]. As a learning theory, the temporal difference was proposed in [10]. Sarsa, State–action–reward–state–action, is another example of simple reinforcement learning proposed in [9]. Although it is very similar to Q-learning, it is an on-policy learning method. Generally, the most significant discovery in reinforcement learning is its combination with a neural network. After deep reinforcement learning becomes available, Mnih *et al.* [6] showed deep Q-learning could outperform humans using the Atari Learning Environment (ALE) [2]. These learning strategies are used in our study.

3   Market Settings and Collusion Metric

The market we employed in this study is based on Bertrand competition model [3]. It allows supply prices to be fixed by each production seller, and the demand quantities for each seller are calculated based on the prices. In every step, all agents submit their bidding price. Then, the quantities for them are calculated by the market. There is only one market in our simulation, and its demands are defined by the equation using the bidding prices of all agents. Because Bertrand competition model is a winner-take-all model (i.e., a seller who submits the lowest sell price gets all demands), the model's demand function is not C^0 function (i.e., the function is a non-smooth function). So, the model's demand function is difficult to analyze using numerical analysis. Thus, we made another demand function as the following.

$\mathcal{N}$ is the set of agents (sellers), and if the number of agents is N, $\mathcal{N} = \{1, 2, 3, \cdots, N\}$. Agent (products seller) i ($\in \mathcal{N}$) set their sell price at time t to $p_{i,t}$ (t means steps in simulations, i.e., $t = 1, 2, 3, \cdots$). Here, we noted the possible price space $\mathcal{P}$ (We assumed all agents set their sell price in the same range), i.e., $\forall i \in \mathcal{N}, \forall t, p_{i,t} \in \mathcal{P}$. $\mathcal{P}$ is usually the continuous non-negative values, i.e., $[0, \infty)$, in the real world, but this can be set of discrete non-negative values, such as $\{1, 2, 3, \cdots, 10\}$, in our simulations. We also defined P_t as the tuple of all agents' price at time t, i.e., $P_t = (p_{1,t}, p_{2,t}, \cdots, p_{N,t})$.

At the step t, all agents publish their sell prices $p_{i,t}(i \in \mathcal{N})$. Then, a sell quantity of agent $i \in \mathcal{N}$ is calculated as:

$$q_{i,t} = \frac{\exp\left(-p_{i,t}/\mu\right)}{\sum_{j \in \mathcal{N}} \exp\left(-p_{j,t}/\mu\right) + \exp\left(-a/\mu\right)} \tag{1}$$

where μ and a are given fixed parameters and $\mu = 5.0$ and $a = 5.0$ in our simulation. Here, μ is a kind of scaling factor, i.e., $p_{j,t}$ depends on μ, and if μ and a become twice, $p_{j,t}$ will be twice to get the same $q_{i,t}$. But, a can affect the market dynamics because the term $\exp\left(-a/\mu\right)$ has effects on the total amount of sold quantities. So, we set a empirically. This equation is based on [4], but we have reduced some variables to facilitate holomorphic analytics and made C^2 function. It is because Bertrand's demand function is not C^0 function which is a winner takes all demand, but if there are multiple winners, they share a pie.

Then, in our simulation, we ignored the production cost because it does not affect the dynamics of markets. The profits of each agent are calculated by $\Pi_{i,t}(P_t) = p_{i,t} \times q_{i,t}$. These settings are very useful for analytics because it has one Nash equilibrium and one cooperative equilibrium, and both equilibria have the same value of $p_{i,t}$ for all agent $i \in \mathcal{N}$.

In the simulation, there was one market handling only one type of goods. Furthermore, we switched two types of markets. Both types have the same calculation process, as mentioned before. In one type of market, all agents can access other agents' bidding prices and quantities. In another type of market, all agents cannot access other agents' bidding prices and quantities. It means that the biddings are shielded, and the price would not be revealed even afterword. We call these two types of agents "open market" and "closed market".

Next, we define a metric for unintentional collusion as:

$$C_t = \frac{1}{|\mathcal{N}|} \sum_{i \in \mathcal{N}} \frac{\Pi_{i,t}(P_t) - \Pi_{i,t}^*}{\Pi_{i,t}^{**} - \Pi_{i,t}^*} \tag{2}$$

where $\Pi_{i,t}^*$ and $\Pi_{i,t}^{**}$ mean the agent i's profits for Nash and Cooperative equilibrium, respectively.

4   Agents

We tested three types of agents, Q-Learning, Sarsa, and Deep Q-Learning agents.

All of them are using one historical price as a state. That is, if the market is an open market, they refer to previous prices of all agents' bids, and if the market is closed, they refer to only the previous prices of themselves. That means if the market is an open market, agent i uses $\{p_{j,t-1} | \forall j \in \mathcal{N}\}$, and if the market is a closed market, agent i uses only $p_{i,(t-1)}$. The reason why we employ only one historical price is the limitation of learning. That is, if we employed multiple historical prices, the state space would be too large to learn and will not converge.

As an action space, i.e., $\mathcal{P}$, we assumed discrete action space $\{p_{i,t}^* + (p_{i,t}^{**} - p_{i,t}^*) \times \frac{i}{10} | i = -1, 0, 1, \cdots, 10, 11\}$ where $p_{i,t}^*$ and $p_{i,t}^{**}$ are Nash and Cooperative equilibrium, respectively. We also employed ϵ-greedy and agents were made to choose their action at random using the following probability: $\epsilon = \epsilon_{end} + (\epsilon_{start} - \epsilon_{end}) \times r^{\frac{t}{decay}}$, where t means steps. In our simulations, $\epsilon_{start} = 0.95$, $\epsilon_{end} = 0.0$, $r = 0.95$, and $decay = 1000$. These values are set empirically. As a reward, we employed a profit coming from the action, i.e., immediate reward. (TD(0))

Other details were varied with each agent as the following. In the following, we note that $s_{i,t}$ is agent i's state at step t, $\mathcal{S}_i$ is agent i's state space, $a_{i,t}$ is agent i's action at step t, $\mathcal{A}_i$ is agent i's action space, $r_{i,t}$ is agent i's reward at step t, i.e., the reward at step t coming from $a_{i,t}$.

Q-Learning   Agent.   Q-Learning   is   the   a   strategy   based   on Q-table [12]. Q-values are updated at each step by:

$$\Delta Q = r_{i,t} + \gamma \max_{a \in \mathcal{A}} Q_i\left(s_{i,(t+1)}, a\right) - Q_i\left(s_{i,t}, a_{i,t}\right), \tag{3}$$

$$Q_i\left(s_{i,t}, a_{i,t}\right) \leftarrow Q_i\left(s_{i,t}, a_{i,t}\right) + \alpha \Delta Q. \tag{4}$$

In our simulation, we set $\alpha = 0.10$, $\gamma = 0.95$. α is the learning rate, and γ is the discount rate in reinforcement learning. These values were set empirically.

Sarsa Agent. Sarsa is State–action–reward–state–action proposed in [9]. This is very similar to Q-Learning, though on-policy learning method. Q-values were updated at each step using:

$$\Delta Q = r_{i,t} + \gamma Q_i\left(s_{i,(t+1)}, a_{i,(t+1)}\right) - Q_i\left(s_{i,t}, a_{i,t}\right), \tag{5}$$

$$Q_i\left(s_{i,t}, a_{i,t}\right) \leftarrow Q_i\left(s_{i,t}, a_{i,t}\right) + \alpha \Delta Q. \tag{6}$$

In our simulation, we set $\alpha = 0.10$, $\gamma = 0.95$. α is the learning rate, and γ is the discount rate in reinforcement learning. These values are set empirically.

Deep Q-Learning Agent. Deep Q-Learning was proposed in [6]. The Q-table in Q-Learning is replaced by a deep neural network such as a multi-layered perceptron (MLP), and this network is called Deep Q-Network (DQN). For updating Q-values, DQN learning was performed. For learning, we used the batch size of 10,000, i.e., learnings of DQN occurred every 10,000 steps, and the learning results applied current DQN every 100,000 steps. We employed ReLU as activation function, 3, 4, or 5 layers (at random), 10, 11, $\cdots$, 20 node per layers (at random), 20% of drop-out, Smooth L1 loss, RMSprop optimizer, and learning rate of 10^{-4}.

5   Simulations

To test the collusion level under some conditions, we performed simulations. Each simulation has 1,000,000 steps. Then, at the end of each simulation, we calculated the final collusion metric by calculating the mean of collusion metrics among the last 10,000 steps in a simulation. In every step, agents bid their price to the market, and quantities for their bidding are given by the market. Then, all agents calculate their profits (rewards) and performed reinforcement learning, such as Q-learning. At the same time, according to the bidding prices, calculations for the collusion metric also happened. Then, after the repeating steps, at the end of the simulation, we calculated the final collusion metric.

In our experiments, we performed 12 patterns of simulations. We change in

- Agent type: Q-Learning, Sarsa, Deep Q-Learning.
- The number of Agents: 2, or 3.
- Market type: Open market, or Closed market.

The number of runs for each pattern is 1,000. Through these experiments, we assess the risk of unintentional collusion by calculating C for each pattern of simulation.

6   Results

Table 1 and Fig. 1 show all the results.

According to this result, when the agents employ Q-learning as a learning strategy, agents are affected by the number of agents more than whether the market is open or closed. The effect of the closed market is very slight. On the other hand, if the number of agents increases, the collusion metric was drastically dropped down. It means that if the agents employ Q-learning, the number of agents of the competitive markets are very important to avoid unintentional collusion.

When the agents employ Sarsa as a learning strategy, the difference between cases of open market and closed markets is very significant. The differences in the collusion metric, which the market type made, was supposed to contribute are around 20%. This difference is bigger than the effect of the number of agents. However, the number of agents is also contributing to the collusion levels.

Table 1. All results. The values represent collusion metric. Each result written in bold is statistically different from others ($p < 0.01$) among results of the same type of agents.

Agents type	# of agents	Open market	Closed market
Q-Learning	2 Agents	**52.49% ± 15.40%**	**50.47% ± 22.17%**
	3 Agents	39.01% ± 10.56%	38.80% ± 17.73%
Sarsa	2 Agents	**53.72% ± 15.18%**	**38.25% ± 28.86%**
	3 Agents	**47.32% ± 8.22%**	**21.31% ± 19.55%**
Deep Q-Learning	2 Agents	58.96% ± 29.87%	58.66% ± 28.99%
	3 Agents	57.15% ± 24.96%	55.69% ± 25.02%
	(4 Agents)	53.90% ± 22.61%	53.80% ± 21.88%

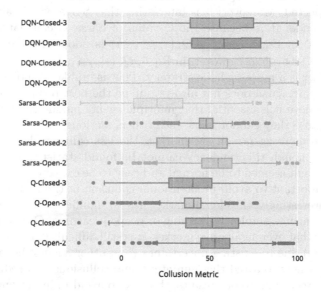

Fig. 1. Box plot of all results.

In the results of deep Q-learning agents, we also put the results from the case with four agents on the markets. It is because deep Q-learning agents can deal with the more dimensional state. The results are interesting. Both effects of a closed market and the number of agents are comparatively small. Basically, closed markets reduce the collusion metric, and the more agents there are, the less collusion metric is. However, the differences among each pattern are very slight. In this result, the case of open market and closed market is not statistically different regardless of the number of agents. Moreover, some other pairs of results are also not statistically different.

Figure 1 shows the box plot of all results. According to the figure, deep Q-learning agents show comparatively significant results on the collusion metric regardless of the market settings or the number of agents. This clearly shows that outperforming learning methods like deep Q-learning have significant risks on unintentional collusion.

It cannot be appropriate to compare the case when the number of agents is 2 and 3 because Nash and cooperative equilibrium are not the same for each case. However, basically, more agents are on the market, less collusion level agents make. On the other hand, interestingly, whether the market is an open market or a closed market did not make as big differences in the case of deep Q-learning as Q-learning or sarsa agents.

7 Discussion

First, the result that deep Q-learning agents outperformed the other agents is easy to be expected. Moreover, it is interesting that Sarsa was weak for closed markets to collude. It is because the Q-value of Sarsa is calculated by using realized actions. In Eq. 3, $\max_{a \in \mathscr{A}} Q_i \left(s_{i,(t+1)}, a \right)$ is adopted for evaluation of future state in Q-learning. However, in Eq. 5, $Q_i \left(s_{i,(t+1)}, a_{i,(t+1)} \right)$ is adopted in Sarsa. The latter is a more realistic strategy. That is, unlike off-policy strategies such as Q-learning, sarsa does not always pursue the best results. Under closed markets, we believe it is essential that multiple agents pursue the best outcome to collude because they cannot know each others' actions.

Second, the more agents on the market, the less collusion level the market would have. Although this tendency cannot be found statistically for deep Q-learning, this result seemed to be normal and easy to be expected. So the number of agents is important to avoid unintentional collusion in the real market.

Thirdly, interestingly, the closed market has no significant effect on the collusion level when agents employ Q-learning or deep Q-learning. One reason we can think of here is that even in an open market, it is still difficult to estimate realized rewards (profits) due to existing uncertainty from other agents' behavior.

The point is how to avoid these unintentional collusions and reduce the collusion metric. According to our results, the way to avoid unintentional collusion we found in this paper is only to increase the number of agents in the market. However, in the actual supply chain, the suppliers of each part are limited and it is not a realistic solution to add more suppliers. Moreover, unfortunately, the closed market is not working to avoid collusion in some situations. As future work, we should try some other attempts to avoid unintentional collusion.

8 Conclusion

In this paper, we addressed the problem of unintentional collusion by auto pricing in a market. First, we defined a new metric for unintentional collusion using Nash and cooperative equilibria in pricing competition in a market. The market's demand function is defined by the sellers' bidding prices.

Second, we run some simulations to calculate each collusion level under some conditions. We changed in the number of seller agents, agent's strategy learning type, and market type, i.e., price opened or closed markets. According to the results, we found that the number of seller agents and agent's strategy learning demonstrates a significant effect on the collusion level in prices. The more agents are put on the market, the less collusion level happens in the market. Moreover, in some situation, the market type, i.e., open market or closed market, also affect the collusion level.

Furthermore, we found that outperforming reinforcement learning, such as deep Q-learning, shows a high risk of collusion. In the future, we hope to find ways to avoid unintentional collusion other than more agents putting on the market.

Acknowledgment. This work was supported by Council for Science, Technology and Innovation (CSTI), Cross-ministerial Strategic Innovation Promotion Program (SIP), "AI Collaboration for Improved Value Chain Efficiency and Flexibility" (Funding agency: NEDO).

References

1. ANAC Organizers: ANAC2019 - Tenth Automated Negotiating Agents Competition (2019). http://web.tuat.ac.jp/~katfuji/ANAC2019/
2. Bellemare, M.G., Veness, J., Bowling, M.: The arcade learning environment: an evaluation platform for general agents. J. Artif. Intell. Res. **47**, 253–279 (2013)
3. Bertrand, J.L.F.: Théorie mathématique de la richesse sociale par Léon Walras: Recherches sur les principes mathématiques de la théorie des richesse par Augustin Cournot. Journal des savants **67**, 499–508 (1883)
4. Granichin, O., Uzhva, D.: Invariance preserving control of clusters recognized in networks of kuramoto oscillators. In: Kuznetsov, S.O., Panov, A.I., Yakovlev, K.S. (eds.) RCAI 2020. LNCS (LNAI), vol. 12412, pp. 472–486. Springer, Cham (2020). https://doi.org/10.1007/978-3-030-59535-7_35
5. Jain, M., An, B., Tambe, M.: An overview of recent application trends at the AAMAS conference: security, sustainability, and safety. AI Mag. **33**, 14–28 (2012). https://doi.org/10.1609/aimag.v33i3.2420
6. Mnih, V., et al.: Human-level control through deep reinforcement learning. Nature **518**(7540), 529–533 (2015). https://doi.org/10.1038/nature14236
7. Mohammad, Y.: yasserfarouk/negmas: Negotiation Multi-Agent System (2019). https://github.com/yasserfarouk/negmas
8. Mohammad, Y., Viqueira, E.A., Ayerza, N.A., Greenwald, A., Nakadai, S., Morinaga, S.: Supply chain management world: a benchmark environment for situated negotiations. In: Baldoni, M., Dastani, M., Liao, B., Sakurai, Y., Zalila Wenkstern, R. (eds.) PRIMA 2019. LNCS (LNAI), vol. 11873, pp. 153–169. Springer, Cham (2019). https://doi.org/10.1007/978-3-030-33792-6_10
9. Rummery, G.A., Niranjan, M.: On-line Q-learning using connectionist systems. University of Cambridge, Department of Engineering Cambridge, England (1994)
10. Sutton, R.S.: Learning to predict by the methods of temporal differences. Mach. Learn. **3**(1), 9–44 (1988). https://doi.org/10.1007/BF00115009
11. Tambe, M.: Security and Game Theory: Algorithms, Deployed Systems, Lessons Learned. Cambridge University Press, Cambridge (2011)
12. Watkins, C.J.C.H., Dayan, P.: Q-learning. Mach. Learn. **8**(3–4), 279–292 (1992). https://doi.org/10.1007/bf00992698

Construct an Artificial Population with Urban and Rural Population Differences Considered: To Support Long-Term Care System Evaluation by Agent-Based Simulation

Shuang Chang[(⊠)] and Hiroshi Deguchi

Tokyo Institute of Technology, Yokohama, Japan
chang@c.titech.ac.jp

Abstract. Bottom-up simulation approaches such as agent-based simulation are attracting attention in Chinese Long-Term Care (LTC) studies. To enable the deployment of agent-based modelling approaches in evaluating LTC systems, a computational base which entails individual and household details is necessary. In this work, we propose a method to construct such an artificial population with the urban and rural population differences considered. Given the situation that nationwide disaggregated records on health issues of households and individuals are not available for the Chinese case, we first propose a method to generate such records based on the first wave of China Health and Retirement Longitudinal Study. Drawn upon above records containing health-related attributes, we then propose a revised combinatorial optimization method to construct an artificial population mirroring a Chinese city including both urban and rural residents. It will be among the first methods in constructing such artificial populations to support agent-based simulation approaches in LTC studies.

1 Introduction

In response to the escalating needs of Long-Term Care (LTC) services attributed to a rapid aging population, China has been putting efforts to develop LTC service systems. LTC models have been piloted in several cities to accelerate the process [16], and empirical assessments of varied design features are becoming critical. Recognizing LTC services as a complex system comprising inextricably connected components, there has been an emerging interest in adopting a complex system perspective to investigate the phenomenon [2,3]. Correspondingly, to complement traditional approaches [6,12,20], an agent-based modelling approach which can evaluate emergent patterns by articulating the underlying dynamic relations explicitly is gaining popularity [15].

To support agent-based simulation approaches which can capture individuals' characteristics and their interactive behaviors against the social context,

T. Uchiya et al. (Eds.): PRIMA 2020, LNAI 12568, pp. 360–367, 2021.
https://doi.org/10.1007/978-3-030-69322-0_25

an artificial baseline population is necessary [5]. Two main streams of methods, synthetic reconstruction and combinatorial optimization [18], have been developed extensively to construct synthetic populations. Iterative proportional fitting (IPF) procedures are well established to estimate the joint-distributions of individual attributes while satisfying a set of constrains. Following the resulted distributions, samples of households and individuals can be drawn by Monte Carlo method [10,13]. In contrast, combinatorial optimization methods first randomly choose a set of households from disaggregated datasets and improve the fit between the resulted and target population through household swapping [17]. Both methods can generate well-fitted synthetic populations but not in the cases when required datasets are unavailable or the parameter space is large [11]. Comparatively, combinatorial optimization methods have less restrictions on constraining tables, introduce less variability in the generated records, and generate individuals nested in households in a more natural way [10].

However, the above methods are not directly applicable for constructing an artificial population in particular to support the deployment of agent-based simulation approaches in evaluating Chinese LTC systems. First, the corresponding Chinese version of nationwide disaggreagated datasets required by above methods are not available. China Health and Retirement Longitudinal Study (CHARLS) [14] can serve as an alternative, but it only sampled those households with a reference person older than 45. Pre-processing procedures are therefore required to generate such records across all age bands. Second, the joint distribution of health-related attributes at aggregated level might not always be available. To evaluate LTC models, not only the basic demographics, but also other factors including health status, living arrangement and care patterns of the elderly, are necessary [8]. Third, a Chinese city may have both urban and rural residents, determined by their *Hukou* status, whose household structure and age structure may differ. A new construction method considering the urban and rural population differences and health-related factors is therefore needed.

Therefore, this work aims to construct an artificial population, which will approximate the population structure of a Chinese city of interested aspects whilst bearing urban and rural population differences. It will serve as a computational base to enable the deployment of an agent-based simulation approach for LTC studies. We first propose a method to generate nationwide disaggregated samples based on the first wave of CHARLS in Sect. 2. Drawn upon such records, we then propose a revised combinatorial optimization method to construct the urban and rural population such that the distribution of selected individual attributes and of household structure fits with that of the target population in Sect. 3.

2   Datasets Preparation

We first process the sectional datasets from the first wave of CHARLS to generate national representative disaggregated individual and household records. These records across all age groups will be used in the subsequent population construction procedures.

2.1 Dataset Description

The baseline samples of CHARLS were chosen from 28 Chinese provinces by multi-stage probability sampling, and 10069 households with a reference person older than 45 were interviewed face-to-face. A broad range of questions on household rosters, socio-economic factors, health-related attributes, healthcare facilities, and so on were surveyed [21]. We first clean and merge CHARLS's sectional files following a conceptual three-level artificial population designed particularly for healthcare system simulations [4]. A list of main household records and their associated lists of individual records are generated. The main attributes are briefly reviewed in below.

Individual Records. Basic individual demographic and socio-economic attributes are drawn directly from survey questions, including age, gender, hukou status (urban or rural), marital status and self-rated health status. ADL (Activities of Daily Living) dependency, a key indicator of LTC needs, is drawn from questions *in how many everyday activities out of six the respondents have any difficulty for more than 3 months, including dressing, showering, eating, using the toilet, incontinence and in-door moving.*

Household Records. Household structure, as lists of household co-residents and other family members, is drawn from *household roster* (non-respondent household members) section and *family information and transfer* (non-household family members) section. Households are classified into eight types based on respondents' marital status and whether they live with their parents (including parents-in-law), siblings, children (including spouse), grandchildren, and/or others. These households are further clustered into three types: households of one generation, two generations and three generations.

2.2 Method

Since CHARLS only sampled households with the reference person older than 45, treated as *main households* in this work, we have to create additional household and individual records to have a household pool containing individuals across all age bands. We first extract and code the information of *main households* respondents' children aged between 20 and 44 and treat them as the reference person of *children households*. Depending on their marital status and number of children they have, we then create new individual records as their household co-residents accordingly by a Monte-Carlo simulation approach. *Children households* records can therefore be linked back to the corresponding *main households* records.

Each household surveyed in CHARLS possesses a weight representing the in verse of sampling probability. Regarding the weight of newly created *children household*, different from the previous work [4] which just used the weight of their main household, we calculate it by multiplying the weight inherited from their main household and the population ratio between those aged above 45 and aged from 20 to 45, for urban and rural residents separately. Then by combining *main households* and *children households*, we get a household pool including nationwide anonymous samples of households and household members, comparable to Sample of Anonymised Records (SAR) in the United Kingdom and Public-Use Microdata Samples (PUMS) in the United States. It is shown to be national representative by comparing with the national census 2000 in terms of the distribution of household types with sampling weights considered [9,19], as plotted in Fig. 1.

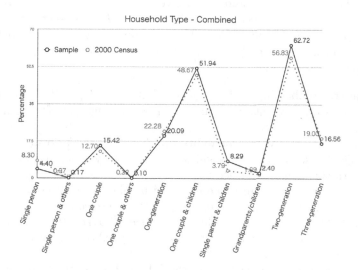

Fig. 1. Number of households of each household type - constructed (sample) vs. national census

We divide the above records by their *Hukou* status, which will be used for constructing urban and rural populations respectively in the following steps.

3   An Algorithm for Population Construction

Using the datasets generated above, we propose a novel method to construct an artificial population. The resulted distribution of interested attributes, i.e., the number of households of each generation type, age pyramids by gender, and the number of individuals of each health status across age groups, will approximate to that of the target population.

Here, health status is defined by 3 categories: *generally healthy, not healthy but don't need assistant in daily activities,* and *need assistant in daily activities.* Accordingly, we have to re-categorize the self-rated health status derived from CHARLS into above categories. Individuals who are with *very good, good,* or *fair* self-rated health condition fall into the first category; who are with *poor* or *very poor* condition whilst *have no ADL items* fall into the second category; and who *have more than 2 ADL items* fall into the last category.

3.1   Method

We now have a national representative set of households H associated with a list of individuals I, for urban or rural residents respectively. We denote the number of households of each household generation type m by num_m, the number of individuals in age group i by a_i, the number of individuals of gender j in age group i by g_{ji}, and the number of individuals with health status s in age group i by h_{si}, where $i = 9$, $j = 2$ and $s = 3$. We denote the constructed and target population by P and D respectively. For instance, $a_i(P)$ represents the number of people in age group i of population P. The procedures to generate the population with an optimization method are given in below and will be repeated until a termination criterion is met.

1. Calculate the probability of choosing each household $H_x \in H$, denoted as p_{H_x}, based on its own weight w_{H_x} and an adjusted weight w_k for its household type k;
2. Select the household with probability p_{H_x} by a Monte-Carlo simulation approach. The household members will be automatically generated as individuals along with this household selection;
3. Repeat steps 1) and 2) until the targeted number of households under each household generation type m, i.e., $num_m(D)$, are selected;
4. Calculate the overall total absolute error *overall TAE* [10], i.e., sum of the discrepancies between the constructed and targeted counts for each attribute category, as shown in Eq. 1;
5. Apply an efficient optimization method DX-NEX [7] to estimate w_k with evaluate(P, D) minimized at each evaluation iteration.

If $num_m(D)$ is smaller than the number of households in the household pool, we will adjust p_{H_x} by multiplying a scaling parameter based on the corresponding household weights.

$$\text{evaluate}(P, D) = \sum_i |a_i(P) - a_i(D)|$$
$$+ \sum_i \sum_j |g_{ji}(P) - g_{ji}(D)| + \sum_i \sum_s |h_{si}(P) - h_{si}(D)| \qquad (1)$$

3.2   Evaluation

We use a district of the capital city of China, with 332708 urban and 405161 rural residents in 119034 and 128701 households respectively, to demonstrate the proposed algorithm. We aim to construct a representative artificial population around 1:10 of the target one. Aggregated statistics for urban and rural residents respectively, including the number of households of each generation type, the age pyramids by gender, and the number of individuals of each health status in age groups above 60, are drawn from the official population census [1].

The simulation results show that the evaluation value, evaluate(P, D), is improved rapidly within around 1500 iterations and kept stable afterwards.

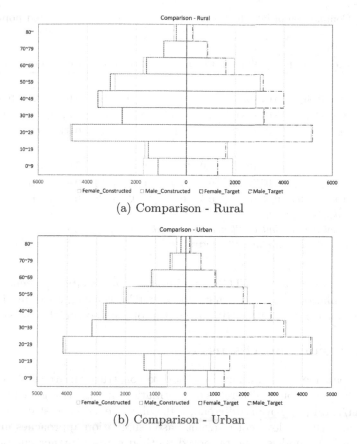

(a) Comparison - Rural

(b) Comparison - Urban

Fig. 2. Comparison of age/gender structure between target and constructed populations

There are no significant discrepancies among different runs, which may shorten the computational time significantly. The household structure is exactly the same to the target population from the algorithm design, thus not illustrated here. The comparison between the generated and targeted population by age and gender structure is illustrated in Fig. 2, for rural and urban residents respectively. It suggests that in general the two populations fit well except for age groups under 20, and for male in age group 40–49. Table 1 compares the resulted distribution of health status across age groups with the target one, and a larger variation in age group 60–69 is observed. This non-satisfactory fit of certain age groups may be explained by the significant differences between the target population at district level and the national one profiled from CHARLS.

The algorithm is implemented by Java, and its outcome is a list of household records with nested lists of individual records with key attributes involved in LTC models. They can be coded into computer programs as computational agents associated with a set of desired attributes to support future simulation works.

Table 1. Comparison of health status between target and constructed populations

Percentage	Urban			Rural		
	Condition 1	Condition 2	Condition 3	Condition 1	Condition 2	Condition 3
Male						
Age: 60–69	0.5 (0.56)	0.02 (0.09)	0.01 (0.01)	0.49 (0.42)	0.05 (0.22)	0.03 (0.02)
Age: 70–79	0.29 (0.2)	0.04 (0.06)	0.02 (0.01)	0.22 (0.17)	0.07 (0.08)	0.04 (0.02)
Age: 80-	0.07 (0.03)	0.02 (0.02)	0.02 (0.02)	0.04 (0.03)	0.03 (0.02)	0.03 (0.01)
Female						
Age: 60–69	0.49 (0.5)	0.03 (0.18)	0.01 (0.01)	0.44 (0.35)	0.07 (0.25)	0.03 (0.01)
Age: 70–79	0.28 (0.16)	0.05 (0.14)	0.02 (0.03)	0.19 (0.12)	0.08 (0.12)	0.04 (0.03)
Age: 80-	0.07 (0.03)	0.03 (0.02)	0.03 (0.03)	0.05 (0.04)	0.04 (0.04)	0.05 (0.04)

Condition 1: *generally healthy*
Condition 2: *not healthy but don't need assistant in daily activities*
Condition 3: *need assistant in daily activities*

For instance, to evaluate an LTC model imported into a city represented by this artificial population, we can simulate the agents' diverse care-seeking behaviors accounted by their different attributes and implemented social contexts.

4   Conclusion and Discussion

This short paper proposed a novel method to construct an artificial population with a special focus on health-related information, living arrangement and Chinese urban/rural population differences. It will serve as the first computational base to enable the deployment of agent-based simulation approaches in evaluating Chinese LTC models. The proposed method can be further customized by other researchers from healthcare fields to construct artificial populations with attributes of their own interests.

There are a few directions to improve and extend this work. First, to improve the fit of certain age groups, we can add randomly generated households to the household pool. By using this expanded household pool, it is expected to reduce the structural discrepancies between records derived from CHARLS and those targeted at district level. Second, the proposed method should be more rigorously evaluated by comparing with other methods. Third, a dynamic population can be generated by simulating various life events with the probability informed from subsequent waves of CHARLS datasets. It will help assess the sustainability of LTC systems from a long-term perspective.

Acknowledgment. This work was supported by JSPS KAKENHI Grant Number 20K18958.

References

1. Beijing Municipal Bureau of Statistics (2020). http://tjj.beijing.gov.cn/tjsj/yjdsj/rk/2020/index.html

2. Atun, R.: Health systems, systems thinking and innovation. Health Policy Plann. **27**(SUPPL. 4), 4–8 (2012)

3. Braithwaite, J.: growing inequality: bridging complex systems, population health and health disparities. Int. J. Epidemiol. 351–353 (2018)

4. Chang, S., Deguchi, H.: A computational base with well-preserved household and age structure for health policy analysis. In: Proceeding of IEEE International Conference on Systems, Man, and Cybernetics, pp. 1150–1155 (2018)

5. Epstein, J.M., Axtell, R.: Growing Artificial Societies: Social Science from the Bottom Up. The Brookings Institution, USA (1996)

6. Feng, Z., Liu, C., Guan, X., Mor, V.: China's rapidly aging population creates policy challenges in shaping a viable long-term care system. Health Aff. **31**, 2764–2773 (2012)

7. Fukushima, N., Nagata, Y., Kobayashi, S., Ono, I.: Proposal of distance-weighted exponential natural evolution strategies. In: 2011 IEEE Congress of Evolutionary Computation (CEC), pp. 164–171, June 2011

8. Gu, D., Vlosky, D.A.: Long-term care needs and related issues in China (2008)

9. Hu, Z., Peng, X.: Household changes in contemporary China: an analysis based on the four recent censuses. J. Chin. Sociol. **2**(1), 9 (2015)

10. Huang, Z., Williamson, P.: A comparison of synthetic reconstruction and combinatorial optimisation approaches to the creation of small-area microdata (2001)

11. Jean-Philippe, A., Gilles, V., Olivier, K.: Generating a located synthetic population of individuals, households, and dwellings. LISER Working Paper Series 2017–07, LISER, May 2017

12. Lei, P., Feng, Z., Wu, Z.: The availability and affordability of long-term care for disabled older people in China: the issues related to inequalities in socialsecurity benefits. Arch. Gerontol. Geriatr. **67**, 21–27 (2016)

13. Norman, P.: Putting iterative proportional fitting on the researcher's desk. Copyright of the School of Geography, University Of Leeds (1999)

14. Peking University. China health and retirement longitudinal study (CHARLS) (2011). http://charls.ccer.edu.cn/en

15. Sturmberg, J., Lanham, H.J.: Understanding health care delivery as a complex system: achieving best possible health outcomes for individuals and communities by focusing on interdependencies. J. Eval. Clin. Pract. **20**(6), 1005–1009 (2014)

16. UNESCAP. Long-term care for older persons in China. SDD-SPPS PROJECT Working Papers Series: Long-Term Care for Older Persons in Asia and the Pacific (2015)

17. Voas, D., Williamson, P.: An evaluation of the combinatorial optimisation approach to the creation of synthetic microdata. Int. J. Popul. Geogr. **6**(5), 349–366 (2000)

18. Williamson, P., Birkin, M., Rees, P.H.: The estimation of population microdata by using data from small area statistics and samples of anonymised records. Environ. Plann. A Econ. Space **30**(5), 785–816 (1998). PMID: 12293871

19. Yi, Z., Wang, Z.: Dynamics of family and elderly living arrangements in China: newlessons learned from the 2000 census. China Rev. **3**(2), 95–119 (2003)

20. Zhan, H., Liu, G., Guan, X., Bai, H.: Recent development in Chinese institutional elder care: changing concepts and attitudes. J. Aging Soc. Pol. **18**(2), 85–108 (2006)

21. Zhao, Y., Hu, Y., Smith, J., Strauss, J., Yang, G.: Cohort profile: the China health and retirement longitudinal study (CHARLS). Int. J. Epidemiol. **43**(1), 61–68 (2014)

Multi-Agent Path Finding with Destination Choice

Ayano Okoso[✉], Keisuke Otaki, and Tomoki Nishi

Toyota Central R&D Labs., Inc., Bunkyo-ku 1-4-14, Tokyo 112-0011, Japan
{okoso,otaki,nishi}@mosk.tytlabs.co.jp

Abstract. Multi-agent path finding problem (MAPF) is a problem to find collision-free paths on a graph for multiple agents from their initial locations to their destinations. MAPF has mainly two types of variants regarding the usage of agent destination; each agent has a unique destination or all agents share common destinations. We propose the MAPF with destination choice problem (MAPF-DC) as a new variant of MAPF. Agents in MAPF-DC could implicitly select the best destinations out of assigned destination candidates partially shared with other agents. Experimental results indicate that the total travel time declines with an increase in the number of destination candidates assigned to each agent.

Keywords: Multi-agent path finding problem · Evacuation route planning problem · Network flow problem

1 Introduction

Multi-agent path finding problem (MAPF) is to find collision-free paths from initial locations to destinations for multiple agents representing robots or vehicles [5,11]. MAPF has been investigated in various research fields [1,3,7,12].

In the standard MAPF, each agent should be assigned a unique destination, as shown in Fig. 1a. In the evacuation route planning problem (evacuation problem) [3,8], a variant of MAPF, all agents evacuate from multiple common destinations, as shown in Fig. 1b. The way of setting the use of destinations (unique or common) depends on particular applications. Sometimes, agents have multiple destinations that may be partially shared with other agents; however, the existing MAPF formulations cannot handle such situations.

In this paper, we propose a *MAPF with destination choice* problem (MAPF-DC) in which each agent may have multiple destinations partially shared with others. Each agent can select any of its own destinations and then move to it, as shown in Fig. 1c. For example, the pink agent has two destinations, **A** and **B**. The set of destinations assigned to each agent (marked in the same color in Fig. 1c) is denoted as a *destination(/exit) candidate*. The pink agent selects the destination **B** because the agent can arrive at the destination **B** earlier than **A** without any collisions. The destination candidate used in MAPF-DC could be useful for various applications, such as in parking lots; drivers can select any

© Springer Nature Switzerland AG 2021
T. Uchiya et al. (Eds.): PRIMA 2020, LNAI 12568, pp. 368–376, 2021.
https://doi.org/10.1007/978-3-030-69322-0_26

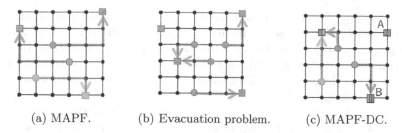

(a) MAPF.   (b) Evacuation problem.   (c) MAPF-DC.

Fig. 1. Comparison of handling destinations. Circles and rectangles with colors denote initial locations and destinations, respectively. Each agent moves to the destination of the same color.

driving exits depending on their will because they aim to exit as quickly as possible.

The solution of MAPF-DC returns the destination and path for each agent. Previous studies have focused on both destination/task assignment and path finding [4,6]; however, these studies required either the assignment of unique destination for each agent before generating paths, or a one-to-one mapping between agents and destinations. In contrast, in MAPF-DC, a destination can be anywhere concerning multiple locations allocated to each agent.

In this paper, we propose a formulation of MAPF-DC by introducing reduction from MAPF-DC to a network flow problem and model it using integer linear programming (ILP) based on the work carried out by Yu et al. [13,14]. The solution implicitly selects the best destination from the candidates. We evaluate the proposed solution through numerical experiments, and the results demonstrate that the total travel time can be reduced by increasing the number of destination candidates assigned to each agent.

2   MAPF with Destination Choice

2.1   Definition

Let $G = (V^G, E^G)$ be an undirected connected simple graph. Let $D \subset V^G$ denote a set of destination vertices. $\mathcal{A} := \{a_1, \dots, a_m\}$ denotes a set of m agents. Each agent a_i is allocated with a task to move from its initial location $o_i \in V^G$ to its destination. Agent a_i has a partially common destination candidate set with other agents $D_i \subseteq D$, and it can reach one of them $d_i \in D_i$. Time is assumed to be discretized $t \in \{0, 1, 2, \dots, \infty\}$, and each time step, an agent can either move to an adjacent vertex or wait at its current vertex, where the action cost is one. Path π_i of agent a_i can be defined as a sequence of vertices $\pi_i := \langle v_1^i, v_2^i, \dots, v_t^i, v_{t+1}^i, \dots, v_{T_i}^i \rangle$ satisfying $v_1^i = o_i$ and $v_{T_i}^i = d_i$, where v_t^i is the vertex visited by a_i at time step t, and T_i is a travel time of a_i until arriving at its destination d_i. Set $\boldsymbol{\pi} := \{\pi_1, \dots, \pi_m\}$ includes paths for all agents.

A *feasible* path of each agent means the path without collisions, that is, each agent does not occupy the same vertex or edge with other agents at the same time. A *solution* of MAPF-DC is defined as a set of *feasible* paths of all agents. An *optimal* solution is a set of feasible paths π^* minimizing a cost function. In the present work, we set the cost function to *sum of travel time* (the total travel time of individual agents). In addition, we define the behavior of agents after they reach their goals as *disappear-at-target* assumption [11], where agents immediately disappear after they have reached their destinations. After an agent disappears at the exit, another agent can use it at different time steps.

MAPF-DC is a generalization of existing formulations given as follows. If every destination candidate set D_i is a singleton set and $D_0 \sqcup D_1 \cdots \sqcup D_m = D$, MAPF-DC coincides with the standard MAPF. If $D_i = D$ under the disappear-at-target assumption, this problem is the same as the evacuation problem.

2.2   Reduction from MAPF-DC to a Network Flow Problem

Here, we explain reduction from MAPF-DC to a network flow problem considering an example illustrated in Fig. 2. Figure 2a demonstrates a simple undirected graph $G = (V^G, E^G)$, where weight $w(e_{u,v}) = 1$ and capacity $c(e_{u,v}) = 1$ for $u, v \in V^G$. $D = \{v_0, v_1\}$ is a set of exit vertices and agents $\mathcal{A} = \{a_0, a_1, a_2\}$ corresponding to respective initial locations v_2, v_3, v_4 are given exit candidate set; $\mathcal{D}_0 = \{v_0\}, \mathcal{D}_1 = \{v_0\}, \mathcal{D}_2 = \{v_0, v_1\}$. In other words, v_0 is common for all agents, and a_1 can additionally choose v_1. To convert G into a network[1], we use a *time-expanded network* generated based on G by inserting the new direction of the time axis. T denotes the time to expand. We create $2T + 1$ copies of vertices from G with index $t = 0, 1, 1', \ldots, T, T'$, as shown in Fig. 2b. Here, v_i^t corresponds to the copy of v_i at a time step of index t. For each edge $(u, v) \in E^G$, a *gadget* represented in Fig. 2c is introduced as an expression that prevents two agents from swapping their locations simultaneously. In a gadget, the capacities of all edges are set equal to one, and the weight of the middle edge represented as a blue arrow is one, while the weights of other edges are zero. To establish a time-expanded network, as illustrated in Fig. 2b, for all vertices copied from G, we add an edge between every two successive copies, such as $(v_i^0, v_i^1), (v_i^1, v_i^{1'}), (v_i^{1'}, v_i^2), \ldots, (v_i^T, v_i^{T'})$, corresponding to the green and yellow arrows. Green edges represent the capacity of a vertex. Here, the weights of edges are zero, and the capacities are one. Similarly, the yellow arrows illustrate the *waiting* action, in which both weight and capacity are one. It should be noted that conversion from a graph to a time-expanded network, as represented in Fig. 2b and 2c, is performed according to Yu et al. [13,14].

Herein, we introduce *aggregation nodes* EX_{in} and EX_{out} in a time-expanded network. Figure 2d represents a time-expanded network ($T = 3$) with aggregation nodes. EX_{in} integrates the initial location vertices of agents sharing the same exit candidate set. We introduce a set of aggregation nodes EX_{out} that bundles exit vertices corresponding to each EX_{in}. In Fig. 2d, agents a_0 and a_1 are bundled, as $\mathcal{D}_0 = \mathcal{D}_1$. Blue lines represent the flow for agents a_0 and a_1, and orange ones denote the flow for agent a_2. The blue circle corresponding to

---

[1] We use the term "network" when the graph is a directed one considering time flow.

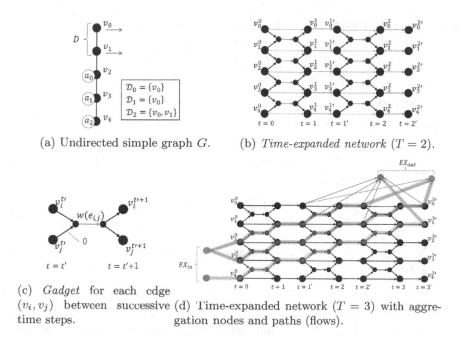

(a) Undirected simple graph G.   (b) *Time-expanded network* $(T = 2)$.

(c) *Gadget* for each edge (v_i, v_j) between successive time steps.   (d) Time-expanded network $(T = 3)$ with aggregation nodes and paths (flows).

Fig. 2. Schematic overview of our reduction method. (Color figure online)

$\mathrm{EX_{in}}$ bundles the initial location vertices of agents a_0 and a_1, while that of $\mathrm{EX_{out}}$ integrates the exit candidate set $\mathcal{D}_0$ (similarly as $\mathcal{D}_1$). Using $2T+1$ copies of exit vertices corresponding to aggregation nodes in $\mathrm{EX_{out}}$, we express the disappear-at-target' assumption by adding edges from each time step of index t' to $\mathrm{EX_{out}}$. It should be noted that the weight and capacity of edges between aggregation nodes and vertices are set equal to zero and one, respectively.

The solutions of MAPF-DC can be obtained by solving a formulated network flow problem in a time-expanded network with aggregation nodes.

2.3 Formulation

We explain the formulation of MAPF-DC converted to a min-cost multi-commodity network flow problem. An instance of MAPF-DC can be defined as $(G, \mathcal{A}, \mathcal{O}, \mathcal{D})$, where $G = (V^G, E^G, w, c)$ is an undirected simple graph with weight $w(e_{u,v}) = 1$ and capacity $c(e_{u,v}) = 1$ for $u, v \in V^G$; $\mathcal{A}$ is a set of agents; $\mathcal{O} = \{o_1, o_2, ... o_{|\mathcal{A}|}\}$ is a set of initial location vertices; $\mathcal{D} = \{\mathcal{D}_1, \mathcal{D}_2, ... \mathcal{D}_{|\mathcal{A}|}\}$ is a family of sets containing destination vertices. Concerning a time-expanded network with aggregation nodes $N^+ = (G, T)$, let $f_k(e) : E^{N^+} \times \mathcal{K} \to \{0, 1\}$ be a flow, where $k \in \mathcal{K}$ is an index of a flow denoted as *flow index*; $\mathcal{K} = \{1, 2, ..., |\mathcal{K}|\}$; $|\mathcal{K}| = |\mathrm{EX_{out}}|$. Then, we denote a set of vertices V^{N^+} and a set of edges E^{N^+} for N^+. For a vertex $v \in V^{N^+}$, the in/out edges are defined as $\delta^-(v) := \{(u, v) \in E^{N^+} \mid u \in V^{N^+}\}$ and $\delta^+(v) := \{(v, u) \in E^{N^+} \mid u \in V^{N^+}\}$, respectively. MAPF-DC can be formulated by ILP as follows:

$$\min_{f} \sum_{k \in \mathcal{K}} \sum_{e \in E^{N^+}} w(e) f_k(e), \tag{1}$$

subject to

$$\sum_{k \in \mathcal{K}} f_k(e) \leq c(e), \quad (\forall e \in E^{N^+}), \tag{2a}$$

$$\sum_{e \in \delta^+(v)} f_k(e) = \sum_{e \in \delta^-(v)} f_k(e), \quad (\forall k \in \mathcal{K}, \forall v \in V^{N^+} \backslash (\text{EX}_{\text{in}} \cup \text{EX}_{\text{out}})), \tag{2b}$$

$$\sum_{e \in \delta^+(v)} f_k(e) = \begin{cases} 1 & (k = h(a_i), \exists a_i \in \mathcal{A}(v)) \\ 0 & (otherwise) \end{cases} \quad (\forall v \in \text{EX}_{\text{in}}), \tag{2c}$$

$$\sum_{e \in \delta^-(v)} f_k(e) = 0, \quad (\forall v \in \text{EX}_{\text{out}}, k \neq h(a_i), \exists a_i \in \mathcal{A}(v)), \tag{2d}$$

$$f_k(e) \in \{0, 1\}, \quad (\forall k \in \mathcal{K}, e \in E^{N^+}), \tag{2e}$$

where $\mathcal{A}(v)$ denotes a set of agents in which their initial locations are aggregated into $v \in \text{EX}_{\text{in}}$, and $h(a_i)$ indicates that a function returns a flow index corresponding to agent a_i. The objective function defined in Eq. (1) is used to formulate total travel time using decision variables. Constraint (2a) is required to satisfy the edge capacity constraints, and constraint (2b) complies with the flow conservation excluding aggregation nodes. Constraint (2c) represents that a flow corresponding to an agent follows the ways of a corresponding flow index. Constraint (2d) indicates that only the flow corresponding to the exit candidate set bundled in an aggregation node can pass the ways corresponding to the flow index. Constraint (2e) is applied to the binary decision variables; $f_k(e) = 1$ when a flow crosses edge $e \in E^{N^+}$ with flow index $k \in \mathcal{K}$, otherwise $f_k(e) = 0$.

To obtain an optimal solution, we must find an optimal extension time T of the time-expanded network. The lower and upper bounds of T are $\max_i |\pi_i^{\text{sp}}|, a_i \in \mathcal{A}$, and $\sum_{a_i \in \mathcal{A}} |\pi_i^{\text{sp}}|$, respectively, where π_i^{sp} denotes the shortest path for $a_i \in \mathcal{A}$ from its initial location to its given destination vertex without considering other agents, and $|\pi_i^{\text{sp}}|$ is defined as the length of a path. The proposed network flow formulation can always obtain solutions with the minimum cost when it has feasible solutions. Accordingly, a solution is optimal when $T = \sum_{a_i \in \mathcal{A}} |\pi_i^{\text{sp}}|$. However, the computation time can be excessively long when the value of T is large, and therefore, we implement an algorithm to obtain a solution by identifying as small T as possible. Specifically, the value of T starts from the lower bound and is increased by $\alpha \in \mathbb{Z}^+$ until a feasible solution is derived.

3   Evaluation

We experimentally compare our proposed method with the existing methods: conflict-based search (CBS) [9] and cooperative A* (CA*) [10].

Table 1. Experimental setups

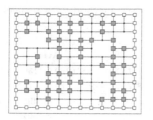

Fig. 3. Sample of a four-sided graph (Color figure online)

Graph size	12×12
The number of agents	10, 20, ..., 70
The size of exit candidate	1, (2, 4, 8, 44 (all))
The probability of obstacles	0%, 20%
The number of trials	30
Timeout	300
MIPgap	0.1
Update parameter α	10

3.1 Experimental Setups

We utilized a four-sided graph as shown in Fig. 3. The white and light blue rectangles represent exit vertices and agents, respectively. We installed obstacles on vertices with the given probability. At each time step, each agent could move to adjacent vertices along edges or stay at current vertices. The initial location of each agent was randomly selected on vertices except exit ones. Experimental setups are summarized in Table 1. MIPgap means an upper bound of the relative error. The number of agents was changed to 10, 20, ..., 70, and exits were randomly assigned $x = 1, 2, 4, 8$, and 44 (all exits) corresponding to the number of elements of $D_i, a_i \in \mathcal{A}$. Each agent could move to any one of them. Only one exit was randomly assigned in CBS and CA*, as these methods did not allow considering multiple destinations. When the success rate was 0%, we terminated the experiment.

All numerical evaluations were performed on a workstation with an Intel Xeon Broadwell CPU at 2.6 GHz with 112 GB of memory and Gurobi 9.0.1 [2].

3.2 Results

Table 2 represents the results of the total travel time compared with the same trials. The values represent the percentage calculated by dividing the total travel time of the proposed method by that of CA * (/CBS), and if the value was negative, the proposed method exhibited shorter total travel time. The values (#) means the number of common trials in which both the proposed method and CA*(/CBS) could obtain a solution within the timeout. When the probability of obstacles or the number of agents were large, the total travel time of the proposed method was shorter than CA*, resulting in up to 9.2% reduction when the number of agents was 70. Therefore, we concluded that the higher was the density in a graph, the better the proposed method performed in terms of generating paths with lower cost. However, compared with CBS, the proposed method resulted in approximately 1.8% longer total travel time.

Table 2. Proportion of the total travel time in the proposed method with respect to CA*/CBS.

		The # of agents							
	obs	10	20	30	40	50	60	70	Average (all)
CA*	0%	0.3 (30)	3.0 (30)	2.1 (30)	0.7 (29)	−2.5 (25)	−3.7 (10)	−4.9 (2)	0.5 (156)
	20%	−0.6 (30)	−1.0 (30)	−3.1 (30)	−6.2 (28)	−6.6 (21)	−8.7 (2)	−9.2 (1)	−3.4 (142)
CBS	0%	0.6 (29)	3.6 (19)	0.0 (1)	−	−	−	−	1.7 (49)
	20%	0.7 (30)	3.5 (18)	3.6 (2)	−	−	−	−	1.8 (50)

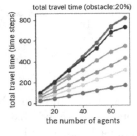

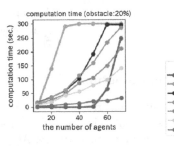

(a) Total travel time.   (b) Computation time.

Fig. 4. Results while varying the number of agents when the probability of obstacles is 20%.

Figure 4a represents the results of the total travel time comparison while varying the number of agents. The results indicated the same tendency regardless the probability of obstacles; therefore, we showed only the results when the probability of obstacles was 20%. *Choice-x* represents the number of exits assigned to each agent. The horizontal and vertical axes represent the number of agents and the total travel time (time steps), respectively. When the number of agents was small, CBS, CA*, and the proposed method (Choice-1) appeared to have almost the same total travel time. In the proposed method, the total travel time declined as the number of assigned exits increased. For example, the total travel time of Choice-2 was 24.3% smaller than Choice-1. These results suggested that it was easy to find vacant exits when there were many choices to select from possible exit candidates, and it could contribute to a shorter total travel time.

Figure 4b shows the results of the computation time comparison. Here, the horizontal and vertical axes represent the number of agents and the computation time, respectively. In most cases, the calculation time of the proposed method was shorter than that of CBS but longer than that of CA*. In the proposed method, the calculation time declined as the number of assigned exits augmented. Analyzing the number of times of expansion corresponding to time T in the time-expanded network, we found that $\max_i |\pi_i^{\mathrm{sp}}| \leq T \leq \max_i |\pi_i^{\mathrm{sp}}| + 3\alpha, a_i \in \mathcal{A}$ in many cases. We did not observe clear correlation between the number of expansions and the number of agents. Accordingly, we found that the solution time of ILP decreased as the number of assigned exits increased, and this effect was dominant concerning the overall computation time.

4 Conclusion

We proposed a generalization of the standard MAPF in terms of the use of destinations. Each agent was assigned multiple destinations partially shared with other agents and can move to any one of them. We named it the MAPF with destination choice problem (MAPF-DC) and formulated it as network flow problems using integer linear programming (ILP). In the proposed formulation, the best destination for each agent is implicitly selected among the destination candidates. The results of the conducted numerical experiments demonstrated that the total travel time could be reduced as a result of increasing the number of destination candidates assigned to each agent. It was shown that the computation time tended to decline as the number of assigned exits increased. As the future research work, we plan to devise a method that would be applicable to an environment of larger scale. Moreover, we will evaluate MAPF-DC in comparison with other alternative methods including destination assignment.

References

1. Dresner, K., Stone, P.: A multiagent approach to autonomous intersection management. J. Art. Intell. Res. **31**, 591–656 (2008)
2. Gurobi Optimization, LLC: Gurobi optimizer reference manual (2018). http://www.gurobi.com
3. Lim, G.J., Zangeneh, S., Baharnemati, M.R., Assavapokee, T.: A capacitated network flow optimization approach for short notice evacuation planning. Eur. J. Oper. Res. **223**(1), 234–245 (2012)
4. Ma, H., Koenig, S.: Optimal target assignment and path finding for teams of agents. In: Proceedings of AAMAS. International Foundation for Autonomous Agents and Multiagent Systems, pp. 1144–1152 (2016)
5. Ma, H., et al.: Overview: generalizations of multi-agent path finding to real-world scenarios. arXiv preprint arXiv:1702.05515 (2017)
6. Ma, H., Li, J., Kumar, T., Koenig, S.: Lifelong multi-agent path finding for online pickup and delivery tasks. In: Proceedings of AAMAS. International Foundation for Autonomous Agents and Multiagent Systems, pp. 837–845 (2017)
7. Okoso, A., Otaki, K., Nishi, T.: Multi-agent path finding with priority for cooperative automated valet parking. In: ITSC, pp. 2135–2140. IEEE (2019)
8. Rodriguez, S., Amato, N.M.: Behavior-based evacuation planning. In: IEEE International Conference on Robotics and Automation, pp. 350–355. IEEE (2010)
9. Sharon, G., Stern, R., Felner, A., Sturtevant, N.R.: Conflict-based search for optimal multi-agent pathfinding. Artif. Intell. **219**, 40–66 (2015)
10. Silver, D.: Cooperative pathfinding. In: AIIDE, vol. 1, pp. 117–122 (2005)
11. Stern, R., Sturtevant, N.R., Felner, A., et al.: Multi-agent pathfinding : definitions, variants, and benchmarks. In: SoCS, pp. 151–158 (2019)
12. Wurman, P.R., D'Andrea, R., Mountz, M.: Coordinating hundreds of cooperative, autonomous vehicles in warehouses. AI Mag. **29**(1), 9 (2008)

13. Yu, J., LaValle, S.M.: Multi-agent path planning and network flow. In: Frazzoli, E., Lozano-Perez, T., Roy, N., Rus, D. (eds.) Algorithmic Foundations of Robotics X. STAR, vol. 86, pp. 157–173. Springer, Heidelberg (2013). https://doi.org/10.1007/978-3-642-36279-8_10
14. Yu, J., LaValle, S.M.: Planning optimal paths for multiple robots on graphs. In: ICRA, pp. 3612–3617. IEEE (2013)

Abductive Design of BDI Agent-Based Digital Twins of Organizations

Ahmad Alelaimat[(✉)], Aditya Ghose, and Hoa Khanh Dam

Decision Systems Lab, School of Computing and Information Technology,
University of Wollongong, Wollongong 2522, Australia
{aama963,aditya,hoa}@uow.edu.au

Abstract. A Digital Twin ideally manifests the same behaviour (in silico) of its physical counterpart. While considerable attention has been paid to the development of Digital Twins for physical devices/systems, the question of developing Twins for organizations has received relatively little attention. This paper seeks to address this gap. The starting point is a log of an organization's externally manifested behaviour that we seek to recreate via a Digital Twin represented as a BDI agent. We present an algorithm to explain the externally visible behaviour of the organization by positing a BDI agent plan library, which, if executed, would manifest the same behaviour. We also present an algorithm to infer the internal behaviour of the agent in terms of event, option, and intention selection functions. The resulting approach suggests that using abduction to generate Digital Twins of organizations in the form of BDI agents can be effective.

Keywords: Rational agents · Digital Twins · Abductive recognition

1 Introduction

Digital Twin technology has been the subject of considerable attention over the past decade. Fundamentally, a Digital Twin provides a test-bed that mimics the behaviour of its physical counterpart based on real-time data, which can form the basis for optimizations, or handle potential deviations before they turn into real-world events.

This paper builds on the following two premises: (1) that Digital Twins of organizations can provide value and (2) that BDI agents are a particularly effective means for representing Digital Twins. Real-life organizations are anthropomorphic entities whose behaviour is complex and unpredictable in some instances. A large body of literature in management anthropomorphizes - attributing human behaviour to non human entities - the organization [1–3]. It makes sense therefore to concentrate on the beliefs of an organization, and its goals and intentions (i.e., internal bahaviour). A software agent with belief-desire-intention (BDI) architecture [4] thus allows us to design Digital Twins of organizations at a significantly fine-grained level. A more fine-grained definition

© Springer Nature Switzerland AG 2021
T. Uchiya et al. (Eds.): PRIMA 2020, LNAI 12568, pp. 377–385, 2021.
https://doi.org/10.1007/978-3-030-69322-0_27

of a Digital Twin therefore is one that also recreates the internal behaviour of the organization, as captured in its execution logs. It is important therefore for Digital Twin developers to understand the underlying complexity of organization behaviour. It may be argued that microscale models - those with sufficient details - of physical spaces are helpful. Nevertheless, they are often unavailable. Considering these challenges, the development of Digital Twins of organizations is far from trivial: It requires deep knowledge of physical space characteristics and dynamics.

Our objective in this work is twofold. First, we characterize the design of Digital Twins of organizations as a behaviour explanation problem, where we are seeking to infer the best explanation of organization visible behaviour on the basis of an abstraction of one of BDI model implementations, known as AgentSpeak(L) [5]. As the second contribution, we characterize the Digital Twin of an organization as a rational software agent having a certain mental attitudes of beliefs, desires, and intentions. Considering anthropomorphic organizations, this offers the best means available for implementing Digital Twins of organizations.

The remainder of this work is structured as follows. First, we formalise the problem of organization visible behaviour explanation using BDI ontology, and propose an algorithm for this purpose in Sect. 2. We consider organization internal behaviour, and propose an algorithm for this purpose in Sect. 3. Experimental results are reported in Sect. 4 before we conclude and outline future work in Sect. 5.

2   Abductive Plan Recognition

Abductive recognition of organization behaviour involves some mechanism takes (1) A set of hypotheses (i.e., plans) that serve as potential explanations, (2) An observed action sequence that we want to explain, and infer an initial high-level goal and composite of plans and subplans, such that the execution of these plans and subplans thus identified generates precisely the observed action sequence given the initial high-level goal thus identified. We define this mechanism as follows.

Definition 2.1 (Abductive plan recognition). Abductive plan recognition problem is a triple $(\text{H}, \text{D}_{\text{All}}, \texttt{explain})$, where:

1. H is a finite set of plans that serve as potential explanations,
2. D_{All} is an observed sequence of actions that we want to explain, and
3. $\texttt{explain}$ is a map from subsets of H to subsequences of D_{All}.

Let D be a subsequence of D_{All}. A hypothesis $\text{h}_t \in \text{H}$ is an explanation of D if $\texttt{body}(\text{h}_t) = \text{D}$. A composite hypothesis (H') is a sequence of hypotheses, each of which explains a subsequence of D_{All}. What we seek to find are plans and subplans that contain the observed actions (i.e., organizations visible behaviour). For theoretical reasons, we need to make an assumption about the completeness of H', such that $\texttt{explain}(\text{H}') = \text{D}_{\text{All}}$.

Algorithm 2.1 (Abductive plan recognition algorithm). Let D_{A11} be an observed sequence of actions and H be a set of potential explanations written on the basis of AgentSpeak(L). A composite hypothesis $H' \in H$ that explains D_{A11} can be computed as follows

```
1:  D_A11 = {d_1,...,d_n}
2:  H = {h_1,...,h_m}
3:  H' = ∅
4:  For h in H: E = E ∪ [triggering(h)]
5:  stack = ∅
6:  while(E ≠ ∅):
7:    e = top(E)
8:    R_e = unify_event(H)
9:    stack.push(R_e)
10:   E = E - {e}
11:   For h_t in stack:
12:     For a_m in body(h_t) and d_n in D_A11:
13:       if(a_m = d_n):
14:         explain(h_t) = [d_n]
15:         H' = H' ∪ [h_t]
16:       if(parent(h_t) ≠ nil):
17:         explain(parent(h_t)) = [d_n]
18:       if(a_m = !g(t)):
19:         e = !g(t)
20:         R_e = unify_event(H)
21:         Foreach h in R_e: parent(h) = h_t
22:         stack.push(R_e)
23:     Endfor
24:   Endfor
25:   stack.clear()
26: Endwhile
```

Algorithm 4.1 starts with parsing the triggering events of hypotheses exist in H. What the function top(E) simply does is selecting the first event in E at each parse step (line 7). Afterwards, it uses unify_event function to retrieve all relevant hypotheses R_e (line 8), and removes the selected event from E (line 9). A nested parsing runs over R_e. At each parse step, the body part of relevant hypothesis is compared with D_{A11} elements (line 12). Depending on the current hypothesis body construct, the algorithm determines if the potential explanation should be added to H' (line 15), or parsing hypothesis subplans (line 18). The algorithm terminates when $E = \emptyset$ (line 6). Note that the algorithm generates a sequence of hypotheses (H'), rather than generalised library of plans (P). Also note that to retain the goal of abductive plan recognition (inferring plans that if carried out to completion, would generate the given behaviour), eliminating redundant plans is key solution. Nevertheless, we need H' to be a sequence of hypotheses for further abduction.

3   Abductive Reasoning Cycle Recognition

Reasoning cycle abduction involves some mechanism takes a sequence of abducted plans H', the set of potential explanations H, i.e., $H' \subseteq H$, and generates preference relations between potential and inferred events, options, and intentions (e,g., if an event is always followed by another event, then this suggest that there is preference relation between both events). For the purpose of explaining organization internal behaviour on the basis of H', we introduce the following notations and definitions.

Definition 3.1 (Regular weak and strict preferences). Let F be a totally ordered set of elements $\{a, b, c, \ldots, z\}$. A regular weak preference, denoted by '$\succeq$', is a binary relation on F. For the ordered pairs (a, b), we use the notation $a \succeq b$ to point out that "a is preferred or indifferent to b". Relation '$\succeq$' is transitive; whenever $a \succeq b$ and $b \succeq c$, then also $a \succeq c$. Relation '$\succeq$' is reflexive. Formally, $\forall a \in F : a \succeq a$. A regular strict preference, denoted by '$\succ$', is another binary relation on F. For the ordered pairs (a, b), we use the notation $a \succ b$ to indicate that "a is strictly preferred to b". Relation $\succ$ is asymmetric. Notationally, $a \succ b \Rightarrow \neg b \succ a$. Also, it is transitive [7].

Definition 3.2 (Abductive S_E). Let $h_j, h_k \in H'$ be two abducted plans such that $\texttt{triggering}(h_j) = e_j$ and $\texttt{triggering}(h_k) = e_k$.

- $e_j \succeq e_k$ *iff* there is an E such that $e_j, e_k \in E$ and $j < k$.
- $e_j \succ e_k$ *iff* $e_j \succeq e_k \wedge \neg e_k \succeq e_j$.
- $S_E(E) = \{e_j \mid e_j \succ E\}$.

Definition 3.3 (Abductive S_O). Let $h_j, h_k \in O_e$ be two applicable plans for the event e.

- $h_j \succ h_k$ *iff* $h_j \in H'$ and $h_k \notin H'$
- $S_O(O_e) = \{h_j \mid h_j \succ O_e\}$.

Definition 3.4 (Abductive S_I). Let $i_j, i_k \in I$ be two intention stacks.

- $i_j \succeq i_k$ *iff* there is an I such that $i_j, i_k \in I$ and $j < k$.
- $i_j \succ i_k$ *iff* $i_j \succeq i_k \wedge \neg i_k \succeq i_j$.
- $S_I(I) = \{i \mid i_j \succ I\}$.

Regular strict preferences here describe how the organization prioritized goal events, selected applicable options, and deliberate - think carefully- about competing intentions based on their appearance in H'. Developed on the arguments above, we now present an algorithm for S_E, S_O, S_I abduction. Reasoning cycle abduction algorithm relies on the fact that two or more events, options, or intentions are competing iff there is a preference relation between them can be detected by inspecting H'.

Algorithm 3.1 (S_E, S_O, S_I Abduction Algorithm). Let H be a set of potential explanations, and H' sequence of abducted explanations. Abductive S_E, S_O, S_I can be computed as follows:

```
1:  H' = [h₁, ..., h_z]
2:  H = {h₁, ..., h_y}
3:  For h in H': E = E ∪ [triggering(h)]
4:  While(E ≠ ∅):
5:     S_E(E) = {e_j | e_j ≻ E}
6:     E = E - {e_j}
7:     R_e = unify_event(H)
8:     O_e = check_context(R_e)
9:     S_O(O_e) = {h_j | h_j ≻ O_e}
10:    I = Construct_intention_stacks(H')
11:    S_I(I) = {i_j | i_j ≻ I}
12: Endwhile
```

Reasoning cycle abduction algorithm aims to explain organization internal behaviour and represent them in terms of event, option, intention selection functions. Clearly, H' is derived by implementing abductive plans recognition algorithm on D_{A11}. As illustrated in Definitions 3.2 and 3.4, goal events and intentions are ordered based on H', where we assume that H' is totally ordered set of hypotheses. Actually, this is based on the assumption that D_{A11} is recorded sequentially. More precisely, since it is possible to order abducted plans based on D_{A11}, it is easy to order goal events and intentions on the same basis. For event selection, what the abductive S_E simply does is selecting the first event in E at each reasoning cycle. Abductive S_O starts with retrieving all relevant plans from H (based on S_E selection), then those whose determined as applicable options are tested for preference relation, as shown in Definition 3.4, abductive S_I requires intentions to be constructed as stacks of plans (see [5] for a representative reference). For intention selection, what the abductive S_I does is selecting the first constructed stack in I at each reasoning cycle. In this sense, one can view I as queue of stacks.

4   Experimental Results

Aiming to establish that the proposed abductive algorithms generate reasonable reliable results, we ran an experiment with Jason's examples[1] and another with amended claim handling event log[2]. Data has been collected using a debugging tool called Mind Inspector [6]. The collected data contains 120 instances, with multiple event, option, and intention selections. The examples visible behaviour have been explained using a collection of hypotheses (up to 20 plans, each of

---

[1] http://jason.sourceforge.net/wp/examples.
[2] http://www.processmining.org/prom/decisionmining.

which with a body consisting of up to 5 subplans). For the selection functions to be abducted, we configured event, option, intention methods of the `Agent` class as described in [6]. An agent equipped with the abducted plan library and customized selection functions has been executed in an environment typical to the used examples.

4.1   Evaluation

We use accuracy measure to evaluate our proposed abductive algorithms. Accuracy is the ratio of correctly simulated actions over the total number of simulated actions. Figure 1 illustrates the accuracy results of the abductive algorithms described above compared to another approaches represented in [8–10], and [11]. Most of these approaches share a common interfering technique, i.e., transforming inferred models (e.g., workflow net) into well-defined plans.

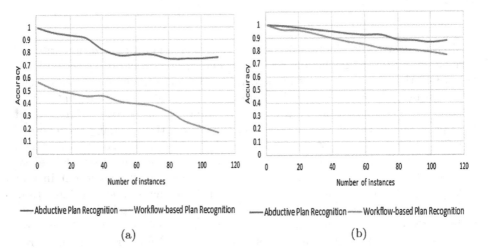

(a)   (b)

Fig. 1. Accuracy results for claim handling (a), and domestic robot (b) examples for different numbers of instances.

As illustrated in Fig. 1, the accuracy results demonstrate the reasonability of our proposed abductive algorithms in both examples. Nevertheless, the reader should keep in mind two important details. First, the more complex the organization mental attitude is, the lower accuracy we can obtain. This is not surprising, because in real-life settings, organizations are driven by a wide range of values that shape their mental attitude. Second, completeness of the observations log plays an important role in explaining organization's internal state. A log that is sufficiently large (i.e., one that includes all possible behaviours) enables selection functions abduction to be more accurate. Compared to the other approaches, our abductive approach performs significantly higher with respect to the two details mentioned above, since it maintains the internal behaviour of the constituent examples. Note that we intentionally modified the selection functions to give different priorities of the queued elements in the claim handling example. For the second experiment as illustrated in Fig. 1(b), the abductive approach performed only slightly better than the workflow-based plan recognition, because what the Domestic Robot does is selecting the first element of each queue (i.e., event, option, intention). Particularly, the robot does not have sophisticated internal attitude.

4.2 Complexity of the Abductive Approach

We ran a number of experiments with the intention of analysing the abductive algorithms for efficiency. Particularly, we aim to test how fast the proposed abductive algorithms could explain a sequence of observations on basis of different practical settings. The experiments have been implemented on an Intel Core i5-6200 CPU (with 8 GB RAM). For any given behaviour, we noticed that there are two parameters that can highly affect the computation time of the abductive algorithms: (1) the number of individual hypotheses, and (2) level of the generated goal-plan tree up to which the abductive plan recognition algorithm will be applied (i.e., depth of search).

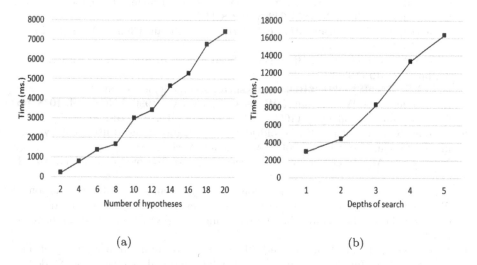

(a)   (b)

Fig. 2. Computing time in millisecond needed for recognition of different number of hypotheses and depths of search.

As illustrated in Fig. 2(a), the computing time is plotted linearly in respect of the number of available hypotheses. Recall that the abductive design of Digital Twins is about finding correct and complete explanation of a given observations. It is necessary therefore to include all available hypotheses. A higher growth rate can be seen with the increasing of search depth, as shown in Fig. 2(b), but this is an extreme case. Naturally, a large number of simple hypotheses would, in real-life settings, explain sophisticated observations or it is more appropriate to not include them there. It is to be noted here that for each run, the abductive plan recognition algorithm generates a different set of plans (a different H'), and thus the S_E, S_0, S_I abduction algorithm generates new preference relations for every run as well.

5   Conclusion

In this work, we addressed the abductive design of Digital Twins of organizations. A number of extensions of this work are of interest, including applications of belief change [14], belief merging [13] frameworks and applications in practical settings such as supply chain management [12].

References

1. Watkins, K.E.: Part five: Do organizations learn? Of course organizations learn!. New Directions Adult Continuing Educ. **1996**(72), pp. 89–96 (1996)
2. Mayer, M.P., Kuz, S., Schlick, C.M.: Using anthropomorphism to improve the human-machine interaction in industrial environments (Part II). In: Duffy, V.G. (ed.) DHM 2013. LNCS, vol. 8026, pp. 93–100. Springer, Heidelberg (2013). https://doi.org/10.1007/978-3-642-39182-8_11
3. Andersen, J.A.: An organization called Harry. J. Organ. Change Manage. **21**(2), 174–187 (2008)
4. Rao, A.S., Georgeff, M.P.: BDI agents: from theory to practice. In: ICMAS, vol. 95, pp. 312–319 (1995)
5. Rao, A.S.: AgentSpeak(L): BDI agents speak out in a logical computable language. In: Van de Velde, W., Perram, J.W. (eds.) MAAMAW 1996. LNCS, vol. 1038, pp. 42–55. Springer, Heidelberg (1996). https://doi.org/10.1007/BFb0031845
6. Bordini, R.H., Hubner, J.F., Wooldridge, M.: Programming Multi-agent Systems in AgentSpeak Using Jason, vol. 8. Wiley, New York (2007)
7. Mas-Colell, A., Whinston, M.D., Green, J.R.: Microeconomic Theory, vol. 1. Oxford University Press, New York (1995)
8. Augusto, V., Xie, X., Prodel, M., Jouaneton, B., Lamarsalle, L.: Evaluation of discovered clinical pathways using process mining and joint agent-based discrete-event simulation. In: Winter Simulation Conference (WSC), pp. 2135–2146. IEEE (2016)
9. Van Dongen, B., van Luin, J., Verbeek, E.: Process mining in a multi-agent auctioning system. In: Proceedings of the 4th International Workshop on Modelling of Objects, Components, and Agents, Turku, pp. 145–160, June 2006
10. Rozinat, A., Zickler, S., Veloso, M., van der Aalst, W.M., McMillen, C.: Analyzing multi-agent activity logs using process mining techniques. In: Asama, H., Kurokawa, H., Ota, J., Sekiyama, K. (eds.) Distributed Autonomous Robotic Systems, vol. 8, pp. 251–260. Springer, Heidelberg (2009). https://doi.org/10.1007/978-3-642-00644-9_22
11. Xu, H., et al.: Automatic BDI plan recognition from process execution logs and effect logs. In: Cossentino, M., El Fallah Seghrouchni, A., Winikoff, M. (eds.) EMAS 2013. LNCS (LNAI), vol. 8245, pp. 274–291. Springer, Heidelberg (2013). https://doi.org/10.1007/978-3-642-45343-4_15

12. Sombattheera, C., Ghose, A., Hyland, P.: A Framework to Support Coalition Formation in Supply Chain Collaboration. In: ICEB, pp. 1–6 (2004)
13. Meyer, T., Ghose, A., Chopra, S.: Social choice, merging, and elections. In: Benferhat, S., Besnard, P. (eds.) ECSQARU 2001. LNCS (LNAI), vol. 2143, pp. 466–477. Springer, Heidelberg (2001). https://doi.org/10.1007/3-540-44652-4_41
14. Ghose, A., Goebel, R.: Belief states as default theories: studies in non-prioritized belief change. In: ECAI, vol. 98, pp. 8–12, August 1998

Beliefs, Time and Space: A Language for the Yōkai Board Game

Dominique Longin[1(✉)], Emiliano Lorini[1], and Frédéric Maris[2]

[1] CNRS, IRIT/LILaC, Toulouse University, Toulouse, France
Dominique.Longin@irit.fr
[2] Université Paul Sabatier, IRIT/ADRIA, Toulouse University, Toulouse, France

Abstract. We present an epistemic language for representing an artificial player's beliefs and actions in the context of the Yōkai board game. Yōkai is a cooperative game which requires a combination of Theory of Mind (ToM), temporal and spatial reasoning to be played effectively by an artificial agent. We show that the language properly accounts for these three dimensions and that its satisfiability problem is NP-complete. This opens up the possibility of exploiting SAT techniques for automating reasoning of an artificial player in the context of the Yōkai board-game. **The full version of this paper can be found in [15].**

1   Introduction

When one wishes to model socio-cognitive agents and, in particular, agents endowed with a Theory of Mind (ToM) who are capable of reasoning about other agents' beliefs, some of the privileged tools are epistemic logic (EL) [12,14] and its extensions by informative and communicative extensions such as public and private announcements [3,13,20]. The latter belongs to the Dynamic Epistemic Logic (DEL) family [9].

The major disadvantage of EL and DEL is that they have most of the time a high complexity thereby making them not very well-suited for practical applications. In particular, it has been shown that extending multi-agent EL by simple notions of state eliminating public announcement or arrow eliminating private announcement does not increase its PSPACE complexity (see, e.g., [7,19]). However, the satisfiability problem of full DEL with public, semi-private and private communicative actions was shown to be NEXPTIME-complete [1]. The situation is even worse in the context of epistemic planning: it is known that epistemic planning in public announcement logic (PAL) is decidable, while it becomes undecidable in full DEL, due to the fact that the epistemic model may grow as a consequence of a private announcement [6].

In [16,17], a variant of epistemic logic with a semantics exploiting belief bases is introduced. It distinguishes explicit belief from implicit belief. The former is modeled as a fact in an agent's belief base, while the latter is modeled as a fact that is deducible from the agent's explicit beliefs. The main advantages of the belief base semantics for epistemic logic compared to the standard possible

© Springer Nature Switzerland AG 2021
T. Uchiya et al. (Eds.): PRIMA 2020, LNAI 12568, pp. 386–393, 2021.
https://doi.org/10.1007/978-3-030-69322-0_28

world semantics based on multi-relational structures (so-called Kripke models) are (i) its compactness, and (ii) its closeness to the way artificial cognitively-inspired agents are traditionally modeled in AI and in the area of knowledge representation and reasoning (KR) by adopting a database perspective [21]. In [18], it is shown that this variant of epistemic logic provides a valuable abstraction for modeling multi-robot scenarios in which each robot is endowed with a ToM whereby being able to ascribe epistemic states to the other robots and to reason about them.[1]

In this paper, we leverage the belief base semantics for epistemic logic to model interaction in the context of the cooperative board-game Yōkai.[2] We consider its two-player variant in which an artificial agent has to collaborate with a human agent to win it and to obtain the best score as possible. Yōkai is an interesting testbed for artificial agents, as it covers a lot of epistemic and strategic reasoning aspects as well as planning and belief revision aspects. The idea of testing the performance of artificial agents in the context of cooperative board-games in which ToM reasoning plays a role is not new. Some works exist about modeling and implementing artificial players for the card game Hanabi [4,10,11]. Yōkai adds to the ToM dimension, which is central in Hanabi, the temporal and spatial dimension. First of all, in Yōkai a player's performance relies on her/its capacity to remember the cards she/it and the other player have seen in the past. Secondly, the players must move cards in a shared space and there are spatial restrictions on card movements that should be taken into account by the players. More generally, the interesting feature of Yōkai, from the point view of KR, is the combination of epistemic, temporal and spatial reasoning that is required to completely apprehend all the game facets and dimensions.

The main novelty of our approach to modeling artificial board-game players is the use of SAT-based techniques. Specifically, the language we present for representing the artificial player's beliefs about the static and dynamic aspects of the game as well as about the human player's beliefs has the same complexity as SAT and can be polynomially translated into a propositional logic language. This opens up the possibility of exploiting SAT techniques for automating reasoning of the artificial player in the context of the Yōkai board-game.

The paper is organized as follows. In Sect. 2, we introduce the specification language for modeling the artificial player's actions and beliefs about the game properties and about the human player's beliefs. It is a timed language for explicit and implicit belief with a semantics exploiting belief bases. The main novelty compared to the epistemic language presented in [17] is the temporal component: the artificial player modeled in the language has knowledge about the current time of the game and beliefs about current and past beliefs of the human player.

---

[1] See also [5,8] for a DEL-based approach to modeling and implementing ToM on social robots.

[2] https://www.ultraboardgames.com/yokai/game-rules.php.

2   A Timed Language for Explicit and Implicit Belief

This section presents a two-agent timed variant of the language and the semantics of the logic of explicit and implicit belief presented in [17]. The two agents are the artificial agent (or machine) $\mathfrak{m}$ and the human user $\mathfrak{h}$. Agents $\mathfrak{m}$ and $\mathfrak{h}$ are treated asymmetrically. Our language allows us to represent (i) $\mathfrak{h}$'s explicit beliefs at different points in a game sequence, and (ii) $\mathfrak{m}$'s actual explicit and implicit beliefs, namely, $\mathfrak{m}$'s explicit and implicit beliefs at the current time point of the game sequence. Following [17], explicit beliefs are defined to be beliefs in an agent's belief base, while implicit beliefs are those beliefs that are derivable from the agent's explicit beliefs.

We first present the static language in which agent $\mathfrak{m}$'s beliefs do not change. Then, we present a dynamic extension in which agent $\mathfrak{m}$'s belief base can be expanded by new information.

2.1   Static Language

Assume a countably infinite set of atomic propositions ATM. We define the language in two steps.

We first define the language $\mathcal{L}_0(ATM)$ by the following grammar in BNF:

$$\alpha ::= p^t \mid \triangle_{\mathfrak{h}}^t \alpha \mid now^{\geq t} \mid \neg\alpha \mid \alpha_1 \wedge \alpha_2 \mid \triangle_{\mathfrak{m}}\alpha,$$

where p ranges over ATM and t ranges over $\mathbb{N}$. $\mathcal{L}_0(ATM)$ is the language for representing agent $\mathfrak{h}$'s timed explicit beliefs and agent $\mathfrak{m}$'s actual explicit beliefs. Specifically, the formula $\triangle_{\mathfrak{h}}^t \alpha$ is read "agent $\mathfrak{h}$ explicitly believes that α at time t", whilst $\triangle_{\mathfrak{m}}$ is read "agent $\mathfrak{m}$ actually has the explicit belief that α". Atomic propositions are assumed to be timed: p^t is read "atomic proposition p is true at time t". Finally, formula $now^{\geq t}$ provides information about the current time point. It is read "the actual time of the game play is at least t".

Then, we define $\mathcal{L}_0^T(ATM)$ to be the subset $\mathcal{L}_0(ATM)$ including only timed formulas, that is:

$$\mathcal{L}_0^T(ATM) = \{p^t : p \in ATM \text{ and } t \in \mathbb{N}\} \cup$$
$$\{\triangle_{\mathfrak{h}}^t \alpha : \alpha \in \mathcal{L}_0(ATM) \text{ and } t \in \mathbb{N}\} \cup$$
$$\{now^{\geq t} : t \in \mathbb{N}\}.$$

Elements of $\mathcal{L}_0^T(ATM)$ are denoted by $x, y, \ldots$

The language $\mathcal{L}(ATM)$ extends the language $\mathcal{L}_0(ATM)$ by a modal operator of implicit belief for agent $\mathfrak{m}$ and is defined by the following grammar:

$$\varphi ::= \alpha \mid \neg\varphi \mid \varphi_1 \wedge \varphi_2 \mid \square_{\mathfrak{m}}\alpha,$$

where α ranges over $\mathcal{L}_0(ATM)$. For notational convenience we write $\mathcal{L}_0$ instead of $\mathcal{L}_0(ATM)$, $\mathcal{L}_0^T$ instead of $\mathcal{L}_0^T(ATM)$ and $\mathcal{L}$ instead of $\mathcal{L}(ATM)$, when the context is unambiguous. The formula $\square_{\mathfrak{m}}\alpha$ is read "agent $\mathfrak{m}$ actually has the implicit belief that α". The other Boolean constructions $\top, \bot, \vee, \rightarrow$ and $\leftrightarrow$ are defined in the standard way. Notice that only formulas from the sublanguage $\mathcal{L}_0$ can be in the scope of the implicit belief operator $\square_m$. Therefore, nesting of this operator is not allowed (e.g.., $\square_m \neg \square_m p^t$ is not a well-formed formula). As we will show at the end of the section, this syntactic restriction on our language is useful to make the complexity of its satisfiability problem the same as the complexity of SAT.

The interpretation of the language $\mathcal{L}$ exploits the notion of belief base. While the notions of possible world and epistemic alternative are primitive in the standard Kripke semantics for epistemic logic [12], they are defined from the primitive concept of belief base in our semantics.

Definition 1 (State). *A state is a tuple $S = (B, V)$ where (i) $B \subseteq \mathcal{L}_0$ is agent m's belief base (or, agent m's subjective view of the actual situation), (ii) $V \subseteq \mathcal{L}_0^T$ is the actual situation, and such that, for every $t, t' \in \mathbb{N}$,*

$$now^{\geq 0} \in V, \tag{1}$$

$$\text{if } now^{\geq t} \in V \text{ and } t' \leq t \text{ then } now^{\geq t'} \in V, \tag{2}$$

$$now^{\geq t} \in V \text{ iff } now^{\geq t} \in B, \text{ and} \tag{3}$$

$$now^{\geq t} \notin V \text{ iff } \neg now^{\geq t} \in B. \tag{4}$$

The set of all states is denoted by $\mathbf{S}$.

Conditions (1) and (2) in the previous definition guarantees time consistency, namely, that the current time should be at least 0 and that if the current time is at least t and $t' \leq t$, then it should be at least t'. Conditions (3) and (4) capture agent m's time-knowledge, namely, the assumption that m has complete information about the current time. Note that the actual situation V includes timed formulas in $\mathcal{L}_0^T$ and not simply atomic propositions from ATM.

The sublanguage $\mathcal{L}_0(ATM)$ is interpreted w.r.t. states as follows:

Definition 2 (Satisfaction). *Let $S = (B, V) \in \mathbf{S}$. Then:*

$$S \models x \iff x \in V,$$
$$S \models \neg \alpha \iff S \not\models \alpha,$$
$$S \models \alpha_1 \wedge \alpha_2 \iff S \models \alpha_1 \text{ and } S \models \alpha_2,$$
$$S \models \triangle_m \alpha \iff \alpha \in B.$$

Observe in particular the set-theoretic interpretation of the explicit belief operator for agent m: agent m actually has the explicit belief that α if and only if α is included in her actual belief base. This highlights the asymmetry between agent m and agent $\mathfrak{h}$ in our semantics. We adopt agent m's *internal* perspective, that is, the point of view of its belief base.[3] On the contrary, agent $\mathfrak{h}$'s explicit beliefs are modeled from an *external* point of view and semantically interpreted in the same way as the other timed formulas in $\mathcal{L}_0^T(ATM)$.

---

[3] See [2] for an in-depth logical analysis of the internal perspective on modeling knowledge and belief.

A multi-agent belief model (MAB) is defined to be a state supplemented with a set of states, called *context*. The latter includes all states that are compatible with agent m's background knowledge.

Definition 3 (Model). *A model is a pair* (S, Cxt), *where* $S \in \mathbf{S}$ *and* $Cxt \subseteq \mathbf{S}$. *The class of all models is denoted by* $\mathbf{M}$.

Note that we do not impose that $S \in Cxt$. When $Cxt = \mathbf{S}$ then (S, Cxt) is said to be *complete*, since $\mathbf{S}$ is conceivable as the complete (or universal) context which contains all possible states.

Definition 4 (Epistemic alternatives). *We define* $\mathcal{R}$ *to be the binary relation on the set* $\mathbf{S}$ *such that, for all* $S = (B, V), S' = (B', V') \in \mathbf{S}$:

$$S\mathcal{R}S' \text{ if and only if } \forall \alpha \in B : S' \models \alpha.$$

$S\mathcal{R}S'$ means that S' is an epistemic alternative for the artificial agent m at S. So m's set of epistemic alternatives at S, noted $\mathcal{R}(S) = \{S' \in \mathbf{S} : S\mathcal{R}S'\}$, includes exactly those states that satisfy m's explicit beliefs.

Definition 5 extends Definition 2 to the full language $\mathcal{L}$. Its formulas are interpreted with respect to models. We omit Boolean cases that are defined in the usual way.

Definition 5 (Satisfaction, cont.). *Let* $(S, Cxt) \in \mathbf{M}$. *Then:*

$$(S, Cxt) \models \alpha \Longleftrightarrow S \models \alpha;$$
$$(S, Cxt) \models \Box_\mathsf{m}\varphi \Longleftrightarrow \forall S' \in Cxt, \text{ if } S\mathcal{R}S' \text{ then } (S', Cxt) \models \varphi.$$

A formula $\varphi \in \mathcal{L}$ is valid in the class $\mathbf{M}$, noted $\models_\mathbf{M} \varphi$, if and only if $(S, Cxt) \models \varphi$ for every $(S, Cxt) \in \mathbf{M}$; it is satisfiable in $\mathbf{M}$ if and only if $\neg\varphi$ is not valid in $\mathbf{M}$. As the following theorem indicates, the satisfiability problem for $\mathcal{L}(ATM)$ has the same complexity as SAT.

Theorem 1. *Checking satisfiability of* $\mathcal{L}(ATM)$ *formulas in the class* $\mathbf{M}$ *is an NP-complete problem.*

SKETCH OF PROOF. Hardness is clear since $\mathcal{L}(ATM)$ extends the propositional logic language. As for membership, we can find a polysize satisfiability preserving translation from $\mathcal{L}(ATM)$ to propositional logic. The translation is divided in three steps. First, we transform the input formula in $\mathcal{L}(ATM)$ into negated normal form (NNF). Secondly, we translate the formula in NNF into a restricted mono-modal language with no nesting of the modal operator. Thirdly, we translate the latter into a propositional logic language in a way similar to the standard translation of modal logic into FOL. We take care of translating a finite theory including axioms corresponding to the four constraints of Definition 1. The axioms have the following form: $now^{\geq 0}$, $now^{\geq t} \rightarrow now^{\geq t'}$ for $t' \leq t$, $now^{\geq t} \leftrightarrow \triangle_\mathsf{m} now^{\geq t}$ and $\neg now^{\geq t} \leftrightarrow \triangle_\mathsf{m} \neg now^{\geq t}$. The theory is finite since we only need to consider instances of the axioms whose symbols occur in the input formula. For example, if $t' \leq t$ and both $now^{\geq t}$ and $now^{\geq t'}$ occur in the input formula, then $now^{\geq t} \rightarrow now^{\geq t'}$ should be included in the theory, otherwise not. ∎

2.2 Dynamic Extension

Let us now move from a static to a dynamic perspective by presenting a extension of the language $\mathcal{L}(ATM)$ with belief expansion operators. Specifically, we introduce the following language $\mathcal{L}^+(ATM)$:

$$\varphi ::= \alpha \mid \neg\varphi \mid \varphi_1 \wedge \varphi_2 \mid \Box_m \alpha \mid [+_m^t \alpha]\varphi,$$

where α ranges over $\mathcal{L}_0$ and t ranges over $\mathbb{N}$. The formula $[+_m^t \alpha]\varphi$ is read "φ holds after agent m has privately learnt that α and that the current time is at least t" or simply "φ holds after agent m has privately learnt that α at time at least t".

Our extension has the following semantics relative to a model:

Definition 6 (Satisfaction relation, cont.). *Let* $S = (B, V) \in \mathbf{S}$ *and* $(S, Cxt) \in \mathbf{M}$. *Then,*

$$(S, Cxt) \models [+_m^t \alpha]\varphi \iff (S^{+_m^t \alpha}, Cxt) \models \varphi$$

with

$$S^{+_m^t \alpha} = (B^{+_m^t \alpha}, V^{+_m^t \alpha}),$$
$$V^{+_m^t \alpha} = V \cup \{now^{\geq t'} : t' \leq t\},$$
$$B^{+_m^t \alpha} = B \cup \{\alpha\} \cup \{now^{\geq t'} : t' \leq t\}.$$

Intuitively speaking, agent m's private learning that α at time at least t simply consists in (i) adding the information α to m's belief base, and (ii) moving the objective time and m's subjective view of time to index t.

As the following proposition indicates, the dynamic semantics given in Definition 6 is well-defined, as it guarantees that the structure resulting from a belief expansion operation belongs to the class $\mathbf{M}$, if the initial structure also belongs to $\mathbf{M}$.

Proposition 1. *Let* $(S, Cxt) \in \mathbf{M}$. *Then,* $(S^{+_m^t \alpha}, Cxt) \in \mathbf{M}$.

Interestingly, adding belief expansion operators to the language $\mathcal{L}$ does not increase the complexity of the corresponding satisfiability problem.

Theorem 2. *Checking satisfiability of* $\mathcal{L}^+(ATM)$ *formulas in the class* $\mathbf{M}$ *is an NP-complete problem.*

SKETCH OF PROOF. The theorem is a consequence of Theorem 1 and the fact that we can a find a polysize reduction of the satisfiability problem for $\mathcal{L}^+(ATM)$ to the satisfiability problem for $\mathcal{L}(ATM)$. The reduction makes use of reduction axioms which allow us to eliminate dynamic operators from the input formula and to obtain a logically equivalent formula in $\mathcal{L}(ATM)$. ∎

Let $EVT = \{+_m^t \alpha : \alpha \in \mathcal{L}_0, t \in \mathbb{N}\}$ be the set of belief expansion events. It is reasonable to assume that such events have executability preconditions that are specified by the following function $\mathcal{P} : EVT \longrightarrow \mathcal{L}(ATM)$. So, we can define the following operator of successful occurrence of an event in EVT:

$$\langle\!\langle +_m^t \alpha \rangle\!\rangle \varphi \stackrel{\text{def}}{=} \mathcal{P}(+_m^t \alpha) \wedge [+_m^t \alpha] \varphi.$$

The formula $\langle\!\langle +_m^t \alpha \rangle\!\rangle \varphi$ has to be read "agent m can privately learn that α at time t and φ holds after the occurrence of this learning event".

In the next section, we will provide a formalization of the Yōkai board-game with the aid of the language $\mathcal{L}^+(ATM)$. We will represent agent m's actions in the game as events in EVT affecting m's beliefs. For every action of m, we will specify the corresponding executability precondition.

3   Conclusion

We have introduced a simple epistemic language for representing an artificial player's knowledge and actions in the context of the cooperative board-game Yōkai. In the extended version of this paper [15]: 1) we explain the rules of Yōkai and clarify the representation and reasoning requirements that are necessary for the artificial player to be able to play the game in a clever way; 2) we have shown that this game requires a combination of Theory of Mind (ToM), temporal and spatial reasoning to be played effectively by the artificial agent; 3) we illustrate how this epistemic language is able to represent strategic reasoning rules. Our approach relies on SAT given the existence of a polysize satisfiability preserving translation of the epistemic language into propositional logic.

Future work will be organized in two steps. First, we intend to specify a belief revision module for the artificial player which spells out how it should change its beliefs after the human player's moves. Secondly, we plan to implement an artificial player based on our formalization and to use existing SAT solvers for automating the reasoning and planning for the artificial player during the game play. We plan to formalize and implement a variety of game strategies for the artificial player, in line with the methodology sketched in [15, Section 4.3], and to the test their performances experimentally.

References

1. Aucher, G., Schwarzentruber, F.: On the complexity of dynamic epistemic logic. In: Proceedings of the 14th Conference on Theoretical Aspects of Rationality and Knowledge (TARK 2013) (2013)
2. Aucher, G.: Private announcement and belief expansion: an internal perspective. J. Logic Comput. **22**(3), 451–479 (2012)
3. Baltag, A., Moss, L., Solecki, S.: The logic of public announcements, common knowledge and private suspicions. In: Gilboa, I. (ed.) Proceedings of the Seventh Conference on Theoretical Aspects of Rationality and Knowledge (TARK 1998), pp. 43–56. Morgan Kaufmann, San Francisco (1998)
4. Bard, N., et al.: The Hanabi challenge: a new frontier for AI research. Artif. Intell. **280**, 103216 (2020)

5. Bolander, T.: Seeing is believing: formalising false-belief tasks in dynamic epistemic logic. In: van Ditmarsch, H., Sandu, G. (eds.) Jaakko Hintikka on Knowledge and Game-Theoretical Semantics. OCL, vol. 12, pp. 207–236. Springer, Cham (2018). https://doi.org/10.1007/978-3-319-62864-6_8
6. Bolander, T., Andersen, M.B.: Epistemic planning for single- and multi-agent systems. J. Appl. Non-Classical Logics 21(1), 656–680 (2011)
7. Bolander, T., van Ditmarsch, H., Herzig, A., Lorini, E., Pardo, P., Schwarzentruber, F.: Announcements to attentive agents. J. Logic Lang. Inf. 25(1), 1–35 (2015)
8. Dissing, L., Bolander, T.: Implementing theory of mind on a robot using dynamic epistemic logic. In: Bessiere, C. (ed.) Proceedings of the Twenty-Ninth International Joint Conference on Artificial Intelligence, (IJCAI 2020), pp. 1615–1621 (2020)
9. van Ditmarsch, H.P., van der Hoek, W., Kooi, B.: Dynamic Epistemic Logic. Kluwer Academic Publishers, Dordrecht (2007). https://doi.org/10.1007/978-1-4020-5839-4
10. Eger, M., Martens, C.: Practical specification of belief manipulation in games. In: Magerko, B., Rowe, J.P. (eds.) Proceedings of the Thirteenth AAAI Conference on Artificial Intelligence and Interactive Digital Entertainment (AIIDE-17), pp. 30–36. AAAI Press (2017)
11. Eger, M., Martens, C., Cordoba, M.A.: An intentional AI for Hanabi. In: IEEE Conference on Computational Intelligence and Games, CIG 2017, pp. 68–75. IEEE (2017)
12. Fagin, R., Halpern, J., Moses, Y., Vardi, M.: Reasoning About Knowledge. MIT Press, Cambridge (1995)
13. Gerbrandy, J., Groeneveld, W.: Reasoning about information change. J. Logic Lang. Inf. 6, 147–196 (1997)
14. Halpern, J.Y., Moses, Y.: A guide to completeness and complexity for modal logics of knowledge and belief. Artif. Intell. 54(2), 319–379 (1992)
15. Longin, D., Lorini, E., Maris, F.: Beliefs, time and space: a language for the Yōkai board game. Research report, IRIT - Institut de recherche en informatique de Toulouse, October 2020. https://hal.archives-ouvertes.fr/hal-02983253
16. Lorini, E.: In praise of belief bases: doing epistemic logic without possible worlds. In: Proceedings of the Thirty-Second AAAI Conference on Artificial Intelligence (AAAI 2018), pp. 1915–1922. AAAI Press (2018)
17. Lorini, E.: Rethinking epistemic logic with belief bases. Artif. Intell. 282, 103233 (2020)
18. Lorini, E., Romero, F.: Decision procedures for epistemic logic exploiting belief bases. In: Proceedings of the 18th International Conference on Autonomous Agents and Multiagent Systems (AAMAS 2019), pp. 944–952. IFAAMAS (2019)
19. Lutz, C.: Complexity and succinctness of public announcement logic. In: Proceedings of the Fifth International Joint Conference on Autonomous Agents and Multiagent Systems (AAMAS 2006), pp. 137–143. ACM (2006)
20. Plaza, J.A.: Logics of public communications. In: Emrich, M., Pfeifer, M., Hadzikadic, M., Ras, Z. (eds.) Proceedings of the 4th International Symposium on Methodologies for Intelligent Systems, pp. 201–216 (1989)
21. Shoham, Y.: Logical theories of intention and the database perspective. J. Philos. Logic 38(6), 633–648 (2009)

Argumentation-Based Explanations of Multimorbidity Treatment Plans

Qurat-ul-ain Shaheen[1](✉)(iD), Alice Toniolo[2](iD), and Juliana K. F. Bowles[2](iD)

[1] IIIA-CSIC, 08193 Barcelona, Spain
qurat@iiia.csic.es
[2] Computer Science, University of St Andrews, St Andrews KY16 9SX, UK
{a.toniolo,jkfb}@st-andrews.ac.uk

Abstract. We present an argumentation model to explain the optimal treatment plans recommended by a Satisfiability Modulo Theories solver for multimorbid patients. The resulting framework can be queried to obtain supporting reasons for nodes on a path following a model of argumentation schemes. The modelling approach is generic and can be used for justifying similar sequences.

Keywords: Multimorbidity · Argumentation schemes · SMT solvers

1 Introduction

Multimorbidity, the presence of two or more chronic conditions in a person, is a major healthcare concern across the globe. In the UK, NICE[1] publishes evidence-based recommendations for treatment, called *Clinical Pathways*, to formalise treatment practices. However, these pathways are based on evidence from single health conditions and rarely consider the presence of comorbidities. Hence, treating multimorbidity involves managing adverse interactions between several drugs corresponding to different conditions. Several efficient approaches have been developed based on Satisfiability Modulo Theories (SMT) solvers [2] to identify safe treatment plans. Medical practitioners are, however, naturally reluctant to use automatic recommendations if they do not understand the underlying reasoning. In this work, we combine the optimising efficiency of SMT solvers with an argumentation framework for explaining their recommendations. While the role of argumentation has been investigated in healthcare [4], explanations in healthcare [8] and multimorbidity [3], the contribution of this paper is a novel approach for modelling graphs and their explanations using argumentation in the context of multimorbidity. The SMT solver provides an optimal solution indicating the safest medical treatment plan for multimorbidity. A set of argumentation schemes captures reasons for these medical treatments as well as possible inconsistencies between recommended plans. We then show how critical questions can be used to query an argumentation framework, where an agent can provide

---

[1] For details see https://www.nice.org.uk.

© Springer Nature Switzerland AG 2021
T. Uchiya et al. (Eds.): PRIMA 2020, LNAI 12568, pp. 394–402, 2021.
https://doi.org/10.1007/978-3-030-69322-0_29

interactive explanations to a medical practitioner. In this paper, we present the argumentation framework and its underlying schemes which can be used in a multi-agent system to uncover explanations of recommended paths.

2 Argumentation and Multimorbidity for NICE Pathways

Clinical pathways are generic flowchart representations. They include guidelines for drug treatments of specific conditions as well as other best practices. We refer to them as *NICE pathways* in this work. Kovalov and Bowles [5] use the SMT solver Z3 [7] to find the safest path across multiple NICE pathways such that adverse drug interactions between all the NICE pathways under consideration are minimised. SMT solvers solve Boolean Satisfiability problems by finding a truth assignment modulo theories and its optimal assignment for some defined objective function. Three types of adverse interactions are considered in [5]: between drugs, between a drug and a disease, and patient intolerance for specific drugs. The approach is scalable to any number of drug alternatives and finds the optimal solution minimising conflicts according to given criteria as opposed to an all or nothing approach. While the solver captures the NICE pathways quantitatively to indicate progression to the next stage of treatment, as a black-box model it does not provide the underlying qualitative intuition. In this paper, our focus is the encoding of this qualitative information in the solver's output.

We adopt the formal representation of [2,5] to represent Pharmaceutical Graphs (PG) which capture the original ordering and branching structure of the NICE pathway in terms of the recommended drug or drug groups. A PG is a directed acyclic graph with a root note for a disease, and where every other node in the graph is associated with a drug or a drug group. For patients with multimorbidities, several event structures are used to model the NICE pathways of each of the conditions they have. A path in the graph represents a complete treatment plan for a single disease, and a combination of paths across diseases is extracted in [5] via an objective function on the basis of a total score for Z3. This score is a combination of medicine efficacy (positive score) and drug interaction conflict (negative score) permitting to identify the optimal treatment plan.

Our definition of PG is based on that of [2], formally considering the unfolding of a PG as an event structure where events are associated with a drug or a group and different treatment options are captured by conflicting events.

Definition 1. *An* event structure *is a triple* $E = (Ev, \rightarrow^*, \#)$ *where Ev is a set of events and* $\rightarrow^*, \# \in Ev \times Ev$ *are binary relations called* causality *and* conflict, *respectively. Causality* $\rightarrow^*$ *is a partial order. Conflict $\#$ is symmetric and irreflexive, and propagates over causality, i.e.,* $(e\#e' \wedge e' \rightarrow^* e'') \Rightarrow e\#e''$ *for all $e, e', e'' \in Ev$. Two events are* concurrent, *written $e \parallel e'$, iff* $\neg(e \rightarrow^* e' \vee e' \rightarrow^* e \vee e\#e')$.

Here we consider PG as the graph formed by the causality relationships of E such that $PG = (Ev, \rightarrow^*)$, and our starting representation of a PG is correspondent to the representation of Z3 input as event structure. We refer to a trace of execution on PG as a sequence of events $Ppath = \langle e_0; \ldots; e_n \rangle$, $Ppath \subseteq PG$, where for each $e_i, e_j \in Ev$ there exists a causal relation $(e_i \rightarrow^* e_j) \in \rightarrow^*$. Hence the output from Z3 is a set of paths for each disease optimising a goal over all sets of event structures under consideration.

In order to compute justifications for this path, we define an argumentation model using a simpler version of ASPIC+ [6] without preferences, strict rules and undercuts. An argumentation framework AF is formed by arguments $\mathscr{A}$ and attacks $\rightarrow: \mathscr{A} \times \mathscr{A}$. An argument $A \in \mathscr{A}$ is constructed from a knowledge base $K \subseteq \mathscr{L}$ where $\mathscr{L}$ is a propositional logic language, and defeasible rules $\mathscr{R}$. $A \in \mathscr{A}$ is a premise in K or a derivation of a conclusion from rules and premises in K. Argument $A1$ attacks $A2$, $A1 \rightarrow A2$, if the conclusion of $A1$ is contrary to a premise (undermines) or to a conclusion (rebuts) of $A2$ determined by a contrariness function$^-: \mathscr{L} \rightarrow 2^{\mathscr{L}}$. The sets of acceptable arguments (i.e., extensions ξ) in an AF is computed according to the preferred semantics. A model of argumentation schemes, stereotypical patterns of reasoning, defines premises, conclusions and critical questions [10]. Schemes are used to derive grounded defeasible rules $\mathtt{k_i} \in \mathscr{R}$ [6]. In our work, attacks will be derived through ASPIC+, while critical questions are used to explore arguments within an extension. $\mathscr{L}$ contains the set of propositions $Props$ in turn divided into subsets $\mathscr{T}_i \subset Props$. A lower case letter refers to a proposition type $t_i \in \mathscr{T}_i$ and we refer to grounded propositions with upper case letters. An argument scheme is defined as $Arg_\gamma : t_0, \ldots, t_j \Rightarrow t_n$ where γ is the name of the scheme and $t_i \in \mathscr{T}_i$ from which we can derive a rule $\mathtt{k_\gamma} : \mathtt{P_0}, \ldots, \mathtt{P_j} \Rightarrow \mathtt{P_n}$, $k_\gamma \in \mathscr{R}$.

3   Argumentation Model

In our model, we adapt PG, input to Z3, for adding explanations and convert it into its equivalent argument representation. Next, we apply a knowledge engineering process to extract the explanations from NICE pathways that were left out by the SMT solver. Lastly, we link the explanations to the respective PG nodes in our final model.

Convert Pharmaceutical Graph to PGraph. Starting from a PG, the event structure representation presented in Sect. 2, we define a *PGraph* as a graph extension of PG. *PGraph* differentiates from its parent PG by having the graph structure marked explicitly in terms of branches required for explanation modelling. A *PGraph* $= (Ev, \rightarrow^*)$ augments the set of events with a new set of nodes where Sb or *StartBranch* is a set of events marking the start of a branch, Eb or *EndBranch* marks the end of a branch. To represent drug groups as sub-branches in PG, we consider a set of nodes Dg or *DrugGroup* named after the drug group which marks the start of the sub-branch. Similarly we have a set of nodes Eg or *EndGroup* to mark the end of the sub-branch. Causality relationships link the new nodes to their respective branches. A path on a PG is then mapped to a path on *PGraph* by accounting for additional marking nodes. In Fig. 1 we show an example of $PG = (Ev, \rightarrow^*)$ for Diabetes from [5] and its correspondent extension *PGraph*. The root node represents the disease (Diabetes), while the remaining nodes represent recommended drugs or drug groups. For example, the node Sulfonylurea indicates that seven drugs belong to this group.

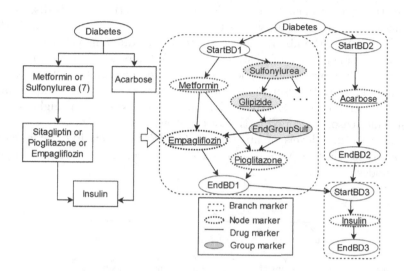

Fig. 1. PG to *PGraph* conversion for diabetes.

Modelling Paths in the Argumentation Model. A casual relation $e \rightarrow^*$ e' in *PGraph* is represented using a Transition Argument Scheme. Transition arguments accumulate the path from start to the current transition using a linear argument structure.

Definition 2. *A Transition Argument Scheme is $Arg_T = \{Given\ e\ in\ a$ PGraph, e' follows from $e\}$ where $e \rightarrow^* e' \in PGraph$.*

This scheme can be represented as $Arg_T : e \Rightarrow e'$, where $e, e' \in \mathscr{T}_{Ev}$ are propositions of type event and $\mathscr{T}_{Ev}$ contains all events Ev of *PGraph*. An inference rule derived through Arg_T can be written as $k_{T_i} : E1 \Rightarrow E2$ with $k_{T_i} \in \mathscr{R}$. A single critical question is defined: **CQ**$_T$ – *Is there a transition to e?* The question undermines the argument on its premise with $\neg e$, and other arguments of type Arg_T can be used to respond.

In order to model different paths taken along *PGraph* as alternative solutions, here we introduce a negation to represent alternatives such that for all concurrent events $e', e'' \in Ev$, $e' \parallel e''$ we have $e' \in \bar{e}''$, $e'' \in \bar{e}'$.

Structured Explanation for Clinical Pathways. We base the explanations of the recommended paths on the drug information provided by NICE. We assess the practical value of this content by talks with experts. Then we manually filter out relevant information and organise it into different levels and types.

Level: The choice of a node in a graph involves decisions at different abstraction levels. For example, starting from the initial node, the medical practitioner needs to choose a branch. Next, they decide which node to transition to and why. This is important because in the treatment plans, moving to the next node in the graph indicates that the previous treatment is no longer effective, so it is discouraged. Once made, the transition as well as the choice of drug or drug group needs to be justified. Hence, the abstraction levels represent different types of decisions to be made. Higher levels of abstraction act as filters for lower levels. As the choice of a node moves from higher to lower level, explanations become more specific and adapt to the user's need for detail. For example, a non-expert might be satisfied with a high-level explanation but a more expert user might press for more specific reasons encoded in the lower levels.

We identify four levels of abstraction for *PGraph* (cf. Fig. 1): a *Branch* contains *Nodes* where a *Node* can be a *Drug* or a composite *Group*, composed of *Drug* nodes.

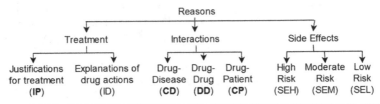

Reasons $\mathcal{T}_{Reas}$	Maps to	$\mathcal{T}_{Type}$	$\mathcal{T}_{Level}$
R1	it is indicated for age less than 55 years	IP	BRANCH
R2	it is the default treatment on the recommended pathway	IP	BRANCH
R3	it is indicated in next stage of treatment if review of previous treatment does not work	IP	NODE
R4	it is contraindicated in	CD	DRUG
R5	it adversely reacts with suggested drug	DD	DRUG

Fig. 2. Type hierarchy for treatment, interactions and side effects with examples for diabetes.

1. *Branch Level*: Given a *PGraph*, the first decision is to choose between alternative branches. This level justifies a transition to a specific branch.
2. *Node Level*: This level allows reasoning about why a transition is taken irrespective of the destination node. In the context of multimorbidity, these reasons allow talking about transitions into the next stage of treatment.
3. *Drug Level*: Reasons about the destination node, i.e. a drug or a drug group.
4. *Group Level*: Reasons about relationships between drugs in a drug family.

In order to identify what level of explanation a reason is attributed to, we define specific propositions in our language $\mathcal{T}_{Level} = \{BRANCH, NODE, DRUG, GROUP\} \subset Props$.

Type: We classify the reasons for choosing or not choosing a drug into four types based on the content. These are distributed across different levels: 1) Clinical pathway; 2) Treatment; 3) Interactions; and 4) Side Effects. The Clinical Pathway type allows the *PGraph* structure itself to be used as justification for a drug choice. Figure 2 shows the sub-classification within the remaining types with those used in this work highlighted in bold. As above, a set of dedicated propositions are used to identify the different type of reason: $\mathscr{T}_{Type} = \{IP, CD, CP, DD, PGraph\} \subset Props$.

Reason: represents the explanation text and is associated with a *Level* and a *Type*. A reason is identified with a proposition type $r_i \in \mathscr{T}_{Reas} \subset Props$. The table in Fig. 2 provides some examples of reasons indicating the proposition type, level and a description.

Argument Schemes for Explanations. The *Explain Argument Scheme* models explanations based on the reasons, types and levels and shows a support or counter reason for giving a drug represented as event e.

Definition 3. *An Explain Argument Scheme Arg_E, is such that given a reason $r \in \mathscr{T}_{Reas}$ with attributes $t \in \mathscr{T}_{Type}$ and $l \in \mathscr{T}_{Level}$ for event e in PGraph, it follows that there is a justification for prescribing e.*

We customize the generic Arg_E to model different types of supporting explanations that can highlight adverse interactions between events in the *PGraph*. We specify additional elements as follows in order to define these schemes. We assume $\mathscr{T}_{Dis} = \{d|d$ is a disease name$\}$, $\mathscr{T}_{Cond} = \{c|c$ is a medical condition expressing patient state$\}$, $\mathscr{T}_{Exp} = \{explain_e|explain_e$ is a proposition representing an explanation for a drug/drug group $e \in \mathscr{T}_{Ev}\}$ and $\mathscr{T}_{Dis}, \mathscr{T}_{Cond}, \mathscr{T}_{Exp} \subset Props$. The general argument scheme is presented as $Arg_E : r, t, l \Rightarrow explain_e$. Four types of schemes Arg_E are defined on the basis of the type of reason: Arg_{EIP} mentions a justification for a treatment; Arg_{EDD} indicates that a drug e_1 is prescribed as another drug e_2 reacting with e_1 has not been prescribed; Arg_{ECD} indicates that e cannot be taken in case of a disease $s \in \mathscr{T}_{Dis}$ but the disease is not present; and Arg_{ECP} includes information on whether e can or cannot be taken in presence or absence of another condition $c \in \mathscr{T}_{Cond}$.

Reasons from Arg_E do not aggregate. A drug can be prescribed as long as there is a single surviving Arg_E to justify it. *Explain* arguments allow a critical question such as: $\mathbf{CQ}_E$ – *Is there an alternative combination of r, t, l for there being a justification for e?* This rebuts the conclusion with $\neg explain_e$, and can be answered with another Arg_E.

Linking the Two Models. The *Give Argument Scheme* links graph and explanations:

Definition 4. *$Arg_G = \{Given$ an event e in PGraph and an explanation $explain_e \in \mathscr{T}_{Exp}$ in favour of e, it follows that e can be prescribed$\}$.*

In order to define formally this scheme, we use $\mathscr{T}_{Pres} = \{give_e | give_e$ is a proposition expressing prescription of $e \in \mathscr{T}_{Ev}\}$. A *Give* argument scheme is then formulated as $Arg_G : e, explain_e \Rightarrow give_e$ where $give_e \in \mathscr{T}_{Pres}$. Two critical questions are defined for this scheme: $\mathbf{CQ}_{G1}$ – *Is there a transition to e?*; and $\mathbf{CQ}_{G2}$ – *Is there an explanation for e?*. Both CQs challenge the premises: CQ_{G1} (same as CQ_T) with $\neg e$ and and CQ_{G2} with $\neg explain_e$ which can be responded with Arg_T and Arg_E, respectively.

General Argumentation Model. So far, we have outlined a number of argumentation schemes to derive defeasible rules $\mathscr{R}$. The knowledge base is defined as $K \subseteq \mathscr{T}_{Dis} \cup \mathscr{T}_{Cond} \cup \mathscr{T}_{Level} \cup \mathscr{T}_{Type} \cup \mathscr{T}_{Reas} \cup \mathscr{T}_{\overline{Ev}}$ where $\mathscr{T}_{\overline{Ev}}$ represents a subset of negated drug/drug group events, s.t. $\neg e \in \mathscr{T}_{\overline{Ev}}, e \in \mathscr{T}_{Ev}$. The components of K are identified as: (i) for $q_i \in (\mathscr{T}_{Dis} \cup \mathscr{T}_{Cond} \cup \mathscr{T}_{\overline{Ev}})$, we assert $q_i \in K$ based on NICE pathways, reflecting the domain properties, which will constitute premises for *Explain* Arguments; (ii) for $q_i \in (\mathscr{T}_{Level} \cup \mathscr{T}_{Type} \cup \mathscr{T}_{Reas})$, we assert $q_i \in K$ as part of the modelling permitting an administrator to tune the explanations returned by the system. $\mathscr{R}$ and K form the basis for an AF to explain an event structure representing a NICE treatment pathway.

Asserting the disease node in the graph activates the graph through the linear structure of *Transition* arguments. At this point we can derive a set of preferred extensions ξ from the argumentation system as described in Sect. 2. A preferred extension is then $\xi_i = \{A_{T_1}, \ldots, A_{T_n}, A_{E_1}, \ldots, A_{E_k}, A_{G_1}, \ldots, A_{G_m}\}$ where $A_{T_i} \in \mathscr{A}$ are arguments about the treatment path, $A_{E_i} \in \mathscr{A}$ are justifications for prescribing the treatment, $A_{G_i} \in \mathscr{A}$ are treatments that can be justifiably prescribed. Hence, ξ_i maps an SMT solver output $Ppath = \langle e_0; \ldots; e_n \rangle$ and additionally incorporates corresponding explanations.

Transition arguments rebut other *Transition* arguments and undermine corresponding *Give* and *Explain* arguments on their *Transition* premises. Consequently, *Give* arguments can be undermined on their *Transition* premise directly and indirectly by undermining one of the premises of their *Explain* arguments.

Example of Argumentation Model. Here we show part of the ASPIC+ model for the Diabetes *PGraph* from Fig. 1. The adverse interactions modelled in this example are only for demonstrative purposes. The example can be extended to include multiple disease *PGraph*s and their explanations by adding corresponding premises, rules and contrariness definitions. The resulting extensions will then include combinations of paths across all graphs, representing the safest path in the context of multimorbidity.

We now show how the AF can be used by an agent to justify prescribed drugs. Assuming the SMT solver gives the optimal path as branch 1 of Diabetes *PGraph* in Fig. 1. We map this to $Ppath = \langle Diabetes; StartBD1; Metformin; Pioglitazone; EndBD1 \rangle$ and get the corresponding preferred extension $\xi_1 = \{A60, A54, A56, A57, .. \}$. Figure 3 shows the attacks in the resulting argument graph for this extension along with a subset of the relevant argument mappings. The arguments included in the extension are highlighted in grey. Assume the agent proposes to give Pioglitazone, $A60$. A user can ask for justifications using some of the critical questions. The agent responds with an argument that can resolve the challenge. For example, if the user asks for a justification about the transition to Pioglitazone, CQ_{G1}, the agent can respond with *Because there is a transition to Pioglitazone from Metformin*, via argument A54. If the user asks about an explanation for this drug, CQ_{G2}, the agent can respond with A56: *Because it is indicated for age less than 55 years (R1)*. The agent can move A57, *Because it is indicated in the next stage of treatment if a review of previous treatment does not work (R3)*, in response to a request for alternative explanations to the drug, CQ_{E1}.

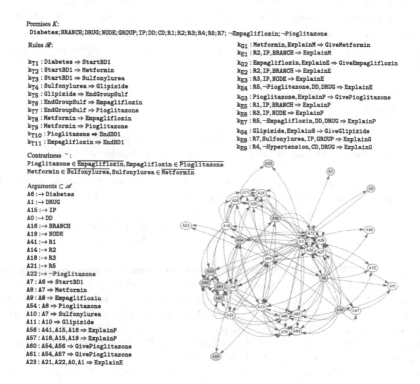

Premises K:
  Diabetes; BRANCH; DRUG; NODE; GROUP; IP; DD; CD; R1; R2; R3; R4; R5; R7; ¬Empagliflozin; ¬Pioglitazone

Rules $\mathscr{R}$:

k_{T1} : Diabetes ⇒ StartBD1
k_{T2} : StartBD1 ⇒ Metformin
k_{T3} : StartBD1 ⇒ Sulfonylurea
k_{T4} : Sulfonylurea ⇒ Glipizide
k_{T5} : Glipizide ⇒ EndGroupSulf
k_{T6} : EndGroupSulf ⇒ Empagliflozin
k_{T7} : EndGroupSulf ⇒ Pioglitazone
k_{T8} : Metformin ⇒ Empagliflozin
k_{T9} : Metformin ⇒ Pioglitazone
k_{T10} : Pioglitazone ⇒ EndBD1
k_{T11} : Empagliflozin ⇒ EndBD1

k_{G1} : Metformin, ExplainM ⇒ GiveMetformin
k_{E1} : R2, IP, BRANCH ⇒ ExplainM
k_{G2} : Empagliflozin, ExplainE ⇒ GiveEmpagliflozin
k_{E2} : R2, IP, BRANCH ⇒ ExplainE
k_{E3} : R3, IP, NODE ⇒ ExplainE
k_{E4} : R5, ¬Pioglitazone, DD, DRUG ⇒ ExplainE
k_{G3} : Pioglitazone, ExplainP ⇒ GivePioglitazone
k_{E5} : R1, IP, BRANCH ⇒ ExplainP
k_{E6} : R3, IP, NODE ⇒ ExplainP
k_{E7} : R5, ¬Empagliflozin, DD, DRUG ⇒ ExplainP
k_{G4} : Glipizide, ExplainG ⇒ GiveGlipizide
k_{G8} : R7, Sulfonylurea, IP, GROUP ⇒ ExplainG
k_{G9} : R4, ¬Hypertension, CD, DRUG ⇒ ExplainG

Contrariness $^-$:
  Pioglitazone ∈ $\overline{\text{Empagliflozin}}$, Empagliflozin ∈ $\overline{\text{Pioglitazone}}$
  Metformin ∈ $\overline{\text{Sulfonylurea}}$, Sulfonylurea ∈ $\overline{\text{Metformin}}$

Arguments $\subseteq \mathscr{A}$
A6 : → Diabetes
A1 : → DRUG
A15 : → IP
A0 : → DD
A16 : → BRANCH
A19 : → NODE
A41 : → R1
A14 : → R2
A18 : → R3
A21 : → R5
A22 : → ¬Pioglitazone
A7 : A6 ⇒ StartBD1
A8 : A7 ⇒ Metformin
A9 : A8 ⇒ Empagliflozin
A54 : A8 ⇒ Pioglitazone
A10 : A7 ⇒ Sulfonylurea
A11 : A10 ⇒ Glipizide
A56 : A41, A15, A16 ⇒ ExplainP
A57 : A18, A15, A19 ⇒ ExplainP
A60 : A54, A56 ⇒ GivePioglitazone
A61 : A54, A57 ⇒ GivePioglitazone
A23 : A21, A22, A0, A1 ⇒ ExplainE

Fig. 3. *AF* for branch 1 of diabetes *PGraph* from Fig. 1.

4 Conclusion and Future Work

We presented an argumentation model to justify the choices on a clinical pathway, as identified by the SMT solver for multimorbid patients. While the solver only encoded drug information in the optimal path, our system delivers additional information extracted from the NICE pathways as well as other sources that justifies each event in the path. Our approach can generalise to explanations of similar graph structures.

A recent approach has integrated argumentation with the Transition-based Medical Recommendation (TMR) model to represent guidelines and their interactions [3]. While they use argumentation for reasoning, we present a novel approach to show how argumentation can add interpretability to a black-box model such as a SMT solver. Although significant work has been invested in making machine learning models more transparent [1], the same focus on making SMT solvers transparent has lacked so far.

The explanations from our model can be used as the basis of an agent dialogue protocol which provides justifications to the user in an interactive way [9], similar to the approach of [8]. Possible future directions include conducting usability studies to see how useful are the generated explanations and formulating the content of the explanations on data collected from patients and medical practitioners.

References

1. Biran, O., Cotton, C.: Explanation and justification in machine learning: a survey. In: Proceedings of the IJCAI 2017 Workshop on Explainable AI (XAI), vol. 8, pp. 8–13 (2017)
2. Bowles, J., Caminati, M., Cha, S., Mendoza, J.: A framework for automated conflict detection and resolution in medical guidelines. Sci. Comput. Program. **182**, 42–63 (2019). https://doi.org/10.1016/j.scico.2019.07.002
3. Čyras, K., Oliveira, T.: Resolving conflicts in clinical guidelines using argumentation. In: Proceedings of Autonomous Agents and Multiagent Systems, pp. 1731–1739 (2019)
4. Hunter, A., Williams, M.: Aggregating evidence about the positive and negative effects of treatments. Artif. Intell. Med. **56**(3), 173–190 (2012)
5. Kovalov, A., Bowles, J.K.F.: Avoiding medication conflicts for patients with multimorbidities. In: Ábrahám, E., Huisman, M. (eds.) IFM 2016. LNCS, vol. 9681, pp. 376–390. Springer, Cham (2016). https://doi.org/10.1007/978-3-319-33693-0_24
6. Modgil, S., Prakken, H.: The ASPIC+ framework for structured argumentation: a tutorial. Argument Comput. **5**(1), 31–62 (2014)
7. de Moura, L., Bjørner, N.: Z3: an efficient SMT solver. In: Ramakrishnan, C.R., Rehof, J. (eds.) TACAS 2008. LNCS, vol. 4963, pp. 337–340. Springer, Heidelberg (2008). https://doi.org/10.1007/978-3-540-78800-3_24
8. Sassoon, I., Kökciyan, N., Sklar, E., Parsons, S.: Explainable argumentation for wellness consultation. In: Calvaresi, D., Najjar, A., Schumacher, M., Främling, K. (eds.) EXTRAAMAS 2019. LNCS (LNAI), vol. 11763, pp. 186–202. Springer, Cham (2019). https://doi.org/10.1007/978-3-030-30391-4_11
9. Shaheen, Q., Toniolo, A., Bowles, J.K.F.: Dialogue games for explaining medication choices. In: Gutiérrez-Basulto, V., Kliegr, T., Soylu, A., Giese, M., Roman, D. (eds.) RuleML+RR 2020. LNCS, vol. 12173, pp. 97–111. Springer, Cham (2020). https://doi.org/10.1007/978-3-030-57977-7_7
10. Walton, D., Reed, C., Macagno, F.: Argumentation Schemes. Cambridge University Press, Cambridge (2008)

The Persistence of False Memory: Brain in a Vat Despite Perfect Clocks

Thomas Schlögl$^{(\boxtimes)}$ ⓘ, Ulrich Schmid ⓘ, and Roman Kuznets ⓘ

TU Wien, Vienna, Austria
thomas.e191-02.schloegl@tuwien.ac.at, {s,rkuznets}@ecs.tuwien.ac.at

Abstract. We extend a recently introduced epistemic reasoning framework for multi-agent systems with byzantine faulty asynchronous agents by incorporating features like reliable communication, time-bounded communication, multicasting, synchronous and lockstep synchronous agents. We use this extension framework for analyzing fault detection abilities of synchronous and lockstep synchronous agents and show that even perfectly synchronized clocks cannot be used to avoid "brain-in-a-vat" scenarios.

1 Introduction

Epistemic reasoning is a powerful technique for modeling and analysis of distributed systems [1], which has proved its utility also for fault-tolerant systems: benign faults, i.e., nodes (termed agents subsequently) that may crash and/or drop messages, have been studied right from the beginning [6]. Recently, a comprehensive epistemic reasoning framework for agents that may even behave arbitrarily ("byzantine" [4]) faulty has been introduced in [2,3]. Whereas it fully captures byzantine asynchronous systems, it is currently not suitable for modeling and analysis of the wealth of other distributed systems, most notably, synchronous agents and reliable multicast communication.

In asynchronous systems, both agents and message transmission may be arbitrarily slow. Notwithstanding the importance of asynchronous distributed systems in general [5], however, it is well-known that adding faults to the picture renders important distributed computing problems like consensus impossible. There is hence a vast body of research that relies on stronger system models that add additional assumptions. One prominent example are *lockstep synchronous systems*, where agents take actions simultaneously at times $t \in \mathbb{N}$, i.e., have access to a perfectly synchronized global clock, and messages sent at time t are received before time $t + 1$. It is well-known that consensus can be solved in such systems with $n \geq 3f + 1$ nodes, if at most f of those are byzantine [4].

Synchronous distributed systems with agents suffering from benign faults such as crashes or message send/receive omissions have already been studied

---

Supported by the Austrian Science Fund (FWF) projects ByzDEL (P33600) and ADynNet (P28182).

T. Uchiya et al. (Eds.): PRIMA 2020, LNAI 12568, pp. 403–411, 2021.
https://doi.org/10.1007/978-3-030-69322-0_30

in [6], primarily in the context of agreement problems, which require some form of common knowledge. By contrast, we are not aware of any attempt on the epistemic analysis of fault-tolerant distributed systems with byzantine agents.

In the present paper,[1] we extend [3] by a comprehensive and modular *extension framework*, which enables to encode and safely combine additional system assumptions typically used in the modeling and analysis of fault-tolerant distributed systems, like reliable communication, time-bounded communication, multicasting, synchronous and lockstep synchronous agents and even agents with coordinated actions. We therefore establish the first framework that facilitates a rigorous epistemic modeling and analysis of general distributed systems with byzantine faulty agents. We demonstrate its utility by analyzing some basic properties of the synchronous and lockstep synchronous agents extension, namely, the agents' fault detection abilities. Moreover, we prove that even the perfectly synchronized clocks available in the lockstep synchronous extension cannot prevent a "brain-in-a-vat" scenario.

2   A Tribute to J. K. Rowling: Harry Potter's View

Given the lack of space, we use the world of the fifth *Harry Potter* book for illustrating our results: The following example consists of three related scenarios that differ in the requirements imposed on communication and agents' behavior, to illustrate asynchronous, synchronous, and lockstep agents.

An evil force that must not be named is trying to lure Harry Potter into a trap by making him believe that Sirius Black is in mortal danger. However, Sirius Black is alive and well, to which multiple people can attest. How can Harry be tricked? We start by describing how it happened in the book, which corresponds roughly to the case of asynchronous agents.

Asynchronous Case. Harry is shown a fabricated vision of Sirius being tortured in the Ministry of Magic (byzantine event). Harry tries to verify the story by contacting Sirius's house via the Floo Network. He essentially broadcasts a message to everyone in the house. But asynchronous agents do not have to be active. Indeed, the only person in the house who responds to Harry is Kreacher the house-elf, who is compromised (byzantine agent). Kreacher confirms to Harry the fake story of Sirius being in danger. Having two seemingly independent confirmations, Harry decides to act and walks right into the trap laid for him. In this example, Harry is fooled by fabricated events and messages. Correct agents fail to disabuse him of this illusion because they are not active at certain crucial moments.

---

[1] Lack of space does not allow us to incorporate the formal treatment of our examples, let alone the fully-fledged extension framework. The interested reader is hence referred to the full version of our paper [7].

Synchronous Case. But what if Harry sent an owl instead? An owl could find Sirius and ensure his action in response. There is still a way to prevent Harry from learning the truth. It is sufficient to intercept the owl on its way from Hogwarts to Sirius. With no guarantee of message delivery, Harry cannot be sure of a response. The lack thereof is consistent with the illusion of Sirius being in trouble. Worse still, another owl with a fake response could be sent confirming the fake story. In this case, Harry sends a message that is never delivered. At the same time, he may receive a fake response that was never sent (by Sirius). Note that maintaining the illusion in this case requires a larger degree of control over the environment, especially the communication channels. Despite all correct agents being active all the time, they cannot help Harry without communicating with him.

Lockstep Case. But what if the communication channels are reliable and time bounded? What if Harry communicated with Sirius using a pair of enchanted coins that magically transmit information from one to the other in a reliable manner? Would this help Harry keep his grip on reality? Unfortunately, even this is not enough, although maintaining the illusion requires even more work in this case. Since a sent message in this case guarantees delivery, Voldemort would have to prevent Harry from sending it. For instance, it would be sufficient to quietly switch the enchanted coin for an ordinary one. Then Harry would think he sent the message without actually sending it. Accordingly, Sirius would not receive the message through his coin, and Harry would interpret the lack of a response as the confirmation of some disaster befalling Sirius.

As we saw, in all three cases, sufficient control of the environment and communication channels would allow to create any illusion necessary and shield the decision maker from reality. This, however, requires the more effort the more robust the agents and their communication are. Perhaps, tellingly, Rowling herself hinted that learning the truth reliably required a more robust form of communication by giving Harry a two-way mirror (which he never used) that would correspond to a lockstep channel of communication with reliable instantaneous delivery and common knowledge of the success of communication.

The ability to create an alternative reality by hijacking all communication to a thinking being is often used in philosophy as a thought experiment called *brain in a vat* to support skepticism, i.e., the belief that it is impossible to distinguish reality from our perception thereof.

Less abstractly, for multi-agent systems with byzantine agents, such as distributed systems, this means that agents cannot safely base their actions on their perceptions since knowledge of what actually happened can never be ascertained that way: as the example above and its formal representation in [7] show, increasing the reliability of agents and communication channels fails to alleviate the problem of separating reality from illusions (unless communication creates common knowledge).

3   A Glimpse of Our Formal Results

We present the essentials of the epistemic reasoning and analysis framework for byzantine multi-agent systems [3].

There is a finite set $\mathcal{A} = \{1, \ldots, n\}$ of **agents**, who generally do not have access to a global clock (unlike **synchronous agents**) and execute a non-deterministic joint **protocol** P. In such a protocol, agent i can perform **actions** ($Actions_i$), e.g., $send(j, \mu)$ of a **message** μ to j, and witness **events** ($Events_i$), in particular, external events e and message deliveries $recv(j, \mu)$ for μ sent by agent j. We collectively refer to events and actions as **haps** denoted by $a, e, \ldots$ The other main player in [3] is the **environment** ϵ executing some *environment protocol* P_ϵ which takes care of scheduling haps, failing agents, and resolving non-deterministic choices in both the joint and environment's protocols (the environment part responsible for the latter is referred to as the **adversary**).

We utilize a discrete-time model, of arbitrarily fine resolution, with time domain $t \in \mathbb{T} := \{0, 1, \ldots\}$. All haps taking place after a **timestamp** $t \in \mathbb{T}$ and no later than $t+1$ are grouped into a **round** denoted $t\frac{1}{2}$ and treated as happening simultaneously. In order to prevent agents from inferring the global time by counting rounds, agents are generally unaware of a round, unless they perceive an event or are prompted to act by the environment. The latter is accomplished by special system events $go(i)$ for each agent i, which are complemented by two more system events for faulty agents: $sleep(i)$ and $hibernate(i)$ signify a failure to activate agent i's protocol and differ in that the latter does not even wake up the agent. None of these **system events** $SysEvents_i$ is directly observable by agents.

The state of the whole system at some time t is the $(n+1)$-tuple $r(t) = (r_\epsilon(t), r_1(t), \ldots, r_n(t))$ consisting of the *environment's history* $r_\epsilon(t)$ and the *local histories* $r_i(t)$. Herein, $r_\epsilon(t) \in \mathscr{L}_\epsilon$ is a sequence of all haps that happened in all the rounds before round $t\frac{1}{2}$. Every $r_i(t) \in \mathscr{L}_i$ is the result of a complex state transition consisting of several phases, which are described below.

Global Haps Format and Faults. There is a global version of every element of *Haps* that provides additional information that is only accessible to the environment. Among it is the timestamp t of every correct action $a \in Actions_i$, which is provided by a one-to-one function $global(i, t, a)$. This is especially crucial for proper message processing, where every sent message is assigned a unique **global message identifier** (GMI). These GMIs enable the direct linking of send actions to their corresponding delivery events. The set of all actions of agent i in the global format is denoted $\overline{GActions_i}$.[2] Both actions and events in the global format are denoted by $A, E, O, \ldots$

Unlike correct actions, correct events witnessed by agent i are generated by the environment ϵ, hence are already produced in the global format $\overline{GEvents_i}$. A byzantine event is an event that was perceived by an agent despite not taking place. In other words, for each correct event $E \in \overline{GEvents_i}$, there is a faulty

---

[2] The horizontal bar here and elsewhere means correctness, i.e., lack of byzantine haps.

counterpart $fake(i, E) \in GEvents_i \setminus \overline{GEvents_i}$ that agent i cannot distinguish from E. An important type of correct global events is delivery $grecv(j, i, \mu, id) \in \overline{GEvents_i}$ of message μ with GMI id sent from agent i to agent j. Since the GMI is part of the global format but cannot be part of the local format because it contains information about the time of sending, this information must be stripped off before updating local histories with the corresponding $recv(j, \mu)$. This is achieved by the function $local$ that converts **correct** haps from the global into the local formats for the respective agents in such a way that $local$ reverses $global$.

To allow for the most flexibility regarding who is to blame for an erroneous action, faulty actions are modeled as byzantine events of the form $fake(i, A \mapsto A')$ where $A, A' \in \overline{GActions_i} \sqcup \{\mathbf{noop}\}$ for a special **non-action noop** in global format. These byzantine events are controlled by the environment and correspond to an agent violating its protocol by performing the action A (in global format), while recording in its local history that it either performs $a' = local(A') \in Actions_i$ if $A' \in \overline{GActions_i}$ or does nothing if $A' = \mathbf{noop}$ (note that performing $A = \mathbf{noop}$ means not acting). The byzantine inaction $fail(i)$ is defined as shorthand for $fake(i, \mathbf{noop} \mapsto \mathbf{noop})$. $BEvents_i$ is the set of all i's byzantine events, corresponding to both faulty events and actions.

Protocols, State Transitions and Runs. The events and actions that occur in each round are non-deterministically chosen by the adversary from the options provided by protocols for agents and the environment. Agent i's **protocol** $P_i \colon \mathcal{L}_i \to 2^{2^{Actions_i}} \setminus \{\varnothing\}$ provides a range $P_i(r_i(t))$ of sets of actions based on i's current local state $r_i(t) \in \mathcal{L}_i$ at time t in run r, from which the adversary non-deterministically picks one. Similarly the environment provides a range of (correct, byzantine, and system) events via its protocol $P_\epsilon \colon \mathbb{T} \to 2^{2^{GEvents}} \setminus \{\varnothing\}$, which depends on a timestamp $t \in \mathbb{T}$ but not on the current state. The protocols P_i and P_ϵ are non-deterministic and always provide at least one option to choose from. It is required that all events of round $t\frac{1}{2}$ be mutually compatible at time t, a property that is called t-coherency. The set of all global states is $\mathcal{G}$.

Agent i's local view of the system after round $t\frac{1}{2}$ is recorded in i's **local state** $r_i(t+1)$, also called i's **local history**, which is agent i's share of the global state $r(t+1) \in \mathcal{G}$. $r_i(0) \in \Sigma_i$ are the **local initial states**, with $\mathcal{G}(0) := \prod_{i \in \mathcal{A}} \Sigma_i$ denoting the set of global initial states. If a round contains neither $go(i)$ nor any event to be recorded in i's local history, then i's history $r_i(t+1) = r_i(t)$ remains unchanged, denying the agent knowledge that the round just passed. Otherwise, i is considered *active* in that round, and $r_i(t+1) = X \colon r_i(t)$, where : stands for concatenation, for the set $X \subseteq Haps_i$ of all actions and events perceived by i in round $t\frac{1}{2}$ (in local format).

These state transitions actually consist of five consecutive phases, which are needed for capturing all conceivable varieties of multi-agent systems:

1. **Protocol phase.** A range $P_\epsilon(t) \subset 2^{GEvents}$ of t-coherent event sets is determined by the environment's protocol P_ϵ. For each $i \in \mathcal{A}$, a range

$P_i(r_i(t)) \subseteq 2^{Actions_i}$ of sets of i's actions is determined by the joint protocol P.

2. **Adversary phase.** The adversary non-deterministically chooses a set $X_\epsilon \in P_\epsilon(t)$ and one set $X_i \in P_i(r_i(t))$ for each $i \in \mathcal{A}$.

3. **Labeling phase.** Actions from X_i are translated into the global format GX_i.

4. **Filtering phase.** Filter functions remove all unwanted or impossible attempted events from X_ϵ and actions from GX_i in round $t\frac{1}{2}$. This is done in two stages: First, $filter_\epsilon$ filters out "illegal" events, resulting in the set $\beta_\epsilon^t(r)$. E.g., in the byzantine asynchronous case, "illegal" constitutes correct receive events for messages that have not been sent, which would violate causality. Other system assumptions would necessitate other types of "illegality." Second, the **standard action filter** $filter_i$ produces the sets $\beta_i^t(r)$ of actions to be actually performed by agent $i \in \mathcal{A}$ in round $t\frac{1}{2}$ by either removing all actions from GX_i when $go(i) \notin \beta_\epsilon^t(r)$ or else leaving GX_i unchanged.

5. **Updating phase.** The events $\beta_\epsilon^t(r)$ and actions $\beta_i^t(r)$ are appended to the global history $r(t)$.

The operations in Phases 2–5 (adversary, labeling, filtering, and updating phases) are grouped into a **transition template** τ that yields a transition relation $\tau_{P_\epsilon,P}$ for any environment and joint protocols P_ϵ and P. Particularly, we use τ^B for the transition template utilizing the byzantine asynchronous event filter $filter_\epsilon^B$ and standard action $filter_i$ (for all $i \in \mathcal{A}$). Given P and P_ϵ, we focus on $\tau_{P_\epsilon,P}$-**transitional runs** r. Each such transitional run begins in some initial global state $r(0) \in \mathcal{G}(0)$ and progresses, satisfying $(r(t), r(t+1)) \in \tau_{P_\epsilon,P}$ for each timestamp $t \in \mathbb{T}$.

As **liveness properties** cannot be ensured on a round-by-round basis, they are enforced by restricting the allowable set of runs via **admissibility conditions** Ψ, which are subsets of the set R of all transitional runs. A **context** $\gamma = (P_\epsilon, \mathcal{G}(0), \tau, \Psi)$ consists of an environment's protocol P_ϵ, a set of global initial states $\mathcal{G}(0)$, a transition template τ, and an admissibility condition Ψ. For a joint protocol P, we call $\chi = (\gamma, P)$ an **agent-context**. A run $r \in R$ is called **weakly χ-consistent** if $r(0) \in \mathcal{G}(0)$ and the run is $\tau_{P_\epsilon,P}$-transitional. A weakly χ-consistent run r is called **(strongly) χ-consistent** if $r \in \Psi$. The set of all χ-consistent runs is denoted R^χ. An agent-context χ is **non-excluding** if any finite prefix of a weakly χ-consistent run can be extended to a χ-consistent run.

Proving the correctness of a protocol for solving a certain distributed computing problem boils down to studying the set of runs that can be generated.

Epistemics. Interpreted systems in the framework [3] are defined as Kripke models for multi-agent environments [1]. Their **states** are given by global histories $r(t') \in \mathcal{G}$ for runs $r \in R^\chi$, for some agent-context χ and timestamps $t' \in \mathbb{T}$. A **valuation function** $\pi \colon Prop \to 2^\mathcal{G}$ determines states where an atomic proposition from $Prop$ is true. This determination is arbitrary except for a small set of **designated atomic propositions**: namely, for $FEvents_i := BEvents_i \sqcup \{sleep(i), hibernate(i)\}$, $i \in \mathcal{A}$, $o \in Haps_i$, and $t \in \mathbb{T}$ such that $t \leq t'$,

- $correct_{(i,t)}$ is true at $r(t')$ iff no faulty event happened to i by timestamp t, i.e., no event from $FEvents_i$ appears in $r_\epsilon(t)$; $correct_i$ is true at $r(t')$ iff no faulty event happened to i yet, i.e., no event from $FEvents_i$ appears in $r_\epsilon(t')$;
- $occurred_{(i,t)}(o)$ is true at $r(t')$ iff i has a **correct** reason to believe $o \in Haps_i$ occurred in round $(t-1)\frac{1}{2}$, i.e., $o \in r_i(t)$ due to $O \in (\overline{GEvents_i} \cap \beta^i_{\epsilon_{t-1}}(r)) \sqcup \beta^{t-1}_i(r)$; $\overline{occurred}_i(o)$ is true at $r(t')$ iff at least one of $\overline{occurred}_{(i,m)}(o)$ for $1 \le m \le t'$ is; finally, $\overline{occurred}(o) := \bigvee_{i \in A} \overline{occurred}_i(o)$.

The following terms are used to categorize agent faults caused by the environment's protocol P_ϵ: agent $i \in A$ is *fallible* if for any $X \in P_\epsilon(t)$, $X \cup \{fail\,(i)\} \in P_\epsilon(t)$; *delayable* if $X \in P_\epsilon(t)$ implies $X \setminus GEvents_i \in P_\epsilon(t)$; *gullible* if $X \in P_\epsilon(t)$ implies that, for any $Y \subseteq FEvents_i$, the set $Y \sqcup (X \setminus GEvents_i) \in P_\epsilon(t)$ whenever it is t-coherent. Informally, fallible agents can be branded byzantine at any time; delayable agents can always be forced to skip a round completely (which does not make them faulty); gullible agents can exhibit any faults in place of all other events. Common types of faults, e.g., crash or omission failures, can be obtained by restricting allowable sets Y in the definition of gullible agents.

Synchronous Agents. Agents who have access to a global clock that can be used to synchronize their actions is a common type of distributed systems. A natural malfunction for such an agent is losing synch with the global clock, however, so *byzantine synchronous agents* can err by both lagging behind and running ahead of the global clock. We implement this feature by means of **synced rounds**: correct agents act in a round $t\frac{1}{2}$ iff the round is synced, whereas a faulty agent may skip a synced round and/or act in between synced rounds. Since it is important for correct agents to be aware of synced rounds, we require agent protocols to issue the special internal action ☺ whenever activated.

Run Modification [3] is a crucial technique for proving agents' ignorance of a fact, by creating an indistinguishable run falsifying this fact. The main interventions we use in our run modifications are as follows:

Definition 1. *For $i \in A$ and $r \in R$, the interventions $CFreeze(r) := (\varnothing, \varnothing)$ and $BFreeze_i(r) := (\varnothing, \{fail\,(i)\})$ freeze agent i with/without fault respectively.*
$$PFake^t_i(r) := \Big(\varnothing, \{fake(i, E) \mid fake(i, E) \in \beta^t_{b_i}(r)\} \quad \cup$$
$$\{fake(i, \mathbf{noop} \mapsto A) \mid (\exists A' \in \overline{GActions} \sqcup \{\mathbf{noop}\}) \, fake(i, A' \mapsto A) \in \beta^t_{b_i}(r)\} \cup$$
$$\Big\{fake(i, E) \mid E \in \overline{\beta}^t_{\epsilon_i}(r)\Big\} \quad \cup \quad \{fake(i, \mathbf{noop} \mapsto A) \mid A \in \beta^t_i(r)\} \quad \sqcup$$
$$\{sleep\,(i) \mid aware(i, \beta^i_{\epsilon_t}(r))\} \quad \sqcup \quad \{hibernate\,(i) \mid unaware(i, \beta^i_{\epsilon_t}(r))\}\Big) \text{ turns all}$$
i's actions and events into indistinguishable byzantine events whereby, whatever actions i may record in its local history, none are actually performed.

Until the end of this section, we assume that P_ϵ and P^S are protocols for the environment and synchronous agents, that $\chi = ((P_\epsilon, \mathscr{G}(0), \tau^S, R), P^S)$ is an agent-context where τ^S uses the synchronous event filter and the standard action filters, and that $\mathcal{I} = (R^\chi, \pi)$ is an interpreted system. We additionally assume that P_ϵ makes a fixed agent i, called the "brain," gullible and all other agents $j \neq i$ delayable and fallible.

Lemma 1 (Synchronous Brain-in-a-Vat Lemma). *Consider the adjustment* $adj = [B_{t-1}; \ldots; B_0]$ *with* $B_m = (\rho_1^m, \ldots, \rho_n^m)$ *where* $\rho_i^m = PFake_i^m$ *for the "brain"* i *and* $\rho_j^m \in \{CFreeze, BFreeze_j\}$ *for other* $j \neq i$, *for* $m = 0, \ldots, t-1$. *For any run* $r \in R^\chi$, *all modified runs* $r' \in R(\tau_{P_\epsilon, PS}^S, r, adj)$ *are* $\tau_{P_\epsilon, PS}^S$*-transitional and satisfy the following properties:*

1. *"Brain" agent* i *cannot distinguish* r *from* r': $r'_i(m) = r_i(m)$ *for all* $m \leq t$.
2. *Other agents* $j \neq i$ *remain in their initial states:* $r'_j(m) = r'_j(0)$ *for all* $m \leq t$.
3. *Agent* i *is faulty from the beginning:* $(\mathcal{I}, r', m) \models \neg correct_i$ *for all* $1 \leq m \leq t$.
4. *Other agents* $j \neq i$ *are faulty by time* t *iff* $\rho_j^m = BFreeze_j$ *for some* m.

Lemma 1 leads to the following introspection and fault detection results:

Theorem 1. *If the agent-context* χ *is non-excluding, the "brain"* i *cannot know*

(a) *that any hap occurred correctly, i.e.,* $\mathcal{I} \models \neg K_i \overline{occurred}(o)$ *for all haps* o;
(b) *that* i *itself is correct, i.e.,* $\mathcal{I} \models \neg K_i correct_i$;
(c) *that another agent* $j \neq i$ *is faulty, i.e.,* $\mathcal{I} \models \neg K_i \neg correct_j$;
(d) *that another agent* $j \neq i$ *is correct, i.e.,* $\mathcal{I} \models \neg K_i correct_j$.

Lockstep Synchronous Agents. In lockstep synchronous distributed systems [5], agents act synchronously in *communication-closed* rounds. In each such round, every correct agent sends a message to every agent, which is received in the same round, and finally processes all received messages, simultaneously at all correct agents. Thus, agents are not only synchronous, but additionally their communication is reliable, broadcast, and synchronous. Our *lockstep round extension* combines 5 different extensions corresponding to the aforementioned properties: (i) byzantine agents [3], (ii) synchronous agents, (iii) reliable communication ensuring that every sent message is eventually delivered, (iv) synchronous communication ensuring that every message is either received instantaneously or not at all, and (v) broadcast communication extension ensuring that every correctly sent message is sent to all agents.

Since, by Lemma 1, even synchronous agents can be fooled by their own (faulty) imagination, it is natural to ask whether a brain-in-a-vat scenario is still possible in the more restricted lockstep synchronous setting. The proof of the possibility of the brain-in-a-vat scenario in an asynchronous setting provided in [3] suggests this not to be the case. However, by considering extension combinations more closely and in more detail, we were able to implement such a scenario despite the additional restrictions.

Thus, even perfect clocks and communication-closed rounds do not exclude brain-in-a-vat scenarios, with the consequence that most introspection results for synchronous systems also hold for lockstep synchronous systems.

Acknowledgments. The authors are grateful to Giorgio Cignarale and Krisztina Fruzsa for inspiring and stimulating conversations. We also thank Ellina for pointing out the most reliable way of magic communication.

References

1. Fagin, R., Halpern, J.Y., Moses, Y., Vardi, M.Y.: Reasoning About Knowledge. MIT Press, Cambridge (1995)
2. Kuznets, R., Prosperi, L., Schmid, U., Fruzsa, K.: Causality and epistemic reasoning in byzantine multi-agent systems. In: Moss, L.S. (ed.) TARK 2019, Volume 297 of Electronic Proceedings in Theoretical Computer Science, pp. 293–312. Open Publishing Association (2019). https://doi.org/10.4204/EPTCS.297.19
3. Kuznets, R., Prosperi, L., Schmid, U., Fruzsa, K.: Epistemic reasoning with Byzantine-faulty agents. In: Herzig, A., Popescu, A. (eds.) FroCoS 2019. LNCS (LNAI), vol. 11715, pp. 259–276. Springer, Cham (2019). https://doi.org/10.1007/978-3-030-29007-8_15
4. Lamport, L., Shostak, R., Pease, M.: The Byzantine generals problem. ACM Trans. Program. Lang. Syst. **4**(3), 382–401 (1982). https://doi.org/10.1145/357172.357176
5. Lynch, N.A.: Distributed Algorithms. Morgan Kaufmann, Burlington (1996)
6. Moses, Y., Tuttle, M.R.: Programming simultaneous actions using common knowledge. Algorithmica **3**, 121–169 (1988). https://doi.org/10.1007/BF01762112
7. Schlögl, T., Schmid, U., Kuznets, R.: The persistence of false memory: brain in a vat despite perfect clocks. Technical report 2011.01057, arXiv, November 2020. arXiv:2011.01057

Box-Office Prediction Based on Essential Features Extracted from Agent-Based Modeling

Koh Satoh[1] and Shigeo Matsubara[2]([⊠])

[1] Kyoto University, Kyoto 606-8501, Japan
[2] Osaka University, Toyonaka 560-8531, Japan
matsubara@sigmath.es.osaka-u.ac.jp

Abstract. In prediction utilizing machine learning techniques, feature selection is significant for increasing the prediction accuracy. Various techniques for feature selection are available, but it is still challenging to provide a set of component features. To overcome this difficulty, we propose to extract essential features through agent-based modeling. Usually, an agent-based model is characterized by a set of parameters. If an agent-based model can mimic the behaviors of the target well, such parameters can be viewed as essential features of capturing the property of the prediction target. To verify the effectiveness of such feature extraction, we focus on opening/gross box-office revenues based on Twitter data and build a regression model that incorporates the information diffusion model as an agent-based model. The experimental results show that our model can extract essential features from Twitter data and predict the gross box-office revenue for 106 movies more accurately than the baseline model.

Keywords: Prediction · Agent-based modeling · Feature selection

1 Introduction

In prediction utilizing machine learning techniques, feature selection is significant for increasing the prediction accuracy. Various techniques for feature selection have been proposed, but a feature that does not appear in the initial set of features cannot be examined. Thus, it is still challenging to provide a set of component features. To overcome this difficulty, we consider agent-based modeling as a method of feature extraction. An agent-based model is characterized by a set of parameters. If a model mimics the behaviors of the target well, such model parameters can be viewed as essential features of the prediction target.

This paper focuses on predicting opening/gross movie box-office revenue as an example case. Many applications of machine learning have been tried to accurately predict box office revenue. Prediction models based on Twitter data has been proposed due to the availability of the data [1]. However, existing models

© Springer Nature Switzerland AG 2021
T. Uchiya et al. (Eds.): PRIMA 2020, LNAI 12568, pp. 412–419, 2021.
https://doi.org/10.1007/978-3-030-69322-0_31

often have difficulty achieving high prediction accuracy, especially for longer-term prediction. A previous study shows that tweet data in the opening week is useful for predicting the box-office revenue in the opening week of a movie's release [1]. The model uses the number and polarity of posts on Twitter in the opening week. However, the model performs poorly for longer-term prediction because gross box-office revenue is difficult to grasp by using only the trend of the opening week.

To solve this problem, we focus on the propagation of posts on Twitter and propose to incorporate the information diffusion model into the prediction model and grasp future trends effective for predicting gross box-office revenue. There are lots of studies about information diffusion [2]. Most of the information diffusion models include a relatively small number of parameters. Suppose we find that a set of parameters can capture the whole period's trend, i.e., estimate the trend over the entire release period from the opening week's data. In that case, these parameters will be essential to achieve the accurate prediction of gross box-office revenue. Thus, to predict the gross box-office revenue, we extract feature values from an information diffusion model and the real data and then apply a multiple regression analysis. There are various diffusion models, but we use a model that acquires parameters representing the speed and scale of information diffusion. Note that the speed and scale of information diffusion cannot be observed without agent-based modeling.

A combination of agent-based modeling and machine learning has been discussed. Machine learning is mainly used in agent-based modeling for two broad cases. A case is the modeling of adaptive agents equipped with experiential learning. Another case is the analysis of outcomes produced by given agent-based modeling. Our approach differs from existing studies in that agent-based modeling is used to extract essential features, which are used for the input of the machine learning model.

We analyze why existing models cannot achieve high prediction accuracy [1]. For an existing prediction model, we consider a model based on using the number of posts about movies and polarity of posts on Twitter. We extend two-class polarity analysis to five-class polarity analysis.

The contributions of this paper are summarized as follows.

- Proposal of a prediction model incorporating the information diffusion parameters as features: Many studies have modeled information diffusion. However, they predict the diffusion of information itself and not related things such as box-office revenue. We utilize a Continuous-Time Independent Cascade (CTIC) Model [2] to obtain features. Our work is built based on that of Asur and Huberman [1], but the introduction of the information diffusion model into a regression model for box-office revenue is new.
- Evaluation of proposed model using movie dataset: We evaluated the proposed model using the obtained features. In the results of experiments using data of 106 movies released from 2017 to 2018, the proposed model increased the coefficient of determination to 0.540 from 0.497 for the existing model.

2   Prediction Model

In this study, we assume the following. (1) If we can obtain the users' behavior on Twitter for the period of theatrical run, we can predict gross box-office revenue accurately. (2) Parameters obtained from the information diffusion model for a movie tell the users' behavior on Twitter during the theatrical run. Some readers may consider that it is possible to skip the estimation of parameters of the information diffusion model and directly predict the gross box-office revenue. We think the prediction of box-office revenue is different from the prediction of non-social targets such as temperature because box-office revenue is a result of aggregated human behaviors. Among various ways to capture such human behaviors, we consider that the intervention of the agent-based model, i.e., the information diffusion model can contribute to obtaining an appropriate abstraction of human behaviors, which enables us to represent the target by using a few parameters.

2.1   Features of Twitter

In this section, we explain features directly obtainable from Twitter: the number of posts and the polarity of contents of posts about target movies on Twitter.

Number of Posts. Previous studies have shown that the number of posts on Twitter about a movie correlates well with the box-office revenue. Asur and Huberman [1] defined the tweet rate as the total number of tweets referring to a particular movie per hour. In this research, we use the number of posts per day for one week after release as seven features, which is the same as Asur and Huberman. Although they did not specify the reason clearly, dividing a week into each day can possibly reflect the rise and fall in the number of posts, so a better model can be created.

Polarity. We improve the polarity classification model by increasing the number of classes from two to five. There are several definitions of polarity, and we choose five classes on the basis of the learning data.

Classification Model. We prepare a dataset of movie reviews acquired from Kaggle.[1] This dataset consists of 156,060 texts, and these data are classified into five classes in accordance with the polarity of the text. Texts are vectorized by the tf-idf method on the dataset and classified by logistic regression. We also specify the parameters in the logistic regression and the ranges in the n-gram as $[0.001, 0.01, 0.1, 1, 10, 100]$ and $[(1,1), (1,2), (1,3)]$, respectively, and select the appropriate parameters by grid search. We used 70% of the dataset for training and the remaining 30% for testing and evaluated the performance of the polarity prediction model. The rate at which the polarity prediction model correctly

---

[1] https://www.kaggle.com.

classified was 64.8%. Even most texts that were not correctly classified turned out to be classified into the neighboring class. The results show that this model effectively classifies data. Thus, we use this model when calculating polarity.

Calculation of Polarity. Next, we show how to calculate the feature related to polarity for each movie. Asur and Huberman classify the polarity of tweets into two classes, Positive and Negative, and calculated the mean polarity (PNratio) by using Eq. (1).

$$Mean\ polarity = \frac{|Tweets\ with\ Positive\ Sentiment|}{|Tweets\ with\ Negative\ Sentiment|} \tag{1}$$

We examined the tweets and found that many tweets should be categorized into the class of neutral polarity. Thus, we classify the polarity of tweets into five classes, Positive, Slightly Positive, Neutral, Slightly Negative, and Negative, and calculated the mean polarity by using Eq. (2).

$$Mean\ polarity = = \frac{2|Positive\ Tweets| + |Slightly\ Pos.\ Tweets|}{2|Negative\ Tweets| + |Slightly\ Neg\ Tweets|} \tag{2}$$

Although the idea is basically the same, we give weight to obviously positive and obviously negative posts. It may be possible to choose three-class categorization or seven-class categorization. As mentioned above, movie review data for building a classifier consist of text and five-star scale rating. Thus, we choose five-class polarity categorization.

2.2   Features of Information Diffusion Model

In this section, we explain features obtainable from an information diffusion model. We focus on the CTIC model [2]. In the CTIC model, the time delay parameter $r_{u,v}$ and the diffusion parameter $\kappa_{u,v}$ are defined for the parent node u and the child node v. The larger/smaller the time delay parameter $r_{u,v}$, the faster/slower the information can be conveyed. Also, the larger/smaller the diffusion parameter $\kappa_{u,v}$, the higher/lower the possibility that information is propagated from the parent node to the child node.

The propagation process in the CTIC model expands at discrete time $t > 0$ and proceeds from the initially infected node set S as follows. The parent node u is thought to be infected at time t. Node u is given an opportunity to infect the uninfected child node v once. The delay time δ is calculated by using the parameter $r_{u,v}$. If child node v is not infected before $t + \delta$ time, u has the opportunity to infect v. The probability of infecting child nodes is $\kappa_{u,v}$. If infection succeeds, v is infected with time $t + \delta$. Propagation is made in order, and the process is terminated when there are no examined nodes.

We employ an infection model as information diffusion, but it does not consider the same person being infected twice. Comparing a case in which the same person may be infected twice with a case in which the same person is infected at most once, the set of the substantially connected persons is larger in the former case than in the latter case, which affects the estimation of the diffusion parameter. In this study, we consider the latter case to keep the discussion simple.

Network Structure. We will build an information diffusion model for each movie. To construct an information diffusion model, we need to construct a virtual network in the process of propagating movie information. In this research, we create a network using Twitter data since it has many users whose preferences reflect people's real-world behavior accurately. To assume the network structure, we need to define the number of nodes and link probability between each node, which are defined below.

Number of Nodes. We assume that the number of nodes is the sum of the number of posts on Twitter one week after a movie's release and count the number of posts including movie titles in text. Also, since the node represents a user, we assume that each user posts once about a movie.

Link Probability Between Each Node. We need to know the existence of links between nodes in order to define the network structure. In this research, we assume users as nodes and links as follow-up relationships on Twitter. If a user posts about a movie, we define the node as infected. The infected parent node gains the opportunity to propagate (infect) the information to the child nodes with the follow-up relationship. Since the follow-up relationship between nodes is difficult to accurately express, we assume that nodes have a follow-up relationship with a certain probability p. The procedure for finding p is as follows.

First, we create an artificial network whose time delay parameter r and propagation parameter κ are known. Saito et al. showed that the value of κ is lower than $1/\bar{d}$ [2]. $\bar{d}$ is the average outgoing degree in the network. They showed that the average outcome of goo[2], which a Japanese blog site, is 6.63. In this research, we conduct experiments on the assumption that the average outcome of Twitter also approaches this value. Specifically, we build a network with $\kappa = 1/6.63 \simeq 0.15$. As r, we build a network with normal time delay ($r = 1.0$).

Next, with respect to an artificial network created using these parameters, we change the probability p to various values and check the existence of a link between each node. Then we build many networks for each probability p. For each network, we estimate the time delay parameter r and the diffusion parameter κ. Finally, we compare the error between the estimated parameter and the true parameter ($r = 1.0$, $\kappa = 0.15$) and calculate p when the error is smallest. We use p as the link probability. Experimental results showed that $p = 0.01$ is optimal, so we will use this value in further experiments.

Parameters of Information Diffusion Model. We will describe the parameters that can be acquired by using the information diffusion model. These parameters are the time delay parameter and the diffusion parameter.

Time Delay Parameter. In the network of movies, convergence will be accelerated if information propagation is fast. If many movies have this property,

---
[2] http://blog.goo.ne.jp.

prediction accuracy is expected to decrease because the model only grasps the trend of the opening week. Therefore, a time delay parameter to grasp future trends is expected to improve prediction accuracy.

Diffusion Parameter. Information is propagated more if the parent node propagates information to the child nodes. Therefore, the diffusion parameter and box-office revenue are considered to positively correlate.

How to Obtain Parameters. Since we defined the network structure above, we map the tweet posts to the network nodes and acquire parameters. Here, we construct a random network using the number of nodes and the link probability. In a random network, links are randomly attached in accordance with the link probability when defining the presence or absence of a link to each node. Also, regarding the time difference, we assume that posts for every day are collected, and a time difference is created each day. As for the parent-child relationship between the nodes, we consider that there is a parent-child relationship when the child node posts after the parent node has posted.

2.3 Regression Analysis

In this section, we describe a method of predicting movie box-office revenue using the features defined in Sects. 2.1 and 2.2. We make predictions using regression analysis. The regression equation is as shown in Eq. (3).

$$Revenue = \beta_0 + \sum_{i=1}^{7} \beta_i * No.\ of\ posts\ on\ i\text{-}th\ day$$
$$+ \beta_8 * Polarity + \beta_9 * r + \beta_{10} * \kappa, \tag{3}$$

where r and κ are the time delay and diffusion parameters, respectively. $\beta_0, \cdots, \beta_{10}$ are coefficients. We also apply regression methods incorporating the regularization term such as Ridge, Lasso, ElasticNet.

3 Experiments

3.1 Datasets

Movie Metadata. We acquired movie metadata used in this research by scraping the Internet Movie Database (IMDb), which is an American movie database site containing various information about movies, movie stars, television programs, television stars, and video games. We used IMDb to obtain titles, weekly box-office revenue after release, and gross box-office revenue for movies released from 2017 to 2018 for which box-office revenue is stated. As a result, we obtained data for 375 movies.

Posts Data Obtained from Twitter. We collected the number of posts for each movie by scraping Twitter. On Twitter, we can search for posts by specifying keywords and periods. To obtain posts about a movie, we specified its title as a keyword. In addition, we specified the period by setting the release date of each movie as the first day, and we regarded all posts that satisfy the condition as the number of posts. We collected data for all 375 movies.

Cleansed Data. When judging the polarity of each movie, it is considered that if the number of posts about a target movie is extremely small, the value will not be correct. Furthermore, if there are too few posts about a movie, we cannot construct an information diffusion model. Therefore, we excluded movies with fewer than 100 posts for one month. Also, we excluded movies whose revenue is less than a million US dollar by following the previous studies. As a result, we obtained data for 106 movies with which to conduct experiments. In total, we analyzed 285,087 tweets.

In Sect. 2, we made the two assumptions. Before examining the prediction accuracy of our model, we experimented with verifying the assumptions. We omit the detailed explanation, but the statistical tests show that the assumptions hold.

3.2   Results of Prediction

We create a movie box-office revenue prediction model by using polarity and parameters obtained from the information diffusion model and evaluate its prediction accuracy. We used the features of the number of posts on the first to seventh days, mean polarity (Eq. (2)), time delay parameter (r), and diffusion parameter (κ).

We built a prediction model for movie box-office revenue using these features and conducted five-folds cross validation. In the evaluation, we used the adjusted coefficient of determination, R'^2, because it is used as a measure of performance in the previous study [1]. Although we should refrain from the naive interpretation of the value, and acceptable values of the coefficient of determination depend on the research fields, textbooks say the following. A value of $0.3 < R'^2 < 0.5$ is generally considered a weak or low effect size, and a value of $0.5 < R'^2 < 0.7$, this value is generally considered a moderate effect size. The prediction results are shown in Table 1.

Table 1. Results of revenue prediction: adjusted coefficient of determination, R'^2

Features	Opening	Gross
#tweet 1 to 7, polarity(2 class)	0.501	0.497
#tweet 1 to 7, polarity(5 class)	0.536	0.533
#tweet 1 to 7, polarity(2 class), r, κ	0.531	0.501
#tweet 1 to 7, polarity(5 class), r, κ	**0.565**	**0.540**

For opening-week box-office revenue prediction, the coefficient of determination is 0.501 for Asur and Huberman's model but 0.565 for our model. For gross box-office revenue prediction, the coefficient of determination is 0.497 for

Asur and Huberman's model but 0.540 for our model. Comparing the coefficients of determination, our model improves prediction accuracy. We consider that our model may not increase accuracy greatly, but it achieved a higher class of performance.

We also applied more advanced regression techniques (Ridge, Lasso, ElasticNet) to our data. In the evaluation, we used the mean squared logarithmic error because it is easy to directly compare the performances and understand its meaning. The prediction results are shown in Table 2. By observing Table 2, applying the advanced regression techniques further improves the performance, but our model still outperforms the previous model.

Table 2. Comparisons of regression techniques for the prediction of gross box-office revenue: mean squared logarithmic error

Features	Linear	Ridge	ElasticNet	Lasso
#tweet 1 to 7, polarity (2 class)	2.165	2.038	1.747	1.759
#tweet 1 to 7, polarity (5 class)	2.135	1.790	1.513	1.545
#tweet 1 to 7, polarity (2 class), r, κ	2.079	1.992	1.774	1.787
#tweet 1 to 7, polarity (5 class), r, κ	2.032	1.756	**1.472**	1.505

4   Conclusions

We proposed a new prediction model using Twitter data that extracts useful features through agent-based modeling and proposed an appropriate prediction model. Specifically, we proposed a prediction model for movie box-office revenue that includes five-class polarity judgment and two parameters, time delay and diffusion, derived from an agent-based model of information diffusion. The experimental results showed that the 5-class polarity and the parameters acquired from the information diffusion model are appropriate for predicting box-office revenue.

Acknowledgments. This work was partially supported by JSPS KAKENHI Grant Number JP19H04170.

References

1. Asur, S., Huberman, B.A.: Predicting the future with social media. In: Proceedings of the 2010 IEEE/WIC/ACM International Conference on Web Intelligence and Intelligent Agent Technology, vol. 01, pp. 492–499. IEEE Computer Society (2010)
2. Saito, K., Kimura, M., Ohara, K., Motoda, H.: Learning continuous-time information diffusion model for social behavioral data analysis. In: Zhou, Z.-H., Washio, T. (eds.) ACML 2009. LNCS (LNAI), vol. 5828, pp. 322–337. Springer, Heidelberg (2009). https://doi.org/10.1007/978-3-642-05224-8_25

Short Duration Aggregate Statistical Model Checking for Multi-Agent Systems

Ramesh Yenda◉ and M. V. Panduranga Rao(✉)◉

Indian Institute of Technology, Hyderabad, India
{cs16resch11005,mvp}@iith.ac.in

Abstract. For analysing large and complex systems, Statistical Model Checking has proved to be an attractive alternative to the more expensive numerical model checking approaches. Statistical Model Checking involves Monte Carlo sampling of execution traces of the system. Stochastic multi-agent systems with very large agent populations add significant simulation overheads that dominate the model checking complexity. This offsets some of the advantage in terms of the speed that statistical model checking offers. To mitigate these simulation overheads, we explore an approach based on sampling agent populations in addition to the Monte Carlo sampling of execution traces.

We argue that this approach is particularly useful for aggregate queries on Multi-Agent systems that are also restricted in the time horizon–for example, bounded until operators in probabilistic temporal languages.

We show that this can result in significant improvement in running times at the expense of only a marginal loss in accuracy and provide empirical evidence for this.

Keywords: Statistical model checking · Multi-Agent systems · Population sampling

1 Introduction

Many natural and man-made systems exhibit stochastic behavior. Probabilistic model checking is a technique for formally analyzing such systems. A particular flavor of this technique involves Monte-Carlo sampling of the runs of a system. Being a sampling based technique, it does not guarantee the same accuracy as exhaustive state space exploration based techniques like Numerical Model Checking [3]. However, this flavor, called Statistical Model Checking, has gained a lot of traction in analyzing large and complex systems where accuracy is not critical and numerical model checking does not scale well [11]. One such class of large and complex systems are Multi-Agent Systems (MAS) [10]. Indeed, statistical model checking for MAS has been investigated in the past [5,6].

For MAS, the time complexity for analysis through statistical model checking has two contributing factors–the SMC algorithm itself, and the generation of the Monte Carlo samples. If the agent population is high, simulating every agent

© Springer Nature Switzerland AG 2021
T. Uchiya et al. (Eds.): PRIMA 2020, LNAI 12568, pp. 420–427, 2021.
https://doi.org/10.1007/978-3-030-69322-0_32

entails a massive computation overhead, indeed, surpassing the SMC algorithm overhead.

In this paper, we propose a simple approach that can significantly reduce the simulation overhead in some important scenarios. We make the case that for a class of expensive queries called *aggregate* queries involving *bounded untils* with small time bounds, a population sampling based approach can result in non-trivial speed-ups. We focus our attention to sampling agent attributes that have a graph structure–an attribute of an agent takes on values by performing walks on an *attribute value* graph.

Our running example is stochastic movement of agents between cities. Thus, the attribute "current city" changes from one city to another, as modeled by nodes of a graph. Presence of an edge between two cities signifies presence of a direct conveyance mode between them. Such scenarios abound in several areas like epidemiology, demographic studies, logistical planning and even traffic management. The query that we ask (in PBLTL) is: what is the expected fraction of the cities that will have an agent population of more than a threshold η before time τ? We show a population sampling based algorithm that yields a significant gain over the naive exhaustive algorithm that simulates every agent.

The paper is arranged as follows. In the next Section, we briefly discuss some prerequisites like Statistical Model Checking and Multi-Agent Systems and previous work related to our work. In Sect. 3, we discuss our approach and in Sect. 4, empirical results.

2   Preliminaries and Related Work

Statistical model checking involves Monte Carlo sampling of the runs of the system being analyzed. The runs, also referred to as *simulations* or *traces*, are inspected to see if they satisfy a (typically probabilistic temporal) logic formula. First proposed by Younes and Simmons [12] for discrete event simulators, this technique has been widely applied to analyze many types of stochastic systems including black-box systems. We refer the interested reader to [1,7] for two excellent surveys of the area.

Multi Agent Systems (MAS) have been used to design and analyze of complex systems constructed out of several independent, interacting and intelligent *agents*. Often, these systems are designed to solve a computational problem that would otherwise be difficult to solve using conventional approaches. In this paper, we restrict our attention to simple stochastic Multi Agent Systems–all agents are homogeneous, with a single attribute of interest (their location) and a common (random walk) algorithm for modifying this attribute. Such a simplistic system is sufficient to illustrate the main idea of this paper.

Given that statistical model checking has been employed for fast analysis of stochastic systems, it is natural to apply these techniques to MAS [4,5]. Of relevance to this work is the idea of in-trace sampling of Herd et al. [6], where they take traces of all agents and perform in-trace sampling and generate coherent fragments for answering queries at different levels of granularity.

The present work uses a probabilistic extension of Bounded Linear Temporal Logic. Following is the syntax of BLTL that is used by the tool:

Definition 1. $\Phi ::= TRUE \mid a \mid \neg \Phi \mid \Phi_1 \wedge \Phi_2 \mid X\Phi \mid \Phi_1 U^{\leq k} \Phi_2$ *where: "a" is an atomic proposition, and* $k \in Q_{\geq 0}$

Consider a system with a (finite) state space $S = \{s_0, s_1, \ldots, s_{|S|-1}\}$. A path $\sigma = (s_0, s'_1, s'_2 \ldots s'_t)$, $s'_i \in S$, is a sequence of states in the execution of the system M over t discrete time units and where each state s'_i corresponding to output of the system at i^{th} time instance i.e. $\sigma[i] = s'_i$. The fact that a path σ satisfies a BLTL formula ϕ is denoted by $\sigma \models \Phi$. Semantics of the BLTL is as follows.

- $\sigma \models TRUE$
- $\sigma \models a$ iff a is true in the state s_0
- $\sigma \models \Phi_1 \wedge \Phi_2$ iff $\sigma \models \Phi_1$ and $\sigma \models \Phi_2$
- $\sigma \models \neg \Phi$ iff $\sigma \nvDash \Phi$
- $\sigma \models X\Phi$ iff $\sigma[1] \models \Phi$
- $\sigma \models \Phi_1 U^{\leq k}\Phi_2$ iff $\exists j \leq k \mid \sigma[j] \models \Phi_2$, and $\forall i < j \mid \sigma[i] \models \Phi_1$

For a BLTL formula Φ, $Pr_{=?}(\Phi)$ is the formula in the probabilistic extension PBLTL–what is the probability that the system satisfies the BLTL formula Φ?

3 Sampling Agent Populations

The simplest agent based system endows its agents with *attributes* and *rules* to modify them. Formally, such a system has a set $\mathcal{A} = \{A_1, A_2, \ldots, A_N\}$ of agents. An agent A_k (for $1 \leq k \leq N$) is endowed with i) a set of $\{\alpha_i\}_{i=1}^r$ (for $1 \leq i \leq r$) attributes, each of which can take a value from a discrete *value set* $\{v_1^{\alpha_i}, v_2^{\alpha_i}, \ldots, v_l^{\alpha_i}\}$, and ii) a set of rules to update these attribute values. Thus, as computation proceeds, these attributes keep changing values as per the update rules.

In general, the attribute value set can be seen to have an underlying graph structure. For example, if an agent's attribute α_i has the value $v_j^{\alpha_i}$ at an instant in computation, it can take the value $v_{j'}^{\alpha_i}$ at the next instant only if there is an edge from $v_j^{\alpha_i}$ to $v_{j'}^{\alpha_i}$ in the underlying graph. For example, consider an application in which an agent has a "current city" attribute, the attribute value graph should capture the connectivity between the cities. That is, this agent can change city at the next instant only if there is a one-hop conveyance link, namely an edge between the cities in the "current city" attribute graph.

Formally,

Definition 2. *An attribute value graph* $G_\alpha = (V, E)$ *for an attribute* α *is a directed graph with vertices* $V = \{v_j^\alpha\}_{j=1}^{|V|}$ *as the values that the attribute can take and a directed edge* $(v_j^\alpha, v_{j'}^\alpha)$ *present if and only if the attribute, when having the value* v_j^α *at a given simulation step, can take the value* $v_{j'}^\alpha$ *at the next step.*

All agents that have attribute α, therefore, perform a walk on G_α. The following atomic propositions are natural for such a multiagent system:

– Individual attribute atomic proposition: $\alpha(A)(t) = v_j^\alpha$ (at time t, the attribute α_i of agent A has the value $v_j^{\alpha_i}$).
– Aggregate attribute atomic proposition: $|\{A \mid \alpha_i(A)(t) = v_j^{\alpha_i}\}| \geq c$ for $c \in \mathbb{N}$ (at time t, the total number of agents with attribute $\alpha_i = v_j^{\alpha_i}$ is at least c).

Clearly, more complex state and path formulas can be composed from these atomic propositions.

Definition 3. *PBLTL formulas constructed out of aggregate propositions are called* aggregate formulas.

For example: $Pr_{=?}(TRUE \quad U^{\leq k} \quad (|\{v_j \mid |\{A \mid \alpha_i(A)(t) = v_j^{\alpha_i}\}| \geq c\}| \geq l))$.

3.1 Sampling Attribute Values

We now focus our attention to one attribute α and the aggregate formula $\eth$

$$\eth = \begin{cases} T & \text{if there exists } l \text{ attribute values } v^\alpha \text{ that are each taken by at least } \eta \text{ agents} \\ F & \text{otherwise.} \end{cases}$$

In the language of PBLTL, then, we are interested in the query $Pr_{=?}[TRUE \quad U^{\leq \tau} \quad \eth]$.

Before we come to the sampling approach, we discuss a naive "non-sampling" algorithm that simulates all the agents for τ steps for each sample generating run. The core idea of the SMC algorithm is to simulate the transitions of all the agents for τ steps. This simulation is repeated, say R times. If in all these simulations, $\Phi = TRUE$ for c times, we declare that $(TRUE \quad U^{\leq \tau} \quad \eth)$ with probability c/R.

3.2 The Sampling Approach

We begin with a few definitions in the context of the attribute value graph that will be useful subsequently.

Definitions: The r-neighborhood of a vertex u at time t, denoted $N_r(u)(t)$, is the set $\{v \mid v$ can be reached from u in at most r steps$\}$. The *area* covered by an r-neighborhood around u is $|N_r(u)(t)|$. A *cylinder* centered at u is the sequence $\langle N_{2r}(u)(t)\rangle_{t=0}^\tau$. Note that the radius does not change with time, and hence the name. A *semi-cone* centered at u is the sequence $\langle N_{2r-t}(u)(t)\rangle_{t=0}^\tau$.

For a given attribute value v^α (i.e., vertex in G_α), agents at a distance of more than τ hops cannot reach v^α within the time horizon τ. Thus, for evaluating the query for the attribute value v^α, we need not simulate the transitions of the agents initially located farther than τ hops from attribute value v^α. Therefore, for a given run of sample generation, we pick some attribute values uniformly at random and simulate only those agents that are located within τ "radius" of these attribute values. Instead of a single attribute value v^α, one can choose a cluster $\mathcal{C} = \{N_\tau(v^\alpha)\}$ of neighboring attribute values for batch simulation. We then wish to find out how many attribute values within the "inner circle" formed by the cluster get agent population more than η within time τ. Clearly, then all the agents in the radius of 2τ have to be simulated, as agents 2τ hops away can reach the cluster. This approach is listed in Algorithm 1.

Algorithm 1. One Run Of The Cylindrical Sampling Based Algorithm

---
1: **procedure** CYLINDERSHAPESAMPLING(G_α, τ, Φ)
2:     Initialize each attribute value v^α (i.e., vertex in G_α) with n_{v^α} agents at time-step $t = 0$.
3:     $S \leftarrow$ GenerateRandomSample(G_α)
4:     //See remarks in the text about the function GenerateRandomSample(G_α)
5:     For each attribute value C in S, construct $N_\tau(C)(0)$
6:     **while** $t \leq \tau$ **do**
7:         Update attributes of agents at distance $\leq 2\tau$ from each attribute value in S.
8:         Check if the query Φ is satisfied
9:         **if** Φ is satisfied **then**
10:             **return** $TRUE$
11:         $t \leftarrow t + 1$

The function $GenerateRandomSample(G_\alpha)$, as the name suggests, picks a "random" sample of vertices in G_α for observation. The exact kind of sampling would depend on the topology of G_α and the update rules for the attribute. For the purpose of illustration, we study a simple situation:

Definition 4. *Random walk on regular-G_α (RWRG) sampling: Sampling vertices uniformly at random on a regular graph G_α, where a) initially all the attribute values had equal number of agents and b) the change of attribute value follows a random walk on G_α.*

A further improvement would be as follows. Instead of simulating agents within the 2τ radius at every time step, one can constrict the radius with time. For instance, after t time steps, it suffices to simulate only those agents that are $2\tau - t$ steps away from the inner circle. This variant is listed in Algorithm 2.

Algorithm 2. One Run Of The Semi-Cone Sampling Based Algorithm

---
Steps 1–6: As in Algorithm 1
Step 7: Update attributes of agents at distance $\leq 2\tau - t$ from each attribute value in S.
Steps 8–11: As in Algorithm 1

Thus, the model checking algorithm would repeatedly invoke one of the above two sampling methods and report the fraction of runs where the formula is satisfied. We remark that this algorithm is effective when the simulation horizon is small, implying short duration simulations, since this keeps the cylinder and semi-cone radii small.

The following theorem regarding accuracy follows from the Chernoff Hoeffding bound.

Theorem 1. *Let every attribute value in graph satisfy the query with a probability p (owing to the RWRG assumption), and let p' be the fraction of attribute values that satisfy the query as estimated by exhaustive simulation (all agents, all attribute values). Further, suppose p and p' are sufficiently close and can be identified with each other. Let $\frac{X}{M}$ be the fraction of samples drawn that satisfy the formula Φ. Then, for $Pr(|p - \frac{X}{M}| \geq \epsilon) \leq \delta$ if M is at least $\frac{\ln 2/\delta}{\epsilon^2}$, for $\epsilon, \delta > 0$.*

This however, is a conservative estimate, since the sampling algorithms discussed simulate agents that are at a distance from the sampled node as well.

Observation 1. *Let the cost of simulating one agent be a constant c. Then the cost of one run of the semi-cone sampling based algorithm is $\sum_S \sum_{C \in S} \sum_{i=0}^{\tau} |N_{(2\tau - i)}| c$, whereas that of the exhaustive simulation is $N \times c$. Therefore, the speedup is $\frac{N}{\sum_S \sum_{C \in S} \sum_{i=0}^{\tau} |N_{(2\tau - i)}|}$. For lower τ, the speed up is more significant. It is also significant for smaller S's, but this would result in a loss in accuracy.*

3.3 Cities and Population Movement

We now illustrate the technique using the example of a large population of agents moving between cities. Naturally, the attribute of interest would be the "current city" of an agent. For simplicity of exposition and pictorial representation, we work with a torus graph with vertices as cities. Agents have an attribute called location that is updated at each time step in such a way that each agent effectively executes a random walk on the graph. We choose an atomic proposition $\eth$ as

$$\eth = \begin{cases} TRUE & \text{if there exist } l \text{ cities with population at least } \eta \\ FALSE & \text{otherwise} \end{cases}$$

and the query $Pr_{=?}[TRUE \; U^{\leq \tau} \; \eth]$.

4 Experiments and Results

In this section, we discuss our experiments and results. We have implemented the experiments in the DyNeMoC framework that we are developing in-house for analyzing dynamical phenomena on graphs through statistical model checking [2, 8, 9]. The tool is implemented in Java and the source code is available at https://github.com/cs16resch11005/FastSMC.

For the experiments, we have used 100×100 torus graph and uniformly distributed 10 million agents. Consequently, an expected 1000 agents are located at each city at time step zero. Subsequently, the agents location attribute is updated as if they are executing a random walk. Simulations are repeated 2335 times which correspond to approximation parameter $\epsilon = 0.03$, and confidence parameter $\delta = 0.03$ as per the Chernoff Hoeffding criterion.

We run experiments for 1, 4 and 8 sample cylinders and semi-cones, $\tau = \{5, 10, 15\}$ and population thresholds $\eta = 980$, 1000, and 1020.

The tool takes this data as input, and simulates random walks of the agents on the torus graph. Each simulation runs for τ time units and checks whether the property is satisfied or not.

In the first experiment, we investigate the performance of the exhaustive simulation technique against the cylindrical and semi-cone algorithms with sample sizes of 1, 4 and 8, holding $\tau = 5$ and the population threshold η as 980. We see from Fig. 1a that the estimated probabilities are comparable. As perhaps would be expected, the probabilities estimates are closer as the number of samples increase.

Figure 1b shows a comparison for the running times of these approaches. Clearly, there is a huge improvement in the running times for the two sampling based algorithms as against the exhaustive simulation approach. These plots indicate that the gains made in terms of running times are very high, at the cost of some loss in accuracy.

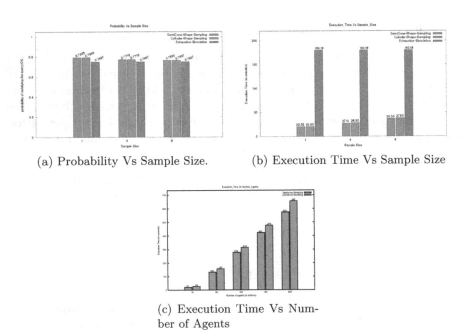

(a) Probability Vs Sample Size.   (b) Execution Time Vs Sample Size

(c) Execution Time Vs Number of Agents

Fig. 1. Experimental Results: Semi-cone: green, Cylinder: Orange, Exhaustive: Blue (Color figure online)

A difference in the running times between the semi-cone sampling and the cylinder sampling technique would be prominently observable with an increase in the number of agents, would also depend on the distribution of the agents on the graph. For example, if there is a larger density of agents in the annulus between the cone and the cylinder, the difference would be stark. Figure 1c gives a comparison of running times between the semi-cone sampling and the cylinder sampling technique as the number of agents increase, all else remaining the same.

References

1. Agha, G., Palmskog, K.: A survey of statistical model checking. ACM Trans. Model. Comput. Simul. **28**(1), 6:1–6:39 (2018)
2. Arora, S., Jain, A., Ramesh, Y., Panduranga Rao, M.V.: Specialist cops catching robbers on complex networks. In: Aiello, L.M., Cherifi, C., Cherifi, H., Lambiotte, R., Lió, P., Rocha, L.M. (eds.) COMPLEX NETWORKS 2018. SCI, vol. 812, pp. 731–742. Springer, Cham (2019). https://doi.org/10.1007/978-3-030-05411-3_58
3. Baier, C., Katoen, J.P.: Principles of Model Checking (Representation and Mind Series). The MIT Press, Cambridge (2008)
4. Herd, B.: Statistical runtime verification of agent-based simulations. King's College of London (2015)
5. Herd, B., Miles, S., McBurney, P., Luck, M.: MC²MABS: a Monte Carlo model checker for multiagent-based simulations. In: Multi-agent-Based Simulation XVI - International Workshop, MABS 2015, Istanbul, Turkey, 5 May 2015, Revised Selected Papers, pp. 37–54 (2015)
6. Herd, B., Miles, S., McBurney, P., Luck, M.: Quantitative analysis of multiagent systems through statistical model checking. In: Baldoni, M., Baresi, L., Dastani, M. (eds.) EMAS 2015. LNCS (LNAI), vol. 9318, pp. 109–130. Springer, Cham (2015). https://doi.org/10.1007/978-3-319-26184-3_7
7. Legay, A., Delahaye, B., Bensalem, S.: Statistical model checking: an overview. In: Barringer, H., et al. (eds.) RV 2010. LNCS, vol. 6418, pp. 122–135. Springer, Heidelberg (2010). https://doi.org/10.1007/978-3-642-16612-9_11
8. Ramesh, Y., Anand, N., Panduranga Rao, M.V.: DyNeMoC: statistical model checking for agent based systems on graphs. In: Baldoni, M., Dastani, M., Liao, B., Sakurai, Y., Zalila Wenkstern, R. (eds.) PRIMA 2019. LNCS (LNAI), vol. 11873, pp. 627–634. Springer, Cham (2019). https://doi.org/10.1007/978-3-030-33792-6_49
9. Ramesh, Y., Anand, N., Rao, M.V.P.: Statistical model checking for dynamical processes on networks: a healthcare application. In: 11th International Conference on Communication Systems & Networks, COMSNETS 2019, Bengaluru, India, 7–11 January 2019, pp. 720–725 (2019)
10. Wooldridge, M.: An Introduction to MultiAgent Systems, 2nd edn. Wiley Publishing, Hoboken (2009)
11. Younes, H.L.S., Kwiatkowska, M., Norman, G., Parker, D.: Numerical vs. statistical probabilistic model checking: an empirical study. In: Jensen, K., Podelski, A. (eds.) TACAS 2004. LNCS, vol. 2988, pp. 46–60. Springer, Heidelberg (2004). https://doi.org/10.1007/978-3-540-24730-2_4
12. Younes, H.L.S., Simmons, R.G.: Probabilistic verification of discrete event systems using acceptance sampling. In: Brinksma, E., Larsen, K.G. (eds.) CAV 2002. LNCS, vol. 2404, pp. 223–235. Springer, Heidelberg (2002). https://doi.org/10.1007/3-540-45657-0_17

Author Index

Alelaimat, Ahmad   377

Baarslag, Tim   317
Balduccini, Marcello   51
Bowles, Juliana K. F.   394
Bundas, Matthew   51

Chang, Shuang   360

da Costa Pereira, Célia   325
Dam, Hoa Khanh   377
Deguchi, Hiroshi   360
Dragoni, Mauro   281

El Zein, Dima   325

Felli, Paolo   259
Fioretto, Ferdinando   100

Garwood, Kathleen Campbell   51
Ghose, Aditya   377
Gianola, Alessandro   259
Greenwald, Amy   343
Griffor, Edward R.   51

Hara, Takanori   334
Heintz, Fredrik   19
Hirano, Masanori   3, 352

Iwata, Tomoharu   334
Izumi, Kiyoshi   3, 352

Jennings, Nicholas R.   182
Jonker, Catholijn M.   231

Kamiyama, Naoyuki   299
Koenig, Sven   248
Koide, Satoshi   116
Kola, Ilir   231
Kuznets, Roman   403

Li, Jiaoyang   248
Longin, Dominique   386
Lorini, Emiliano   386

Mahesar, Quratul-ain   199
Maris, Frédéric   386
Matsubara, Shigeo   412
Matsushima, Hiroyasu   3, 352
Miyamoto, Kensuke   84
Miyashita, Yuki   150
Mohammad, Yasser   68, 343
Montali, Marco   259
Mukai, Taisei   352
Müller, Jörg P.   317

Nakadai, Shinji   343
Nguyen, Khoa   34
Nguyen, Thanh Hai   51
Nishi, Tomoki   116, 368

Okoso, Ayano   116, 368
Oren, Nir   199
Otaki, Keisuke   116, 368

Panduranga Rao, M. V.   420
Parizi, Mostafa Mohajeri   215
Peng, Jiahao   133
Pereira, Célia da Costa   281
Präntare, Fredrik   19

Sakaji, Hiroki   3
Satish Kumar, T. K.   248
Satoh, Koh   412
Schlögl, Thomas   403
Schmid, Ulrich   403
Schumann, René   34
Sebe, Sînziana-Maria   317
Shaheen, Qurat-ul-ain   394
Shimizu, Hitoshi   334
Sileno, Giovanni   215
Smith, Ken   150
Son, Tran Cao   51
Sugawara, Toshiharu   133, 150
Surynek, Pavel   248

Tabakhi, Atena M.   100
Teixeira, Milene Santos   281
Tielman, Myrthe L.   231
Toniolo, Alice   394

van Engers, Tom   215
van Riemsdijk, M. Birna   231
Vasconcelos, Wamberto W.   199

Wang, Yixiang   165
Watanabe, Norifumi   84
Wu, Feng   165, 182

Yamada, Hiroaki   299
Yenda, Ramesh   420
Yeoh, William   100

Zhang, Han   248
Zilberstein, Shlomo   182

Printed in the United States
By Bookmasters

Printed in the United States
By Bookmasters